Building Websites with Microsoft Content Management Server

Lim Mei Ying

Joel Ward

Stefan Goßner

Building Websites with
Microsoft Content Management Server

First edition: December 2004

Published by Packt Publishing Ltd.
32 Lincoln Road
Olton
Birmingham, B27 6PA, UK.

ISBN 1-904811-16-7

www.packtpub.com

Cover Design by www.visionwt.com

Credits

Author

Lim Mei Ying
Joel Ward
Stefan Goßner

Technical Reviewers

Andreas Klein
Luke Nyswonger
Aaron Rinaca

Commissioning Editor

Douglas Paterson

Technical Editors

Richard Deeson
Douglas Paterson

Layout*

Ashutosh Pande
Nanda Padmanabhan

Indexer*

Ashutosh Pande

Proofreader

Chris Smith

Cover Designer

Helen Wood

* Services provided by www.editorialindia.com

About the Authors

Lim Mei Ying has plenty of real-world experience setting up MCMS systems at the enterprise level. As a systems analyst for SingTel, she has spent many hours figuring out the dos and don'ts of Microsoft's extensive product and enjoys finding new ways to solve MCMS related problems. She contributes actively to the newsgroup community, and is a Microsoft Most Valuable Professional. Mei Ying lives on the sunny island of Singapore.

Thanks to my husband, Louis, for the much needed support throughout the many months of writing. Special thanks to my family and friends for their encouragement.

Joel Ward works for Booz Allen Hamilton as a web developer. Once destined to be an architect, he switched tracks midway through college and instead graduated with a degree in Integrative Arts from Penn State University. His professional career has taken him on a journey through design, programming, usability, and accessibility.

Joel has enjoyed working with MCMS since its first release in 2001. Over the years, Joel has been active in the newsgroups and has been recognized as a Microsoft Most Valuable Professional for his work in the MCMS community.

He enjoys a good challenge, which includes working on projects that use ASP.NET and MCMS. His interest in technology and collaboration has motivated him to help coordinate a .NET user group at Booz Allen.

Joel lives in the Commonwealth of Virginia in the United States. You can visit his website at `http://www.wardworks.com/joel/`.

I would like to thank my wife, Ann-Marie, for supporting (a.k.a. putting up with) me all of these months while I was working on the book. I would also like to thank my family, friends, and co-workers for the help and encouragement that they provided during this wonderful endeavor!

Stefan Goßner works for Microsoft as an Escalation Engineer in the Developer Support department. He provides customers with technical solutions to problems related to Microsoft Internet Server Products. Stefan has breadth and depth in all areas of MCMS. His contributions to the newsgroup have helped many people to implement MCMS solutions in corporations around the globe, to the point where it has been said that if you don't know Stefan, then you're probably new to MCMS. He lives in Munich, Germany.

I would like to thank my girlfriend, Michaela, for the support throughout the months of writing, reviewing and coding for the book. Also many thanks to my friends in the MCMS product team in the U.S.

Shared Acknowledgements

We the authors would also like to thank the following people for supporting us and helping us along the way:

Our editors: Douglas Paterson and Richard Deeson, and the rest of the team at Packt for accepting our book proposal and for the wonderful work they have done in bringing this book to life.

Special acknowledgements go to the Microsoft folks who provided technical reviews of our book: Pat Miller, Mark Harrison, Andreas Klein, Arpan Shah, Luke Nyswonger and Jason Ren. A special thanks to Pat and Jason for their input on caching—the caching chapter would not be the same without you!

We would also like to express our gratitude to Aaron Rinaca from Booz Allen Hamilton. Your insightful reviews and suggestions have made a significant contribution to the quality of the book. Thank you!

Table of Contents

Chapter 15: Building Custom Placeholder Definitions and Placeholders

Chapter 16: Extending the Workflow

Introduction

Building Websites with Microsoft Content Management Server presents the fundamentals of Microsoft Content Management Server 2002 (MCMS) to propel you over the learning curve. Once you have mastered the basics, we build on that to help you to become an MCMS expert.

Learning should be fun. Plus, we suspect that your boss or client is expecting a prototype of the website within yet another incredible deadline. We have carved up the entire book in 24 lessons, each filled with working examples that build on top of one another so that you can get a site up and running from scratch in a very short time.

We provide lots of opportunities for you to get your programming feet wet in the form of numerous exercises. As you progress through the book completing these exercises, you will build up a single website allowing you to gain experience of all the key stages of website development. After we have walked you through the examples step-by-step you will have a fully functional site built entirely by you.

Fingers and mouse ready? Have fun getting to know your new Content Management Server!

What This Book Covers

Chapter 1 introduces Microsoft Content Management Server (MCMS) and gives you a tour of the features that ship with the product. *Chapter 2* guides you through the installation process for MCMS and prepares you for the chapters ahead.

MCMS uses SQL Server 2000 to host the database for storing content. *Chapter 3* shows how to connect MCMS to a SQL Server database using the Database Configuration Application (DCA). In *Chapter 4*, you will learn about the Server Configuration Application (SCA) and use it as an administrative tool to modify server-wide settings.

Chapter 5 provides the basic guidelines on how to transform websites from sketches on a storyboard to reality. You will design and build the containers that define the structure of a website for a fictitious gardening society, Tropical Green. In this chapter, you will create the Visual Studio .NET solution that's used for organizing the code files built throughout the book.

Templates are used to generate pages in MCMS. *Chapter 6* takes you step-by-step through the creation of a template. In *Chapter 7*, you will learn how to add editable areas called placeholders to the template and create postings based on it.

You will learn the how to debug an MCMS project and how that relates to debugging a regular ASP.NET web application in *Chapter 8*.

Chapter 9 shows how you can build summary pages by either assigning a posting as the default posting of a channel or by using a channel rendering script.

In *Chapter 10*, you will look at the integrated workflow solution available in the product. This chapter explores the various user roles that take part in the approval cycle and explains how a newly created posting moves along the workflow process. You will explore the user interface from an author's viewpoint in *Chapter 11* and use Web Author Console to create and manage postings.

MCMS ships with a rich Publishing Application Programming Interface (PAPI). *Chapter 12* gives you an overview of the various libraries and gets you started on building your own customized web applications. In *Chapter 13*, you will use the PAPI to create dynamic navigation controls that are managed by content contributors. You will construct a horizontal menu bar, a vertical menu bar that supports JavaScript, a breadcrumb, and a navigation tree.

Once you have learned the basics of the PAPI, you will move on to perform more complex customizations. In *Chapter 14* you will look at how easy it is to create your own custom placeholder controls. In *Chapter 15*, you will learn how to build a custom placeholder definition-placeholder pair.

Chapter 16 looks at how you can extend the default workflow model and shows how you can customize and configure it to simulate existing business processes in today's workplace.

The Web Author is not the only way for authors to upload content. Authors who are familiar with Word can continue to use it for creating and updating pages on the website. In *Chapter 17*, you will see how the Authoring Connector integrates Microsoft Word with MCMS.

Some websites require guest users to view areas of the site while restricting access to confidential information and, of course, authoring. In *Chapter 18*, you will set up a member's-only segment of the website, using forms to authenticate members and authors. You will also open up public areas of the site to visiting guests.

The author's experience can be enhanced further by tailoring the Web Author Console to include functions that help them do their jobs better. *Chapter 19* discusses various techniques for modifying the design and behavior of the authoring console.

Chapter 20 presents the concept of connected templates and pages. You will learn how connected templates and pages allow authors to upload their content only once and share it across different parts of the website without the need to maintain each copy separately

Before you can finish your new website, you will need to create a home page. In *Chapter 21* you will delve into a few ways to aggregate content for the home page.

Site performance is an important success factor for websites. *Chapter 22* covers caching and how it can be used to improve the performance of your website. As MCMS websites are extensive and dynamic, it is important to build pages without creating long wait times for visitors, and we show how this is done here.

Chapter 23 demonstrates how information stored in the content repository can be migrated across various MCMS setups using the Site Deployment Manager. You will also look at the Site Deployment API. You will write scripts that automate the process of deploying the content from one MCMS server to another.

Chapter 24 shows how you can apply mapped host headers to allow multiple websites to be hosted on the same MCMS server. You will also see how you can use SSL to ensure that the authentication mechanism for the member's segment of the website is secure.

Lastly, *Appendix A* discusses the finer points of upgrading an existing MCMS 2001 website to MCMS 2002, and *Appendix B* provides a list of references mentioned throughout the book.

What You Need for This Book

This book has been written for ASP.NET developers with a sound grasp of C#. To use this book you need to have access to the following:

- Visual Studio .NET Professional or higher (2002 or 2003 version)

- Microsoft Content Management Server 2002 Developer/Enterprise Edition. You can use the Standard Edition, but some features will not be available. A 120-day evaluation version of Enterprise Edition is available from `http://www.microsoft.com/cmserver`.

To install and run Microsoft Content Management Server 2002, you will need the following:

- The .NET Framework 1.0 or 1.1

- One of the following operating systems: Windows Server 2003, Windows 2000 Professional, Windows 2000 Server, or Windows XP Professional

- An installation of SQL Server 2000 Developer or Enterprise editions.

Conventions

In this book you will find a number of styles of text which distinguish between different kinds of information. This section provides some examples of these styles, and an explanation of their meaning.

There are three styles for code. Code words in text are shown as follows: "Pass the path of any object as an input parameter of the `Searches.GetByPath()` method to retrieve the requested object".

If we have a block of code, it will be set as follows:

```
HierarchyItem hItem =
cmsContext.Searches.GetByPath("/Channels/TropicalGreen/MysteryObject");

if(hItem is Channel)
{
    //Object is a Channel
}
else if(hItem is Posting)
{
    //Object is a Posting
}
```

When we wish to draw your attention to a particular part of a code block, the relevant lines will be made bold:

```
private CmsHttpContext cmsContext;
private void Page_Load(object sender, System.EventArgs e)
{
    // Put user code to initialize the page here
    cmsContext = CmsHttpContext.Current;
    if(!Page.IsPostBack)
```

3

```
    {
      GetPlantFactSheets();
    }
}
```

New terms and **important words** are introduced in a bold-type font. Words that you see on the screen, in menus, on dialog boxes and so on, appear in our text like this: "clicking the Next button moves you to the next screen".

> General tips, suggestions, or important notes appear in a box like this.

Troubleshooting tips and suggestions appear in the following format:

The option for the component I want to install is grayed out and I can't select it.

That's because you do not have the pre-requisites required by that component. For example, if you did not install Microsoft Visual Studio, you will not be able to install the Developer Tools. To find out what's missing, click on the component and read the description on the right-hand side of the dialog.

Any command-line input and output is written as follows:

```
sn -k "c:\TropicalGreenGACKey\TropicalGreenKey.snk"
```

Reader Feedback

Feedback from our readers is always welcome. Let us know what you think about this book, what you liked or may have disliked. Reader feedback is important for us to develop titles that you really get the most out of.

To send us general feedback, simply drop an e-mail to feedback@packtpub.com, making sure to mention the book title in the subject of your message.

If there is a book that you need and would like to see us publish, then please send us a note in the Suggest a title form on www.packtpub.com or e-mail suggest@packtpub.com.

If there is a topic that you have expertise in and you are interested in either writing or contributing to a book, then see our author guide on www.packtpub.com/authors.

Customer Support

Now that you are the proud owner of a Packt book, we want you to get the most from your purchase. Packt's Customer Support is here to try to make sure that happens, and there are a number of ways we can help you.

Downloading the Example Code for the Book

Visit http://www.packtpub.com/support, and select this book from the list of titles to view any example code or extra resources available for download for this book.

The downloadable files contain instructions on how to use them.

Errata

Although we have taken every care to ensure the accuracy of our books' contents, mistakes do happen. If you find a mistake in one of our books – be it a mistake in text or a code error – we would be grateful if you could report this to us. By doing this you can save other readers from frustration, and also help to improve subsequent versions of this book.

To report any errata you find, visit http://www.packtpub.com/support/, select your book, click on the Submit Errata link, and enter the details of your errata. Once your errata have been verified, your submission will be accepted and added to the list of existing errata. The existing errata can be viewed by selecting your title from http://www.packtpub.com/support/.

Questions

You can contact us at questions@packtpub.com if you are having a problem with any aspect of the book, and we will do our best to address it.

1

Overview of Microsoft Content Management Server

You probably already have a live website running, or at least, are planning to start one. Take this simple test to find if your website would benefit from a content management tool:

- Would you like your website to have a consistent look and feel throughout?
- Would you benefit from being able to apply a new look and feel to the website without reloading all of your information?
- Do you wish you could share content across pages without duplicating it all over the place?
- Do you want to avoid getting feedback from users about incorrect information posted online?
- Would you like to be able to pull out all pages that meet certain criteria, such as being newly created in the last 10 days?
- Would you like to give your content authors a simple, user-friendly interface to create web content with?
- Do you need to find out exactly where in the publishing process a page could be at any point in time?

If you answered 'yes' to any of the above questions, your website could benefit from a content management application. Microsoft Content Management Server is one of the most comprehensive applications on the market providing you with a ready-to-use publishing solution.

Like many packaged solutions, MCMS has been marketed to various organizations in different ways giving you different ideas about how this product could fit into your organization. If you are evaluating the software, you may be required to provide an analysis of what the product can and cannot do. And if you have already purchased it, your boss is likely to ask you to provide solutions to real problems, and fast. Before you begin, it's important that you get a good idea of what MCMS really is.

In this chapter, we provide you with a quick overview of what MCMS is all about. We also explain some core concepts behind the inner workings of the Server. In the coming chapters, we will examine how MCMS works in greater detail.

Why Content Management?

The dot-com boom years saw many companies creating a presence on the Internet. Product brochures, company profiles, quarterly reports, and organizational charts found their way from filing cabinets and wall charts to web pages.

Who did all that work? A team of technical people in every organization was responsible for cranking out web pages as fast as their fingers could type and they gained the name of webmasters. It was a job that was popular when the Internet started. Webmasters were the resident gurus in hacking out scripts and HTML: in fact these skills are often prerequisites for the position.

As websites grew in importance and size, it came to the point where a single webmaster (or even a team of webmasters) was not able to cope with the large volume of information that needed to make its way online.

Content started to become unmanageable. While a single team of webmasters could manage the website in its infant stages, it was clear that either processes had to be changed or super-webmasters would have to be recruited to keep the site going as it grew.

Frustrated with being at the mercy of overworked webmasters, some content providers or authors took up the task of trying to publish their own content online. Without a proper content management system, this usually meant that authors had to take on the role of the webmaster and learn the dark art of web publishing. They went through boot camps that taught them how to use various web editing tools. Most authors did not have programming backgrounds. It was often a hair-tearing, time-consuming and difficult process.

Why Webmasters Could not Sleep at Night

Some of the problems faced by webmasters:

Bottlenecks and Looming Schedules

The webmaster was the only person who knew how to convert documents and other materials to decent web pages. Everyone who needed to get their material published online relied on them.

By the time the material arrived on the webmaster's desk, there was not much time to get the information online. A good part of the day was spent on making the document web-friendly and getting it to look like the thousands of other web pages. As the number of contributors grew, it was not surprising to find that webmasters could not keep up with the volume of change and soon became a bottleneck in the workflow process.

Online Content Became Out-of-Date

The webmaster's in-tray was full of backlogged work. As long as the task remained outstanding, the website continued to display out-dated information. The poor employee was already working overtime, busy cranking as many pages as his or her poor sore fingers could crunch out.

Inconsistent Look and Feel

As the website gained popularity, so did its scope. Gradually, every department in the organization wanted to have a presence on the website. Each department had its own boss. Each boss had a different idea on how the design of the web pages representing their department should appear. Different teams of webmasters were assigned to create each site. Without any way to govern the look and feel, the website started to look more and more like grandmother's patchwork quilt with each sub-web having its own individual identity.

Duplication of Content all over the Website

Content was duplicated all over the place. Updating content often meant scouring the entire website for the duplicates and amending the changes page by page. Say, the opening hours of a shop has been changed. Uh-oh, looks like another late night at the office. Among the thousands of pages on the website, which ones contain the shop's operating hours?

The Solution—Content Management Servers

An emerging technology that has gained popularity in recent years is that of content management systems (CMS). They come in many flavors and designs, the most common of which are web content management systems, designed to manage the process of uploading content from the desktop to the website.

Microsoft Content Management Server 2002 is one such solution.

Microsoft Content Management Server has been around since 1997. It was first built by NCompass Labs, a Vancouver-based business that was one of the first players in the Content Management field. The version was called **NCompass Resolution**.

It started out as an enterprise-class web solution that empowered corporations to install and deploy fully functional content management system without help of external services.

In 2001, it was sold to Microsoft. However, traces of its origins with NCompass can still be found in the package.

It is a solution that can help you with almost all aspects of content management, from template development, content authoring, site management, and deployment, to data storage and retrieval. MCMS can efficiently handle the smallest of websites with tens of pages to large enterprise solutions that contain hundreds of thousands of pages. It also offers tight integration with Microsoft's suite of products including its ubiquitous word processor, Microsoft Word.

The Components of MCMS

Microsoft Content Management Server 2002 runs on the Windows platform (Windows 2000 Professional, Windows 2000 Server, Windows XP, and Windows Server 2003). It makes use of Internet Information Services (IIS) to deliver dynamic web pages and Microsoft SQL Server 2000 as its content repository.

Authoring is performed using either the browser-based component (Web Author), or Microsoft Word (when installed with Authoring Connector).

Developers use Visual Studio .NET to develop ASP.NET template files, a special kind of web form that defines the layout and behavior of each dynamically generated web page. Templates in the content repository are managed using MCMS Template Explorer, an add-on within Visual Studio .NET. The MCMS Publishing Application Programming Interface (API) is used for retrieving and updating content in the repository.

Several administrative interfaces are provided for managing the site structure and global settings: Site Manager, Database Configuration Application, and the Server Configuration Application.

Content is transported from one server to another using the Site Deployment Manager, and custom scripts are built using the Site Deployment API. Site Stager can be used to generate a static image of an ASP-based MCMS website (but does not work with ASP.NET-based MCMS sites).

The following diagram shows the architecture and how the components connect with each other. The subsections that follow briefly describe what each module does.

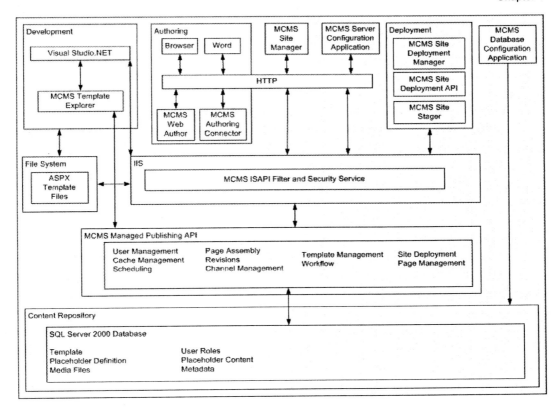

MCMS is a Content Server

MCMS uses Internet Information Services (IIS) to serve MCMS-driven websites. IIS is the engine that receives and processes HTTP requests from clients: MCMS does not get involved with any of that. It does, however, have a part to play in how content is transformed from data in the backend database to HTML pages—called postings in MCMS—for the browser.

MCMS 2002 works together with IIS 5.x (Windows 2000 and XP platforms) as well as IIS 6.0 (Windows Server 2003)

To understand this better, let's follow the path of a single HTTP request and see how IIS and MCMS work together to render content.

How MCMS Renders Content

When visitors to your site request a page, they send its URL to the web server. For example, this could be: http://www.TropicalGreen.net/PlantCatalog/hibiscus.htm. The HTTP request is first received by IIS.

MCMS has two ISAPI filters, which are then applied:

- **Resolution HTML Packager** (REHTMLPackager.dll) is the first filter to intercept requests. It ensures that client-side scripts are handled correctly when a user wishes to compare two different versions of a single posting. It does this by injecting a JavaScript routine on the fly, modifying the output of the page doing the comparison.

- **MCMS ISAPI Filter** (ReAuthFilt.dll) checks the incoming URL against the MCMS repository to see if the request is for an MCMS object. Non-CMS objects are handled by IIS just as they would be without MCMS.

> ISAPI stands for Internet Server Application Program Interface. It is a set of calls that hook into IIS and monitor events while the client reads a page from the server. They filter every request until they find one they need to process.
>
> In versions of MCMS prior to MCMS 2002 Service Pack 1a, the MCMS ISAPI Filter was called the **Resolution Filter** instead. This was a throwback to the NCompass Resolution product that was the predecessor to MCMS.

Should the MCMS ISAPI Filter find that the request is for an MCMS object, it proceeds to check to see if the user requesting the object has rights to it. If so, it transforms the incoming URL. The transformed URL contains information that maps to an object in the MCMS database and takes this form (for clarity, this URL has been split onto multiple lines):

```
http://www.tropicalgreen.net/Templates/Plants.aspx
?NRMODE=Published
&NRORIGINALURL=%2fTropicalGreen%2fPlantCatalog
&NRNODEGUID=%7bA9261BA7-A58B-4760-850D-512CCF77BAC8%7d
&NRCACHEHINT=NoModifyGuest
```

It's not a pretty URL but it conveys a lot of information. The request is then passed to IIS and ASP.NET to process the web form, which in the above case is Plants.aspx. The MCMS HTTP modules (registered in the web application's web.config file) query the database for an object with a key that matches the value in the NRNODEGUID (the unique identifier or GUID), NRMODE, NRORIGINALURL, and NRCACHEHINT parameters and create a so-called CmsHttpContext giving the code in the web form access to the associated repository items. The form will render the content according to these repository items.

> The posting's unique identifier is also known as its GUID, or globally unique identifier. GUIDs make excellent database keys. They are unique and prevent clashes when merging two sets of data together.

With these instructions, control is passed over to IIS. IIS sends the response back to the browser that made the request. All these processes are carried out transparently. The visitor to the website would not be aware that any URL transformation has taken place.

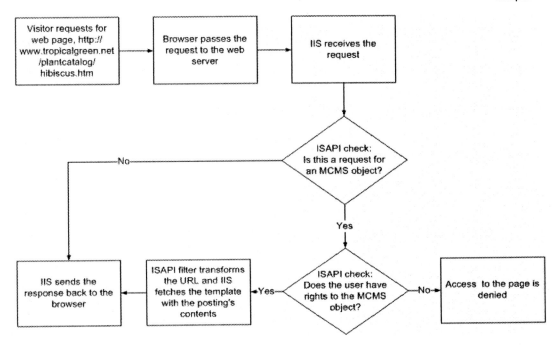

And that is how MCMS delivers pages.

Naturally, MCMS makes use of caching—an important concept that is used to boost its performance by minimizing database queries. For a more detailed explanation on how MCMS processes requests with caching, read Chapter 22.

How to Locate the MCMS ISAPI Filters

The filter is installed globally on your MCMS server. To see it:

1. Select Start | Administrative Tools | Internet Services Manager (If this does not appear, you may need to turn on this option in your Start Menu options, or you can access the Administrative Tools through the Control Panel.)

2. Right-click on the node representing your server and select Properties from the pop-up menu.

3. In the properties dialog, select the ISAPI Filters tab. You should see a dialog similar to the following screenshot.

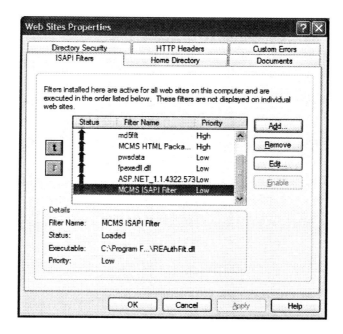

I can't find the filter in the ISAPI Filter section

You have to install MCMS first (see Chapter 2). The filters are applied on a global level (on your web server). Check that you are looking at the properties of the server (represented by the icon of a computer:⊞) and not the individual website.

Security Service

Not everyone should be given access to author the website or view confidential information. MCMS provides security checks through the Security service (see Chapter 10 for a detailed discussion of security).

A service named AESecurityService runs on all servers loaded with MCMS. The AESecurityService ensures that authentication is working correctly. When it is stopped, it is not possible to author your website as the web authoring tool will not be displayed. It is also responsible for maintaining the disk cache. If you stop the service, the disk cache is cleared.

You can see the presence of the AESecurityService by selecting Start | Administrative Tools | Services (or by going to the Control Panel). By default, it is configured to start automatically when Windows loads.

MCMS Is a Content Repository

As we've said, MCMS connects to a backend SQL Server 2000 database. All MCMS objects—such as content entered by authors—are stored in this database.

One of the greatest sources of confusion for developers is that web pages rendered by MCMS do not have a "physical" form. If you search your server's hard drive for the `about+us.htm` file or the `summary.htm` in the WoodgroveNet sample site that ships with the CD (or can be downloaded from the Microsoft website at `www.microsoft.com/cmserver`), you won't find any.

The reason is because the pages are not stored in the file system. Chunks of information are stored in the content repository (namely SQL Server database) instead. They are assembled on the fly when requested, based on the logic coded by developers using the template files discussed in the earlier section *How MCMS Renders Content*.

Template files are a special kind of a web form. They are stored in the file system and contain the logic that governs the look and feel of the pages and how they behave. As a developer, you will work with template files to write all code-behind scripts and HTML. We discuss template files in Chapter 6.

MCMS Integrates with Visual Studio .NET

MCMS provides native support for Visual Studio .NET. It's the preferred tool for developers to construct the template files necessary for creating websites built with MCMS.

We will be assuming that you are working with Visual Studio .NET throughout the book. While it is technically possible to use other development environments to create the code and template files, you will not benefit from several conveniences that result from the integration of MCMS and Visual Studio .NET, such as integration with the MCMS Template Explorer.

.NET Framework

It's easy to find developers who can work with MCMS because it supports the popular Microsoft .NET framework, and you can develop websites using either C# or VB.NET. In this book, we present all code samples in C#.

Integration with other Microsoft Server Products

There are also connectors available for you to integrate MCMS with other Microsoft Server products like Commerce Server and SharePoint Portal Server.

Publishing API

Microsoft does not recommend direct updates to the MCMS database: documentation on how the database is updated is not even available. You should not attempt to do this yourself as doing so may cause your system to become unusable.

Instead, Microsoft has provided a set of library files, known as the Publishing Application Programming Interface (PAPI). This provides a safe and structured way to retrieve, update, and delete the contents of the database.

As a developer, you may have a natural inclination towards working with the database directly by writing Transact-SQL scripts to do additions, updates, and deletions. You may find that working with the MCMS PAPI requires some getting used to. However, because the PAPI contains pre-packaged code, you would not need to write much of the code yourself, saving you valuable time. All you need to do is to call the appropriate functions when and where you need them.

The same PAPI is used internally within the MCMS Web Author application.

There are two versions of the PAPI shipped with MCMS 2002:

- The managed .NET framework version
- The unmanaged COM version

The COM version exists mainly for backward compatibility and works primarily with ASP-based template files. You will use this set of library files if you work with templates that were migrated from an existing MCMS 2001 website. When starting a website from scratch, it is highly recommended to develop with the ASP.NET version of the API. Not only does it provide better performance, it offers many new features that are not available with the COM version. In addition it is most likely that Microsoft will remove the COM-based API from the next version of MCMS. So to ensure compatibility with future versions, you should use the managed PAPI rather then the COM-based PAPI.

The PAPI is one of the central features of MCMS. We will make use of it extensively throughout the book.

MCMS Is a Web Authoring Tool

There are several ways authors can get their content from the desktop to the Web. They can enter content through:

- A web browser using the **Web Author**
- Microsoft Word with **Authoring Connector**

Web Author

MCMS provides data-entry components that have rich editing capabilities. These run on web pages, so all authoring can be done through the browser. There is no need to learn other web editing tools. In fact, it allows authors to copy and paste pre-formatted text as well as drag and drop attachments.

Business users are in total control over when and where the content is updated on the website. At the click of the Approve button, the material is made available online in real time—bypassing the need to have the material sent to a webmaster.

Authoring Connector

User-friendly web content management systems do not require authors to know any scripting languages. Microsoft Content Management Server goes the extra length to ensure tight integration with Microsoft Word. Authors don't have to leave the authoring environment they are already comfortable with, doing everything from the familiar Word interface, and with a few clicks of the mouse, their material can be published online.

What Authors can do with MCMS Web Authoring Tools

As a web authoring tool, you will find many basic features embedded within MCMS.

A Rich Editing Experience

Authors can write into rich text boxes and format text directly from Web Author. They can use familiar functions like applying bold, underline, and italics to selected text.

Content Scheduling

It is possible to schedule when pages should be made live or expired. A publish date could be scheduled such that the information is uploaded to the system but made available only at midnight. Similarly, expiry dates may be set to remove the content at a specified time. This automation makes things really convenient for authors who would otherwise have to add or remove the content manually at the appropriate times.

Content Reuse

Reusing content in multiple places on the website is easy, and avoids having to maintain separate versions and the consequent need to manually copy from one page to another.

Link Management

Links that reference expired or deleted pages are immediately removed. Say goodbye to broken links on your websites. Of course, only links that point to MCMS objects are managed.

Publishing Workflow

The product provides an integrated workflow solution that can be used to ensure the accuracy and integrity of the content that gets posted online.

The workflow is completely extensible. In Chapter 16 we show you how it can be customized to follow almost any business process in the organization.

Versioning

In real websites, content may change frequently. MCMS tracks changes to content by keeping each copy as a separate version. You can query the system to find out how the web page appeared on the live site at particular date and time. You can also compare two versions of a page to see what portions have been added or deleted since the last change.

Template-Based Publishing

Templates govern the look and feel of web pages and define their behavior. The use of templates drives the process of creating content to the business users. Webmasters are no longer needed to handcraft web pages one at a time. Business users enter content within specified text boxes, click the Save button and a web page is automatically created based on the selected template.

> Do webmasters need to look for new jobs? Contrary to popular belief, they are still needed. Instead of uploading content to websites, they have moved up the value chain. Their job now is to create and design the templates with the text boxes that authors use to upload content. In this way, the technical wizards get to do what they are best at, leaving the work of creating and uploading content to the subject-matter experts.

MCMS is a Website Manager

There are several tools available for site administrators to manage MCMS.

Site Manager

Once called Site Builder back in MCMS 2001, this was renamed to Site Manager in MCMS 2002 to better reflect what it does in the new version. Site Manager is the tool that enables Site Administrators and Channel Managers to work with container objects in MCMS. However, it does not allow the addition or editing of content: that is the job of the Web Author.

Server Configuration Application

We explore the Server Configuration Application in Chapter 4. There are some global settings that are applied to MCMS that can be configured using the Server Configuration Application.

Database Configuration Application

This is the tool that links an MCMS Server to a SQL Server 2000 database. Although you can only have one database behind each MCMS Server, you can switch from one database to another using the Database Configuration Application. Chapter 3 provides a detailed discussion of the Database Configuration Application.

MCMS Enables Deployment of Content Across Systems

MCMS provides several means for you to share content with other MCMS systems as well as non-MCMS systems.

Site Deployment

The MCMS Site Deployment Manager, part of the Site Manager application, packages selected objects in an MCMS site into distributable object files. This way, you can transport an entire MCMS site (or a selected portion of it) from one MCMS server to another.

Site Deployment Scripts

You can also write scripts based on the Site Deployment APIs to automate the process of incremental deployments from one MCMS server to another.

Custom Web Services

There are many occasions where you may want to extract content and use it in applications outside MCMS. With ASP.NET being the preferred development platform, developers can create web services based on the Publishing API. Web services are excellent tools for use in syndicating content across systems.

Web services can also be used as a means for external applications to interact with content stored in the content repository. For example, a billing application can trigger the creation of postings through a web service.

Site Stager

Site Stager takes a snapshot of the pages of your website and creates static images of them. It is useful for creating offline versions of ASP-based sites.

> Site Stager does not work for ASP.NET-based sites.

What Microsoft Content Management Server Is Not

Unfortunately, the words "Content Management" have been used by people to mean too many things. We will now clear up some misconceptions by telling you what MCMS is not.

MCMS Is Not a Document Management System

Document Management Systems focus on individual files. You upload documents to a website, check them out when you need to work with them and check them back in when you are done.

MCMS's focus is on the entire web page, not the individual files. Here, documents are called attachments or resources and you manage the web page in its entirety. For example, when a web page is approved, all attachments within it are collectively approved at the same time.

MCMS Is Not a Portal Management System

Portals are made up of portlets or mini-pages that provide information drawn from a wide variety of applications or other websites. They typically provide users with the ability to manage what they see on their portal. Users drag and drop portlets into neat little columns and subscribe to their content. An example of a popular portal is My Yahoo!

MCMS does not provide portal management features. You won't find out of the box solutions for personalization and membership. However, these features can be added with other Microsoft software like Commerce Server or Sharepoint Portal Services that offer integration with MCMS.

MCMS Is Not a Team Collaboration Tool

If you are looking for solutions with team calendaring, discussion forums, or list-bots, this solution may not be the one for you. While you could fashion templates to deliver these features, there aren't any immediate out of the box solutions that will do this.

> If you are looking for document management, portal management, or collaboration tools, have a look at Microsoft SharePoint Portal Server. It's a product that complements MCMS and provides these features out of the box

Microsoft Content Management Server really is a great tool for managing web pages and content. Over the course of the rest of this book, we demonstrate how to use MCMS to solve today's typical content-management problem scenarios.

MCMS Objects

Throughout the book, we will be using several key terms describing the various data objects employed by MCMS. They can be broadly classified under two categories:

- Containers for holding logical groupings of objects
- Objects, which can be postings (pages), page resources, templates, and even users

The diagram below shows the relationship between containers and objects.

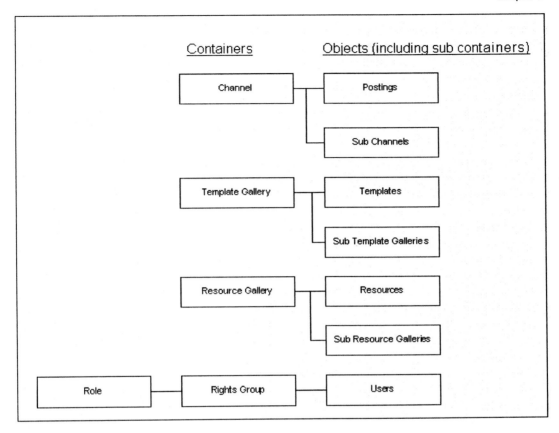

Channels

Channels are like folders in Windows Explorer. They organize postings and other sub-channels in very much the same way files are organized in folders. Usually, the channel hierarchy determines the URL of the web page, but we will find out about exceptions to this in Chapter 5.

In MCMS, channels are represented by this icon:

Postings

In MCMS, a posting is a web page, but not your traditional web page of course. Postings are assembled on the fly by piecing together data stored in the database and the template file.

Postings are represented by this icon:

Resource Galleries

Resource galleries store resources (and other sub-resource galleries). This is the icon that represents a resource gallery:

Resources

Resources are objects that are inserted into a posting. These can be anything from images or Word documents to plain text documents. MCMS stores resources as BLOBs in the content repository.

> BLOBs (Binary Large Objects) are arrays of bytes. Most relational databases today store data in predefined data types (e.g. integers, characters, bits, decimals, dates, etc.). When the database encounters data that doesn't fit into these predefined molds, it gives us the option to store them in raw binary formats—or blobs. Usually, this happens when we try to store entire files like GIF and JPEG images within the database.

MCMS does not have a particular icon for resources. The icon used to represent a resource depends on its file type.

Template Galleries

Template galleries store templates (and other sub-template galleries). In MCMS, they are represented by this icon:

Templates

Templates shape the content stored in the content management system and are used by authors to generate postings (web pages) that have the same form and shape. In MCMS, they are represented by this icon:

Roles and Rights Groups

Rights groups are logical groupings of users. In MCMS, there are eight different types of rights groups, each corresponding to one of the following roles: administrators, channel managers, template designers, resource managers, moderators, editors, authors, and subscribers. Unlike other container type objects, rights groups can't be nested. You can, however, assign both NT/Active Directory (AD) users and NT/AD groups to a rights group.

Users

Users are members of rights groups. In MCMS, users are represented by this icon: and groups by this icon:

Summary

This chapter has worked through the basic concepts behind MCMS 2002. We've seen that MCMS is made up of a content server, uses SQL Server 2000 as a content repository, and has modules that provide integration with Visual Studio .NET. For authors, it provides both a browser interface and integration with Word for a user-friendly authoring experience. In addition, it has website management capabilities.

Next, we discussed the main objects in MCMS: channels, postings, resource galleries, resources, template galleries, templates, rights groups, and users.

Throughout the course of the book, you will find that despite the large number of modules that make up the product, MCMS is really very easy to use. You will use the knowledge you gain from the book in virtually every MCMS project that you work on.

Now that we have covered the basic concepts, we are ready to move on and lay the foundations for the TropicalGreen website that we will build in the remaining chapters of the book.

2

Installing Microsoft Content Management Server 2002 for the Developer

In this chapter, we walk you through the set-up process for a single developer working on a single workstation or server. Should you get stuck along the way, the troubleshooting guide at the end will help you to get past common problems encountered in the installation process.

We are going to use MCMS 2002 with Service Pack 1a in this book. If you have the earlier Released To Manufacturing version (RTM) of MCMS 2002, you can install the RTM version and then upgrade it. We will cover both installation scenarios below, though we recommend you get your hands on a full SP1a version if you can.

Pre-Installation Checklist for the Developer

To help you get started, we have put together a checklist that should be followed in order to get MCMS up and running on your workstation or server. Depending on your existing operating system, the steps involved in the installation vary.

MCMS 2002 can be installed on any of these operating systems:

- Microsoft Windows Professional 2000
- Microsoft Windows Server 2000/ Microsoft Windows Advanced Server 2000
- Microsoft Windows XP Professional
- Microsoft Windows Server 2003 Standard or Enterprise Edition (MCMS 2002 is not supported on Web Edition or DataCenter Edition)

The pre-installation checklist is shown below. Don't be alarmed by its length. You probably have most of the software installed; we just want to be on the safe side and list everything so that you will not miss anything out.

- Ensure that the computer meets the minimum hardware requirements
- Run Windows Update to have:
  - The latest security fixes applied
  - Internet Explorer 6.0 Service Pack 1 or above
  - The latest Service Pack for the .NET Framework
- Configure Internet Information Services
- Install Microsoft Visual Studio .NET (2002 or 2003)
- Install Microsoft SQL Server 2000
- Apply the latest Service Pack for SQL Server 2000
- Decide on an MCMS System Account
- Create the MCMS Database
- Decide and/or create the MCMS Web and Server Configuration Application Entry Points (Windows 2000 Server and Windows Server 2003 only)
- Install Internet Explorer Web Controls
- Install Visual J# Redistributable
- Set the maximum size for uploaded resources and site deployment (Windows Server 2003 only)
- Ensure that the account running the ASP.NET process has impersonation privileges

Ensuring that the Computer Meets the Minimum Hardware Requirements

Microsoft recommends that your development PC should have:

- A Pentium III-compatible or higher processor
- At least 1GB of RAM
- 2GB free disk space
- A CD-ROM Drive

Don't worry if your machine does not meet all the above requirements if you are setting up a development environment. Although these are the recommended settings, MCMS can run on machines with much lower specifications. Just bear in mind that on lower-end machines MCMS may run a bit slower and Site Deployment may not have sufficient memory to complete its job.

We have developed MCMS sites on a Pentium III computer with only 256MB of RAM. While this works fine, performance, of course, is not as great as it would be on a higher-end machine.

Working on a lower-end machine might be OK for development, but don't take that risk when building a production server.

Does your machine have what it takes? If so, place a little check mark against this step on the list and let's move on.

Running Windows Update

To install MCMS you will need to have, depending on your operating system, at least:

- Service Pack 2 for Windows 2000
- Service Pack 1 for Windows XP

Microsoft recommends running Windows Update before installing, and then on a regular basis to ensure that service packs, patches, and other security fixes for Windows are applied. Visit http://windowsupdate.microsoft.com or select the Tools | Windows Update option from Internet Explorer. Windows Update will not only install the latest service packs for your specific version of Windows and the .NET Framework, but also any critical security updates and hotfixes.

It is always a good idea to have the latest service packs installed on your server. This will not only fix some of the bugs that shipped with the original software, but will also keep certain viruses and hackers at bay.

Configuring Internet Information Services (IIS)

Depending on your version of Windows, the steps to configure IIS vary.

Computers Running Windows 2000 (all editions) or Windows XP Professional

If you already have Windows up and running, check to see if you have the correct settings selected for IIS.

1. From the Control Panel, choose to Add/Remove Programs.
2. In the Add/Remove Programs dialog, click Add/Remove Windows Components.
3. The Windows Components Wizard appears. Ensure that Internet Information Services (IIS) is checked. Highlight it and click Details...
4. The Internet Information Services (IIS) Details dialog opens. Ensure that the following components are selected:

   - Common Files
   - FrontPage 2000 Server Extensions
   - Internet Information Services Snap-In
   - World Wide Web Server

5. If you're missing any of these components or any other components not required to install MCMS, but needed for other reasons, check them now.

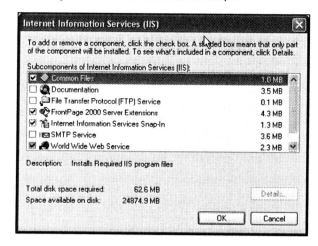

6. Click OK to close the Internet Information Services (IIS) Details dialog.

7. Click Next to apply the configuration changes you requested. You may be asked to insert the Windows installation CD.

8. Click Finish to close the Windows Components Wizard.

Computers Running Windows Server 2003

When you first install Windows Server 2003, most of the components are disabled. This security feature forces you to consider the settings applied to your machine carefully and makes it less likely that hackers and viruses will be able to use your computer as a conduit for mayhem.

In order for MCMS to function correctly on Windows Server 2003, you need to activate several IIS components:

- ASP.NET
- ASP
- Server-side Includes

Here's how you can check if these components are installed and activated:

1. From the Control Panel, choose to Add or Remove Programs.

2. In the Add or Remove Programs dialog, click Add/Remove Windows Components.

3. The Windows Components Wizard appears. Ensure that the following components are selected:

- ASP.NET (found within Application Server)
- Active Server Pages (found within Application Server | Internet Information Services | Web Service)
- Server Side Includes (found within Application Server | Internet Information Services | Web Service)

4. Click Next when you have selected all the necessary components. Follow the on-screen instructions to complete the installation.

5. Close the Add or Remove Programs dialog when the installation completes.

Ensuring that Internet Explorer is Version 6.0 or Above

Microsoft Content Management Server 2002 requires Internet Explorer of at least version 6.0 for accessing the online administration modules. If you ran Windows Update earlier you should already have the latest version of Internet Explorer.

> Clients accessing the server for authoring need at least Internet Explorer 5.0 when using Web Author or Site Manager or Internet Explorer 5.5 when using Authoring Connector.
>
> Other browsers like Netscape Navigator or Internet Explorer for Macintosh are only supported as browsers used by visitors to your site to view the MCMS content. They cannot be used for authoring.

To check your Internet Explorer version:

1. Point to Start | Programs | Internet Explorer.
2. On the Internet Explorer Toolbar, point to Help | About Internet Explorer.
3. Ensure that the version number is 6.0 or above.

If you have a lower version of Internet Explorer, upgrade it with the latest versions of the browser directly from Microsoft at http://www.microsoft.com/ie/, or by using Windows Update.

Installing Microsoft Visual Studio .NET 2002 or 2003

Since this is a development machine, Visual Studio .NET must be installed. Needless to say, we need it for writing and compiling the code for the website we intend to create. The .NET Framework is automatically installed with Visual Studio .NET. MCMS supports both .NET Framework version 1.0 and .NET Framework version 1.1. Visual Studio .NET should be installed before installing MCMS, otherwise you will need to run through certain installation steps again after installing Visual Studio .NET.

You can use Visual Studio .NET 2002 to develop with .NET Framework version 1.0 only. Use Visual Studio .NET 2003 to develop with either the .NET Framework version 1.0 or version 1.1.

We will use Visual Studio .NET 2003 and .NET Framework 1.1 in this book.

> For a production machine, install the .NET Framework without Visual Studio .NET. The .NET Framework for both versions 1.0 and 1.1 can be found on Microsoft's website (www.microsoft.com).

Applying the Latest Service Pack for .NET Framework 1.0

If .NET Framework 1.0 is your choice, ensure that you have installed at least Service Pack 2, which can be found in the Dotnet directory on the RTM CD, via the Microsoft website, or via Windows Update.

To find out which Service Pack has been installed on your computer:

1. Open Windows Explorer or My Computer, browse to `<Windows Install Drive>/<Windows Install Folder (WinNT or WINDOWS)>/Microsoft.NET/Framework/v1.0.3705/`.
2. Right-click on the file `mscorcfg.dll` and select Properties.
3. Click the version tab and view the last set of digits in the File Version. The version of the ASP.NET service pack is reflected in the first digit of the last decimal. For example, if the version number is `1.0.3705.288`, you have applied Service Pack 2.

If you are using .NET Framework 1.1, then MCMS does not require any service packs but in general you should install the latest service pack for all products when they become available (remember to read the release notes of each service pack and perform the necessary backups before you install it!).

Installing Visual Source Safe

If you plan to work with multiple developers on the same project, install Visual Source Safe (VSS) for source-code versioning and control. Visual Source Safe is shipped together with Visual Studio.NET Enterprise Architect and Visual Studio.NET Enterprise Developer editions. Alternatively, should you already have an existing Visual Source Safe server that you wish to use, run the `NetSetup.exe` file found in the `Microsoft Visual Studio/VSS/` directory on the server that contains the VSS database.

You can also use a different source-control system if you like. We recommend choosing one that integrates into Visual Studio .NET.

Installing Microsoft SQL Server 2000

By now you probably know that MCMS uses SQL Server 2000 as its storage repository.

MCMS and SQL Server 2000 do not have to sit on the same box to work together. You can connect MCMS to a SQL Server installed on a separate machine in your network. In fact, if you are going to have multiple developers work on the same MCMS website project, they usually share a common MCMS database during development.

> You can download a 120 day trial version of SQL Server 2000 from the official SQL Server website (`http://www.microsoft.com/sqlserver`).

There are a few things to watch out for when installing or configuring SQL Server 2000 for use with MCMS 2002:

1. Choose to Create a new instance of SQL Server, or install Client Tools.

2. Install both Server and Client Tools, and choose the Default installation option rather than specifying a name for your SQL server.

3. Choose to do a custom install. When selecting sub-components, ensure that Full-Text Search (found within Server Components) is selected.

4. Use the default setting on the next dialog, which asks for the user account to use for SQL Server.

5. Decide on the Authentication Mode. Microsoft recommends that when possible, you use Windows Authentication. It provides several benefits over SQL authentication including validation and encryption of passwords, auditing, and password expiration. Choose Mixed Mode if you need to support SQL Server Authentication to the database e.g. for backwards compatibility.

6. Accept the default Collation settings. That would be dictionary order, case-insensitive, for use with 1252 character sets.

7. On the Network library dialog, ensure that both Named Pipes and TCP/IP Sockets are enabled. You can check these settings on an existing installation of SQL Server, by accessing the Server Network Utility (select Start | Programs | Microsoft SQL Server | Server Network Utility).

Applying the Latest Service Pack for SQL 2000

MCMS requires SQL Server Service Pack 3a or higher.

Find out which service pack has been installed on your server:

1. Point to Start | Programs | Microsoft SQL Server | Query Analyzer.

2. Connect to the SQL Server.

3. Type the following statement in the SQL Query Analyzer window:

```
Use master
Select ServerProperty('productlevel')
```

4. Press F5 to execute the query.

You should get results similar to the following figure:

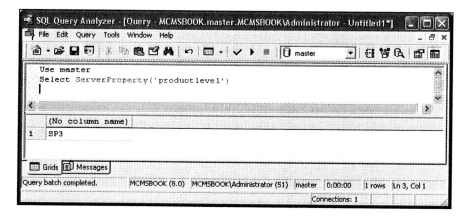

Results showing SP1, SP2, or RTM imply that you need to download and install the latest SQL Server patch from the official Microsoft SQL Server website (http://www.microsoft.com/sql). For SP3a, the download comes as a package containing three files: You only need to install the one called sql2ksp3.exe. Although MCMS works with instances of SQL Server with at least SP3 applied, we strongly suggest that you go with SP3a if possible.

I have SP3a applied but the T-SQL statement returns SP3 instead.

In order to differentiate between SP3 and SP3a, check the CSDVersion key, which specifies the number of the most recent service pack installed. To get the CSDVersion key of your SQL Server, execute the following T-SQL statement:

```
EXECUTE master.dbo.xp_instance_regread N'HKEY_LOCAL_MACHINE',
N'SOFTWARE\Microsoft\MSSQLServer\MSSQLServer\CurrentVersion',
N'CSDVersion'
```

SQL Servers patched with SP3 have a CSDVersion of 8.00.760 and SQL Servers patched with SP3a have a CSDVersion value of 8.00.761.

Deciding on an MCMS System Account

The system account is used to browse the active directory/domain and grant rights to the database and file-system assets. You can get away by using an account that does not have rights to read the active directory/domain (which may be the case if you are planning to use a local system account). However, when it comes to assigning users to an MCMS group, you would have to enter their names one by one without any means to select from a list.

Decide on an MCMS System Account. This account should fulfill the following criteria:

- Read access to the MCMS install directory.

- Rights to browse the Active Directory Service containing users who would be accessing MCMS (optional).
- Ideally a dedicated account just for MCMS, and not used for any other reason.
- Log on locally rights to the machine. Don't worry about this setting for now. The Database Configuration Application will prompt you to configure it later in the installation process.

Scribble the user account that you would like to use here. If the account has not been created yet, create it now.

My MCMS System Account is (DOMAIN\AccountName):

_____(Reminder: Keep the password to yourself!)

If you are using a local system account, replace DOMAIN with the local computer name.

Creating the MCMS Database in SQL Server 2000

We will now create the SQL Server database that we will use as the content repository for the Tropical Green website we are building. In this book, we will name the database TropicalGreen. You can of course, give it any valid name you choose.

1. Point to Start | Programs | Microsoft SQL Server | Enterprise Manager.
2. Expand the nodes Microsoft SQL Servers | SQL Server Group | [server name] (Windows NT).
3. Right-click on the Databases node and select New Database from the pop-up menu.
4. The Database Properties dialog appears. Name the new database TropicalGreen. Click OK.

Assigning Users and Specifying Role Membership to the MCMS Database

In addition, depending on the authentication mode used, you will have to assign users and specify their role membership.

1. Expand the node inside Databases that represents the newly created database. Right-click Users. Select New Database User... from the pop-up menu.
2. The Database User Properties dialog appears. Use the following matrix below to determine the Login Name and Database role membership required for each authentication mode. Use Windows Authentication if possible, but in some cases SQL Authentication may be required by your particular setup.
3. In the Name field, if the user does not appear or belong to any groups in the drop-down list, select <New> and create a new user. This is required for successful connection to the database later.

Authentication Mode	User Account	Database Role Membership
Windows Authentication	MCMS System Account (the Windows account created earlier on the domain or local machine)	db_datareader (read from all tables in the database)
		db_datawriter (write to all tables in the database)
		db_ddladmin (execute statements that manage the tables and other objects in the database)
	The Windows account of the user logged in to run the Database Configuration Application later – e.g. your personal Windows account	db_owner
SQL Authentication	SQL account that will be used to connect to the database	db_owner

4.   When you are done, click OK to close the dialog.
5.   Close Enterprise Manager.

Once MCMS has been successfully installed and the DCA configured and run successfully for the first time, you can downgrade the accounts above to have fewer rights. We will discuss the post-installation rights required for each user in Chapter 3.

Creating the MCMS Web and Server Configuration Application Entry Points (Windows 2000 Server and Windows Server 2003 only)

If you are developing on Windows 2000 Professional or Windows XP Professional, skip on down to *Installing Internet Explorer Web Controls*. Only the Server editions of Windows support the creation of more than one website.

MCMS requires two web entry points:

- A virtual site for hosting Microsoft Content Management Server
- A virtual site for hosting the Server Configuration Application

Virtual Site for Hosting MCMS Managed Websites

MCMS runs perfectly well on the default website. The default website is created when Internet Information Services (IIS) was installed, uses Port 80, and makes use of the primary IP Address of the server.

You can of course, start a fresh work area. To do so, you would need to create another website using Internet Services Manager. This will work in most situations, although Microsoft officially only supports the Default website to be used with the MCMS Developer Tools for VS.NET.

If you would like to create a new virtual site, use the Internet Services Manager to set it up:

1. In the Control Panel, open Administrative Tools | Internet Services Manager.

2. On the left panel, right-click the node representing your server. Select New | Web Site from the pop-up menu.

3. The Web Site Creation Wizard dialog appears. Click Next to continue.

4. Give a description to the website (for example, TropicalGreen for our site). Click Next to continue.

5. Enter an appropriate port number for the website. Unless you have strong reasons, it is a good idea to stick to the default and use port 80. Click Next to continue.

6. Specify a path for the website home directory (e.g. c:\tropicalgreen). Use Windows Explorer to create the folder if it does not exist—the MCMS installer will not do it for you. Click Next.

7. On the Web Site Permissions screen, allow:

   • Read

   • Run Scripts

8. Select additional permissions if required. Click Next.

9. The wizard announces that the website has been successfully created. Click Finish.

Do you see the text (Stopped) next to the newly created virtual site as shown below?

 TropicalGreen (Stopped)

That is because there is another site on your server, which uses the same port number and IP address.

To solve this conflict, give a different port number or a different IP address to one of the websites. You can also choose to stop the conflicting website by right-clicking on the node in Internet Services Manager and select the Stop option, then start the TropicalGreen website by right-clicking on it and selecting Start.

Virtual Site for Hosting the Server Configuration Application

The Server Configuration Application (SCA) is a management module used to set global settings in MCMS. Needless to say, you would not want public users to access this website and change the settings of your MCMS server. As an added precaution, you would probably want to decouple the administration site from the public site to minimize the impact of changes done to either. So it is not surprising that Microsoft recommends creating a separate website to host the SCA.

If the IIS Admin website is already installed on the server, we recommend that you use that virtual server to host the SCA as it should already be secured with only the necessary features enabled. If it is not created or not locked down, follow the steps below.

The steps for creating the virtual site to host SCA are the same as those for creating the virtual site that hosts MCMS apart from a couple of differences:

- Give it a meaningful description, for example, SCA Entry Point.

- Try not to use port number 80 for the SCA entry point; pick another number, like 8000. Make sure not to choose a port number used by other services running on the same machine, like HTTPS (443), FTP (21), or SQL Server (1433/1434).

- Prohibit anonymous access to the website by un-checking the Allow anonymous access to this Web Site option (available on the Web Site Home Directory tab of the Properties page).

- To help ensure strict security, download the Microsoft IIS Lockdown tool from http://support.microsoft.com/default.aspx?id=325864. Unzip the files to a suitable folder on your hard drive. Copy iislockd.ini and urlscan_cms.ini from the support folder of your installation CD into the folder containing the unzipped files. Run iislockd.exe and select Content Management Server when prompted for a template.

Additional Security Measures for SCA

As this is an administration website, it is good practice to allow only administrators logged on to the local machine (and perhaps a few others) to access the site. With Internet Services Manager still open, right-click on the website that represents the entry point for the SCA and select Properties from the pop-up menu. Internet Services Manager will display the Properties dialog.

Among the various buttons and tabs available on the screen, select the Directory Security tab. In the middle section labeled IP addresses and domain name restrictions, click the Edit... button to bring up the IP Address and Domain Name Restrictions dialog.

Check the Denied Access radio button. Click Add... and add the IP 127.0.0.1 of type Single Computer (this IP address represents the local machine) to the exception list. Click OK to save the changes and close the dialog.

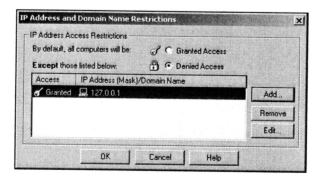

When you have created both virtual websites, close Internet Services Manager.

Installing Internet Explorer Web Controls

Internet Explorer Web Controls are a set of components that provide rich browsing capabilities. In this set of controls, you will find Tree Views, Tab Controls, Multi-Page controls and Toolbars. All these enhance the browsing experience of authors, providing them with a user interface that acts more like a regular Windows program than a web browser.

You can find the installation file for Internet Explorer Web Controls in the webControls folder on the MCMS RTM CD. Double-click the iewebcontrols.msi file and follow the instructions given by the installation wizard. If you're installing the full SP1a or evaluation version of MCMS, you can download the Web Controls at:

http://www.microsoft.com/downloads/details.aspx?FamilyID=fac6350c-8ad6-4bca-8860-8a6ae3f64448&DisplayLang=en.

Installing the Visual J# Redistributable

The Visual J# Redistributable is required for Site Manager (and Site Stager) to work properly with MCMS 2002 SP1a. The version of the Visual J# Redistributable you need depends on the version of the .NET Framework you have installed.

Before installing, check to see if you have the Visual J# Redistributable already installed. From the Control Panel, select the Add or Remove Programs option and look for any instances of the Visual J# Redistributable Package that you may have installed previously.

If you are using .NET Framework version 1.0, download the Visual J# Redistributable Package 1.0 at http://go.microsoft.com/fwlink/?LinkId=14506.

If you are using .NET Framework version 1.1, download the Visual J# Redistributable Package 1.1 at http://go.microsoft.com/fwlink/?LinkId=16283.

If you have both versions of the .NET Framework installed on your machine, you must install *both* of the Visual J# Redistributable packages.

Setting the Maximum Size for Uploaded Resources and Site Deployment (Windows Server 2003 only)

If you are installing MCMS on Windows Server 2003 you need to increase the default maximum size for uploaded resources and site deployment files. Otherwise when you attempt to upload any image, attachment, or deployment package larger than 200KB, you will raise HTTP 403 errors.

1. Open Internet Services Manager (select Start | Administrative Tools | Internet Information Services).
2. Right-click on the node representing your server and select Stop Internet Services. Click OK.
3. Open the metabase.xml file located in the %windir%\system32\inetsrv\ folder.
4. Search for the text ServerBindings and look for a line like this after it:

```
ServerComment = "(Name of website)"
```

For example, if you are using the default website, you would see:

```
ServerComment = "Default Web Site"
```

5. Take note of the Location attribute of the <IIsWebServer> element surrounding the matching <ServerBinding>. The Location attribute has the format /LM/W3SVC/Instance ID. Record the instance ID. For example, if the Location attribute appears as /LM/W3SVC/1, then the instance ID would be 1.

6. Press *Ctrl+F* and search for the tag <MBProperty>. Between the <MBProperty> and </MBProperty> tags, add the following code:

```
<IIsWebDirectory
Location ="/LM/W3SVC/(InstanceID)/ROOT/NR/System/ResUpload"
AppFriendlyName="ResUpload"
AppIsolated="2"
AppRoot="/LM/W3SVC/(InstanceId)/Root/NR/System/ResUpload"
AspMaxRequestEntityAllowed="51200000">
</IIsWebDirectory>

<IIsWebDirectory
Location ="/LM/W3SVC/(InstanceID)/ROOT/NR/System/SDUpload"
AppFriendlyName="SDUpload"
AppIsolated="2"
AppRoot="/LM/W3SVC/(InstanceId)/Root/NR/System/SDUpload"
AspMaxRequestEntityAllowed="51200000">
</IIsWebDirectory>
```

7. Replace (InstanceID) with the value of the instance ID found in Step 5. Set AspMaxRequestEntityAllowed to the maximum file size you allow for upload. In this example, we have set it to 50 MB.

Ensuring that the Account Running the ASP.NET Process has Impersonation Privileges

A new security setting, "Impersonate a client after authentication" or seImpersonatePrivilege, was introduced in Windows 2000 Server Service Pack 4 as part of Microsoft's effort to increase security in its operating systems. MCMS requires the account that runs the ASP.NET process to have seImpersonatePrivilege to work correctly. Follow the steps outlined below for machines running Windows 2000 Server with at least SP4 applied, Windows Server 2003, or Windows XP with at least SP2 applied.

1. From the Control Panel, select Administrative Tools | Local Security Policy.

2. In the Security Settings tree, expand the Local Policies node.

3. Select User Rights Assignment. On the right hand-panel, right-click Impersonate a client after authentication and select Properties.

4. In the Impersonate A Client After Authentication properties dialog, ensure that the account running the ASP.NET process is listed. Otherwise, click Add User or Group and add the user to the list. The user running the ASP.NET process depends on the operating system. Refer to the following table for the account to look for.

Operating System	User
Windows 2000 Server	ASPNET
Windows Server 2003	ASPNET
Windows XP	ASPNET
Windows 2000 Domain Controllers with .NET Framework 1.1	IWAM_<MachineName>

5. Close all opened dialogs.

Considerations for Windows XP with Service Pack 2

An additional security setting added to Service Pack 2 for Windows XP prevents COM components from being activated by the internet guest account. This is required for Site Manager to run. To fix this issue:

1. From the Control Panel, select Administrative Tools | Component Services.
2. Expand the Component Services | Computers menu. Right-click My Computer and select Properties.
3. Click on the COM Security tab.
4. In the Launch and Activation Permissions section of the dialog, click Edit Default...
5. Ensure that the internet guest user account (by default, this is the IUSR_<MachineName> account) has been added to the list. Otherwise, add it in.
6. Close all opened dialogs.

Installing Microsoft Content Management Server 2002 with SP1a

The computer is now prepared and set up for Microsoft Content Management Server.

If you have the Microsoft Content Management Server 2002 CD, take a look at its label. Does it say Microsoft Content Management Server 2002 SP1a? If your CD does not have **SP1a** after the title, it is likely to be the **Released to Manufacturing (RTM)** version. For installation of RTM versions, follow the instructions in the next section, *Installing from the Released To Manufacturing Version of MCMS*.

Otherwise, if you are evaluating the software, you can download the 120-day evaluation version of MCMS with SP1a from the Microsoft site (http://www.microsoft.com/cmserver/).

At the time of writing, SP1a is the latest service pack available. This is the version used throughout the book. By the time you read this, newer Service Packs may be available. The installation steps may differ from version to version. Check out the ReadMe files that come with the CD or download to get the latest instructions.

To begin, insert the CD into the CD-ROM drive, or run the Evaluation version download by double-clicking it to expand the files and start the setup. The splash screen should appear quickly.

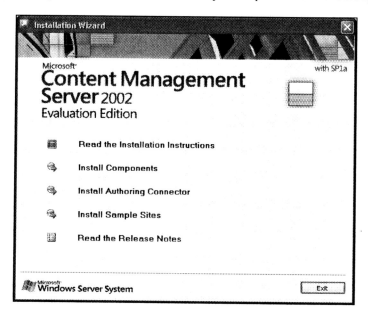

If you are using the CD and for some reason the splash screen does not appear, open Windows Explorer, navigate to the CD's root folder and double-click on the setup.exe file.

On this screen, you can choose to visit the official MCMS website, or read the release notes or the installation help file. These are resources that you may want to visit later to learn more about the product. This screen also provides options to install Authoring Connector and Sample Sites. Select Install Components.

You will be presented with the dialog to enter your name, organization, and product key. Evaluation and MSDN copies of the software should have the product key already filled in.

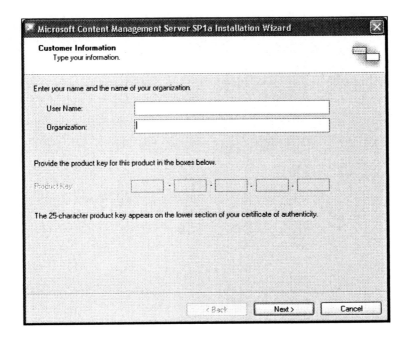

The next screen shows the **End-User License Agreement (EULA)**. Once you have accepted the EULA, you are asked to choose the type of installation.

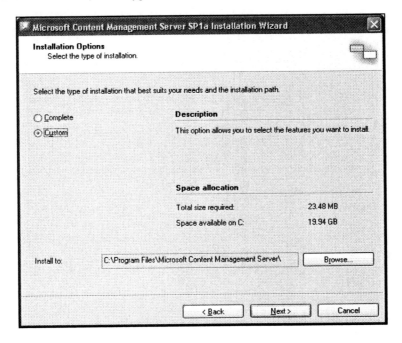

You can opt to do a complete installation or a custom installation. In order to see what components are available, select a Custom installation. Before clicking Next, also decide the directory and folder MCMS will be installed in. Click the Browse... button to select an alternative location if you need to. By default, setup will suggest the Program Files directory of the drive that runs the operating system. It is recommended to have at least 500 MB of free disk space on this drive, but MCMS requires about 50 MB for its installation files (not including space for the database). When you have made your selection, click Next.

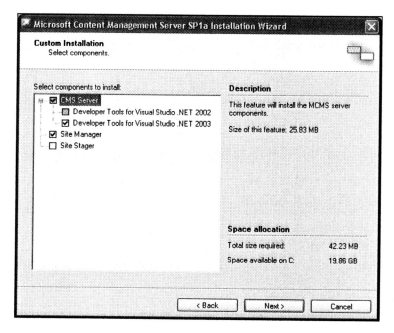

The next screen shows a list of components available for installation, and you need to select those you would like to install on your machine. By default, CMS Server is pre-selected. Make sure the following boxes are checked:

- CMS Server
- Developer Tools (pick the one that corresponds with your version of VS.NET)
- Site Manager

Leave the Site Stager option unchecked. Select it only if you need to use it for staging postings based on ASP templates, which would interest you only if you are upgrading from an MCMS 2001 website. Site Stager is not supported when using ASP.NET templates, and we expect Site Stager to disappear in the next version of MCMS. Click Next.

The option for the component I want to install is grayed out and I can't select it.

That's because you do not have the pre-requisites required by that component. For example, if you did not install Microsoft Visual Studio, you will not be able to install the Developer Tools. To find out what's missing, click on the component and read the description on the right-hand side of the dialog.

The wizard presents a confirmation screen where you can review the components that will be installed. Click Install and relax while the wizard performs the installation. This process will take approximately 5 to 15 minutes depending on your system's capabilities and may require a reboot if replaced components are in use.

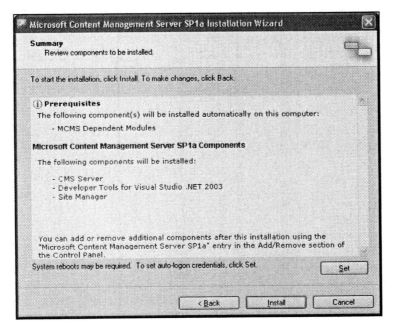

Once the installation has been completed, you will be presented with the Installation Completed dialog. This dialog tells you the location of the installation log file. Refer to this log file to review any error messages generated by the wizard.

> For the MCMS 2002 SP1a installation, the installation log file will be saved as
> `C:\Documents and Settings\<Username>\Local Settings\Temp\`
> `CMS2002SP1aSetup(<timestamp>).log`.

Uncheck the Launch Database Configuration Application after Installation is completed option and click Finish. We will run the **Database Configuration Application (DCA)** in the next chapter.

Installing from the Released To Manufacturing version of MCMS

Microsoft Content Management Server made its way to the market in October 2002, before Windows Server 2003 and Visual Studio .NET 2003 appeared on the scene. As a result, the **Released To Manufacturing (RTM)** version did not have all the pre-requisites necessary to run on the new platforms. If your CD contains MCMS without SP1a, the installation steps vary from those described above.

> The label on the CD for the RTM version does not indicate the presence of any Service Packs. If you received your CD in October 2002, chances are you have the RTM version.

To start the wizard, insert the CD and wait for the splash screen to appear or run the `setup.exe` program found in the root folder of the CD. Select Install Components. The next screen presents a set of three options:

- Install MCMS Components
- Install Authoring Connector
- Install Sample Site

Notice that the option to install the sample site is grayed out. That is only available if you have an existing installation of MCMS on the machine. Select Install MCMS Components.

The Installation Wizard starts and prepares itself. When it is ready it presents you with a welcome message. Click Next. Now you are presented with the EULA. Accept it and click Next.

The following screen asks which components you wish to install. The choice you make here depends on the operating system and the version of Visual Studio you are using. To make your decision easier, we have put together a matrix that shows which combination to choose.

> Visual Studio .NET 2003 will not work with the MCMS 2002 RTM version Developer Tools. If you would like to use Visual Studio .NET 2003, install the version of MCMS 2002 packaged with SP1a, or install the RTM version of MCMS 2002 and upgrade it to SP1a to enable Visual Studio .NET 2003 integration.

When you have made your selection using the following table, click Next.

Operating System	Visual Studio 2002 (.NET 1.0)	Visual Studio 2003 (.NET 1.1)
Windows 2000 Professional Windows Server 2000 Windows Advance Server 2000 Windows XP Professional	CMS Server Developer Tools	CMS Server
Windows Server 2003	This configuration is not recommended by Microsoft	CMS Server

At this stage, the Installation Wizard carries out some preliminary checks to see if you have the pre-requisites for MCMS. If you've followed through the check-list at the beginning of the chapter, you should breeze past this stage. If you are missing any components, you will be informed. Exit the installation wizard, go back to the relevant step above and perform it before running setup again.

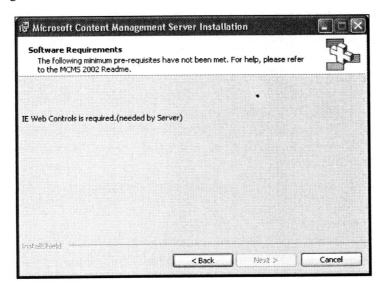

Enter your name, organization, and product key and click Next. Evaluation copies have the product key pre-filled. If you have misplaced your product key, check your certificate of authenticity. It is not typically printed on the CD.

The next screen shows you the Disk Cache configuration. For now, accept the default settings and click Next. We will show you how to alter these values and how to pick the best configuration for your system in Chapter 4.

The wizard informs you that it has all the information it needs to install the program. Uncheck the Launch Database Configuration Application after Installation is completed checkbox. Click Install.

When the wizard completes the installation, it presents you with the InstallShield Wizard Completed dialog. Click Finish.

Applying SP1a on the RTM version of MCMS

As a developer, you are probably aware of the benefits of applying service packs. Service Pack 1a includes plenty of bug fixes as well as the components and features that enable MCMS 2002 to integrate fully with both Windows Server 2003 and the .NET Framework 1.1. You will need SP1a to install the rest of the components like Site Manager and the Developer Tools for Visual Studio .NET 2003.

MCMS 2002 Service Pack 1a is available as a self-extracting zip file. You can download it from the official MCMS website (http://www.microsoft.com/cmserver). Double-click the zip file to extract it. When it's done extracting, you will be presented with a list of choices on a splash screen. Select Install Components.

Setup continues by examining your current configuration. When it's ready, it presents the end-user license agreement. Choose to agree and you will be shown the list of components that will be upgraded. Click Upgrade and wait while the installation wizard runs. If all goes well, you will get the Installation Completed screen. Click Finish to close the wizard.

Installing Site Manager and Developer Tools with Sp1a

If you are using Visual Studio .NET 2003, you will find that you are still lacking the Developer Tools for Visual Studio .NET 2003. Notice, also, that Site Manager has yet to be installed. Interestingly, you've just installed that Service Pack successfully and these components are still missing. Or are they really?

To find these "missing" components, open the Control Panel and select the Add/Remove Programs icon. From the Add/Remove Programs screen, highlight Microsoft Content Management Server SP1a and click the Change/Remove button.

Select Modify and click Next to move on to the Custom Installation Dialog, which lists the components that can be installed, including the ones we missed earlier. Check these boxes:

- CMS Server
- Developer Tools (pick the one that corresponds with your version of Visual Studio .NET)
- Site Manager

After you have made your selection, click Next. The wizard presents a confirmation screen where you can review the components that will be installed. Click Install to start the installation process. When the wizard has installed all the selected components, click Finish to close the dialog.

What has been Installed on My Computer?

And that's it! You have just passed the first phase of the installation process. Let's take a look at what has been installed on your computer.

For the MCMS 2002 SP1a installation, the installation log file will be saved as:

```
C:\Documents and Settings\<Username>\Local
Settings\Temp\CMS2002SP1aSetup(<timestamp>).log
```

For the MCMS 2002 RTM version installation, the installation log file will be saved in the folder:

```
C:\Program Files\Microsoft Content Management Server\LogFiles\
```

New Additions to the Start Menu

Click the Start button and expand Programs. You should see a new entry, Microsoft Content Management Server. Expand that and you should find three new options:

- Database Configuration Application (discussed in Chapter 3)

- MCMS Help
- Site Manager

A fourth option will be added after you run the DCA for the first time in Chapter 3:

- Server Configuration Application (discussed in Chapter 4)

If you have chosen to install Site Stager, you will see it listed there as well.

Additional Items in the File System

Open Windows explorer and browse to the installation directory (this is located in the `<Install drive>/Program Files/Microsoft Content Management Server/` directory, unless you changed it during the installation).

Look at the list of folders and files added. We will show you what some of the files do and which are customizable as we move through the book.

New Service Available

From the Control Panel, select Administrative Tools | Services. Look for the newly added AESecurityService.

New Keys in the System Registry

Most of the keys related to MCMS 2002 are located in the `HKEY_LOCAL_MACHINE/SOFTWARE/NCompass` directory. You should not need to change any of these settings manually, but you may be interested to take a look at them.

> To open the Registry Editor, point to Start | Run. Type regedit and click OK.

Throughout the rest of the book, we will see how these components work together to create a powerful engine that manages web content effectively and efficiently.

Frequently Asked Questions

Sometimes, the Installation Wizard coughs up fur balls and refuses to continue until you feed it the right medicine. We have put together solutions to the common problems that have perplexed fellow developers in the past.

Is it possible to install MCMS on a central server and have all our developers connect to it?

No, this is not possible. Each and every developer requires a local instance of MCMS on their machines. We discuss the extra steps required to establish a multi-developer environment in chapter 3.

I am a developer for both MCMS 2001 and MCMS 2002. Can I install both versions on my computer?

Again, this is not possible. MCMS 2002 and MCMS 2001 share different versions of the same library files, so they cannot co-exist on the same computer. This includes the Site Builder and Site Manager client applications, so only one or the other can be installed at the same time. This also includes service pack versions, so an MCMS 2002 Site Manager instance will not work with an MCMS 2002 SP1a server installation.

The only solution in this situation is to use a product like VMware or VirtualPC to host multiple virtual machines on your system for each version of MCMS that you require.

Can I do silent installations of MCMS?

Unfortunately this isn't possible. You need to be present to answer the questions asked by the Installation wizard. No provision has been made for unattended installation.

The Installation Wizard says Microsoft Java VM 5.0 or higher required when I attempt to install Site Manager and/or Site Stager. I cannot find this as a download anywhere. Where can I get this?

This message appears because you're installing from the RTM version of MCMS 2002 on Windows XP Professional or Windows Server 2003. Here's the good news: You don't need Microsoft Java Virtual Machine (VM) to install these components. MCMS SP1a ships with a version of Site Manager and Site Stager that does not use the Java VM. Leave these components out when running the installation and follow the steps outlined in the *Installing from the Released To Manufacturing Version of MCMS* section to install these components when upgrading to SP1a.

The Installation Wizard can't recognize Visual Studio 2003 although it's been installed on my computer. It says: Microsoft Visual Studio .NET not found (needed by Dev Tools).

You need MCMS 2002 with at least SP1 or above to support Visual Studio 2003. Either install the RTM version without the developer tools and install SP1a afterwards or install using the SP1a version of MCMS 2002 from CD or the downloaded executable.

Where can I find out more information about installing MCMS?

See the MCMS Product Documentation on the Microsoft website at:

`http://www.microsoft.com/cmserver/default.aspx?url=/cmserver/techinfo/prod uctdoc/.`

Summary

Congratulations! Your system is now equipped with one of the most powerful content-management servers on the market. In the next chapter, we will take you through the second phase of the installation process: Connecting your newly installed Content Management Server to SQL Server 2000 using the Database Configuration Application.

3

The Database Configuration Application

In the previous chapter, you installed the server and developer tool components of MCMS. This chapter will show you the next step: using the DCA to link MCMS to a database.

Behind every Microsoft Content Management Server is a Microsoft SQL Server 2000 database, and the utility that links them together is the Database Configuration Application (DCA).

We take you behind the scenes for an in-depth look at what the DCA does. In addition, we demonstrate the use of the DCA to switch from one database to another.

The DCA Links MCMS Server to the Database

Running the DCA will perform the following functions:

- Tell MCMS which SQL Server and database in the network to use
- Encode and store the ODBC Connection string, which includes the user name and password used for SQL authentication.
- Write initial settings to the registry and database, including information about the Web Entry Points and the MCMS System Account, as well as the first administrator of the server

If your chosen database is empty, the DCA will carry out an additional task:

- Import the required tables, stored procedures, and the database schema

The DCA Toggles between Databases

The DCA can be used to connect the MCMS server to any existing networked MCMS database.

At any time, an MCMS Server can connect to exactly one database.

Let's say you are working on MCMS websites for two different clients. Their websites have different configurations. You build two separate MCMS databases to cater for this purpose. You have only one development server, your trusty old desktop. Here's when the DCA can be useful, allowing you to switch between the different databases.

Or perhaps you have received a support call from a client running an MCMS website you created, and you need to analyze the content of the website to see if that is contributing to the problem. The client sends you the project files along with the backup of the entire database. All you need to do is to restore both the executables and the database, use the DCA to point your server to the database, and you are ready to go.

Another case is if you are working primarily on a development server. For some reason, you need to look at the contents of the staging server. You would use the DCA to switch from the database on the development server to the database on the staging server.

There are many other scenarios where using the DCA to switch from one database to another would be necessary.

> In the previous version of MCMS (2001) you could use SQL Server 7.0 to house the MCMS content repository. This is no longer supported for MCMS 2002.
>
> This does not mean that you are not able to access other content in such databases from your MCMS applications! As with any traditional web application you can store content in any database you like, but you will have to organize and manage this content yourself with your own application(s); the content cannot be natively retrieved using MCMS.

Running the DCA for the First Time

In the previous chapter, we installed the MCMS Server. Now we need to connect it to the SQL Server 2000 database that will store our website content.

First, start the DCA by pointing to Start | Programs | Microsoft Content Management Server | Database Configuration Application. The DCA starts by presenting a splash screen. Click Next.

The DCA will then ask if you wish to support ASP-based content (Mixed Mode) or purely ASP.NET content.

> Don't confuse this with the ability to run ASP-based applications. Legacy ASP-based applications can run alongside MCMS on the same server regardless of this setting.

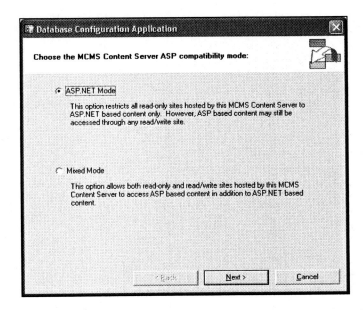

Which option do you choose? The rule of thumb is: Unless you're planning to upgrade a website from MCMS 2001 to MCMS 2002, choose ASP.NET mode. In ASP.NET mode, you write all MCMS templates using the ASP.NET framework. There will be no difference in performance regardless of your choice here. ASP.NET, by virtue of its new and improved engine provides a more secure model. Selecting it now enforces the rule that your system will support only ASP.NET-based templates.

Mixed mode provides backwards compatibility with ASP template files created with the earlier version, MCMS 2001. In mixed mode, templates can be scripted using either the ASP framework or the ASP.NET framework. It is most likely that Microsoft will drop support for ASP-based templates in the next version of MCMS.

> Warning: The decision you make now is irreversible. The only way to change the compatibility mode later is to re-install MCMS.

Select ASP.NET Mode and click Next.

The next screen asks for the location of the website that will be hosting MCMS sites.

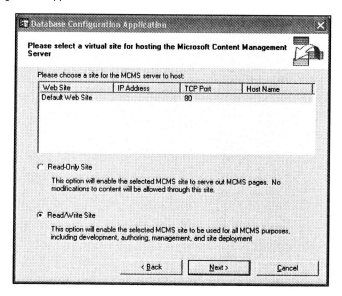

Highlight the MCMS Web Entry point created in the pre-installation steps. If you are running Windows 2000 Professional or Windows XP Professional, select the Default Web Site.

The two radio buttons at the bottom of the dialog give you the option to choose whether or not you want the site to be read-only or read/write. Since we are setting up an environment for development, we will need to work with the authoring module, deployment modules, and management modules, so select Read/Write Site, and click Next. We are now asked to select the SCA Web Entry Point.

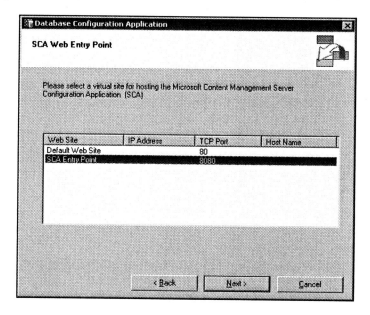

If you are developing on Windows 2000 Professional or Windows XP Professional, just select the Default Web Site. Otherwise, choose the SCA Web Entry Point created in the pre-installation steps or select the administration website on your server if it is installed.

Click Next, and the DCA evaluates the site chosen to host the SCA Web Entry Point. You will receive a warning if the SCA Web Entry Point chosen is less than ideal:

- The selected virtual site hosts a Microsoft Content Management Server. You have selected to use the same site as an MCMS Web Entry Point.

- The selected virtual site grants access by default. See the section, *Additional Security Measures for SCA* in Chapter 2 for details.

- The selected virtual site allows anonymous access. You did not uncheck the Allow anonymous access to this Web Site option in the Web Site Home Directory tab of the site's Properties page in Internet Services Manager.

- The selected virtual site is using port 80. Configure it to use another port number.

If you are using Windows 2000 Professional or Windows XP Professional, you will receive this warning no matter what, as you are only allowed to have one virtual site in IIS.

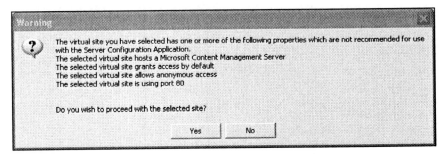

Click Yes to ignore the warning. DCA will proceed.

After the Web Entry Points have been selected, the DCA prompts you for the MCMS System Account. This is the account that you scribbled down in Chapter 2, in the pre-installation step, *Deciding on an MCMS System Account*. The syntax for the user account is DOMAIN\accountname.

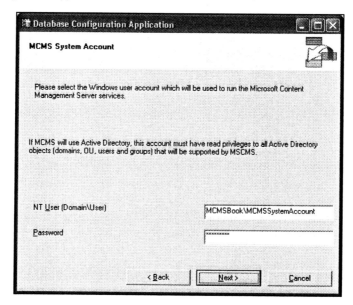

When you have entered the NT User account and password, click Next.

I keep getting the message Unable to authenticate user. Please make sure the account and password are valid. Note: Blank passwords are not valid. I'm running DCA on Windows XP Professional. The username and password entered are correct and not blank. What did I do wrong?

You need to change the security policy on your Windows XP box. To do this:

1. Start the Microsoft Management Console (MMC) by pointing to Start | Run...

2. In the Open field, enter mmc.exe and click OK.

2. Add the Group Policy snap-in.

3. Expand Local Computer Policy | Computer Configuration | Windows Settings | Security Settings | Local Policy | Security Options.

4. Change the option Network access: Sharing and security model for local accounts to Classic – local users authenticate as themselves.

Once this is done, DCA will be able to recognize the username and password that you have entered.

If the MCMS System Account does not have logon locally rights, DCA will prompt you to grant it: The selected user does not have the logon locally right. This right MUST be granted for the DCA to complete. Grant it now? Answer Yes if you get this prompt.

At this point, the DCA will warn you that it is about to stop the World Wide Web Publishing Service: In order to continue, the IIS service and all dependent services must be stopped. Do you want to stop IIS now? Answering No will exit this program. [Yes/No] Click Yes and IIS Admin Service and all dependent services will stop.

Click Select Database to tell MCMS which database in the network to connect to. In this book, we will use the database named TropicalGreen. You can of course, select any appropriate name for your database.

Next, DCA presents the Select Database dialog. Since this is the first time we are running the DCA, it's no surprise to find the currently selected database field empty. We need to fill that in.

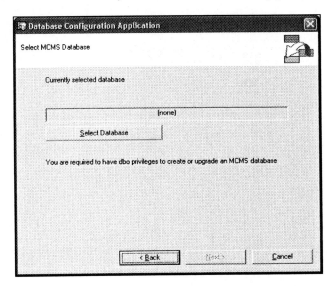

Click Select Database. You are presented with the SQL Server Login dialog as shown in the following figure:

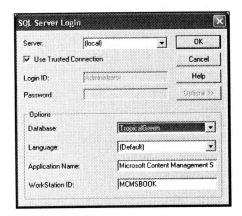

SQL Server can be installed on any machine accessible on the network or the (local) machine. In the Server field, select the name of the server that hosts the SQL Server.

Check the Use Trusted Connection option to use the MCMS System Account to connect to the database. Uncheck it to specify your own SQL user account and password.

Select the database to connect to. After clicking the Options >> button, the dialog expands to reveal more fields. Fill in the blanks using the following table as a guide. Click OK to close the SQL Server dialog box.

Field	Description
Database	Select the database that will act as the content repository for MCMS. We named our database TropicalGreen in Chapter 2. This drop-down list shows only the databases where the MCMS system account or the user shown in the Login ID field has db_owner rights. If you cannot find the database listed in the dropdown, chances are the user chosen to connect to the SQL Server is not a db_owner of it.
	Note: Do not use the (Default), master, tempdb, or msdb databases, or any databases that already contain custom data for other applications.
Language	Choose the language that is supported by the database.
Application Name	This information is used mainly for SQL Server auditing purposes. Unless you have turned that on, the values entered here do not matter.
Workstation ID	

At this point, you may receive an Error verifying rights message. Follow the steps outlined in the section *Assigning Users and Specifying Role Membership to the MCMS Database* in Chapter 2 for the remedy.

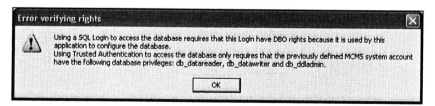

Click Next on the Select MCMS Database dialog to continue. DCA confirms the selection of an empty database and notices that our selected database does not contain the tables, stored procedures, and other settings required by MCMS—it is a fresh setup. It warns us with: The selected database is empty. Do you wish to install the MCMS schema into this empty database?

By 'empty' the DCA means that it cannot find the MCMS tables. Should you select a database that contains existing tables created by you for other applications, DCA will still consider it as empty.

Click Yes to move on to the next screen. Verify that the chosen database is correct and click Next to populate the database. Note that if you have chosen an existing database with other tables, DCA will add all the tables and objects required by MCMS, introducing an unwelcome clutter. In addition, service packs, migration tools, and hot fixes may delete tables not recognized by MCMS, so it is best to use a brand-new database exclusively for MCMS.

Populating the database should be a fairly fast process that lasts about a minute or so.

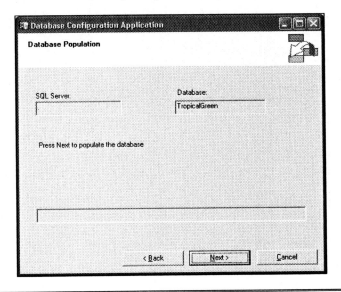

DCA refuses to populate the database. It keeps saying, Must declare the variable @InsertedParentGuid.

This is because the collation or locale setting of the selected database is case sensitive. The database assumes Abc is not the same as ABC. Refer to the SQL Server documentation to find out how you can change the Collation settings of your database.

While attempting to commit changes, DCA throws out one of these errors: ActiveX Component can't create object or Automation error. The specified procedure cannot be found or Run-time error '91' – Object variable or With block variable not set.

You are missing Windows Script 5.6. Fix this either by re-installing Internet Explorer 6.0 with SP1 or by downloading the component directly from Microsoft's website.

Once the database is populated, DCA prompts us for an Administrator account. This account will have full privileges on the MCMS website. You can use this account to log into MCMS and add more administrators later. Most likely you will enter the account name and password of your current Windows login in the format DOMAIN\accountname.

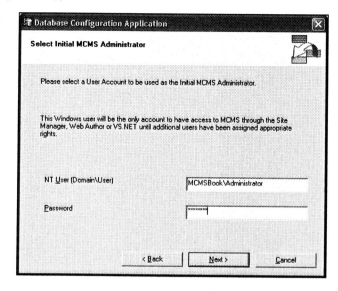

DCA commits the changes and configures Microsoft Content Management Server. When it's ready, DCA asks how you would like to configure Site Stager Access. The decision must be made regardless of whether you have installed the Site Stager component. There are two reasons for this:

1. DCA configures access rights to certain files based on the choice you make here. These access rights are not configured again if you choose to install Site Stager later.
2. If you do not restrict Site Stager access now, instances of Site Stager on client machines would have access to the MCMS server.

Select Yes-Restrict Access to local server machine and click Next.

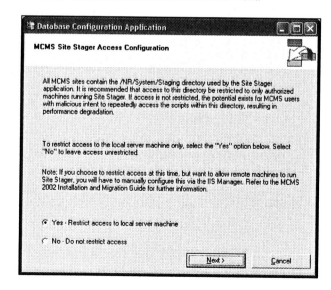

If you are using a local instance of SQL Server and you do not already have the SQL Server Agent Service up and running, a message pops up saying that the SQL Server Agent must be started on the SQL Database. Click Yes.

If you are using a remote instance of SQL Server, you will see a message to remind you to have the SQL Server administrator start the SQL Server Agent.

The SQL Server Agent must run to execute background cleanup tasks on a daily scheduled basis.

And that is it. We have reached the end of the installation process. You can choose to view the log file to review all the above steps. The DCA log file (DCALog.txt) can be found in the MCMS installation directory under the LogFiles folder. The DCA adds further messages to this text file each time it executes.

Uncheck the Launch SCA Now option and press Finish.

Final Steps

After the DCA has successfully linked MCMS to the database, you can optionally revise the rights assigned to the account used to connect to the database:

Authentication Mode	User Account	Database Role Membership
Windows Authentication	MCMS System Account	Remove db_ddladmin rights for the MCMS System Account. The MCMS system account requires db_ddladmin rights only if you are planning to do MCMS site deployment import actions using this account. If this is not a requirement, you may remove this right and leave only the following rights: • db_datareader • db_datawriter • CMSSystem For details on site deployment see Chapter 23.
	The Windows account of the user logged in to run the Database Configuration Application—such as your personal account	Remove the account used to run the DCA from the database. Giving a user that ran the DCA db_owner access to the database means that he or she has permissions to perform the actions of all database roles available (somewhat like being an administrator). This is only required when running the DCA. After you have set up the link between MCMS and the database, you can remove the account from the database if you do not expect the user to run the DCA again.
SQL Authentication	SQL Server Account that will be used to connect to the database.	Remove db_owner rights to the SQL Account specified in the DCA. Assign the following rights to the account instead: • db_datareader • db_datawriter • CMSSytem If you are planning on performing site deployment functions then you will also need to assign the db_ddladmin right to the account.

What is the CMSSystem role?

If you decide to change the user assigned to the MCMS System Account or SQL Server account at a later time, you will find that there is an additional Database Role Membership, CMSSystem, that you must choose.

You must assign the MCMS System Account or SQL Server account to the CMSSystem role in SQL Server. This role does not appear until the DCA has run and populated a blank database with the MCMS tables and stored procedures.

If you do not choose the CMSSystem role, the MCMS Server Configuration Application will not function properly and your MCMS website may throw HTTP 404 (page not found) errors.

Connecting to an Existing MCMS Database

If you already have an MCMS 2002 database, say from another server, you can point MCMS to it instead of an empty database.

Before proceeding, ensure that the MCMS database has been assigned rights as listed in the section *Assigning Users and Specifying Role Membership to the MCMS Database* in Chapter 2.

Start the Database Configuration Application by pointing to Start | Programs | Microsoft Content Management Server | Database Configuration Application. Click Next to get past the splash screen.

DCA asks if it may stop the World Wide Web Publishing Service. Answer Yes. The next screen is the Select Database dialog. There, you will find the name of the database that your MCMS server is currently connected to. To change this database, click Select Database. Fill in the details of the Server location, Database Name and credentials used to authenticate with the server in the SQL Server Login dialog.

Should the selected database be an existing database, DCA would warn you by asking: The selected database already contains the schema for MCMS. Do you wish to continue with this existing MCMS database? Answer Yes.

The next screen asks if you wish to add a Content Management Server Administrator. This question is always asked regardless of whether the database contains records of existing administrators. To add on to the existing list, click Yes and enter the name of a new administrator.

Should you forget the password to the single administrator of your MCMS system, the Add Initial MCMS Administrator dialog would be your life saver. You can add names of new administrators without having to re-install your entire MCMS Server.

You will be prompted to start the SQL Server Agent if it is not already running. After DCA has completed the configuration, click Finish to close it.

Refer Appendix A for details on the upgrade process for upgrading a database from MCMS 2001.

DCA—Behind the Scenes

The DCA is a neat tool that does many tasks through the use of a friendly user interface. At the same time, it hides the complexity of having you add these settings yourself. Let's look under the hood and see what the DCA has done for you.

New Virtual Directories in Internet Service Manager

You can view the new virtual directories from Internet Services Manager. From the Control Panel, select Administrative Tools | Internet Information Services. Look at the new virtual directories created under the Web Entry Points.

> Recall from Chapter 2 that a **Web Entry Point** is a Microsoft Internet Information Services (IIS) website that Microsoft Content Manager (MCMS) 2002 recognizes as configured to support MCMS content. MCMS checks all requests coming to that site to determine if they are MCMS requests or not.

The MCMS Web Entry Point has two new virtual directories:

- NR (mapped to the folder `<install drive>\Program Files\Microsoft Content Management Server\Server\IIS_NR`)
- MCMS (mapped to the folder `<install drive>\Program Files\Microsoft Content Management Server\Server\MCMS`)

The SCA website has a single new virtual directory:

- NRConfig (mapped to `<install drive>\Program Files\Microsoft Content Management Server\Server\NRConfig`)

These were created by selecting the Web Entry Points when running the DCA for the first time.

Additional Database Tables

If you open SQL Server Enterprise Manager, you will see a host of tables required by MCMS that have been added to the TropicalGreen database. Note that writing data to MCMS tables manually is an activity that is not supported by Microsoft! You could break the system by modifying the data without using the Publishing API.

Additional Stored Procedures

With Enterprise Manager still open, click on the Stored Procedures node of the TropicalGreen database. Like all good database applications, MCMS leverages the efficiency of stored procedures to read and write data.

Most of the stored procedures are stored in encrypted format and not readable. You will get the following error message when double-clicking on them.

Background Processing

Within Enterprise Manager, expand the Management | SQL Server Agent node, and click Jobs. A new job has been added to the list. By default, DCA names the new job BGP- followed by the name of the database. For example, if your database is called TropicalGreen, the job will be named BGP-TropicalGreen.

This job will run the necessary background processes on a scheduled basis (by default, this is set to run once a day at 1.00 am) to perform housekeeping duties on the database.

Double-click on the job to open the Properties dialog and select the Steps tab. You see that five tasks are performed by this batch job:

- Process expired pages deletes pages that have expired. This includes all page revisions of the expired pages. By default the job is configured to skip this step. Often it is necessary to keep expired content in the database to reactivate it later or to perform other actions on these items. For this reason this job step is deactivated by default. Otherwise, you may end up with 'missing' pages that have been deleted because they have expired.

- Purge content for deleted pages checks to see if there exists content tied to deleted pages that has not been removed. If it finds any, it removes it.

- Update gallery based resources verifies that the BLOBs are linked to the correct resource gallery item. If there are any discrepancies, it corrects them.

- Purge deleted rights groups from container ACLs looks for traces of containers related to user roles that have been deleted. If it finds any, it removes them.

- Purge data for deleted resources removes attachments and resources that are no longer in use within pages in the system.

> In order for this job to run on a scheduled basis, SQL Server Agent must be started on the Database Server.

Click Cancel to close the Properties dialog. Close Enterprise Manager.

Additional Keys in the Registry

DCA stores some of the answers you give to its questions in the registry. Information such as the connection string, whether or not the Web Entry Point is read-only, and so on can be found in the keys located within the \HKEY_LOCAL_MACHINE\SOFTWARE\NCompass hive of the registry.

Registry values should never be changed directly unless you are absolutely sure about what you are doing. In Chapter 4, we will see how we can use the Server Configuration Application to change some of these values, so you would never normally need to dive into editing the registry at all.

Addition to the Start Menu

Click the Start Menu button and expand Programs. You should see an entry, Microsoft Content Management Server. Expand that and you should find one new option, Server Configuration Application, which will be discussed in the next chapter.

Summary

Running the DCA is the second phase of our MCMS configuration process. The DCA is an application that is used to link MCMS to a backend SQL Server 2000 database. Once the MCMS Server has been set up, developers often use the DCA to toggle between databases when working with different websites.

Now that the DCA has been successfully run, we are almost ready to finish configuring MCMS. The last step is to review the settings in the SCA, which is the subject of the next chapter.

4

The Server Configuration Application

In the previous chapters, you installed MCMS and connected it to a back-end SQL Server database using the Database Configuration Application (DCA).

During the process, you made some basic decisions regarding the way MCMS is configured to run. These and many more settings can be configured using a web interface known as the Server Configuration Application (SCA).

As a developer, you are likely to use the SCA very often to configure options, tune the cache settings, and look for pockets of information that are necessary for setting up your websites. This chapter is designed to walk you through the available options. However, nothing beats getting hands-on experience. Right now, we don't have a website to see the effect these values have on the system. Along the way, we will refer you to chapters that provide a step-by-step guide on how to work with these options on a live website.

Starting the SCA

Start the SCA by pointing to Start | Programs | Microsoft Content Management Server | Server Configuration Application.

The URL behind this shortcut is:

`http://localhost:<Port Number>/NRConfig` (e.g. `http://localhost:8080/NRConfig`).

The port number is that of the SCA web entry point (see Chapter 2).

I can't find the entry for Server Configuration Application on my Start Menu bar.

The option is not available immediately after installing MCMS; it appears only after you have run the DCA successfully at least once.

I keep getting a prompt to enter my username and password when starting the SCA. Even though I enter a correct set of credentials, MCMS keeps telling me that I am Not authorized to view this page.

You must be an administrator of the machine that is running SCA. The files that are used to run the SCA can be found in <install directory>/Microsoft Content Management Server/Server/NRConfig. When you installed MCMS, these files were configured to allow only members of the local administrator group to read and execute. If you are running Windows XP Professional, you may get this error if you are using Simple File Sharing, the default setting in Windows XP.

To disable Simple File Sharing:

1. From the desktop, right-click on My Computer.

2. Go to Tools | Folder Options. Choose the View tab.

3. Scroll down to the bottom of the list and deselect the Use simple file sharing (recommended) checkbox.

4. Click Ok.

The SCA is made up of two sections. The upper section contains information on the current MCMS Server and the database it is connected to. The lower section is organized into tabs:

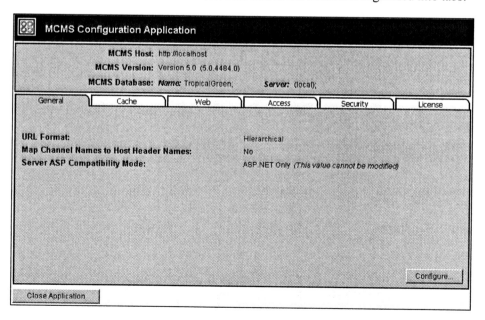

Tab	Description
General	This tab gives access to information about the URL format to be used and whether or not to map host header names to channel names (discussed in Chapter 5). It also tells you the ASP compatibility mode MCMS is running in.
Cache	This tab gives access to information on the location of the local disk cache and its maximum size. It also allows you to configure the size of the memory node cache and also gives you the option to clear it.
Web	This tab lists all virtual websites that are found on the server with options to configure them as an MCMS Web Entry Point
Access	This tab lists all domains that have been configured to be used by MCMS for authentication purposes.
Security	This tab lists the MCMS System Account, Guest access settings, and Web Browser cookie settings
License	This tab displays licensing information including the user name, organization, product ID, and license type.

Launching SCA from a Remote Machine

Out of the box, the SCA runs only from a browser on the local CMS server machine. Special provisions must be made to create a secure network connection (SSL) before you can run it off a remote machine. Without SSL you will get the error message below:

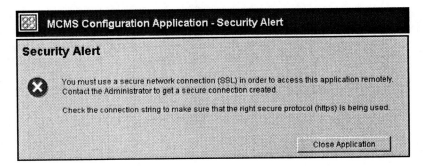

This restriction safeguards you from unauthorized access to information managed by SCA. As you work through this chapter, you will see the list of options that can be configured and the effect each one has on the system. Should hackers sniff the network and get hold of unencrypted data passed over the wire, they might get information about your MCMS configuration including the username and password for the MCMS system account.

Additional security on the SCA is always a good thing. As far as possible, restrict access to just administrators who have local access to the server. Although it is not best practice, there are occasions where the need for remote access to the SCA arises.

About the MCMS Host, Version, and Database

The upper section of the SCA provides you with information regarding the MCMS Host, Version and, Database.

MCMS Host

This entry shows the currently used protocol and server name to access the SCA.

MCMS Version

MCMS 2002 is the fifth version of MCMS. Your version number should begin with 5.x. If it's 4.x, you've got MCMS 2001.

Version Number	MCMS Service Pack Level
5.0.1581.0	No service pack installed
5.0.2284.0	Service Pack 1
5.0.4484.0	Service Pack 1a

MCMS Database

Do you remember the connection to the database that was created in Chapter 3? Well, the information that is stored in there is retrieved by the SCA and lets you easily find out which database you are currently connected to.

> Switching between databases can become confusing. Which database are you currently working with? Check this section of the SCA for the answer.

- **db Type** is short for database (db) type. For MCMS 2002, this value would always be 'SQL Server'. This field was removed in MCMS SP1a.
- **db Name** is the name of the database that MCMS is connected to. In our case, the database's name is TropicalGreen.
- **db Server** is the name of the server that hosts the SQL Server database.

You should always use the DCA/SCA to change any of these values.

> Developers often ask for the code that is used by the SCA to retrieve this information. The code can be found in ASP pages located within the NRConfig folder in the installation directory. The pages access the registry and database records using an undocumented library component (ServerConfigurationAPI.dll). Because ASP files by nature are not compiled, you can view the code that is used to retrieve the information. However, you should not use them within your own applications as doing so would break warranty and support boundaries with Microsoft.

General Settings

When you start the SCA, the first tab opened is the General tab. Here, you can:

- Configure URL Format
- Map Channel Names to Host Header Names

It also shows what Server ASP Compatibility Mode was selected the first time you ran the DCA.

URL Format

MCMS supports two URL formats:

- Hierarchical URLs
- Unique ID-based URLs

Hierarchical URLs

By default, MCMS runs using the Hierarchical option. This means that you can request web pages using a familiar URL format similar to a directory structure. For example, if PageA is located under ChannelA, its URL is: http://hostname/ChannelA/PageA.

These are friendly URLs. You get to see how objects are logically arranged, like a file directory. URLs in this format are easy to remember. They are best used for websites where you want people to remember or even guess the location of pages.

For those of us who are used to working with file-based websites (for example, sites created with FrontPage or Dreamweaver), it does not make sense to have any other way of representing a URL. Why then, do we have Unique ID Based URLs?

Unique ID-Based URLs

Unique ID-Based URLs use a specially generated key known as a GUID to form part of the URL. They typically look like this:

http://hostname/NR/exeres/89837A11-28FF-4E8A-975C-7D1C5BF7B823.htm

where {89837A11-28FF-4E8A-975C-7D1C5BF7B823} is a GUID that acts as a key to represent a specific object in the database.

A popular reason for choosing this style of formatting is to prevent links to your website from other websites or from users' bookmarks from getting broken. Since the URLs are independent of the name and location of the object, the URL remains the same regardless of how the name changes later. You can also move an object from container to container and the URL does not change. It is for this reason that, internally, MCMS formats URLs based on Unique IDs. Even if you have chosen to use Hierarchical URLs, MCMS will convert page requests into Unique ID-based URLs and process them from there. This prevents MCMS-managed links from breaking internally even if you use Hierarchical URLs!

This option is also used by websites that choose to hide the way objects are organized within the site for security or privacy purposes. For example, you may have a page that has the following

URL: http://www.tropicalgreen.net/Secrets/Research/ManEatingPlant.htm. With this URL, it's very easy for people to move back up the folder structure. Once you know that a Secrets folder exists, there is nothing to stop you from entering: http://www.tropicalgreen .net/Secrets. Even if access restrictions have been put in place on the Secrets folder, its existence could be a secret in itself. This is not a problem with unique ID-based URLs because all the reader knows of the Man Eating Plant is its strange looking GUID.

MCMS has built-in security measures. People who are not supposed to see the contents of a particular folder will not see them. We give you the details on how this works in Chapter 10. Although the choice you make here affects the way MCMS generates the URLs of objects, you can access objects using either method. For example, in the address bar of the browser enter:

http://www.tropicalgreen.net/Secrets/Research/ManEatingPlant.htm

or its corresponding Unique ID-based URL:

http://www.tropicalgreen.net/NR/exeres/89837A11-28FF-4E8A-975C-7D1C5BF7B823.htm

Using either URL, MCMS would fetch you the page that you are looking for.

Configuring the URL Format

To configure the URL Format:

1. With the SCA opened, click on the General tab. Click Configure...
2. The General Configuration Dialog opens. In the URL Format field, there are two options you can choose:
   - Hierarchical
   - Unique ID Based
3. When you have made your selection, click OK to close the dialog.

Map Channel Names to Host Header Names

This setting allows you to host more than one MCMS website on a single server. We discuss this feature in depth in Chapter 5, including the correct way to set it up.

Cache Settings

Caching improves the performance of MCMS. The cache speeds up access to content that has already been requested in the past by storing an offline copy on the MCMS server machine, which saves a trip to the database. MCMS uses two modes of caching:

- Local Disk Cache
- Memory Cache

The SCA provides the means to configure the location and maximum size of the local disk cache as well as the maximum number of nodes in the memory cache.

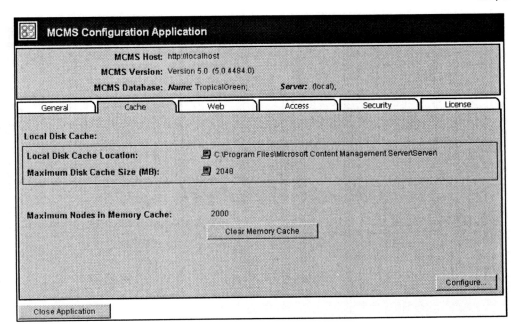

Deciding on the actual values is an art in itself and requires much trial and error before settling on the optimum for your site. We discuss both caching techniques and how to derive the cache values in chapter 22. For now, we will simply show you how these values can be configured.

Configuring Cache Settings

Before we configure the settings, let's review what each setting does.

Local Disk Cache Location

By default, MCMS chooses the location: `<install directory>/Microsoft Content Management Server/Server/` as the directory to store cached files. There are two ways to change this:

- Enter the path directly in the field Local Disk Cache Location.
- Click the Browse button and choose the location of the cache from the Disk Cache Location Browser.

Maximum Disk Cache Size

The default value for the maximum disk cache size is 2048 MB or 2 GB. There are two options:

- Use Global Default: Represented by a globe icon ⊕. When this is selected, all MCMS Servers that share the same MCMS database will share the same maximum disk cache value. Choose this option when you want machines running on a web farm to share values. To change the global value, click Set Global... A dialog appears with a prompt to enter an appropriate value in the Maximum Disk Cache Size field. The size entered is in megabytes. Once updated, all MCMS servers pointing to the same database and configured to use the global default value would automatically use the new value.

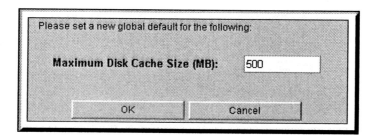

- Use Local Override: Represented by a computer icon . This is the default setting. The maximum disk cache setting is unique to this computer and does not share its value with other computers pointing to the same MCMS database.

Maximum Nodes in Memory Cache

This indicates the maximum number of nodes (or MCMS objects) that will be stored in the server's memory. The default value is 2000. You can change this value by updating the Maximum Nodes in Memory Cache field. As with the maximum disk cache size, you can choose to use the global default settings or use a local override setting.

Clear Memory Cache

The Cache tab also provides a button for clearing the memory cache. This is required when:

- The memory cache is not synchronized with the database
- Tuning the performance of the server

We will reveal more about these scenarios in Chapter 22. Bear in mind that each time you clear the memory cache, MCMS needs to build it up again. With an empty cache, all requests for objects will go directly to the database, affecting the performance of the server.

To clear the memory cache, simply click the Clear Memory Cache button. There isn't any warning or confirmation dialog—the cache clears immediately. You should receive a message that The Microsoft Content Management Server memory cache has been successfully cleared. Only the local memory cache is cleared. So if you need to clear the memory cache on all servers on a web farm, you need to perform this action on each server.

There isn't a similar button on the SCA for emptying the disk cache. To clear the disk cache, you will have to:

1. From the Control Panel, choose Administrative Tools | Services.

2. Stop the World Wide Web Publishing Service.

3. Stop the AESecurityService.

4. If all goes well, all the files in the rdonlyres folder found in the local disk cache location are deleted—if items are left, you can safely remove them now.

5. Start World Wide Web Publishing Service.

6. Start AESecurity Service.

7. Close the Services Console.

And you will have emptied your disk cache.

Now that we have reviewed the options, we return the cache settings to their default values:

1. With the SCA opened, select the Cache tab. Click Configure....
2. You will be presented with the Cache Configuration Dialog:

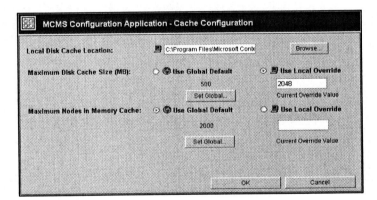

3. When you have made your selection, click OK to close the Cache Configuration dialog.

Web Settings

Internet Information Server (IIS), installed on all versions of Windows Server, is capable of supporting multiple virtual websites on a single server. Each of these websites can be used as a web entry point to serve content managed by MCMS. The Web Settings page shows a list of websites found on your server. It displays the website's name, assigned IP address, and port number and host name. The last column indicates whether or not the website has been configured to be an MCMS web entry point. There are three possible values:

Value	Description
Yes – Read Only	This website can serve content managed by MCMS. Authors cannot modify content, and Administrators cannot connect to the site using Site Manager.
Yes – Read Write	This website can serve content managed by MCMS. Authors can modify content using the Web Author or the Publishing API. Administrators can connect to the site using Site Manager.
No	This website cannot serve content managed by MCMS.

You should see at least one website with Yes marked next to it since you selected a website as an MCMS web entry point when you ran the DCA for the first time. Subsequent execution of the DCA does not provide you with the option to select more websites. If you need to add/remove web entry points, the SCA is the place to do it. Click the Configure... button to add or remove web entry points.

It is possible to configure multiple web entry points. This is a common practice for organizations that require a public viewing website that is Read Only and a separate site for authoring as Read Write. This configuration provides additional security where authors, protected by a corporate firewall, can make modifications to the content. The public can access the same content, but on a different site with read-only permissions.

Another common application for multiple web entry points is the scenario where you need to get a search engine to crawl an authenticated website. You could have one web entry point configured to use Windows authentication and another using forms authentication. The forms-authenticated website is used for browsing and the Windows-authenticated website is used as an entry point for a search crawler (like SharePoint) that cannot deal with forms authentication.

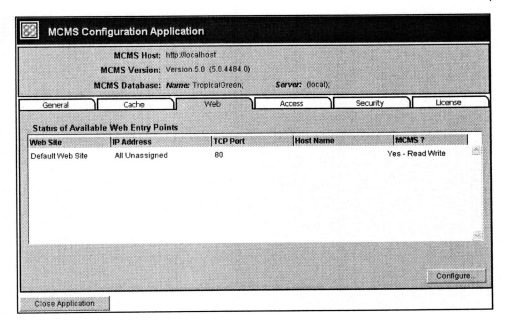

Access Settings

The Access tab displays a list of supported domains. MCMS 2002 supports two types of domains:

- Windows NT Domains
- Windows Active Directory Domains

Take a look at the list of supported Windows NT Domains. The domains of the system account and the initial administrator are listed. These were added during the first run of the DCA.

Only users who belong to the specified domains will have access to the MCMS server.

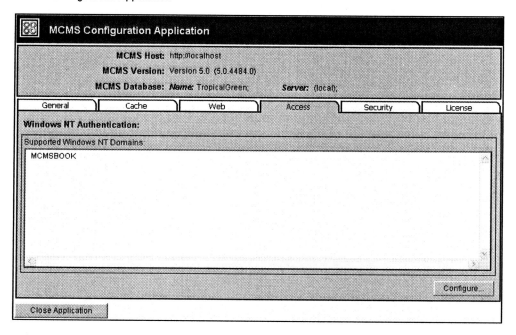

Modifying the List of Domains

With the SCA opened, select the Access tab. Click Configure....

Adding a New Domain

In the field Supported NT Domains enter the NETBIOS/OS name of the domain you wish to add to the list. Click Add.

Alternatively, click Browse to see what domains are available on the network. You will receive a warning that the Windows NT Domain browser can take a significant amount of time to load if there are a substantial number of domains to display. Click OK.

The list of Visible NT Domains displays a list of domains that can be contacted by your server, while the list of Other Supported Windows NT Domains contains domains that were once contactable by your server but are currently unavailable.

Check the domains you wish to add to the list.

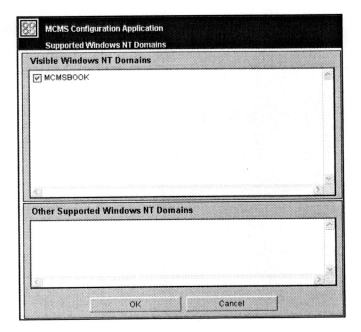

Removing Support for a Domain

Uncheck the domains you wish to remove from the list. Click OK to close the Access dialog.

MCMS 2001 supported LDAP (Lightweight Directory Access Protocol). This was because Microsoft Site Server, a product that has a membership directory that could be integrated with MCMS 2001, used LDAP. As Site Server is becoming obsolete, Microsoft made the decision to remove native support for LDAP authentication in MCMS 2002. However, you can still use LDAP by implementing your own custom authentication system.

Security Settings

The fifth tab in the series is the security tab. It lets you configure the:

- System Account
- Guest Access
- Web Browser Cookie Settings

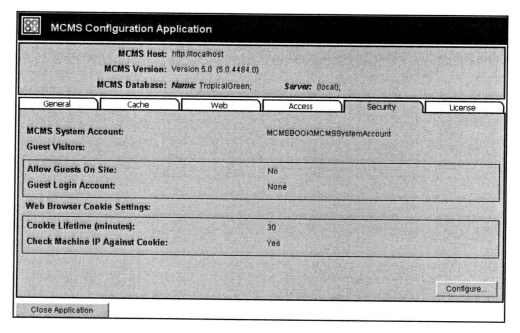

MCMS System Account

One of the things you did when running the DCA for the first time was to specify the MCMS System Account.

The System Account is used for:

- Connecting to the Windows domain or active directory. This is used when browsing the active directory to list users.
- Trusted connections when reading/writing to the back-end SQL Server 2000 database. Only needed when selected to use trusted connections in the DCA.
- Reading the MCMS cache directories.

If, for any reason, the account is not configured correctly or is not given sufficient access privileges to do its work, MCMS will not operate properly.

Configuring the System Account

1. From the SCA, click the Security tab. Click Configure.... The Security Configuration dialog opens.

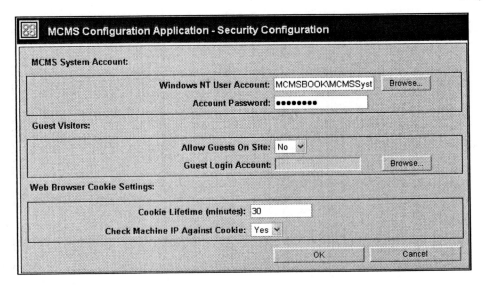

2. In the section for the MCMS System Account:

    • Either enter the name of the Windows NT User Account that would be used as the system account (format: DOMAIN\UserName)
      or
      Click the Browse... button next to the Windows NT User Account field.

    • You will be warned that the Windows NT user browser can take a significant amount of time to load if there are a substantial number of users to display. Click OK.

    • From the list of Window NT domains, select the system account domain.

    • Select the system account from the list of Windows NT Users. If the existing system account does not have the rights to browse the selected Windows Domain/Active Directory, MCMS will not be able to produce this list of users. As a consequence, you won't be able to select the account from the graphical interface.

    • Click OK.

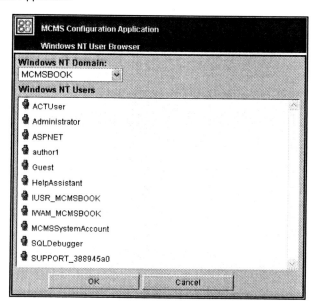

3. Enter the password for the system account.

4. Click OK to close the Security Configuration dialog.

When the Password of the System Account Changes

Bear in mind that changes to the password of the system account are not automatically reflected in the SCA. If for some reason the password to the system account changes, you will have to manually enter the new password via the SCA. Otherwise, MCMS would not have access to key resources. You will be notified with this error message when running Site Manager or within the event log:

> The CMS System Account username or password is incorrect. Please correct this via the SCA. See the Application Event Log for details.

To avoid this problem, Microsoft recommends using a dedicated user account for the system account that is configured not to expire passwords. Otherwise, using your own password or that of another co-worker's account would subject the system account to the same security policies such as changing the password once every other month. To reset the password, open the SCA. A warning message tells you that the system account credentials cannot be used to log into MCMS. Click Configure... and enter the new password and/or user name.

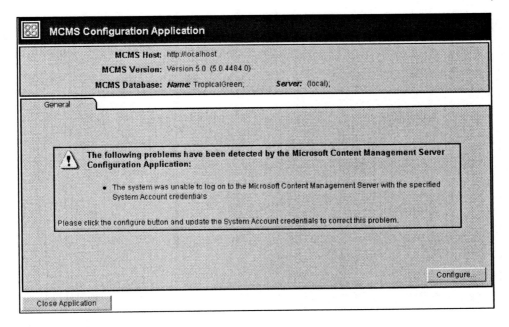

Configuring Guest Access

This is where you can set MCMS to allow visitors to view the site without entering a user name or password. MCMS identifies these visitors as guests. Clearly, most public websites are set up for guests such that authentication is not required to view content. By default, however, MCMS does not allow unauthenticated visitors to enter the website. As setting up a guest account involves more than specifying an account in the SCA, we cover this in Chapter 10.

Web Browser Cookie Settings

Cookie settings apply when you use forms-based authentication—one of the modes of authentication available with MCMS 2002. In forms-based authentication, users enter their user name and password on a web form. When MCMS determines that the credentials entered are correct, two things happen:

1. MCMS issues a cookie to the user.
2. As the user continues surfing the site, requesting web pages, the browser will automatically send this cookie back to MCMS, which uses it to validate each request.

The concept is quite similar to visiting some theme parks. To enter the park, you buy an entrance ticket. Each time you want to enter an attraction within the park, you show your ticket to the gatekeeper. So long as your ticket is valid, you may visit as many attractions as you are entitled to. In MCMS, the cookie acts as your ticket to the content stored in its repository. The default MCMS cookies are stored on the user's computer in memory (session cookies). If you look inside your temporary folder, you will not find the cookie there. Therefore, each time you close your browser and open it again, you must re-enter your user name and password. If you create your own login form you can set the option to create a persistent cookie rather than a session cookie.

83

Cookie Lifetime

Because cookies are stored on the user's computer, there should be some form of lifetime limit. Otherwise, the user would have access to the resources for as long as he or she leaves their browser open. Among other possibilities, unauthorized personnel may gain access to a co-worker's opened session while they are out for lunch or in the bathroom. The cookie lifetime determines how long a cookie remains valid. By default, this is set to 30 minutes. After 30 minutes of inactivity, the cookie would expire. Users would be forced to re-enter their user name and password before accessing content. In MCMS 2001, the default value for cookie lifetime was 720 minutes or 12 hours.

Cookie Validation by Machine IP

Each cookie contains the IP Address of the user. When set to Yes (the default value), MCMS checks the cookie to ensure that the IP address does not change. Should it detect a change of IP address, the user would be requested to re-enter their user name and password. This provides an additional layer of security, preventing a hacker (on a computer with a different IP address) from hijacking the session of an authenticated user.

There are occasions when you would want to turn this option off. Some Internet Service Providers change the IP address of users each time a HTTP request is made. Also if the request passes a proxy array, the IP address seen by the server can be that of any of the array members. So if you require internet users to authenticate themselves before visiting your website, it is best to leave this option unchecked. Otherwise, a portion of users would have to continuously enter their credentials each time they request a page.

License Settings

The License tab displays the:

- User Name
- Company Name
- Product ID
- License Type

These values were entered when installing MCMS. You can't change them unless you re-install the software. The License Type indicates which edition of MCMS was installed. Except for the Standard Edition (which offers a trimmer version of MCMS), all other versions function exactly the same way. The differences are purely on paper and are related to legal issues. Ensure that you have the license for the copy that you are running.

Summary

In this chapter, you learned about which settings are managed by the Server Configuration Application, and a little about how and why each setting is important. In later chapters, we will return to the SCA to make changes and explain more about the importance of each feature.

5
Setting Up a Website from Scratch

You have formed a great team of developers, met with the end users, gathered their requirements, and even completed the initial drafts of the project specifications. Everything is on schedule and happening quickly. Now people are looking to you and your team to build that website.

No sweat, you say. This can't be too difficult. There's a sample that ships with Microsoft Content Management Server 2002. All you need to do is to rename the sample site, move some objects around and voilà! The site will work.

But what happens if your requirements don't exactly match those of the sample site? You need to list pictures next to abstracts in the summary page and implement a navigation scheme that uses pop-up menus instead of trees. Your product page requires a different template. The differences are endless. Getting it to morph into the website as described in your requirements specifications proves to be a major re-coding session.

Instead of showing you the sample site as a place to begin with, we prefer to start right from the beginning—the step after you have installed MCMS on your development machine: An empty database, a non-existent project, a clean start.

Laying the Foundations

Let's begin building the foundation for the TropicalGreen site. We assume that you have the specifications of the project and the task at hand will be to construct the website.

Here are the main ingredients to the foundation:

- Design and build the channel structure
- Design and build the template and resource gallery structure
- Create the web project
- Build the home page
- Set the authentication mode

Designing and Building the Channel Structure

It is always a good idea to draw out the entire channel structure for the website before you begin. This is because the ways channels are arranged in the hierarchy defines their addresses (or URLs).

The scenario we are describing uses the Hierarchical URL format, discussed in the previous chapter: `http://localhost/ChannelName/PostingName.htm`

Have a look at the channel structure of a typical website shown below.

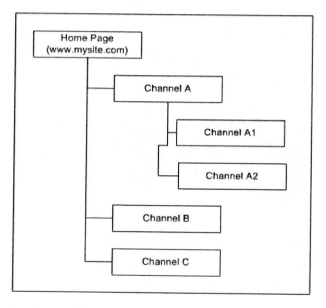

Channel A sits directly below the Home Page. This gives it the URL `http://www.mysite.com/ChannelA/`.

Channel A1 sits below Channel A. So it has the URL `http://www.mysite.com/ChannelA/ChannelA1/`.

The deeper the channel is within the hierarchy, the longer its address. Burying your channels under more layers of channels makes navigation more complex. If you can, avoid creating complicated nested hierarchies.

> The Three-Click Rule of web design recommends that visitors should get to their destination within three clicks from the home page. While it may be considered unrealistic by some, it raises a valid point: Users are easily confused by complicated navigation embedded many levels deep. Avoid building channel hierarchies that are more than three levels deep if you plan on applying this rule to your website. Keep it shallow!

If you really need to nest your channels within a mountain of other channels, explore other navigation aids like a BreadCrumb or a Navigation Tree (see Chapter 13). A powerful search engine also helps users get information quickly.

Channel Naming Guidelines

Since the channel's name is used to generate URLs, they should be short and sweet, and channel names have a maximum length of 100 characters. Anything above 100 characters in length is truncated by MCMS.

The character length limitation applies only for names. If you need to give your channels longer names or names that include characters outside those permitted for URLs, use the Display Name property instead.

When planning the site navigation structure, bear in mind that certain characters are forbidden for use within channel names.

Only the characters listed below are allowed. Other characters are not.

- a-z
- A-Z
- 0-9
- [ ] ( )
- . –
- space

There is also the restriction that you can't end the channel name with a period. Neither can you use two consecutive periods. This makes a whole lot of sense when you consider that all names are transformed into addresses and are required to have a valid URL syntax.

One last note about names: Avoid using spaces. MCMS converts spaces to + signs, so that Plant Catalog becomes Plant+Catalog. Don't confuse your visitors with URLs that contain spaces. Think about it; if you want to find out more about TropicalGreen, which of these do you find easier to type, remember, and is better eye candy? `http://tropicalgreen/PlantCatalog` or `http://tropicalgreen/Plant+Catalog` or in the URL-encoded form `http://tropicalgreen/Plant%20Catalog`.

Do yourself and your visitors a favor and avoid spaces in channel names!

Can a channel contain multiple sub-channels that share the same name?

Although MCMS allows administrators to create channels that have the same name within the same parent container—don't do it. Doing this will just confuse you later when trying to access the content in your repository. When attempting to retrieve a channel based on its path, MCMS will return the first channel it sees. The only way to retrieve the other one with the duplicate name would be to use its unique-ID-based URL

It's All for Display

With so many restrictions on channel names, where can we store the 'friendly' name that should be displayed as the text of hyperlinks pointing to this channel? Well, that's what the Display Name is for. All channels have a Display Name along with the standard Name property. The Display Name, as the name suggests, is used for display purposes. You can store almost all characters in display names. Names full of spaces and otherwise illegal characters, or French names, Japanese names, Swahili names—you name it, it stores it. Just don't sneak in control characters (ASCII values 1-31); that won't work.

There's a generous limit of 250 characters for a display name. You shouldn't need to have a name that long. Even the world's longest place name (and domain name if you add ".com" to the end) Llanfairpwllgwyngyllgogerychwyrndrobwyll-llantysiliogogogoch (It does exist! It's the name of a town in North Wales) contains only 60 characters (Add four more to include .com). If you do find one and it's still pronounceable in a single breath, drop us an e-mail, we'd be interested to know.

The Channel Structure

Since we now know that the channel hierarchy determines the navigation structure, let's build our channels based on the storyboard of the TropicalGreen site:

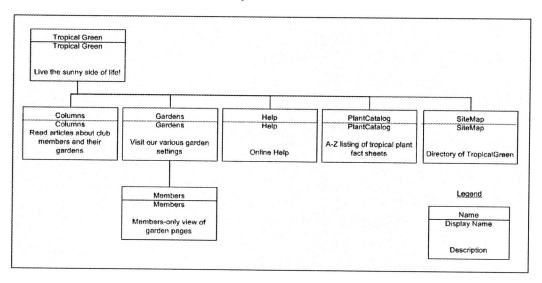

Armed with this blueprint, let's begin building channels.

Building Channels with Site Manager

We'll use Site Manager to build the containers for the TropicalGreen site. Let's start with the topmost channel, the TropicalGreen channel.

1. From the Start menu, select Programs | Microsoft Content Management Server | Site Manager. If you are running Site Manager for the first time or have applied the SP1a service pack, you may be prompted for a server name. Enter localhost and the port number of the MCMS Web Entry Point if you changed it from the default. Click OK to continue.

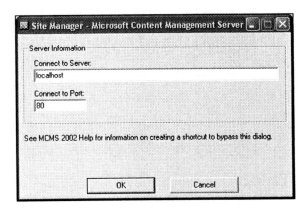

How can I bypass the Server Information dialog?

To bypass the Server Information dialog you need to specify the server name and port number in the shortcut that points to Site Manager:

Right-click on the shortcut to Site Manager and select Properties.

The value in the Target field contains the file path and name of the Site Manager executable (nrclient.exe) followed by the URL to the login.asp script. Modify the URL to the login.asp script to match the server name and port number of the MCMS server you wish to work with. This can be localhost or a remote server. For example:

```
"c:\Program Files\Microsoft Content Management Server\Client\nrclient.exe"
http://localhost:80/NR/System/ClientUI/login.asp
```

or:

```
"c:\Program Files\Microsoft Content Management Server\Client\nrclient.exe"
http://www.tropicalgreen.net:4321/NR/System/ClientUI/login.asp
```

Click OK to close the properties window.

The next time you click on the shortcut to Site Manager, the Server Information dialog will be skipped. If you manage multiple MCMS servers, you can create multiple Site Manager shortcuts, each with a different server name and port number.

2. Log in as the administrator. In Chapter 2, you gave yourself administrator privileges, so select Logon as <yourusername> and click Start on the Site Manager login page.

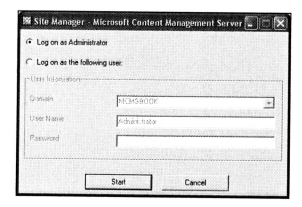

3. In the channel tree, right-click on the channel called Channels. A pop-up menu appears. Select the New Channel option.

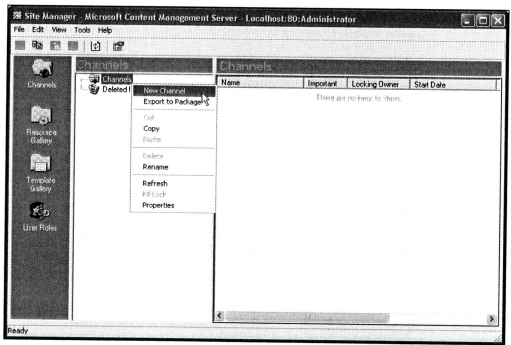

4. In the New Channel dialog, set the Name to TropicalGreen and the Display Name to Tropical Green.

5. Give it a simple Description: Live the sunny side of life!

6. Click OK.

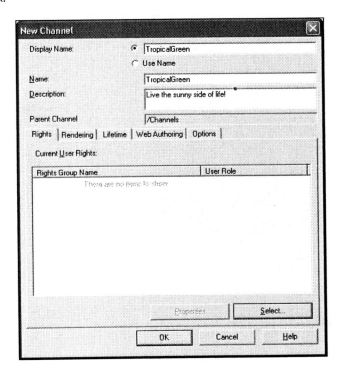

7. The TropicalGreen channel is created.

You probably noticed several other properties in the New Channel dialog beside Name and Display Name. The table below contains descriptions for these properties.

Property	Description
Name	See section Channel Naming Guidelines for an explanation of theName.
Display Name	See section It's all for Display for an explanation of the Display Name.
Description	This gives you a space to describe in less than 500 characters what this channel is about.
Rendering	This sets properties to define the page that is delivered to visitors when someone requests the channel, rather then one of the postings inside the channel. More about this in Chapter 9.

Property	Description
Lifetime	This sets the lifespan of the channel. You can adjust the start and stop dates. A channel will not appear on the published site if the current date is not between these two dates.
	By default, the start date is set to be immediate and the stop date to never.
	Never is a long time. Internally the end date is set to 1st Jan 3000. That's a pretty long lifespan for a system to have; for our generation, medical breakthroughs not withstanding, this is as good as never.
Web Authoring	You can set the default template and resource galleries here. Again, we'll discuss these fields more in Chapter 9.
Options	This gives you the option to flag the channel as an:
	Important channel
	Hidden channel (hide it from the navigation)
	It also gives you the option to set some parameters that affect how search engines index the channel.
	The Web Robots Can Crawl Links option and Web Robots can Index this channel's Navigation option work together to create the tag `<meta name="ROBOTS" content="FOLLOW,INDEX">` when both are turned on.

There is one more tab for Channel User Rights. This is where you can set permissions on the channel level.

Based on our blueprint, there are quite a few channels to create. Refer to the blueprint to create each of them below the TropicalGreen channel such that the listing of channels appears as shown in the following figure:

Designing and Building the Template and Resource Gallery Structure

We know from Chapter 1 that template galleries store templates, and resource galleries store resources (such as images, attachments, and video files).

Designing the Gallery Structure for Authors

The people who benefit most from a well designed gallery structure are the authors; without a well designed gallery structure they would have to search through the entire MCMS database looking for the right template or resource to use when creating or updating a posting. Therefore, organize templates and resources in ways that are intuitive to authors. We give some tips on how you can do this in the following sections.

Organizing by Website Structure

The most instinctive way to design galleries is to group them according to the website structure. Let's try this for the TropicalGreen website.

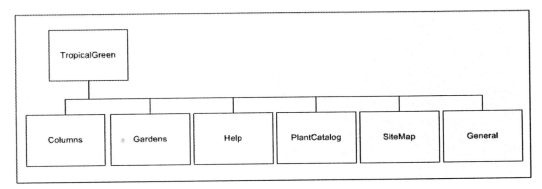

> Unlike channels, galleries do not have a Display Name property.

If you've read the last section, this design should look familiar to you. It's basically a cut and paste from the channel structure we designed earlier. We added a gallery called General to hold templates/resources that don't fall into any of the categories.

With this design, authors are likely to find the templates or resources they need just by understanding the channel structure. They first think of the channel they want to post to, then look for the corresponding template or resource in the gallery.

This works fine for our little gardening society. However, for a large organization with many departments, each with an individual substructure, this design may not work. For such cases, it could be more intuitive to group templates and resources by departments (or functional areas).

Organizing by Functional Areas

In larger organizations it may be more practical to cluster galleries by departments.

Here's how it works for the TropicalGreen site. We first identify the people who will be adding content to the website. From your interviews with the committee, you know that there are only two groups of people:

- The Communications Department
- The Research Department

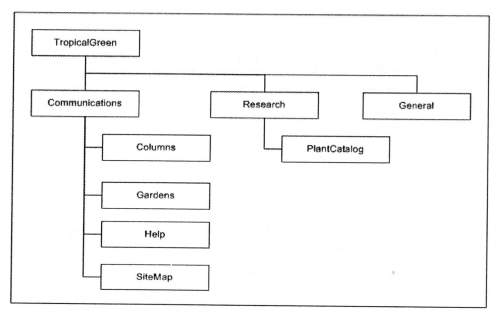

We create a gallery for each group of users and then place sub-galleries under each of the main galleries that correspond with the content that they will contain. So the Communications department will have templates or resources for the Columns section in their gallery, and so on.

As before, we add a gallery named General to contain any templates/resources that do not fall into any of the existing categories.

In this book, to keep the structure as simple as possible, we will create our template and resource galleries based on the structure of the website.

Building Template Galleries with Site Manager

Like before, we'll use Site Manager to build the template galleries. Let's start with the topmost channel, the TropicalGreen template gallery.

1. Within Site Manager, select Template Gallery in the panel on the left hand of the screen.
2. In the template gallery tree, right-click on the gallery called Templates.
3. A pop-up menu appears. Select New | Gallery.

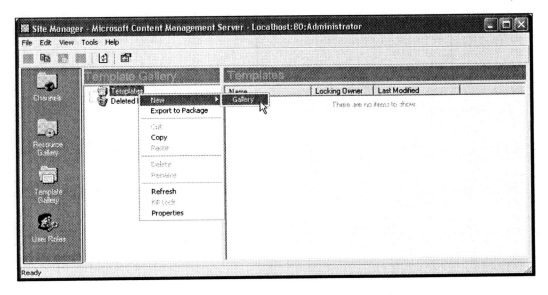

4. In the New Template Gallery dialog, set the Name to TropicalGreen.
5. Give it a simple Description, e.g. Contains templates for TropicalGreen.
6. Click OK.

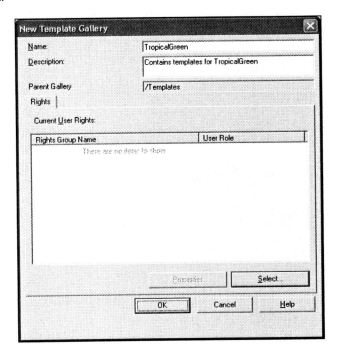

7. The TropicalGreen template gallery is created.

8. Repeat steps 1-6 and create the following galleries below the new TropicalGreen template gallery.

Template Gallery Name	Template Gallery Description
General	Contains generic templates for TropicalGreen
Columns	Contains templates for the Columns section
Gardens	Contains templates for the Gardens section
PlantCatalog	Contains templates for the Plant Catalog section

Compared with channels, template galleries do not have many properties you can set: You can only set the Name and Description.

Property	Description
Name	See section *Channel Naming Guidelines* (which also applies to template galleries) for an explanation of the Name.
Description	Gives you a place to describe (in less than 255 characters) details such as what this template gallery contains, who has rights to use the templates within, and so on.

Like channels, template galleries have a Current User Rights tab where you can set permissions on who should have rights to use the templates within the gallery. We will discuss this in Chapter 10. The complete template gallery structure is shown in the following figure.

Building Resource Galleries with Site Manager

Like template galleries, resource galleries are created using Site Manager:

1. In Site Manager, select Resource Gallery in the bar on the left hand of the screen.

2. In the resource gallery tree, right-click on the gallery called Resources.

3. A pop-up menu appears. Select New | Gallery.

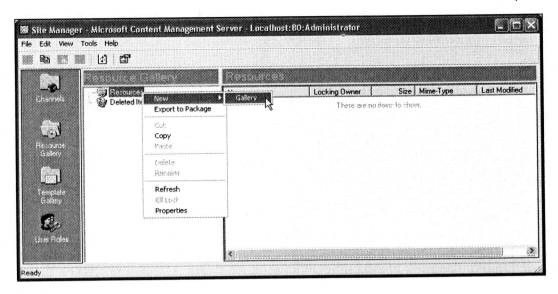

4. In the New Resource Gallery dialog, set the Name to TropicalGreen.

5. Give it a simple Description, e.g. Contains resources for TropicalGreen.

6. Click OK.

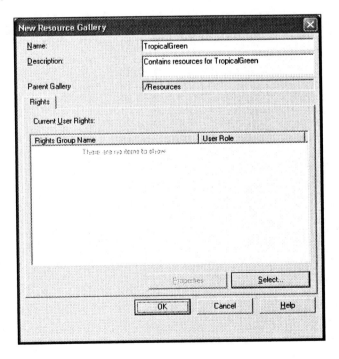

The TropicalGreen resource gallery is created. Repeat steps 1-6 and create the following galleries below the new TropicalGreen resource gallery.

Resource Gallery Name	Resource Gallery Description
General	Contains generic resources for TropicalGreen
Columns	Contains resources for the Columns section
Gardens	Contains resources for the Gardens section
PlantCatalog	Contains resources for the Plant Catalog section

The complete resource gallery structure is shown below.

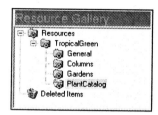

Like template galleries, only the Name and Description properties for resource galleries can be set:

Property	Description
Name	See section *Channel Naming Guidelines* (which also applies to resource galleries) for an explanation of the Name.
Description	Gives you a space to describe in less than 255 characters what this resource gallery contains and who has rights to use the resources within.

Creating the TropicalGreen Project in Visual Studio .NET

If you've gone through the earlier sections of this chapter, you have now created the structure in MCMS for channels and galleries. Now, let's get on with the final bit: Creating the project file for TropicalGreen.

This is a two step process:

1. Create the TropicalGreen Project in Visual Studio .NET
2. Set up folders within the TropicalGreen project to organize our template files, stylesheets, and other project files.

Using Visual Studio .NET to Create the TropicalGreen Project

1. From the Start Menu, select Programs | Microsoft Visual Studio .NET. | Microsoft Visual Studio .NET.

2. From the toolbar, select File | New | New Project.

3. The New Project dialog appears. Select Content Management Server Projects | Visual C# Projects. Choose MCMS Web Application.

4. Set the location to: http://localhost/TropicalGreen.

5. Click OK.

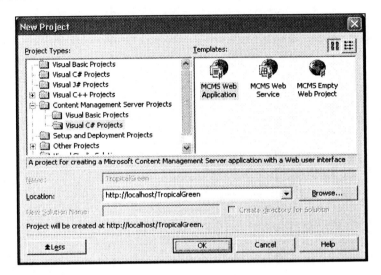

6. The TropicalGreen project is created in the %sysdir%/inetpub/wwwroot/tropicalgreen directory.

> If Content Management Server Projects is not listed in this dialog, the MCMS developer tools are not installed or not registered correctly. Visual Studio .NET needs to be installed before MCMS. This problem also occurs when Visual Studio .NET is re-installed without re-installing the MCMS developer tools as well.

Creating Folders for Template Files and Stylesheets in the TropicalGreen Project

1. In the Solution Explorer, right-click the TropicalGreen project. Select Add | New Folder.

2. Name the new folder Templates. A new folder for storing templates is created.

3. Repeat steps 1-2 to create a folder named Styles. The Styles folder will store all stylesheets.

4. Repeat steps 1-2 to create a folder name Images. The Images folder will store all *.gif and *.jpg files used by the template files.

5. Repeat steps 1-2 to create a folder named UserControls. The UserControls folder will store all user control files (*.ascx).

The solution should contain the folders as shown in the following figure:

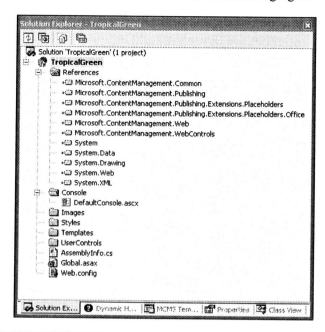

When attempting to create an MCMS Project, Visual Studio .NET returns the error: Could not create virtual directory 'http://localhost/project/CMS' in location (install directory)\Microsoft Content Management Server\Server\IIS_CMS\.

Only local websites can be enabled as MCMS projects. Check that you are creating the project in the location: `http://localhost/projectname` and not `http://localhost/projectname/` (note the last slash) or `http://servername/projectname` or `http://domainname/projectname`.

Only the default website running on port 80 is officially supported by the MCMS developer tools. But you can make them work with other websites if you ensure that the port number of the website being accessed is unique. Other websites on the same server (including those that have been stopped) must not have the same port number.

Also if using a website other than the default website, there are a couple of things that you will have to do to get Visual Studio to work correctly:

Look up the registry hive at the location `HKEY_LOCAL_MACHINE/SOFTWARE/NCompass/Resolution ContentServer/Configuration/0/EntryPoints`.

Each MCMS Web Entry Point has a numbered key there. Look for the key your website is using. For example, the second website could have the `InstanceId` of 1027671297 as shown in the following diagram:

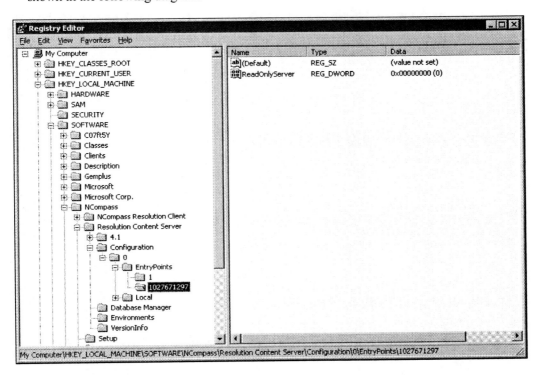

In the `<Install folder>\Microsoft Content Management Server\DevTools` folder, make a backup copy of `DeveloperTools.xml`, then open the original version and comment out the following code:

```
<!--<CMSENVIRONMENT>
<SERVER BaseUrl="http://localhost" InstanceId="1" />
<TEMPLATE QueryString="" />
</CMSENVIRONMENT>-->
```

Below the code, add a `<CMSEnvironment>` tag with the `InstanceId` set to that of the Web Entry Point located in the previous step:

```
<CMSENVIRONMENT>
<SERVER BaseUrl="http://localhost" InstanceId="1027671297" />
<TEMPLATE QueryString="" />
</CMSENVIRONMENT>
```

What the MCMS Project Creation Wizard Does

The MCMS Project Creation Wizard does several things:

- Adds References to MCMS libraries
- Adds references to Assemblies and HttpModules to the web.config file
- Creates a Default Console, which you can use for your templates
- Adds the CMS virtual directory to the template project

In the next sections, we highlight the more important tasks it has done with regards to the above four areas.

Adds References to MCMS Libraries

If you still have the TropicalGreen project file opened, expand the References node.

A MCMS project contains the following references:

- Microsoft.ContentManagement.Common
- Microsoft.ContentManagement.Publishing
- Microsoft.ContentManagement.Publishing.Extensions.Placeholders
- Microsoft.ContentManagement.Publishing.Extensions.Placeholders.Office
- Microsoft.ContentManagement.Web
- Microsoft.ContentManagement.WebControls

You can find all these libraries in the <Install folder>\Microsoft Content Management Server\Server\bin directory.

Adds References to Assemblies and HttpModules in the Web.config File

Have a look at the web.config file. In there you will see that some assemblies have been added between the <compilation> and </compilation> tags. These are:

```
<compilation defaultLanguage="c#" debug="true">
<assemblies>
    <add assembly="Microsoft.ContentManagement.Common,
        Version=5.0.1200.0,
        Culture=neutral,
        PublicKeyToken=31bf3856ad364e35" />
    <add assembly="Microsoft.ContentManagement.Publishing,
        Version=5.0.1200.0,
        Culture=neutral,
        PublicKeyToken=31bf3856ad364e35" />
    <add assembly =
        "Microsoft.ContentManagement.Publishing.Extensions.Placeholders,
        Version=5.0.1200.0,
        Culture=neutral,
        PublicKeyToken=31bf3856ad364e35" />
    <add assembly =
        "Microsoft.ContentManagement.Publishing.Extensions.Placeholders.Office,
        Version=5.0.1200.0,
        Culture=neutral,
        PublicKeyToken=31bf3856ad364e35" />
```

```
    <add assembly="Microsoft.ContentManagement.Web,
         version=5.0.1200.0,
         Culture=neutral,
         PublicKeyToken=31bf3856ad364e35" />
    <add assembly="Microsoft.ContentManagement.WebAuthor,
         version=5.0.1200.0,
         Culture=neutral,
         PublicKeyToken=31bf3856ad364e35" />
    <add assembly="Microsoft.ContentManagement.WebControls,
         version=5.0.1200.0,
         Culture=neutral,
         PublicKeyToken=31bf3856ad364e35" />
    <add assembly="Microsoft.Web.UI.WebControls,
         version=1.0.2.226,
         Culture=neutral,
         PublicKeyToken=31bf3856ad364e35" />
</assemblies>
</compilation>
```

When compiled, these assemblies are automatically linked to the project and guarantee that all ASPX pages within the project have access to the assemblies.

> Notice that the assemblies are added in two places. Once beneath the References node of the project and again in the web.config file. Why are the assemblies added twice?
>
> When you add the reference to the References node, you allow code-behind files (think *.cs) to access the assemblies. When the reference is added to the web.config file, all ASPX files (think *.aspx) have access to the assemblies.

Scroll down to the bottom of the web.config file. Notice that an entire section, between <httpModules> and </httpModules> tags, has been added. These are the assemblies that handle and filter client requests.

```
<httpModules>
<add type="Microsoft.ContentManagement.Web.Security.CmsAuthorizationModule,
         Microsoft.ContentManagement.Web,
      version=5.0.1200.0, Culture=neutral,
      PublicKeyToken=31bf3856ad364e35"
      name="CmsAuthorizationModule" />
<add type="Microsoft.ContentManagement.Web.CmsEndRequestModule,
         Microsoft.ContentManagement.Web,
      version=5.0.1200.0,
      Culture=neutral,
      PublicKeyToken=31bf3856ad364e35"
      name="CmsEndRequestModule" />
<add type="Microsoft.ContentManagement.Publishing.Events.PostingEventsModule,
         Microsoft.ContentManagement.Publishing,
      version=5.0.1200.0,
      Culture=neutral,
      PublicKeyToken=31bf3856ad364e35"
      name="CmsPosting" />
<add type="Microsoft.ContentManagement.Web.Caching.CmsCacheModule,
         Microsoft.ContentManagement.Web,
      version=5.0.1200.0,
      Culture=neutral,
      PublicKeyToken=31bf3856ad364e35"
      name="CmsCacheModule" />
</httpModules>
```

Creates a Default Console for your Templates

Now look at the Solution Explorer. Notice that there is a folder there called `Console`. In it, you will find a user control, `DefaultConsole.ascx`. This console will be used by all your templates to provide authoring functions.

Creates a Link to the CMS Virtual Directory

There's one last thing that the wizard does for you. Open the Internet Information Services (IIS) Manager and navigate to the TropicalGreen virtual directory. Expand it. Do you see a virtual directory called `CMS`? Right-click on this CMS virtual directory. It points to the `IIS_CMS` directory in `<Install folder>\Microsoft Content Management Server\Server`. Within the folder are files that provide MCMS-related functionality.

Setting the Authentication Mode

For ease of development, we're going to use Integrated Windows Authentication. This means that the credentials used to authenticate you with the MCMS server are the same as used when you signed on to Windows. It's a single-sign-on feature and is a convenient solution for our testing.

Configuring Internet Information Services for Integrated Windows Authentication

To configure Integrated Windows authentication:

1. Open Internet Information Services Manager.
2. In the Tree on the left-hand panel, right-click on the TropicalGreen virtual directory. Select Properties from the pop-up menu.
3. The TropicalGreen Properties dialog appears. Select the Directory Security tab. In the Anonymous access and authentication control section, click on the Edit... button.
4. The Authentication Methods dialog opens. Ensure that the Integrated Windows authentication option is checked. Also ensure that Anonymous access and Basic authentication are *not* checked. Click OK.

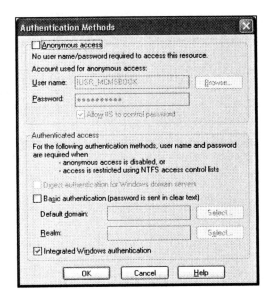

5. Click OK to close the TropicalGreen Properties dialog.

6. In the Tree on the left-hand panel, right-click on the MCMS virtual directory. Select Properties from the pop-up menu.

7. The MCMS Properties dialog appears. Select the Directory Security tab. In the Anonymous access and authentication control section, click on the Edit... button.

8. The Authentication Methods dialog opens. Ensure that the Anonymous access option *is* checked. Click OK to close the Authentication Methods dialog.

9. Click OK to close the MCMS Properties dialog.

10. Repeat steps 6-9 for the NR virtual directory.

Verify Settings in the Web.Config File

Next, we need to check the web.config file. Open the web.config file and scroll to the section that contains the <authentication> tag. By default, the MCMS creation wizard sets the authentication mode to Windows.

```
<!-- AUTHENTICATION This section sets the authentication policies of the
application. Possible modes are "Windows", "Forms", "Passport" and "None" -->
<authentication mode="Windows" />
```

We will change this setting in Chapter 18 when we turn on Guest access and use forms to authenticate members of the TropicalGreen society.

Setting up a Multi-Developer Environment

Your box is successfully set up with an empty shell of the TropicalGreen website. Now, what happens if a co-worker wants to work on this project together with you?

The very first thing they will need to do is to set up their machine as described in Chapters 2-4. Every developer needs to have a local instance of MCMS, because the MCMS developer tools for Visual Studio .NET cannot access a remote MCMS server.

Next, upload the project you created previously on your machine to a Visual Source Safe database. You can use another source control program if you prefer, but we will specifically cover the steps for using Source Safe here. Other source control programs, like **Rational ClearCase** or **Merant PVCS**, should have similar setup procedures.

Visual Source Safe manages your source code. All ASP, ASP.NET pages, image files, XML files, and other files used within the project can be stored inside Visual Source Safe and checked in or checked out by developers. This ensures that at any one time, only one developer is working on the file. It also has a version control system. You can roll back changes, and make comparisons to see which lines of code were amended and when. We choose Visual Source Safe because it is fully integrated with Visual Studio .NET.

Where can I get a copy of Visual Source Safe?

Visual Source Safe ships with the Enterprise Architect and Enterprise Developer editions of Visual Studio .NET. In order to follow the rest of this section, you will need to have a Visual Source Safe server set up. For details on how this is done, visit the Microsoft Visual Source Safe site (`http://msdn.microsoft.com/vstudio/previous/ssafe/`).

Ensure that DCA Points to the Common Development Database

Open the MCMS Database Configuration Application and use it to point to the database server used by the central development machine. For more information on how this is done, see Chapter 3.

Add the Existing Project to Visual Source Safe

Because Visual Source Safe is tightly integrated with Visual Studio .NET, adding the TropicalGreen solution created earlier to the Source Safe Database requires only a few steps:

1. With the solution opened in Visual Studio .NET, select File | Source Control and choose the Add Solution to Source Control option from the toolbar.
    You may receive a warning saying that you will no longer be able to open the project using FrontPage Web Access. Just click Continue if so.

2. The next screen requests your username, password, and the location of the source safe database. When you have supplied these values, click OK.

3. In the Add to SourceSafe project dialog, give a name to the Visual Source Safe project. This is just a folder in the Visual Source Safe database that stores your project. In this case, an appropriate name would be TropicalGreen.root. Click OK.

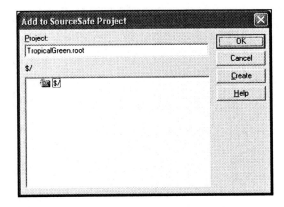

4. You get a warning saying that the project does not exist in Visual Source Safe. Click Yes to create it.

The project is now under source control. All developers, including you, will now need to check files out from the Source Safe database to work on them and check in after the changes are finished so other developers may check them out.

Opening a Source-Controlled Project for the First Time

Once your co-worker has completed the setup of MCMS on their work machine, several things need to be done:

1. Start Visual Studio .NET.

2. From the toolbar, select Source Control | Open From Source Control...

> If all the options are grayed out, it means that you have not installed the Visual Source Safe Client tools. The setup file will be located at Microsoft Visual Studio/VSS/ NetSetup.exe on the server that contains the Visual Source Safe database.

3. If you are prompted for your login and password, enter the credentials provided by the Visual Source Safe Administrator.

   Click the Browse... button to look for the Visual Source Safe database. By default, the database is installed in the /Microsoft Visual Studio/VSS/ directory and referenced by the srcsafe.ini file of the host server. The administrator can create a separate srcsafe.ini in a separate directory. Do check with him or her first before proceeding.

   Click OK.

4. The Create Local Project from SourceSafe dialog appears.

    Next to the field Create a new project in this folder click the Browse... button. Set the working directory to the directory of the virtual directory (in our case this is c:\inetpub\wwwroot\TropicalGreen). This is where the Visual Studio .NET solution file (*.sln file) would be stored on your local computer.

    In the SourceSafe project to download field, navigate through the tree and browse to the TropicalGreen project folder.

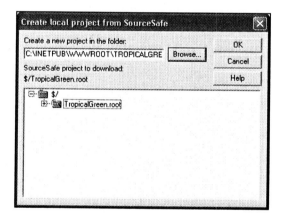

    When you have made your selection, click OK. You have now mapped the project store in the Source Safe database to a local directory. From now on, solution files downloaded from this project in Visual Source Safe will be stored in this folder.

5. The Open Solution dialog appears. Highlight the TropicalGreen.sln file and click Open.

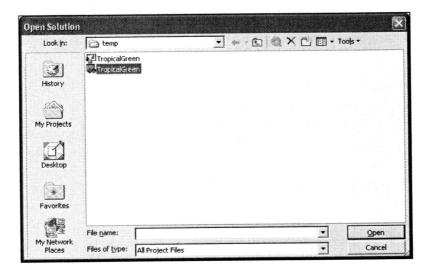

6. The Set Project Location dialog appears. In the Enter Working Copy Location Here field, ensure that the value is `http://localhost/TropicalGreen`. Click OK. The project files (`*.csproj` and all files associated with it) are downloaded to the folder bound to this virtual directory.

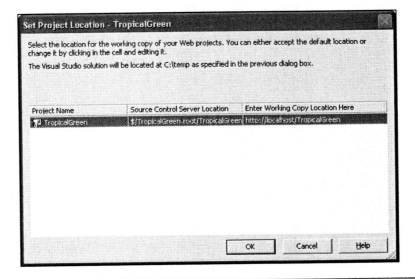

I get this error message while opening the Solution from Visual Source Safe: Could not get root template gallery.

There are a few possible reasons for this. A common one is that the developer opening the solution does not have at least Template Designer rights to the root template gallery.

If the machine is running Windows Server 2003 or Windows 2000 with Service Pack 4 or higher, then ensure that the user running Visual Studio .NET has the Impersonate a client after authentication privilege. You can find this setting by opening Local Computer Policy from Administrative Tools. Expand the node Local Policies and click on Security Options. Ensure that the Impersonate a client after authentication option is checked.

Lastly, you could be attempting to open an MCMS project located on a remote server. This is not possible. The MCMS developer tools can only work against the local server. MCMS projects have to be duplicated on every developer's machine and worked on locally. That's one reason why you need a tool like Visual Source Safe to centrally manage your code files.

---

7. Since the project was not created by MCMS, there are a few steps that you will have to do manually:

   o Open Internet Services Manager. Right-click the TropicalGreen virtual directory and select New | Virtual Directory from the pop-up menu. Click Next > to close the Virtual Directory Creation Wizard Welcome screen.

   o Set the following settings on the new virtual directory:

Property	Property Value
Alias	CMS
Directory	`<install directory>/Microsoft Content Management Server/IIS_CMS`
Allow	Read
	Run Scripts (such as ASP)

   o Click Next. The CMS Virtual Directory is created.

When attempting to create the CMS virtual directory on a Windows XP box, I get an error message saying that "The alias you have given is not unique".

A bug in Windows XP causes virtual directories to disappear from the IIS 5.1 Snap-in (`http://support.microsoft.com/?id=308179`). The virtual directory is there, but you can't see it.

Because the MMC creates a web application instead of a virtual directory by default, right-click on the CMS web application directory and select Properties from the pop-up menu. Open the Virtual Directory tab and locate the Application Settings. Click the Remove button. Click OK to close the properties dialog. Notice that the icon used to represent the CMS virtual directory changes from to .

> A missing CMS virtual directory is a common problem encountered by many developers. If this step is not carried out, you will find that certain components, such as the Web Author, fail to work.

Repeat these steps for every developer machine. After the mapping between the local solution and Visual Source Safe has been successfully established, you can safely open the solution from your machine just like any other Visual Studio .NET project.

Summary

In this chapter we looked at how the site navigation structure is determined by how channels are arranged in the hierarchy. We also looked at how the way galleries are arranged can make the job of looking for templates and resources easier for authors.

We used Site Manager to create channels, template galleries, and resource galleries for the TropicalGreen site. We discussed the properties that can be set and some tips and guidelines to follow when creating containers.

Finally, we created the TropicalGreen project and created the folders required for storing the code that we will be writing later. We showed you what went on under the hood when the wizard set up the MCMS project file. We finished up with a discussion on how Visual Source Safe can be used for source control when working with multiple developers on the same project.

Now you have built the foundations necessary to set up an environment to allow different developers to work together with you on your website. In the coming lessons, we will program the functionality and create the content of your TropicalGreen website.

6

Creating Templates and Postings

Before content management systems, websites had teams of webmasters who were in charge of putting up content. There were some problems in getting all pages to adopt a common look. Typically, a single file would be passed around as the "template" and programmers filled in the parts marked for content. As the site expanded, the task of updating pages was usually delegated to the people who provided the content. Maintaining the look and feel of the site became increasingly difficult as more people got involved in the content publishing process.

Microsoft Content Management Server provides a solution to this problem by fixing the look and feel across a website in predefined templates, which cannot be changed by authors. Pages based on the same template are alike in both design and layout. They serve as special web forms that support editable text regions for authors to enter content. In this way, developers concentrate on the programming aspect of the job, leaving the task of providing content to the subject experts.

Something About Templates

Templates predetermine the layout, design, and behavior of a page.

You can use a single template to create multiple pages that share the same design elements. In our TropicalGreen website, we will have a template called Plant. There are thousands of species of plants in the tropics. Each plant's web page will use the Plant template and so although the content for each plant's page is different, the look and feel will be the same because they share the same template. And if you decide to remove the plant's picture from each and every single web page, all you have to do is to amend that single template and thousands of plant postings are updated.

In MCMS, templates are made up of:

- MCMS template files on the web server
- Template gallery items in the CMS repository

Each template file is linked to a related template gallery item.

MCMS Template Files

MCMS template files dictate the overall look and feel of the web pages, how the content is positioned, the colors and fonts used, etc. They can be either ASP.NET web forms (`*.aspx`) or ASP files (`*.asp`). More importantly, they give developers full flexibility in programming the behavior of the web page. Since they are regular `*.aspx` or `*.asp` files, they enjoy the full benefits of ASP.NET/ASP programming. All the tools that ASP.NET/ASP provides can be used to create powerful templates in MCMS.

Template Gallery Items

Template gallery items are stored in the MCMS repository. They contain additional information about the template such as its name, its description, what placeholder definitions have been defined for the template, which custom properties should be available to authors of postings, and which gallery it belongs to. In addition, the template gallery item contains the information about which template file it is bound to.

Before We Begin

In this chapter, we will create the Plant template. We will create the template file and the template gallery item. Our first template will simply be used to generate web pages. At the end of this chapter we will use the template to generate the first plant fact sheet (or posting). The material in Chapter 7 extends our work to include editable regions (placeholders) for authors to enter content.

The Plant template will be used later to create fact sheets about plants used as a resource for hobbyists wishing to find out more about certain plants. Club members are avid gardeners. They often exchange gardening tips with fellow members. Younger green thumbs look up the information posted in the plant fact sheet to tap into the wealth of experience that has been posted by fellow gardeners.

Typically, before you begin creating templates, you would have planned the entire site structure and storyboard of the site. The complete draft of the blueprint would have been discussed with stakeholders and printed out. As our focus is on the technical aspect of the project, we won't be discussing that here.

At this point, we do not need to worry about the content (information about plants). We will concentrate only on the skeletal structure of the template.

The resulting skeleton is shown on the next page. We will use this shell to provide several key lessons to give us a solid framework on which to build the rest of the site.

Creating the Plant Template File

In Chapter 2, we installed the Developer Tools that integrate MCMS with Visual Studio.NET. We will use the add-ons to create the template file in Visual Studio .NET.

1. Open the TropicalGreen Solution in Visual Studio .NET. Point to Start | Programs | Microsoft Visual Studio .NET | Microsoft Visual Studio .NET. On the Start Page, click Open Project. Browse to the location of the TropicalGreen.sln file and click Open.

2. In Solution Explorer, right-click on the Templates folder created in Chapter 5. Select Add | Add New Item from the pop-up menu. The Add New Item dialog opens.

3. In the Categories column, select Content Management Server. Select the MCMS Template File option that appears in the Templates column.

   In the Name input field enter Plant.aspx. Click Open. A new template file is created.

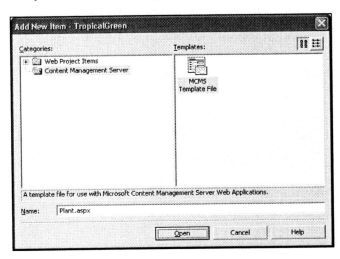

4. The MCMS template file you added looks just like a regular ASP.NET web form.

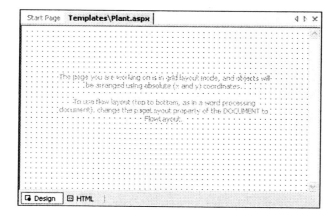

Editing the Template File

On adding the MCMS template file to the project, Plant.aspx file opens and is ready for editing.

5. The dots indicate gridlines. The page is currently using grids to position objects—the default setting for web forms created using Visual Studio .NET to allow positioning of controls using drag and drop.

    Using GridLayout means that all controls and text will be at fixed positions. This can cause problems in combination with MCMS when content entered by authors into Placeholder controls is longer than expected and overlaps with other content later. To prevent this from happening, change the layout to FlowLayout.

    Right-click anywhere within the page. Select Properties in the pop-up menu. Change the value of Page Layout from GridLayout to FlowLayout. The grid disappears.

6. Switch to HTML view by right-clicking anywhere on the page and selecting View HTML Source in the pop-up menu (or press *Ctrl + Page Down*). Enter the HTML table below as you see it between the <form> and </form> tags. The table provides the basic format for the page with the logo and horizontal menu at the top of the page and the vertical menu on the right-hand side. The rest of the space is for the main body or content. Text markers for content (e.g. (Space for Console)) will be replaced later in this chapter and in subsequent chapters.

```
<table width="100%" border="0" cellspacing="0" cellpadding="0" height="100%">
<tr>
    <td width="100%" colspan="2" valign="top" bgcolor="#FFCC00">
      <IMG src="/tropicalgreen/images/Logo.gif">
    </td>
    <td rowspan="10" valign="top">
      (Space for Console)
    </td>
</tr>
<tr bgcolor="#66CC33">
    <td colspan="2">(Space for Top Menu)</td>
```

```
  </tr>
  <tr>
    <td valign="top">
    (Space for Main Body)
    </td>
    <td class="RightMenuBar" width="20%" valign="top" height="100%"
                          align="center" rowspan="2" bgcolor="#669900">
    (Space for Right Menu Bar)
    </td>
  </tr>
  </table>
```

7. The logo of the TropicalGreen club can be obtained from the code download section in the book's companion site. Download the `logo.gif` file and add it to the solution in the Images folder of the TropicalGreen project

8. Your developer's instinct is probably prompting you to test the template code. Switch over to Design View and see what you have created. Click on the Design tab at the bottom of the Visual Studio designer, or right-click anywhere on the page and select View Design. Or, for those of us who like shortcuts, press *Ctrl + Page Down*.

This is plain for a template file but it covers the essence of it. We'll add in the cosmetic effects later.

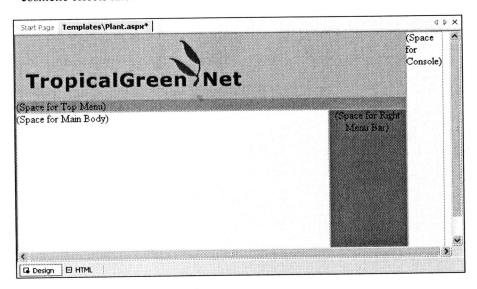

Adding the Default Console

Note that we have reserved a cell on the right of the table for the console. We will be introduced to the Web Author console in the next few chapters. For now, add it into the template file. To add the Default Console:

1. In Design view, drag and drop the `DefaultConsole.ascx` file into the table cell that contains the words (Space for Console). You can find `DefaultConsole.ascx` in the

/Console/ folder of the solution. This widget was added by the wizard when you created the TropicalGreen Project.

2. Delete the words (space for console). In Design View, your template file should now look like the screenshot below.

3. Make it a habit to press *Ctrl + S* or press the **Save** button once in a while when writing your code to save your work. If you have not done so, save now.

4. Build the solution by pressing *Ctrl + Shift + B*.

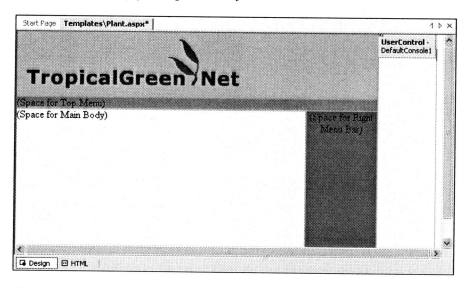

We're halfway there. Let's create the second part of a template—the template gallery item (or the part that resides in the content repository).

Creating a Template Gallery Item

Creating an ASPX template file as we did in the previous section is only half the story. We still need to create an entry in the MCMS repository (or the template gallery item) to let MCMS know about the template file we've created.

Viewing the MCMS Template Explorer

An additional window appears in Visual Studio .NET for projects that are MCMS enabled: the MCMS Template Explorer.

The MCMS Template Explorer (shown on the next page) provides a graphical interface to manage template galleries and template gallery items. In Chapter 4, we created template galleries using Site Manager. We can do the same using the MCMS Template Explorer in Visual Studio .NET.

This is a good feature that nicely integrates Visual Studio .NET with MCMS. It gives template designers the ability to use a single tool to maintain templates. They don't have to use Site

Manager to maintain template galleries; all required tasks to create and update templates can be performed from within Visual Studio .NET.

If the MCMS Template Explorer Window does not appear on the screen, you can bring it to the surface by pointing to View | Other Windows | MCMS Template Explorer from the Visual Studio .NET toolbar.

Should the option to open the MCMS Template Explorer not be available, chances are, your project is not MCMS-enabled. You can choose to:

1. Select Project | Enable as MCMS Project from the toolbar.

2. Delete the project and follow the steps outlined in Chapter 2.

Creating the Plant Template Gallery Item

In the MCMS Template Explorer, right-click on the template gallery named PlantCatalog that was created in Chapter 5.

Select New Template from the pop-up menu, and name the new template Plant.

Look at the icon next to the newly created template. It looks like a broken object with a red check next to it:

The broken template indicates that the template gallery item is not linked to a physical template file. The red check means that you have checked out the template gallery item. No one else can change the template gallery item while it's checked out to you.

Linking the Template Gallery Item to the ASPX Template

We need to link the template gallery item to the template file created earlier. This is an important step. Miss it and your template would not have a physical form.

Right-click on the newly created Plant template in MCMS Template Explorer and select Properties. The Properties window of the template gallery item appears. For now, zoom in to the TemplateFile field and set it to point to the /TropicalGreen/Templates/Plant.aspx file we have just created, as shown below. To save typing effort, click on the ellipsis and browse to the Plant.aspx template file.

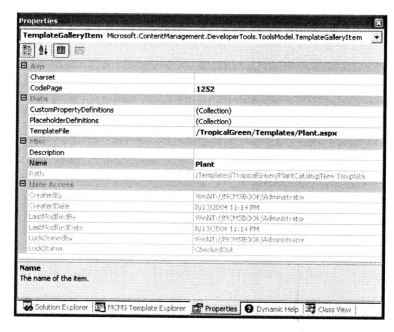

Look at the icon that represents the template gallery item—it is no longer showing as broken:

That's because the template gallery item is now linked to a template file.

Saving the Template Gallery Item

Your changes are not committed to the database yet. To do so, right-click on the Plant template and select Save. Alternatively, click the **save** icon in the MCMS Template Explorer. Notice that the name of the template changes from bold text to regular text. If the template name is in bold, it means recent changes haven't been saved to the database yet.

> Use the **save** button to commit changes to the database while the template is checked out to you.

Checking In the Template Gallery Item

In the Template Explorer, right-click the Plant template and select Check In. The red check beside the icon of the template gallery item disappears after you have checked in the template.

The Check-In and Check-Out functions of the MCMS Template Explorer are useful when you are working with other developers on the same project. When a developer needs to amend the properties of a template gallery item, he or she has to check it out first. When the template gallery item is checked out, no one else can change any of its properties. In this way, the developer can safely make any changes to the object without worrying that someone else is unwittingly overwriting any work. Keep in mind this does not reserve the template ASPX file, just the template gallery item in the MCMS database.

Remember to check in the template gallery item when you are done with the changes, or the template will be checked out indefinitely. You don't want to get urgent phone calls from co-workers when you go on vacation as no one else can work on the template!

> Checking in a template gallery item automatically saves it to the database.

And we are done! The template is now complete. We are ready to create our first posting.

Creating the First Posting

Creating the first posting is a chicken-and-egg problem. Postings are created by clicking the Create New Posting option in the Web Author Console. If we don't have any postings within the channel in the first place, we don't have a posting with a Console to use. How then, do we create the first posting?

The good news is that channels can be accessed from a browser just like postings. For any channel that does not contain a posting MCMS renders a default channel rendering script, called the channel cover page. This cover page also contains a console.

Opening the Built-In Channel Rendering Script

To see this in action, open Internet Explorer and enter `http://localhost/TropicalGreen/ PlantCatalog` in the address bar. If you get a login screen, type in the username and password of the Windows account you are using. You will get the page as shown overleaf. This is the built-in channel rendering script.

The built-in channel rendering script is just a regular old-style Active Server Page called `Cover.asp`. You can find it at `(Install Location)\Microsoft Content Management Server\Server\IIS_NR\Shared`.

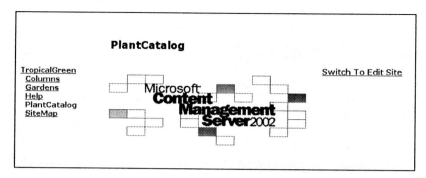

The Channel Cover Page can also be viewed by accessing `http://localhost/channels`.

Creating a New Page

Look at the Web Author Console on the right-hand side of the built-in channel rendering script. We use the buttons presented in the Console to create a new page.

1. Click Switch to Edit Site in the Web Author Console. You are now in edit mode. The Web Author shows you several options that are available to you.

2. In the Web Author Console, click Create New Page.

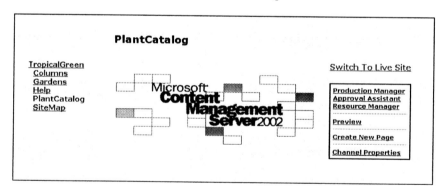

3. The Select Template Gallery dialog appears. Select the template gallery PlantCatalog. If you can't see the PlantCatalog template gallery, expand the number of items in the page to All.

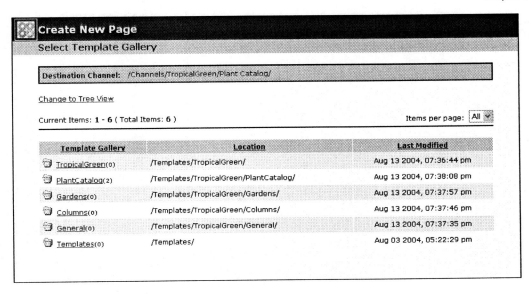

4. Select the Plant template by clicking on the hand icon (<image>) in the second column.

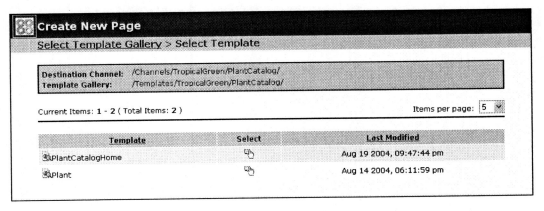

5. A posting based on the Plant template is displayed. For now, we have not added any editable regions to the template so there is nothing we can do to change its appearance. Click Save New Page in the Web Author Console.

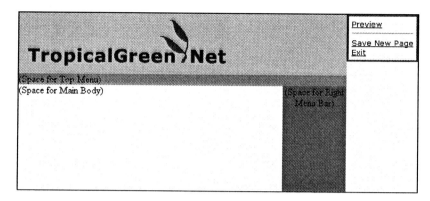

6. The Save New Page dialog appears. Set the Name and Display Name of the new page to Hibiscus.

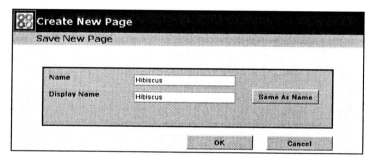

7. Towards the bottom of the Web Author Console, click Submit. The posting is immediately published to the live site. Clicking Switch To Live Site allows you to view the published posting, which should look something like that shown below.

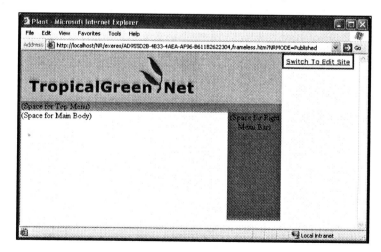

Observe the URL in the address bar: `http://localhost/NR/exeres/AD955D2B-4B33-4AEA-AF96-B611B2622304,frameless.htm?NRMODE=Published`. The GUID in the middle may be different but no matter how you look at it, it's ugly. In an earlier chapter, we discussed how MCMS adds instructions to a URL. This is the URL with the added instructions. MCMS converts all those clean URLs (like `http://localhost/tropicalgreen/plantcatalog`) to this ugly URL for its own use.

The Difference between a Template File and a Regular ASP.NET Web Form

When you add an MCMS template to an MCMS template project, the wizard does a few things behind the scenes. Back in Visual Studio .NET, open `Plant.aspx` and toggle to HTML View by selecting View | HTML Source from the toolbar or pressing *Ctrl + Page Down*.

At the top of the HTML code, you will see a page-level Register directive to register the `Microsoft.ContentManagement.WebControls` namespace and assign it an alias of `cms`. `Microsoft.ContentManagement.WebControls` contains classes that are required to support all out-of-the-box Placeholder controls.

```
<%@ Register TagPrefix="cms"
             Namespace="Microsoft.ContentManagement.WebControls"
             Assembly="Microsoft.ContentManagement.WebControls,
             Version=5.0.1200.0,
             Culture=neutral,
             PublicKeyToken=31bf3856ad364e35" %>
```

Further down, in the HTML head section, you will find the `RobotMetaTag`:

```
<cms:RobotMetaTag runat="server" id="RobotMetaTag1"></cms:RobotMetaTag>
```

To understand what the `RobotMetaTag` does, look at the source code of a posting:

1. View the posting created earlier by entering its URL into the address bar of your browser (e.g. http://localhost/tropicalgreen/plantcatalog/hibiscus.htm).

2. Right-click on the browser window and select View Source from the pop-up menu.

The `RobotMetaTag` writes out two lines of code within the `<HEAD>` tags of the generated posting.

The first line is:

```
<meta name="ROBOTS" content="FOLLOW,INDEX">
```

By default, most Search Crawlers will index all pages of a site. You can prevent a page from being indexed by setting the content attribute of this tag to `"noindex"`. A value of `"nofollow"` prevents pages that are linked to this page from being indexed. The value of the content attribute takes its cue from the `Web Robots Can Crawl Links` (`IsRobotFollowable` in the PAPI) and `Web Robots can Index this Channel's Navigation` (`IsRobotIndexable` in the PAPI) properties of the posting.

The second line looks like this:

```
<base href="(fully qualified path of the template file with querystring)">
```

A live example of that would be:

```
<base href="http://www.tropicalgreen.net/Templates/Plant.aspx?
NRORIGINALURL=%2fNR%2fexeres%2f994840E6-823F-4B7C-824F-
237CD81B28FA%2cframeless%2ehtm&FRAMELESS=true&
NRNODEGUID=%7bF3658973-8735-484E-845D-22C7A70D4070%7d&
NRCACHEHINT=ModifyLoggedIn">
```

The `<base>` tag provides support for relative links within the template. For example, you may have an image that is coded as `<img src="myImage.gif">`. Without the `<base>` tag, the browser will look for the image based on the path of the generated web page. In our Plants example, this could be anything from `/shrubs/myImage.gif` to `/Cactus/myImage.gif`. As we can't predict the path of the page, it makes more sense to look for `myImage.gif` based on the path of the template file.

Warning: The `<base>` tag causes internal bookmarks to go awry.

Secret: Any regular ASP.NET web form can be used as an MCMS template file. If your template file hosts placeholder controls, add the above page level Register directive. Should you need to prevent a search engine from indexing the postings generated by this template or have relative links within your page, add both the `RobotMetaTag` and the page level registration.

Summary

Congratulations—you've now created your first template! Templates ensure that a consistent look and feel is applied across pages that are generated from it. They also act as special kinds of web forms where authors can enter content in special editable regions without needing to know how to create a web page.

Templates are made up of two distinct parts:

- Template files
- Template gallery items

Template files are created and managed in Visual Studio .NET in MCMS-enabled projects. Developers define the layout, design, and behavior of the page by writing code in template files.

MCMS provides an add-on to Visual Studio .NET called MCMS Template Explorer. Developers use the MCMS Template Explorer to create MCMS template gallery items in the MCMS repository. Once created, template gallery items are linked to template files.

You created the first posting based on the Plant template and viewed it from the browser. Because this is the first posting in the website, we used the Web Author Console available from the built-in channel rendering script to access the Create New Page function.

The Plant template is at its bare minimum. In the next chapter, we will add placeholders, which are editable regions where authors can upload content.

7
Working with Placeholders

One of the most compelling reasons to deploy a content management solution is to empower authors to manage their own content. Placeholders are an integral part of the solution, providing editable regions within which authors can enter the content. If you have attended a sales presentation on any content management system, the sales person would have shown you how easily content can be entered into rich text boxes without the author needing to understand HTML tags and codes.

Of course, placeholders do more than provide user-friendly interfaces for authors. They also offer an excellent way to organize and structure content into compartments. For example, instead of storing a page with text and tags mixed together in an inseparable heap, you could store the abstract in a placeholder, the story in a second placeholder, and the summary in a third placeholder. In fact, every chunk of information you divide your page into can be given a corresponding placeholder. A page can have as many placeholders as you require, and there is unlikely to be any performance hit unless you have much more than 30 in a page. The more finely the page is divided, the more granular control you have over its content.

With content organized neatly into containers, it can be easily re-purposed, re-used, re-located, and managed across pages and websites. You can, with significantly less effort, do things like:

- Revamp the look and feel of the website without having to go through the painful exercise of re-entering and re-formatting its content.

- Extract portions of a page (e.g. the title and abstract) for display on a summary page or for distribution to other applications.

- Share content across multiple pages. Common information, like a legal disclaimer, can be stored in a single placeholder. All pages that require the information can read it from a central location where it only needs to be updated once.

It would be tempting to say that content management provides a clean separation between the presentation/layout of the page and the content (often referred to as structured content). That's not always the case. As long as HTML mingles together with content, a complete separation cannot be achieved.

Ideally, content would be entered by the author devoid of any information regarding its presentation. In this way, the same chunk of information can be re-used across any page that needs it. For example, an employee's contact number could be displayed on both the intranet and the extranet.

XML (Extensible Markup Language) offers promising breakthroughs in this area. It provides a means to cleanly separate content from design elements, because a corresponding XSL (Extensible Style sheet) can transform XML content into a presentable format. However, until web editing tools evolve to the stage when the average author can write in XML as he or she would with a regular word editor, the challenge to keep text free of design tags remains.

Using Placeholders

In order for content to be managed effectively by the system, it has to be broken down into chunks. For example, the Plant page could have sections for:

- A picture of the plant
- A description of the plant
- A research paper about the plant

The template captures these chunks of content using embedded placeholders, which are part of the content collection mechanism.

In essence, there are three parts to a placeholder:

1. The Placeholder Control
2. The Placeholder Definition
3. The Placeholder Object

The term "placeholder" is often used loosely to describe how the page is divided into slices of information. Developers often get confused about its meaning. They start creating a placeholder but are not sure if that means building a control, creating a definition or working with the object through code. The following section aims to clear up some common misconceptions developers have about the meaning of the word "placeholder" with regards to MCMS.

Placeholder Controls

The visible part of the placeholder is the placeholder control. In authoring mode, it acts as an input control for authors to enter content. In presentation mode, it displays whatever is stored in the placeholder.

All placeholder controls inherit from the `BasePlaceholder` class, which is part of the MCMS Object Model and is installed together with MCMS. Apart from that, they are not too different from the controls you find in the Toolbox in Visual Studio .NET.

The properties of a placeholder control govern how the control behaves in authoring and publishing time. For example, the HtmlPlaceholderControl has a property that controls whether the author is allowed to switch to HTML view and reveal the source of the content they are editing, a function similar to the HTML view function in Visual Studio.

MCMS ships with three placeholder controls:

- HtmlPlaceholderControl (a control that accepts HTML)
- SingleImagePlaceholderControl (a control that accepts a single image)
- SingleAttachmentPlaceholderControl (a control that accepts a single attachment)

One of the best things about MCMS is that it allows you to create your own custom placeholder controls that are tailored for your needs. For example, if you need a date-time picker and none of the controls that were shipped in the box provides the desired functionality, you can easily write your own. We will be creating some custom placeholder controls in Chapter 14.

> The placeholder control discussed in this section does not refer to the ASP.NET PlaceHolder control found in the web forms section of the Toolbox in Visual Studio .NET (notice "PlaceHolder" with a capital "H"). The control named "PlaceHolder" in the Toolbox is used as a container object to store other controls and is not used to manage MCMS content. It has a totally different application from MCMS placeholder controls.

Placeholder Definitions

Placeholder definitions have a collection of properties that outline how the placeholder behaves. This includes the type of media to be accepted by the placeholder, the format that the content has to be in, and other constraints a placeholder might have. These properties can be set through the Placeholder Definition Editor in Visual Studio .NET.

For example, you could configure an HtmlPlaceholder control to allow only text to be entered—in which case formatting tags like bold, italics, and underlines are not allowed. These settings are stored in the placeholder definition. When the content is saved into the repository, all tags that don't meet the requirements of the definition are stripped away.

Or, perhaps the placeholder used to store the plant's picture should only accept image files from the resource gallery, and not allow authors to upload their own images. This feature is controlled by a flag in the ImagePlaceholderDefinition, named MustUseResourceGallery. When turned on, it instructs the placeholder control to not allow any image file that is not stored in the resource gallery. Out of the box, MCMS ships with six placeholder definitions:

- HtmlPlaceholderDefinition: Definition for a placeholder that holds content with support for HTML markup tags
- XmlPlaceholderDefinition: Definition for a placeholder that supports native XML
- AttachmentPlaceholderDefinition: Definition for a placeholder that holds a single attachment
- ImagePlaceholderDefinition: Definition for a placeholder that holds a single image

129

- `OfficeAttachmentPlaceholderDefinition`: Definition for a placeholder that holds a single attachment uploaded through Microsoft Word
- `OfficeHtmlPlaceholderDefinition`: Definition for a placeholder that holds content with support for HTML markup tags uploaded through Microsoft Word

Like custom placeholder controls, you can create custom placeholders based on custom placeholder definitions if any of the above definitions are not able to fulfill your website's requirements. We will demonstrate creating custom placeholder definitions in Chapter 15.

Placeholder Objects

Each placeholder object is bound to a specific placeholder definition. Placeholder objects expose methods and properties to access the content of a placeholder in a specific posting.

In this chapter we will explore the three placeholder objects that ship with MCMS 2002:

- `HtmlPlaceholder`
- `AttachmentPlaceholder`
- `ImagePlaceholder`

Before We Begin

Template designers usually start by planning what goes into a page. In our example website, each fact sheet contains the plant's description, research paper, and picture as detailed in this table

What	Description	Placeholder to Use
Description	How does the plant grow? Where does it come from? What does it thrive on? All these questions and more describe the plant's characteristics and behavior.	HtmlPlaceholder The description forms the bulk of the content on the page and would consist of formatted text. The HtmlPlaceholder is well suited for this purpose.
Research Paper	Some club members are scientists active in the research community. Occasionally, they write a paper related to the plant. This document is attached to the fact sheet.	AttachmentPlaceholder We will not have more than one document for each plant. Hence, the AttachmentPlaceholder is an excellent choice here.
Picture of Plant	For the curious, images of the plant are uploaded. Never seen a Hibiscus flower before? Look at the picture.	ImagePlaceholder Since we are storing a link to a single image, we will use the ImagePlaceholder to handle the plant's picture.

As you divide the page into chunks of information, you define the data structure of the site and add placeholder definitions to the template gallery item as you move along. The template designer adds a placeholder definition to the template for each of these pieces of information.

Work on the layout of the page typically starts after the blueprint of the entire site has been agreed upon by all stakeholders. Next, developers enter the scene and add the placeholder controls to the template file.

Here's a draft that outlines a possible arrangement of placeholder controls on the Plant template.

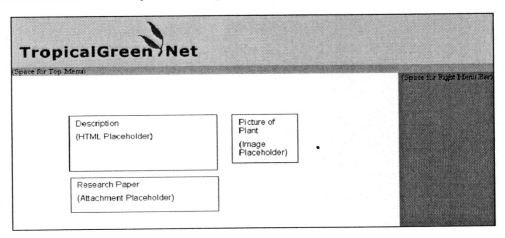

Lumping the details of the plant in a single area called Description works out well for this tutorial. In actual work scenarios, you may want to consider chopping it up into finer pieces in order to manage the content better.

Drafting the Prototype

It's a good idea to draft the layout of the page in simple HTML before you begin coding. That will give you a graphical guide to where the placeholders controls would go.

1. Within the TropicalGreen solution, open the Plant.aspx template file created in Chapter 6 in HTML view.

2. In the space marked (Space for Main Body), enter the following code. Make sure to remove the text marked (Space for Main Body) when you are done.

```
<br>
 (Space for Plant Common Name)<br>
<br>
<table>
<tr>
   <td class="BodyText"><br>
      <H2>Description</H2>
   (Space for Description)<br>
```

131

```
        </td>
        <td vAlign="top" rowSpan="3">(Space for Image of Plant)</td>
    </tr>
    <tr>
        <td>
            <H2>Research Paper</H2>
          <br>
          (Space for Research Paper)
          </td>
    </tr>
    </table>
    <br><br><br>
```

3. Save and you are done.

The resulting template file appears as shown below in Design view.

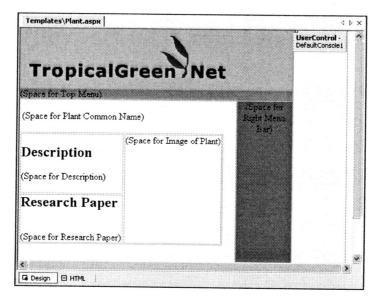

HtmlPlaceholder

The best known of all placeholders is the HtmlPlaceholder. It was built to store chunks of HTML formatted content.

You find the HtmlPlaceholder most commonly used in pages with unstructured content where images are mixed with text, or with text that requires formatting styles applied, and so on. It is also the only out-of-the box placeholder with the capability of storing chunks of HTML text, so it is not surprising to find the HtmlPlaceholder is one of the most common placeholders in MCMS-managed sites.

We will use the HtmlPlaceholder for the Plant's description. In order to add an HtmlPlaceholder to the Plant Template, we need to add the:

- HtmlPlaceholderDefinition to the template gallery item
- HtmlPlaceholderControl to the template file

Adding an HtmlPlaceholderDefinition

Let's add an HtmlPlaceholderDefinition for the plant's description.

1. In the MCMS Template Explorer, right-click the Plant template object and select Check Out.
2. With the Template checked out, right-click on it again and select Properties.
3. Click your mouse on the PlaceholderDefinitions property field. Click on the ellipsis (...) that appears.

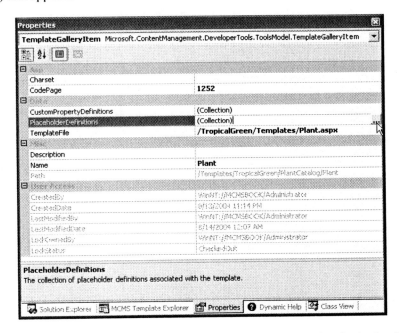

4. The Placeholder Definition Collection Editor opens. If this dialog looks familiar to you, that's because it is the same Collection Editor that is used to manage Collections like items in a DropDownList/CheckBoxList control.
5. Click Add. This adds a new HtmlPlaceholderDefinition to the collection. If you click on the arrow next to the Add button, you will see a list of available placeholder definitions that ship with MCMS. Since the HtmlPlaceholderDefinition is the first on the list, it's the default definition added when you click Add.

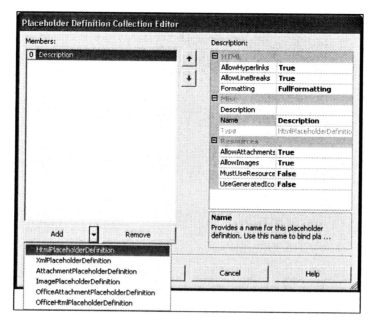

6. Click your mouse on the fields and look at the description in the Properties panel for an explanation of what each means. We examine each field in detail in the next section. Since the Description is rich in nature, we will give authors the ability to turn text into hyperlinks and add any kind of HTML formatting. Give the properties of the HtmlPlaceholderDefinition the following values:

Property	Property Value
AllowHyperlinks	True
AllowLineBreaks	True
Formatting	FullFormatting
Description	<Leave this blank>
Name	Description
AllowAttachments	True
AllowImages	True
MustUseResourceGallery	False
UseGeneratedIcon	False

The fastest way to toggle between values is to double-click on the field. You can also click on the field, click on the drop-down list, and select the value that you want.

You may have noticed the up and down arrows in the middle of the dialog. Usually, you would use these arrows to sort the items in the Members column but, in the Placeholder Definition Editor, the arrows have been disabled. That's because the MCMS does not provide the functionality to sort placeholder definitions; the placeholder definitions are always listed in the order you added them.

When you are done, click OK to close the Placeholder Definition Collection Editor.

You have just added the first placeholder definition. MCMS now knows that it is supposed to store content in a placeholder named Description. We won't check the template gallery item in just yet as we will be adding more placeholder definitions as we work through this chapter.

Properties of the HtmlPlaceholderDefinition

When working with the HtmlPlaceholderDefinition earlier, you saw its list of properties. Most are self-explanatory (like whether or not hyperlinks are allowed). Nevertheless, here is a no-holds-barred examination of the HtmlPlaceholderDefinition's properties.

Property	Description
AllowHyperlinks	Set this to true when you want to allow hyperlinks in the placeholder content. Disabling hyperlinks would not strip away any tags but the "Edit Hyperlink" button on the authoring toolbar would be disabled.
AllowLineBreaks	This is used in conjunction with the Formatting property to determine what tags are allowed in the content. See the following section (*Formatting Content*) for a full explanation on how this affects the tags allowed.
Formatting	Choose between: • NoFormatting • FullFormatting • TextMarkup • HtmlStyles • TextMarkupAndHtmlStyles See the *Formatting Content* section below for a full explanation on what each item means.
Description	The text entered here is displayed as default content of the placeholder when the posting is created for the first time. Holds a maximum of 500 characters. Usually used to describe what the placeholder does and provide instructions to authors.
Name	The name of the placeholder is also its identifier. It has to be unique within a placeholder definition collection in a Template. Holds a maximum of 100 characters. The naming restrictions described in Chapter 6 apply here as well.
Type	Read-only. Fixed to be HtmlPlaceholderDefinition. Basically tells you what kind of object this is.

`AllowAttachments`	Set to true to allow attachments in the content. Attachments can be anything from items in the resource gallery to files uploaded from the author's desktop. No tags are stripped on save when this property is set to false. However, the formatting toolbar will have the insert attachment button disabled.
	Note that once this is set to `true`, there is no restriction on the type of files that can be uploaded.
`AllowImages`	Set to true to allow images or pictures in the content. If `false`, all `<img>` tags would be stripped from the content on save.
`MustUseResourceGallery`	Set to false to allow authors to upload attachments and images from their desktops. Usually set to true to restrict the author's choice to items available in the resource gallery, preventing the uploading of unapproved material.
`UseGeneratedIcon`	Set to true to display attachments as an icon.

Icons Used to Represent Attachments

When the `UseGeneratedIcon` property is set to true, attachments are displayed as icons instead of a text hyperlink. The generated icon follows the image associated with the file type of the attachment on the server (not the client machine!) and includes the file's name. For example, a generated icon for a rich-text document (`*.doc`) looks like this:

hibiscus.doc

and documents with no associated icon look like this:

hibiscus.unknown

You can have more control over the icon that is used by MCMS; if you do not set up common icon types on the server, attachments will appear with the generic icons as shown above. One way to associate a document with an icon is to install the software on the MCMS machine. That would incur additional licensing costs for the software (e.g. Microsoft Office).

A more effective way would be to change the icon associated with a file type. To do so:

1. Open Windows Explorer.
2. From the toolbar, select Tools | Folder Options.
3. Open the File Types tab.
4. In the list of registered file types, select the file type you wish to associate a new icon with. If the file type is not listed, click New to add the extension to the list.
5. Click Advanced. In the Edit File Type dialog, click Change Icon... Browse to the icon file you wish use. You don't have to change other properties such as the Actions.
6. Click OK to close the opened dialogs.

7. Restart the AESecurityService using the Services Manager for the icons to show up.

Formatting Content

The HtmlPlaceholder only accepts commonly used markup tags. Using the HtmlPlaceholderDefinition, you can restrict the sets of markup tags that would be accepted. Markup tags are classified into 6 categories:

- **Flow**: <Address> <Blockquote> <Center> <Div> <Hr> <Nobr> <Pre> <Q> <Span> <Wbr>
- **Heading**: <Dir> <H1> <H2> <H3> <H4> <H5> <H6> <Marquee> <Menu>
- **List**: <Li> <Ol> <Ul>
- **Table**: <Caption> <Col> <Colgroup> <Table> <Tbody> <Td> <Tfoot> <Th> <Thead> <Tr>
- **Markup**: <B> <Em> <I> <Strong> <S> <Strike> <Tt> <Abbr> <Acronym> <Cite> <Code> <Del> <Dfn> <Ins> <Kbd> <Samp> <Var> <Bdo> <Rt> <Ruby> <Blink>
- **Font**: <Font>

The options in the Formatting field are used in conjunction with the AllowLineBreaks field to determine which set of tags are allowed in the placeholder.

AllowLineBreaks	Formatting	Flow	Heading	List	Table	Markup	Font
True	FullFormatting	✓	✓	✓	✓	✓	✓
False	FullFormatting	✓	✓	✗	✗	✓	✓
True	HTMLStyles	✓	✓	✓	✗	✗	✗
False	HTMLStyles	✓	✓	✗	✗	✗	✗
True/False	TextMarkup	✗	✗	✗	✗	✓	✗
True	TextMarkupAndHTMLStyles	✓	✓	✓	✗	✓	✗
False	TextMarkupAndHTMLStyles	✓	✓	✗	✗	✓	✗
True/False	NoFormatting	✗	✗	✗	✗	✗	✗

When the placeholder content is saved to the repository, the tags that don't meet the above criteria are stripped out when the content is saved. For example, if a placeholder definition is configured to allow NoFormatting, which does not allow any HTML tags, code such as the following:

```
<b>text in bold</b>
```

would be stripped down to remove the <b></b> tags:

```
text in bold
```

HtmlPlaceholderControls

The `HtmlPlaceholderControl` contains a WYSIWYG text editor as shown below.

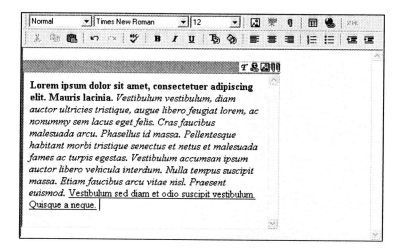

> **WYSIWYG—What you see is what you get**—editors are popular in content management systems. They allow authors to see the formatting of text as it would appear on the website when the content is published.

You have seen this at work in almost all web-editing tools: Bold plain text simply by selecting a block of text and clicking on the bold button. Spice up your page with a jazzy image by clicking on the insert image button. And that's just a slice of what you can do. With it, authors can enter text and apply standard formatting such as bold, italics, and underline using basic word processing skills. They do not need expert knowledge of HTML tags to crunch out web pages and work within a familiar environment to create and publish content to the site.

In MCMS 2002, the `HtmlPlaceholderControl` looks similar to the one that was shipped with MCMS 2001—that's because *it is* the same control. It still relies on ActiveX technology to deliver the formatting toolbar. It continues to provide the same basic functions for formatting text—with a few exceptions:

1. The toolbar of the `HtmlPlaceholderControl` no longer has a video button.
2. At the time the time of printing, it does not support a DHTML version of the Placeholder control. Previously, developers had the option of activating a DHTML version of the `HtmlPlaceholderControl` so that authors do not need to download and install the ActiveX Control version. It was also available as an alternative for users authoring from a Macintosh computer.

Every page with an embedded `HtmlPlaceholderControl` loads a formatting toolbar. In order for the toolbar to appear correctly the browser needs to meet the following requirements:

1. ActiveX Controls must be allowed.

2. JavaScript must be enabled.

We will explore the toolbar in Chapter 11. For now, let's take a closer look at the `HtmlPlaceholderControl` in design mode by adding a control to our Plant template file.

> If you do not need to display the contents of the placeholder on the page, you could simply remove the placeholder control. So long as you do not delete the corresponding placeholder definition, you will not delete the contents as was the case in MCMS 2001.

Adding an HtmlPlaceholderControl

We will now add `HtmlPlaceholderControl` to our template file so that authors can update a plant's description.

If you have not done so, open the TropicalGreen solution in Visual Studio .NET.

The quickest way to add the control would be to drag and drop the `HtmlPlaceholderControl` from the Toolbox. Switch to Design view (toggle between HTML and Design view by pressing *Ctrl + Page Down*). Open your toolbox (*Ctrl + Alt + X*) and select the **Content Management Server** category.

Drag and drop the HtmlPlaceholderControl into the cell that contains the words (`Space for Description`). Delete the words (`Space for Description`).

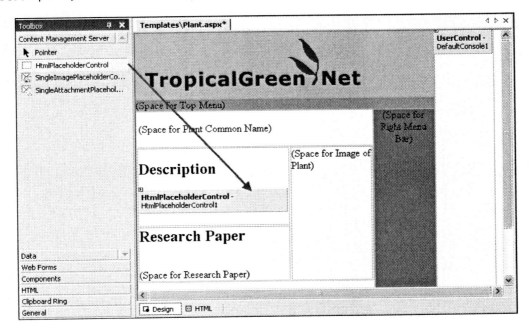

In a single action, Visual Studio .NET has added several lines of code. To see what was done under the covers, switch to HTML view. At the top, a new page registration directive has been added.

```
<%@ Register TagPrefix="cms"
Namespace="Microsoft.ContentManagement.WebControls"
Assembly="Microsoft.ContentManagement.WebControls, Version=5.0.1200.0,
Culture=neutral, PublicKeyToken=31bf3856ad364e35" %>
```

`Microsoft.ContentManagement.WebControls` contains classes that support all placeholder controls. Moving down the page, look at the cell that you dropped the control into; you see this:

```
<cms:HtmlPlaceholderControl id="HtmlPlaceholderControl1"
runat="server"></cms:HtmlPlaceholderControl>
```

That is the HTML tag that you would have to key in if you did not drag and drop.

Linking the Placeholder Control to the Placeholder Definition

Still in Design view, right-click on the `HtmlPlaceholderControl`. Select Properties. There is one property that is common among all placeholder controls: `PlaceholderToBind`.

The `PlaceholderToBind` property links the placeholder control to its corresponding `PlaceholderDefinition`. It's the equivalent of the `TemplateFile` property for template objects.

Place your mouse pointer over the `PlaceholderToBind` property. Click on the little arrow that appears on the right to open the drop-down list. Since we have only created a single placeholder definition, Description, that's the only choice we have.

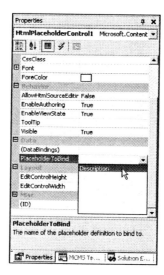

For now, set the following values:

Property	Property Value
CssClass	BodyText
	Note: At the end of the chapter (*Linking a Stylesheet to the Template File*), we will show you how to link a stylesheet to the template file.
EditControlHeight	400
EditControlWidth	400
ID	PlantDescription
PlaceholderToBind	Description

Save your work and build the solution.

Properties of an HtmlPlaceholderControl

There are some properties that are common across all placeholder controls. That's because they are inherited from the base class, BasePlaceholderControl (part of the Microsoft.ContentManagement.WebControls namespace). You can find the complete list in the product documentation. Here, we look at those that are commonly used.

Properties Common Across all Placeholder Controls

These properties are available not just for the HtmlPlaceholderControl, but also for placeholder controls, including customized ones.

Property	Description
BorderColor	Defines the color of the border surrounding the placeholder control.
BorderStyle	Defines the style of the border. Choose between NotSet, None, Dotted, Dashed, Solid, Double, Groove, Ridge, Inset, and Outset.
BorderWidth	Specifies the width of the border surrounding the image.
	When rendered, the values of the border properties are included as attributes of a <span> element containing the placeholder control. A border with the color #FF0000 (red), dotted with a width of 1px would be rendered as:
	`<span id="PlantDescription" style="border-color:#FF0000;border-width:1px;border-style:Dotted;">Contents of Description Placeholder</span>`
BackColor	Defines the background color of the placeholder control.
Font	Defines the font used in the placeholder control.
ForeColor	Defines the color of the font used in the placeholder control.
	You would probably not use the BackColor, Font, or ForeColor properties. Chances are you would be managing the appearance of the content using a stylesheet, which offers a more elegant way of defining how the page looks. Note, these properties are not available for the SingleAttachment PlaceholderControl or SingleImagePlaceholderControl.

Property	Description
CssClass	If you are using a stylesheet, specify the class that governs the contents of the placeholder here.
EnableAuthoring	Set this to true to enable authors to update the contents of the placeholder. A value of false renders the placeholder control read-only.
EnableViewState	Set this to true to have the template file remember the field's value across postbacks. If your template file does not require postbacks, you can set this to false to reduce the amount of data wired across the network.
ToolTip	The value entered here appears as a descriptive text box when a mouse pointer is placed over the placeholder. MCMS adds a Title attribute to the <span> element surrounding the placeholder. `<span id="PlantDescription" title="Value of Tooltip property">Contents of Description Placeholder</span>`
Visible	When this is set to true, the placeholder appears on the page. Hides the placeholder when false. Developers often use it to hide the placeholder when no content has been entered.
PlaceholderToBind	Links the placeholder control to its corresponding PlaceholderDefinition.
ID	The unique identifier of the placeholder control.

Properties Unique to the HtmlPlaceholderControl

The following properties only apply to the HtmlPlaceholder Control.

Property	Description
AllowHTMLSourceEditing	When set to true, allows authors to switch to HTML view and edit code.
EditControlHeight	Defines the height of the control (in pixels) in authoring mode.
EditControlWidth	Defines the width (in pixels) of the control in authoring mode. Together with the EditControlHeight property, determines how much window space is given to the author.

The more space you give authors, the happier they are. Ideally, for placeholders that contain a huge chunk of information, like the plant's description, the authoring space should stretch across the entire screen for maximum viewing. One thing about the HtmlPlaceholderControl is that you cannot define the height and width as a percentage of the page. When deciding the values of the EditControlHeight and EditControlWidth properties, think about the screen resolution your authors are using. Authors using an 800 x 600 resolution would have less screen space than those using a 1024 x 768 resolution, so do not make the size of the HtmlPlaceholderControl too large or too small.

AttachmentPlaceholder

Another useful placeholder available out of the box is the AttachmentPlaceholder. The AttachmentPlaceholder stores a link to a single document contained in the MCMS content repository. This document could exist in the resource gallery or it could be uploaded directly from the author's hard disk.

You will find it useful for a page that has a specific area containing links to documents and files for users to download and view. An HtmlPlaceholder could be used as a substitute. Authors could simply click on the Add Attachment button and add attachments to the HtmlPlaceholderControl. But doing so would mean that authors could attach an unlimited number of files and mix them together with the text/HTML (which may or may not be what you are looking for), and there would be no way to specify how the links are organized and laid out on the page.

The AttachmentPlaceholder offers the benefit of holding a link to one document only. In this way, you can control the number of attachments on the page by adding to the template the exact number of placeholders you require. The layout of the displayed hyperlinks is determined by the way you place them on the template: Authors won't get a chance to mess up the design of the page. It's also easier to work with when using the **Publishing Application Programming Interface (PAPI)** as we shall see later in Chapter 12.

Like the HtmlPlaceholder, the AttachmentPlaceholder requires you to define both a placeholder definition and placeholder control to work correctly.

Adding an AttachmentPlaceholderDefinition to the Template

We will now add an AttachmentPlaceholderDefinition to the Plant template to store the single research paper contributed by members.

With the Plant template checked out in Template Explorer, right-click on it and select Properties. Click on the PlaceholderDefinition field and open the Placeholder Definition Collection Editor. Click on the arrow next to the Add button. Select the AttachmentPlaceholderDefinition. Give the new Placeholder Definition the following properties:

Property	Property Value
Description	Research Paper on the Plant
Name	ResearchPaper
MustUseResourceGallery	False
UseGeneratedIcon	True

Click OK to close the Placeholder Definition Editor.

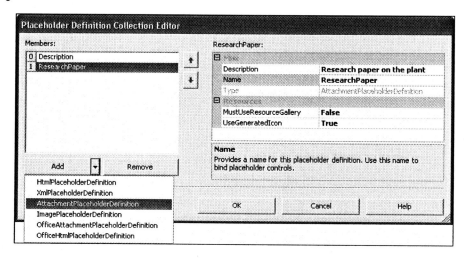

AttachmentPlaceholderDefinition Properties

The AttachmentPlaceholderDefinition has considerably less properties than the HtmlPlaceholderDefinition.

Property	Description
Description	Like the HtmlPlaceholderDefinition, the description holds up to 500 characters. It does not show up anywhere in the out-of-the-box solution, but you can always use the PAPI to retrieve this value for your own use. It is often used to describe what the placeholder is used for.
Name	See the Name property for the HtmlPlaceholderDefinition.
Type	Read-only. Contains the value AttachmentPlaceholderDefinition.
MustUseResourceGallery	See the MustUseResourceGallery property for theHTML Placeholder Definition.
UseGeneratedIcon	See the UseGeneratedIcon property for the HTML Placeholder Definition.

SingleAttachmentPlaceholderControl

In the days of the webmaster, creating a hyperlink to a file required the author to first upload the file to the web server, take note of its URL and use a web editing tool to create a hyperlink on the page. More often than not, this process was repeated multiple times in the creation of a page that might contain links to many dozens of files. It was a tedious process that tested the patience of most webmasters.

The SingleAttachmentPlaceholderControl is helpful to authors because it makes things easier for them by creating links to files in a single step. In authoring mode, it presents itself as a simple input field with three small buttons at the top as shown opposite. Clicking on the Add or Edit Attachment button on the placeholder control leads you to a dialog that prompts you to link to an existing resource gallery item or to upload a chosen file to the content repository and generates the

URL. The middle button shows a dialog where you can edit the properties of the attachment, and the last button removes the attachment.

> Note, however, that if you intend to link to a resource in the resource gallery, you will still have to perform the additional step of uploading the resource to the gallery first.

In presentation mode, the placeholder renders the hyperlink to the linked file in the form of text or a generated icon, based on the value of the UseGeneratedIcon property of the corresponding Placeholder Definition.

Adding a SingleAttachmentPlaceholderControl

Let's add a SingleAttachmentPlaceholderControl to the Plant template. The control will be used to upload a single document about the plant.

In Design view, drag and drop the SingleAttachmentPlaceholderControl from the toolbox to the Plant template file in the table cell that contains the words (Space for Research Paper), and then delete these words.

Right-click on the SingleAttachmentPlaceholderControl and select Properties. In the Properties window, set the following property values:

Property	Property Value
EnableAuthoring	True
PlaceholderToBind	ResearchPaper
ID	PlantResearchPaper

When you are done, save Plant.aspx. The Plant template file now appears as shown overleaf in Design view.

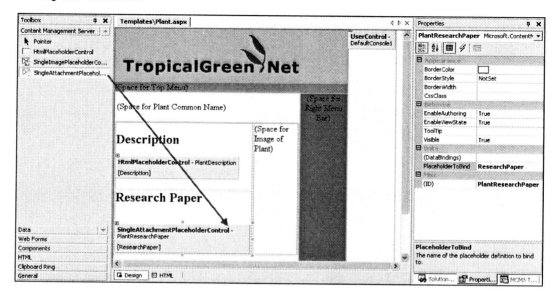

ImagePlaceholders

It has been said that a picture is worth a thousand words. It is common to add to a page an accompanying picture of its subject, which could take the form of a picture of a product, employees, a place or almost anything you can think of. Usually, the web designer would designate a place on the page for the image to be displayed. For example, a news article may display a picture of the story's subject next to its abstract.

You could use an HtmlPlaceholder to store the image. However, one major advantage of using an ImagePlaceholder is that as a developer, you get to control the size of the image. Images uploaded by authors would be automatically resized to fit the width and height specified.

You also ensure that authors do not mix text together with the image, thus making it easier to extract the image later for use on other pages.

The ImagePlaceholder is similar to the AttachmentPlaceholder with one major exception— it holds a link to an image instead of a file. And like the file in the AttachmentPlaceholder, this could either be an image from the resource gallery or an image uploaded from the author's desktop.

Adding an ImagePlaceholderDefinition to the Template

Now let's add an Image Placeholder to store a link to a picture of the plant.

As before, open the Placeholder Definition Editor by clicking on the ellipsis of the PlaceholderDefinitions field in the properties page of the Plant template object.

On the Placeholder Definition Editor, click on the down arrow next to the Add button. Select ImagePlaceholderDefinition. Set the following property values:

Property	Property Value
AllowHyperlinks	True
Description	Picture of the plant
Name	PlantPicture
MustUseResourceGallery	False

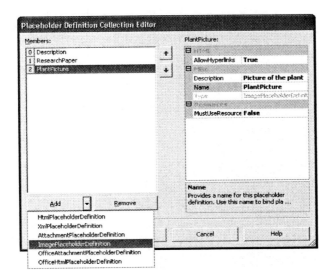

Click OK to close the Placeholder Definition Editor. This is the last change we will be doing to the template object, so let's check it in. In MCMS Template Explorer, right-click the Plant template object and select Check In from the pop-up menu.

ImagePlaceholderDefinition Properties

The ImagePlaceholderDefinition shares common properties with the AttachmentPlaceholderDefinition. It has an additional property (AllowHyperLinks) that allows the image to be hyperlinked.

Property	Description
AllowHyperLinks	When this is set to true, the image will be clickable. It will point to a URL set by authors in the SingleImagePlaceholderControl.
Description	See the Description property for the Attachment Placeholder Definition.

| Type | Read-only. Has the value `ImagePlaceholderDefinition`. |
| `MustUseResourceGallery` | See the `MustUseResourceGallery` property for the HTML Placeholder Definition. To allow authors to upload their own images, this property must be set to false. |

SingleImagePlaceholderControl

Like the `SingleAttachmentPlaceholderControl`, the `SingleImagePlaceholderControl` allows authors to upload a single image or link to an existing image in the resource gallery. It provides three buttons at the top, one for adding an image, a second for editing the image properties, and the third for removing the image.

Adding a SingleImagePlaceholderControl

Now let's add a `SingleImagePlaceholderControl` for authors to upload the picture of the plant.

With the Plant template file (`Plant.aspx`) opened in Design mode, drag and drop the SingleImagePlaceholderControl from the toolbox to the Plant template file in the table cell that contains the words (Space for Image of Plant), and then delete these words.

Open the properties page of the SingleImagePlaceholderControl by right-clicking on it and selecting Properties. Set the following property values:

Property	Property Value
ID	PlantPic
`EnableAuthoring`	True
`PlaceholderToBind`	PlantPicture
`DisplayWidth`	150px

Save `Plant.aspx` and you are done.

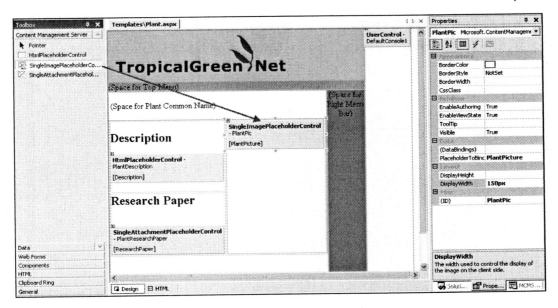

SingleImagePlaceholderControl Properties

Apart from the properties that are common across other placeholder controls, the SingleImagePlaceholderControl has two additional properties that govern its appearance.

Property	Description
DisplayHeight	Specifies the height of the image in pixels
DisplayWidth	Specifies the width of the image in pixels

The DisplayHeight and DisplayWidth property values are used together to fix the size of the image. If the referenced image is smaller/bigger than the specified height and width, it is expanded/shrunk accordingly. Be careful when uploading images with different height to width ratios, they will get distorted.

When the image is rendered on the page, the values are used for the style attributes in the <img> tag. For example, when the DisplayHeight is set to 100px and the DisplayWidth to 200px, the image is rendered as:

```
<img src="/nr/rdonlyres/guid/mypicture.gif" style="height:100px;width:200px;" >
```

The Completed Page

Now that we have added the placeholders, save and build the solution. To see the resulting page in authoring mode:

1. Save and build the TropicalGreen solution.
2. In Internet Explorer, navigate to `http://localhost/tropicalgreen/plantcatalog`.
3. Click on the Switch To Edit Site link in the Web Author Console.
4. Click Edit.

The first time an author opens a posting that contains an `HtmlPlaceholderControl` for editing, they will be prompted to install the ActiveX control for the "Microsoft CMS HTML Editor" . The author must have Power User or Administrator rights on the Windows machine in order to install this control. If you get the following dialog box, click Yes:

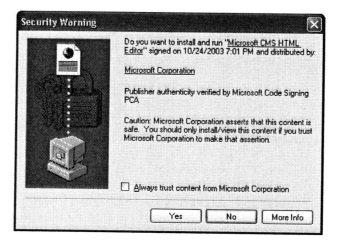

Here's what you will see:

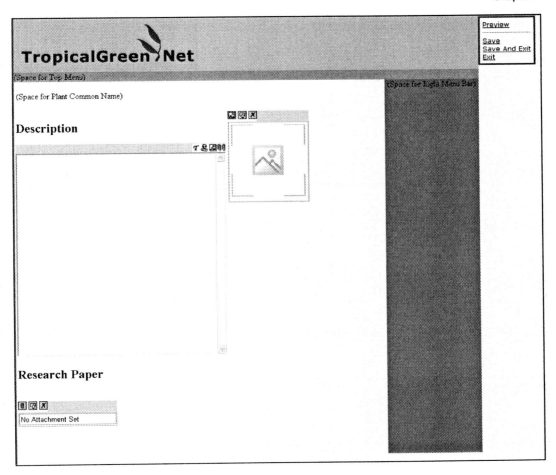

The posting that we created earlier now has an `HtmlPlaceholderControl` for entering the description, a `SingleAttachmentPlaceholderControl` for uploading a single research paper, and a `SingleImagePlaceholderControl` for uploading the plant's image.

Linking a Stylesheet to the Template File

Like other web forms, you could embed style information within HTML tags or web controls used in the template file. For example, the code below sets the level-1 header to bold, with an orange color and 14 points type size:

```
<H1 style= "color:#993300;font-weight:bold;font-size:14pt">Testing</H1>
```

The drawback to this approach is that it applies the styles only to the particular tag. For the style to be consistently applied to all level-1 headings, it has to be duplicated on all `<H1>` tags.

Alternatively, you could insert the style information between <head> tags like this:

```
<head>
    <style>
        H1{color:#993300;font-weight:bold;font-size:14pt}
    </style>
</head>
```

Embedding the style as inline code between the <head> tags ensures that all similar tags on the page use the style defined. However, using this method, the style information must be duplicated on all template files that require it.

The nice thing about linking to a stylesheet is that it allows you to update the look and feel of all template files that are linked to it by modifying a single document. We will create a cascading stylesheet (CSS) for the TropicalGreen site and link it to the Plant.aspx template file:

1. In the Solution Explorer, right-click on the Styles folder and select Add | Add New Item. Add a new Style Sheet and name it styles.css.

2. styles.css opens and is ready for editing. Enter the following styles:

```
Body{font-family:Verdana,Arial;font-size:11pt}
A{color:#0000ff;font-size:10pt;font-weight:bold}
.TopMenu{font-weight: bold;font-size:11pt;color:#CCFF99;text-
                                             decoration:none;}
.RightMenu{font-size:11pt;color:#CCFF99;text-decoration:none;font-
                                             weight:bold}
H1{color:#993300;font-weight:bold;font-size:14pt}
H2{color:#FF6600;font-weight:bold;font-size:12pt}
.BodyText{font-family:Verdana,Arial;font-size:10pt}
```

3. Save styles.css.

4. Drag styles.css from Solution Explorer and drop it onto the Plant.aspx web form in Design view.

5. Switch to HTML view.

6. Between the <head> tags, look for the <LINK> tag shown below:

```
<LINK href="../Styles/Styles.css" type="text/css" rel="stylesheet">
```

7. Notice that the URL to the stylesheet is a relative link and not an absolute link. When linking stylesheets to template files, you *should* use absolute links. The reason being, when viewing a posting, e.g. http://localhost/mysite/channelA/channelB/myPage.htm based on a template file that has a relative link, the server won't be able to load styles.css because it would be looking for it in http://localhost/mysite/channelA/Styles/Styles.css. Change the value of the href attribute to point to an absolute URL:

```
<LINK href="/tropicalgreen/Styles/Styles.css" type="text/css"
                                             rel="stylesheet">
```

8. Save Plant.aspx.

We could have chosen to set the RenderBaseHref property of the RobotMetaTag control to true instead of setting an absolute URL. When the <base> tag is rendered, it ensures that relative links on the page work correctly too.

Navigate to `http://localhost/tropicalgreen/plantcatalog` again. Click **Switch to Edit Site** and click **Edit**. The resulting page reflects the newly applied stylesheet as shown below.

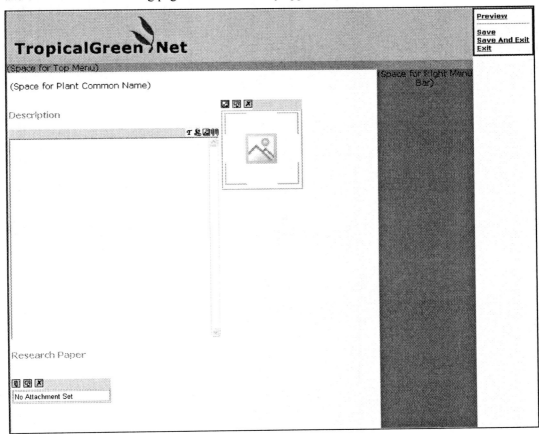

Summary

In this chapter we discussed what placeholders are and how they can be used to divide content into manageable chunks. Placeholders consist of three basic elements:

- The placeholder control
- The placeholder definition
- The placeholder object

We looked at the properties of the `HtmlPlaceholder`, the `AttachmentPlaceholder`, and the `ImagePlaceholder` and their corresponding placeholder definitions. We added placeholders of each type onto the Plant template file. Using the Placeholder Definition Editor, we added corresponding placeholder definitions for each placeholder control and linked them using Template Explorer. As a result, we now have editable areas for authors to write content to.

Finally, we looked at how stylesheets can be applied correctly to a template file by using absolute links instead of relative links.

In Chapter 11, we will look at the Web Author Console interface and put on our author's hat to generate plant fact sheets from the Plant template.

8

Debugging Template Files

At some point in time, you are going to find a bug in your application. Ideally, we would write applications that have zero defects. However, despite our best efforts at writing perfect code, chances are, the application is not going to behave as you expect the first time you run it.

Creating quality code is appreciated by everyone and an important part of that is a process of rigorous testing and debugging before release. The debugging techniques discussed in this chapter are similar to those that apply to regular ASP.NET web applications with several key differences, which we will highlight as we work through each section. Each method discussed is equally effective in debugging a solution.

Before We Begin

If you have been following us so far, your code should be bug free, as the sample code has been thoroughly tested. In order to demonstrate debugging, we will now introduce a bug into the template code.

To add a bug to the Plant template file:

1. Open the TropicalGreen solution in Visual Studio .NET.

2. Open the Plant.aspx template file.

3. In HTML view, replace the text markers (Space for Plant Common Name) with the following code:

```
<h1>
    <asp:Literal id="PlantCommonName" runat="server"></asp:Literal>
</h1>
```

4. To preview the layout of the page, toggle to Design view.

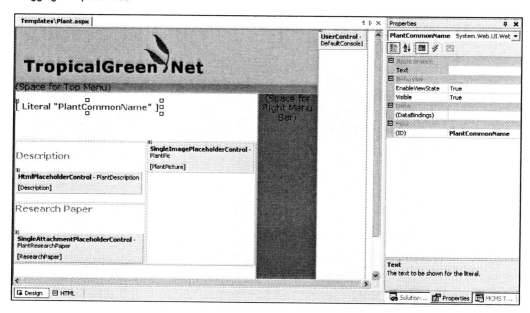

5. Double-click on the template file in Design view. This will bring you to the
Page_Load() event of the code-behind file. First, add the required namespace at the
top of the code:

```
using System;
using System.Collections;
using System.ComponentModel;
using System.Data;
using System.Drawing;
using System.Web;
using System.Web.SessionState;
using System.Web.UI;
using System.Web.UI.WebControls;
using System.Web.UI.HtmlControls;
using Microsoft.ContentManagement.Publishing;

namespace TropicalGreen.Templates
{
    . . . code continues . . .
}
```

In the Page_Load() section, enter:

```
private void Page_Load(object sender, System.EventArgs e)
{
    // Put user code to initialize the page here
    string pageDisplayName = CmsHttpContext.Current.Channel.DisplayName;
    PlantCommonName.Text = pageDisplayName;
}
```

6. Save and build the solution.

When the template file loads, it writes the DisplayName of the channel to the Text property of the
PlantCommonName Literal control. That is not correct because we should show the DisplayName of

the posting instead. The channel's DisplayName will always be Plant Catalog—that is not the name of the plant. This is the bug we are introducing and the one we are going to catch.

Now that we have a bug, let's enable debugging on our project.

> Note that this is a design bug, not a code bug. Therefore, you will be able to build the project without any problems.

Enable Debugging on the TropicalGreen Project

Your project should be ready for debugging without having to change any settings. However, double-check the project options to ensure that it is properly set up for debugging. To do so:

1. Open the web.config file of the TropicalGreen solution.

2. Look for the <compilation> tag. Ensure that the debug attribute has been set to true.

```
<compilation defaultLanguage="c#" debug="true">
    <assemblies>
        . . . code continues . . .
    </assemblies>
</compilation>
```

3. Save and close the web.config file.

And we are ready to start debugging. There are two ways to go about debugging an MCMS web application: the correct way and the wrong way.

Debugging the Template File: The Wrong Way

One MCMS developer was overheard asking another how to debug a template file. To which, the reply was "We don't debug. Use `Response.Write`."

While introducing `Response.Write` statements before and after every block of problem code can help you determine which variable is holding the wrong values, it is an outdated debugging technique left over from ASP days. You have to go guess which block of code or variable is causing problems and you get no clue as to how the code is being called within routines or what's really happening.

Another popular technique that works when debugging regular ASP.NET web applications might lead an MCMS developer to set TropicalGreen as the Start Up project and make the template file the start page. We'll see why this doesn't work in the following section.

Attempting to Test the Plant.aspx Template File: The Wrong Way

Let's try setting the Plant template file as the start page and see what happens:

1. In Solution Explorer, right-click on the TropicalGreen project. Select Set as StartUp Project in the pop-up menu.
2. Right-click on the `Plant.aspx` file and select Set As Start Page
3. From the Visual Studio toolbar, select Debug | Start (or press *F5*).

Here's what you will see:

```
Server Error in '/TropicalGreen' Application.
```

This operation requires the context of a Posting. The request must have a valid Posting Url or QueryString so that the CmsHttpContext.Posting will not be null.

Description: An unhandled exception occurred during the execution of the current web request. Please review the stack trace for more information about the error and where it originated in the code.

Exception Details: Microsoft.ContentManagement.WebControls.WebAuthorException: This operation requires the context of a Posting. The request must have a valid Posting Url or QueryString so that the CmsHttpContext.Posting will not be null.

Source Error:

```
Line 38:              //
Line 39:              InitializeComponent();
Line 40:              base.OnInit(e);
Line 41:      }
Line 42:
```

Source File: c:\inetpub\wwwroot\tropicalgreen\templates\plant.aspx.cs   **Line:** 40

Stack Trace:

```
[WebAuthorException: This operation requires the context of a Posting.  The request must have a valid Posting Url
   Microsoft.ContentManagement.WebControls.BasePlaceholderControl.initializePlaceholderObject() +96
   Microsoft.ContentManagement.WebControls.BasePlaceholderControl.initializeBinding() +64
   Microsoft.ContentManagement.WebControls.BasePlaceholderControl.Page_Init(Object sender, EventArgs e) +11
   System.EventHandler.Invoke(Object sender, EventArgs e) +0
   System.Web.UI.Control.OnInit(EventArgs e) +67
   TropicalGreen.Templates.Plant.OnInit(EventArgs e) in c:\inetpub\wwwroot\tropicalgreen\templates\plant.aspx.cs:
   System.Web.UI.Control.InitRecursive(Control namingContainer) +241
   System.Web.UI.Page.ProcessRequestMain() +174
```

Version Information: Microsoft .NET Framework Version:1.1.4322.573; ASP.NET Version:1.1.4322.573

This is the error message that appears:

> This operation requires the context of a Posting. The request must have a valid Posting Url or queryString so that CmsHttpContext.Posting will not be null.

You've got to like ASP.NET. Its error messages are very descriptive. There are times when we wonder why, since it knows what went wrong, it doesn't also fix itself.

The reason this method of debugging doesn't work is because templates cannot be called directly from a browser. They need to be called in the context of a posting.

Attempting to enter `http://localhost/tropicalgreen/templates/plant.aspx` in your browser calls for a template file directly and you would get the same error message as above. However, entering `http://localhost/tropicalgreen/plantcatalog/hibiscus.htm` calls for a posting and gives you the page based on the Plant template.

The conclusion is: You can't test the Plant template by simply setting that as the start page of the project. While this technique works for regular ASP.NET web applications, it won't work for an MCMS web application.

Debugging the Template File: The Correct Way

To debug a template file correctly, we need to start the debugger from a posting instead of a template file. However, postings do not appear as physical pages within the Solution Explorer so it is not as straightforward as setting the posting as a start page.

There are three ways of getting the debugger to start from a posting:

1. Create a debug page that points to a posting.
2. Start the Debugger from a URL.
3. Attach the Debugger to the ASP.NET Worker Process (`aspnet_wp.exe` on Windows 2000 and Windows XP or `w3wp.exe` on Windows Server 2003).

Debugging with a Debug Start Page

One way to debug is to create a debug page. The debug page is simply an HTML file that contains hyperlinks to a posting that uses the template you wish to debug.

Creating the Debug Page

Let's create a dummy page that links to the plant catalog. First, if you haven't already, stop debugging by going to the Visual Studio .NET toolbar and selecting Debug | Stop Debugging.

When debugging stops, go to the Solution Explorer and right-click the TropicalGreen project. Select Add | Add New Item.

Select the Web Project Items category and create a new HTML Page called `DebugStartPage.htm`. The new file opens and is ready for editing.

Enter the text:

Navigate to TropicalGreen Plant Catalog and debug.

Convert the text into a hyperlink by highlighting it and selecting Format | Convert to HyperLink from the Visual Studio .NET toolbar or pressing *Ctrl + L*. Set the URL to:

```
http://localhost/tropicalgreen/plantcatalog
```

Use Insert | Hyperlink in Visual Studio .NET 2002.

Setting the Debug Page as the Start Page

In Solution Explorer, right-click `DebugStartPage.htm` and select Set As Start Page in the menu.

When you are done, save `DebugStartPage.htm`.

Debugging the Plant Template using the Debug Start Page

Now that we've created the Debug page, let's proceed to test our template through the Visual Studio .NET debugging environment.

First, add a breakpoint. In Design view, double-click the `Plant.aspx` file. That will take you to the `Page_Load()` event handler of the code-behind file.

160

Go to the line that says:

```
PlantCommonName.Text = pageDisplayName;
```

Place a breakpoint on that line of code. You can do this using one of the following ways:

1. Right-clicking on the line and selecting Insert Breakpoint
2. Pressing *F9*
3. Left-clicking on the left-margin

The line of code is highlighted by a red bar with a circle in the margin as shown below.

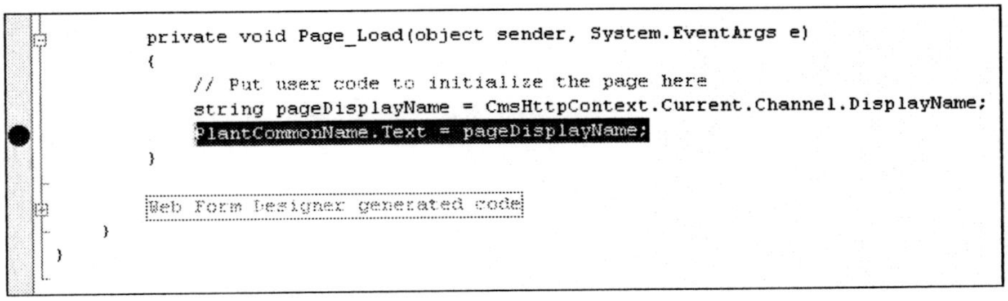

```
private void Page_Load(object sender, System.EventArgs e)
{
    // Put user code to initialize the page here
    string pageDisplayName = CmsHttpContext.Current.Channel.DisplayName;
    PlantCommonName.Text = pageDisplayName;
}

Web Form Designer generated code
```

Starting the Debugger

From the Visual Studio .NET toolbar, select Debug | Start (or press *F5*). The browser opens with the debugstartpage.htm file we created earlier. Click on the Navigate to TropicalGreen PlantCatalog and debug hyperlink. Visual Studio .NET stops the application and goes into debug mode. More importantly, it stops at the breakpoint that you inserted.

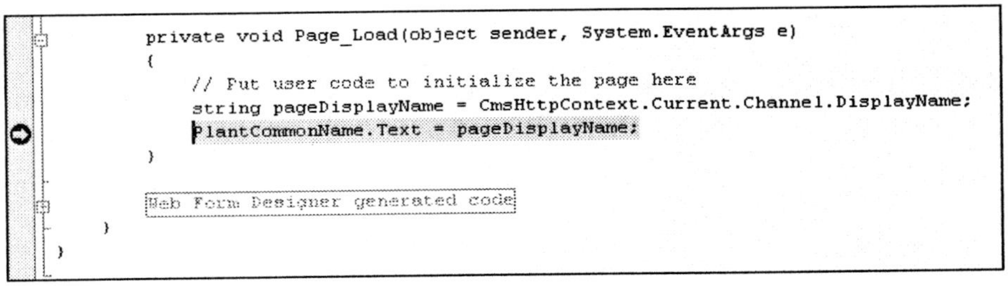

```
private void Page_Load(object sender, System.EventArgs e)
{
    // Put user code to initialize the page here
    string pageDisplayName = CmsHttpContext.Current.Channel.DisplayName;
    PlantCommonName.Text = pageDisplayName;
}

Web Form Designer generated code
```

You can view the values of the variables by placing your mouse cursor over them. Place your mouse cursor over the pageDisplayName variable. A tooltip appears with the words Plant Catalog. Now we know that pageDisplayName is holding the wrong value.

```
        private void Page_Load(object sender, System.EventArgs e)
        {
            // Put user code to initialize the page here
            string pageDisplayName = CmsHttpContext.Current.Channel.DisplayName;
            PlantCommonName.Text = pageDisplayName;
        }                                           ┌────────────────────────────────┐
                                                    │pageDisplayName = "Plant Catalog"│
                                                    └────────────────────────────────┘
        ┌──────────────────────────────────┐
        │Web Form Designer generated code  │
        └──────────────────────────────────┘
    }
}
```

The best part about debugging within Visual Studio .NET is the ability to place breakpoints anywhere in your code-behind files. You enjoy the full features of the debugger such as the **command** and **watches** windows.

> There are many debugging features available in Visual Studio .NET. We won't attempt to explain all of them. The aim of this section is to show you how to reach a breakpoint in the template file. From there, you can make use of any available debugging tool to debug your application. To find out more about debugging in a Visual Studio .NET environment, see:
>
> http://msdn.microsoft.com/library/default.asp?url=/library/en-us/vsdebug/html/vc_Debugging_Your_Application_home_page.asp.

Stopping the Debugger

To stop debugging, simply close the browser. Or you could select Debug | Stop Debugging from Visual Studio .NET's toolbar.

Debugging by Starting from a URL

The debug start page provides a way to debug template files. However, it requires a dummy page to be created in the project. Another way is to configure Visual Studio .NET to begin debugging from a URL instead of a project file:

1.   In Solution Explorer, right-click on the TropicalGreen project and select Properties.
2.   In the left-hand panel, select Configuration Properties | Debugging.
3.   Set Debug Mode to URL. Click Apply.
4.   In the Start URL field, enter http://localhost/tropicalgreen/plantcatalog/.
5.   Click OK.

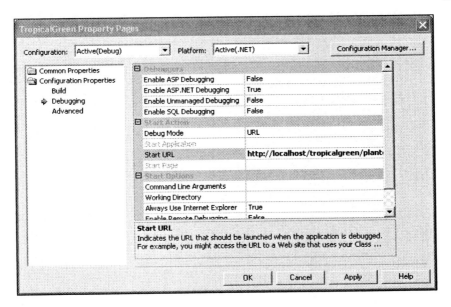

When you press *F5* or select Debug | Start from the toolbar, the browser now opens from `http://localhost/tropicalgreen/plantcatalog/`.

Debugging by Attaching the Debugger to the ASP.NET Worker Process

All web pages are served by the ASP.NET worker process (`aspnet_wp.exe` on Windows 2000 and Windows XP or `w3wp.exe` on Windows Server 2003). Another popular method of debugging standard ASP.NET web applications is to attach the debugger to the ASP.NET worker process, and this works for MCMS projects too. Using this method, you don't have to create a dummy page containing hyperlinks to all parts of your website.

Attaching the Debugger

From the Visual Studio .NET toolbar, select Debug | Processes. The Processes dialog opens:

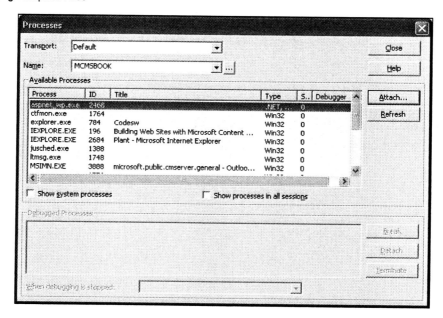

In the list of Available Processes, select the ASP.NET worker process. For Windows 2000 and Windows XP systems, select aspnet_wp.exe and for Windows Server 2003, select w3wp.exe. Click Attach.... The Attach Processes dialog opens. Ensure that the Common Language Runtime option is checked. Click OK to close the Attach to Process dialog.

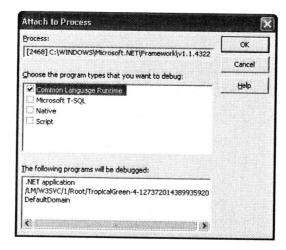

Click Close to close the dialog.

I'm using Windows Server 2003 and there are multiple w3wp.exe processes running. How do I determine which one to use?

One fast and easy way to identify the running w3wp.exe processes is to use the iisapp.vbs script located in the c:\windows\system32 directory.

On your Windows Server 2003 machine, open a command prompt and type:

```
cd c:\windows\system32
```

Then type:

```
iisapp.vbs
```

and hit the *Enter* key. This makes it is simple to find the right process. The output looks like this:

```
W3WP.exe PID: 3676   AppPoolId: DefaultAppPool
```

If you have more than one w3wp.exe listed, you can figure out which app is yours by reviewing the process ID (PID) and the IIS application pool (AppPoolId).

Debugging the Template File

Open Internet Explorer and browse to http://localhost/tropicalgreen/plantcatalog. Since we have just created the one plant posting for Hibiscus, the page will load the Plant.aspx template.

As the Page_Load event handler of the Plant.aspx template file is called, the debugger stops at the specified breakpoint. From here, you can use any of the debugging features available.

Stopping the Debugger

To stop debugging, select Debug | Stop Debugging or press *Shift + F5*. This resets the process's debug settings as well, so if you want to debug the template again you will have to attach it again.

Solving the Problem

Now that we know where the bug is, we can solve the problem. Stop any ongoing debugging process if you have not done so. In the code-behind file of the Plant.aspx template file, change the following code, from:

```
PlantCommonName.Text = CmsHttpContext.Current.Channel.DisplayName;
```

to:

```
PlantCommonName.Text = CmsHttpContext.Current.Posting.DisplayName;
```

Save and build the solution.

Removing Breakpoints

The fastest way to remove a breakpoint is to click on the red circle that appears at the margin or to place the cursor at the highlighted line and press *F9*.

Selecting Debug | Clear All Breakpoints or Pressing *Ctrl + Shift + F9* removes all breakpoints in the solution.

Summary

In this chapter, we covered the basics of debugging an MCMS template file. We started by showing you one way to debug your code that turns out not to work for MCMS projects. Setting the template file as the start page does not work for MCMS web applications.

The correct way is to set a posting, not a template file, as a start page. In order to debug a template file correctly, you must choose between creating a dummy debug start page and attaching the debugger to the ASP.NET worker process. You can use either method to debug an MCMS project; both are equally effective in tracing bugs.

9

Default Postings and Channel Rendering Scripts

We can create many fact sheets for our Plant Catalog, but none of them can be found unless people know the URLs. A summary page (also known as an index page, default page, or cover page) is a page that typically lists pages within a given section. In this chapter, we introduce the concept of default postings and channel rendering scripts and the use of these techniques to create a summary page. Our summary page will list the plants from A-Z and provide hyperlinks to the corresponding fact sheets.

Making a summary page is nice, because if someone only knows the existence of the plant catalog, they can access the fact sheets without having to know the exact name of the plant that they are looking for. Another benefit of using generated summary pages is better link management. Before the days of content management, webmasters manually updated hyperlinks to a summary page. It was a manual and tedious process that often led to HTTP 404 (file not found) errors when pages were deleted but the summary page still contained a link to them. With dynamically generated summary pages, only working links are shown to visitors. The following figure shows the summary page for the Plant Catalog channel that we will be building in this chapter.

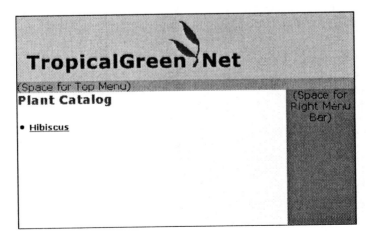

Traditionally, the summary page is returned when the URL requested matches the directory. For example, when a user requests http://website/FolderA/, the summary page that lists all the pages available within FolderA is displayed. In MCMS, FolderA corresponds to a channel; in our case, the PlantCatalog channel. We will show you how you can designate a posting as the summary page by assigning it to be the default posting of a channel. We will also provide an alternative that achieves the same results by using a channel rendering script.

Default Postings

Channels and folders are not pages. When users request a URL that matches a channel or a folder, what should they see? The idea of assigning a default posting to a channel is very much like the concept of default.htm files in Microsoft Internet Information Services (IIS). In MCMS, every channel object has a DefaultPostingName property. When a request that matches the URL of a channel is made, the posting with a name that matches the value stored in the channel's DefaultPostingName property will be displayed.

There are two ways to go about assigning default postings to a channel. You could:

- Use Site Manager. This is the easiest and fastest method, which we will explore in this chapter.
- Use the Publishing Application Programming Interface (or PAPI; see Chapter 12 for information about using the PAPI).

Using Site Manager to Assign the Default Posting Name

Let's use Site Manager to assign a Default Posting Name to the Plant Catalog channel.

1. Open Site Manager. Log in using your current Windows credentials. You need to belong to a group that has the rights to assign properties to channels, such as MCMS administrator or channel manager. We discuss MCMS roles and rights in Chapter 10.
2. By default, the Channels panel is displayed when Site Manager first starts. Expand the TropicalGreen channel to reveal its sub-channels. Right-click on the PlantCatalog channel and select Properties from the pop-up menu.
3. In the PlantCatalog Properties dialog box, on the Publishing tab, look at the section labeled Channel Rendering. Click Select...

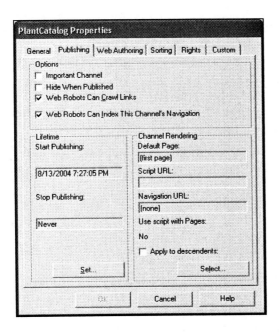

4. The Select Channel Rendering dialog opens. In the Default Page section, select the Use page with this name option. Enter Summary in the text box. Ensure that the Script URL field is blank. We choose the name "Summary" because later on, we are going to create a corresponding posting named "Summary" in the Plant Catalog channel. You can also enter the name of any other posting within the channel and use it as the default posting.

5. Click OK to close the Select Channel Rendering dialog.

6. Click OK to close the PlantCatalog Properties dialog.

And you're done. When the URL matches that of the channel, the server looks for a page named Summary and, when found, delivers it.

When There Are No Postings in the Channel with the Default Posting's Name

Wait a minute, what if the channel does not contain a posting that goes by the default posting's name? When that happens, it shows the first posting it finds in the channel. The first posting is the one that has the highest position in the posting collection. This is defined by the posting's SortOrdinal property. The posting with the highest SortOrdinal value is the first posting.

> The SortOrdinal of a posting is a number that describes the position of the posting relative to other postings/channels in the same channel. The higher the SortOrdinal number, the higher the posting is in the hierarchy. If the default page is not set, the posting with the highest SortOrdinal property automatically becomes the default.

A newly created posting is assigned the lowest SortOrdinal value of 0. In the case where all your postings share the same SortOrdinal value, MCMS picks a posting from the collection at random and you can't predict which posting would be returned.

If there are no postings at all, the channel will revert to the MCMS default cover page.

When More Than One Posting Has the Default Posting's Name

And what happens when there are two or more postings have the same name as the default posting? For example, you could have two published postings in the PlantCatalog channel that are named Summary. Again, the channel returns the posting named Summary (or whatever the DefaultPostingName is set to) with the highest SortOrdinal value.

Coding the Summary Page

Now that we have assigned a Default Posting Name to the PlantCatalog channel, we need to create a posting of that name. Our summary page will be based on a template that lists the plants from A-Z. To do so, we will follow these steps:

1. Build the PlantCatalog_Summary.aspx template file

2. Create the PlantCatalogHome template object and link it to the PlantCatalog_Summary.aspx template file

3. Create a new posting with the name Summary.

The PlantCatalog_Summary Template File

Let's start by creating the template file.

Add a new web form (not an MCMS template file) to the Templates folder of the TropicalGreen project. Name the file PlantCatalog_Summary.aspx. Change the Page Layout to FlowLayout.

With the PlantCatalog_Summary.aspx template file opened in HTML view, link styles.css to the web form by adding the following line between the <head> tags.

```
<LINK href="/tropicalgreen/Styles/Styles.css" type="text/css"
rel="stylesheet">
```

Now enter the following code between the <form> tags. This code provides the basic structure of the page, including the top banner, space for the default console, and visual markers for other controls. Enter the text as you see it, including the words in each table cell.

```
<table width="100%" border="0" cellspacing="0" cellpadding="0" height="100%">
<tr>
    <td valign="top">
     <h1>(Space for Header)</h1>
     (Space for Table)
    </td>
     <td valign="top">
        (Space for Console)
     </td>
</tr>
</table>
```

Toggle to design, drag and drop the following controls, and delete the text markers when you have done so.

Control	Drag From	Drop On	Properties	Used For
Table	Toolbox | Web Forms	Table cell with the words (Space for Table)	ID = CatalogTable	A table that contains rows of plant fact sheets arranged alphabetically from A-Z
DefaultConsole.ascx	Solution Explorer | Console | DefaultConsole.ascx	Table cell with the words (Space for Console)	Keep the default property values	The Web Author Console that contains the action buttons used to manage postings
Literal	Toolbox | Web Forms	Table cell with the words (Space for Header)	ID = litHeader	The subject of the page

Double-click on the form to open its code-behind file (PlantCatalog_Summary.aspx.cs) and add the following code above the namespace declaration. Doing this will enable us to use all the classes in the Microsoft.ContentManagement.Publishing namespace without having to type in the entire namespace.

```
using System;
using System.Collections;
using System.ComponentModel;
using System.Data;
using System.Drawing;
```

```
using System.web;
using System.web.SessionState;
using System.web.UI;
using System.web.UI.WebControls;
using System.web.UI.HtmlControls;

//add reference to Microsoft Content Management Server
using Microsoft.ContentManagement.Publishing;

namespace TropicalGreen.Templates
{
    public class PlantCatalog_Summary : System.web.UI.Page
    {
        . . . code continues. . .
    }
}
```

Ensure that both the CatalogTable variable and the Page_Load() event handler have been defined. Visual Studio .NET automatically adds these declarations when you double-click on the web form.

```
protected System.web.UI.WebControls.Table CatalogTable;
private void Page_Load(object sender, System.EventArgs e)
{
// Put user code to initialize the page here
}
```

In the Page_Load event handler, add the code as shown below.

```
private void Page_Load(object sender, System.EventArgs e)
{
    // Put user code to initialize the page here

    //Get the current CmsHttpContext
    CmsHttpContext cmsContext = CmsHttpContext.Current;

    //Get the current channel
    Channel currentChannel = cmsContext.Channel;

    //display the display name of the channel in the header
    litHeader.Text = currentChannel.DisplayName;

    //get the collection of postings in the current channel
    PostingCollection postings = cmsContext.Channel.Postings;

    //sort the postings from A-Z
    postings.SortByDisplayName(true);

    //iterate through each posting in the collection
    //and add a table row to the CatalogTable
    foreach(Posting plant in postings)
    {
        if(currentChannel.DefaultPostingName != plant.Name)
        {
            CatalogTable.Rows.Add(AddPlant(plant));
        }
    }
}
```

We first get a reference to the current context in the cmsContext variable. When you enter CmsHttpContext.Current and press the period (.) key, IntelliSense introduces a long list of objects that can be accessed. The one we are interested in is the current channel the visitor is viewing (the PlantCatalog channel) which is held in the cmsContext.Channel property.

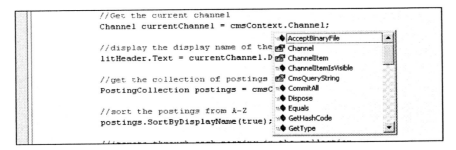

Since we are generating a list of plants, we need to iterate through all postings beneath the PlantCatalog channel. Within the foreach statement, a new row is added to the CatalogTable using the AddPlant() method defined next.

Beneath the Page_Load() event handler, define the AddPlant() method. This method accepts a Posting object and returns a new table row containing a hyperlink to the corresponding plant type page and a short description.

```
private TableRow AddPlant(Posting plant)
{
    TableRow row;
    TableCell cell;
    HtmlAnchor plantLink;

    plantLink = new HtmlAnchor();
    plantLink.InnerText = HttpUtility.HtmlEncode(plant.DisplayName);
    plantLink.HRef = plant.Url;

    row = new TableRow();
    cell = new TableCell();
    cell.Controls.Add(new LiteralControl("&#8226; "));
    cell.Controls.Add(plantLink);
    row.Cells.Add(cell);

    return (row);
}
```

Basically, this section of code will generate the following HTML code programmatically:

```
<tr>
    <td>
        &#8226;
        <a href="/TropicalGreen/PlantCatalog/<postingName>.htm">
            [Posting Name]
        </a>
    </td>
</tr>
```

Finally, save PlantCatalog_Summary.aspx and build the solution.

That's the first half of the template. The next half consists of the template object that links to the template file that we have just created.

The PlantCatalogHome Template Object

We need to create a template object in the content repository that links to the `PlantCatalog_Summary.aspx` template file.

1. In the MCMS Template Explorer, add a new template to the PlantCatalog template gallery.
2. Name the new template `PlantCatalogHome`.
3. Set the `TemplateFile` property of the `PlantCatalogHome` template to point to the newly created `Templates/PlantCatalog_DefaultPage.aspx` file.
4. Check-in the template object.

The Summary Posting

Earlier, we set the Default Posting Name for the PlantCatalog channel to Summary. Now that we have the both the template file and template object built, we are ready to create this Summary posting. To do so:

1. Navigate to `http://localhost/tropicalgreen/plantcatalog` in Internet Explorer. Because we don't have any postings that match the Default Posting Name value, the first posting in the channel is displayed.
2. Click Switch to Edit Site.
3. Click Create New Page.
4. In the Select Template dialog, browse to the PlantCatalog template gallery and select the PlantCatalogHome template.
5. When the new page is displayed in the browser, click Save New Page.
6. In the Save New Page dialog, set both the name and display name of the page to Summary. Click OK.
7. Click Submit to make it available on the live site.

We now have a summary page by setting a posting to be the default page of the channel.

Viewing the Summary Posting

When you next visit `http://localhost/tropicalgreen/plantcatalog`, the summary page gets displayed instead of a plant fact sheet.

Notice how the list of fact sheets is automatically generated as rows in a table. Right now, we only have the Hibiscus fact sheet listed. Each time a fact sheet is added or deleted, the summary page is automatically updated, providing current information to visitors.

Plant Catalog   Switch To Edit Site

• Hibiscus

Next, we will show you another way to create the summary page—one that does not require the use of postings. Instead we will use a channel rendering script.

Channel Rendering Scripts

A channel rendering script is so named because it is the page that gets displayed (or rendered) when the URL matches that of a channel.

The beauty of channel rendering scripts is that they work even though the channel has no postings. Using a channel rendering script, you cut two steps from the process—creating the template gallery item and creating the posting.

Channel rendering scripts are usually used to display a page that shows how the channel is positioned in the web hierarchy when no postings exist for the user to peruse. Another popular use of channel rendering scripts is in the implementation of framed sites as we shall see later.

Creating a Channel Rendering Script

Channel rendering scripts provide an alternative to assigning a default posting to the channel. Let's use this technique to create the summary page.

Normally, you would simply create a new web form and build the channel rendering script from scratch. Since we have already built a working script when creating the default posting, we will reuse what we have done so far and simply make a copy of the PlantCatalog_Summary.aspx template file.

1. Make a copy of the PlantCatalog_Summary.aspx web form and store it in the Template folder. You can do this by dragging and dropping the file in Solution Explorer using the right mouse button. Rename the copy ChannelRenderingScript.aspx.

2. Look for all occurrences of the string PlantCatalog_Summary and replace it with ChannelRenderingScript in both the ChannelRenderingScript.aspx page and its code-behind file. Use the Edit | Find and Replace feature with the .aspx page in HTML view and the .aspx.cs page in code view.

3. Double-click on the web form in design view. You are brought to the Page_Load event handler.

4. Modify the text displayed in the litHeader Literal control to indicate that this web form is different from the one that we have created earlier. Also, because there is no longer a designated default posting, you can comment out the lines that check for the default posting name in the Page_Load event handler.

```
private void Page_Load(object sender, System.EventArgs e)
{
    // Put user code to initialize the page here

    //Get the current CmsHttpContext
    CmsHttpContext cmsContext = CmsHttpContext.Current;

    //Get the current channel
```

```
Channel currentChannel = cmsContext.Channel;

//display the display name of the channel in the header
litHeader.Text = currentChannel.DisplayName + " Generated from
                ChannelRenderingScript.aspx";

//get the collection of postings in the current channel
PostingCollection postings = cmsContext.Channel.Postings;

//sort the postings from A-Z
postings.SortByDisplayName(true);

//iterate through each posting in the collection
//and add a table row to the CatalogTable
foreach(Posting plant in postings)
{
    //if(currentChannel.DefaultPostingName != plant.Name)
    //{
        CatalogTable.Rows.Add(AddPlant(plant));
    //}
}
}
```

5. Save the `ChannelRenderingScript.aspx` page and build the solution.

Using Site Manager to Assign the Channel Rendering Script to the Channel

Now we will use Site Manager to assign our newly created channel rendering script to the PlantCatalog channel.

1. In Site Manager, right-click on the PlantCatalog channel, select Properties from the pop-up menu, and in the Publishing tab of the PlantCatalog Properties dialog click Select...

2. This time, we are interested in the Channel Rendering section of the dialog. Set the Script URL to /tropicalgreen/templates/ChannelRenderingScript.aspx. For now, we will set the Use Channel script with Pages option to no. Later, we will turn this option to yes and see how it is used in the implementation of a framed site.

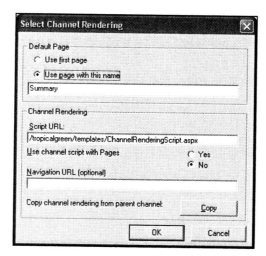

3. Click OK to close the Select Channel Rendering Dialog, and OK again to close the PlantCatalog Properties dialog.

What you have just done is to instruct MCMS to render `ChannelRenderingScript.aspx` whenever a request for `http://localhost/tropicalgreen/PlantCatalog/` is made.

Valid Script URLs

The Script URL property takes in a relative path; you can't enter an absolute path such as `http://localhost/tropicalgreen` as the colon character ":" is not accepted and you will get the error message shown below. So all channel rendering scripts must reside in the same web space as the MCMS website you are building.

Furthermore, the Script URL property only accepts valid URLs. A valid URL is one that is:

*   Less than 2000 characters
*   Starts with the character '/'. Although you are allowed to enter a path without a slash, you will get an `Invalid URI: The hostname could not be parsed` error message when accessing the URL of the channel from the browser.
*   Contains only the characters 0-9, A-Z, a-z, . ( ) \ - _ { } & ' $ @ ~ ! ^ # /
*   Does not contain two consecutive periods (..) or end with a period

If you entered an illegal character, you will get an error message:

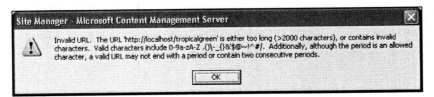

Testing the Channel Rendering Script

The next time you visit `http://localhost/tropicalgreen/plantcatalog`, the channel rendering script executes and displays the summary page. The page named Summary appears in the list of plant fact sheets. To remove it, simply delete it using Site Manager.

When a Channel Rendering Script Meets a Default Posting

When both the channel rendering script and the default posting properties are assigned values, the channel rendering script is executed. For example, when testing the channel rendering script we saw how the script was displayed in place of the Summary posting even though we did not remove the default posting assignment.

To understand this better, consider the several methods provided by the PAPI that retrieve the URL of a `ChannelItem`. They are:

*   `ChannelItem.Url`

- `ChannelItem.UrlModePublished`
- `ChannelItem.UrlModeUnpublished`
- `ChannelItem.UrlModeUpdate`
- `ChannelItem.UrlInnerChannelItem.UrlInnerPlain`

Let's add some code to the channel rendering script to display the values of each of these properties.

1. Double-click on the `PlantCatalog_Render.aspx` page in design mode to get to the `Page_Load` event handler of its code-behind file.

2. Add the highlighted lines of code:

```
public class ChannelRenderingScript : System.Web.UI.Page
{
    protected System.Web.UI.WebControls.Table CatalogTable;
    protected System.Web.UI.WebControls.Literal litHeader;

    private void Page_Load(object sender, System.EventArgs e)
    {
        // Put user code to initialize the page here

        //Get the current CmsHttpContext
        CmsHttpContext cmsContext = CmsHttpContext.Current;

        //Get the current channel
        Channel currentChannel = cmsContext.Channel;

        //display the URL of the channel in different modes
        Response.Write(currentChannel.Url + "<br>");
        Response.Write(currentChannel.UrlModePublished + "<br>");
        Response.Write(currentChannel.UrlModeUnpublished + "<br>");
        Response.Write(currentChannel.UrlModeUpdate + "<br>");
        Response.Write(currentChannel.UrlInner + "<br>");
        Response.Write(currentChannel.UrlInnerPlain + "<br>");

        . . . code continues . . .
    }
```

3. Save and build the solution.

When you navigate to `http://localhost/tropicalgreen/plantcatalog`, you get an additional six lines of text that display the URL returned by each property. The table below shows the possible set of results.

Property	URL Format
`Url`	Returns a string depending on the current mode: `Published`, `UnPublished`, or `Update`.
`UrlModePublished`	`/NR/exeres/5AB16268-78AD-418B-B86A-4A7AFE97BBE1.htm` when the URL Format is set to Unique ID based; `/TropicalGreen/PlantCatalog/` when the URL Format is set to Hierarchical.
`UrlModeUnpublished`	`/NR/exeres/5AB16268-78AD-418B-B86A-4A7AFE97BBE1.htm?NRMODE=Unpublished`
`UrlModeUpdate`	`/NR/exeres/5AB16268-78AD-418B-B86A-4A7AFE97BBE1.htm?NRMODE=Update`

Property	URL Format
UrlInner	/NR/exeres/5AB16268-78AD-418B-B86A-4A7AFE97BBE1,frameless.htm?varA=x
	Any querystrings that are passed to the page are retained in the UrlInner property.
	The frameless keyword is a flag for MCMS to return the inner page without the frameset. It was added to prevent recursive loading of the frameset. Otherwise, you would find frames loading within frames.
UrlInnerPlain	/NR/exeres/5AB16268-78AD-418B-B86A-4A7AFE97BBE1,frameless.htm
	UrlInnerPlain is similar to UrlInner but strips away all querystrings.

The last two properties (UrlInner and UrlInnerPlain) provide the URL of the ChannelItem, ignoring the channel rendering script. If for some reason, you have set both the channel rendering script and the default posting properties to contain values, you can bypass the channel rendering script by using the values returned by the UrlInner and/or UrlInnerPlain properties in your script to link to the ChannelItem.

The UrlInner property is used when building framed pages—the topic of our next discussion.

> A ChannelItem can be either a Posting or a Channel.

Channel Rendering Scripts are used to 'Frame' a Page

Frames can be considered a bane or a boon. When applied correctly, frames fix certain portions of the page such that they get displayed consistently at the same spot on all pages. Usually, navigation elements like menu bars and banners are placed in frames.

However, not all browsers can read frames. The page does not get displayed correctly for people using older browsers, surfing from their television sets, or viewing the website from mobile phones. Users of assistive technology may have trouble with framed websites, and government accessibility guidelines may prohibit or dissuade the use of frames. Also, printing is not as straightforward—users would have to focus their mouse on the frame that contains the content before clicking on the print button. Major search crawlers may not be able to index a framed site correctly. All these issues and some others have gotten many developers to feel that frames are not worth the trouble. Most prefer to go the route of using HTML tables or CSS layers to position navigation elements even if it means reloading them on each page request.

Nevertheless, frames exist today and remain a choice available to website designers. MCMS provides support for frames and to illustrate how frames work in MCMS, we are going to write a framed version of the TropicalGreen Plant Catalog.

Writing a Channel Rendering Script for a Framed Site

First, we decide how the page will look like framed up. We will have a banner on the top and a navigation page on the right-hand side. The content of each posting will be displayed on the left, as shown in the diagram:

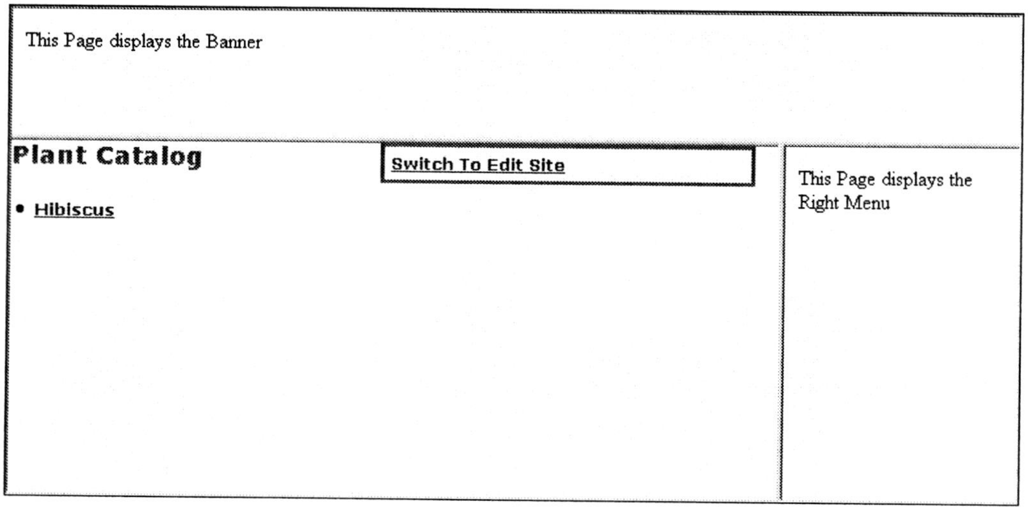

```
This Page displays the Banner




Plant Catalog           ┌─────────────────────┐    This Page displays the
                        │  Switch To Edit Site │    Right Menu
  • Hibiscus            └─────────────────────┘
```

The Banner Page

Add a web form item to the Templates folder of the TropicalGreen Project. Name the new form Banner.aspx. Add some temporary text to the page, like This Page displays the Banner.

The Right Menu Page

Add another web form to the Templates folder. Name the second form RightMenu.aspx. Add some text to the page, like This Page displays the Right Menu.

For now, we use these pages to represent the top banner and right-hand menu bars.

The Page that Defines the Framesets

Add a third web form file item to the Templates folder. Name the new form PlantCatalog_Frames.aspx. Switch to HTML View. Add the following line of code at the top of the page below the <%@ Page language="c#" %> line:

```
<%@ Import Namespace="Microsoft.ContentManagement.Publishing"%>
```

Because we are using framesets, we don't need the <body> tags. *Remove* the following code generated by Visual Studio.

```
<body MS_POSITIONING="GridLayout">
<form id="PlantCatalog_Frames" method="post" runat="server">
</form>
</body>
```

Replace them with <frameset> tags, which define the layout of the frames that will hold the banner, right menu and default posting (Summary).

```
<frameset rows="100,*">
    <frame src="/tropicalgreen/templates/Banner.aspx">
    <frameset cols="*, 180">
     <frame src="<%=CmsHttpContext.Current.ChannelItem.UrlInner%>">
        <frame src="/tropicalgreen/templates/RightMenu.aspx">
    </frameset>
</frameset>
<noframes>
<p>Sorry, this site requires frames.</p>
</noframes>
```

Save all files and build the solution.

Setting the Default Posting and Script Url Properties

Use Site Manager to set the /tropicalgreen/templates/PlantCatalog_Frames.aspx file as the
Script Url for the PlantCatalog channel. Assign Summary to be the default posting of the channel.

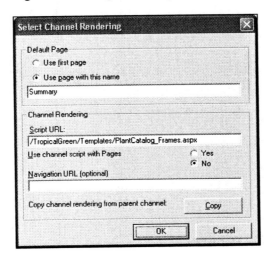

By setting the default posting of the PlantCatalog Channel to Summary, the
ChannelItem.UrlInner property returns the URL of the Summary Page.

Viewing the Framed Page

View http://localhost/tropicalgreen/plantcatalog. You should see the page as shown in
the following diagram.

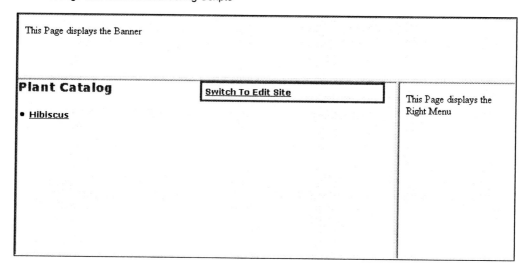

Frames pages typically use both the channel rendering script and the default posting properties of the channel. It takes both to frame a page and we just did that for the TropicalGreen Plant Catalog.

Using Channel Script with Pages

Try accessing the Hibiscus fact sheet by entering its URL directly on the browser's address bar. For example `http://localhost/tropicalgreen/plantcatalog/hibiscus.htm`. Notice that the plant fact sheet opens without the frames. In order for the frames to be rendered for all the fact sheets, we need to apply the channel rendering script on all postings. We do that by setting the Use Channel Script with pages option to Yes in the Channel Properties dialog we saw earlier.

In Site Manager, for the PlantCatalog channel, in the Select Channel Rendering Dialog, set the Use channel rendering script with Pages option to Yes.

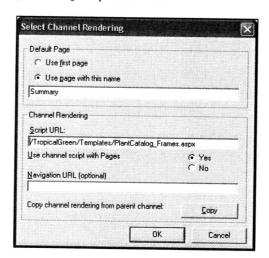

Now when you open the Hibiscus fact sheet, the page renders with the frames applied. However, if you click on the link to any of the fact sheets from the summary page, you will find that the page opens within a frame.

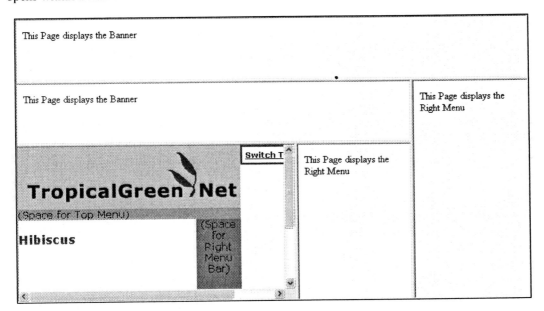

To solve the frames opening within frames problem, open the `PlantCatalog_Summary.aspx.cs` page, modify the `AddPlant()` method to use the `Posting.UrlInner` property instead of the `Posting.Url` property. The `Posting.UrlInner` property returns the URL of the posting without frames applied. Using it prevents the plant fact sheets from opening up as framed pages within framed pages.

```
private TableRow AddPlant(Posting plant)
{
    TableRow row;
    TableCell cell;
    HtmlAnchor plantLink;

    plantLink = new HtmlAnchor();
    plantLink.InnerText = HttpUtility.HtmlEncode(plant.DisplayName);
    plantLink.HRef = plant.UrlInner;

    row = new TableRow();
    cell = new TableCell();
    cell.Controls.Add(new LiteralControl("&#8226; "));
    cell.Controls.Add(plantLink);
    row.Cells.Add(cell);

    return (row);
}
```

Navigation URL

There is one more property that we have not yet discussed and that is the Navigation URL property. The Navigation URL property exists for backward compatibility with pages that were migrated from MCMS 2001 sites. It takes over the Navigation Template property of MCMS 2001. Unless you are working with ASP-based Templates, you can ignore this property. We won't be discussing ASP-based templates in this book.

If you are working with ASP-based templates, refer to the following articles available on Microsoft's website:

- Microsoft Content Management Server 2001 Product Documentation
  http://www.microsoft.com/cmserver/default.aspx?url=/cmserver/techinfo/doc_help.htm

- Preparing to Migrate to MCMS 2002 and ASP.NET
  http://msdn.microsoft.com/library/en-us/dnmscms02/html/cms_2002migrationnet.asp

Wrapping up the Summary Page

We won't be working with framed pages for the rest of the book. We will, instead, use the channel rendering script that we created earlier. In this section, we will polish ChannelRendering.aspx to include both the banner and the right menu bar and clean up code that we don't need.

1. Open ChannelRendering.aspx in HTML view.

2. Modify the HTML code to display the banner, space for the top menu bar, and space for the right menu bar. We will develop the menu bars in Chapter 13.

```
<table width="100%" border="0" cellspacing="0" cellpadding="0" height="100%">
<tr>
    <td width="100%" colspan="2" valign="top" bgcolor="#FFCC00">
    <IMG src="/tropicalgreen/images/Logo.gif">
    </td>
    <td rowspan="10" valign="top">
<uc1:DefaultConsole id="Defaultconsole1" runat="server"></uc1:DefaultConsole>
    </td>
</tr>
<tr bgcolor="#66CC33">
    <td colspan="2">(Space for Top Menu)</td>
</tr>
<tr>
    <td valign="top">
    <h1> <asp:Literal id="litHeader" runat="server"></asp:Literal></h1>
    <asp:Table id="CatalogTable" runat="server"></asp:Table>
    </td>
    <td class="RightMenuBar" width="20%" valign="top" height="100%"
        align="center" rowspan="2" bgcolor="#669900">
    (Space for Right Menu Bar)
    </td>
</tr>
</table>
```

3. Right-click anywhere in the web form and select View Code to open the code-behind file, ChannelRenderingScript.aspx.cs.

4. Comment out the lines of code added earlier to display just the DisplayName of the channel as well as the values returned by the different Channel properties.

```
public class ChannelRenderingScript : System.Web.UI.Page
{
    protected System.Web.UI.WebControls.Table CatalogTable;
    protected System.Web.UI.WebControls.Literal litHeader;

    private void Page_Load(object sender, System.EventArgs e)
    {
        // Put user code to initialize the page here

        //Get the current CmsHttpContext
        CmsHttpContext cmsContext = CmsHttpContext.Current;

        //Get the current channel
        Channel currentChannel = cmsContext.Channel;

        //display the display name of the channel in the header
        litHeader.Text = currentChannel.DisplayName;

        //display the URL of the channel in different modes
        //comment out this block of code
        /*Response.Write(currentChannel.Url + "<br>");
        Response.Write(currentChannel.UrlModePublished + "<br>");
        Response.Write(currentChannel.UrlModeUnpublished + "<br>");
        Response.Write(currentChannel.UrlModeUpdate + "<br>");
        Response.Write(currentChannel.UrlInner + "<br>");
        Response.Write(currentChannel.UrlInnerPlain + "<br>");*/

        . . . code continues . . .
    }
}
```

5. Open the PlantCatalog_Summary.aspx.cs page, and change the AddPlant() method back to use the plant.Url property instead of plant.UrlInner:

   plantLink.HRef = plant.Url;

6. Save and build the solution.

7. Finally assign ChannelRenderingScript.aspx to the Script URL property of the PlantCatalog channel and set the Use script with Pages property to No (refer the *Using Site Manager to Assign the Channel Rendering Script to the Channel* section).

Now, when you navigate to http://localhost/tropicalgreen/plantcatalog, you will see the screen as shown below. We will re-use ChannelRenderingScript.aspx throughout the book for displaying summary pages of other channels in the TropicalGreen site.

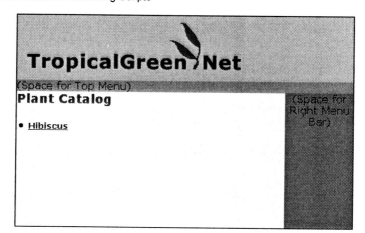

Tips and Tricks

I don't want to have a summary page. On my site, we need to ensure that the default posting is the most recent posting added to the channel; how can we do that?

The trick is to set the sortordinal property of the posting to equal the number of postings such that the most recent posting always has the highest sortordinal value. Another method is to set the Default Posting Name to be that of the last posting added to the channel. You can do this by writing a script in the Workflow Event Handlers (discussed in Chapter 16) to update these properties whenever a new posting is created and approved.

How can I display the contents of placeholders in my summary page? For example, I would like to have the plant's image displayed alongside its name.

Use the code in Chapter 12 to get the contents of the placeholder you wish to display and add them to the code used to generate the summary.

Summary

In this chapter, we have created a summary page using channel rendering scripts and default postings in addition to the Plant template created in Chapter 6. You have made use of code-behind files to add logic that gathers collections of channels and postings so that users can access them. You have also learned that with proper coding, any time new channels or postings are added, the navigation page automatically reflects them. Next, we explored how channel rendering scripts and default postings can be used together to create a framed page. Lastly we set up a generic channel rendering script that can be used throughout the TropicalGreen site.

10
Understanding the MCMS Publishing Workflow

Content publishing is a people-driven process. After the developer has set up the structure of the website, created the templates, and ensured that the applications work, contributors, or authors begin creating content. They fill the site with the pages and files that make up the site. Finally, a gatekeeper, usually a supervisor or manager eyeballs the content provided by authors before it is published on the site. Even if you are running a fully automated site that draws content from multiple sources, at some point in time, there are people involved in the process.

The way content gets published at your organization may differ. Despite the differences, there is always a standard way of doing things, processes that people follow, and rules to play by.

You do not have to create a publishing process (called a **workflow** in MCMS) from scratch. MCMS offers a simple approval workflow out of the box. Before we get to that, let's take a look at the user roles defined in the system.

The Eight User Roles in MCMS

In every workflow system, there are actors who play out the processes. MCMS provides eight different user roles. Each of these user roles comes with unique responsibilities and is given specific rights.

- **Subscribers** are visitors to the site. They have read-only access to those areas of the site to which they have been granted access.
- **Authors** are sometimes known as content contributors or providers. They create postings and edit them. When their work is ready, they usually submit it to an editor/moderator for review.
- **Editors** have all the powers of an author. In addition, they can approve or decline content that authors submit to them and send the posting up the workflow process.
- **Moderators** have all the power of an author. In addition they can approve or decline changes to the posting's properties or location.

- **Resource Managers** don't directly participate in the workflow process of channels and postings. Their primary responsibility is to upload, replace, or delete resources in pre-created resource galleries.

- **Template Designers** are usually developers working on the project whose job is to build templates and set up the website structure.

- **Channel Managers** have full rights over the channels, resource galleries, and template galleries they have been assigned to. In addition, they can assign pre-created rights groups to channels, template galleries, and resource galleries.

- **Administrators** are super users. Anything that can be done in MCMS can be done by the administrator. Administrators are the only group of people who can manage rights groups.

The relationship between user roles, rights groups, and users is this: All rights groups are assigned to exactly one of the user roles above. And within these rights groups are collections of MCMS users who are given specific and identical rights to the system, based on the user roles they are linked to. For example, if we include our user account as a member of the rights group belonging to the Administrator user role, we automatically receive full administrative rights to the site.

Users are never directly assigned to one of the user roles listed above. Only rights groups can be assigned to a user role. Users will then be added to the rights group—either directly or by adding an NT group or Active Directory security group that contains user accounts.

> There is only one rights group for administrators, which is added when MCMS is first installed. You cannot add more groups or remove the default group. You can, however, add members to the existing Administrator group.

Rights Groups Organize Users

Rights groups organize collections of users. Unless you are using the Standard Edition of MCMS, you can add as many user accounts to each rights group as you need.

> The Standard Edition of MCMS allows up to 15 non-subscriber accounts and an unlimited number of subscriber accounts.

A single user can be a member of multiple rights groups. For example, Jane from the Marketing department could belong to both the MarketingAuthors rights group and the MarketingSubscribers rights group.

Users can be either local Windows accounts or domain users. They can also be NT groups or Active Directory security groups. In a production environment, it's better to work with domain security groups and users. Using domain security groups and users offers several benefits:

- It facilitates single sign-on. Users can access the site based on the credentials of the account they use to access the network (usually the same one they use to log on to Windows) without having to enter a separate user name and password. This is especially useful for intranet setups where guest access is disabled.

- It is easier to export and import rights group and their members from one server to another within the same domain.

Rights Groups are Assigned to Containers

Containers offer the finest granular level for controlling object permissions. Rights groups are assigned to specific channels, resource galleries, and template galleries. For instance, assigning John to be a subscriber of the PlantCatalog channel gives him access to read all postings in the channel. It does not make him a subscriber of all other postings in the site.

> Unfortunately, you cannot define rights on a page level such that John has access only to the Hibiscus posting and not the other postings in the same channel.

The user role of the rights group determines the permissions granted to the user. The table below gives a detailed breakdown of the rights defined for each user role and container type. Remember, administrators have rights to do everything in this list.

Container Object	Linking a rights group to these containers means giving rights to	User Role						
		Channel Manager	Template Designer	Resource Manager	Moderator	Editor	Author	Subscriber
Channel	View all immediate postings	Yes	Yes	No	Yes	Yes	Yes	Yes
	Create postings	Yes	Yes	No	Yes	Yes	Yes	No
	Edit/delete all immediate postings	Yes	Yes	No	Yes	Yes	Yes[+]	No
	Submit postings	Yes	Yes	No	Yes	Yes	Yes[+]	No
	Approve/decline postings	Yes	Yes	No	Yes	Yes	No	No
	Create sub-channels	Yes	Yes	No	No	No	No	No
	Edit selected channel's properties	Yes	Yes	No	No	No	No	No
	Delete selected channel	Yes	Yes	No	No	No	No	No
	Assign rights groups to selected channel	Yes	Yes	No	No	No	No	No

Container Object	Linking a rights group to these containers means giving rights to	User Role						
		Channel Manager	Template Designer	Resource Manager	Moderator	Editor	Author	Subscriber
Resource Gallery	View all immediate resources	Yes	Yes	Yes	Yes	Yes	Yes	Yes
	Add resources to postings	Yes	Yes	Yes	Yes	Yes	Yes	No
	Import resources	Yes	Yes	Yes	No	No	No	No
	Edit/delete all immediate resources	Yes	Yes	Yes	No	No	No	No
	Create sub-resource galleries	Yes	Yes	No	No	No	No	No
	Edit selected resource gallery's properties	Yes	Yes	No	No	No	No	No
	Delete selected resource gallery	Yes	Yes	No	No	No	No	No
	Assign rights groups to selected resource gallery	Yes	Yes	No	No	No	No	No
Template Gallery	View all immediate templates	Yes	Yes	No	Yes	Yes	Yes	Yes
	Create templates	Yes	Yes	No	No	No	No	No
	Edit/delete all immediate templates	Yes	Yes	No	No	No	No	No
	Submit template	Yes	Yes[+]	No	No	No	No	No
	Create sub-template galleries	Yes	Yes	No	No	No	No	No
	Edit selected template gallery's properties	Yes	Yes	No	No	No	No	No
	Delete selected template gallery	Yes	Yes	No	No	No	No	No
	Assign rights groups to selected template gallery	Yes	Yes	No	No	No	No	No

+ only if the posting/template is not locked by another user

The Complete Publishing Workflow when a Posting is Created

The MCMS publishing workflow is defined by the user roles of the rights groups assigned to each channel. Of the eight user roles, only authors, editors, and moderators actively participate in the publishing workflow.

The full workflow is experienced when a new posting is created in a channel that has been assigned members from all three user roles—authors, editors, and moderators:

1. The publishing workflow begins when an author creates a posting.

2. On completing the posting, the author submits it to an editor for approval.

3. The editor checks the work done by the author. If satisfied, the editor approves the posting. Otherwise, the editor can choose to decline the posting, in which case the posting will be assigned back to the author who would have to make the necessary amendments and submit the posting again.

4. Once the editor approves the posting, it is submitted to a moderator for final approval. The moderator's job is different to that of an editor. While the editor approves the posting's contents, moderators review the posting's properties such as its display name, start date, end date, and location. In subsequent updates to the posting, a moderator's approval may not be required if the posting's properties have not changed values.

5. Like editors, moderators can choose to approve or decline a posting. Declined postings are sent back to the author for rework and must be re-submitted. Approved postings are published to the live site where they can be viewed by subscribers.

Each role is optional. You can simplify the process simply by removing user roles from the channel. Recall from Chapter 6 that when you created the Hibiscus posting, you did not have to get an editor or moderator to approve the posting. That's because there were no editors or moderators assigned to the PlantCatalog channel at the time.

The following diagram is a graphical representation of the entire process.

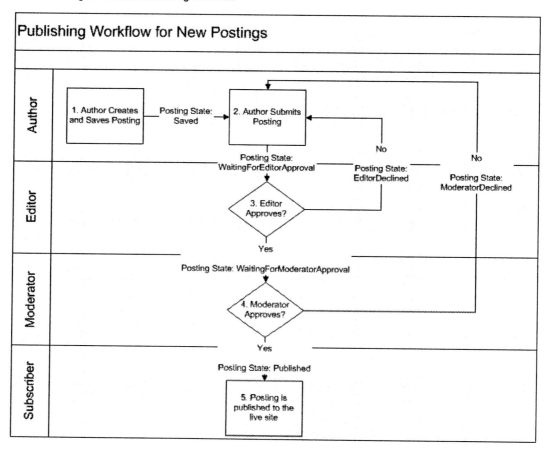

Before We Begin

In this chapter, we will play the role of an author, an editor, and a moderator in turn to experience first-hand how the publishing process in MCMS works. These are the steps that we will take to set up and test the workflow:

1. Prepare the environment by creating user accounts to represent authors, editors, and moderators for the TropicalGreen site and change our browser settings to allow us to log in using different user accounts.

2. Create three rights groups: one for the authors, a second for the editors, and the third for the moderators.

3. After creating the rights groups, we will assign the TropicalGreen users as members.

4. Next, we will specify the channels, resource galleries, and template galleries that each rights group has access to.

Finally, we will test the workflow process by assuming the identities of an author, followed by an editor and a moderator.

Creating Local Accounts for TropicalGreen Users

Let's create user accounts for authors, editors, and moderators to simulate the users of the TropicalGreen site. Typically, in an actual work scenario, these accounts will already exist in the domain and you won't have to create them. In this book, we will use local Windows accounts for the convenience of testing the workflow design on the local machine.

We create four local Windows user accounts, representing two authors, an editor, and a moderator.

1. From the Desktop, right-click on the My Computer icon and select Manage from the popup menu.

2. The Computer Management application will open. Expand the Local Users and Groups node.

Right-click the Users folder and select New User. The New User dialog appears. Create the following accounts giving each of them appropriate passwords.

User Name	Full Name
Author1	Author 1
Author2	Author 2
Editor1	Editor 1
Moderator1	Moderator 1

3. Close the New User dialog.
4. Close the Computer Management application.

Setting up the Environment for Testing

Since we are testing the workflow from a single machine, we need to configure Internet Explorer to prompt for a login ID and password so that we can log in with different user accounts and simulate the roles of each actor.

1. Open Internet Explorer. Select Tools | Internet Options.
2. The Internet Options dialog appears. Click on the Security tab.
3. Select the Local Intranet content zone. Click Custom Level.
4. In the settings list, scroll right to the bottom. In the User Authentication | Logon option, check the Prompt for user name and password option.
5. Click OK. A prompt appears with the message Are you sure you want to change the security settings for this zone? Click Yes.
6. Click OK to close the Internet Options dialog.

> In Chapter 18, we implement **Forms Authentication**, which allows the user ID and password to be entered on the page without the prompt.

At the end of the chapter, remember to set the Logon option back to its original setting (usually Automatic logon only in Intranet zone) to remove the prompts.

Creating Rights Groups

In this section, we will create a new authors rights group for a group of researchers working on the TropicalGreen site. There is only one way to create rights groups and that is to use Site Manager.

To create a rights group, open Site Manager and log in with an account that has administrator rights. Click on the User Roles icon.

The User Roles icon does not appear in Site Manager.

You must log into Site Manager with an MCMS Administrator account. Only members of the MCMS Administrators user role have the ability to create, update, and delete other rights groups.

In the User Roles panel, right-click on the user role you wish to create a rights group for. In our case, we want to create a new authors group. Right-click on the Authors user role and select New Rights Group from the pop-up menu.

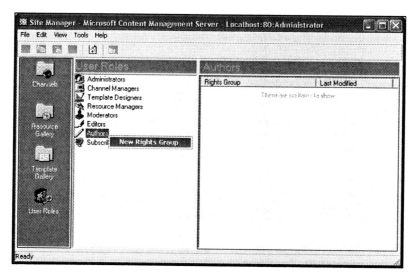

A rights group named New Rights Group is created and appears in the Authors list.

Right-Click on New Rights Group and select Rename from the pop-up menu (or press *F2*). Name the rights group as Researchers. You have now successfully created a new authors rights group with this name.

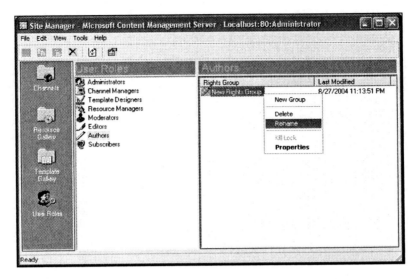

An optional descriptive text can be assigned to a rights group. Right-click on the Researchers rights group and select Properties. The General tab of the properties window provides a text box where you can enter a string of up to 256 characters. The text entered here can be seen by other administrators, channel managers, and template designers. It's a good place to enter remarks and notes that provide some form of documentation about the group's background. Click OK to close the Properties dialog. Repeat and create rights groups for the remaining roles.

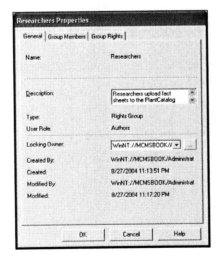

Role	Rights Group Name
Editors	Press Secretary
Moderators	Communications

Assigning Users to Rights Groups

Now that we have created rights groups, we can assign users as members. In this section, we will assign the local Windows account created (Author1), as a member of the Researchers rights group.

To begin, open the Properties dialog by right-clicking on the Researchers rights group and selecting Properties from the pop-up menu. In the properties dialog for the Researchers rights group, select the Group Members tab. You should find there are currently no members assigned to the group. Click Modify...

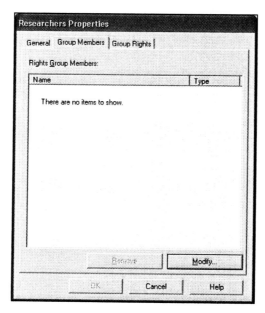

The Modify Members dialog appears. On the NT Domains panel located on the left-hand side, select the NT Domain that represents your local computer (usually in the form of WinNT://computername).

I don't see my local computer listed in the list of domains!

You will need to run the Server Configuration Application (SCA) to add your local computer to the list of domains on the Access tab. See Chapter 4 for more information.

In the pull-down menu on the right, you can choose to:

- Select from list of all groups, which shows a list of the first 1000 groups in the selected NT Domain.

- Select from list of all groups and users, which shows a list of the first 1000 groups and users in the selected NT Domain. Site Manager may take a long while to render the entire list if there is a sizeable number of groups and users in the selected domain.

- Manually enter groups and users, which provides a text box where you enter the name of the group or user.

After choosing either the Select from list of all groups or the Select from list of all groups and users options, nothing shows up in the display list. I get the message "There are no items to show".

This means that the MCMS system account does not have rights to browse the selected domain. If the system account is a local account, then the domain needs to allow anonymous users to enumerate (browse and list) its collection of domain users/groups. Otherwise, if you are using a domain account, the selected domain must be trusted to the domain in which the system account belongs to.

Choose to Manually enter groups and users. This is the fastest way to add users as you do not have to wait for the system to retrieve a list of groups and users. It is also useful when working with domains that have more than 1000 members, a number that is beyond what the Display List dialog is designed to show.

In the Group or User Name field, enter Author1. Click Add. Author1 appears in the list of Rights Group Members at the bottom panel.

When you have finished adding Author1, add Author2. Click OK to close the Modify Members dialog. Click OK again to close the Properties dialog. Repeat to add the members to the remaining rights groups.

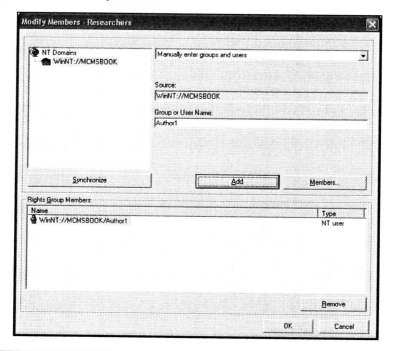

Role	Rights Group Name	Members
Authors	Researchers	WinNT://computername/Author1
		WinNT://computername/Author2
Editors	Press Secretary	WinNT://computername/Editor1
Moderators	Communications	WinNT://computername/Moderator1

Assigning Rights Groups to Containers

By default, rights groups are denied access to all objects in MCMS. There are two ways to go about assigning rights groups to containers:

- The Properties dialog of the selected container
- The Properties dialog of the selected rights group

Method 1: The Properties Dialog of the Selected Container

You can assign rights groups to any container from the container's Properties dialog in Site Manager. To illustrate this, let's grant the Researchers rights group permission to post content to the PlantCatalog channel.

While you are logged in as an Administrator in Site Manager, click on the Channels icon on the left-hand panel. Expand the TropicalGreen channel and then right-click on the PlantCatalog channel. Select Properties from the pop-up menu.

In the Properties dialog, select the Rights tab. Click Modify....

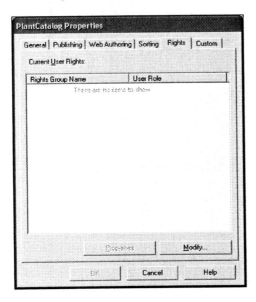

The Select User Rights for Channel dialog appears. Select Authors from the Look In drop-down list. A list of all author rights groups is displayed. Select the Researchers rights group and click the Add button.

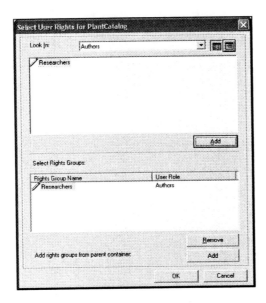

Click OK to close the dialog. A warning message pops up:
Although there are author and/or editor rights groups assigned to this channel, there are no

moderator rights groups. Any page placed in this channel will have its publication details auto-approved once its content is approved. Is this OK?

This means that any changes or updates to posting properties done by authors or editors are automatically published without having to go through additional approvals from a moderator. We will see how this works in a coming section (*An Authors-Only Workflow*). For now, click Yes. Click OK to close the Properties dialog.

Method 2: The Groups Rights Tab

Another way of assigning permissions to a rights group is to start from the Groups Rights tab of the rights group. Let's give our group of researchers more rights to more channels and to use resources and templates as well.

You can access the Groups Rights tab from the Properties dialog of the rights group. While logged in as an administrator in Site Manager, click the User Roles icon on the left panel. In the User Roles column, select Authors. A list of available Author rights groups is displayed on the right-hand side.

Right-click the Researchers rights group and select Properties from the pop-up menu. The Properties dialog appears.

Select the Group Rights tab. Expand the list by using the "+" sign so you can see all container objects below each level, as in the following figure. The red crosses indicate objects the group does not have access to. If you click on any of the red crosses, they change to green checks.

Authors require rights to channels to create, edit, and delete postings. They also need rights to template galleries so that they can create postings from templates stored there. Authors require rights to resource galleries containing resources they can add to postings.

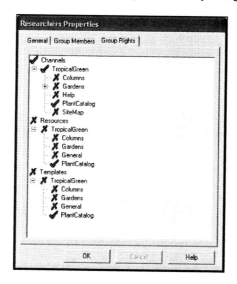

Ensure that green checks appear next to:

- The Channels, TropicalGreen, and PlantCatalog channels
- The PlantCatalog resource gallery
- The PlantCatalog template gallery

When you have finished assigning rights to the Researchers rights group, click OK to close the Properties dialog.

> Instead of setting permissions one by one, you can right-click on a parent container node and select the Propagate Rights to Children option. All child nodes will adopt the permission settings of the parent node.

An Authors-Only Workflow

We now have an author group assigned to the PlantCatalog channel. A workflow is automatically enforced on the PlantCatalog channel without any additional programming.

An authors-only workflow provides the simplest and most straightforward route to getting a posting published. Authors update placeholder content and save as many times as they need to without affecting the content on the live site. Upon clicking Submit, the latest working copy of the posting becomes available on the live site.

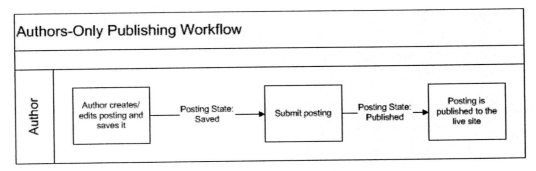

Let's see the authors-only workflow in action for the PlantCatalog channel.

Log in as Author1

Browse to http://localhost/TropicalGreen/PlantCatalog. Since we have configured the browser to prompt for a user name and password, a login dialog appears. Enter the credentials of the author:

- UserName = Author1
- Password = [the password you have set for Author1]
- Domain (optional) = localhost

Edit the Hibiscus Posting as Author1

The TropicalGreen plant catalog will appear. Select the Hibiscus fact sheet. Click the Switch To Edit Site link.

Notice the options on the Web Author Console. These are the actions an author can perform on the currently displayed posting (in this case, the Hibiscus posting). Compared with what we are used to seeing on the console for an administrator, the number of buttons available has shrunk: The Approval Assistant, Resource Manager, and Channel Properties buttons are no longer available.

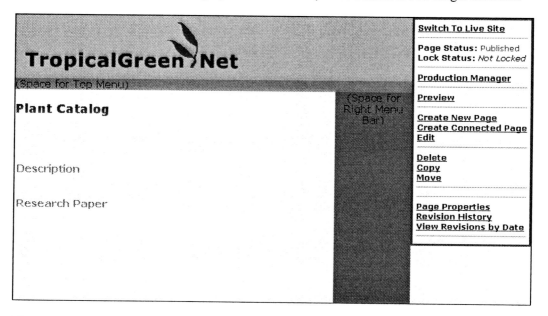

Click Edit. Usually, you would make some amendments to the placeholder content. For now, you don't have to do anything; we will simply assume that some changes have been made. Simply click Save And Exit. Note that:

- The Page Status changes from Published to Saved.
- The Version now states that the Page has Live Version.
- The Lock Status is WinNT://computername/author1.
- The Submit button is available.
- There are no Approve or Decline buttons.

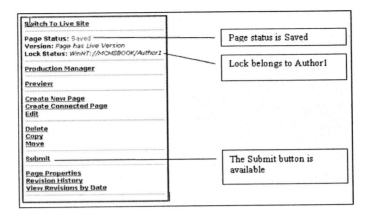

The Submit button is enabled only if the posting is in any of the following states:

- `Saved`
- `EditorDeclined`
- `ModeratorDeclined`

> Up to now, we have only discussed the New and Saved states. We will discuss the
> EditorDeclined and ModeratorDeclined states in the coming sections.

Authors Can Only Edit Postings They Own

The Lock Status contains the identity of the person that owns the posting. The owner is the person who has created a new page or the last person to save an existing page.

As long as the Lock Status indicates that Author1 is the owner, no other author can edit the posting. If you log in as another author, the Edit button will be missing from the console.

Attempting to Edit a Locked Posting

Let's login as Author2 and see what happens if we try to edit a posting that Author1 is working on.

Open a new instance of Internet Explorer. In the address bar, enter `http://localhost/tropicalgreen/plantcatalog/Hibiscus.htm`. At the network login prompt, enter:

- User Name = Author2
- Password = [the password you have set for Author2]
- Domain (optional) = localhost

Click Switch to Edit Site.

The options available on the Web Author Console have decreased. Missing from the Console are:

- Edit
- Create Connected Page

- Delete
- Move

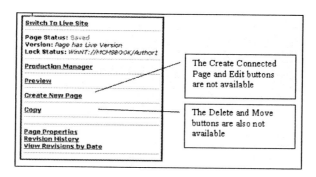

There is no way Author2 can modify the contents of the posting while it is locked by Author1.

The lock exists to prevent other authors from editing the contents of a posting when someone else is working on it. Consider the case where Author1 receives new updates about the Hibiscus plant and starts to write new content into the posting and saves the changes. The lunch bell rings and Author1 leaves the work unfinished while on lunch. Author2 receives a separate update on the Hibiscus plant fact sheet. If the lock was not there to stop them, they would just go ahead and proceed to edit it. Being a faster worker, Author2 could save their work and submit it for publishing. When Author1 returns from lunch, all their hard work from the morning would be overwritten by Author2. That is a recipe for trouble.

Unlocking a Posting

What happens if Author1 decides during lunch break to take off for the rest of the week and not return? Author2 may have to wait a very long time before being able to work on the posting.

Fortunately, MCMS offers at least two ways to unlock a posting.

1. You could get an editor, moderator, template designer, channel manager, or administrator to edit the posting. Users belonging to any of these roles can edit a posting regardless of who is holding the lock. When they do so, they become the owners of the lock. If they choose to approve the posting, thereby publishing it, the lock would be automatically released.

2. Write a script that makes use of the Posting.ReleaseOwnership() method available in the Publishing Application Programming Interface (PAPI). We show how this is done when customizing the Web Author Console in Chapter 18.

Submitting a Posting

The posting remains locked as long as it is not published. While the posting remains unpublished, the working version will not be viewable by subscribers. Subscribers only see the current live version. Let's submit the posting.

Toggle back to the screen for Author1. Click the Submit button. Observe the following changes:

- The status changes to Published. The posting is now available to Subscriber users for viewing.
- The lock status is changed to Not Locked. If Author2 were to log in and attempt to edit the posting, it would now be possible.

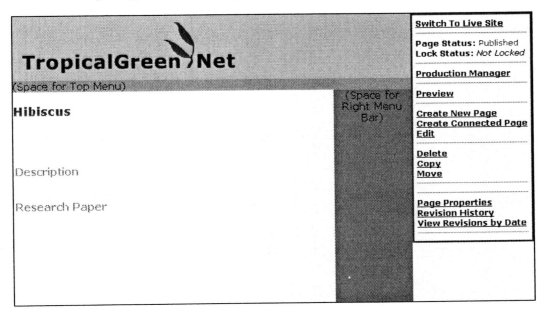

Authors, editors and moderators do not have the rights to use Site Manager. If they attempt to log on, Site Manager returns an error message: The user attempting to log on does not have sufficient rights to access the specified MCMS server using the MCMS Site Manager.

An Author-Editor Workflow

With editors included in the workflow, changes to placeholder content, custom properties, or the posting name (but not display name) by the author do not get published immediately after clicking the Submit button. The content has to be approved by a member of the assigned Editor rights group before it gets published. Postings that are declined by the editor have to be resubmitted by the author.

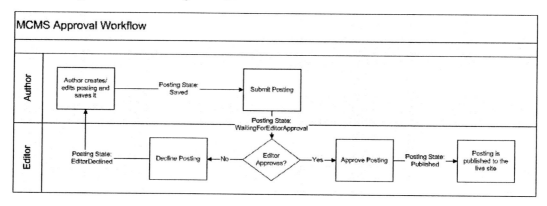

Assign Editors to the PlantCatalog Channel

Before proceeding with the rest of this section, grant the Press Secretary user group rights to the Channels, TropicalGreen, and PlantCatalog channels, the PlantCatalog resource gallery, and PlantCatalog template gallery using any of the methods described in the *Assigning Rights Groups to Containers* section earlier.

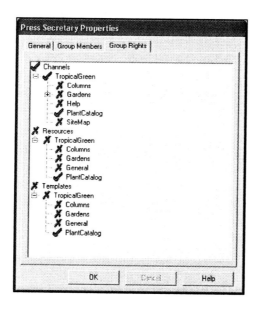

Author Submits a Posting to the Editor

Start the workflow from the author's perspective. Open Internet Explorer and browse to http://localhost/TropicalGreen/PlantCatalog/Hibiscus.htm. In the login prompt, enter the credentials of Author1. Click Switch To Edit Site and edit the content of the Hibiscus plant fact sheet. When you are ready, submit the changed posting by clicking on the Submit button.

Notice that the posting does not immediately get published as the system recognizes that there are editors assigned to the channel. Thus the posting's status changes from Saved to Waiting For Editor Approval. Now, whenever changes to the posting's content are made, an editor has to approve the posting before it is published.

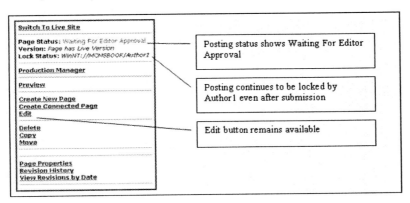

The Edit button remains available even though the posting has been submitted to an editor for approval. Author1 can continue to update the posting while waiting for Editor1 to approve the posting. The lock continues to belong to Author1. No other authors (Author2 included) can edit the posting. However, once Author1 saves the update, the posting's state changes from Waiting For Editor Approval to Saved. In the Saved state, the editor will not be able to approve the posting, and Author1 must re-submit the posting before it can be approved.

Since the Hibiscus posting has a live version, it will continue to be available to subscribers while the version in production is waiting for editor approval.

Can an editor edit a posting that has been locked by an author?

Editors, moderators, channel managers, template designers, and administrators are not bound by locks on postings. As long as they have rights to the channel, they can edit a posting regardless of its lock status.

What Editors See in the Web Author Console

Open a new instance of Internet Explorer. Browse to `http://localhost/TropicalGreen/PlantCatalog/Hibiscus.htm`. A prompt appears requesting you to log in. Enter the credentials for the editor:

- UserName = Editor1
- Password = [the password you have set for Editor1]
- Domain (optional) = localhost

Click on the Switch to Edit Site link. Open the Hibiscus posting that was amended by Author1.

Notice that two new buttons appear on the Web Author Console:

- Approve
- Decline

These buttons are available to editors when the posting's status is Waiting For Editor Approval. At this point, the editor can choose to either Approve the posting or Decline it.

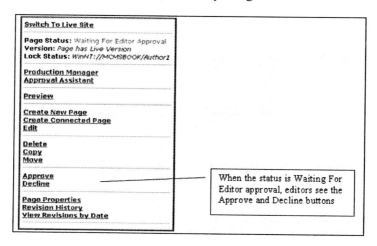

Editor Declines Posting

Click Decline. Note that Page Status changes from Waiting For Editor Approval to Editor Declined.

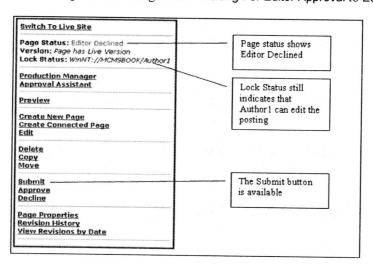

Usually, the editor would follow up with an e-mail to notify the author that the work was rejected. In Chapter 16 we will extend the workflow to automate the e-mail notification process.

Because the locked status is still with Author1, that author can edit the posting again and submit it back to the editor for approval.

Interestingly, when Editor1 declines a posting, the Submit button becomes available. This just means that the editor is able to take on the role of an author and re-submit the posting back to himself or herself, or another editor.

Editor Approves Posting

Let's imagine that Author1 has reworked the content of the Hibiscus plant fact sheet. They have re-submitted the posting and it's waiting for editor approval again.

Still on Editor1's screen, click on the Approve button. Several things happen:

- The posting gets published if the start time has been reached. Otherwise, the status changes to Approved (for future start times) or Expired (for past end times).
- The Approve and Decline buttons disappear.
- The lock on the posting is released. The Lock Status now says Not Locked.

Submissions could be from any author assigned to the PlantCatalog channel. It does not matter which author submits the posting. Editors can approve the work of any author in the channels where they have rights to. Similarly, if Author1 submits the posting for approval, any editor assigned to the channel can approve the posting.

Editor Edits Posting

Editors can edit a posting's content regardless of its Lock Status. Notice that even though the Lock Status indicates that Author1 is holding on to the lock, the Edit button remains available to Editor1.

To see this, have Author1 edit and save the posting first. Don't submit the posting just yet. Then, toggle over to Editor1's screen and click Edit. Make some changes to the posting. When you are done updating the posting, click Save and Exit. A few changes are reflected on the Web Author Console:

- The posting's status changes to Saved.
- The Lock Status indicates that Editor1 has locked the posting.
- The Submit button is available.

An interesting point to note is that Editor1 now holds the lock. This makes sense because Editor1 just edited the posting.

Usually, having the lock owned by the editor does not pose a problem. Problems may arise when Editor1 decides to decline the posting at this stage. Editor1 would find that none of the authors assigned to the channel can edit the posting because Editor1 has the lock.

Some editors may find this behavior confusing. They expect authors to pick up where they left off after declining the posting. So when authors tell them that they, the editors, are holding onto the lock, what should they do?

Unfortunately, the only way for the editor to release the lock is to approve the posting. And when they do so, all content gets published on the live site. That defeats the purpose of the editor declining the posting in the first place. There's no immediate way of tackling this problem with the out-of-the-box workflow. In Chapter 19, we show you how this problem can be solved by customizing the Web Author Console.

Editor Submits Posting

After an editor saves an edited posting or declines it, the Submit button is enabled. This gives the editor the flexibility of taking on the role of an author. After the editor submits the posting, it would be in a Waiting For Editor Approval state again.

While on the Editors screen, click Edit followed by Save and Exit. Click on the Submit button.

Notice that:

- The Posting's status changes to Waiting For Editor Approval.
- At the same time, the Approve and Decline buttons are still available. The editor can choose to approve or decline their own work or get another editor to do so.

Click Approve. The posting gets published.

Having editors approve postings that they have submitted may seem pointless. Why not just do away with the Submit button and have only the Approve button? The reason is because, in some cases, you may need to have another editor to review the work before it gets published. In Chapter 19, we show you how you can customize the console to hide or show buttons. These techniques let you hide the Approve button for the editor that submits the posting. This will ensure that editors will not be able to approve postings that they have submitted.

Editors Do Not Get Triggered When Authors Change the Properties of a Posting

So far, we have seen how changes made by authors to placeholder content require editor approval before being published.

What happens when the author changes the properties of a posting without amending placeholder content?

1. Toggle over to Author1's screen, which should be showing the Hibiscus posting in edit site view. Ensure that the posting's status is Published.
2. Click Page Properties. The Page Properties dialog opens.
3. Check the Important Page option.
4. Click Save. The Page Properties dialog closes.

Notice that although you have just made some changes to the posting's properties, the page status remains Published.

That is because changes to the properties (with the exception of the name, description, and custom properties) of the posting do not require any approval from editors. In Author-only, Editor-only and Author-Editor workflows, all updates to a posting's properties are applied with immediate effect without needing anyone to approve them.

For posting property values to become part of the workflow process, we need to consider a third group of people, moderators.

An Author-Editor-Moderator Workflow

We have worked out the scenarios as the posting moves along the workflow process from the author to the editor. Let us now shift our focus onto the last group of people that influence the workflow, moderators.

Moderators Approve Changes to Posting Properties, not Content

In most MCMS workflow diagrams, moderators are placed right after editors in the workflow process. While not entirely wrong, it may give the misleading impression that a three-level workflow process can be achieved simply by assigning moderators to a channel.

The truth is that they are not always activated. Moderators are triggered only when:

- New postings are created
- Postings are moved or copied to a different location
- Properties of the posting have been amended, such as:
    o Name
    o Display Name
    o Start Date
    o End Date
    o Important Page
    o Hide When Published
    o Web Robots Can Crawl Links
    o Web Robots Can Index This Page

They are not triggered when:

- Changes are made to placeholder content within the posting
- Changes are made to custom property values of a posting

The actual workflow is a little more complicated:

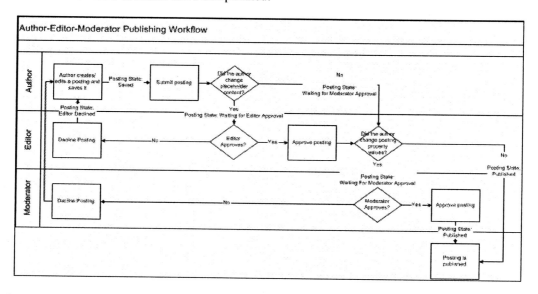

Assign Moderators to the PlantCatalog Channel

To see the effect moderators have on the workflow, grant the Communications Moderator user rights group access to the `PlantCatalog` channel, template gallery, and resource gallery as shown:

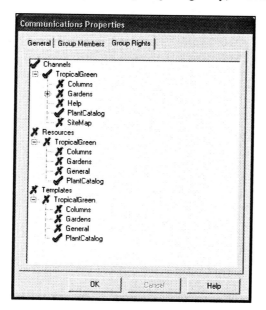

Author Submits a Posting

Browse to `http://localhost/TropicalGreen/PlantCatalog/Hibiscus.htm` and log in as
Author1. Do the following:

1. Click Switch to Edit Site.
2. Click Edit followed by Save and Exit.
3. Click Page Properties and un-check the Important Page option in the page.

Submit the posting when you are done.

Note the change in the Page Status from Saved to Waiting For Editor Approval. This is expected
since we have assigned editors to approve content for the `PlantCatalog` channel.

Also, the Version: Page has Live Version message has disappeared. This means the posting is
saved but there is no live version anymore. Subscribers to the website will not be able to view the
Hibiscus posting.

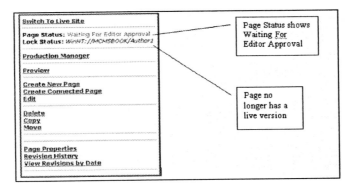

Postings waiting for moderator approval are not available on the Live Site.

When a posting is waiting for moderator approval, subscribers can't access it even though
it could already have a live version. This is a design limitation.

MCMS provides versioning for placeholder content but not for posting properties. This
means that only one set of properties are kept for every posting and so when the
properties change and require moderator approval, the entire posting has to be pulled out
of production.

Only after a moderator approves the posting will it be available on the live site. This is
the biggest drawback to including moderators in the workflow process.

Editor Approves a Posting

In a separate instance of Internet Explorer, browse to `http://localhost/TropicalGreen/PlantCatalog` and log in as Editor1. On the `PlantCatalog` summary page, you will need to switch to edit site view to see the Hibiscus posting now, as there is no longer a live version available.

1. Click Switch To Edit Site.
2. Click on the link to the Hibiscus posting.

With the Hibiscus posting opened in edit site view, click Approve.

Note that the status changes from Waiting For Editor Approval to Waiting For Moderator Approval. At the same time, the Approve and Decline buttons disappear. That is because Editor1 does not have the right to approve the posting while it is in a Waiting For Moderator Approval state.

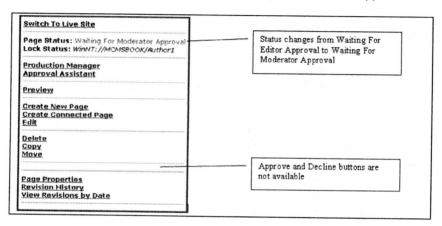

What Moderators See in the Web Author Console

Open a new instance of the browser and browse to `http://localhost/TropicalGreen/PlantCatalog`. Log in as Moderator1 with the following credentials:

- UserName = Moderator1
- Password = [the password you have set for Moderator1]
- Domain (optional) = localhost

On the Plant Catalog summary page, click Switch to Edit Site. Click on the Hibiscus posting, which was previously approved by Editor1.

The Approve and Decline buttons are enabled for Moderator1 and the Page Status reflects that the posting is Waiting For Moderator Approval.

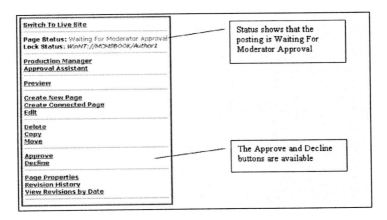

Moderator Declines Posting

Choose to Decline the posting. The status of the posting changes to Moderator Declined.

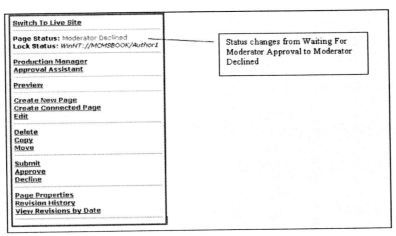

At this point, the moderator should follow up with an e-mail to inform the author/editor that the posting has been declined. We will show how to automate this process when we extend the workflow in Chapter 16.

Moderator Approves Posting

Click on the Approve button. Since we have scheduled the posting to be published immediately (or before the current date and time), the posting's state changes to Published. Otherwise, the status would be Approved or Expired depending on its start and end dates.

At the same time, any lock on the posting would be released.

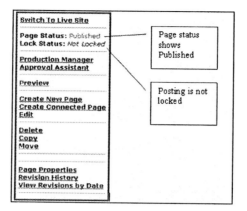

Moderator Edits Posting

In MCMS 2002, moderators can edit postings too. The previous version did not allow moderators to edit a posting's content. Be aware that if the moderator decides to edit content, the lock status changes to that of the moderator. Authors will not have the rights to edit the posting while it is locked by a moderator.

Using Moderator1's account, and with the Hibiscus posting opened in edit site view, click Edit followed by Save and Exit. The Submit button becomes available.

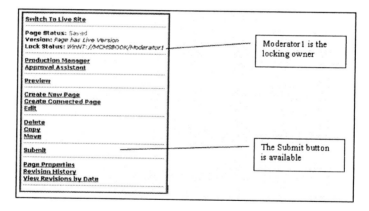

Moderator Submits Posting

Just like editors, moderators can choose to either submit, approve, or decline the posting after editing it.

With the Hibiscus posting opened by Moderator1 in edit site view, click the Submit button to send it for approval.

Because editors have been assigned to the PlantCatalog channel, the status of the posting changes to Waiting For Editor Approval.

The Approve and Decline buttons disappear from the Web Author Console. That is because moderators cannot approve changes to placeholder content. In order to publish the posting, log in as Editor1 and approve the posting.

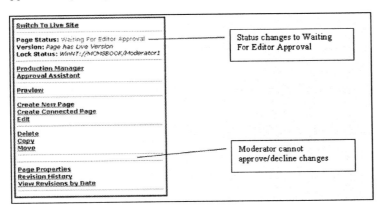

When the Workflow Skips Moderators

We have seen how the workflow moves from authors to editors and lastly to moderators. What happens if the author amends the content of an existing posting but not its properties?

Log in as Author1 and amend the Hibiscus fact sheet. Once you are satisfied with the changes, submit the posting. As expected, the status of the posting changes from Saved to Waiting For Editor Approval.

Log in as Editor1, navigate to the Hibiscus fact sheet. Approve the posting. Notice that the posting's status changes from Waiting For Editor Approval directly to Published! The workflow seemed to have completely bypassed the moderators.

This is a common cause of confusion, especially when you are thinking of moderators as a third level of approval.

Just remember that once a posting has a live version, moderators are triggered only if there are changes to the posting's properties or if a posting has changed location resulting from a copy or move operation.

In this case, only placeholder content was changed, therefore editor approval was sufficient to get the posting published.

When the Workflow Skips Editors

Log in as Author1 and open the Hibiscus posting for editing. Click on the Page Properties button. The Page Properties dialog opens. Check the Important Page flag (or uncheck it if it already checked) and save the changes.

This time, the posting's status went straight from Saved to Waiting For Moderator Approval. The workflow decided to bypass the editors this time and move the posting directly to the moderator.

This time, the placeholder content was not updated, only the properties of the posting were updated. Hence, the posting did not require editor approval before it got published. Log in to `http://localhost/TropicalGreen/PlantCatalog` as Moderator1, click Switch To Edit Site, and approve the Hibiscus posting.

Deleting Postings

Did you notice that the Delete button is available to anyone who has the right to edit the posting?

While lots of care has been taken to ensure that creation and editing of postings goes through the proper workflow processes, deletion of postings requires absolutely no approval.

So be warned—your postings can disappear when careless authors, editors, moderators, channel managers, or administrators decide to click on the Delete button. In Chapter 19 we will show you how to protect your postings from such accidental deletion.

One Last Thing

Remember to set the Internet Explorer Logon option back to its original setting (usually Automatic logon only in Intranet zone).

Summary

In this chapter we learned how the out-of-the-box workflow processes operate in MCMS. You have seen how authors create and submit their work to editors. You should have an idea of how editors can be employed to approve the content of postings. Lastly, you have seen firsthand how the workflow changes when moderators are added into the picture. Moderators approve changes to a posting's properties and location, while editors approve changes to a posting's placeholder content.

In reality, workflow systems are typically more complicated than the examples shown in this chapter. In Chapter 16, we show you how the workflow can be extended to cater for almost any scenario that exists in the workplace today.

11

Authoring with Microsoft Content Management Server

Now that the basic components of your website are in place, including the Plant template and the PlantCatalog channel rendering script, we are ready to add content to the site.

The MCMS Web Author is a powerful tool for managing content in an MCMS website. It's a complete package that includes:

- A Web Author Console that lists a series of action buttons for managing postings and channels
- Dialogs to aid the authoring process

We will start by looking at the Web Author Console and its various options. Next, we will see how easy it is for authors to edit/create postings, insert images, add attachments, and publish changes. We will move on to look at how the Web Author provides useful tools for editors and moderators to manage unfinished postings and postings that are in the approval workflow. To complete the section, we will play the role of resource managers and add, edit, replace, and delete resources from resource galleries.

> Authoring with MCMS is not limited to the Web Author. In Chapter 17, we use Authoring Connector to upload content directly from Microsoft Word.

How Users Edit Postings

MCMS follows the in-context content management model. Instead of a detached administration area, users navigate to the actual channel or posting in order to add and edit content. So, to add a new posting, a content contributor would:

1. Navigate to the channel where the posting should be added
2. Switch to edit mode
3. Create a new posting
4. Save the posting and submit it to the next level in the publishing workflow

The posting is approved by another user with appropriate rights.

The content contributor can be anyone who maps to an author, editor, moderator, template designer, channel manager, or administrator user role.

Back in Chapter 6 we coded a template from scratch and created a sample posting in the PlantCatalog channel called Hibiscus. That is probably the first time you saw the Web Author in action. However, besides creating an empty posting we did not add any content or additional postings. In this chapter we will add some content to our Hibiscus posting and add a few more postings to the PlantCatalog channel. Along the way, we will cover a majority of the various functions available from the Default Web Author Console.

The Default Web Author Console

MCMS comes with a Default Web Author Console. The web user control file, DefaultConsole.ascx, is located in the ConsoleControls folder of an MCMS web application. You may remember that we included the Default Console on our Plant template and PlantCatalog channel rendering script in Chapter 6. The Web Author Console is used to create and edit content, plus it is used for workflow actions like submitting and approving.

The Web Author Console can be used out of the box, or it can be customized or replaced with your own console, which we will try out in Chapter 19. This chapter will cover the functionality of the default Web Author Console, explaining what each option does in detail.

In order to see and use the Web Author Console, you must be logged in to the MCMS website. Since we have been running our development machine as an administrator, you will have sufficient rights to see all of the functions.

The Web Author hides/shows options depending on a combination of factors such as the:

- Current mode (live site, edit site, and so on)
- Status of the posting you are currently working on
- User role(s) you are mapped to

Investigating the Web Author Console

To start, open Internet Explorer and enter http://localhost/tropicalgreen/plantcatalog /hibiscus.htm in the address bar and click Go. The following screenshot shows where we left off in Chapter 7. Apart from the headings, the Hibiscus posting has no content.

Take a look at the right-hand side. The green box with a hyperlink that says Switch To Edit Side is the Default Web Author Console. It was added to the Plant template file when we built it in Chapter 6. You have used it several times when working with postings in the PlantCatalog channel. In this chapter, we will walk you through each available option.

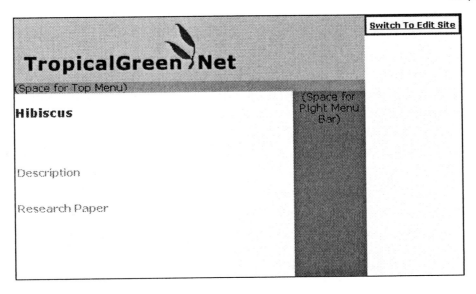

Switching To Edit Site

Click the Switch To Edit Site hyperlink. Notice how the Web Author Console expands on the right side of the posting. As an administrator, you see the full range of buttons available.

- **Switch to Live Site** brings you back to the Live site.
- **Page Status** shows you where the posting is in the workflow.
- **Lock Status** tells you who is currently editing the posting

- **Production Manager** lists all postings owned by the current user that are not published, approved, or expired.

- **Approval Assistant** lists all postings waiting for approval by the current user.

- **Resource Manager** provides an interface to add, replace, and delete resources.

- **Preview** allows you to see how the posting will look like after being published.

- **Create New Page** creates a new posting in the current channel.

- **Create Connected Page** creates a connected posting in a specified channel.

- **Edit** allows you to change the content of the placeholders of the current posting.

- **Delete** removes the current posting from the repository.

- **Copy** creates a duplicate posting of the current posting in a specified channel.

- **Move** transfers the current posting to a specified channel.

- **Page Properties** provides an interface to manage the property values (including custom property values) of the current posting.

- **Revision History** lists all available historical revisions of the current posting.

- **View Revisions by Date** shows you the historical revision of the current posting from a specified date and time.

- **Channel Properties** provides an interface to manage the property values (including custom property values) of the current channel.

Since we created and approved the Hibiscus posting in a previous chapter, the console shown above is for a posting that has already been published and is available on the live site. In the next section we will go over the differences in the console for a posting that has not been published yet as we create a few new postings for the TropicalGreen site.

> The terms 'posting' and 'page' are used interchangeably in MCMS. We typically use the term posting, but often you will see the term page used, as in the Web Author Console.
>
> In MCMS 2001, postings and pages were handled as different objects, but in MCMS 2002 Microsoft removed the confusion over postings and pages by hiding the page object from the developer and end users. But pages are still there in the system—they are just not accessible via the **MCMS Publishing Application Programming Interface (PAPI)** or Site Manager.

The console for a channel without a default posting is slightly different. In such cases, you can toggle between the live and edit sites, access the Production Manager, Resource Manager, and Approval Assistant, as well as create new postings and access the channel properties page. You cannot perform actions that relate to postings, such as edit.

```
┌─────────────────────────────┐
│ Switch To Live Site         │
│ ........................... │
│ Production Manager          │
│ Approval Assistant          │
│ Resource Manager            │
│ ........................... │
│ Preview                     │
│ ........................... │
│ Create New Page             │
│ ........................... │
│                             │
│                             │
│ Channel Properties          │
└─────────────────────────────┘
```

In addition, depending on the rights of the currently logged in user, you may not see all of the options. The table below lists the Web Author Console options and their availability for each user role in the context of a posting.

	Subscriber	Author	Editor	Moderator	Resource Manager	Template Designer	Channel Manager	Administrator
Switch to Edit Site	Yes*	Yes	Yes	Yes	No	Yes	Yes	Yes
Production Manager	Yes*	Yes	Yes	Yes	No	Yes	Yes	Yes
Approval Assistant	No	No	Yes	Yes	No	Yes	Yes	Yes
Resource Manager	No	No	No	No	Yes+	Yes	Yes	Yes
Preview	Yes*	Yes	Yes	Yes	No	Yes	Yes	Yes
Create New Page	No	Yes	Yes	Yes	No	Yes	Yes	Yes
Create Connected Page	No	Yes	Yes	Yes	No	Yes	Yes	Yes
Edit	No	Yes	Yes	Yes	No	Yes	Yes	Yes
Delete	No	Yes	Yes	Yes	No	Yes	Yes	Yes
Copy	Yes*	Yes	Yes	Yes	No	Yes	Yes	Yes
Move	No	Yes	Yes	Yes	No	Yes	Yes	Yes
Submit	No	Yes	Yes	Yes	No	Yes	Yes	Yes
Approve	No	No	Yes	Yes	No	Yes	Yes	Yes
Decline	No	No	Yes	Yes	No	Yes	Yes	Yes
Page Properties	Yes**	Yes	Yes	Yes	No	Yes	Yes	Yes
Revision History	Yes**	Yes	Yes	Yes	No	Yes	Yes	Yes

	Subscriber	Author	Editor	Moderator	Resource Manager	Template Designer	Channel Manager	Administrator
View Revisions by Date	Yes**	Yes	Yes	Yes	No	Yes	Yes	Yes
Channel Properties	No	No	No	No	No	Yes	Yes	Yes

A subscriber would only see the Switch To Edit Site option if they are also part of an Author, Editor, Moderator, Resource Manager, Template Designer, Channel Manager, or Administrator role group for another channel. If they are merely a subscriber, they will not see the Web Author or any of its options.

** Read-only access.

+ Only if the Resource Manager user has subscriber rights to the channel will they see the link to the Resource Manager along with all of the other rights of a subscriber. Otherwise they will not have access to the Web Author at all, only the ability to use Site Manager.

Before we make any changes to our Hibiscus posting, let's have a quick overview of each option in the Default Console when the posting is seen in edit site view.

Switch to Live Site

This will return you to the Live Site view. If the current posting has a published version you will be taken to that version. If no published version of the current posting exists, you will be taken to the channel rendering script or default posting of the current channel.

Page Status

Page Status is a read-only value that shows you where the posting is in the publishing workflow. It displays one of these values:

Status	Meaning
Published	The posting has been published and is available on the live site to subscribers.
Saved	The posting has been edited and the changes have been saved. There isn't a published version of it on the live site. Subscribers are not able to view it.
Saved (Page has Live Version)	The posting has been edited and the changes have been saved. A previously published version of the posting does exist and is available to subscribers on the live site.
Waiting For Editor Approval	The posting has been submitted and is currently waiting for an editor to approve it.
Waiting For Moderator Approval	The posting has been submitted and is currently waiting for a moderator to approve it.
Approved	The posting has gone through the approval process but its start date has been set to a time in the future.

Status	Meaning
Editor Declined	An editor has declined the posting.
Moderator Declined	A moderator has declined the posting.
Expired	The posting has gone through the approval process but its end date has been set to a time in the past.

Lock Status

Lock Status shows the user name of the last user to edit and save the posting. Authors cannot edit a posting if it is being locked by another user. Once the lock on a posting is released, the Lock Status shows the value Not Locked.

Production Manager

The Production Manager is a helpful tool for managing the postings you are working on but have not completed. If you have postings you have saved but not submitted to the next level in the publishing workflow, they will appear in the Production Manager. This shows postings from anywhere in the site, not just the current channel.

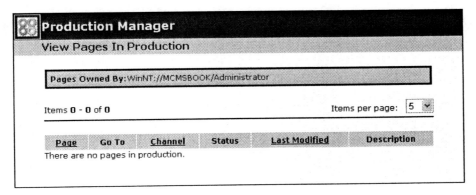

See the *Managing Workflow* section in this chapter for more details on the Production Manager.

Approval Assistant

Editors and moderators will find the Approval Assistant to be an invaluable tool for tracking and locating postings that are currently waiting for their approval.

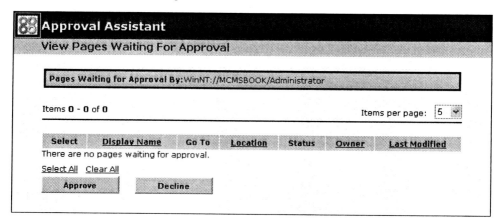

See the *Managing Workflow* section in this chapter for more details on the Approval Assistant.

Resource Manager

The Resource Manager provides a web interface for resource managers to add and remove content in the resource galleries.

Authors and editors will add these resources as attachments to their postings. See the section *Managing Resources* later in this chapter for more details on the Resource Manager.

The following screenshots show the Resource Manager. This screen shows it in the View As Tree mode:

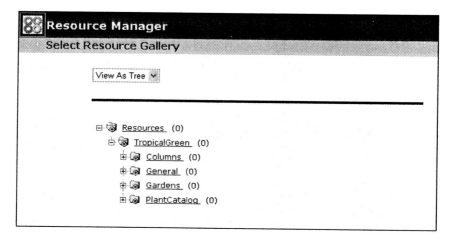

This screen shows that we currently do not have any resources added to the PlantCatalog resource gallery.

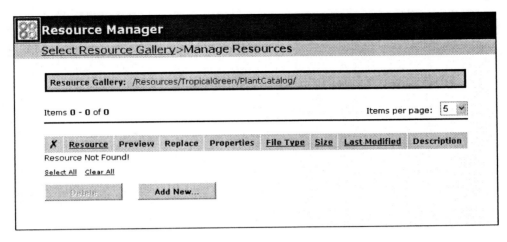

Preview

The Preview link will open the current posting or channel in a new window. This preview shows how the current posting or channel cover page looks like to a subscriber. The Web Author Console does not appear.

Create New Page

Creating new postings is one of the most frequently used functions of the Web Author Console.

When you click on the Create New Page link, the Web Author presents you with a dialog to select the template gallery and then the template you will use for your new posting. Once the template has been selected, the posting will change from edit site view:

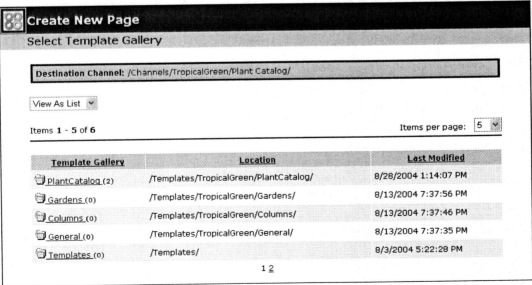

to authoring view:

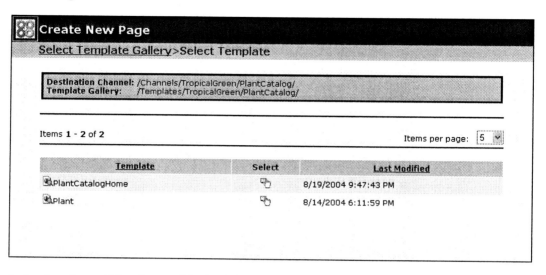

Authoring view will be discussed in detail in the following section.

The list shows only template galleries the user has rights to. This can be a problem in the View As Tree mode, as certain template sub-galleries may be hidden if the parents of those template galleries are not accessible to the user. In that case, View As List mode may be a better choice.

In addition, if the user has subscriber rights but not authoring rights, then the template gallery name(s) will be grayed out.

Create Connected Page

This will open the Create Connected Page dialog box. Connected postings share the content of all their placeholders, so if content is updated in one posting it will be reflected in all postings connected to it.

See Chapter 20 for more information on connected postings and connected templates. Briefly, you first choose the destination channel:

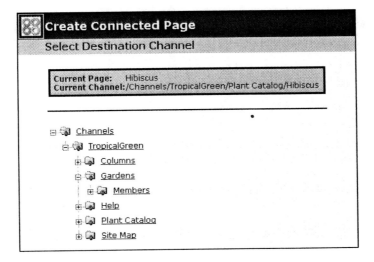

then select the connected template the posting will be based on:

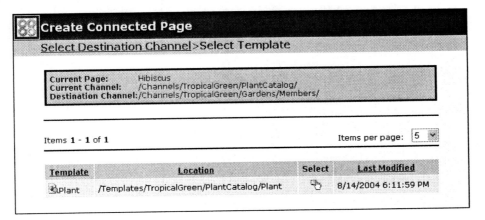

Edit

Another frequently used function on the console is Edit. If you have author rights or above for the current channel, you will see a link to edit the current posting. Clicking on it will bring you from edit site view to authoring view (see the *Editing the Hibiscus Posting* section below for details on the authoring view).

Delete, Move, Copy

The Delete option will delete the current posting from the MCMS repository. Unlike the delete function in Site Manager, the Web Author delete function will permanently purge the posting from the system. There's no 'undelete' function available to recover a deleted item.

> Items deleted from the Site Manager by pressing *Delete* are sent to the Deleted Items bin where they may be recovered, as long as the bin is not emptied.
> Items deleted from the Site Manager using *Shift + Delete* cannot be recovered, just like items deleted from the Web Author Console.

The Move option will move the current posting to another channel. Depending on the rights of the new channel, the posting may need to be re-approved by a moderator after being moved.

The Copy option will create a copy of the current posting in another channel. Depending on the rights of the new channel, the posting may need to be approved by an editor and/or moderator after being copied. This is not the same as creating a connected posting. The new posting will have no connection to the old posting, so if content is modified on one posting the other posting will not reflect the changes.

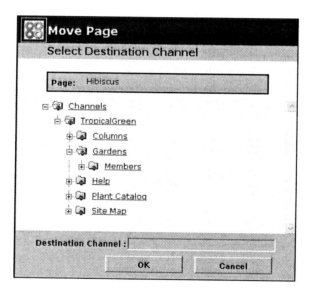

Page Properties

This link will open the Page Properties dialog box in a new window. This dialog allows you to change the properties of the posting.

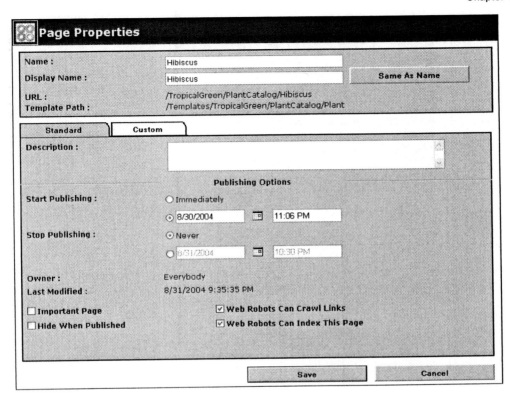

Page properties include the following on the Standard tab:

Property	Description
Name	The name of the posting. This value is used as part of the hierarchical URL,
Display Name	Text accessible through the DisplayName property. Usually used in navigation dialogs to give a friendly name to the user.
URL	The URL of the current posting. This field is read-only.
Template Path	Full path of the template used for the current posting. This field is read-only.
Description	Field to hold a short description about the current posting.
Start Publishing	Date and Time the current posting will appear on the Live Site.
Stop Publishing	Date and Time the current posting expires, will be removed from the Live Site.
Owner	If a user is listed as Owner, the posting is locked by that user and it cannot be edited by another user. If Everybody listed as Owner, any user can edit the posting. This field is read-only.
Last Modified	Date and time that the posting was last changed. This field is read-only.
Important Page	A property that can be used by the navigation page of the site to display a listing of important postings.

Property	Description
Hide When Published	A property automatically used by the navigation of the site to hide the current posting from being listed. By default, MCMS will not return postings marked as hidden in any collection while in published mode.
Web Robots Can Crawl Links, Web Robots Can Index This Page	Selected by default. Determines whether web crawlers for search engines are allowed to index the current posting or explore links in the current posting. Only works if the MCMS `RobotMetaTag` server control has been included in the `<head>` section of the template. E.g. `<cms:robotmetatag id="RobotMetaTag1" runat="server"></cms:robotmetatag>`.

The Custom tab of the Page Properties dialog box lists all custom properties that have been defined for the template of the current posting. Here you can change values for any of the custom properties. See Chapter 13 for more information about custom properties and how they can enhance your site.

Revision History

You can use the Revision History function to view previous versions of the current posting. The Revision History will display a list of all previously approved revisions, including the current version. If the current posting is unapproved it will be listed as such. If previous versions of the posting have been removed from the database (by using the Clear Revision History function of the Site Manager), then there may not be any revisions listed.

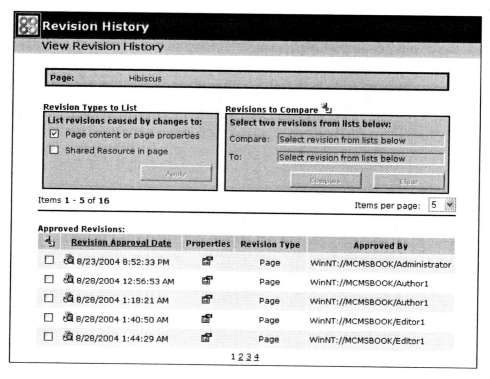

You can check two revisions and click Compare. This will open up a new window and highlight differences between the two revisions by Appearance, Source code, or Properties.

Unfortunately, you cannot roll back to a previous version. You can only view the differences. However, as a developer you can use the MCMS PAPI to access previous version content and create your own rollback feature for your website. That feature could then be added to the Web Author Console as a new option.

> The sample code for reverting a page to its previous version is available at
> http://www.gotdotnet.com/Community/UserSamples/Details.aspx?SampleGuid=580
> 1E02F-AF3A-413F-8985-A773336D84D8

See the *Revisions* section later in the chapter for more details on the Revision History.

View Revisions by Date

This option allows you to view how the current posting appeared on a specific date and time.

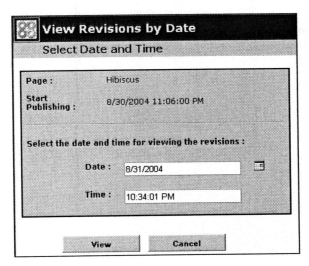

See the *Revisions* section later in the chapter for more details on viewing revisions by date.

Channel Properties

Only Channel Managers and Administrators will see this option. This link will open the Channel Properties dialog box in a new window. The Channel Properties dialog looks similar to the Page Properties dialog.

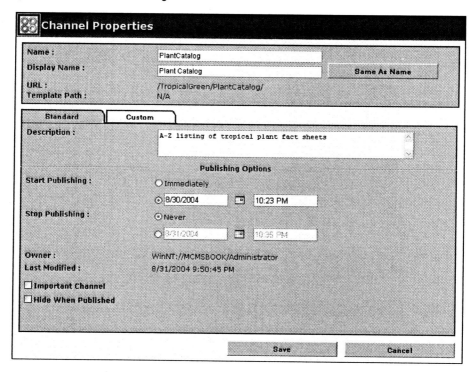

Channel properties include the following on the Standard tab:

Property	Description
Name	The name of the channel. Value is used as part of hierarchical URL.
Display Name	Text accessible through the Display Name property. Usually used in navigation dialogs to give a friendly name to the user.
URL	The URL of the current channel. This field is read-only.
Template Path	Not applicable to a channel.
Description	Field to hold a short description about the current channel.
Start Publishing	Date and Time the current channel will appear on the live site.
Stop Publishing	Date and Time the current channel will expire and get removed from the live site.
Owner	The user who currently owns the channel. Unlike postings and templates, owning the channel does not mean that other users can't modify it. Users with rights to create new postings or modify the channel's properties can do so regardless of the value stored here.
Last Modified	Date and time the channel was last changed.
Important Channel	A property that can be used by the navigation of the site to display a listing of important channels.

Property	Description
Hide When Published	A property automatically used by the navigation of the site to hide the current channel from being listed. By default, MCMS will not return channels marked as hidden in any collection while in published mode.

The Custom tab of the Channel Properties dialog box lists all custom properties that have been defined for the channel in Site Manager. Here you can change the value for any of the custom properties. See Chapter 13 for more information about custom properties and how they can enhance your site.

That covers all of the options available in the edit site view. Now let's start using the Web Author!

Editing the Hibiscus Posting

You should still be on the Hibiscus posting and in edit site view.

Start Editing

Click Edit and the Web Author Console will switch to the authoring view. You will see:

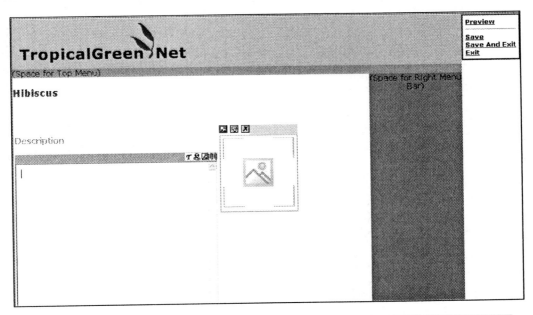

The HTML Placeholder does not show up correctly. I see the area for entering content but the Toolbar is missing.

The HTML placeholder requires each author to download and install a Microsoft ActiveX control. If your authors are having problems downloading the control from the MCMS server, you could do one of the following:

- Ensure that the user is a member of the local administrator or power-user security group on the computer and attempt to load the page again. If the browser does not prompt to download and install the control, it could mean that there is a previous version of the control that was not successfully installed. To remove the earlier installation of the control:

  1. Select Tools | Internet Option from the Internet Explorer menu bar.
  2. Look for the Temporary Internet files section of the General tab. Click Settings…
  3. In the Settings dialog, click View Objects.
  4. Delete any instances of MCMS Html Editor and Microsoft Html Editor Toolbar. These are older versions (pre-SP1) of the control. The most recent name of the control (after SP1) is Microsoft CMS HTML Editor Toolbar.
  5. Close all open instances of Internet Explorer.

- Check to see if there are any security policies in place in the organization that prevent users from downloading ActiveX controls. If there are, you can manually install and register both classes used by the control:

  1. Select Start | Run…
  2. In the Run dialog, enter cmd to open the Windows Command Prompt.
  3. In the prompt enter the following statements, replacing the folder paths to each file with the one that matches your system.

```
REGSVR32 "c:\Program Files\Microsoft Content Management Server\Server\
    IIS_CMS\WebAuthor\Client\PlaceholderControlSupport\ncbmprdr.dll"

REGSVR32 "c:\Program Files\Microsoft Content Management Server\Server\
    IIS_CMS\WebAuthor\Client\PlaceholderControlSupport\nrdhtml.dll"
```

  4. Close the Windows Command Prompt window.

Once in authoring view, you will be able to add content to the three placeholders we added to the Plant template (Description, ResearchPaper, and PlantPicture).

Adding HTML Content

Place your mouse cursor over the placeholder under the label Description. Click in the placeholder. You are now ready to add some content!

Type a few words about the Hibiscus plant.

The icons that appear at the top right-hand corner of the placeholder field may look like buttons, but they are actually just indicators of the formatting options that are available. Mouse-over each icon to read a description of the available functionality.

Notice that when you are typing into the Description placeholder, the toolbar at the top of your Internet Explorer window comes to life:

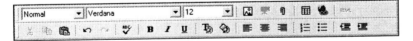

This toolbar acts much like the formatting toolbar in Microsoft Word. Depending on the options set by the template designer, certain buttons may be enabled to do some or all of the following:

- Change the style (e.g. Normal, Heading, Formatted, List, etc.)
- Change the font face and font size
- Add images, attachments, tables, hyperlinks
- Edit the HTML source code (this is the only option not available to us now, as we did not enable it)
- Cut, copy, and paste content
- Undo or redo
- Check spelling (only if Microsoft Office is installed on the local machine)

- Make text bold, italic, and underlined
- Change the foreground or background color
- Align left, center, or right
- Start a numbered or bullet list
- Increase and decrease indent

In our Description placeholder, nearly all options are available because we set it to allow full formatting, allow images, allow line breaks, and allow hyperlinks back in Chapter 7. Feel free to test any of these buttons.

> You can drag and drop attachments and images from Windows Explorer directly to the HTML placeholder.

Inserting Tables

Let's insert a table. Click the Insert Table button . A little dialog appears as shown below.

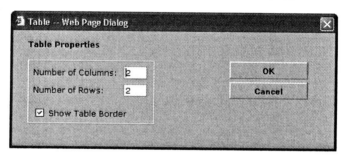

Set the following values and click OK when you are done.

Field Name	Value
Number of Columns	2
Number of Rows	2
Show Table Border	Checked

A table with 2 rows, 2 columns, and a border is inserted into the Description placeholder with default text in each cell. You can replace the text in each cell with custom text/images and use the other formatting options in the toolbar to change the way they look.

The Insert Table function offers basic features that get you started. If you need to do complex actions such as merging and splitting cells, you can choose to:

- Switch to HTML view (if the template designer has enabled this option) and edit the table's HTML source code.
- Use external editors such as Microsoft Word that provide rich table editing capabilities. Tables created from Word can be copied and pasted onto the HTML placeholder.
- Consider using alternative controls that provide richer table editing features as compared to the out-of-the-box HTML placeholder such as the Telerik r.a.d.editor for MCMS 2002.

> You will find more information on the Telerik r.a.d.editor for Microsoft Content Management Server at http://www.telerik.com/mcms/

- To delete a table, click on the table's borders when the cursor turns into a cross-hair. Eight white squares surround the border. Press the *Delete* key. The table is removed.

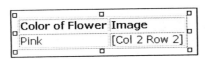

Editing Hyperlinks

You can convert any text or image in the HTML placeholder to a hyperlink. To do so, simply highlight the text/image you wish to convert and click on the Edit Hyperlink button 🖱.

We will set the word shrub to open the web page at the address `http://www.google.com/search?q=define:shrub` (Google's collection of definitions for the word shrub), in a new window.

1. In the `Description` HTML placeholder, highlight the word shrub.
2. From the MCMS authoring toolbar, click Edit Hyperlink.
3. In the Edit Hyperlink dialog, set the following values:

Field Name	Value	Attribute of the `<A>` tag
Hyperlink Address	`http://www.google.com/search?q=define:shrub`	`Href`
Tooltip	Definition of shrub	`Title`
Open Link In	New Unnamed Window	`Target`

4. Click OK.

The word shrub now links to the specified address.

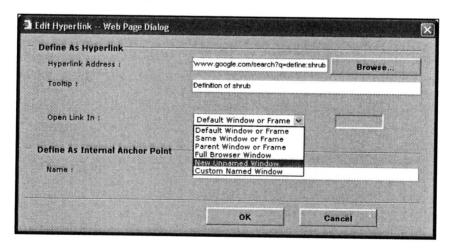

The hyperlink could point to the URL of an existing channel or posting. In such cases, you don't have to manually key in the full address and you can just click on the Browse... button. You will be brought to the Internal Links dialog where you can select the channel or posting you wish to link to. The dialog allows you to link only to channels and postings you have read access to.

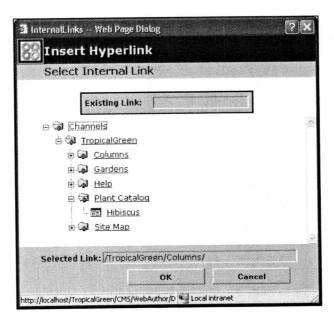

Once you have inserted the hyperlink to a channel or posting, MCMS manages the link for you. When the object has expired, or if the user does not have access to it or if it has been deleted, the text will continue to be displayed but the user will not be able to click on the link. Internally, MCMS converts these links from `<a href= "(some url)">` to `<a zref="(some url)">`.

How can I remove a hyperlink?

Highlight the text you wish to unlink in the placeholder and click on the Edit Hyperlink button. Set both the Hyperlink Address and Name fields to a blank string and click OK. You will get a warning saying:

You did not specify a Hyperlink Address or a Name. As a result the selection in the placeholder will receive no anchor tag. Do you want to proceed?

Click OK. The selected text will no longer be a hyperlink.

Mapping the Buttons on the Authoring Toolbar to the HTML Placeholder Definition Properties

The table overleaf maps the HTML Placeholder Definition properties to the options available on the toolbar. The template designer decides what tags and styles are allowed on the control by setting the properties of the HTMLPlaceholderDefinition on the template object.

HTML Placeholder Definition Properties	Style	Font Face	Font Size	Insert Image	Insert Video	Insert Attachment	Insert Table	Edit HyperLink	Bold	Italic	Underline	Foreground Color	Background Color	Align Left	Align Center	Align Right	Numbered List	Bulleted List	Decrease Indent	Increase Indent
Formatting = NoFormatting																				
Formatting = FullFormatting	✓	✓	✓				✓		✓	✓	✓	✓	✓	✓	✓	✓	✓	✓	✓	✓
Formatting = TextMarkup									✓	✓	✓									
Formatting = HtmlStyles	✓													✓	✓	✓	✓	✓	✓	✓
Formatting = TextMarkupAnd HtmlStyles	✓								✓	✓	✓			✓	✓	✓	✓	✓	✓	✓
AllowHyperlinks = true								✓												
AllowAttachments = true						✓														
AllowImages = true				✓																

Adding Pictures

To add a picture to our Hibiscus posting, we will use the `PlantPicture` `SingleImagePlaceholderControl`. Pictures are inserted into HTML Placeholders following similar steps.

The single-image placeholder has three buttons at the top for inserting, editing, and deleting the image.

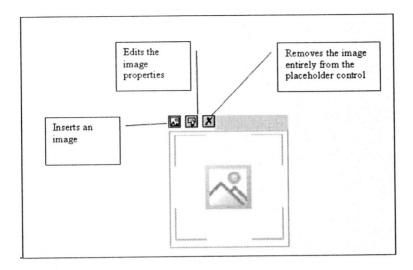

Let's insert a picture of the Hibiscus plant:

1. Click on the Add or Edit Image icon [icon] in the PlantPicture single-image placeholder. This brings up the Insert Image dialog where you can select the source.

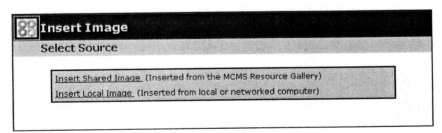

2. Choose Insert Local Image.
3. Click Browse... and choose a GIF or JPEG file on your machine. If you have downloaded the resource files from this book's companion site, use the hibiscus.jpg file.
4. If the file already has a GIF or JPEG/JPG extension, then you can leave the File Type option alone. MCMS will automatically detect the types of files that have extensions. Otherwise, if your file does not have an extension, select a File Type from the drop-down list.
5. Set the Alternate Text to Hibiscus flower. You can also choose to make the image a hyperlink, but we will leave it blank for this example.
6. Click Insert. The image is inserted into the PlantPicture single-image placeholder.

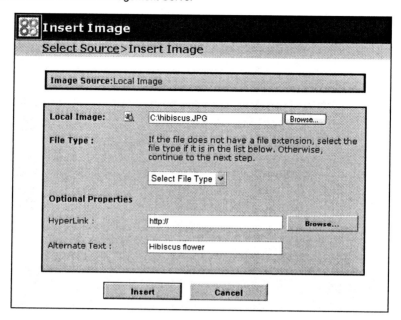

Insertion of local images and attachments is allowed only if the template designer has set
MustUseResourceGallery property of the corresponding placeholder definition to false.

Adding Attachments

Attachments are files that are linked to a posting. You can attach files in either an
HtmlPlaceholderControl or an AttachmentPlaceholderControl. Let's insert an attachment to
the ResearchPaper AttachmentPlaceholderControl. The process for adding attachments to the
Description HtmlPlaceholderControl is very similar.

The AttachmentPlaceholderControl has three buttons at the top for inserting an attachment,
editing the attachment's properties, and removing the attachment from the placeholder.

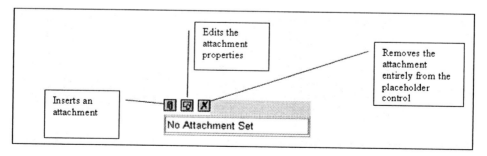

To insert an attachment:

1. Scroll down to the bottom of the posting and click on the Add or Edit Attachment icon ▣ of the placeholder control bound to the ResearchPaper attachment placeholder.

2. Choose Insert Local Attachment and then the Insert Attachment dialog will appear (we will show you how to add a shared resource later in the chapter when we discuss resource galleries).

3. Click Browse... and choose a Word document or PDF file from your machine. If you have downloaded the resource files from this book's companion site, use the hibiscus.doc file.

4. As with images, if the file already has a DOC or PDF extension, then you can leave the File Type option alone. MCMS will automatically detect the types of most files.

5. Set the Display Text to Hibiscus in depth.

6. Click Insert. The document is inserted as an attachment.

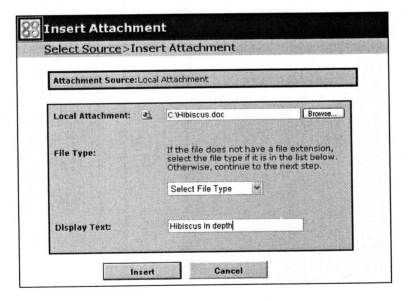

At this point, all three placeholders should be filled with content and your posting should look something like this:

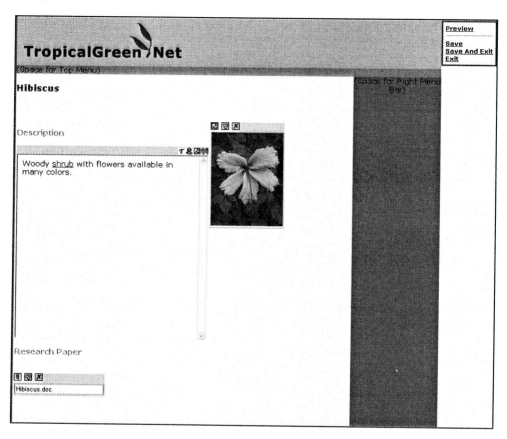

Now that we are done adding content to the posting, we need to save and exit. Notice the options in the Web Author Console:

- **Preview** opens a new window with a preview of the content as it would appear after saving. This gives you an idea how the posting will look like on the live site before you commit the changes to the database.

- **Save** will save any changes you have made, but keep you in authoring view. Since there is no Microsoft Word-like auto-save in MCMS it is a good idea to periodically save your changes to the site.

- **Save And Exit** saves the changes to the current posting and return to edit site view. From here, you can edit the posting again, or submit it to the workflow so the changes will eventually appear on the live site.

- **Exit** discards all changes done in the current edit session and ends editing the current posting. You will be asked to confirm the exit. Once you exit, you will not be able to go back to retrieve the changes, so they are lost forever.

When you click Save And Exit your changes are saved to the database and the posting state is changed to Saved.

Publishing the Changed Posting

Now that the Hibiscus posting has been saved, your posting should look something like this:

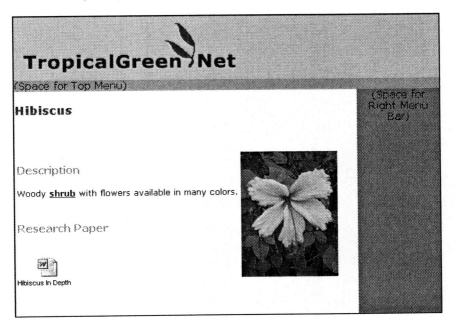

If a posting has been saved but not submitted to the next level of the publishing workflow, the edit site mode console will look a little different. As an administrator, you will see the Submit, Approve, and Decline buttons. Other users may not see them, depending on their rights.

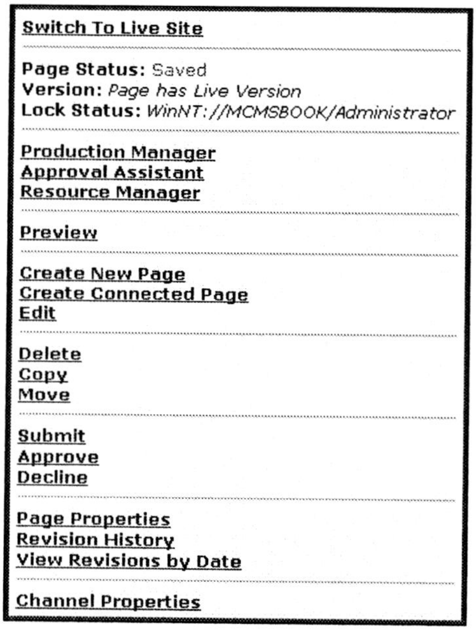

```
Switch To Live Site

Page Status: Saved
Version: Page has Live Version
Lock Status: WinNT://MCMSBOOK/Administrator

Production Manager
Approval Assistant
Resource Manager

Preview

Create New Page
Create Connected Page
Edit

Delete
Copy
Move

Submit
Approve
Decline

Page Properties
Revision History
View Revisions by Date

Channel Properties
```

Submit, Approve, and Decline were covered in detail in Chapter 10. Click Approve and then Switch To Live Site. Your changes have been saved, approved, and now appear on the live site!

Creating a New Plant Posting

Now that you have seen how to add content to an existing posting, let's pull it all together and make a few more postings in the PlantCatalog channel.

1. First, click on Switch To Edit Site to bring the Web Author Console back into view.
2. Choose Create New Page. This brings up the list of template galleries.
3. Choose the PlantCatalog template gallery. This will bring up the Select Template view of the Template Gallery explorer.

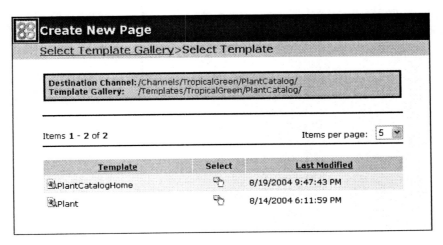

4. Choose the Plant template by clicking on the Select icon .

You will now have an empty plant posting! Fill in each placeholder with the following content:

Property	Values
Description	The banana needs no introduction. Its sweet yellow fruit is often pictured in the hands of a hungry monkey.
Plant Picture	*Leave this empty for now.*
Research Paper	Any file on your computer, or the banana.doc file from the companion website
Research Paper Display Text	Banana tree in depth

Since this posting was created from scratch, the Web Author Console will appear like so:

```
Preview
Save New Page
Exit
```

- **Preview** opens a new window with a preview of the content. The posting is not yet saved to the site, so you can get an idea of what the posting will look like before you commit it to the database.
- **Save New Page** saves the current posting to the site. First, you will be asked to provide the Name and Display Name properties of the new posting. Fill them out and click Save. The posting is added to the site and committed to the database. You can now edit the posting again, or submit it to the next level in the publishing workflow.
- **Exit** discards all content and exits from creating a new posting. You will be asked to confirm the exit. Once you exit, you will not be able to go back to retrieve the content you just entered, so it is lost for ever.

You are now ready to save and submit the new posting.

1. Click Save New Page. The Save New Page dialog will appear.
2. Set the name to BananaTree and the Display Name to Banana Tree.
3. Click OK to commit the changes and close the Save New Page dialog.

Don't submit or approve the posting just yet. Repeat the steps to create a few more plant postings using the following content.

Description Placeholder	PlantPicture Placeholder	ResearchPaper Placeholder	Name	Display Name
The health benefits of eating the inner leaves of the Aloe Vera have made it popular. Also used to make gels and cream known to have rejuvenating properties.	*Leave it blank for now.*	*Leave it blank for now.*	AloeVera	Aloe Vera
Named after Admiral Louis de Bougainvillea. The plant has petal-like leaves that grow in tight clusters giving off vibrant bursts of color.			Bougainvillea	Bougainvillea
If you have a pet monkey, teach it to climb the tree to get your coconuts! Or simply wait for its delicious fruit to fall.			CoconutTree	Coconut Tree
[TOP SECRET] Rumor has it that scientists have discovered a man eating plant growing in a certain basement... don't say we didn't warn you and if anybody asked, you didn't hear it from us.			ManEatingPlant	Man Eating Plant

Managing Workflow

Earlier in the chapter we briefly reviewed two options in the Web Author Console: the Production Manager and the Approval Assistant. Now we will try out both of those features so you can get a feel for how they work.

Using the Production Manager

To begin, navigate to the `PlantCatalog` channel at `http://localhost/tropicalgreen/plantcatalog/` and click the Switch To Edit Site link. Then click the link to the Production Manager. Earlier, we created five new plant fact sheets. Since we didn't submit or approve them, they are still in the production line. You should see each posting listed in the Production Manager.

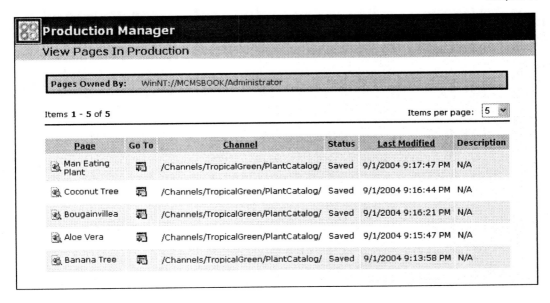

There are two options you have from this dialog:

- **Preview Page** opens a new browser window with a preview of the posting.
- **Go To Page** opens the posting in the parent browser window.

These options make it easy to find postings you need to finish. Let's continue work on the Banana Tree posting and submit it to the workflow:

1. Click the Go To Page icon for the Banana Tree posting in the Production Manager. The Production Manager closes and the Banana Tree posting appears in the parent browser window.
2. Click Edit and insert the following text in the Description HTML placeholder: "One of the hardest tropical trees to grow."
3. Click Save And Exit.
4. Click Submit.

The Banana Tree posting is now in the workflow. Use the Production Manager to go to each of the four other postings we have created earlier and submit them.

Next we will explore the Approval Assistant.

Using the Approval Assistant

We are using the administrator account, but assume for a moment that it was an author who submitted the Banana Tree posting to the workflow. That's most likely how your site will work. Now we will pretend we are an editor coming in to review and hopefully approve our new posting.

Navigate to the PlantCatalog channel at http://localhost/tropicalgreen/plantcatalog/ and click the Switch To Edit Site link. Then click the link to the Approval Assistant. You should now see the Approval Assistant with a list of postings you submitted in the previous section.

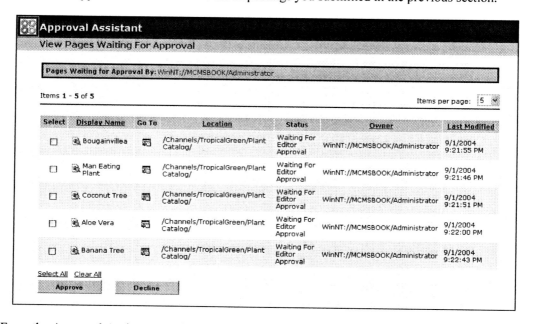

From the Approval Assistant you have the same two options as in the Production Manager:

- **Preview Page** opens a new browser window with a preview of the posting.
- **Go To Page** opens the posting in the parent browser window. From there you can Edit, Approve, or Decline the posting as you normally would using the Web Author Console.

In addition, there is a third option for those approvers who are in a hurry. You can click the Select box next to each posting that you want to approve or decline. This means you can approve or decline a bunch of postings all at once. Let's give it a try:

1. Click Select All.
2. Click Approve.

All the postings in the list will get approved and the Approval Assistant will be refreshed. A message There are no pages waiting for approval will appear in the Approval Assistant if there are no postings left for review. Go ahead and close the Approval Assistant.

From the Plant Catalog page, click on the Banana Tree posting and you will see that the Page Status has changed to Published.

Since we are running the site as administrator, we skipped over the editor and moderator workflow process. Normally, if your channels have both editors and moderators, both would need to approve new postings. In this case, the administrator trumped both the editor and moderator and was able to approve a posting in a single step.

Revisions

One nice feature of the default Web Author Console is the ability to see past versions of a particular posting. This can be accomplished by both the Revision History and View Revisions by Date options in the Web Author Console.

Using the Revision History

First, navigate to the `http://localhost/tropicalgreen/plantcatalog/bananatree.htm` page and click on Switch To Edit Site. Then click on the Revision History link. The Revision History should only have one revision listed.

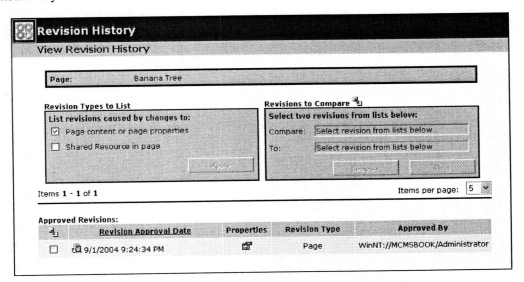

We need to change the posting and re-approve it. Close the Revision History and do the following:

1. Click Edit.
2. In the Description placeholder, replace hardest with easiest and insert the word, fruit: One of the easiest tropical fruit trees to grow.
3. Click Save And Exit.
4. Click Approve. The posting is published.

Click the Revision History link again. Now there are two versions of the Banana Tree posting. In the Revision History window, click the checkbox next to each revision.

You can compare a previous approved version with the currently unapproved version, if it exists.

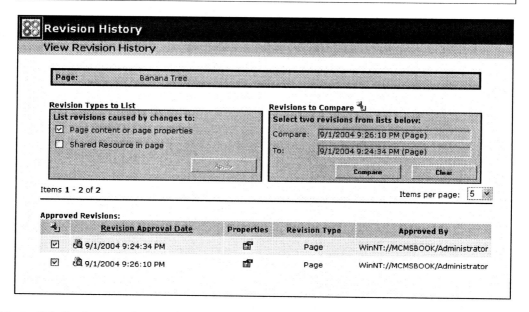

Next, click the Compare button. A new window will open and the Appearance tab will be selected. Scroll down to see highlights of the added and removed content.

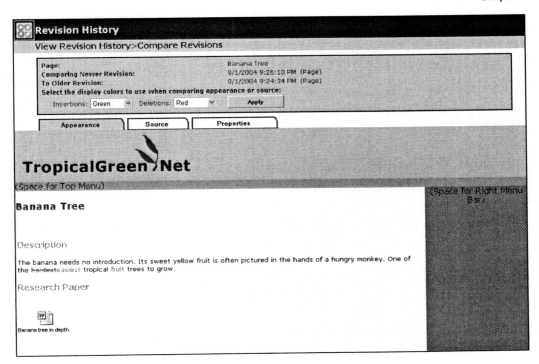

You can also click on the Source and Properties tabs to see differences in the HTML source code and posting properties, respectively.

> Unfortunately, there is no way to roll back changes to a previous version using the default Web Author Console. This functionality would need to be added by custom coding
>
> The sample code for reverting a page to its previous version is available at
> http://www.gotdotnet.com/Community/UserSamples/Details.aspx?SampleGuid=580 1E02F-AF3A-413F-8985-A773336D84D8

When you are done exploring the Revision History dialog, close both windows, and return to the parent browser window of the Banana Tree posting.

Viewing Revisions by Date

Another useful feature of the default Web Author Console is the View Revisions by Date feature. While viewing the Banana Tree posting, click on View Revisions by Date.

View Revisions by Date

Select Date and Time

Page :   Banana Tree

Start Publishing :   9/1/2004 9:13:58 PM

Select the date and time for viewing the revisions :

Date :   9/1/2004

Time :   9:36:45 PM

View   Cancel

Choose a date and time right after the Start Publishing date/time listed in the dialog. Click View. A new browser window will open with a view of the posting at that particular date and time.

When you are done exploring the View Revisions by Date dialog, close both windows and return to the parent browser window of the Banana Tree posting.

Clearing the Revision History

As time goes by, the number of revisions made to postings in the system increases. It may come to a point where you may want to housekeep the revisions to maintain a small database.

Revision histories are cleared using Site Manager:

1. Open Site Manager and log in with an account that has MCMS Administrator access.
2. From the toolbar, select Tools | Clear Revision History...
3. In the Clear Revisions dialog, select a date and time to mark the earliest revisions you wish to keep. Any revisions made before the selected date and time are deleted.

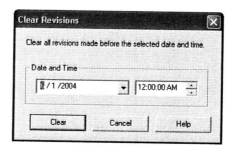

4. Click Clear.
5. Click Yes to confirm.

The deletion of revisions is done on the entire site. It is not possible to target revisions on individual postings.

Only administrators are able to access the Clear Revision History function in Site Manager.

Managing Resources

There are two ways to upload file attachments:

- As attachments from the author's desktop machine
- As part of a collection of resources in resource galleries

It is always convenient for authors to upload files as attachments from the author's computer. This convenience, however, comes at a price: MCMS creates a unique entry in the repository for each attachment uploaded. So even if you upload the same image file for five different postings in your website, MCMS creates five different entries of that same image in the database.

For a more efficient way to handle shared files managed by authors, they can be stored in resource galleries. Resource galleries serve as central storage locations for resources. Using the same resource gallery item within postings creates hyperlinks that link to the same entry in the content repository. In this way, the same resource could be used in thousands of postings and MCMS would maintain only one single instance of it.

When you replace a resource in a resource gallery, all postings that use the resource immediately show the new version of the resource. This is definitely a great advantage from the point of view of authors. Imagine if the boss came over to your desk one day and said "Our designers have created an updated look for our products. Update all our web pages with this new picture," and sent you a floppy containing the new image file of the company's redesigned product. If you had stored the image in the resource gallery, all you would need to do is replace it once. Job done, you get to go home. Otherwise, you would probably spend the rest of the day (and night) at the office poring through your code and postings just to do that one thing.

Up to this point you may have noticed references to resources, shared images, and the resource gallery. In Chapter 5, we set up the resource galleries using Site Manager, but we haven't done much with them so far.

Adding Resources to the Resource Gallery

Before we proceed, download the image files for each plant from the book's companion website and store them in an appropriate location on your hard disk. We are going to add these files to the PlantCatalog resource gallery. There are two ways to do this:

1. Use the Resource Manager function available in Web Author. This is useful for adding files one at a time.
2. Use Site Manager. This is useful for adding multiple files at the same time.

Using Web Author to Add a Resource

Switch back to your browser window and click on the Resource Manager link. Expand the TropicalGreen resource gallery and select the PlantCatalog resource gallery.

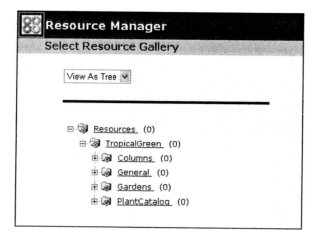

Click Add New... to bring up the Add Resource dialog. Click the Browse... button, find the BananaTree.jpg image file that you downloaded earlier, and click Open. Set the Display Name to Banana Tree. Enter a short description: Picture of the Banana Tree used by plant fact sheets. Click OK to close the dialog.

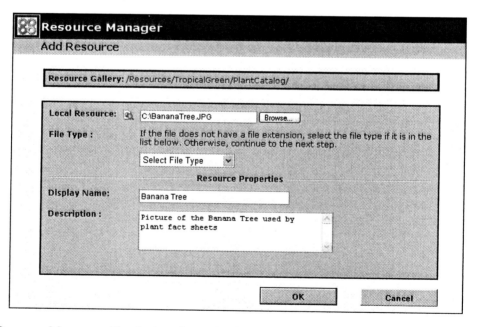

The Resource Manager will refresh and you should see your Banana Tree image listed.

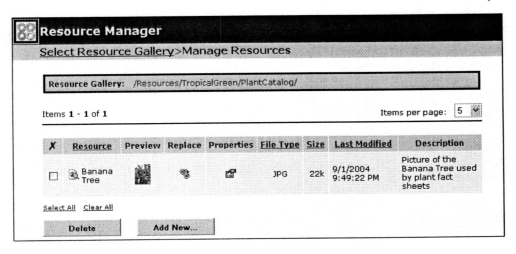

Using Site Manager to Add Resources

We have a few more image files to add to the Plantcatalog resource gallery. Instead of adding them one by one using the Web Author, upload them using Site Manager.

1. Open Site Manager and log in as an MCMS administrator or a resource manager (who has access to the Plantcatalog resource gallery).

2. Click on the Resources icon in the left panel.

3. In the Resources panel, expand the nodes: Resources | TropicalGreen | PlantCatalog. Keep the Site Manager window opened.

4. Open Windows Explorer and place the window above the Site Manager window.

5. Browse to the folder that contains the image files you have downloaded.

6. Press *Ctrl* and click to select the following image files:

    *   AloeVera.jpg
    *   Bougainvillea.jpg
    *   CoconutTree.jpg

7. Drag the selected image files and drop them onto the Plant Catalog resource gallery in Site Manager.

The three files you have selected are added to the Plantcatalog resource gallery.

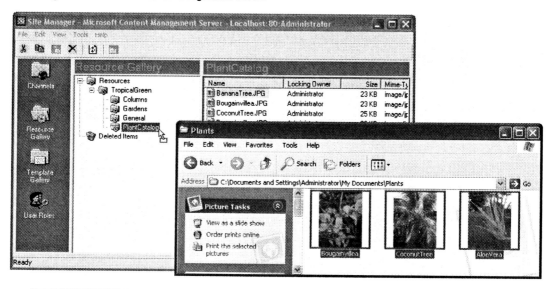

I've accidentally selected the wrong resource gallery. Can I move resources without affecting my postings?

The answer is, yes. To move resources from one resource gallery to another, use Site Manager. Simply drag the resources to be moved and drop them into the new resource gallery. Postings will not be affected by this operation.

Using Shared Resources in Postings

Now when you need to insert an image into a posting you can choose the Insert Shared Image option and use the resource gallery version of the image. This can also be done for any resource type using an attachment or HTML placeholder, including Word documents, PowerPoint slideshows, and Adobe PDF files.

Let's add a picture of the banana tree to the Banana Tree posting:

1. Navigate to http://localhost/tropicalgreen/plantcatalog/bananatree.htm and click Switch To Edit Site.
2. Click Edit.
3. Click on the Add or Edit Image icon ![] in the Plant Picture placeholder.
4. Choose Insert Shared Image. The Select Resource Gallery dialog appears.
5. Choose the PlantCatalog resource gallery.
6. Click the Select icon ![] for the Banana Tree JPG image.
7. Set the Alternate Text to Banana Tree.

8. Click Insert. The Resource Gallery will close and the plant image will be inserted into the Plant Picture placeholder.

9. Click Save And Exit and then Approve the posting.

Your Banana Tree posting now contains a shared resource!

Replacing Resources

The great benefit of using the resource galleries to hold resources is that now you can replace any instances of the same resource with a click of the button. When you use the Replace 🔁 feature in the Resource Manager, any instance of that resource in any posting is automatically updated. In addition, for large resources this helps keep the size of your database down by eliminating duplicate resource files.

To replace an image file in the PlantCatalog resource gallery:

1. With the Banana Tree posting opened in edit site view, click on the Resource Manager link in the Web Author Console.

2. In the Select Resource Gallery dialog, select the PlantCatalog resource gallery.

3. Select the Replace button for the Banana Tree.

4. In the Replace Resource dialog, click Browse... and select banana.jpg from your computer.

5. Click OK.

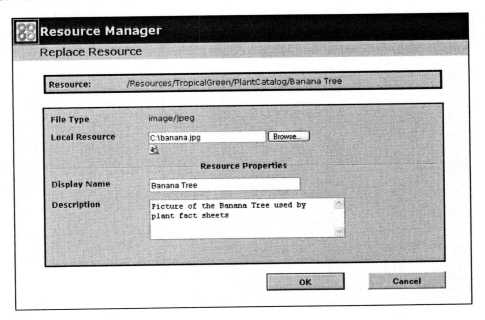

The BananaTree.jpg file has now been replaced with banana.jpg. You did not have to edit the posting and get it approved again.

Replacement does not mean deleting a resource and uploading a resource with the same name. Resource managers sometimes delete a resource by mistake and attempt to correct it by uploading a 'replacement' resource of the same name. Unfortunately, this remedy does not work. MCMS recognizes resources by their GUIDs. The new resource that is uploaded may have the same name and even the same content, but it will have a different GUID from the one that has been deleted.

Deleting Resources

Resources can be deleted using either Web Author or Site Manager.

Be careful when deleting resources. The system does not check to see if the resource is being used within postings. If you delete a resource that has been linked to a posting, the posting will continue to show the link to the resource. However, the link will be broken and lead to HTTP 401 forbidden access or 404 file not found errors when a subscriber clicks on it.

I'm logged in as the administrator and the deleted resource continues to appear on my posting. However, subscribers to my website get HTTP 401 or 404 errors when accessing the resource.

Under the hood, MCMS does not actually delete the physical resource file. It is stored in an internal folder called "Archive Folder", accessible only to administrators. That's why administrators have no problems viewing postings with deleted resources.

When all historical revisions of postings no longer link to the resource, the background process will delete them permanently from the system.

Delete Resources using Web Author

Unlike adding resources, you can delete multiple resources in a single step.

1. Click on the Resource Manager link in the Web Author Console.
2. Select the resource gallery that contains the resources you wish to delete.
3. Click on the checkbox next to the resources to be deleted. You can select multiple resources by checking more than one box.
4. Click Delete and the resources are removed permanently.

Delete Resources using Site Manager

Site Manager can be used to delete resources. To do so:

1. In Site Manager, select the resource gallery that contains the resources you wish to delete.
2. In the list of resources, select the ones to be deleted.
3. Right-click and select Delete (or press *Delete*).

The resources you have selected are moved to the Deleted Items bin. The nice thing about using Site Manager to delete resources is that if you delete a resource by mistake, you can still recover it from the Deleted Items bin.

Summary

In this chapter we looked at the various functions available from the Web Author. Web Author is the main way that your users will add and edit content on your website. We saw the lists of actions available from the Web Author Console, which provide a range of actions that you can perform on channels and postings.

We went on to edit the Hibiscus posting, experiencing first-hand what authoring with the HTML placeholder, single-image placeholder, and single-attachment placeholder is like. We added text, inserted tables, created hyperlinks, added images and attachments to our postings, and published the changes to the live site.

Next, we created more postings for the PlantCatalog channel and saw how the Production Manager and Approval Assistant help us to keep tabs on the items that are moving along the publishing workflow, giving us a list of postings in production as well as postings that are waiting for our approval.

We used Revision History to compare two versions of the same posting. It provides a useful visual guide to authors who need to keep track of changes to posting content. We are also able to look at a snapshot of the posting at a specific date and time using the View Revisions by Date function.

Finally, we made use of the Resource Manager to upload, replace, and delete resources. We also explored alternative ways of managing resources using Site Manager.

There may be options you'd like to add to the Web Author Console. We will go over a few ways of doing that later, in Chapter 19.

12

The Publishing Application Programming Interface

As a developer you will make use of the Publishing Application Programming Interface (PAPI) in almost all sites built with MCMS. The PAPI is a collection of .NET and COM libraries through which you can programmatically retrieve and update content stored in the repository. Furthermore, you can perform custom actions, build interfaces between content and legacy applications, and even create housekeeping batch jobs. The more you know about what is available in the PAPI, the better equipped you will be to make programming design decisions and write better code. Having an understanding of what the PAPI provides will be indispensable to you as an MCMS developer.

In this chapter, we will take a brief look at the namespaces, properties, methods, and events that are available out of the box.

There are a total of ten .NET namespaces available for developers to work with. It would be a mammoth undertaking to describe what each one does in detail in a single chapter. As a start, we will concentrate on using the PAPI to retrieve the most commonly required objects from the repository. We will walk you through the remaining classes in the coming chapters.

The PAPI gives us lots of flexibility in designing our MCMS site. With it, we can customize the product to meet business requirements. Already, we had a sneak preview of the PAPI in Chapter 9 when we built summary pages for the PlantCatalog channel. That's just a sliver of what the PAPI can do for you. The PAPI can also be used to build navigation controls, modify the default workflows, build custom controls, change the default dialogs provided in Web Author, and much more. It is a powerful feature and a key ingredient of every MCMS website.

The PAPI is available in two implementations:

- .NET classes
- A COM object

The COM version of the PAPI is available for backward compatibility with sites that were built in MCMS 2001 using ASP-based templates. The .NET version of the PAPI has capabilities similar to the COM version but provides extra functionality. It also has the advantage of being managed and executed by the Common Language Runtime. Lastly, the COM-based PAPI will probably not be available in the next version of MCMS. In this book, we use only the .NET classes.

> The Site Deployment API discussed in Chapter 23 is only available with the COM-based PAPI as it is intended to be used from Visual Basic scripts, which do not have a native interface to managed classes.

Setting Up the Work Area

In this chapter, we will set up a specific work area to play around with the PAPI. Within the work area, we can test the properties, methods, and events of the PAPI without affecting the functionality of the site.

The work area will reside in the TropicalGreen project that we have created earlier in a dedicated folder named PAPI. Within this folder we will create three web forms:

- AccessObjects.aspx will be used to demonstrate how containers at the root level are accessed through code. From the root, we will navigate to other objects, moving up and down the hierarchy as we do so.

- Searches.aspx will be used to show a more targeted and optimized way of retrieving objects from the MCMS repository. Rather than navigating from the root container through all levels to the object, we can jump straight to the object that we wish to retrieve.

- Placeholders.aspx will be used to illustrate how placeholder content can be retrieved programmatically.

Let's set up the work area:

1. Create a new folder in the TropicalGreen project.
2. Name the folder *PAPI*.
3. In the PAPI folder, add three new web forms.
4. Name the web forms as below:
   o AccessObjects.aspx
   o Searches.aspx
   o Placeholders.aspx
5. Set the Page Layout to FlowLayout for all three web forms.
6. Drag and drop styles.css from the Styles folder into each web form.
7. Save and build the TropicalGreen solution.

The Namespaces

All managed libraries provided with MCMS begin with the `Microsoft.ContentManagement` prefix. You can find the assembly files for each of these namespaces in the `<Install Directory>/Microsoft Content Management Server/Server/bin` directory.

- `Microsoft.ContentManagement.Publishing` provides the core classes of the PAPI, so it's not surprising to find that it is the most commonly used of all the namespaces. You use its classes to work with channels, postings, template galleries, templates, resource galleries, and resources. It's the namespace that houses the biggest collection of classes.

- `Microsoft.ContentManagement.Events` contains classes that work with the MCMS event model. It is most commonly used to customize the publishing workflow. We will discuss this namespace in detail in Chapter 16 when we implement a customized workflow for the TropicalGreen website.

- `Microsoft.ContentManagement.Extensions.Placeholders` contains classes that get/set content from the out-of-the-box placeholders for use on web-based template files. We will explore how the methods and properties of the classes in this namespace can be used to retrieve placeholder content at the end of this chapter.

- `Microsoft.ContentManagement.Extensions.Placeholders.Office` is similar to the `Microsoft.ContentManagement.Extensions.Placeholder` namespace except that it contains classes that work with Authoring Connector (see Chapter 17).

- `Microsoft.ContentManagement.Web` contains classes that work with ASP.NET web applications. In particular, the `CmsHttpApplication` class is used to implement ASP.NET output caching (see Chapter 22).

- `Microsoft.ContentManagement.Web.Caching` contains classes that govern the caching behavior of postings (Chapter 22).

- `Microsoft.ContentManagement.Web.Security` contains classes that are used when implementing custom authentication methods such as forms authentication (see Chapter 18).

- `Microsoft.ContentManagement.WebControls` contains classes that support helper controls like the placeholder controls used in template files. It also provides the `BasePlaceholderControl` class for the creation of custom placeholder controls (see Chapter 14).

- `Microsoft.ContentManagement.WebControls.ConsoleControls` contains classes that work with the Web Author Console (see Chapter 19).

- `Microsoft.ContentManagement.WebControls.Design` contains classes for the design-time behavior of the placeholder control being used during development in Microsoft Visual Studio .NET.

Accessing Objects

The `Microsoft.ContentManagement.Publishing` namespace contains the core classes that are used heavily throughout an MCMS site. The first item you need to be familiar with is the `CmsHttpContext` class.

MCMS creates a `CmsHttpContext` object for every request to a posting or channel. The object lasts for the length of a single request. When the user navigates away to another page, another instance of `CmsHttpContext` is created.

You can never programmatically create new instances of the `CmsHttpContext` object, but you can get a reference to the current one. The `CmsHttpContext` object is important as it is used by the PAPI as the entry point to other objects like channels, postings, template galleries, templates, resource galleries, and resources.

The following diagram shows how the principal MCMS objects can be accessed from the `CmsHttpContext` object. Directly from the `CmsHttpContext` object, you can access the root channel, root template gallery, and root resource gallery objects. From there you can access collections of channels, postings, template galleries, templates, resource galleries, and resources.

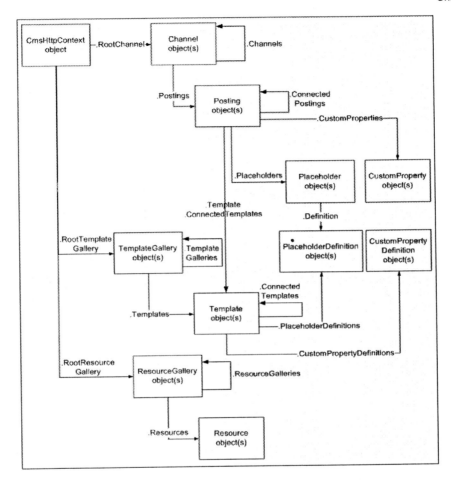

In this section we will build a web form, AccessObjects.aspx, that demonstrates how the following tasks can be accomplished:

- First, we will get a reference to the current CmsHttpContext.
- After that we will make use of the retrieved current CmsHttpContext to access the root channel.
- Following this, we will get the property values of the root channel and display their values in a table.
- Then we will move down the hierarchy to retrieve objects lower down the hierarchy.
- Once we reach the bottom, we will switch directions and move up the hierarchy.
- Finally, we will show you a faster method of getting objects by their relative paths.

Here's what `AccessObjects.aspx` will look like when completed:

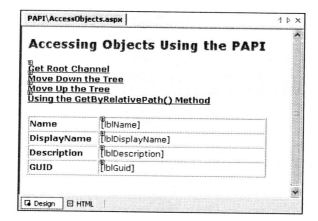

Getting a Reference to the Current CmsHttpContext

The only way to get the `CmsHttpContext` is to get a reference to the context that is currently being used. In the code-behind file of the `AccessObjects.aspx` web form, import the `Microsoft.ContentManagement.Publishing` namespace:

```
using System;
using System.Collections;
using System.ComponentModel;
using System.Data;
using System.Drawing;
using System.Web;
using System.Web.SessionState;
using System.Web.UI;
using System.Web.UI.WebControls;
using System.Web.UI.HtmlControls;
//Add reference to the PAPI
using Microsoft.ContentManagement.Publishing;

namespace TropicalGreen.PAPI
{
    . . . code continues . . .
}
```

Now declare `cmsContext` to be a variable of type `CmsHttpContext`. For convenience's sake, we will make it available throughout all methods in the web form. To do so, add this line of code within the class declaration:

```
. . . code continues . . .
public class AccessObjects : System.Web.UI.Page
{
    private CmsHttpContext cmsContext;
    private void Page_Load(object sender, System.EventArgs e)
    {
        // Put user code to initialize the page here
    }

    #region Web Form Designer generated code
    . . . code continues . . .
    #endregion
}
```

In the `Page_Load()` event handler, assign `cmsContext` to hold a reference to the current `CmsHttpContext` by storing the object returned by the `CmsHttpContext.Current` property.

```
private void Page_Load(object sender, System.EventArgs e)
{
    // Put user code to initialize the page here
    cmsContext = CmsHttpContext.Current;
}
```

Save and build the solution. You have stored a reference to the current `CmsHttpContext` in the `cmsContext` variable.

Getting the Root Channel

Now that we have created a reference to the current `CmsHttpContext`, we can proceed to access objects in the MCMS repository.

The `CmsHttpContext` contains a `RootChannel` property that returns the root channel. Because the root channel is created by the system when MCMS is first installed and it cannot be renamed or deleted, the `RootChannel` property will always return a reference to /Channels/.

With `AccessObjects.aspx` opened in HTML view, add a header for the form's title between the `<form>` tags.

```
<form id="Form1" method="post" runat="server">
    <h1>Accessing Objects Using the PAPI</h1>
</form>
```

Toggle to Design view. Drag a `LinkButton` from the Web Forms tab of the toolbox on to the form. Set the ID of the `LinkButton` to btnGetRootChannel and the Text property to Get Root Channel.

The diagram below shows the layout of the form in Design view.

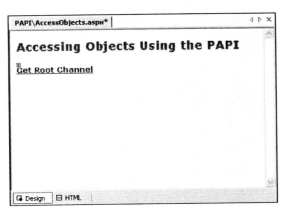

Double-click on btnGetRootChannel. You are taken to the btnGetRootChannel_Click() event handler. Call the GetRootChannel() method, which we will define right after this:

```
private void btnGetRootChannel_Click(object sender, System.EventArgs e)
{
    //call the GetRootChannel() method
    Channel rootChannel = GetRootChannel();
}
```

The `GetRootChannel()` method returns a reference to the root channel. It does so by retrieving the `RootChannel` property of the current `CmsHttpContext`. Add the `GetRootChannel()` method directly below the `btnGetRootChannel_Click()` event handler.

```
private Channel GetRootChannel()
{
    //Return the root channel
    return cmsContext.RootChannel;
}
```

> You can also get references to the root resource and template galleries by using the `RootResourceGallery` and `RootTemplateGallery` properties.

Getting the Values of Object Properties

Retrieving the property values of an object is fairly straightforward. We will display the `Name`, `DisplayName`, `Description`, and `GUID` property values of the root channel item we just retrieved.

With `AccessObjects.aspx` opened in Design view, select Table | Insert | Table... from the toolbar and insert a table with four rows and two columns. Set the `class` property of the table to `BodyText`. For each cell in the left-hand column of the table, add the words `Name`, `DisplayName`, `Description`, and `GUID` and make the text bold. Drag four labels from the Web Forms section of the Toolbox and drop them on to the form, placing one in each cell in the right-hand column of the table. Give the `ID` of each Label one of the following values: `lblName`, `lblDisplayName`, `lblDescription`, and `lblGuid`; and remove the `Text` values. The diagram below shows the table in Design view.

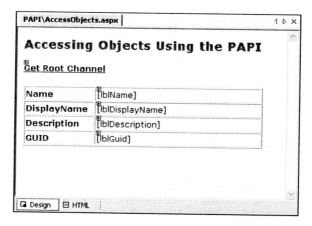

In Design view, double-click on `btnGetRootChannel` to get to the `btnGetRootChannel_Click()` event handler.

Add a call to the `DisplayProperties()` method, which we will define in a moment.

```
private void GetRootChannel_Click(object sender, System.EventArgs e)
{
    //call the GetRootChannel() method
    Channel rootChannel = GetRootChannel();
```

```
//Display the properties of the ChannelItem in the text box
DisplayProperties(rootChannel);
}
```

The `DisplayProperties()` method retrieves the `Name`, `DisplayName`, `Description`, and `Guid` of the requested channel item and displays their values in the labels in the table. Add the `DisplayProperties()` definition directly below the `btnGetRootChannel_Click()` event handler.

```
private void DisplayProperties(ChannelItem ci)
{
    string name; //Stores the Name of the ChannelItem
    string displayName; //Stores the DisplayName of the Channel Item
    string description; //Stores the Description of the Channel Item
    string guid; //Stores the Guid of the Channel Item

    //Retrieve the property values from the ChannelItem

    //Get the Name
    name = ci.Name;

    //Get the DisplayName
    displayName = ci.DisplayName;

    //Get the Description
    description = ci.Description;

    //Get the GUID
    guid = ci.Guid;

    //Assigns the retrieved property values to the
    //.Text property of the respective TextBoxes
    lblName.Text = name;
    lblDisplayName.Text = displayName;
    lblDescription.Text = description;
    lblGuid.Text = guid;
}
```

Save and build the solution. Open Internet Explorer and navigate to `http://localhost/tropicalgreen/papi/accessobjects.aspx`. Click on the Get Root Channel link button. The properties of the root channel are displayed in the labels as shown in the next diagram.

In the diagram, we have chosen to display only four properties: `Name`, `DisplayName`, `Description`, and `Guid`. The `ChannelItem` object has many more properties than these. The tricky part is finding out what properties an object has.

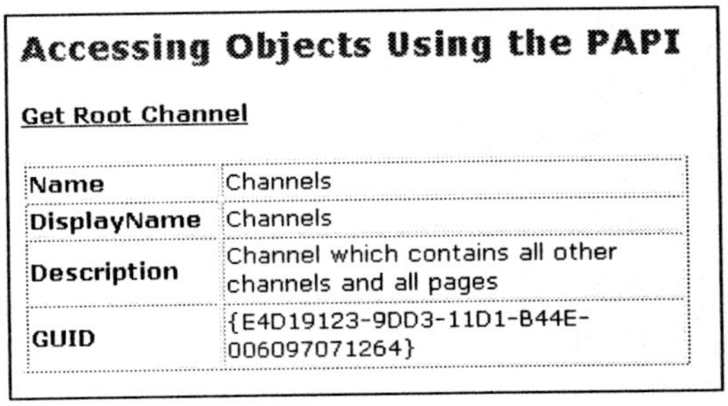

Accessing Objects Using the PAPI

Get Root Channel

Name	Channels
DisplayName	Channels
Description	Channel which contains all other channels and all pages
GUID	{E4D19123-9DD3-11D1-B44E-006097071264}

> The online MCMS help file has a complete list of properties and methods of an object. Look in particular at the Developer Reference section.

If you are using Visual Studio .NET, IntelliSense shows up a list of properties and methods associated with the object the moment you press the period. For example, when you type in the period after the ci variable in the DisplayProperties() method, a list of all properties and methods for a ChannelItem object is listed in a window:

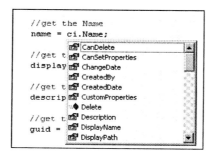

> IntelliSense is useful for checking your work as you type. If the list of properties does not appear when you press the period, chances are you made a typo when declaring the variable.

Moving Down the Hierarchy

Once you get a reference to the root channel, you can use the Channels collection to move down the tree and access any channel item (a channel or a posting) in the MCMS repository. If you have been following the tutorials so far, the Channel structure resembles this:

Channels

- TropicalGreen
    - PlantCatalog

    … other channels …

We will write code that programmatically moves from the root channel down to the PlantCatalog channel. To show that we have indeed retrieved the PlantCatalog channel, we will display its property values on the screen.

In Design view, add a LinkButton after btnGetRootChannel. Set the ID property to btnMoveDownTree and the Text property of the btnMoveDownTree to Move Down the Tree.

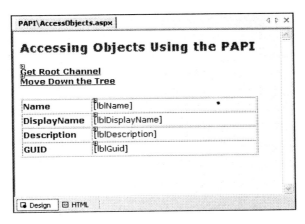

Double-click on btnMoveDownTree in Design view to get to the btnMoveDownTree_Click() event handler. Here, we will call the MoveDownTree() method (defined later). Following which, we will call the DisplayProperties() method to display the property values of the channel object returned by MoveDownTree().

```
private void btnMoveDownTree_Click(object sender, System.EventArgs e)
{
    //Moving down the tree
    Channel plantCatalog;

    //Call the MoveDownTree() method
    plantCatalog = MoveDownTree();

    //Display the properties of the ChannelItem in the text box
    DisplayProperties(plantCatalog);
}
```

The MoveDownTree() method takes us two levels down from the root channel to the PlantCatalog channel. It starts from the root channel and uses the Channels property to get a collection of sub-channels directly under the root. To access the TropicalGreen channel from the collection, we specify its name in square brackets:

```
tropicalGreen = root.Channels["tropicalgreen"];
```

The logic is repeated to get the PlantCatalog channel from the collection of channels below the TropicalGreen channel.

Add the MoveDownTree() method directly below the btnMoveDownTree_Click() event handler:

```
private Channel MoveDownTree()
{
    //Getting the PlantCatalog channel starting from the root channel
    Channel root;
    Channel tropicalGreen;
    Channel plantCatalog;

    //Start from the root channel
    root = GetRootChannel();

    //Move down one level to the TropicalGreen channel
    tropicalGreen = root.Channels["tropicalgreen"];

    //Move down another level to the PlantCatalog channel
```

```
    plantCatalog = tropicalGreen.Channels["plantcatalog"];

    return plantCatalog;
}
```

Save and build the solution.

Browse to `http://localhost/tropicalgreen/papi/accessobjects.aspx` and click on the Move Down the Tree link. Notice that the values in the labels have changed to show the properties of the PlantCatalog channel, indicating that we have moved two levels down the channel hierarchy from the root.

Accessing Objects Using the PAPI

Get Root Channel
Move Down the Tree

Name	PlantCatalog
DisplayName	Plant Catalog
Description	A-Z listing of tropical plant fact sheets
GUID	{3E5EF7C1-0532-4EE4-B3B1-392E47601E2E}

Similarly, you can use the `TemplateGalleries` and `ResourceGalleries` properties of the `TemplateGallery` and `ResourceGallery` objects to access template and resource hierarchies.

Moving Up the Hierarchy

Now that we have moved two levels down the channel hierarchy, we will switch directions and move back up one level: from the PlantCatalog channel to the TropicalGreen channel, just to see how it's done.

In Design view, add another `LinkButton`, below the `btnMoveDownTree` button, and set its `ID` property to `btnMoveUpTree` and its `Text` property to Move Up the Tree.

```
PAPI\AccessObjects.aspx                                    ◁ ▷ ✕

Accessing Objects Using the PAPI

Get Root Channel
Move Down the Tree
Move Up the Tree

 Name          [lblName]
 DisplayName   [lblDisplayName]
 Description   [lblDescription]
 GUID          [lblGuid]


 ⌨ Design    ⊡ HTML
```

In Design view, double-click on btnMoveUpTree to get to the btnMoveUpTree_Click() event handler. We will first call the MoveDownTree() method to retrieve the PlantCatalog channel. After moving down the hierarchy, we will call the MoveUpTree() method (defined right after this) and display the properties of the returned channel by calling the DisplayProperties() method.

```
private void btnMoveUpTree_Click(object sender, System.EventArgs e)
{
    Channel plantCatalog;
    Channel parentOfPlantCatalog;

    //Call the MoveDownTree() method first to move down the channel
    //hierarchy to get the PlantCatalog channel
    plantCatalog = MoveDownTree();

    //Call the MoveUpTree() method
    parentOfPlantCatalog = MoveUpTree(plantCatalog);

    //Display the properties of the parent channel of the PlantCatalog channel
    //which should be, the TropicalGreen channel
    DisplayProperties(parentOfPlantCatalog);
}
```

Next, we will define the MoveUpTree() method, which returns the parent channel object of a specified channel passed in as an input parameter. To get the parent of a channel object, we use the Parent property. In our example, the parent of the PlantCatalog channel is the TropicalGreen channel. Let's add MoveUpTree() directly below the btnMoveUpTree_Click() event handler.

```
private Channel MoveUpTree(Channel childChannel)
{
    Channel parentChannel;

    //Get the parent channel of childChannel
    parentChannel = childChannel.Parent;

    return parentChannel;
}
```

Save and build the solution. Browse to http://localhost/tropicalgreen/papi/ AccessObjects.aspx and click on the Move Up the Tree link. Notice that the properties of the TropicalGreen channel (parent of the PlantCatalog channel) are retrieved.

Accessing Objects Using the PAPI

<u>Get Root Channel</u>
<u>Move Down the Tree</u>
<u>Move Up the Tree</u>

Name	TropicalGreen
DisplayName	Home
Description	Live the sunny side of life!
GUID	{77B99A68-36EC-484D-84EC-181A6F9053EF}

Using GetByRelativePath() to Access other Objects

While iterating through the list of channels returned by the `Channels` collection is one way to get to other channels in the hierarchy, there are faster ways to do this.

The PAPI provides a method called `GetByRelativePath()` for all channels, postings, template galleries, templates, resource galleries, and resources. Once you have retrieved a reference to an object (for example, the TropicalGreen channel), you can use the `GetByRelativePath()` method to get any other channel by passing in its relative path. A relative path, unlike an absolute path, never begins with a forward slash (/) character.

For moving down the hierarchy, use expressions like this:

- `ChannelName`: (e.g. `PlantCatalog` for moving down one level from the TropicalGreen channel)
- `ChannelName/ChannelOrPostingName`: (e.g. `TropicalGreen/PlantCatalog` to move down two levels from the root channel)

And to move up the hierarchy, add two consecutive periods followed by a forward slash `../` before the path (in the same way as you would move up a directory from the command prompt), like this:

- `../ChannelName`: (e.g. `../Columns` will get the Columns channel from the PlantCatalog channel)

Let's repeat our attempt to navigate to the PlantCatalog channel from the root channel and see how the `GetByRelativePath()` method shortens the number of steps significantly.

With `AccessObjects.aspx` opened in Design view, add another `LinkButton` below `btnMoveUpTree`, and set its `ID` property to `btnGetByRelativePath` and its `Text` property to Using the GetByRelativePath() Method.

278

Double-click on btnGetByRelativePath. You will be brought to the
btnGetByRelativePath_Click() event handler. First we will retrieve the root channel. From the
root channel, instead of moving down to the PlantCatalog channel one level at a time, we will use
its relative path, tropicalgreen/plantcatalog/ and the GetByRelativePath() method to
retrieve it. Add the following code to retrieve the properties of the PlantCatalog channel and
display its properties.

```
private void btnGetByRelativePath_Click(object sender, System.EventArgs e)
{
    //Getting the PlantCatalog channel starting from
    //the current channel
    Channel root;
    Channel plantCatalog;

    root = GetRootChannel();
    plantCatalog = root.GetByRelativePath("tropicalgreen/plantcatalog/")
                as Channel;

    //Display the properties of the Channel Item in the text box
    DisplayProperties(plantCatalog);
}
```

Save and build the solution. Look at the results by browsing to
http://localhost/tropicalgreen/papi/AccessObjects.aspx and clicking on the Using the
GetByRelativePath() Method link.

The property values of the PlantCatalog channel are displayed, showing that we have successfully retrieved it using the `GetByRelativePath()` method to get it from the root.

Getting the Current Channel or Posting

The `CmsHttpContext` provides the `Channel` property to retrieve the currently requested channel. It works when used within template files or channel rendering scripts. When a visitor views a posting, or when a channel with a channel rendering script is viewed, the `Channel` property returns a reference to the channel the user is currently accessing. For example, if you are viewing a plant fact sheet, the `Channel` property returns a reference to the PlantCatalog channel. Using the `Channel` property is a nice shortcut. You don't have to start from the root channel and iterate downwards to get the object you need. You may remember that we used the `Channel` property in the channel rendering script when we built the summary page in Chapter 9.

Besides getting the current channel, you could also get a reference to the posting that's being viewed or the current channel item as the code snippet below shows.

```
//Get the current CmsHttpContext
CmsHttpContext currentContext = CmsHttpContext.Current;

//Get the current channel
Channel currentChannel;
currentChannel = currentContext.Channel;

//Get the current posting
Posting currentPosting;
currentPosting = currentContext.Posting;

//Get the current channel item
ChannelItem currentChannelItem;
currentChannelItem = currentContext.ChannelItem;
```

What's the difference between the objects returned by the `CmsHttpContext.Current.Channel`, `CmsHttpContext.Current.Posting`, and `CmsHttpContext.Current.ChannelItem` properties?

The difference is in the object type. For example, if you request a posting, say `http://localhost/tropicalgreen/plantcatalog/hibiscus.htm`, the `Channel` property returns a reference to the PlantCatalog channel. Both `Posting` and `ChannelItem` properties return a reference to the Hibiscus posting.

Now, if you were to view the URL of a channel, say `http://localhost/tropicalgreen/plantcatalog`, which makes use of a channel rendering script, the `Channel` property will still return a reference to the PlantCatalog channel but the `Posting` property will return a null (since you aren't looking at a posting) and `ChannelItem` will return the PlantCatalog channel.

Using the Searches Class to Reference Any Object

The PAPI provides a handy shortcut with the Searches class. You can use objects from the Searches class to get direct access to any object, without needing to iterate from the root. There are three ways of doing this:

- Using the path of the object
- Using the GUID of the object
- Using the URL of the object

> Template galleries, templates, resource galleries, and resources are not accessible using the Searches.GetByUrl() method. Instead, use the Searches.GetByPath() or Searches.GetByGuid() method to reference these objects.

Before proceeding with the rest of this section, open Searches.aspx. In HTML view, between the `<form>` tags, add a header for the page title.

```
<form id="Form1" method="post" runat="server">
  <h1>Accessing Objects using the Searches Class</h1>
</form>
```

Switch to Design view. Select Table | Insert | Table... from the toolbar and insert a table that has four rows and two columns. Set the class property of the table to BodyText. In the left-hand column, enter the words Path/GUID/URL:, Name:, and GUID: into the first, third, and forth rows. Make the words bold.

For the cells in the right-hand column, add a textbox in the first cell. Set the ID property to txtPathGuidUrl and the width to 300. Next to the txtPathGuidUrl textbox, add a button (btnGet). Set the Text property of the button to Get.

In the second column of the second row, insert a RadioButtonList for selecting the search mode. Set the ID property to rdoMethods and add three ListItems to the RadioButtonList Items collection and set their Text and value property values to:

- GetByPath
- GetByGuid
- GetByUrl

In the last two cells, add two labels with ID values of lblName and lblGuid. Remove the Text values. Add a button below the table with an ID value of btnReset and a Text value of Reset.

The following diagram shows how the form looks in Design view.

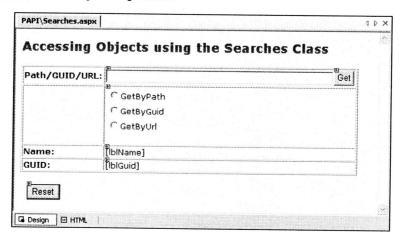

In the code-behind file, add the line to import the `Microsoft.ContentManagement.Publishing` namespace:

```
using System;
using System.Collections;
using System.ComponentModel;
using System.Data;
using System.Drawing;
using System.Web;
using System.Web.SessionState;
using System.Web.UI;
using System.Web.UI.WebControls;
using System.Web.UI.HtmlControls;

//Add reference to the PAPI
using Microsoft.ContentManagement.Publishing;

namespace TropicalGreen.PAPI
{
    . . . code continues . . .
}
```

Toggle to Design view and double-click on the `btnGet` button to get to the `btnGet_Click()` event handler. Enter the following code, which uses the `Searches.GetByPath()`, `Searches.GetByGuid()` and `Searches.GetByUrl()` methods to retrieve a reference to the requested object. Unlike the earlier examples, you do not have to perform any iterations.

```
private void btnGet_Click(object sender, System.EventArgs e)
{
    //Using the Searches object
    CmsHttpContext cmsContext = CmsHttpContext.Current;
    string inputValue = txtPathGuidUrl.Text;
    Channel channelObject = null;

    switch(rdoMethods.SelectedItem.Text)
    {
        case "GetByPath":
            //getting the PlantCatalog channel using it's path
            channelObject = cmsContext.Searches.GetByPath(inputValue) as Channel;
            break;

        case "GetByGuid":
            //getting the PlantCatalog channel using it's guid
```

```
            channelObject = cmsContext.Searches.GetByGuid(inputValue) as Channel;
            break;

        case "GetByUrl":
            //getting the PlantCatalog channel using its Url
            channelObject = cmsContext.Searches.GetByUrl(inputValue) as Channel;
            break;
    }

    if(channelObject!=null)
    {
        DisplayProperties(channelObject);
    }
    else
    {
        lblName.Text = "object not found!";
    }
}
```

The `Searches.GetByPath()` and `Searches.GetByGuid()` methods return an object of type `HierarchyItem`. `HierarchyItem` is the base class of the `ChannelItem`, `ResourceGalleryItem`, and `TemplateGalleryItem` classes. In order to access the properties of the channel, we need to recast the object returned by the `Searches` class to a `Channel` using the `as` operator. If the returned object is not a channel, `channelObject` will contain a null value. Using the `as` operator to covert types is the preferred method since a null reference that arises from a mismatch in types is easier to handle in code.

You could do the same thing by recasting the returned `HierarchyItem` object to a `Channel` object:

```
    channelObject = (Channel) cmsContext.Searches.GetByPath(inputValue);
```

However, this will cause run-time exceptions should the returned object not be a channel.

The `Searches.GetByUrl()` method returns an object of type `ChannelItem`, which is the base class of the channel and posting classes.

In addition, the methods return null values if the path/URL/GUID that you specified:

- Does not exist
- Points to objects you do not have access to

As different users in the system are assigned different rights to containers, you can never be sure when the methods will return a null value.

For these reasons, it is always a good idea to check for null exceptions when writing code. For example, in the example above, we surrounded our code with an `if` statement that checks to see if `channelObject` is null.

```
    if(channelObject!=null)
    {
        DisplayProperties(channelObject);
    }
    else
    {
        lblName.Text = "object not found!";
    }
```

In this way, we can avoid the nasty Object reference not set to an instance of an object exception and elegantly handle cases where the object cannot be found.

Add the DisplayProperties() method below the btnGet_Click() event handler. We retrieve the Name and Guid of the ChannelItem and display their values in labels. A try-catch statement wraps around the code block. Any messages from exceptions are written to lblName.

```
private void DisplayProperties(Channel c)
{
    try
    {
        string name; //stores the Name of the Channel Item
        string guid; //stored the Guid of the Channel Item

        //retrieve the property values from the Channel Item
        name = c.Name;
        guid = c.Guid;

        //assigns the retrieved property values to the
        //Text property of the respective TextBoxes
        lblName.Text = name;
        lblGuid.Text = guid;
    }
    catch(Exception ex)
    {
        lblName.Text = ex.Message;
    }
}
```

Toggle back to Design view and double-click on the btnReset button to get to the btnReset_Click() event handler. When the btnReset button is clicked, we want to clear the form by setting the textbox and labels to contain empty strings and clear the selection made in the RadioButtonList.

```
private void btnReset_Click(object sender, System.EventArgs e)
{
    //Resets the screen
    txtPathGuidUrl.Text = "";
    rdoMethods.ClearSelection();
    lblName.Text = "";
    lblGuid.Text = "";
}
```

Save and build the solution.

Searches.GetByPath()

Pass the path of any object as an input parameter of the Searches.GetByPath() method to retrieve the requested object. Let's run the code sample above to display the properties of the PlantCatalog channel using the Searches.GetByPath() method:

1. From the Browser, navigate to:
   http://localhost/tropicalgreen/papi/searches.aspx.

2. In the Path/GUID/URL field, enter the path of the PlantCatalog channel,
   /channels/tropicalgreen/plantcatalog.

3. Select the GetByPath option.

4. Click Get.

The properties of the PlantCatalog channel are retrieved as shown in the diagram below.

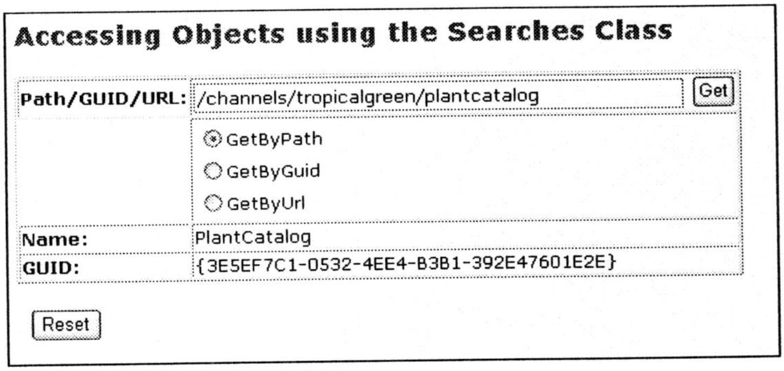

```
Accessing Objects using the Searches Class

Path/GUID/URL:  /channels/tropicalgreen/plantcatalog        [Get]

                ⦿ GetByPath
                ○ GetByGuid
                ○ GetByUrl
Name:           PlantCatalog
GUID:           {3E5EF7C1-0532-4EE4-B3B1-392E47601E2E}

[Reset]
```

You can retrieve channels, postings, template galleries, templates, resource galleries, and resources using their paths as the code snippet below shows.

```
CmsHttpContext cmsContext = CmsHttpContext.Current;
Searches searchObject = cmsContext.Searches;

//Getting the PlantCatalog channel using its path
Channel channelObject;
channelObject = searchObject.GetByPath("/Channels/TropicalGreen/PlantCatalog")
as Channel;

//Getting the Hibsicus posting using its path
Posting postingObject;
postingObject =
searchObject.GetByPath("/Channels/TropicalGreen/PlantCatalog/Hibiscus") as
Posting;

//Getting the PlantCatalog template gallery using its path
TemplateGallery templateGalleryObject;
templateGalleryObject =
searchObject.GetByPath("/Templates/TropicalGreen/PlantCatalog/") as
TemplateGallery;

//Getting the Plant template using its path
Template templateObject;
templateObject =
searchObject.GetByPath("/Templates/TropicalGreen/PlantCatalog/Plant") as
Template;

//Getting the PlantCatalog resource gallery using its path
ResourceGallery resourceGalleryObject;
resourceGalleryObject =
searchObject.GetByPath("/Resources/TropicalGreen/PlantCatalog") as
ResourceGallery;

//Getting the BananaTree.JPG resource using it's path
Resource resourceObject;
resourceObject =
searchObject.GetByPath("/Resources/TropicalGreen/PlantCatalog/BananaTree.JPG)
as Resource;
```

The Searches.GetByPath() method returns a HierarchyItem object. You can work with it without recasting it but you will be limited to the skeletal properties and methods of the

HierarchyItem class. The as operator converts the returned HierarchyItem object to the higher-order object type.

If you do not know the object type returned, you can use the is operator to find out. The code below shows how to use the is operator to decide if the object named MysteryObject is a channel or a posting.

```
HierarchyItem hItem =
cmsContext.Searches.GetByPath("/Channels/TropicalGreen/MysteryObject");
if(hItem is Channel)
{
    //Object is a Channel
}
else if(hItem is Posting)
{
    //Object is a Posting
}
```

The Path of an object is case insensitive. /Channels/TropicalGreen/ will fetch the same results as /channels/tropicalgreen. Paths always begin with a forward slash, /. Because root channels and galleries cannot be renamed or deleted, the starting point of the path is always the same for each kind of object as listed below.

Object Type	Path Always Begins With
Channels and Postings	/Channels/
Template Galleries and Templates	/Templates/
Resource Galleries and Resources	/Resources/

The path of an object is made up of the names of all its parents separated by the slash character (/) and its own name. Because MCMS does not restrict the names of objects to be unique, you may end up having two or more objects sharing the same path value. When that happens, MCMS will only be able to retrieve one or possibly none of the items. To resolve this issue, avoid giving objects under the same parent the same name. However, if you really need to do so, the only ways around this are to use the Searches.GetByGuid() method or use their unique-ID-based URLs with the Searches.GetByUrl() method.

Searches.GetByGuid()

You can get a reference to an object by passing its GUID to the Searches.GetByGuid() method.

To see this in action in our example above:

1. Copy the GUID of the PlantCatalog channel from the GUID label (returned from the previous result) to the clipboard. (Don't use the GUID in the image opposite, as the GUID for your system will be different.)
2. Click the Reset button to clear the results from the previous search.
3. Paste the GUID from the clipboard into the Path/GUID/URL textbox.
4. Select the GetByGuid option.
5. Click Get to retrieve the object again.

```
Accessing Objects using the Searches Class

Path/GUID/URL: {3E5EF7C1-0532-4EE4-B3B1-392E47601E2E}     [Get]

                ○ GetByPath
                ◉ GetByGuid
                ○ GetByUrl
Name:           PlantCatalog
GUID:           {3E5EF7C1-0532-4EE4-B3B1-392E47601E2E}

[Reset]
```

The `Searches.GetByGuid()` method is by far the most efficient of all the search mechanisms we have discussed. The GUID is the unique key used to identify each and every object in the content repository. When retrieving objects using their GUID, the PAPI does not need to perform expensive queries and lookups. It simply zooms in to the specified row in the table and returns the results. The code snippet below shows how you would use the `Searches.GetByGuid()` method to get a reference to the PlantCatalog channel.

```
//Getting the PlantCatalog channel using it's guid
//GUIDs are unique. The GUID for the PlantCatalog channel would be different
//for your system.
Channel channelObject = cmsContext.Searches.GetByGuid(
                "{3E5EF7C1-0532-4EE4-B3B1-392E47601E2E}") as Channel;
```

You probably won't remember the GUID of an object off hand. The `Searches.GetByGuid()` method is often used in cases where you are passing a GUID from one method to another, extracting the GUID from query strings on a page or from unique-ID-based URLs.

The `Searches.GetByGuid()` method also has the added advantage that, unlike the path or URL of an object, the GUID of an object does not change even if it is been moved from one container to another. It remains the same throughout the lifespan of the object. Therefore, should you choose to hard-code the GUID into your application, you would not have to worry about getting null values or broken links from objects that have moved.

> For optimal performance, use the `Searches.GetByGuid()` method over the `Searches.GetByPath()` and `Searches.GetByUrl()` methods.

A GUID has the format {FFFFFFFF-FFFF-FFFF-FFFF-FFFFFFFFFFFF}, where F is a hexadecimal digit (0-9, A-F). If you pass in a value that is not of this format, an exception of type `CmsInvalidInputException` is raised. Without an exception handler that catches this exception, you would see the following error message in your browser:
Server error. Contact the site administrator.

> It is worth noting that developers often forget the opening and closing braces when passing GUIDs to functions in code.

Searches.GetByUrl()

We can also pass in the URL of the object to the `Searches.GetByUrl()` method to retrieve it:

1. Click the Reset button to clear the results from the previous search.
2. Enter the URL of the PlantCatalog channel in the Path/Guid/Url textbox, http://localhost/tropicalgreen/plantcatalog.
3. Select the GetbyUrl option.
4. Click Get.

And the properties of the PlantCatalog channel are displayed yet again:

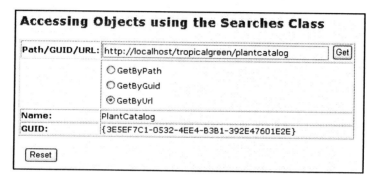

Valid URLs include absolute paths that begin with a forward slash:

```
/tropicalgreen/plantcatalog
```

and fully qualified URLs such as:

```
http://localhost/tropicalgreen/plantcatalog
```

It is not possible to retrieve resource galleries, resources, template galleries, and templates using the `Searches.GetByUrl()` method.

Accessing Placeholder Content

We have seen how to retrieve specific postings using the classes in the `Microsoft.ContentManagement.Publishing` namespace. To get at the content stored within a posting, we need to use another namespace, `Microsoft.ContentManagement.Extensions.Placeholders`.

In Chapter 7, we added placeholders to the PlantCatalog template. We created plant fact sheets based on the Plant template and stored content within its placeholders. Now, let's use the PAPI to read and display the stored content. The available placeholders found in each plant fact sheet are:

- `ResearchPaper (AttachmentPlaceholder)`
- `Description (HtmlPlaceholder)`
- `PlantPicture (ImagePlaceholder)`

In order to access the placeholder content, we first create a drop-down list containing a list of all our postings. When the Get Fact Sheet Content button is clicked, we retrieve the contents of the placeholders of the selected posting. This is an interesting example because it shows you how to iterate through a collection of postings. Open `Placeholders.aspx`. In HTML view, add a heading between the <form> tags for the page title.

```
<form id="Form1" method="post" runat="server">
    <h1>Getting Content Stored in Placeholders</h1>
</form>
```

Switch to Design view, drag and drop a `Label`, a `DropDownList` and a `Button`. Set the ID property of the label to `lblInstructions` and the Text property to `Select a Plant Fact Sheet:` and its `CssClass` property to `BodyText`. Set the ID of the `DropDownList` to `ddlFactSheets`. Set the ID of the button to `btnGetFactSheetContent` and the Text property to `Get Fact Sheet Content`.

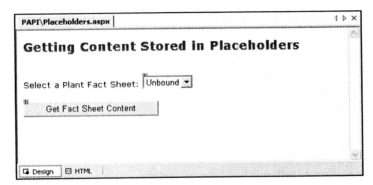

Double-click anywhere on the form in Design view to get to its code-behind file. Above the namespace declaration, import the MCMS PAPI namespaces. Importing the `Microsoft.ContentManagment.Publishing.Extensions.Placeholders` namespace allows us to call methods and properties of the specialized placeholder classes without typing in the entire namespace.

```
using System;
using System.Collections;
using System.ComponentModel;
using System.Data;
using System.Drawing;
using System.Web;
using System.Web.SessionState;
using System.Web.UI;
using System.Web.UI.WebControls;
using System.Web.UI.HtmlControls;

//Add reference to the PAPI
using Microsoft.ContentManagement.Publishing;
using Microsoft.ContentManagement.Publishing.Extensions.Placeholders;

namespace TropicalGreen.PAPI
{
    . . . code continues . . .
}
```

We will populate the ddlFactSheets DropDownList with a list of plant fact sheets when the page loads for the first time by calling the GetPlantFactSheets() method (defined later) in the Page_Load() event handler. Also remember to add the call to the cmsContext above Page_Load().

```
private CmsHttpContext cmsContext;
private void Page_Load(object sender, System.EventArgs e)
{
    // Put user code to initialize the page here
    cmsContext = CmsHttpContext.Current;
    if(!Page.IsPostBack)
    {
        GetPlantFactSheets();
    }
}
```

The GetPlantFactSheets() method gets a reference to the PlantCatalog channel using the Searches.GetByPath() method. A foreach statement loops through each posting in the PlantCatalog channel and adds them as ListItem objects to the ddlFactSheets DropDownList.

Add the GetPlantFactSheets() method directly below the Page_Load() event handler.

```
//Displays the available fact sheets in a dropdownlist control
private void GetPlantFactSheets()
{
    //Get a reference to the PlantCatalog channel
    string path = "/Channels/tropicalgreen/plantcatalog/";
    Channel plantCatalog = cmsContext.Searches.GetByPath(path) as
    Channel;

    //Populate the drop down list with
    //all the fact sheets in the PlantCatalog channel
    foreach(Posting factSheet in plantCatalog.Postings)
    {
        if(factSheet.Template.Name == "Plant")
        {
            ListItem li = new ListItem();
            li.Text = factSheet.DisplayName;
            li.Value = factSheet.Guid;
            ddlFactSheets.Items.Add(li);
        }
    }
}
```

Toggle back to Design view. Double-click on the btnGetPlaceholderContent button to get to the btnGetPlaceholderContent_Click() event handler. We will use the Searches.GetByGuid() method to access the selected posting and pass it as an input parameter to three methods: GetAttachmentPlaceholderContent(), GetHtmlPlaceholderContent(), and GetImagePlaceholderContent().

```
private void btnGetPlaceholderContent_Click(object sender, System.EventArgs e)
{
    //The guid is the value of the selected item.
    string guid;
    guid = ddlFactSheets.SelectedItem.Value;

    //Get a reference to the selected fact sheet
    Posting factSheet;
    factSheet = cmsContext.Searches.GetByGuid(guid) as Posting;

    GetAttachmentPlaceholderContent(factSheet);
    GetHtmlPlaceholderContent(factSheet);
    GetImagePlaceholderContent(factSheet);
}
```

Add the `GetAttachmentPlaceholderContent()`, `GetHtmlPlaceholderContent()`, and `GetImagePlaceholderContent()` methods below the `btnGetPlaceholderContent_Click` event handler. These methods don't do anything for now, but we need them for our page to compile.

We will fill them with code in the coming sections.

```
//Retrieves and displays the contents of the AttachmentPlaceholder
private void GetAttachmentPlaceholderContent(Posting p)
{
}

//Retrieves and displays the contents of the HtmlPlaceholder
private void GetHtmlPlaceholderContent(Posting p)
{
}

//Retrieves and displays the contents of the ImagePlaceholder
private void GetImagePlaceholderContent(Posting p)
{
}
```

The AttachmentPlaceholder

The `AttachmentPlaceholder` class, as the name suggests, provides access to the properties and the content stored within the `AttachmentPlaceholder` object.

The commonly used properties of the `AttachmentPlaceholder` class are:

Property	Description
AttachmentText	Contains the text entered in the Display Text field when you added the attachment. If no Display Text is found, it returns the name of the file uploaded.
IconUrl	Contains the URL of the icon used to represent the attachment. Returns a value only if the `UseGeneratedIcon` of the corresponding `AttachmentPlaceholderDefinition` is set to true.
Name	Holds the name of the placeholder as defined in the corresponding placeholder definition.
Url	Provides the address of the uploaded file in the content repository.

In HTML view, add a second-level heading below the `btnGetPlaceholderContent` button.

```
<form id="Placeholders" method="post" runat="server">
<P>
    <h1>Getting Content Stored in Placeholders</h1>
    <br>
    <asp:Label Runat="server" ID="lblInstructions" CssClass="BodyText"
Text="Select a Plant Fact Sheet:"></asp:Label>
    <asp:DropDownList id="ddlFactSheets" runat="server"></asp:DropDownList>
    <br>
    <br>
    <asp:Button id="btnGetFactSheetContent" runat="server" Text="Get Fact
Sheet Content"></asp:Button>
    <h2>AttachmentPlaceholder</h2>
</form>
```

Toggle to Design view and insert a table with four rows and two columns below the header. Set the `class` property of the table to `BodyText`. Fill the left-hand side columns with the names of the properties we will be getting: `Name`, `AttachmentText`, `IconUrl`, and `Url`. Bold each of the names.

Drag and drop four labels onto the cells on the right-hand column of the table for displaying property values. Give each label one of the following IDs: APH_Name, APH_AttachmentText, APH_IconUrl, and APH_Url according to the text description to its left. Remove the Text values. The form appears as shown below in Design view.

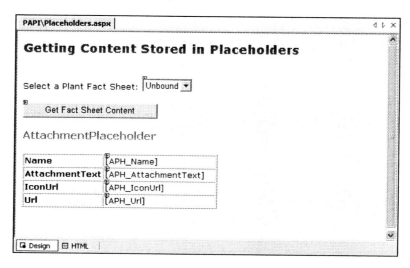

In the code-behind file, modify the GetAttachmentPlaceholderContent() method to retrieve the ResearchPaper AttachmentPlaceholder object of the selected posting. We will display its properties in the Labels.

```
//Retrieves and displays the contents of the AttachmentPlaceholder
private void GetAttachmentPlaceholderContent(Posting p)
{
    //Get a reference to the ResearhPaper AttachmentPlaceholder
    AttachmentPlaceholder researchPaper;
    researchPaper = p.Placeholders["ResearchPaper"] as
    AttachmentPlaceholder;

    if(researchPaper!=null)
    {
        //Write out the contents of the AttachmentPlaceholder
        APH_AttachmentText.Text = researchPaper.AttachmentText;
        APH_IconUrl.Text = researchPaper.IconUrl;
        APH_Name.Text = researchPaper.Name;
        APH_Url.Text = researchPaper.Url;
    }
    else
    {
        APH_Name.Text = "Placeholder not found!";
    }
}
```

Save and build the solution. To run the code:

1. Open Internet Explorer and navigate to
   http://localhost/tropicalgreen/papi/placeholders.aspx.

2. Select a fact sheet from the drop-down list.

3. Click Get Fact Sheet Content.

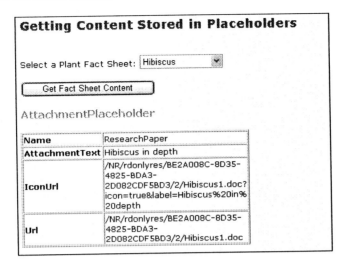

The Name property shows that we are accessing the contents of the ResearchPaper placeholder object. AttachmentText contains whatever we entered as the description of the uploaded file. Notice that the Url of the attachment starts with /NR/rdonlyres, followed by the GUID, a number, and the file name. The value returned by the IconUrl property resembles this:

```
/NR/rdonlyres/BE2A008C-8D35-4825-BDA3-
2D082CDF5BD3/2/Hibiscus1.doc?icon=true&label=Hibiscus%20in%20depth
```

If you look at it carefully, it consists of the URL of the attachment, followed by two query string parameters—icon and label. Of interest is the label parameter. It contains the value of the AttachmentText property and is used as the text beneath the icon when rendered by MCMS.

> Open a new browser window. Copy the value of the IconUrl property and paste it into the address bar. Change the value of the label query string parameter to I love plants. Ensure that http://localhost has been added at the start of the URL. Click Go, and watch the text displayed with the icon change.

Differentiating between a Local Resource and a Shared Resource

You can determine whether or not the resource was uploaded as a local attachment or as a shared resource from the Resource Gallery by parsing the Url property of the AttachmentPlaceholder. Because the URL of a file referenced by the AttachmentPlaceholder always contains the GUID of the resource, we can use it to see if it belongs to a resource gallery. The code snippet below shows how you can do this:

```
//Detecting if a file belongs to a resource gallery
string url;
string[] arrUrl;
string guid;
```

```
url = researchPaper.Url;
arrUrl = url.Split('/');
guid = arrUrl[3];

//Add the starting and ending braces to the guid to make it valid
guid = "{" + guid + "}";

Resource r = CmsContext.Searches.GetByGuid(guid) as Resource;
if(r!=null)
{
    //file is a resource gallery item
    string resourceName = r.Name;
    string resourceDisplayName = r.DisplayName;
    string resourceDisplayPath = r.DisplayPath;
    string resourceFileExtension = r.FileExtension;
    int resourceSize = r.Size;
    string resourceType = r.MimeType;
    string url = r.Url;
    sring urlThumbnail = r.UrlThumbnail;
}
else
{
    //File is a local attachment
}
```

Should the file be a resource from the resource gallery, you can access the properties and methods of the resource such as Resource.Size, Resource.MimeType, and so on.

> You can apply this technique on the ImagePlaceholder to determine whether the image is a resource gallery item or a local image.

The HtmlPlaceholder

The HtmlPlaceholder class provides you with the properties required to access the contents of the HtmlPlaceholder. The main properties are:

Property	Description
Name	Returns the name of this HtmlPlaceholder object.
Html	Retrieves the contents of the HtmlPlaceholder as it is stored.
FilteredHtml	Returns the same content as the Html property but applies the restrictions set in the corresponding HtmlPlaceholder definition.
Text	Returns the same content as the Html property but removes all HTML tags, returning only text content. This includes tags, which are *not* replaced with newline characters.

To retrieve the contents of the Description HtmlPlaceholder of the Plant template, we will add another HTML table that displays the contents of the AttachmentPlaceholder. Toggle to HTML view and add a level-two heading just before the closing </form> tag:

```
<form>
. . . code continues . . .
        <h2>HtmlPlaceholder</h2>
</form>
```

Switch to Design view and insert a table with four rows and two columns below the level-two header. Set the Class property of the table to BodyText. In the cells on the left-hand side of the table, enter the property names of the HtmlPlaceholder whose values we will be retrieving: Name, Text, FilteredHtml, and Html. Make the text bold.

Drag and drop a Label onto each cell on the right-hand side of the table. Give each Label one of the following IDs according to the corresponding text description to its left: HPH_Name, HPH_Text, HPH_FilteredHtml, and HPH_Html. Remove the Text values.

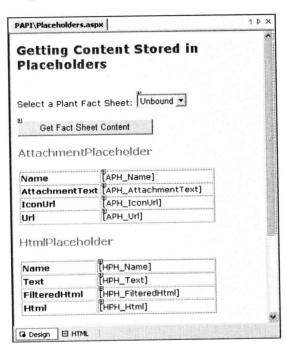

In the code-behind file, add code to the GetHtmlPlaceholderContent() method to retrieve and display the contents of the Description HtmlPlaceholder. The logic used to retrieve the contents of the HtmlPlaceholder is similar to that used for the AttachmentPlaceholder. We use the Server.HtmlEncode() method so that angled brackets around HTML tags are correctly displayed in the browser.

```
private void GetHtmlPlaceholderContent(Posting p)
{
    //Get a reference to the Description HtmlPlaceholder
    HtmlPlaceholder description;
    description = p.Placeholders["Description"] as HtmlPlaceholder;

    if(description!=null)
    {
        //Write out the contents of the HtmlPlaceholder
        HPH_Name.Text = description.Name;
        HPH_Text.Text = Server.HtmlEncode(description.Text);
        HPH_FilteredHtml.Text =
            Server.HtmlEncode(description.FilteredHtml);
        HPH_Html.Text = Server.HtmlEncode(description.Html);
```

```
    }
    else
    {
        HPH_Name.Text = "Description Placeholder not found!";
    }
}
```

Save and build the solution. When you run the code, you will find that Name returned the value Description indicating that we are retrieving the contents of the Description HtmlPlaceholder. Text contains whatever we entered in the description placeholder minus the HTML tags. FilteredHtml and Html contain the same values. They will return different values only when you change the HtmlPlaceholderDefinition after you have saved the posting.

HtmlPlaceholder	
Name	Description
Text	Woody shrub with flowers available in many colors.
FilteredHtml	\<P>Woody \<A title="Definition of a shrub" href="http://www.google.com/search?q=define:shrub" target="_blank">shrub\</A> with flowers available in many colors.\</P>
Html	\<P>Woody \<A title="Definition of a shrub" href="http://www.google.com/search?q=define:shrub" target="_blank">shrub\</A> with flowers available in many colors.\</P>

The ImagePlaceholder

The ImagePlaceholder class provides properties required to read the contents of the ImagePlaceholder. The main properties are given in the following table.

Property	Description
Name	Holds the name of the placeholder as defined in the corresponding placeholder definition.
Alt	Contains the alternative text of an image.
Href	Holds the URL of the hyperlink surrounding the image.
Src	Contains the URL of the image.

Putting it all together, here's how the properties are used when the image is rendered:

```
<a href="ImagePlaceholder.Href">
    <img src="ImagePlaceholder.Src" alt="ImagePlaceholder.Alt">
</a>
```

The anchor tags \<a>\</a> are omitted if the image is not hyperlinked to anything.

To retrieve and display the contents of the PlantPicture ImagePlaceholder, add another table. In HTML view, before the closing \</form> tag, add a level-two heading.

```
<form>
. . . code continues . . .
        <h2>ImagePlaceholder</h2>
</form>
```

Switch to Design view. Insert a table with four rows and two columns below the level-two heading. Set the `class` property of the table to `BodyText`. In the cells on the left-hand side of the table, enter the property names of the `ImagePlaceholder` whose values we will be retrieving: `Name`, `Alt`, `Href`, and `Src`. Make the text bold.

Drag and drop a `Label` onto each cell on the right-hand side of the table. Give each `Label` one of the following IDs according to the corresponding text description to its left: `IPH_Name`, `IPH_Alt`, `IPH_Href`, and `IPH_Src`. Clear the `Text` values.

In the code-behind file, amend the `GetHtmlPlaceholderContent()` method. The logic to retrieve the property values of `ImagePlaceholder` mirrors that for the `AttachmentPlaceholder` and `HtmlPlaceholder` classes.

```
private void GetImagePlaceholderContent(Posting p)
{
    //Get a reference to the PlantPicture ImagePlaceholder
    ImagePlaceholder plantPicture;
    plantPicture =p.Placeholders["PlantPicture"] as ImagePlaceholder;
    if(plantPicture!=null)
    {
        //Write out the contents of the ImagePlaceholder
        IPH_Name.Text = plantPicture.Name;
        IPH_Alt.Text = plantPicture.Alt;
        IPH_Href.Text = plantPicture.Href;
        IPH_Src.Text = plantPicture.Src;
    }
    else
```

```
    {
        IPH_Name.Text = "PlantPicture placeholder not found!";
    }
}
```

Save and build the solution. When you next click on the Get Plant Fact Sheet Content button, you will retrieve the contents of the PlantPicture ImagePlaceholder, as indicated by the Name property. Alt contains whatever we entered for Alternate Text in the Image Properties dialog in Web Author. Href contains the link entered in the HyperLink field of the Image Properties dialog in Web Author. Finally, Src returns the URL of the uploaded image.

ImagePlaceholder	
Name	PlantPicture
Alt	Hibiscus flower
Href	
Src	/NR/rdonlyres/BE2A008C-8D35-4825-BDA3-2D082CDF5BD3/1/hibiscus.JPG

> There is one more placeholder class that ships with MCMS, the XmlPlaceholder class. We will discuss the XmlPlaceholder class in detail in Chapter 14 when we build custom placeholder controls.

Detecting when Placeholders are Empty

Did you notice that when you did not upload a file to the ResearchPaper AttachmentPlaceholder earlier, the label that says Research Paper still showed up on the screen?

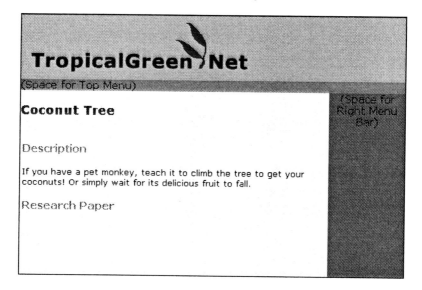

The label also shows up if we left the description placeholder empty. Usually, you would want to hide the headings when authors have not uploaded any content to the placeholder as, otherwise, the page just looks unfinished. Now let's amend the Plant template file to check for empty placeholders and hide the labels accordingly.

Detecting when an AttachmentPlaceholder is Empty

When an attachment has not been uploaded to the AttachmentPlaceholder, the Url property returns an empty string.

We will hide the table row that displays the header for the ResearchPaper AttachmentPlaceholder when it is empty. First, open the Plant.aspx template file in HTML view and convert the table row to a server control by setting the runat attribute to server and giving it an ID of trResearchPaper:

```
. . . code continues . . .
<table>
. . . code continues . . .
      <tr runat="server" id="trResearchPaper">
      <td>
          <H2>Research Paper</H2>
              <cms:SingleAttachmentPlaceholderControl
                  id="PlantResearchPaper"
                  runat="server"
                  PlaceholderToBind="ResearchPaper">
              </cms:SingleAttachmentPlaceholderControl>
      </td>
   </tr>
</table>
. . . code continues . . .
```

Switch to Design view and double-click on the web form to get to its code-behind file. Add the following namespaces above the namespace declaration.

```
. . . code continues . . .
//Add reference to the PAPI
using Microsoft.ContentManagement.Publishing;
using Microsoft.ContentManagement.WebControls;
using Microsoft.ContentManagement.Publishing.Extensions.Placeholders;

namespace TropicalGreen.Templates
{
      . . . code continues . . .
}
```

Within the Page_Load() event handler, we add an if statement that checks the mode that we are currently working in. We only want to hide the table row when not in authoring view. Next, we get a reference to the ResearchPaper AttachmentPlaceholder and pass it as an input parameter to the IsAttachmentPlaceholderEmpty() method, which we will define later. If no attachments were found in the placeholder, we will hide the table row.

```
private void Page_Load(object sender, System.EventArgs e)
{
      // Put user code to initialize the page here
      . . . code continues . . .

      //The Table Row is initialized to be displayed
      trResearchPaper.Visible = true;
      //Only perform the check when not in Authoring view
      WebAuthorContext wac = WebAuthorContext.Current;
```

```
if(wac.Mode != WebAuthorContextMode.AuthoringNew &&
    wac.Mode != WebAuthorContextMode.AuthoringReedit)
{
    //Get a reference to the current posting
    Posting currentPosting = CmsHttpContext.Current.Posting;

    //Get a reference to the ResearchPaper AttachmentPlaceholder
    AttachmentPlaceholder researchPaper;
    researchPaper = currentPosting.Placeholders["ResearchPaper"] as
        AttachmentPlaceholder;

    //Check to see if any attachments have been uploaded
    if(IsAttachmentPlaceholderEmpty(researchPaper))
    {
        //no attachments have been uploaded
        trResearchPaper.Visible = false;
    }
}
}
```

The `IsAttachmentPlaceholderEmpty()` method accepts an `AttachmentPlaceholder` object as an input parameter. It checks to see if the placeholder contains a link to a file by looking at the `Url` property of the `AttachmentPlaceholder` object. If it does not contain a link to a file, then the `Url` property returns an empty string. Add the `IsAttachmentPlaceholderEmpty()` method below the `Page_Load()` event handler.

```
private bool IsAttachmentPlaceholderEmpty(AttachmentPlaceholder aph)
{
    //Detecting to see if a file has been uploaded to the
    //AttachmentPlaceholder
    bool attachmentPlaceholderIsEmpty;

    if(aph.Url=="")
    {
        //Nothing has been uploaded!
        attachmentPlaceholderIsEmpty = true;
    }
    else
    {
        //A file has been uploaded
        attachmentPlaceholderIsEmpty = false;
    }
    return attachmentPlaceholderIsEmpty;
}
```

This method can now be used to hide certain controls like headers when the `AttachmentPlaceholder` does not contain a file. You can also use this sort of test for validating that a mandatory `AttachmentPlaceholder` has been filled in. Save and build the solution and view the Coconut Tree Plant posting (a posting without an attachment) to see how the attachment label is now hidden.

Detecting when an HtmlPlaceholder is Empty

We can apply the same logic to hide the table cell that contains the header and placeholder for the plant's description when no content has been added to that placeholder.

However, there are some issues to consider when deciding whether or not a `HtmlPlaceholder` is empty or not. Basically, you can do one of two things:

1. Check the `Html` or `FilteredHtml` property for empty strings

2. Check the Text property for empty strings

Checking the Html or FilteredHtml Property for empty strings

You could check to see if the Html or FilteredHtml properties contain empty string values. However, this does not always give the expected result.

Consider this: an author writes content into the HtmlPlaceholder, but later decides to delete it. The author opens up the posting in edit site mode and deletes whatever is in the HtmlPlaceholder control. When the author saves the posting again, the content is deleted; or is it?

MCMS does not remove the contents of the HtmlPlaceholder completely. It leaves behind a space coded as <p> </p>. When this happens, the Html and FilteredHtml properties do not return an empty string.

When using the Html property for deciding whether or not an HtmlPlaceholder has content, check whether either one of the following two conditions is fulfilled.

- The Html property returns an empty string.
- The Html property returns the value <p> </p>.

To avoid this problem, some template designers allow HTML source formatting on HtmlPlaceholderControls. When the author wishes to delete all content, they must click on the HTML button on the authoring toolbar and delete HTML content, tags and all. However, some argue that this releases the genie from the bottle and gives authors too much control over the formatting of the content to solve a technical problem.

Checking the Text Property for empty strings

What about the Text property? It is true that should the HtmlPlaceholder contain the <p> </p> tags, the Text property will return an empty string.

However, you will also get an empty string if the content of the Placeholder consists of tags only. For example, if the HtmlPlaceholder has the tags <img src="myimage.gif">, the Text property will also return an empty string since an image is not text content.

Nevertheless, we have to choose one option and using the Text property is better suited for the Plant template file because we don't expect our authors to upload image-only or tags-only content (if your authors might, check the Html property value as well).

Let's see this in action within our plant fact sheets. Open Plant.aspx in HTML view and convert the table cell that holds the heading for the Description and the description placeholder into a server control:

```
. . . code continues . . .
<table>
<tr>
    <td class="BodyText" runat="server" id="tdDescription"><br>
        <H2>Description</H2>
        <cms:HtmlPlaceholderControl id="PlantDescription"
        runat="server"
            EditControlWidth="400" EditControlHeight="400"
            PlaceholderToBind="Description">
        </cms:HtmlPlaceholderControl><br>
        <br>
    </td>
. . . code continues . . .
```

```
</table>
    . . . code continues . . .
```

Switch to Design view and double-click on the web form to get to the `Page_Load()` event handler. Add the highlighted code as shown below.

```
private void Page_Load(object sender, System.EventArgs e)
{
    . . . code continues . . .

    //The Table Rows/Cells are initialized to be displayed
    trResearchPaper.Visible = true;
    tdDescription.Visible = true;

    //Only perform the check when not in Authoring view
    WebAuthorContext wac = WebAuthorContext.Current;
    if(wac.Mode != WebAuthorContextMode.AuthoringNew &&
        wac.Mode != WebAuthorContextMode.AuthoringReedit)
    {
        //Get a reference to the current posting
        Posting currentPosting = CmsHttpContext.Current.Posting;

        //Get a reference to the ResearchPaper AttachmentPlaceholder
        AttachmentPlaceholder researchPaper;
        researchPaper = currentPosting.Placeholders["ResearchPaper"] as
                AttachmentPlaceholder;

        //Check to see if any attachments have been uploaded
        if(IsAttachmentPlaceholderEmpty(researchPaper))
        {
            //no attachments have been uploaded
            trResearchPaper.Visible = false;
        }

        //Get a reference to the Description HtmlPlaceholder
        HtmlPlaceholder description;
        description = currentPosting.Placeholders["Description"] as
                HtmlPlaceholder;

        //Check to see if content has been added to the HtmlPlaceholder
        if(IsHtmlPlaceholderEmpty(description))
        {
            //No content has been added
            tdDescription.Visible = false;
        }
    }
}
```

The `IsHtmlPlaceholderEmpty()` method checks to see if the `HtmlPlaceholder` passed in as an input parameter contains any content. It does this by checking the values returned by the `Html` and `Text` properties. Add `IsHtmlPlaceholderEmpty()` directly below the `IsAttachmentPlaceholderEmpty()` method.

```
private bool IsHtmlPlaceholderEmpty(HtmlPlaceholder hph)
{
    //Detecting if the HtmlPlaceholder has content
    bool htmlPlaceholderIsEmpty;

    if(hph.Text.Trim()=="")
    {
        //The placeholder does not contain content!
        htmlPlaceholderIsEmpty = true;
    }
    else
    {
```

```
        //There is content
        htmlPlaceholderIsEmpty = false;
    }

    return htmlPlaceholderIsEmpty;
}
```

Detecting when an ImagePlaceholder is Empty

An `ImagePlaceholder` is empty if the `src` property returns an empty string as demonstrated by the code snippet below.

```
private bool IsImagePlaceholderEmpty(ImagePlaceholder iph)
{
    //Detecting if the Image Placeholder contains an image
    bool imagePlaceholderIsEmpty;

    if(iph.Src=="")
    {
        //no image found!
        imagePlaceholderIsEmpty = true;
    }
    else
    {
        //An image has ben uploaded
        imagePlaceholderIsEmpty = false;
    }

    return imagePlaceholderIsEmpty;
}
```

We don't have headings that describe the `ImagePlaceholder` on our plant template file, so we won't need to implement this check. Nevertheless, feel free to try it out on your own.

Summary

We have covered quite a bit of material in this chapter. We saw that the `CmsHttpContext` object serves as a gateway to all objects in the MCMS content repository. It allows us access to channels, postings, template galleries, templates, resource galleries, and resources. Our first example made use of iteration techniques to get references to channels. We started from the root channel and worked our way down and up the channel hierarchy. We saw how the `GetByRelativePath()` method could be used to shorten the number of iterations required.

We went on to work on a second example using the `Searches` class to get references to objects anywhere in the hierarchy without performing any iterations. With the path, URL, or GUID of an object, we can use the `GetByPath()`, `GetByGuid()`, and `GetByUrl()` methods of the `Searches` class to get a reference to the object.

Our third example accessed the contents of placeholders programmatically. We explored the various properties for each of the three placeholder classes: `AttachmentPlaceholder`, `HtmlPlaceholder`, and `ImagePlaceholder`. We retrieved the values that we entered previously in our plant fact sheets and displayed them on our custom web form. Finally, we learned how to detect when a placeholder is empty. The information provided in this chapter is sufficient to get you through the rest of the book, and should be sufficient for most websites' requirements.

13
Building Navigation Controls

Navigation is a hot topic among web designers. It's easy to get caught up in the many debates that are circling around about the design and functional aspects of website navigation. While working out the do's and don'ts of good navigation is important, our focus for this chapter is on the code. We aren't going to worry about whether a menu looks best on the top, left, right, or middle of the page. We are not going to discuss the pros and cons of popups versus plaintext menus. We leave that battle to the web designer (the person who provides the artistic view) and the information architect (the person who decides how the navigation scheme flows from the home page).

Instead, we'll show you how to write the code. Static menus are easy to build. Simply hard-code the menu items within the navigation controls and you're ready to go. The drawback of embedding links in code is that once URLs change, developers have to be called in. Would you or your coworkers volunteer for another late night in the office changing links? We think not.

We want our navigation controls to be dynamic and preferably managed by content contributors. Whenever channels are added or deleted, or if the URLs change, the navigation should be updated along with it. To do this, we will use the Publishing API (PAPI) to programmatically read off the channel structure.

Common Navigation Controls

We will tackle four common forms of navigation for the Tropical Green site. Your website may have a similar navigation scheme. Even if it's not entirely the same, you should be able to customize the solutions here to fit your needs. Navigation is usually highly customized for the site it is intended for; a one-size-fits-all solution simply does not exist. The techniques discussed here can be easily re-used to build the navigation controls you require.

- **The top menu bar** will be used as our starting point. With it, we'll cover the basic aspects of walking through the channel structure using the PAPI as well as picking out menu items that belong to the top from the list of available channels.

- **The left or right menu bar** is similar to the top menu bar but with the items arranged vertically. It is common for menu bars to have some form of client-side scripting, like JavaScript scripts, for a richer user experience. We will demonstrate how a client-side script can enhance a navigation generated by server-side script code in a right-hand menu. When the mouse cursor is placed over the first-level menu item, we want the second-level menu items to appear in a popup.

- **The BreadCrumb Control** is made up of a series of links that connect to one another, like this:

  Home > Plant Catalog > Hibiscus

  While reading the contents of the fact sheet, visitors can click on the Plant Catalog hyperlink anytime to get back to the Plant Catalog summary page. This control is essentially the "You Are Here" sign that tells visitors exactly where they are.

- **The Site Map Control** uses the TreeView control that ships with MCMS 2002 to generate a dynamic view of the entire site. Most smaller sites have a page that lists all the pages available on the site. The choice of display varies from site to site. A common representation is a tree which gives a hierarchical view of the site, showing how each page relates to the others.

Putting it all together, we have the Plant template, complete with navigation menus:

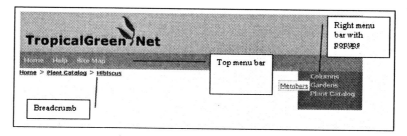

The tree is accessed from the Site Map link located at the top menu bar. When completed, it will look like this:

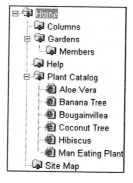

In building these controls, we have tried as far as possible to use menus like those used on real websites. The controls you see here are simplified versions of navigation schemes used on websites we have built, with some of the components changed for simplicity. The pop-up menu for the right-hand menu uses the built-in pop-up object that comes with the Internet Explorer. The TreeView control used in the site map is the one that ships with MCMS 2002. Using these ready-to-go solutions lets us concentrate on the MCMS aspects of the problem. On an intranet, these solutions work well. Nevertheless, you can easily plug in your own customized JavaScript routines to get the menus to work across different browser types and versions.

Web User Controls Promote Design Consistency

The top and right menu bars are to be consistently applied on every single web page. The problem is: How can these sets of code be duplicated without having to maintain separate copies of each one on each template that uses it?

What was done in the good old ASP (Active Server Pages) days was to use include files. These were inserted into our regular ASP code using include directives:

```
<!--#include file="TopMenu.asp"-- >
```

Here, `TopMenu.asp` would be an active server page that contained code that displays the banner.

Developers would have placed that line of code within ASP pages. Although the code could be managed from a single file, it became a nightmare when that include file started to contain other include files, which in turn included other files. Things got really messy and confusing and it was very easy for the entire site to become unmanageable.

Fortunately, ASP.NET has made things a lot simpler with the introduction of Web User Controls.

Web User Controls behave similarly to include files: you create the component once and you can use it on any web form within the same project file. Just drag and drop the Web User Control on the web form and you're done.

Unlike include files (which are just scripts that run whenever the ASP page is executed), Web User Controls expose functionality in the form of properties, methods, and events. This allows a cleaner design and more efficient code re-use.

For the Tropical Green website, we will embed our navigation controls in Web User Controls to ensure that they can be consistently applied across all templates and in channel rendering scripts.

A Simple Menu—Creating the Top Menu Web User Control

The top menu consists of a row of items consisting of three options displayed horizontally at the top of the screen:

- Home
- Help
- Site Map

In this exercise we create a Web User Control that consists of a table containing the top menu bar.

We will start by adding a new Web User Control to the project. In Solution Explorer, right-click the `UserControls` folder. (The `UserControls` folder was created in Chapter 5.) Select Add | Add Web User Control in the pop-up menu. Name the new Web User Control `TopMenu.ascx`.

The control appears in Design view. Toggle to HTML view and add a table at the top of the page. The table consists of a single row with no cells. We will write the logic to define the cells of this row in the code-behind file later.

```
<%@ Control Language="c#" AutoEventWireup="false" Codebehind="TopMenu.ascx.cs"
    Inherits="TropicalGreen.UserControls.TopMenu"
    TargetSchema="http://schemas.microsoft.com/intellisense/ie5"%>

<asp:Table CellPadding="10" ID="Menu" CssClass="TopMenuBar" Runat="server">
<asp:TableRow></asp:TableRow>
</asp:Table>
```

Switch to Design view and double-click on the Web User Control to open its code-behind file.
Above the class declaration, import the `Microsoft.ContentManagement.Publishing` namespace.

```
namespace TropicalGreen.UserControls
{
    using System;
    using System.Data;
    using System.Drawing;
    using System.Web;
    using System.Web.UI.WebControls;
    using System.Web.UI.HtmlControls;

    //Add reference to the PAPI
    using Microsoft.ContentManagement.Publishing;

    /// <summary>
    ///     Summary description for TopMenu.
    /// </summary>
    public abstract class TopMenu : System.Web.UI.UserControl
    {
        . . . code continues . . .
    }
}
```

And in the `Page_Load()` event handler, add the code below. As usual, we start by getting a
reference to the current `CmsHttpContext`. From there, we access the TropicalGreen channel and
add it to the top menu as a link to the home page. We then list all sub-channels directly beneath
TropicalGreen as menu items.

```
private void Page_Load(object sender, System.EventArgs e)
{
    // Put user code to initialize the page here

    //Get a reference to the current CmsHttpContext
    CmsHttpContext cmsContext = CmsHttpContext.Current;

    //Get a reference to the TropicalGreen channel
    Channel tropicalGreen;
    string path = "/Channels/tropicalgreen/";
    tropicalGreen = cmsContext.Searches.GetByPath(path) as Channel;

    //Add the TropicalGreen channel as a link to the home page
    AddMenuItem(tropicalGreen.DisplayName, tropicalGreen.Url);

    //Iterate through each sub channel directly
    //beneath the tropicalgreen channel
    foreach(Channel subChannel in tropicalGreen.Channels)
    {
        //for each sub channel, create a menu item
        AddMenuItem(subChannel.DisplayName, subChannel.Url);
    }
}
```

The `AddMenuItem()` method accepts the `DisplayName` and the `Url` of the channel. It constructs the
horizontal menu by adding cells containing hyperlinks to the first row of the table that will hold
the menu. Enter the `AddMenuItem()` method directly below the `Page_Load()` event handler.

```
//Adds cells to the first row of the Menu Table
//to form a horizontal menu
private void AddMenuItem(string displayName, string url)
{
    //create an anchor for the hyperlink
    HyperLink anchor = new HyperLink();
    anchor.NavigateUrl = url;
    anchor.Text = displayName;
    anchor.CssClass = "TopMenu";

    //add the anchor to the cell
    TableCell td = new TableCell();
    td.Controls.Add(anchor);

    //add the cell to the first row of the Menu table
    Menu.Rows[0].Cells.Add(td);
}
```

Add the `TopMenu.ascx` Web User Control to the Plant template. Open the `Plant.aspx` template file in Design view. Drag `TopMenu.ascx` from Solution Explorer and drop it onto the cell that says (Space for Top Menu). Delete the text (Space for Top Menu). Do the same for the `ChannelRenderingScript.aspx` template.

Save and build the solution and you are done.

To see the results of the code, view the Plant Catalog by accessing `http://localhost/tropicalgreen/plantcatalog` from Internet Explorer.

We have successfully constructed a top menu that lists *all* the Channels beneath TropicalGreen as menu items; but that's not what we want. We only want three items—Home, Help, and Site Map. Also, the first item in the list says Tropical Green instead of Home. That isn't informative as it doesn't tell visitors where the link leads. We need to change the display name of the channel to read Home—when visitors see that, they will immediately know that clicking on the link brings them back to the home page.

Changing the Display Name of the TropicalGreen Channel

Let's start by changing the display name of the TropicalGreen channel from Tropical Green to Home. We will use Site Manager to do this.

- Open Site Manager.
- Right-click on the TropicalGreen channel and select Properties.
- In the Display Name field, enter Home.
- Click OK to commit the changes and close the Properties dialog.

Next, browse to `http://localhost/tropicalgreen/plantcatalog/`.

Notice that the first item in the top menu bar now shows Home. While this is a simple exercise, it demonstrates that channel managers and administrators can modify the display name of channels and postings without affecting the functionality of the site.

> Modifying the Name property of a channel or posting may affect the site as it changes the URL of the channel or posting.

Using Channel Custom Properties to Differentiate Between Top and Right Menu Items

Short of hard-coding the menu items, we need to figure out how to filter out channels that should not be included in the top menu. Fortunately, channels have a built-in collection, known as custom properties. Custom properties give us the space to provide additional information about channels. In this example, we will use them to indicate where the channel belongs—the top or right menu.

> We could have marked the channels that appear on the top menu using available flags such as the IsImportant property of the channel. However, doing so would mean that we couldn't then use such properties for other more intuitive purposes.

We will add a custom property to indicate which channels belong to the top menu and which ones to the right menu. Creation or deletion of channel custom properties can only be done within Site Manager. Once created, the PAPI and Web Author Console provide the interfaces to update a custom property value.

Using Site Manager to Add a Channel Custom Property

Let's create a custom property named MenuLocation that stores a value of Top or Right to indicate whether the channel appears as a menu item on the top of the page or at the right. If you have not done so, open the Site Manager. Log in as an administrator. Right-click on the PlantCatalog channel and select Properties. In the Properties dialog, select the Custom tab. Click New..... The Add Custom Property dialog opens.

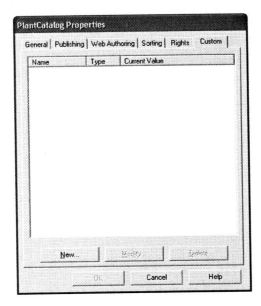

In the Add Custom Property dialog, enter the following values:

Property	Value
Name	MenuLocation
Type	Selection

Watch how the input controls at the bottom panel transform when you change the property type from Text to Selection. To add the values Top and Right to the Allowed Values list, click New....

Highlight Right and click Set as Current to make it the currently selected value of the MenuLocation custom property. When you are done, close both the Add Custom Property and PlantCatalog Properties dialogs.

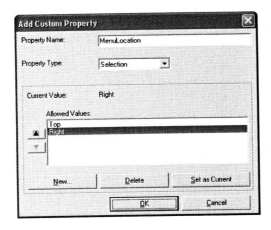

> Once the Name property has been set, you can't change it. Also, each allowed value can only store string values of up to 45 characters in length.

Repeat for the sub-channels directly below and including the TropicalGreen channel. Set the custom property values of each channel based on the following table:

Channel Name	Custom Property Name	Set as Current Value
TropicalGreen	MenuLocation	Top
Columns		Right
Gardens		Right
Help		Top
PlantCatalog		Right
SiteMap		Top

Each channel now has a tag that indicates whether it belongs to the top or right menu.

Modifying Channel Custom Property Values

Once custom properties have been created for channels, you can modify the values assigned to them using either Site Manager or the Web Author Console. Let's use the Web Author Console to see how we can change the custom property value of the PlantCatalog channel.

Browse to the Plant Catalog page (http://localhost/tropicalgreen/plantcatalog) and switch to Edit site. In the Web Author Console, click Channel Properties. In the Channel Properties dialog, click on the Custom tab. The allowed values of the MenuLocation custom property are shown in the drop-down list. Make sure Right is selected and click Save to commit the change to the repository.

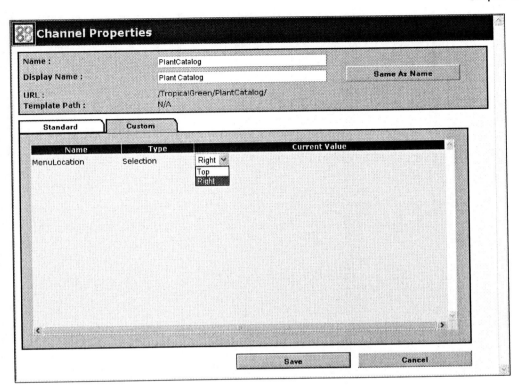

Filtering the Top Menu

Now that we have created a custom property to tag the channels, we can re-write the
TopMenu.ascx Web User Control to filter out channels that don't belong to the top menu.

Method 1: Using Searches.GetChannelsByCustomProperty

The fastest way to code this is to call the Searches.GetChannelsByCustomProperty() method; a
member of the CmsHttpContext.Searches class. It accepts two parameters:

- The Name of the Custom Property
- The value of the Custom Property (optional)

It returns a ChannelCollection object.

Passing in the name of the custom property alone returns a ChannelCollection of all channels in
the system that have the custom property defined. Passing in both the name and value retrieves all
channels that have the custom property defined and match the specified custom property value.

Open the TopMenu.ascx file and double-click the web form to open the code-behind file.

Modify the Page_Load() event handler to use the Searches.GetChannelsByCustomProperty()
method to retrieve a collection of all the channels that have the custom property MenuLocation
with the value of Top.

```
private void Page_Load(object sender, System.EventArgs e)
{
    //Put user code to initialize the page here
    //Get a reference to the current CmsHttpContext
    CmsHttpContext cmsContext = CmsHttpContext.Current;

    //We comment out these lines as the TropicalGreen channel is
    //fetched as part of the collection when we use the
    //Searches.GetChannelsByCustomProperty() method
    /* Channel tropicalGreen;
    string path = "/Channels/tropicalgreen/";
    tropicalGreen = cmsContext.Searches.GetByPath(path) as Channel;

    //Add the TropicalGreen channel as a link to the home page
    AddMenuItem(tropicalGreen.DisplayName, tropicalGreen.Url); */


    //Get a collection of all Channels with the
    //MenuLocation custom property value of "Top"
    ChannelCollection topChannels =
        cmsContext.Searches.GetChannelsByCustomProperty ("MenuLocation",
                                                          "Top");

    foreach(Channel subChannel in topChannels)
    {
        //for each sub channel, create a menu item
        AddMenuItem(subChannel.DisplayName, subChannel.Url);
    }
}
```

Save and build the solution and open `http://localhost/tropicalgreen/plantcatalog/`. The menu displays as shown in the following diagram with only the top menu items.

Performance Considerations

However, using the `Searches.GetChannelsByCustomProperty()` method is expensive. As far as possible, it is best to avoid using it. In order to retrieve the collection of channels that share the same custom property and custom property values, it had to search the entire repository.

We wanted to retrieve two channels to be added to the top menu. In order to get these channels, the `Searches.GetChannelsByCustomProperty()` method searches the entire collection of custom properties in the MCMS repository and fetches out the ones that have a named property with the value specified.

For a small site, like Tropical Green, the method returns results within a reasonable timeframe (the wait time is not noticeable). As the site grows, the `Searches.GetChannelsByCustomProperty()` method gets slower and slower to the point where it starts to affect the performance of the site.

In the next example, we will use a more effective method to retrieve a specific collection of channels based on custom property values.

Method 2: Checking the Custom Property Values of Each Channel

While `Searches.GetChannelsByCustomProperty()` provides a convenient solution, it's not always the most efficient. In this section, we look at a better way to retrieve the collection of channels that have the custom property `MenuLocation` with a value of `Top`.

Rather than use `Searches.GetChannelsByCustomProperty()`, we check the custom properties of each sub-channel directly beneath TropicalGreen. This approach fares better on larger sites. Let's see how this is done.

In the `Page_Load()` event handler of the `TopMenu,ascx.cs` file, replace all of the current code with the revised code shown below. It iterates through each of the sub-channels below the TropicalGreen channel and checks to see if a custom property named `MenuLocation` exists. If it does and if it holds the value `top`, we add it to the menu. Modify the code in the `Page_Load()` event handler so that it looks exactly as shown below.

```
private void Page_Load(object sender, System.EventArgs e)
{
    // Put user code to initialize the page here
    //get a reference to the current CmsHttpContext
    CmsHttpContext cmsContext = CmsHttpContext.Current;

    //Get a reference to the TropicalGreen channel
    Channel tropicalGreen;
    string path = "/Channels/tropicalgreen/";
    tropicalGreen = cmsContext.Searches.GetByPath(path) as Channel;

    //Add the TropicalGreen channel as a link to the home page
    AddMenuItem(tropicalGreen.DisplayName, tropicalGreen.Url);

    //Iterate through each sub channel directly
    //beneath the TropicalGreen channel
    foreach(Channel subChannel in tropicalGreen.Channels)
    {
        //Check to see if the channel has a
        //custom property named MenuLocation
        CustomProperty menuLocation =
        subChannel.CustomProperties["MenuLocation"];

        if(menuLocation != null)
        {
            //Check that the value stored in the
            //MenuLocation custom property has the value "top"
            if(menuLocation.Value.ToLower()=="top")
            {
                AddMenuItem(subChannel.DisplayName, subChannel.Url);
            }
        }
    }
}
```

When the channel does not have a custom property of the particular name/index, a null value is returned. As in the above code, it's a good idea to check for nulls to avoid run-time errors.

Save and build the solution.

The end result of this revised code achieves the same thing as before: We still get the items we want displayed on the top menu. However, this solution is better than using the Searches.GetByChannelCustomProperty() method because instead of searching the entire MCMS repository for channels that have the specified custom property name and value, it only looks within the sub-channels directly below TropicalGreen. It does not matter how large the site is, the number of lookups done is limited to the range you are searching and performance remains relatively unaffected by the number of channels and custom properties in the entire site.

Menus with JavaScript—Creating the Right Menu Web User Control

Navigation menus come in all shapes and sizes and many extend beyond the first level. Developers often face an uphill task attempting to generate multi-leveled menus. The immediate problem is getting the script to iterate through several levels of channels and postings, and when that has been done, there is the challenge of integrating client-side scripts (like JavaScript) with ASP.NET.

This is the problem we're going to tackle in this section. The right menu bar that we are creating generates two levels of menus. The items displayed here include:

- Columns
- Gardens
  - Members Only
- Plant Catalog

We will use JavaScript to create popups that display the sub-menu items when the mouse is placed over the first-level menu items.

Why place the menu on the right and not the left? Well, we don't really have a preference. We picked right because it's less conventional and our fictitious panel of Tropical Green web committee members had a preference for right over left.

The nice thing about coding with Web User Controls is that you can always change the position by dragging and dropping the control from right to left, or wherever you wish to place it.

The methods used to build multi-level menus vary widely from site to site. It is common for developers to download ready-to-use JavaScript menus off the Internet and integrate them into their own solutions. For this example, we are going to use a built-in pop-up object that's available in Internet Explorer 5.5 and above.

Let's say that the menu structure looks like this:

- Menu 1
- Menu 2
  - Sub-Menu A
  - Sub-Menu B

  o Sub-Menu C

The first-level menu items are displayed vertically in the form of a table. When a mouse pointer is placed over the menu item for Menu 2, a pop-up menu appears with listings to Sub-Menu A, Sub-Menu B and Sub-Menu C.

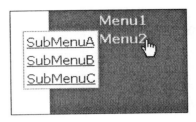

To achieve this, we use the `window.createPopup()` method built into Internet Explorer (version 5.5 and above only). The following code snippet shows how to use it to create a pop-up menu:

```
<script language="javascript">
var oPopup = window.createPopup();
oPopup.document.body.innerHtml = "contents of popup";

//x = x-coordinate of popup
//y = y-coordinate of popup
//width = width of popup
//height = height of popup
//obj = element in which the x and y-coordinates are relative to
oPopup.show(x,y,width,height,obj);
</script>
```

What we need to do is to replace the string, `contents of popup`, with the list of second-level menu items and call it when a mouse cursor is placed over the first-level menu items.

> Warning: This solution works well in an intranet environment where the browser version is controlled and can be guaranteed to be at least Internet Explorer 5.5 and above. Being a built-in function of the browser, it's also simple to follow. You can easily replace the JavaScript used here with scripts that provide cross-browser functionality.

The First-Level Menu Items

Add a new Web User Control to the project: In Solution Explorer, right-click the UserControls folder and select Add | Add Web User Control from the pop-up menu. Name the new Web User Control RightMenu.ascx.

Toggle to HTML view. Add a server-side table and give it the ID RHMenu.

```
<%@ Control Language="c#" AutoEventWireup="false"
Codebehind="RightMenu.ascx.cs" Inherits="TropicalGreen.UserControls.RightMenu"
TargetSchema="http://schemas.microsoft.com/intellisense/ie5"%>
<asp:Table ID="RHMenu" Runat="server">
</asp:Table>
```

Double-click on the on Web User Control in Design view to get to the code-behind file. Above the class declaration, import the Microsoft.ContentManagement.Publishing namespace.

```
namespace TropicalGreen.UserControls
{
    using System;
    using System.Data;
    using System.Drawing;
    using System.Web;
    using System.Web.UI.WebControls;
    using System.Web.UI.HtmlControls;

    //Add the reference to the PAPI
    using Microsoft.ContentManagement.Publishing;

    /// <summary>
    ///    Summary description for RightMenu.
    /// </summary>
    public abstract class RightMenu : System.Web.UI.UserControl
    {
        . . . code continues . . .
    }
}
```

And in the Page_Load() event handler, add the following code:

```
private void Page_Load(object sender, System.EventArgs e)
{
    // Put user code to initialize the page here
    CmsHttpContext cmsContext = CmsHttpContext.Current;

    //Get a reference to the TropicalGreen channel
    Channel tropicalGreen;
    string path = "/Channels/tropicalgreen/";
    tropicalGreen = cmsContext.Searches.GetByPath(path) as Channel;

    //Iterate through each sub channel directly
    //beneath the TropicalGreen channel
    foreach(Channel subChannel in tropicalGreen.Channels)
    {
        //Check to see if the channel has a
        //custom property named MenuLocation
        CustomProperty menuLocation =
            subChannel.CustomProperties["MenuLocation"];

        if(menuLocation != null)
        {
            //Check that the value stored in the
            //MenuLocation custom property has the value "right"
            if(menuLocation.Value.ToLower()=="right")
            {
                AddMenuItem(subChannel);
            }
        }
    }
}
```

The code is very similar to that of the previous example when we built the top menu, the main difference being that we check that the MenuLocation custom property holds a value of Right instead of Top.

Add the AddMenuItem() method below the Page_Load() event handler. It displays the list of menu items vertically by adding rows to the table. In addition, the method accepts the first-level channel as an input parameter. This makes it easier for us to get the second-level menu items later.

```
//Adds a new row to the table, displaying the menu items
//vertically
private void AddMenuItem(Channel menuItem)
```

```
    {
        TableRow tr = new TableRow();
        TableCell td = new TableCell();
        HyperLink anchor = new HyperLink();

        anchor.NavigateUrl = menuItem.Url;
        anchor.Text = menuItem.DisplayName;
        anchor.CssClass = "RightMenu";

        td.Controls.Add(anchor);
        tr.Cells.Add(td);

        RHMenu.Rows.Add(tr);
    }
```

Each generated TableRow looks like this:

```
<tr>
  <td>
    <a href="(Channel_Url)" class="RightMenu">
    (Channel_DisplayName)
    </a>
  </td>
</tr>
```

The Second-Level Menu Items

Now that we coded the first level-menu items, we are ready to move down to the second level.

Add the following code to the AddMenuItem() method.

```
//Adds a new row to the table, displaying the menu items
//vertically
private void AddMenuItem(Channel menuItem)
{
    TableRow tr = new TableRow();
    TableCell td = new TableCell();
    HyperLink anchor = new HyperLink();

    anchor.NavigateUrl = menuItem.Url;
    anchor.Text = menuItem.DisplayName;
    anchor.CssClass = "RightMenu";

    td.Controls.Add(anchor);
    tr.Cells.Add(td);
    RHMenu.Rows.Add(tr);

    //Create the second level menu items
    if(menuItem.Channels.Count>0)
    {
        //Add a mouse over event
        //when the mouse is place over the first level items,
        //the ShowMenu JavaScript function is called
        anchor.Attributes.Add("onmouseover","javascript:ShowMenu('" +
                        menuItem.Name + "',1);void 0;");

        //The division that contains the table of
        //second level menu items
        HtmlGenericControl div = new HtmlGenericControl("div");
        div.ID = "menu" + menuItem.Name;
        div.Attributes.Add("style","display:none");

        //The table that contains the second level menu items
        Table tblSubMenu = new Table();
        tblSubMenu.Attributes.Add("style",
            "border:1px solid DarkGray; font-family:Verdana; font-size:11pt");
```

319

```csharp
tblSubMenu.BackColor = System.Drawing.Color.FromArgb(255,255,204);

//Iterate through each sub Channel
//Create a new row/cell pair for each item
foreach(Channel subMenuItem in menuItem.Channels)
{
    TableRow trSubMenu = new TableRow();
    TableCell tdSubMenu = new TableCell();

    //Create a hyperlink to the sub Channel
    HyperLink subAnchor = new HyperLink();
    subAnchor.Text = subMenuItem.DisplayName;
    subAnchor.Attributes.Add("style","color:#006600");
    subAnchor.NavigateUrl = "javascript:void 0";
    subAnchor.Attributes.Add("onClick",
        "javascript:window.top.location='" + subMenuItem.Url + "'");

    tdSubMenu.Controls.Add(subAnchor);
    trSubMenu.Cells.Add(tdSubMenu);
    tblSubMenu.Rows.Add(trSubMenu);
}

div.Controls.Add(tblSubMenu);
td.Controls.Add(div);
}
else
{
    //There are no sub menus for this channel.
    anchor.Attributes.Add("onmouseover",
        "javascript:ShowMenu('" + menuItem.Name + "',0);void 0;");
}
}
```

Essentially, what the code does is embed the list of second-level menu items inside a <div> tag. The style="display:none" attribute in each <div> tag keeps the sub-menu items hidden from view. The HTML output for each generated row with sub-menu items is shown below. The highlighted section shows the HTML code of the second-level menu items between <div> and </div> tags.

```html
<tr>
  <td>
    <a href="(Channel_Url)" class="RightMenu"
      onmouseover="javascript:ShowMenu((Channel_Name))">
    (Channel_DisplayName)
    </a>

    <div id="menu(Channel_Name)" style="display:none">
      <table style=" border:1px solid DarkGray; font-
        family:Verdana; font-size:11pt">
        <tr>
          <td>
            <a href="javascript:void 0;" onClick="javascript:
              window.top.location='(URL of sub channel)'
              style="color:#006600">
              (DisplayName of sub channel)
            </a>
          </td>
        </tr>
      </table>
    </div>

  </td>
</tr>
```

We have created both the first-level and the second-level menu items, but the script is not complete yet. We need to add in the JavaScript that shows the sub-menu items in a popup when the mouse cursor is placed over the first-level menu items. The complete JavaScript function is shown below.

The ShowMenu() method accepts two input parameters—the name of the menu (menuName) and a flag to indicate whether the menu reveals any sub-menus (showSubMenu).We first create the pop-up object. Next, we set the contents of the pop-up object using the contents of the <div> element embedded within the first-level menu item created in the previous step. Then we determine the exact width and height required for the popup to display its contents. Finally, we reveal the popup.

```
<script language="JavaScript">
function ShowMenu(menuName,showSubMenu)
{
    var oPopup = window.createPopup();
    if(showSubMenu==0)
    {
        oPopup.show();
        oPopup.hide();
    }
    else
    {
        var obj;

        obj = eval('ID of Control_menu' + menuName);
        oPopup.document.body.innerHTML = eval('ID of control_menu' +
                                   menuName + '.innerHTML');

        var popupBody = oPopup.document.body;
        oPopup.show(0,0,0,0);
        var realWidth = popupBody.scrollWidth;
        var realHeight = popupBody.scrollHeight;
        oPopup.hide();

        oPopup.show(-realWidth,0,realWidth,realHeight,obj);
    }
}
</script>
```

When the page is rendered on the browser, ASP.NET re-writes the ID of the <div> object as (ID of control)_menu(channel name). For example, the ID of the <div> object attached to the Gardens channel is RightMenu1_menuGardens. Therefore we can't embed this JavaScript directly into the template file as we would usually do for a regular HTML page as the script requires us to code the ID of the control, a variable that is determined by the developer who drags and drops the control to the template file. If we hard-code the ID now, the script will not work should the developer change the ID of the control on the template file and forget to change it in the script. For this reason, it makes sense for the code-behind file to dynamically generate the entire JavaScript.

In the Page_Load() event handler, add the following code:

```
private void Page_Load(object sender, System.EventArgs e)
{
    // Put user code to initialize the page here
    CmsHttpContext cmsContext = CmsHttpContext.Current;

    //Get a reference to the TropicalGreen channel
    Channel tropicalGreen;
    string path = "/Channels/tropicalgreen/";
    tropicalGreen = cmsContext.Searches.GetByPath(path) as Channel;
```

```
        //Iterate through each sub channel directly
        //beneath the TropicalGreen channel
        foreach(Channel subChannel in tropicalGreen.Channels)
        {
            //Check to see if the channel has a
            //custom property named MenuLocation
            CustomProperty menuLocation =
                subChannel.CustomProperties["MenuLocation"];

            if(menuLocation != null)
            {
                //Check that the value stored in the
                //MenuLocation custom property has the value "right"
                if(menuLocation.Value.ToLower()=="right")
                {
                    AddMenuItem(subChannel);
                }
            }
        }

        //Add javascript to show/hide second level menu items
        System.Text.StringBuilder sb = new System.Text.StringBuilder();
        sb.Append("<script language=\"Javascript\">");
        sb.Append("function ShowMenu(menuName,showSubMenu){\n");
        sb.Append("var oPopup = window.createPopup();\n");
        sb.Append("if(showSubMenu==0)\n");
        sb.Append("{\n");
        sb.Append("oPopup.show();oPopup.hide();\n");
        sb.Append("}\n");
        sb.Append("else{");
        sb.Append("var obj;\n");
        sb.Append("obj = eval('" + this.ID + "_menu' + menuName);\n");
        sb.Append("oPopup.document.body.innerHTML = eval('" +
            this.ID + "_menu' + menuName + '.innerHTML');\n");
        sb.Append("var popupBody = oPopup.document.body;\n");
        sb.Append("oPopup.show(0,0,0,0);\n");
        sb.Append("var realWidth = popupBody.scrollWidth;\n");
        sb.Append("var realHeight = popupBody.scrollHeight;\n");
        sb.Append("oPopup.hide();\n");
        sb.Append("oPopup.show(-realWidth, 0, realWidth, realHeight,obj);\n");
        sb.Append("}\n");
        sb.Append("}\n");
        sb.Append("</script>");

        Page.RegisterClientScriptBlock("ShowMenu",sb.ToString());
    }
```

It looks cryptic at first. What we have done is to use a StringBuilder object (from the System.Text namespace) to create the JavaScript. The ID of the Web User Control is determined by the value returned by this.ID. We then added the script to the page using the Page.RegisterClientScriptBlock() method, which injects the JavaScript between the page's <head> tags when the page loads.

> For the script to work correctly, the channels must not have spaces or single quotes in their names.

Now we can add the RightMenu Web User Control to the Plant template. Open the Plant.aspx template file in Design view. Drag RightMenu.ascx from Solution Explorer and drop it onto the cell that says (Space for Right Menu Bar). Delete the text (Space for Right Menu). Do the same for the ChannelRenderingScript.aspx template. Save your work and build the solution.

Open the Hibiscus plant posting. You should see both the top and right menus. Place your mouse cursor over Gardens. Did you get a pop-up menu as shown below?

Working with External URLs

While it's nice to be able to iterate through collections of channels and postings in MCMS to generate menus, most of us will encounter situations where the URL links to pages that are neither channels nor postings. This could be anything from legacy web applications to external pages residing on other servers/websites.

Take for example, the Tropical Green website. What if we needed to place a link to www.microsoft.com/cmserver on the top menu? www.microsoft.com/cmserver is not part of our MCMS website. When we iterate through the sub-channels beneath TropicalGreen, we aren't going to get this listing.

There are several ways to go about this.

- We could hard-code the URL such that it appears on the menu.
  Hard-coding is always the easiest option. But there are administrative overheads in keeping the links updated. What if the address for the www.microsoft.com/cmserver/ site changes?
- We could create a channel within the Tropical Green website that does nothing more than to redirect to www.microsoft.com/cmserver/ when requested.

Creating Channels that Lead to External URLs

The trick is to use a channel rendering script. Here's how it's done:

In Site Manager, set the Script URL of the Help channel to /tropicalgreen/templates/redirect.aspx (for details about channel rendering scripts see Chapter 9).

Create another custom property for the Help channel. This time, make it accept Text input and give it the name URL and the value http://www.microsoft.com/cmserver/.

Custom Property	Value
Name	URL
Value	http://www.microsoft.com/cmserver
Property Type	Text

Create a new web form in the Templates folder of the TropicalGreen solution. Name it Redirect.aspx. Double-click on Redirect.aspx in Design mode to access its code-behind file.

Add the reference to the MCMS PAPI at the top of the file. In the Page_Load() event handler add code that redirects the page to the address found in the URL custom property of the channel. When you have added the code, save and build the solution.

```
using System;
using System.Collections;
using System.ComponentModel;
using System.Data;
using System.Drawing;
using System.Web;
using System.Web.SessionState;
using System.Web.UI;
using System.Web.UI.WebControls;
using System.Web.UI.HtmlControls;

//Add the reference to the PAPI
using Microsoft.ContentManagement.Publishing;

namespace tropicalgreen.Templates
{
    /// <summary>
    /// Summary description for Redirect.
    /// </summary>
    public class Redirect : System.Web.UI.Page
    {
        private void Page_Load(object sender, System.EventArgs e)
        {
            // Put user code to initialize the page here
            CmsHttpContext cmsContext = CmsHttpContext.Current;
            Channel currentChannel = cmsContext.Channel;

            string url = currentChannel.CustomProperties["URL"].Value;
            Response.Redirect(url);
        }

        #region Web Form Designer generated code
        . . . code continues . . .
        #endregion
    }
}
```

As Help is a channel that has a MenuLocation custom property value of Top, it appears as a menu item in the top menu bar. When you click on it, the Redirect.aspx channel rendering script runs and redirects you to the www.microsoft.com/cmserver/ website.

Save and build the solution and try out the Help link. You will be taken to the MCMS website.

A BreadCrumb Control

A menu that displays two levels of navigation works well on some sites. Others require the generation of multiple levels, sometimes all the way down to the last child in the hierarchy. An example of this is a BreadCrumb control.

This control gives visitors a visual clue as to their location in the website. When showing the Plant Catalog page, the BreadCrumb displays:

Home > Plant Catalog

When showing the Hibiscus plant fact sheet, the BreadCrumb changes to:

Home > Plant Catalog > Hibiscus

It's the "You Are Here" sign helping visitors to orientate themselves and not get lost in your site. Visitors can click on any of the crumbs and jump to the parent sections of the current page.

> The term breadcrumb is used because it resembles the trail left by the fictional characters Hansel and Gretel and essentially helps you to find your way back.

Add a new Web User Control to the project. In Solution Explorer, right-click the UserControls folder. Select Add | Add Web User Control in the pop-up menu. Name the new Web User Control `BreadCrumb.ascx`.

Double-click on the on Web User Control in Design view to get to the code-behind file. Above the class declaration, import the `Microsoft.ContentManagement.Publishing` namespace and the `System.Web.UI` namespace.

```
namespace TropicalGreen.UserControls
{
    using System;
    using System.Data;
    using System.Drawing;
    using System.Web;
    using System.Web.UI.WebControls;
    using System.Web.UI.HtmlControls;

    //Add the reference to the PAPI
    using Microsoft.ContentManagement.Publishing;


    //Namespace for the HtmlTextWriter
    using System.Web.UI;

    /// <summary>
    ///     Summary description for BreadCrumb.
    /// </summary>
    public abstract class BreadCrumb : System.Web.UI.UserControl
    {

        . . . code continues . . .
    }
}
```

Within the `BreadCrumb` class we will override the `Render()` method of the base class. Overriding the `Render()` method gives you full control over the markup created by the Web User Control. You can pass HTML code to the `HtmlTextWriter`, which writes to the output stream. In this case, the HTML is strung together by adding the crumb of the current posting and the crumbs returned by the `CollectChannel()` method, which we will code right after this. This approach is a little different from the `TopMenu` and `RightMenu` Web User Controls where we created tables and coded logic in the `Page_Load()` event handler. Add the `Render()` method directly below the `Page_Load()` event handler.

```
protected override void Render(HtmlTextWriter writer)
{
    string startHtml = "";
    CmsHttpContext cmsContext = CmsHttpContext.Current;
```

```
        //Add the leaf
        Posting currentPosting = CmsContext.Posting;
        if(currentPosting !=null)
        {
            startHtml = BuildCrumb(currentPosting.Url, currentPosting.DisplayName,
                                   false);
        }

        //Start with the current channel and go backward
        Channel currentChannel = CmsContext.Channel;
        startHtml = CollectChannel(currentChannel,startHtml);

        writer.Write(startHtml);
    }
```

The CollectChannel() method starts from the current channel and works its way back up the root channel. It starts off with the first crumb, for instance if you are on the Hibiscus page:

Hibiscus

Then it moves up to its parent to get the second crumb, inserting a > sign between the two crumbs:

Plant Catalog > Hibiscus

It repeats this until it reaches the root. The channel just beneath the root is the TropicalGreen channel, which is also our site's home page:

Home > PlantCatalog > Hibiscus

Add the CollectChannel() method below the Render() method.

```
    private String CollectChannel(Channel c, string html)
    {
        while(!c.Parent.IsRoot)
        {
            html = BuildCrumb(c.Url, c.DisplayName, false) + html;
            c = c.Parent;
        }

        //The channel just beneath the root has the URL to the Home Page
        html = BuildCrumb(c.Url,c.DisplayName, true) + html;
        return html;
    }
```

The BuildCrumb() method creates the crumb, which is essentially a hyperlink. Add the BuildCrumb() method below the CollectChannel() method.

```
    private string BuildCrumb(string url, string displayName, bool isStartPoint)
    {
        string crumb = "";
        if(!isStartPoint)
        {
            crumb = " &gt; ";
        }

        crumb += "<a href = '" + url +"'>";
        crumb += displayName;
        crumb += "</a>";

        return crumb;
    }
```

Open the Plant.aspx template file in Design view. Drag BreadCrumb.ascx from Solution Explorer and drop it onto the form, somewhere below the top menu. Save and build the solution and you're done! When you next view a plant fact sheet, you will see the BreadCrumb control as shown below. You can click on any of the crumbs to move back up the trail.

Generating the Entire Site Map—A TreeView Control

TreeViews are good for displaying a hierarchical view of channels and postings. People instinctively know how to work through a TreeView—present one in front of your user and they know how to expand and collapse the folders to get its contents. We use the TreeView control that ships with MCMS to create a site map of the TropicalGreen site. In order to do that, we will write a recursive function (that is, a function that calls itself) to walk through the entire collection of channels and postings. A simple recursive function is shown below.

```
public void EatPizza()
{
    InsertIntoMouth(Pizza);
    bool hungry = IsStomachGrowling();
    while(hungry)
    {
        EatPizza();
    }
}
```

`EatPizza()` continues to call itself as long as the `IsStomachGrowling()` function returns a value of true. We will apply this technique to generate a site map of the Tropical Green site. Add a new Web User Control in the UserControls folder of the TropicalGreen project. Name the new control `SiteMapTree.ascx`. In the Toolbox, right-click on the Web Forms tab and select Add/Remove Items (or Customize Toolbox for Visual Studio .NET 2002 developers).

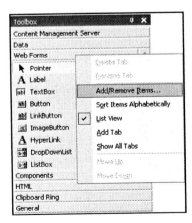

The Customize Toolbox dialog may take a while to load. When it opens, select the .NET Framework Components tab. Click on the Namespace column to sort the components by their namespaces. Scroll through the list and look for the TreeView control, which is part of the `Microsoft.Web.UI.WebControls` namespace (or press t to jump to the components that begin with 't'). Place a checkmark against the TreeView control and click OK.

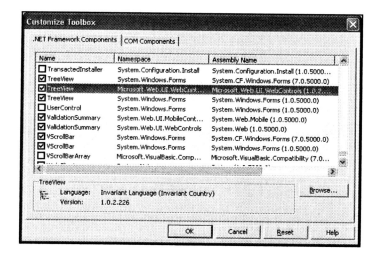

The TreeView control appears in the Web Form toolbox as a little tree icon 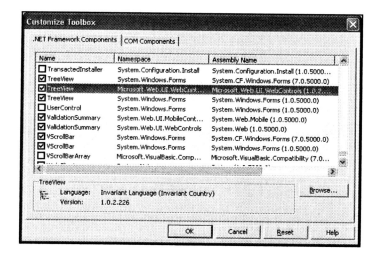. It is probably at the bottom of the list; you may need to scroll to see it. Drag and drop the `Treeview` control onto the `Treeview.ascx` form. Right-click on the TreeView control and select Properties from the pop-up menu. In the Properties dialog, set the values in the table.

Property Name	Property Value
ID	Tree
DefaultStyle	font-size:10pt;font-family:arial
HoverStyle	background-color:orange
SelectedStyle	background-color:green

Open the TreeNodeType Collection Editor by clicking on the ellipsis (...) in the TreeNodeTypes property. We will use the TreeNodeType element of the TreeView object to define two types of nodes in our sitemap.

- **Container**: Represented by the image of a channel icon
- **Leaf**: Represented by the image of a posting icon

Start by creating the node for a `container` based on the property values below. The images (`channelclose.gif`, `channelopen.gif`, and `posting.gif`) can be downloaded from the download section of the book's companion site. Once you have downloaded them, create a new folder below the `images` folder of the TropicalGreen project. Name the new folder `treeicons` and use it to store the downloaded images.

Property Name	Property Value
Type	ContainerNode
ImageUrl	/tropicalgreen/images/treeicons/channelclose.gif
SelectedImageUrl	/tropicalgreen/images/treeicons/channelopen.gif
ExpandedImageUrl	/tropicalgreen/images/treeicons/channelopen.gif

Next, create the node for a Leaf. Because we are not changing the image assigned to the leaf when it is selected or expanded, we just need to assign a value for the ImageUrl property. Create the node TreeNodeType by setting the following properties:

Property Name	Value
Type	LeafNode
ImageUrl	/tropicalgreen/images/treeicons/posting.gif

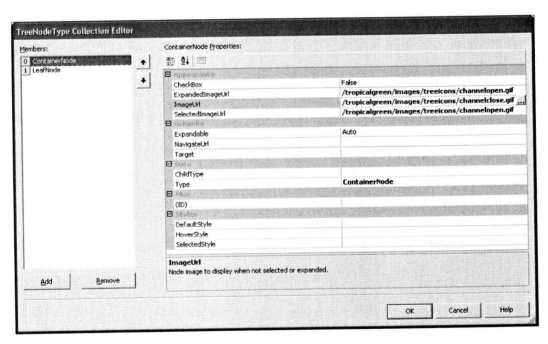

When you have created the nodes, close the TreeNode Type dialog.

Double-click anywhere on the Web User Control in Design mode. You are brought to the code-behind file. Start by adding the namespaces above the class declaration for the SiteMapTree class:

- Microsoft.ContentManagement.Publishing to access the MCMS PAPI

- `Microsoft.Web.UI.WebConrols` to access methods and properties of the TreeView control

```
namespace TropicalGreen.UserControls
{
    using System;
    using System.Data;
    using System.Drawing;
    using System.Web;
    using System.Web.UI.WebControls;
    using System.Web.UI.HtmlControls;

    //Add reference to the PAPI
    using Microsoft.ContentManagement.Publishing;
    //Add the namespace to the TreeView's class
    using Microsoft.Web.UI.WebControls;

    /// <summary>
    ///     Summary description for SiteMapTree.
    /// </summary>
    public abstract class SiteMapTree : System.Web.UI.UserControl
    {
        . . . code continues . . .
    }
}
```

Adding the First Node

The first node on our site map is the TropicalGreen channel. In the `Page_Load()` event handler, we will use the `Searches` object to get a reference to the TropicalGreen channel and create a `TreeNode` object by calling the `CreateNode()` method (defined next) and adding it to the tree.

```
private void Page_Load(object sender, System.EventArgs e)
{
    // Put user code to initialize the page here
    //Get a reference to the current CmsHttpContext
    CmsHttpContext cmsContext = CmsHttpContext.Current;

    //Start from the tropicalgreen channel
    Channel tropicalGreen = cmsContext.Searches.GetByPath
                            ("/Channels/TropicalGreen/") as Channel;

    //Add the tropicalgreen node to the tree
    TreeNode node = CreateNode(tropicalGreen);
    Tree.Nodes.Add(node);
}
```

The `CreateNode()` method accepts a `ChannelItem` (either a channel or a posting) as an input parameter. The node is built based on:

- `TreeNode.ID` or the `Guid` of the channel or posting
- `TreeNode.Text` or the `DisplayName` of the channel or posting
- `TreeNode.NavigateUrl` or the `Url` of the channel or posting

If the `ChannelItem` is a channel, the node type needs to be set to `ContainerNode`. Should it be a posting, the node type will have to be `LeafNode`. Add the `CreateNode()` method below the `Page_Load()` event handler.

```
//Create a new TreeNode object based on the ChannelItem
private TreeNode CreateNode(ChannelItem channelItem)
{
```

```
TreeNode node = new TreeNode();
node.ID = channelItem.Guid;
node.Text = channelItem.DisplayName;
node.NavigateUrl = channelItem.Url;
if(channelItem is Channel)
{
    node.Type = "ContainerNode";
}
else
{
    node.Type = "LeafNode";
}
node.Expandable = ExpandableValue.Auto;
node.Expanded = true;

    return(node);
}
```

Building the Rest of the Tree Recursively

In order to build the rest of the tree, we will start from the first node and walk through each sub-node and any sub-sub-nodes, and so on until the last leaf has been reached, when we add them all to the tree.

To get things started, add a call to the CreateTree() method in the Page_Load() event handler. Pass in the first channel (TropicalGreen) and the first node object created earlier as arguments. This is the starting point of the recursion.

```
private void Page_Load(object sender, System.EventArgs e)
{
    // Put user code to initialize the page here
    //Get a reference to the current CmsHttpContext
    CmsHttpContext cmsContext = CmsHttpContext.Current;

    //Start from the tropicalgreen channel
    Channel tropicalGreen = cmsContext.Searches.GetByPath
                            ("/Channels/TropicalGreen/") as Channel;
    //Add the tropicalgreen node to the Tree
    TreeNode node = CreateNode(tropicalGreen);
    Tree.Nodes.Add(node);

    CreateTree(tropicalGreen,node);
}
```

When the TropicalGreen channel is added as the start point, the tree looks like this:

```
+ TropicalGreen
```

The CreateTree() method creates a sub-node for each sub-channel/posting found within the TropicalGreen channel. Add the CreateTree() method below the CreateNode() method.

```
//The CreateTree() method is a recursive function that walks the
//entire tree, creating a node for every channel/posting
private void CreateTree(Channel channel, TreeNode parentNode)
{
    foreach(ChannelItem channelItem in channel.AllChildren)
    {
        TreeNode subNode = CreateNode(channelItem);
        parentNode.Nodes.Add(subNode);

        if(channelItem is Channel)
        {
            CreateTree((Channel)channelItem, subNode);
        }
```

```
        }
    }
```

After the first recursion, the second-level items are added and the tree looks like this:

```
+ TropicalGreen
    + Plant Catalog
```

And for each sub-channel, the `CreateTree()` method calls itself again. After the second recursion, the third-level items are added and the tree appears like this:

```
+ TropicalGreen
    + Plant Catalog
        - Aloe Vera
        - Banana Tree
        - Bougainvillea
        - Cocount Tree
        - Hibiscus
        - Man Eating Plant
```

The process repeats itself for each sub-item beneath TropicalGreen until the entire tree is built. That completes the code for the Tree. When you are done, save your work!

Creating the SiteMap Page

Now that we have created a Web User Control to display the site map, there are two other tasks that remain to be done:

1. Create a web form to make use of the Web User Control we have just created.
2. Set the Script Url property of the Site Map channel to point to this web form.

First, add a new MCMS web form to the `Templates` directory of the TropicalGreen project. Name the file `siteMap.aspx`. Once it opens, change the Page Layout to FlowLayout.

Toggle to HTML view and add the following code between the `<form>` tags.

```
<table width="100%" border="0" cellspacing="0" cellpadding="0" height="100%">
<tr>
    <td width="100%" colspan="2" valign="top" bgcolor="#FFCC00">
        <IMG src="/tropicalgreen/images/Logo.gif">
    </td>
    <td rowspan="10" valign="top">
        (Space for Console)
    </td>
</tr>
<tr bgcolor="#66CC33">
    <td colspan="2">(Space for Top Menu)</td>
</tr>
<tr>
    <td valign="top">
      (Space for Main Body)
    </td>
    <td class="RightMenuBar" width="20%" valign="top" height="100%"
align="center" rowspan="2" bgcolor="#669900">
      (Space for Right Menu Bar)
    </td>
</tr>
</table>
```

Switch to Design view, and drag and drop `styles.css` onto the web form. Next, drag and drop `TopMenu.ascx` into the cell that says (Space for Top Menu), `RightMenu.ascx` into the cell that says (Space for Right Menu Bar), and DefaultConsole.ascx into the cell that says (Space for Console). When you are done, delete the text markers.

Drag SiteMapTree.ascx from Solution Explorer and drop it onto the cell that says (Space for Main Body). Save and build the solution. Close any open files.

Next, open Site Manager and log in with an account that has administrator or channel manager rights. Open the properties page of the SiteMap Channel and set the Script Url property to /tropicalgreen/templates/sitemap.aspx. Save and build the solution and you're done!

To view the site map, open http://localhost/tropicalgreen/sitemap/.

The completed page looks like this:

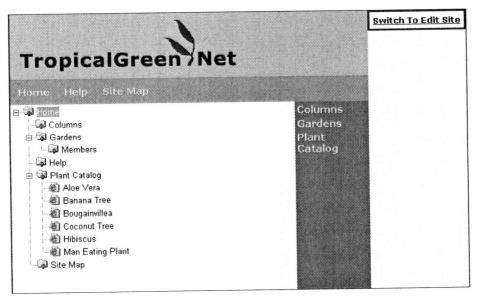

Recursion is always an expensive operation to perform. As the site grows (and we're sure it will), the time it takes to render the entire tree grows along with it. It is best practice to implement ASP.NET output caching (discussed in Chapter 22) before the size of the tree gets out of hand.

Summary

Navigation is a central theme behind every website. In this chapter, we have looked at four common types of navigation. We built a simple top menu using the PAPI. We used custom properties to differentiate between menu items that belong to the top and items that go to the right. For the right menu, we integrated some client-side scripts for a richer user experience.

Next, we showed how links to sites not within the current website can be included by including additional channels. We created an all-purpose channel rendering script that looks at a custom property value of the channel to redirect the user to the appropriate external website.

We went on to demonstrate how navigation can be extended beyond any required level with the breadcrumbs and the site map through loops and recursions. With the essential techniques learned in this chapter, you should be able to implement the design elements required for just about any kind of navigation control.

14

Customizing Placeholder Controls

The ability to create custom placeholder controls is by far one of the most exciting advancements in MCMS 2002. Previous versions of MCMS shipped with the standard placeholder controls that you saw in Chapter 7 but there was very little that could be done to change the way they behaved.

To recap, the default MCMS placeholder controls provide basic authoring features. To add files, authors use the SingleAttachmentPlaceholderControl. The SingleImagePlaceholderControl is used for images, and for everything else there is the HtmlPlaceholderControl, which can also include attachments and images. On the face of it, you may not find any compelling reasons to take the extra time to build custom placeholder controls.

What if, instead of giving authors free play over the number of characters entered in the placeholder, you need to impose a restriction on the number of characters entered? Or perhaps you would like to give authors the convenience of using a date picker to fill a placeholder with a selected and date and time. And what do you do when you need authors to pick from a selection of items and store the selected values as XML? The default placeholder controls certainly can't do all that. Fortunately, we are using MCMS 2002 where all this and more can be achieved by building custom placeholder controls.

In this chapter, we will create four custom placeholder controls:

- A single-line TextBox placeholder control that imposes a limitation on the number of characters entered
- A version of the SingleImagePlaceholderControl that allows authors to set the alignment of the image
- A version of the SingleAttachmentPlaceholderControl that accepts a Flash file, and instead of showing it as a link or icon, plays the Flash animation on the browser
- A CheckBoxList placeholder control that saves data as XML

Each placeholder control will be created using a difference technique. You could build custom placeholder controls using one of three methods:

1. Write a placeholder control from scratch by deriving from the BasePlaceholderControl class

2. Expand the functionality of existing placeholder controls by inheriting from their classes (which in turn inherit from the `BasePlaceholderControl` class)

3. Do some quick prototyping of placeholder controls derived from the `SingleAttachmentPlaceholderControl` and `SingleAttachmentPlaceholderControl` using the `PresentationTemplate` property

Before We Begin

To begin, we will create a new project, `TropicalGreenControlLib`, and add it to the TropicalGreen Solution.

Creating the TropicalGreenControlLib Project

1. Open `TropicalGreen.sln` in Visual Studio.

2. In Solution Explorer, right-click the TropicalGreen solution (don't mix it up with the TropicalGreen project inside the TropicalGreen solution). Select Add | New Project from the pop-up menu.

3. Create a new Visual C# Web Control Library. Name it `TropicalGreenControlLib`. Find a suitable location (e.g. `c:\`) to contain the project files. Click OK.

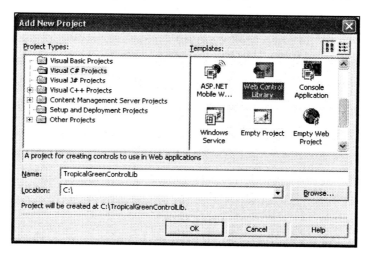

4. Delete the `WebCustomControl1.cs` file that was created by the wizard. We won't be using it.

Why do we create a separate Web Control Library project instead of adding on to the existing TropicalGreen project?

Web Custom Controls are compiled into dynamically linked libraries (with the extension `*.dll`). By separating our custom controls from the main TropicalGreen project file, we are creating a DLL file that contains only components that are meant for reuse across projects. Had we not done so, the DLL would contain the compiled code of all the TropicalGreen code-behind files and other excess baggage.

Adding References to the TropicalGreenControlLib Project

Next, we will add references to the assemblies that are required for developing custom placeholder controls.

Right-click the References folder of the TropicalGreenControlLib project in Solution Explorer and select Add Reference. The Add Reference dialog opens.

Ensure that the .NET tab is selected. Scroll through the list of components and select System.Design.dll. Click Select to add it to the list headed Selected Components.

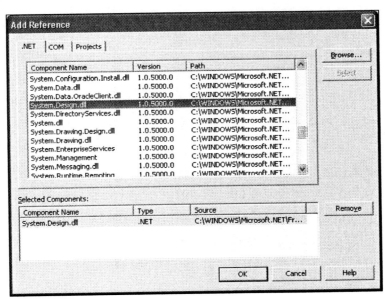

Click Browse... to open the Select Component dialog. Browse to \server\bin\ under the MCMS installation folder. Select:

- Microsoft.ContentManagement.Common.dll
- Microsoft.ContentManagement.Publishing.dll
- Microsoft.ContentManagement.Publishing.Extensions.Placeholders.dll
- Microsoft.ContentManagement.WebControls.dll

Hold down the *Ctrl* key and left-click to select more than one library at the same time. Click Open to add each one to the list. When all the library files have been added, click OK to close the Add Reference dialog.

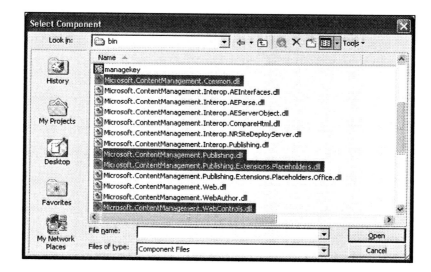

Deriving from the BasePlaceholderControl Class

One technique of building custom placeholder controls is to create Web Custom Controls that inherit directly from the BasePlaceholderControl class. This is probably the most popular and also the best documented method. The result is a set of Web Custom Controls that can be distributed to any MCMS web project that requires them.

Don't confuse Web Custom Controls with the Web User Controls we built in Chapter 13. The table below lists the differences between the two.

Web Custom Control	Web User Control
Re-usable across multiple projects. Compiled into a library file that can be referenced by any project. If you are building a control that could be used across multiple projects, consider using Web Custom Controls instead of Web User Controls.	Good for use only within the project file. If we wanted to share it with another project, we would have to duplicate the code.
Generally harder to create. All logic has to be coded from within a code-behind file.	Relatively easy to create. Designer interface allows drag and drop of existing controls to create a composite control.

About the BasePlaceholderControl Class

All custom placeholder controls are directly or indirectly inherited from the BasePlaceholderControl class (which in turn is inherited from the ASP.NET WebControl class) and are members of the Microsoft.ContentManagment.WebControls namespace.

The BasePlaceholderControl class contains methods that determine how all placeholder controls behave in both presentation and authoring modes.

Methods for Creating Child Controls

`CreatePresentationChildControls()` creates child controls that will be displayed in presentation mode. It accepts a `BaseModeContainer` object (`presentationContainer`) as an input parameter and has no return value. The `BaseModeContainer` object acts as a container for child controls that are seen in presentation mode. It has the following syntax:

```
protected override void CreatePresentationChildControls(BaseModeContainer
presentationContainer)
{
    //add code to load controls into the presentationContainer here
}
```

`CreateAuthoringChildControls()` creates controls which will be displayed in authoring mode. Like the `CreatePresentationChildControls()` method, it accepts a `BaseModeContainer` object (`authoringContainer`) that acts as the container for controls that are seen and used by authors.

```
protected override void CreateAuthoringChildControls(BaseModeContainer
authoringContainer)
{
    //add code to load controls into the authoringContainer here
}
```

Methods for Loading Placeholder Content

`LoadPlaceholderContentForPresentation()` populates the placeholder control with content that would be seen in presentation mode.

```
protected override void
LoadPlaceholderContentForPresentation(PlaceholderControlEventArgs e)
{
    //add code to load content to the controls in presentation mode
}
```

The input parameter, `PlaceholderControlEventArgs`, has a single property:

- `Posting`, which returns the posting that is currently being saved

`LoadPlaceholderContentForAuthoring()` populates the placeholder control with content that would be seen by authors in authoring mode.

```
protected override void
LoadPlaceholderContentForAuthoring(PlaceholderControlEventArgs e)
{
    //add code to load content to the controls in authoring mode
}
```

Method for Saving Placeholder Content

`SavePlaceholderContent()` is the method used to write the content in the placeholder control to the repository.

```
protected override void
SavePlaceholderContent(PlaceholderControlSaveEventArgs e)
{
    //add code to save content from placeholders to the repository
}
```

The input parameter, `PlaceholderControlSaveEventArgs`, has two properties:

- `Posting` returns the posting that is currently being saved.

- `IsTemporarySaveForPreview` is a Boolean that returns a value `true` when the content is being saved because the user has clicked on the Preview button, and `false` when the content is saved permanently to the database. It is usually used when your code has to perform certain actions on preview. For example, you may need to store the placeholder content of the posting in an external database for indexing when the posting is saved. You typically won't need to do this for a temporary save when the author previews the posting.

All five methods need to be implemented in a custom placeholder control that inherits from the `BasePlaceholderControl` class. Otherwise the project will not compile.

Building a Single-Line TextBox Placeholder Control

Let's begin by creating a really simple placeholder control from scratch. It's easiest to start with a control based on a familiar web page element: the single-line `TextBox` placeholder control.

You could simulate the creation of a single-line text box by setting the `HtmlPlaceholder` to not allow any formatting, line breaks, images, or hyperlinks. Then you would end up with a control that looks like this:

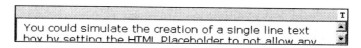

The problem begins when the text grows beyond the width of the control. Text starts to wrap and the control behaves more like a `TextArea` than a single-line `TextBox` control. Another problem with this approach is that you can't set the maximum length of acceptable text. Authors can add as much content as they like, which is not always a good thing.

To tackle these problems, we will build a custom placeholder control that appears as a single-line `TextBox` when in authoring mode. The `TextBox` will limit the number of characters an author can enter by having its `MaxLength` property set.

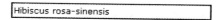

In presentation mode, it appears as a `Label` displaying contents saved to the repository:

Hibiscus rosa-sinensis

Creating the TextBoxPlaceholderControl Class

To begin, right-click the TropicalGreenControlLib project in Solution Explorer. Select the Add | Add Class option. Name the new class file `TextBoxPlaceholderControl.cs`.

Add the following namespaces above the `TropicalGreenControlLib` namespace declaration.

```
using System;
using System.Web.UI.WebControls;
using Microsoft.ContentManagement.Publishing;
using Microsoft.ContentManagement.Publishing.Extensions.Placeholders;
```

```
using Microsoft.ContentManagement.WebControls;
using Microsoft.ContentManagement.WebControls.Design;

namespace TropicalGreenControlLib
{
    . . . code continues. . .
}
```

Inheriting from the BasePlaceholderControl Class

Get the TextBoxPlaceholderControl class to inherit from the BasePlaceholderControl class by adding a colon followed by the BasePlaceholderControl class name.

```
public class TextBoxPlaceholderControl : BasePlaceholderControl
{
    . . . code continues . . .
}
```

In order for the control to compile at this stage, we need to add empty implementations for five methods of the BasePlaceholderControl class. Add the following code after the TextBoxPlaceholderControl() constructor:

```
protected override void CreateAuthoringChildControls(BaseModeContainer
                                                      authoringContainer)
{
}

protected override void CreatePresentationChildControls(BaseModeContainer
                                                         presentationContainer)
{
}

protected override void
LoadPlaceholderContentForAuthoring(PlaceholderControlEventArgs e)
{
}

protected override void
LoadPlaceholderContentForPresentation(PlaceholderControlEventArgs e)
{
}

protected override void SavePlaceholderContent(
                                PlaceholderControlSaveEventArgs e)
{
}
```

The code now compiles without errors. However, it does not do much of anything yet!

Next, we will declare the variables for holding references to controls that are loaded in both authoring and presentation mode.

In authoring mode, we will display a single-line TextBox control where authors can enter up to 100 characters of text. This TextBox control is referenced by the editTextBox variable. The maxLength variable stores the maximum number of characters the TextBox control will hold and the MaxLength property allows developers to get and set its value.

In presentation mode, the content stored in the placeholder will be shown in a Label control. For this purpose, we will declare a presentationLabel variable, which holds the reference to the Label control.

Insert the following code below the TextBoxPlaceholderControl() constructor:

```
private TextBox editTextBox;
private Label presentationLabel;

private int maxLength;
public int MaxLength
{
    get { return maxLength; }
    set { maxLength = value; }
}
```

Set maxLength to have a default value of 100 in the TextBoxPlaceholderControl() constructor.

```
public TextBoxPlaceholderControl()
{
    //
    // TODO: Add constructor logic here
    //

    //set the default maximum number of characters allowed in the TextBox
    maxLength = 100;
}
```

Specifying the Supported Placeholder Definition Type

The SupportedPlaceholderDefinitionType class specifies the placeholder definition type that the placeholder control supports and is used by the PlaceholderToBind property in the Properties window of the control in Visual Studio .NET. When template designers expand the dropdown associated with the PlaceholderToBind property, it shows list of placeholders of the specified SupportedPlaceholderDefinitionType.

We would like the single-line TextBox custom placeholder control to support placeholders that are based on the HtmlPlaceholderDefinition. To do so, add the type attribute above the class declaration:

```
[SupportedPlaceholderDefinitionType( typeof(HtmlPlaceholderDefinition) )]
public class TextBoxPlaceholderControl : BasePlaceholderControl
{
    . . . code continues . . .
}
```

It's a good idea to associate your custom placeholder control with its supported type. Leaving it out gives template designers the ability to select any placeholder defined in the template. For example, if we have left out that line of code, template designers will see all placeholders defined for the template regardless of their placeholder definition types. They may accidentally pick an AttachmentPlaceholder instead of an HtmlPlaceholder. When that happens, authors are going to hit errors as they attempt to save HTML content to an AttachmentPlaceholder.

Implementing the CreateAuthoringChildControls() Method

To create the TextBox for authoring, add editTextBox to the authoring container in the CreateAuthoringChildControls() method using the following code. We shall first create a new instance of the TextBox control class and set its properties. The last line adds editTextBox to the authoring container.

```
protected override void CreateAuthoringChildControls(BaseModeContainer
                                                     authoringContainer)
{
```

```
editTextBox = new TextBox();
editTextBox.Width = base.Width;
editTextBox.TextMode = TextBoxMode.SingleLine;
editTextBox.CssClass = base.CssClass;
editTextBox.MaxLength = maxLength;
authoringContainer.Controls.Add(editTextBox);
}
```

Implementing the LoadPlaceholderForAuthoring() Method

Next, we will load editTextBox with content stored in the repository. The
LoadPlaceholderContentForAuthoring() method decides which content gets displayed in the
TextBox. We want to read the content of the HtmlPlaceholder that is bound to the current
placeholder control instance and write it to our TextBox child control. To do this, modify the
LoadPlaceholderContentForAuthoring() method as follows:

```
protected override void
LoadPlaceholderContentForAuthoring(PlaceholderControlEventArgs e)
{
    EnsureChildControls();
    editTextBox.Text = ((HtmlPlaceholder)this.BoundPlaceholder).Html;
}
```

This first calls the EnsureChildControls() method, guaranteeing that the TextBox control has
been created before we write content to it. If we skip this, we could end up with errors if the
LoadPlaceholderContentForAuthoring() method attempts to write to a control that has not yet
been created.

Next, the content in the repository is read from the HtmlPlaceholder bound to the current
placeholder control and written to the TextBox control. The second line in the above snippet does
this for us:

```
editTextBox.Text = ((HtmlPlaceholder)this.BoundPlaceholder).Html;
```

this.BoundPlaceholder returns a reference to the placeholder defined in the PlaceholderToBind
property of the placeholder control, which we will set later when we add the control to the
template file. Because we know that we are definitely working with an HtmlPlaceholder object
(the SupportedPlaceholderDefinitionType was set to only allow associations to
HtmlPlaceholder), we will cast it as such and use the Html property to get its contents.

Implementing the SavePlaceholderContent() Method

To write the content back to the repository we need the code for our SavePlaceholderContent()
method. The SavePlaceholderContent() method takes the value entered by authors in the
textbox control and writes it into the repository when the page is saved. Modify the
SavePlaceholderContent() method as follows:

```
protected override void
            SavePlaceholderContent(PlaceholderControlSaveEventArgs e)
{
    EnsureChildControls();
    ((HtmlPlaceholder)this.BoundPlaceholder).Html = editTextBox.Text;
}
```

Again, we call the EnsureChildControls() method to guarantee that the TextBox control has
been created. Once we get the contents of the TextBox, we write it back to the HtmlPlaceholder
the control is bound to.

> If we stopped here and did not implement the remaining methods, we would have created a write-only placeholder control that appears only in authoring view and not in presentation view.

Implementing the CreatePresentationChildControls() Method

As discussed before, the `CreatePresentationChildControls()` method allows us to add controls to the `presentationContainer` collection. All controls added to this collection will be displayed when the posting is in presentation mode. Modify the `CreatePresentationChildControls()` method to create a new `Label`, set its `CssClass` property, and add it to the presentation container:

```
protected override void CreatePresentationChildControls(BaseModeContainer
                                                         presentationContainer)
{
    presentationLabel = new Label();
    presentationLabel.CssClass = base.CssClass;
    presentationContainer.Controls.Add(presentationLabel);
}
```

Implementing the LoadPlaceholderContentForPresentation() Method

The `LoadPlaceholderContentForPresentation()` method has to fill the `Label` with the content that was stored in the MCMS content repository for the `HtmlPlaceholder`. We will first call the `EnsureChildControls()` method to ensure that the `Label` control has been completely loaded by the form before assigning values to it. Next, we will get the contents stored in the `HtmlPlaceholder` and assign it to the `Text` property of the `Label` control. Modify the `LoadPlaceholderContentForPresentation()` method as shown below:

```
protected override void
LoadPlaceholderContentForPresentation(PlaceholderControlEventArgs e)
{
    EnsureChildControls();
    presentationLabel.Text = ((HtmlPlaceholder)this.BoundPlaceholder).Html;
}
```

We have completed the `TextBoxPlaceholderControl` class. Save and build the solution. Before we can use it, we need to add the `TextBoxPlaceholderControl` to the Toolbox.

Adding the Custom Control to the Toolbox

The Toolbox may show different tabs depending on which view you are currently looking at and the configuration settings of Visual Studio .NET. Open any web form or template file (for example, `Plant.aspx`) and switch to Design view.

> You can also right-click anywhere within the Toolbox and select Show All Tabs to display all tabs regardless of the view you are working on.

To add the `TextBoxPlaceholderControl` to the Toolbox:

1. In the Toolbox, right-click the toolbar and select Add Tab.
2. Name the new tab TropicalGreen Controls.

3. In the Toolbox, right-click the TropicalGreen Controls tab and select **Add/Remove Items** in the pop-up menu (or **Customize Toolbox...** if you are working with Visual Studio .NET 2002).

4. In the Customize Toolbox dialog, click the **.NET Framework Components** tab. Click Browse and browse to: `<Project Path>/TropicalGreenControlLib/bin/Debug/ TropicalGreenControlLib.dll`.

5. Click Open to add the control.

6. Click OK to close the Customize Toolbox dialog.

You should see a little control appear in the Toolbox as shown below.

Adding an HtmlPlaceholderDefinition

Before we add the `TextBoxPlaceholderControl` to the Plant template file, we need to add a new `HtmlPlaceholderDefinition` to the Plant template object.

Using the MCMS Template Explorer, check out the Plant template object and add a new `HtmlPlaceholderDefinition` with the following property values (see Chapters 6 and 7 if you forgot how to edit the Plant template object):

Property	Value
Type	HtmlPlaceholderDefinition
AllowHyperLinks	false
AllowLineBreaks	false
Formatting	NoFormatting
Description	Enter the plant's scientific name
Name	ScientificName
AllowAttachments	false
AllowImages	false
MustUseResourceGallery	false
UseGeneratedIcon	false

Be sure to commit the changes to the repository by saving the Plant template (right-click the template and select **Save**) when you have added the new definition. Keep the template checked out for the moment.

Adding the Textbox Placeholder Control to the Plant Template File

Once the `TextBoxPlaceholderControl` has been added to the Toolbox, you can add it to template files by dragging and dropping it.

Let's do this now for the Plant template file:

1. Open `Plant.aspx`.
2. Switch to Design view.
3. Drag and drop the `TextBoxPlaceholderControl` onto the form, below the `PlantCommonName` Literal control. Set the properties of the control to:

Property	Value
CssClass	BodyText
PlaceholderToBind	ScientificName
Width	300px
Font-Italic	true
ID	PlantScientificName

4. Save `Plant.aspx` and build the TropicalGreen solution.

Test the new `TextboxPlaceholderControl` by editing any of the plant fact sheets that are based on the Plant template. If everything goes smoothly, you should get a single-line `TextBox` control in authoring mode as shown in the diagram below:

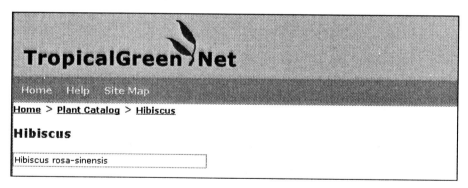

The `TextBox` does not allow you to enter more than 100 characters, and it changes to a `Label` in presentation mode:

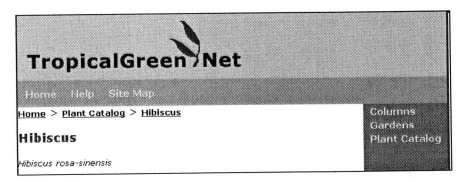

Populating a Custom Control with Default Content

Instead of showing an empty TextBox when a page is created, you may add a default value. This is especially useful when you want to give authors an indication of what should be entered in the box.

You see this at work when you work with the default HtmlPlaceholderControl. When a new posting is created, the initial content of the HtmlPlaceholderControl is the value entered in the Description property of its corresponding HtmlPlaceholderDefinition.

To populate a custom placeholder control with a default value, we need to implement the OnPopupulatingDefaultContent() method. This method is not required for the code to compile and is called just once: when the posting is created using the **Create New Page** console action.

Add the following code within the class declaration of TextboxPlaceholderControl.cs, below the SavePlaceholderContent() method.

```
protected override void
OnPopulatingDefaultContent(PlaceholderControlCancelEventArgs e)
{
    string description;
    description =
        ((HtmlPlaceholder)this.BoundPlaceholder).Definition.Description;
    editTextBox.Text = description;
}
```

The code populates the TextBox with the value of the Description property from the placeholder definition when a new posting is created. OnPopulatingDefaultContent() is called only when the posting is new. When the posting is opened for re-editing, the method is not called again.

Save and build the solution. When you next create a new posting based on the Plant template, you will see that the `TextBoxPlaceholder` control contains default text:

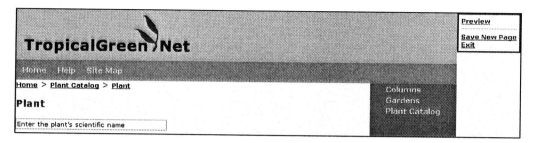

Deriving from the MCMS Placeholder Controls

Was building the `TextBoxPlaceholderControl` a lot of work? You bet it was. You wrote lines and lines of code just to add a `TextBox` in authoring mode and a `Label` in presentation mode.

What if you just wanted to modify the way an existing placeholder control works? For example, perhaps you simply wanted to add a property that sets the alignment of an image inserted in the `SingleImagePlaceholderControl`. Would you like to create your own version of the `SingleImagePlaceholderControl` from scratch? That would work but most developers would prefer not to.

Fortunately, those nice people at Microsoft did not seal the `SingleImagePlaceholderControl` class, and we can inherit directly from it. When we do, we immediately get all the features already built into it. All we need to do is to modify the parts we want to enhance.

> The example that follows uses the `SingleImagePlaceholderControl` class. You can also create variations of the `SingleAttachmentPlaceholderControl` and the `HtmlPlaceholderControl` by inheriting their classes in your code.

In this example, we will be creating the `AlignedImagePlaceholderControl`, a version of the `SingleImagePlaceholderControl`, with an additional `ImageAlignment` property that provides developers with the option of setting the `align` attribute of the image, as shown in the screenshot.

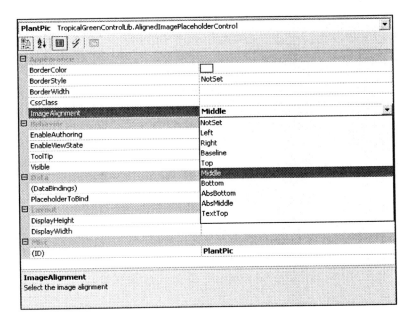

The default behavior for images is that text is aligned to the bottom of the image, like this:

This is a plant

If you would like the text to be aligned with the top or middle of the image, you need to set the `align` attribute of the rendered `<img>` tag.

In order to do this, we will replace the `SingleImagePlaceholderControl` that was used for the `PlantPicture` placeholder earlier on with the new `AlignedImagePlaceholderControl`.

Building the AlignedImagePlaceholderControl

Add a new class file to the TropicalGreenControlLib Project. Name the new class file `AlignedImagePlaceholderControl.cs`.

At the top of the namespace declaration, import the namespaces of the classes we need.

```
using System;
using System.IO;
```

```
using System.Web.UI.WebControls;
using System.ComponentModel;
using Microsoft.ContentManagement.Publishing;
using Microsoft.ContentManagement.Publishing.Extensions.Placeholders;
using Microsoft.ContentManagement.WebControls.Design;
using Microsoft.ContentManagement.WebControls;

namespace TropicalGreenControlLib
{
    /// <summary>
    /// Summary description for AlignedImagePlaceholderControl.
    /// </summary>
    public class AlignedImagePlaceholderControl
    {
        public AlignedImagePlaceholderControl ()
        {
            //
            // TODO: Add constructor logic here
            //
        }
    }
}
```

Inherit from the `AlignedImagePlaceholderControl` class (not from the `BasePlaceholderControl` class!).

```
public class AutoCssPlaceholderControl : SingleImagePlaceholderControl
{
    public AlignedImagePlaceholderControl()
    {
        //
        // TODO: Add constructor logic here
        //
    }
}
```

If you used your control as it is now, you'd get nothing more than another copy of the `SingleImagePlaceholderControl`.

Next, we will add a public property called `ImageAlignment` and a corresponding private variable `imageAlignment`. The public property will be used by developers to set the alignment of the image. The private variable `imageAlignment` is assigned an initial value of `NotSet` and is used by the public property within its get and set accessors. Add the `ImageAlignment` public property directly below the `AlignedImagePlaceholderControl()` constructor.

```
private ImageAlign imageAlignment = ImageAlign.NotSet;

[Bindable(true)]
[Category("Appearance")]
[Description("Select the image alignment")]
public ImageAlign ImageAlignment
{
    get
    {
        return imageAlignment;
    }
    set
    {
        imageAlignment = value;
    }
}
```

Now that we have formulated a way for developers to specify the image alignment, we need to apply this property value to the image itself. When displayed on a posting, the image is rendered as follows:

```
<img src="myimage.jpg">
```

What we need to do is to insert the align attribute like this:

```
<img src="myimage.jpg" align="middle">
```

We will do this by overriding the base Render() method. We first check to see that the code is running in one of the presentation modes: published, authoring preview, unpublished, and unpublished preview (in the other modes, we just display whatever the SingleImagePlaceholderControl renders, which is essentially the box for uploading the image). Next, we capture the original output of the SingleImagePlaceholderControl by calling the base Render() method. Following which, we inject the align attribute and its value into the <img> tag. Finally, the modified content is written back to the page.

Add the overridden Render() method directly below the ImageAlign public property.

```
protected override void Render(System.Web.UI.HtmlTextWriter output)
{
if ((WebAuthorContext.Current.Mode ==
        WebAuthorContextMode.PresentationPublished) ||
    (WebAuthorContext.Current.Mode == WebAuthorContextMode.AuthoringPreview) ||
    (WebAuthorContext.Current.Mode ==
        WebAuthorContextMode.PresentationUnpublished) ||
    (WebAuthorContext.Current.Mode ==
        WebAuthorContextMode.PresentationUnpublishedPreview))
    {
    //Get the output of the original SingleImagePlaceholderControl's
    // Render method
    TextWriter tempWriter = new StringWriter();
    base.Render(new System.Web.UI.HtmlTextWriter(tempWriter));

    //Use standard string manipulation to insert the new attribute
    string orightml= tempWriter.ToString();
    string newhtml;
    newhtml = orightml.Replace("<img ","<img align="+imageAlignment.ToString()
                                                                +" ");

    output.Write(newhtml);
    }
    else
    {
        base.Render(output);
    }
}
```

The AlignedImagePlaceholderControl class is complete. You do not have to implement the other methods as these have already been created within the parent SingleImagePlaceholderControl class. Save and build the TropicalGreen solution.

Adding the AlignedImagePlaceholderControl to the Plant Template File

Add the AlignedImagePlaceholderControl to the Toolbox following the steps we used earlier in the chapter. Drag and drop it to the Plant.aspx template file, below the PlantPicture placeholder control. Delete the `PlantPicture` placeholder control. Give the `AlignedImagePlaceholderControl` the following property values.

Property	Value
ID	PlantPic
PlaceholderToBind	PlantPicture
ImageAlignment	Middle

Place some text before the `AlignedImagePlaceholderControl`. The image must be placed next to text for you to see the effects of adding the `align` attribute. Add the words This is a picture before the control as shown below.

Save the Plant template file and build the solution.

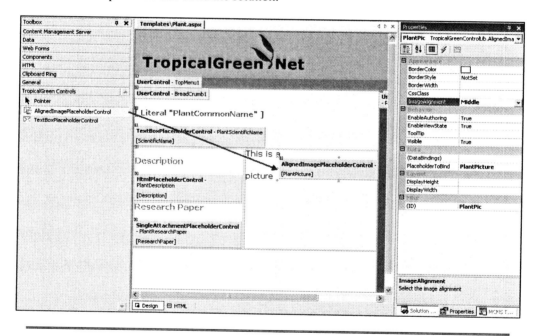

Duplicate controls appearing in your Toolbox? That means that you have added different versions of the controls.

To remove the duplicate entries:

1. Right-click within the TropicalGreen Component tab and select Add/Remove Items.
2. In the Customize Toolbox dialog, select the .NET Framework Components tab. Sort the components list by Namespace.
3. Scroll down the list till you find the TropicalGreenControlLib Namespace.

4. If you expand the Assembly Name field, you will find a set of controls that have an older version number. Uncheck those controls to remove them from the list.

5. Click OK to close the Customize Toolbox dialog.

The duplicate entries are removed!

You can prevent duplicate entries from appearing within your Toolbox by manually setting the version of the TropicalGreenControlLibrary library within the AssemblyInfo.cs class. Just fill in (or remove) the * in the statement:

```
[assembly: AssemblyVersion("1.0.*")]
```

Open an existing plant fact sheet that has a picture, like the Hibiscus fact sheet. Notice that the paragraph now appears in the middle of the image instead of at the bottom. That's because we have set the ImageAlignment property of its AlignedImagePlaceholderControl to middle.

Wrapping up the AlignedImagePlaceholderControl

Now that we have seen how the ImageAlignment property of the AlignedImagePlaceholderControl works, we have no need for the additional text that we placed next to the PlantPicture placeholder earlier. Delete any text that you have typed into the template file. In our case, we will simply delete the words This is a picture.

Using PresentationTemplates

We are going to show you a secret feature of MCMS that provides an even faster way to prototype custom placeholder controls. The secret is—PresentationTemplates.

Well, it is not quite a secret. The feature was built into the product towards the end of the development cycle. As a result, the documentation team was not able to write much about it before the product shipped, so very little is known about it until now. With PresentationTemplates, you can determine the way content is displayed in presentation mode. Let's look at how you could use PresentationTemplates for the SingleAttachmentPlaceholderControl.

> PresentationTemplates can only be used with the
> SingleAttachmentPlaceholderControl and the SingleImagePlaceholderControl.

For example, you may need to customize the SingleAttachmentPlaceholderControl to display Flash content. Flash is a common format used by web designers to display high-impact animation. An author who uploads a Flash file expects the animation to be played on the browser when visitors view the page. The AttachmentPlaceholderControl usually will not do this. Left to its own, it simply displays a hyperlink to the Flash file.

MyFlash.swf

To play Flash animation on the browser, you need to use the Flash plug-in developed by Macromedia. The HTML code that needs to be embedded in the page sent to the browser is:

```
<object classid="clsid:d27cdb6e-ae6d-11cf-96b8-444553540000"
  codebase="http://fpdownload.macromedia.com/pub/shockwave/cabs/flash/
                                                  swflash.cab
  #version=7,0,0,0" width="200" height="200"
  id="MyFlash" align="middle" VIEWASTEXT>

  <param name="allowScriptAccess" value="sameDomain" />
  <param name="movie" value="MyFlash.swf" />
  <param name="quality" value="high" />
  <param name="bgcolor" value="#ffffff" />
  <embed src="MyFlash.swf" quality="high" bgcolor="#ffffff"
      width="200" height="200" name="MyFlash" align="middle"
      allowScriptAccess="sameDomain" type="application/x-shockwave-flash"
      pluginspage="http://www.macromedia.com/go/getflashplayer" />
</object>
```

You could render the HTML by creating a custom placeholder that derives from the SingleAttachmentPlaceholderControl and overrides the CreatePresentationChildControls() and LoadPlaceholderContentforPresentation() methods. That would work, but you can achieve the same results without programming by using PresentationTemplates.

Building a Presentation Template for Flash Content

To begin, in the MCMS Template Explorer, add an AttachmentPlaceholderDefinition to the Plant template object with the following properties:

Property	Value
Type	AttachmentPlaceholderDefinition
Name	Flash
MustUseResourceGallery	False
UseGeneratedIcon	False

Make sure to save the Plant template object by right-clicking the object and selecting **Save** in the Template Explorer. Keep the object checked out for the moment.

Open the `Plant.aspx` template file in Design view. Drag and drop a `SingleAttachmentPlaceholderControl` onto the template file, below the `PlantPicture` placeholder. Set the properties of the `SingleAttachmentPlaceholderControl` to:

Property	Value
ID	FlashPH
PlaceholderToBind	Flash

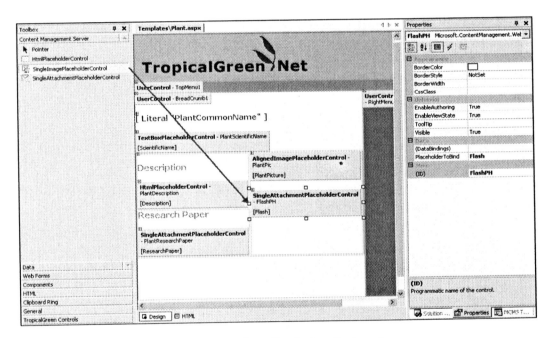

Switch to HTML view and scroll to the section of code that displays the `SingleAttachmentPlaceholderControl`. You should see code as shown below.

```
<cms:SingleAttachmentPlaceholderControl id="FlashPH" runat="server"
PlaceholderToBind="Flash">
</cms:SingleAttachmentPlaceholderControl>
```

There isn't anything unusual about these lines of code, it's the usual code used to render the `SingleAttachmentPlaceholderControl`.

Here's when it starts to get interesting. Insert the following lines of code between the opening and closing tags of the `<cms:SingleAttachmentPlaceholderControl>`. We will use `<PresentationTemplate>` tags to define how the attachment is displayed in presentation mode.

```
<cms:SingleAttachmentPlaceholderControl id="FlashPH" runat="server"
PlaceholderToBind="Flash">
    <PresentationTemplate>
```

```
<object classid="clsid:d27cdb6e-ae6d-11cf-96b8-444553540000"
codebase=
"http://fpdownload.macromedia.com/pub/shockwave/cabs/flash/swflash.cab
#version=7,0,0,0" width="200" height="200"
id="MyFlash" align="middle" VIEWASTEXT>

<param name="allowScriptAccess" value="sameDomain" />
<param name="movie" value="<%# Container.AttachmentUrl %>" />
<param name="quality" value="high" />
<param name="bgcolor" value="#ffffff" />
<embed src="<%# Container.AttachmentUrl %>" quality="high"
    bgcolor="#ffffff" width="200" height="200" name="MyFlash"
    align="middle" allowScriptAccess="sameDomain"
    type="application/x-shockwave-flash"
    pluginspage="http://www.macromedia.com/go/getflashplayer" />
</object>
</PresentationTemplate>
</cms:SingleAttachmentPlaceholderControl>
```

The control is complete. Save your work.

> One of the advantages of using this method is that you don't have to build the solution because you did not add any files or make any changes to the code-behind files.

When the control is displayed in presentation mode, the content between the `<PresentationTemplate>` tags is rendered. In other modes, like authoring, the content is ignored. Edit the posting; you should see the regular `SingleAttachmentPlaceholderControl` as shown below. Upload a Flash file into the Attachment Placeholder. You can download a sample Flash file (`MyFlash.swf`) from the code download section of the book's companion website.

When in presentation mode, instead of showing the link to the file, the Flash movie is played.

The `PresentationTemplate` uses the notation `<%# Container.AttachmentUrl %>` to access the `AttachmentUrl` property of the `AttachmentPlaceholderControl` and render it inside the custom presentation-mode code of the placeholder control. You can use the same method to access the properties shown in the following table. The `PlaceholderControl` property is used to access the `AttachmentPlaceholder` object itself, allowing access to all other properties and methods of this placeholder control.

Placeholder Control	Property Name
`SingleAttachmentPlaceholderControl`	`AttachmentText`
	`AttachmentUrl`
	`PlaceholderControl`
`SingleImagePlaceholderControl`	`AlternateText`
	`DisplayHeight`
	`DisplayWidth`
	`ImageUrl`
	`NavigateUrl`
	`PlaceholderControl`

The `PresentationTemplate` tags get your control up and running in the shortest possible time. However, if you are planning to use the control on more than one template, it would be a better idea to build a custom placeholder control, rather than duplicating the code all over the place, which makes it more difficult to maintain later.

Creating Custom Placeholder Controls for the XmlPlaceholder

`XmlPlaceholder` is another placeholder type that comes with MCMS we haven't yet worked with.

In traditional web development in HTML, formatting is mixed together with content. For example, by displaying a table we could show the zones that a certain plant thrives in.

```
<table>
    <th>Where the Plant can be Grown</th>
    <tr>
        <td>Zone 10</td>
    </tr>
    <tr>
        <td>Zone 11</td>
    </tr>
</table>
```

Plant fact: Have you seen a live cactus in Antarctica? Or a banana tree in Iceland? Tropical plants love the sun. Gardeners grow their plants according to the Hardiness Zone Map (`www.usna.usda.gov/Hardzone/`) developed by the United States Department of Agriculture. The map divides the world into different zones. Based on this map, gardeners can find out which plant types grow best in the zone they live in.

In our example, our plant grows in zone 10 (Florida, California) and zone 11 (Hawaii and Mexico).

Given this HTML table, how would you extract the zones? Developers used to parse and extract information stored in HTML documents. To add to the confusion, the table is often embedded within the <body> tags of an HTML document that's littered with dozens of other tags. This onerous task was often known as screen-scraping. Developers still cringe at the thought of writing code to scrape documents. Well, that's history now. Today, we have XML.

XML is a markup language. It resembles HTML, but it focuses on the structure and relationships of data rather than how it looks. Here's the same piece of information represented as XML:

```
<Zones>
    <Zone>Zone 10</Zone>
    <Zone>Zone 11</Zone>
</Zones>
```

The <Zone> tags provide a structured way of marking zones 10 and 11. It's now clear to the computer how to retrieve the zoning information (just look for <zones> and everything between that is a <zone>).

By itself, XML does not do anything. If you tried displaying it on the browser, it would probably appear as text, angle brackets and all. We need to write code to understand and display it. That's easy to do. ASP.NET comes with native support for XML so we won't have to write our own parsers. You can find entire libraries supporting XML within the system.xml namespace.

> The best thing about XML is that it's platform independent. Any system that is capable of receiving text files or strings can work with XML. This makes XML particularly attractive for applications that require information flows between different systems.

XML provides an excellent way of separating data from content. You could store data as XML, then apply logic within the custom placeholder control to display it by means of transforms (written in the stylesheet language XSLT) or otherwise.

Properties of the Xml Placeholder Definition

The XmlPlaceholder object comes with an XmlPlaceholderDefinition that has the following properties:

Property	Description
Description	Holds a maximum of 500 characters. Does not show up anywhere in the out-of-the-box solution, but you can always use the API to retrieve this value for your own use. It's often used to describe what the placeholder is used for.
ManageCmsUrls	This property controls whether URLs pointing to an MCMS resource inside the XML structure should be automatically adjusted when the object is moved, expired, or deleted. If it is set to false, the URLs remain static and MCMS will not attempt to modify them.
	This feature was disabled in pre-SP1 releases of MCMS. It is only available after applying MCMS SP1 or SP1a (or above).
	Before SP1 the placeholder always behaved as if the value of this property was set to false.
Name	The name of the placeholder is also its identifier. It has to be unique within a placeholder definition collection in a template. Holds up to 100 characters. The naming restrictions described in Chapter 5 apply here as well.

Property	Description
CheckForValidity	When set to true, validates the contents of the Placeholder with the XML Schema specified in the XsdUrl property. Should the XML be invalid, an exception is raised and the error message is displayed on the Error Console when the page is saved.
CheckForWellFormedness	When set to true, checks that the XML content is well-formed: • All opened tags have an end tag. • Attributes are quoted e.g. `<a href="www.tropicalgreen.com"></a>`. • The XML document contains a single root element. Should the XML be malformed, an exception is raised and the error message is displayed on the Error Console when the page is saved.
XsdUrl	The path of the Xml Schema that is used to validate the placeholder's content when the CheckForValidity property is set to true. e.g.: `c\inetpub\wwwroot\tropicalgreen\MySchema.xsd`.

Building a CheckBoxListPlaceholderControl

MCMS does not ship with an XmlPlaceholderControl, so there is no control from which we could inherit and override methods as we have shown for the SingleImagePlaceholderControl. We have to create a custom placeholder by deriving from BasePlaceholderControl and implementing all necessary methods for authoring and presentation mode.

Since a plant may grow in more than one zone, a friendly way for authors to enter this information would be with a list of checkboxes as shown below. Authors mark the zones best suited for the plant by placing check marks within the boxes.

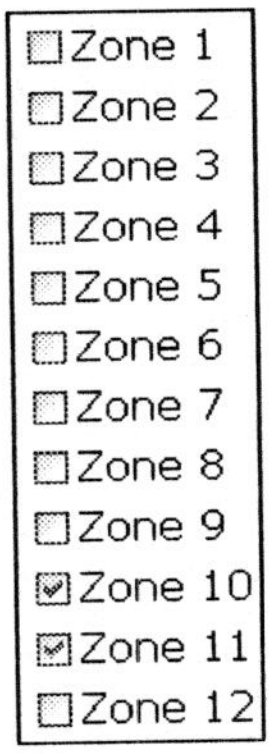

```
☐ Zone 1
☐ Zone 2
☐ Zone 3
☐ Zone 4
☐ Zone 5
☐ Zone 6
☐ Zone 7
☐ Zone 8
☐ Zone 9
☑ Zone 10
☑ Zone 11
☐ Zone 12
```

When the plant page is viewed by visitors, the list of zones is transformed into a table.

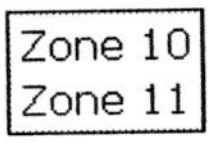

```
Zone 10
Zone 11
```

Behind the scenes, our control will store the information as XML. Here's what's being captured by the placeholder:

```
<Zones>
    <Zone>Zone 10</Zone>
    <Zone>Zone 11</Zone>
</Zones>
```

Let's create the `CheckBoxListPlaceholderControl`. We will first add a new class file to the `TropicalGreenControlLib` project and name it `CheckBoxListPlaceholderControl.cs`. Import the required namespaces of classes within the code above the namespace declaration of the class.

```
using System;
using System.Web.UI.WebControls;
using System.Xml;
using Microsoft.ContentManagement.Publishing;
using Microsoft.ContentManagement.Publishing.Extensions.Placeholders;
using Microsoft.ContentManagement.WebControls;
using Microsoft.ContentManagement.WebControls.Design;

namespace TropicalGreenControlLib
{
    . . . code continues . . .
}
```

Specify that the `CheckBoxListPlaceholderControl` supports only the `XmlPlaceholderDefinition` and inherits from the `BasePlaceholderControl` class.

```
[SupportedPlaceholderDefinitionType( typeof(XmlPlaceholderDefinition))]
public class CheckBoxListPlaceholderControl : BasePlaceholderControl
{
    . . . code continues . . .
}
```

Next, we will declare the two variables used throughout the class file:

- `zoneList` refers to the `CheckBoxList` that is shown in authoring mode.
- `tblZones` refers to the table presented to visitors in presentation mode.

Add the declarations above the `CheckBoxListPlaceholderControl` constructor.

```
//Authoring controls
CheckBoxList zoneList;

//Presentation controls
Table tblZones;

public CheckBoxListPlaceholderControl()
{
    //
    // TODO: Add constructor logic here
    //
}
```

In the `CreateAuthoringChildControls()` method, we will create a `CheckBoxList` object for authoring. We will add the `CheckBoxList` control to the `authoringContainer` so that it is displayed in authoring mode. Add the `CreateAuthoringChildControls()` method below the `CheckBoxListPlaceholderControl()` constructor.

```
protected override void CreateAuthoringChildControls(BaseModeContainer
                                                     authoringContainer)
{
    zoneList = new CheckBoxList();
    zoneList.CssClass = base.CssClass;
    BuildZoneList();
    authoringContainer.Controls.Add(zoneList);
}
```

The BuildZoneList() method function adds the twelve zones to the checkbox list control. We made it easy here and generated the choices for the CheckBoxList control by adding the word Zone to a counter. In a real-world scenario, you would probably have to retrieve the items from an external data source like an XML file or database table. Enter the BuildZoneList() method below the CreateAuthoringChildControls() method.

```
private void BuildZoneList()
{
    int zoneNumber;
    for(zoneNumber=1;zoneNumber<=12;zoneNumber++)
    {
        zoneList.Items.Add(new ListItem("Zone " + zoneNumber,
                                        "Zone " + zoneNumber));
    }
}
```

The LoadPlaceholderForAuthoring() method loads the CheckBoxList with content from the repository by retrieving the stored XML from the placeholder and looping through each node. If the value of the node matches that of a ListItem, we select it to indicate that the zone has been selected. Add the LoadPlaceholderForAuthoring() method below the CreateAuthoringChildControls() method.

```
protected override void
LoadPlaceholderContentForAuthoring(PlaceholderControlEventArgs e)
{
    EnsureChildControls();
    XmlDocument xmlZone = new XmlDocument();
    string xml;

    xml = ((XmlPlaceholder)this.BoundPlaceholder).XmlAsString;

    try
    {
        xmlZone.LoadXml(xml);
    }
    catch
    {
        xmlZone.LoadXml("<Zones></Zones>");
    }

    foreach(XmlNode zoneNode in xmlZone.DocumentElement.ChildNodes)
    {
        ListItem zone =zoneList.Items.FindByValue(zoneNode.InnerText);
        zone.Selected = true;
    }
}
```

The SavePlaceholderContent() method does the job of writing the content back to the repository on saving. It needs to add an XmlDocument object with a root element of <Zones>. For each zone marked by the author, an XML element (<zone>) is to be inserted into the XmlDocument. Add SavePlaceholderContent() method below LoadPlaceholderContentForAuthoring() method.

```
protected override void
SavePlaceholderContent(PlaceholderControlSaveEventArgs e)
{
    EnsureChildControls();

    XmlDocument xmlZone = new XmlDocument();
    XmlNode zoneParentNode = xmlZone.CreateElement("Zones");
    xmlZone.AppendChild(zoneParentNode);
    foreach(ListItem zone in zoneList.Items)
    {
        if(zone.Selected == true)
        {
            XmlNode zoneNode = xmlZone.CreateElement("Zone");
            zoneNode.InnerText = zone.Text;
            zoneParentNode.AppendChild(zoneNode);
        }
    }
    ((XmlPlaceholder)this.BoundPlaceholder).XmlAsString =
    xmlZone.InnerXml.ToString();
}
```

The CreatePresentationChildControls() method adds the zone table to the presentation container. Enter the CreatePresenationChildControls() method below the SavePlaceholderContent() method.

```
protected override void CreatePresentationChildControls(BaseModeContainer
                                                        presentationContainer)
{
    tblZones = new Table();
    tblZones.ID = "TblZones";
    tblZones.CssClass = base.CssClass;
    tblZones.BorderWidth = Unit.Pixel(1);
    presentationContainer.Controls.Add(tblZones);
}
```

The LoadPlaceholderContentForPresentation() method needs to loop through the XML collection and add a row to the zone table for each zone stored. Add the LoadPlaceholderContentForPresentation() method below the CreatePresentationChildControls() method.

```
protected override void
LoadPlaceholderContentForPresentation(PlaceholderControlEventArgs e)
{
    EnsureChildControls();

    XmlDocument xmlZone = new XmlDocument();
    string xml;
    xml = ((XmlPlaceholder)this.BoundPlaceholder).XmlAsString;
    if(xml.Length>0)
    {
        xmlZone.LoadXml(xml);
        foreach(XmlNode zoneNode in xmlZone.DocumentElement.ChildNodes)
        {
            TableRow row = new TableRow();
            TableCell cell = new TableCell();
            cell.Text = zoneNode.InnerText;
            row.Cells.Add(cell);
            tblZones.Rows.Add(row);
        }
    }
}
```

The Placeholder control is complete. Save CheckBoxListPlaceholder.cs and build the TropicalGreen solution.

Adding an XmlPlaceholderDefinition

Let's add the corresponding XmlPlaceholderDefinition to the Plant template to store the zone information.

Open the Properties page of the Plant template object in the MCMS Template Explorer and add an XmlPlaceholderDefinition. Give the new placeholder definition the following properties:

Property	Value
Type	XmlPlaceholderDefinition
Name	Zones
Description	Plant Zones
ManageCmsUrl	true
CheckForValidity	true
CheckForWellFormedness	true

When you are done, click OK to close the Placeholder Definition Editor and check in the Plant template (right-click and select Check In).

Testing the CheckBoxListPlaceholderControl

Add the CheckBoxListPlaceholderControl to the TropicalGreen Controls section of the Toolbox and drag and drop it onto the Plant.aspx template file, below the PlantDesription placeholder. Give it an ID of PlantZones and set the PlaceholderToBind property to Zones. Save Plant.aspx.

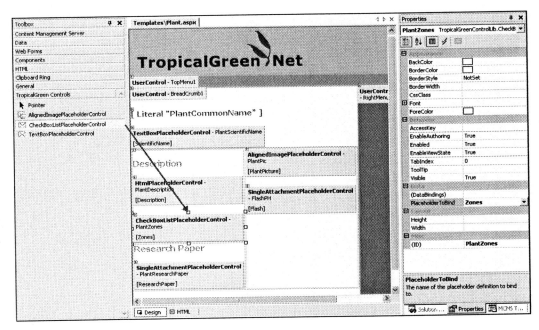

Edit any of the Plant fact sheets. Place a check mark against some zones. Save the page and see how the selected zones appear as a table in presentation mode.

Summary

Custom placeholder controls provide you with maximum flexibility in how your content is entered and stored. MCMS ships with only three placeholder controls (HtmlPlaceholderControl, SingleAttachmentPlaceholderControl, and SingleImagePlaceholderControl) but it provides you with the necessary tools to create your own customized controls. You can also download placeholder controls from the Internet and use them in your own projects.

In this chapter, we created a TextBoxPlaceholderControl by writing a control derived from the BasePlaceholderControl class.

Next, we explored how we could create a new placeholder that inherits the SingleImagePlaceholderControl class in order to apply alignment to our plant picture.

We also saw how quick prototyping of controls can be done when we derived from the SingleAttachmentPlaceholderControl to make a Flash movie appear in a posting.

Finally, we created our first XML placeholder control, a CheckBoxListPlaceholderControl, and saw how XML can be entered, stored, and retrieved from XmlPlaceholders.

Building Custom Placeholder Definitions and Placeholders

Customization does not stop at placeholder controls. You can change the way content is defined, stored, and retrieved by creating your own custom placeholder and placeholder definition classes.

We explored the placeholder definitions that ship with MCMS in Chapter 7 and saw how they are used to provide a set of rules to constrain the format of content that gets saved to the content repository. For example, the Formatting property of the HtmlPlaceholderDefinition can be set to NoFormatting to ensure that the content does not contain any block or in-line HTML tags.

Every placeholder definition has a corresponding placeholder class so, when creating your own placeholder definition, you must build a placeholder class to pair with it. A placeholder object based on this class provides a logical representation of the content and is used within code to retrieve/save data in the MCMS repository. An example of this is the standard HtmlPlaceholder. Using the HtmlPlaceholder object, we can get or set the Html property value of a specific posting through code.

In this chapter, we will create a custom placeholder definition/placeholder pair, called the HtmlStrippingPlaceholderDefinition and HtmlStrippingPlaceholder respectively. Together, they behave somewhat like the HtmlPlaceholderDefinition/HtmlPlaceholder pair. Our custom placeholder definition will be used to filter HTML tags. However, instead of using the Formatting property that uses a pre-defined collection of tags, it will have its own Tags property where developers can specify the tags to be included in or excluded from the placeholder content.

Why Build Custom Placeholder Definitions?

The standard placeholder definition and placeholder classes are usually sufficient to cater for most kinds of content ranging from HTML to XML. Usually, you would not need to write your own custom placeholder definition/placeholder pair.

Even if you do find a situation where you may need to modify the properties and attributes of the placeholder, customizing the placeholder control to massage the data as authors save or retrieve content for display would usually suffice.

The choice of implementation is yours. Generally it is more common to find solutions based on custom placeholder controls as they are easier to build and distribute than custom placeholder definitions and placeholders.

Consider writing a custom placeholder definition and/or placeholder when you want to:

- Expand or change the list of constraints and properties of the basic placeholder definitions that ship with the product
- Provide an API that includes the business logic to retrieve and save the content in placeholders

Before We Begin

We will create a new project to hold the placeholder definition classes built in this chapter.

> Classes for custom placeholder controls and custom placeholder definitions should not be compiled into the same DLL.

In the TropicalGreen solution, create a new Visual C# Project using the Class Library template. Name the new Project TropicalGreenPlaceholderDefinition. Set the location to a suitable folder on your disk e.g. c:\. Delete the file class1.cs, which was added by the wizard. We will not be using this file.

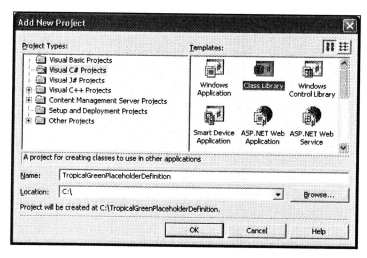

Adding the Required References to the Project

In Solution Explorer, right-click on the References tab of the new project and select Add Reference. Click Browse... and add the following library files:

- `Microsoft.ContentManagement.Common.dll`
- `Microsoft.ContentManagement.Publishing.dll`

The library files are in the `\server\bin\` directory under your MCMS installation folder.

Setting the Version of the Project

Later, we will be adding the `TropicalGreenPlaceholderDefinition.dll` file to the global assembly cache (required for custom placeholder definitions). To prevent the version number from increasing with each build, open `AssemblyInfo.cs` and set the Assembly Version to 1.0.0.0:

```
[assembly: AssemblyVersion("1.0.0.0")]
```

Save and close the `AssemblyInfo.cs` file.

The reason for fixing the version is to ensure that when rebuilding the project later, the version number does not change. We want to avoid having problems registering multiple versions of the library in the global assembly cache.

The HtmlStrippingPlaceholderDefinition / HtmlStrippingPlaceholder Pair

Imagine the situation where you needed to allow authors to work with `<table>` tags and to do so you set the `Formatting` property of the `HtmlPlaceholderDefinition` to `FullFormatting`.

The authors were happy. They could now apply almost all kinds of tags without any restrictions. Some chose to use orange fonts by using `<font color=orange>` tags instead of the black headings defined in the main stylesheet. Others merrily copied formatted text from Word documents into the `HtmlPlaceholderControl`. Someone even ventured a `<marquee>` tag.

The look and feel of each page strayed further and further from the predefined stylesheet. Editors and moderators got called for an explanation on how the dozens of unapproved styles and colors were finding their way into the pages.

The problem is that the standard `HtmlPlaceholderDefinition`/`HtmlPlaceholder` pair can't allow `<table>` tags but disable `<font>` and other tags that mess up the look and feel of the page.

What you need is a custom `HtmlStrippingPlaceholderDefinition`. One that has a property that allows you to set a list of allowed tags so that all tags not found in the list are stripped away from the content when saved. For example, you could specify `<table>`, `<tr>`, `<td>`, and `<b>` as allowed tags. Thus, when the following content is entered into the placeholder the `<font>` tag is stripped away when the content is saved, leaving the other tags in place:

```
<table>
<tr>
    <td>
        <b>
            <FONT color=red face="Times New Roman">
            Your local plant nursery.
            </FONT>
        </b>
    </td>
</tr>
```

```
</table>
```

This results in:

```
<table>
<tr>
    <td>
        <b>
            Your local plant nursery.
        </b>
    </td>
</tr>
</table>
```

> Like just about all programming tasks, there are many ways to solve this problem. In this case, you could also write a custom placeholder control (Chapter 14) or a workflow extension (Chapter 16) to remove all unwanted tags when the content is saved.

The HtmlStrippingPlaceholderDefinition

Add a new class file to the TropicalGreenPlaceholderDefinition project. Name the new class file HtmlStrippingPlaceholderDefinition.cs.

Import the namespaces for the classes used within the code above the namespace declaration:

```
using System;
using Microsoft.ContentManagement.Publishing;
```

Note the namespace declaration, TropicalGreenPlaceholderDefinition. We will need to use this later when adding the assembly to the **Global Assembly Cache (GAC)**.

The PlaceholderDefinition base class will be the starting point for most custom placeholder definitions. To inherit from it, add a colon followed by PlaceholderDefinition after the HtmlStrippingPlaceholderDefinition class declaration.

```
namespace TropicalGreenPlaceholderDefinition
{
    /// <summary>
    /// Summary description for HtmlStrippingPlaceholderDefinition.
    /// </summary>
    public class HtmlStrippingPlaceholderDefinition : PlaceholderDefinition
    {

    }
}
```

> You can also inherit from the XmlPlaceholderDefinition class. However, you should not inherit directly from the HtmlPlaceholderDefinition, AttachmentPlaceholderDefinition, or ImagePlaceholderDefinition classes. While technically possible, inheriting from these classes is not supported by Microsoft and you may run into problems.

The code will not compile until you have implemented the CreatePlaceholder() method. In this case, the CreatePlaceholder() method returns a new HtmlStrippingPlaceholder object based on the linked `HtmlStrippingPlaceholder` class, which we will define later. Add the `CreatePlaceholder()` method below the `HtmlStrippingPlaceholderDefinition()` constructor:

```
public override Placeholder CreatePlaceholder()
{
    return new HtmlStrippingPlaceholder();
}
```

Next, we will define a `Tags` property that contains a list of tags to keep or remove. Each tag needs to be separated by a vertical pipe character, '|'. For example, a|b|i indicates that all <a></a>, <b></b>, and <i></i> tags will be removed or kept (whether they are removed or kept depends on the value of the `TagAction` property defined later).

Add the following code below the `CreatePlaceholder()` method.

```
private string m_strTags;
public string Tags
{
    get
    {
        BeginRead();
        return m_strTags;
    }
    set
    {
        BeginWrite();
        m_strTags = value;
        EndWrite();
    }
}
```

Notice that the get and set accessors have calls to the following methods belonging to the base `PlaceholderDefinition` class: `BeginRead()`, `BeginWrite()` and `EndWrite()`.

Before reading the value of `m_strTags` in the get accessor, we call `BeginRead()`, which performs extra checks to see if the properties of the current `PlaceholderDefinition` object can be read. `BeginRead()` will generate an exception if:

- The template containing the placeholder definition object has been marked for deletion by calling the `Template.Delete()` method but the delete has not been committed to the database.

- The placeholder definition object has been marked for deletion by calling the `PlaceholderDefinition.Delete()` method but the delete has not been committed to the database.

Likewise, the `BeginWrite()` method is called before modifying the `Tags` property value. The `BeginWrite()` method locks the template containing the placeholder definition object. If the template already has a published version, the method creates an unpublished version of the template before updating the property of the placeholder definition object.

It also checks to see if the placeholder definition object can be updated. You won't be able to modify the properties of placeholder definition objects if:

- The placeholder definition object has been marked for deletion or has been deleted.
- The parent template of the placeholder definition object has been marked for deletion or has been deleted.
- It was retrieved using the placeholder definition property.
- You do not have the rights to modify the template.
- You are not executing the request in the Update mode.

When m_strTags has been assigned a new value, a call to EndWrite() is made to save the value in the m_strTags property of the current placeholder definition object.

After that, we will add a TagAction property, which will contain a value that specifies what should be done with HTML markup tags that match the tags specified in the Tags property.

To do this we will first define an enumeration called Action. The enumeration contains two possible values:

1. Keep: Tags specified in the Tags property are retained. All other tags are removed.
2. Remove: The opposite of Keep. Tags specified in the Tags property are removed. All other tags are retained.

Add the Action enumeration below the Tags() property:

```
public enum Action
{
    Keep,
    Remove
}
```

Next, we will create the TagAction property. The private variable m_eAction has a default value of Action.Remove. As in the Tags property, we call BeginRead(), BeginWrite(), and EndWrite() methods within the get and set accessors. Directly below the enum Action declaration, add the TagAction property:

```
private Action m_eAction = Action.Remove;
public Action TagAction
{
    get
    {
        BeginRead();
        return m_eAction;
    }
    set
    {
        BeginWrite();
        m_eAction = value;
        EndWrite();
    }
}
```

The HtmlStrippingPlaceholderDefinition class is complete. Remember to save your work.

The HtmlStrippingPlaceholder

Add a new class file to the `TropicalGreenPlaceholderDefinition` project. Name the class file `HtmlStrippingPlaceholder.cs`.

As usual, import the namespaces of the classes used within the code by adding these statements above the namespace declaration:

```
using System;
using Microsoft.ContentManagement.Publishing;
using System.Text.RegularExpressions;
```

The `HtmlStrippingPlaceholder` should inherit from the base `Placeholder` class. Add a colon followed by `Placeholder` after the `HtmlStrippingPlaceholder` class declaration:

```
namespace TropicalGreenPlaceholderDefinition
{
    /// <summary>
    /// Summary description for HtmlStrippingPlaceholder.
    /// </summary>
    public class HtmlStrippingPlaceholder : Placeholder
    {
        public HtmlStrippingPlaceholder()
        {
        }
    }
}
```

The `Html` property is used to retrieve and save the HTML content stored in the placeholder. Add the following code for this property after the `HtmlStrippingPlaceholder()` constructor:

```
public string Html
{
    get
    {
        return RetrieveContent();
    }
    set
    {
        object strValue = StripTags(value) as object;
        BeginWrite("Html", ref strValue);
        SaveContent(strValue as string);
        EndWrite("Html");
    }
}
```

The `get` accessor calls the `RetrieveContent()` method of the base `Placeholder` class, which returns the placeholder data stored in the content repository.

The `set` accessor is a little more complex. First we strip out all unwanted tags by calling the `StripTags()` method (defined later) and store the result in an object named `strValue`.

Then we call the `BeginWrite()` method. Although this method from the `Placeholder` class shares the same name as the `BeginWrite()` method of the `PlaceholderDefinition` class, they have totally different meanings. The purpose of the `BeginWrite()` method of the `Placeholder` class is to raise the pre-publishing events used when customizing the workflow as discussed in Chapter 10. It accepts two parameters:

1. The name of the property that is being updated
2. A reference to the value of the property

In this example, the name of the property is Html and its value is stored in the variable strValue. We call the BeginWrite() method as follows:

```
BeginWrite("Html", ref strValue);
```

To store the property value in the content repository, we call the SaveContent() method.

We call the EndWrite() method at the end of the set statement to trigger post-publishing event handlers for a customized workflow. It accepts only the name of the property that is being updated. In this example, the name of the property we are updating is Html. We call it like this:

```
EndWrite("Html");
```

> When writing setter methods for custom placeholder classes, always wrap the call of the SaveContent() method with the BeginWrite() and EndWrite() method calls.

Next, we will write the StripTags() method, which is split into two parts. The first handles the case where we want to remove the markup specified in the Tags property of the HtmlStrippingPlaceholderDefinition. The second covers the case of keeping the tags.

> We make use of regular expressions to find the tags in the content. For an introduction to regular expressions visit this website: http://www.regular-expressions.info.

Case 1: Remove the Specified Tags and Keep All Other Tags

In the first case, we handle situations where the Action property has been set to a value of Remove. A single regular expression captures all the instances of markup in the Tags property and removes them from the content. Add the StripTags() method below the Html public property.

```
private string StripTags(string Html)
{
HtmlStrippingPlaceholderDefinition definition = this.Definition as
HtmlStrippingPlaceholderDefinition;
    if(definition.TagAction==HtmlStrippingPlaceholderDefinition.Action.Remove)
    {
        string strRegExp = "<[\\s|/]*(" + definition.Tags + ")\\b[^>]*>";
        Regex r = new Regex(strRegExp, RegexOptions.IgnoreCase |
                                       RegexOptions.Compiled);
        return r.Replace(Html,"");
    }
}
```

Case 2: Keep the Specified Tags and Remove All Other Tags

In the second case, we handle the case where the Action property contains the value Remove. Again, we use a regular expression to look for all matching tags. This routine may look complex at first but it's really quite simple. Let's say the stored HTML is:

<b>Lorem ipsum</b> <u>dolor sit amet</u>, <i>consectetuer adipiscing elit.</i>

And suppose the Tags property of the HtmlStrippingPlaceholderDefinition stores b|i which means that we want to remove all tags that do not match <b></b> and <i></i>.

To solve this, we write two nested `for` loops. The first loop grabs a collection of all tags in the HTML. A regular expression matches everything between the opening and closing angle brackets of an HTML tag. Based on the stored HTML above, the first loop therefore iterates through `<b>,</b>,<u>,</u>,<i>,</i>` in that order.

The second loop compares each tag found in the first loop with the ones listed in the `Tags` property. If it matches one of the tags defined in the `Tags` property, then the tag is retained. Otherwise, the code replaces it with an empty string. In the stored HTML above, all tags apart from the `<b>`, `</b>`, `<i>`, and `</i>` tags are removed. Result: the `<u>` and `</u>` tags will be deleted.

Add the second part of the `if-else` block to the `StripTags()` method.

```
private string StripTags(string Html)
{
    HtmlStrippingPlaceholderDefinition definition = this.Definition as
    HtmlStrippingPlaceholderDefinition;
    if(definition.TagAction==HtmlStrippingPlaceholderDefinition.Action.Remove)
    {
        string strRegExp = "<[\\s|/]*(" + definition.Tags + ")\\b[^]*>";
        Regex r = new Regex(strRegExp, RegexOptions.IgnoreCase |
                                       RegexOptions.Compiled);
        return r.Replace(Html,"");
    }
    else
    {
        //The regular expression <[^]*> matches evetything between the opening
        //and closing brackets of a HTML tag
        string strRegExpForAllTags = "<[^]*>";
        Regex reAllTags = new Regex(strRegExpForAllTags, RegexOptions.IgnoreCase
                                       |RegexOptions.Compiled);
        //The regular expression <[\\s|/]* definition.Tags \\b[^]*
        //matches all tags specified in the Tags property
        string strRegExp = "<[\\s|/]*(" + definition.Tags + ")\\b[^]*>";
        Regex reKeepTags = new Regex(strRegExp, RegexOptions.IgnoreCase |
                                       RegexOptions.Compiled);

        string strRetVal = Html;
        //The first for loop iterates through all HTML tags in the content
        for(Match matchTag = reAllTags.Match(strRetVal);
            matchTag.Success;
            matchTag=matchTag.NextMatch())
        {
            bool bFound = false;
            //The second for loop compares the tag with the
            //list in the Tags property
            for(Match matchRequestedTag =
                reKeepTags.Match(matchTag.Groups[0].Value);
                matchRequestedTag.Success;
                matchRequestedTag.NextMatch())
            {
                bFound = true;
                break;
            }
            //The tag does not match any of the tags in the Tags property,
            //so remove it
            if(bFound==false)
            {
                strRetVal = strRetVal.Replace(matchTag.Groups[0].Value,"");
            }
        }
        return strRetVal;
    }
}
```

The `HtmlStrippingPlaceholder` is complete. Save and build the project.

Making the Placeholder Definition Available to Template Designers

Before template designers can use the placeholder definition, we must perform two tasks:

1. Register the assembly for the placeholder definition in the Global Assembly Cache.
2. Add an entry for the PlaceholderDefinition in the `Microsoft.ContentManagement.Publishing.config` file.

Registering the Placeholder Definition Assembly in the GAC

We will perform the usual process of putting an assembly into the GAC:

1. Create a new directory to store the `StrongName` key (e.g. `c:\TropicalGreenGACKey`).

2. Select Start | Programs | Microsoft Visual Studio .NET | Visual Studio .NET Tools | Visual Studio .NET Command Prompt. At the prompt, run the following command:
`sn -k "c:\TropicalGreenGACKey\TropicalGreenKey.snk"`

3. Switch over to the `TropicalGreenPlaceholderDefinition` project (NOT TropicalGreen), open the `AssemblyInfo.cs` file, and update the `[assembly]` tag.
`[assembly:`
`AssemblyKeyFile("c:\\TropicalGreenGACKey\\TropicalGreenKey.snk")]`
Save and build the `TropicalGreenPlaceholderDefinition` project.

4. Toggle back to the Command Prompt, and run the following command to add the `TropicalGreenPlaceholderDefinition.dll` to the global assembly cache:
`gacutil -I "c:\TropicalGreenPlaceholderDefinition\bin\debug\`
`          TropicalGreenPlaceholderDefinition.dll"`
As we are still developing the code, we register the debug version of the library, which provides information useful when debugging. When the code is done, you would want to create a release version of the library and deploy that instead.

    If all goes well, you will receive the message `Assembly successfully added to the cache`. Close the Command Prompt.

5. Open `c:\windows\assembly` (or `c:\winnt\assembly` if you are working in Windows 2000) in Explorer. Look for `TropicalGreenPlaceholderDefinition`. Right-click and select Properties. Write down the public key token or copy it to the clipboard—we'll need it in a moment. Close the Properties window.

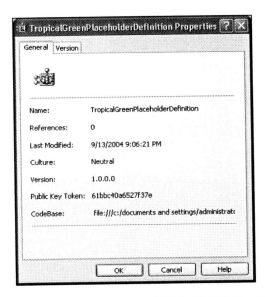

To remove the assembly from the GAC, open the Visual Studio .NET Command prompt and enter: `gacutil -u TropicalGreenPlaceholderDefinition`

Adding the HtmlStrippingPlaceholderDefinition to the Publishing.config File

The `Microsoft.ContentManagement.Publishing.config` file is located in `\Server\Config` under the MCMS installation folder.

Open the file with Visual Studio .NET or Notepad. At the end of list of `<PlaceholderDefinitionTypes>`, add the following line:

```
<PlaceholderDefinitionType
Assembly="TropicalGreenPlaceholderDefinition,
Version=1.0.0.0,
Culture=neutral,
PublicKeyToken=61bbc40a6527f37e"
ClassName=
    "TropicalGreenPlaceholderDefinition.HtmlStrippingPlaceholderDefinition" />
```

Remember to replace the `PublicKeyToken` with the one recorded in the previous step. Save and close the file.

Adding the HtmlStrippingPlaceholderDefinition to the Template

First, close and re-open Visual Studio .NET, and then open the `TropicalGreen` solution. In Template Explorer, check out the `Plant` template. Right-click and select Properties. Click on the ellipsis in the PlaceholderDefinitions field to open the Placeholder Definition Collection Editor.

Click on the arrow next to the Add button and select the HtmlStrippingPlaceholderDefinition. Set the following properties:

Property	Value
Name	WhereToBuy
Action	Remove
Tags	font|h1

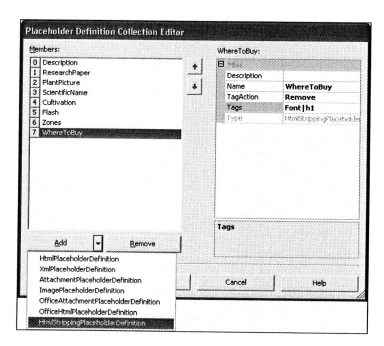

Make sure to check in the Plant template object before continuing.

The HtmlStrippingPlaceholderDefinition is not available in the Placeholder Definition Editor.

If the HtmlStrippingPlaceholderDefinition is not listed, chances are, Visual Studio .NET could not load it. When that happens, check the application event log. There are several reasons why the Placeholder Definition does not get loaded.

1.   The Class is not a PlaceholderDefinition

You will see an error message that resembles this:

The type TropicalGreenPlaceholderDefinition.HtmlStrippingPlaceholder found in the configuration file 'C:\Program Files\Microsoft Content ManagementServer\Server\config\ Microsoft.ContentManagement.Publishing.config' is not a valid PlaceholderDefinition type

It means that you have specified a class that is not a `PlaceholderDefinition`. Check that the `Microsoft.ContentManagement.Publishing.config` file is correctly updated to reference the placeholder definition instead of the placeholder. In this example, the Placeholder Definition Editor was attempting to load the `HtmlStrippingPlaceholder`, which is not a placeholder definition (it's a placeholder). Use `HtmlStrippingPlaceholderDefinition` instead.

2. The Class Name is Incorrect

When you specify a class name that does not exist, you will get the following error:

Failed to get type 'TropicalGreenPlaceholderDefinition.HtmlStrippingPlaceholderDefinition' from assembly 'TropicalGreenPlaceholderDefinition, Version=1.0.0.0, Culture=neutral, PublicKeyToken=9c16545464bbfddd' (c:\winnt\assembly\gac\tropicalgreenplaceholderdefinition\1.0.0.0__9c16545464bbfddd\tropicalgreenplaceholderdefinition.dll).

First, check that the class name has been specified correctly with no typos. Also, ensure that the classes for the placeholder definition are contained in a separate library file to the classes that define custom placeholder control classes.

3. The Public Key Token is Incorrect

If you specified a public key token that does not correspond with the assembly that was registered in the GAC, you will get the error message below:

Failed to load assembly 'TropicalGreenPlaceholderDefinition, Version=1.0.0.0, Culture=neutral, PublicKeyToken=9030e866aa61b5fb'.

Assembly.Load() details: System.IO.FileLoadException: The given assembly name or codebase, 'TropicalGreenPlaceholderDefinition, Version=1.0.0.0, Culture=neutral, PublicKeyToken=9030e866aa61b5fb', was invalid.

Look at the properties of the library in the GAC (see the section, *Registering the Placeholder Definition Assembly in the GAC*) and check that you have entered the correct public key token with no typos.

4. The Version Number or Namespace is Incorrect

For situations where the version number or namespace of the placeholder definition does not match that registered with the GAC, you will get this error message:

Failed to load assembly 'TropicalGreenPlaceholderDefinition, Version=1.0.0.0, Culture=neutral, PublicKeyToken=9030e866aa61b5fb'.

Assembly.Load() details: System.IO.FileNotFoundException: File or assembly name TropicalGreenPlaceholderDefinition, or one of its dependencies, was not found.

It is most likely caused by typos in the version number or namespace of the placeholder definition. Check that the values entered in the `Microsoft.ContentManagement` `.Publishing.config` file have the same values as the ones registered in the GAC.

The HtmlStrippingPlaceholderControl Class

We can't use `HtmlPlaceholderControl` because it only supports `HtmlPlaceholderDefinition` and not the `HtmlStrippingPlaceholderDefinition` that we have built.

To get around this, we will build a simple placeholder control that appears as a `TextBox` in authoring view. Authors can enter HTML content into the `TextBox` as shown below:

```
<table border="1">
<tr>
    <td>
          Notice that the content appears within a TextBox
in authoring view and a Literal in presentation view.
    </td>
</tr>
</table>
```

In presentation view, the contents of the `HtmlStrippingPlaceholder` are displayed in a `LiteralControl`.

Notice that the content appears within a TextBox in authoring view and a Literal in presentation view.

To keep things simple, we have chosen to use a `TextBox` as the input control for the `HtmlStrippingPlaceholderControl`. You can use more advanced and user-friendly controls, such as a third-party WYSIWYG control like the standard Telerik.RAD editor (not the MCMS placeholder version) or the Ektron eWebEditPro editor.

Open the `TropicalGreenControlLib` project (created in Chapter 14). Add a new class file and name it `HtmlStrippingPlaceholderControl.cs`.

In the Reference section of Solution Explorer for the `TropicalGreenControlLib` project, add a reference to the `TropicalGreenPlaceholderDefinition` project created using the Project tab.

As before, import the namespaces of the classes that are used within the code, including the `TropicalGreenPlaceholderDefinition` namespace.

```
using System;
using System.Web.UI;
using System.Web.UI.WebControls;
using TropicalGreenPlaceholderDefinition;
using Microsoft.ContentManagement.WebControls;
using Microsoft.ContentManagement.WebControls.Design;

namespace TropicalGreenControlLib
{
    /// <summary>
    /// Summary description for HtmlStrippingPlaceholderControl.
    /// </summary>
    ///
}
```

Next, inherit from the `BasePlaceholder` class:

```
public class HtmlStrippingPlaceholderControl : BasePlaceholderControl
{
}
```

Specify that `PlaceholderControl` can only be bound to `HtmlStrippingPlaceholderDefinition` by denoting it in the `SupportedPlaceholderDefinitionType` above the class declaration:

```
[SupportedPlaceholderDefinitionType(typeof(HtmlStrippingPlaceholderDefinition))]
    public class HtmlStrippingPlaceholderControl : BasePlaceholderControl
{
}
```

Declare the variables that will be used throughout the code. `htmlEditControl` references a `TextBox` which would be used for entering HTML content in authoring mode. `htmlPresentationControl` references a `LiteralControl` that displays the contents of the placeholder in presentation and preview modes. Add the following variables directly below the `HtmlStrippingPlaceholderControl()` constructor:

```
private TextBox htmlEditControl;
private LiteralControl htmlPresentationControl;
```

Next, create a helper function, `BoundStrippingHtmlPlaceholder`. This function comes in handy when we need to get a reference to the `Placeholder` object linked to the `PlaceholderControl` through the `PlaceholderToBind` property. Add the `BoundStrippingHtmlPlaceholder` function below the variables.

```
private HtmlStrippingPlaceholder BoundStrippingHtmlPlaceholder
{
    get
    {
        return(HtmlStrippingPlaceholder)this.BoundPlaceholder;
    }
}
```

Next, we will add the `CreateAuthoringChildControls()` method, which creates a multi-line `TextBox` with a height of 200 units and width of 500 units. This is the box used by authors to enter

HTML content. The `TextBox` is added to the `authoringContainer`. Add the following code below the `BoundStrippingHtmlPlaceholder` function:

```
protected override void CreateAuthoringChildControls(BaseModeContainer
                                                     authoringContainer)
{
    this.htmlEditControl = new TextBox();
    this.htmlEditControl.ID = "AuthoringControl";
    this.htmlEditControl.Height = 200;
    this.htmlEditControl.Width = 500;
    this.htmlEditControl.TextMode = TextBoxMode.MultiLine;
    authoringContainer.Controls.Add(this.htmlEditControl);
}
```

The `LoadPlaceholderForAuthoring()` method populates the `AuthoringControl` `TextBox` with data stored in the content repository. It accesses the content using the `Html` property of the `StrippingHtmlPlaceholder` object. If an error occurs, the message is written to the `TextBox`. Add the following code below the `CreateAuthoringChildControls()` method:

```
protected override void
LoadPlaceholderContentForAuthoring(PlaceholderControlEventArgs e)
{
    EnsureChildControls();
    try
    {
        this.htmlEditControl.Text = this.BoundStrippingHtmlPlaceholder.Html;
    }
    catch(Exception ex)
    {
        this.htmlEditControl.Text = "<error>" + ex.Message + "</error>";
    }
}
```

The `SavePlaceholder()` method saves the content entered in the `htmlEditControl` `TextBox` into the `StrippingHtmlPlaceholder` object bound to the control. Add the following code below the `LoadPlaceholderContentForAuthoring()` method:

```
protected override void
SavePlaceholderContent(PlaceholderControlSaveEventArgs e)
{
    EnsureChildControls();
    try
    {
        this.BoundStrippingHtmlPlaceholder.Html = this.htmlEditControl.Text;
    }
    catch (Exception ex)
    {
        throw(ex);
    }
}
```

The `CreatePresentationChildControls()` method creates a `LiteralControl` used for displaying the contents of the placeholder and adds it to the `presentationContainer`. Add the following code below the `SavePlaceholderContent()` method:

```
protected override void CreatePresentationChildControls(BaseModeContainer
                                                        presentationContainer)
{
    this.htmlPresentationControl = new LiteralControl();
    this.htmlPresentationControl.ID = "PresentationControl";
    presentationContainer.Controls.Add(this.htmlPresentationControl);
}
```

Finally, the `LoadPlaceholderForPresentation()` method loads content from the repository into the `LiteralControl` for display. Add the following code below the `CreatePresentationChildControls()` method:

```
protected override void
LoadPlaceholderContentForPresentation(PlaceholderControlEventArgs e)
{
    EnsureChildControls();
    try
    {
        this.htmlPresentationControl.Text =
               this.BoundStrippingHtmlPlaceholder.Html;
    }
    catch (Exception ex)
    {
        this.htmlPresentationControl.Text = ex.Message;
    }
}
```

The `HtmlStrippingPlaceholderControl` is complete. Save and build the solution.

Next, we will add the HtmlStrippingPlaceholderControl to the Toolbox. Remember that we did this in the section *Adding the Custom Control to Toolbox* in Chapter 14. Follow the steps outlined in that section to add the `HtmlStrippingPlaceholderControl` to the Toolbox.

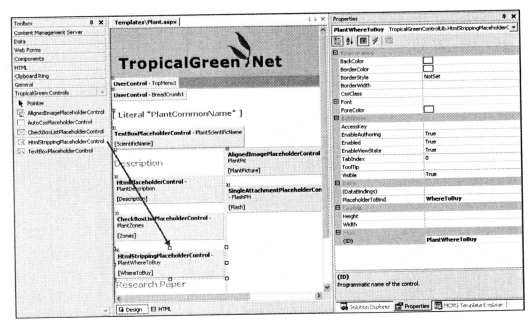

Once you have done this, open the `Plant.aspx` template file in Design view. Drag and drop the `HtmlStrippingPlaceholderControl` onto the template file, above the **Research Paper** heading. Set the following property values:

Property	Value
ID	PlantWhereToBuy
PlaceholderToBind	WhereToBuy

Save `Plant.aspx`.

Trying it Out

Navigate to `http://localhost/tropicalgreen/plantcatalog/hibiscus.htm` and switch to edit site view. Choose to edit the posting. You should see the `HtmlStrippingPlaceholderControl` as a `TextBox` as shown below.

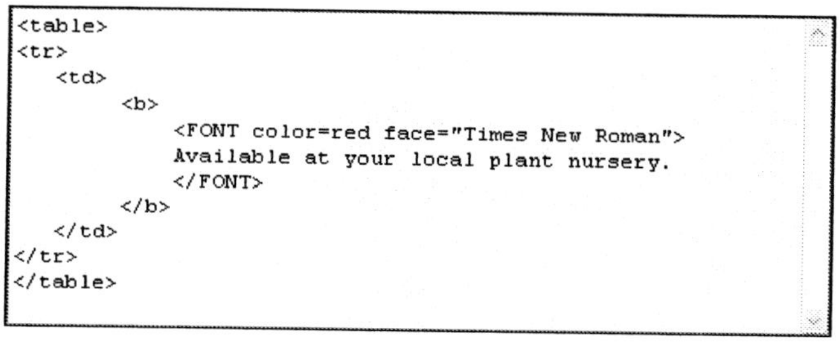

```
<table>
<tr>
    <td>
        <b>
            <FONT color=red face="Times New Roman">
            Available at your local plant nursery.
            </FONT>
        </b>
    </td>
</tr>
</table>
```

Enter some content with HTML:

```
<table>
<tr>
    <td>
        <b>
            <FONT color=red face="Times New Roman">
            Available at your local plant nursery.
            </FONT>
        </b>
    </td>
</tr>
</table>
```

Save the posting. Notice that the `<FONT>` tags are removed from the content!

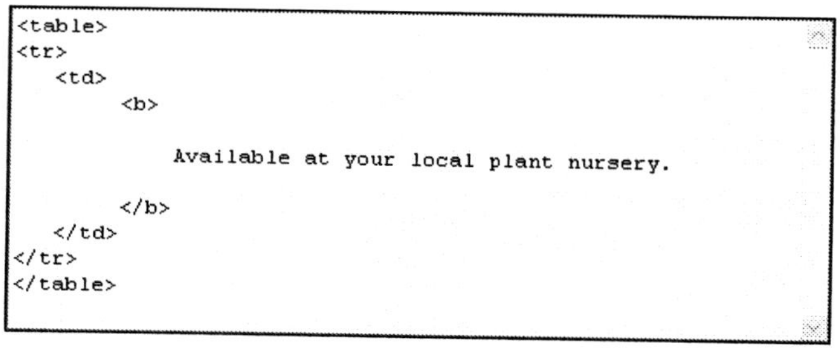

```
<table>
<tr>
    <td>
        <b>

            Available at your local plant nursery.

        </b>
    </td>
</tr>
</table>
```

Summary

MCMS gives you the flexibility to customize all aspects of the content creation process—from the moment content is entered into a placeholder to how it stored in the content repository. On top of customizing placeholder controls, you can also create customized versions of placeholder classes and placeholder definitions.

In this chapter, we looked at how a custom placeholder definition/placeholder pair is created. We developed a custom placeholder definition (HtmlStrippingPlaceholderDefinition) that allows developers to define the tags they wish to keep or remove in the placeholder (HtmlStrippingPlaceholder).

We went on to register the assembly of the custom placeholder definition with the Global Assembly Cache and added an entry to the Publishing.config file to make our placeholder definition available in the Placeholder Definition Editor dialog.

Finally, we created a custom placeholder control (HtmlStrippingPlaceholderControl) that utilizes our custom placeholder definition/placeholder pair. We entered HTML tags that are not specified in the list defined by the developer and saw how the HtmlStrippingPlaceholder removed these tags when the content gets saved.

16
Extending the Workflow

In Chapter 10, we saw how postings are routed from the author to the editor and finally to the moderator before being published. You have also seen how the basic workflow can be altered by adding or removing rights groups from channels. This basic solution may be sufficient for simple workflows. More often than not, you will find that the business processes in organizations today require more than the standard solution provides.

Common workflow extension requests include:

- **E-mail notification**: You need to have the system send e-mail to inform staff that there are postings awaiting their approval.

- **Canceling an operation**: You need to have the system prevent certain events from happening.

- **Preventing deletes**: You need to program the system to allow only specific people to delete postings through the Web Author Console.

- **Updating property values**: You may want to write values to custom properties or posting properties on behalf of a user for certain operations.

- **Cleaning up HTML**: You need to clean out HTML imported from Word documents, removing any unwanted tags. This can also be done using placeholder definitions or controls.

- **Audit tracking**: You have been asked to build an audit trail to record the transactions that have taken place.

- **Multiple editor approval**: You need to build a three-level workflow involving an author, an editor, and a senior editor.

Any website you code will probably have some of these additional requirements. To address such tasks, MCMS ships with a set of publishing events that can be used to extend and customize the workflow. It provides access to the core events that take place in the basic workflow cycle. You can customize the event handlers by adding your own business logic to tailor the workflow to meet the needs of just about any workflow scenario in your workplace.

In this chapter, we will provide working examples of e-mail notification, canceling an operation, and preventing deletes. Once you've worked through the chapter, you should have a good idea of how to set about the other tasks in the above list. You also might find the samples at www.gotdotnet.com useful, or those in Microsoft's online book called *Integration Techniques and*

Strategies for Internet Business, which you can find by searching the www.microsoft.com website. Plus, there are third-party products available that can help enhance your workflow, such as K2.net (http://www.k2workflow.com/solutions/collaboration/cms.aspx) and Teamplate Workflow Wizard (http://www.teamplate.com/internal/product/cmsworkflowwizard.asp).

Before We Begin

In order for us to customize the workflow event modules, we need to register the MCMS Publishing Events module in the web.config file. To do so:

1. Open the TropicalGreen solution in Visual Studio .NET.

2. Open the web.config file.

3. Ensure that the following line is present within the <httpModules> tag. If the project was created using the MCMS Project Creation wizard, the Publishing Events modules will have already been registered. Otherwise, add it in.

```
<add
type="Microsoft.ContentManagement.Publishing.Events.PostingEventsModul
e, Microsoft.ContentManagement.Publishing, Version=5.0.1200.0,
Culture=neutral, PublicKeyToken=31bf3856ad364e35" name="CmsPosting" />
```

MCMS Publishing Events

MCMS Publishing Events are actions that are triggered as a result of an action on a posting. Two events are fired for every operation: a **pre-event** (fired before the operation is performed) and a **post-event** (fired after the operation has been completed but before it is committed to the MCMS repository). The table below lists the available pre-event and post-event handlers associated with each action. Pre-events are identified by the suffix "ing", and post-events, by the suffix "ed".

Action	Pre-event	Post-event
Any change to a posting	Changing	Changed
Approve	Approving	Approved
Create	Creating	Created
Custom Property Changed	CustomPropertyChanging	CustomPropertyChanged
Decline	Declining	Declined
Delete	Deleting	Deleted
Move	Moving	Moved
Placeholder Content Changed	PlaceholderPropertyChanging	PlaceholderPropertyChanged
Property Changed	PropertyChanging	PropertyChanged
Submit	Submitting	Submitted

Registering Event Handlers

To get a good idea of the order in which workflow events are raised, let's register all the events in the TropicalGreen project.

Open the code-behind file of the Global.asax file of the TropicalGreen project. First, add using statements to import namespaces from the MCMS PAPI and System.IO above the TropicalGreen namespace declaration.

```
using System;
using System.Collections;
using System.ComponentModel;
using System.Web;
using System.Web.SessionState;
using Microsoft.ContentManagement.Publishing;
using Microsoft.ContentManagement.Publishing.Events;
using Microsoft.ContentManagement.Publishing.Extensions.Placeholders;
using System.IO;

namespace TropicalGreen
{
    /// <summary>
    /// Summary description for Global.
    /// </summary>
    public class Global : System.Web.HttpApplication
    {
        public Global()
        {
            InitializeComponent();
        }
    }
    . . . code continues . . .
}
```

Within the class declaration, below the Global() constructor, add the event handlers. You can get the complete set of code from the code download section of the book's website.

```
protected void CmsPosting_Approved( Object sender, ChangedEventArgs e ) {}

protected void CmsPosting_Approving( Object sender, ChangingEventArgs e ) {}

protected void CmsPosting_Changed( Object sender, ChangedEventArgs e ) {}

protected void CmsPosting_Changing( Object sender, ChangingEventArgs e ) {}

protected void CmsPosting_Created( Object sender, CreatedEventArgs e ) {}

protected void CmsPosting_Creating( Object sender, CreatingEventArgs e ) {}

protected void CmsPosting_CustomPropertyChanged( Object sender,
Microsoft.ContentManagement.Publishing.Events.PropertyChangedEventArgs e ) {}

protected void CmsPosting_CustomPropertyChanging( Object sender,
PropertyChangingEventArgs e ) {}

protected void CmsPosting_Declined( Object sender, ChangedEventArgs e ) {}

protected void CmsPosting_Declining( Object sender, ChangingEventArgs e ) {}

protected void CmsPosting_Deleted( Object sender, ChangedEventArgs e ) {}

protected void CmsPosting_Deleting( Object sender, ChangingEventArgs e ) {}

protected void CmsPosting_Moved( Object sender, MovedEventArgs e ) {}
```

```
protected void CmsPosting_Moving( Object sender, MovingEventArgs e ) {}

protected void CmsPosting_PlaceholderPropertyChanged( Object sender,
Microsoft.ContentManagement.Publishing.Events.PropertyChangedEventArgs e ) {}

protected void CmsPosting_PlaceholderPropertyChanging( Object sender,
PropertyChangingEventArgs e ) {}

protected void CmsPosting_PropertyChanged( Object sender,
Microsoft.ContentManagement.Publishing.Events.PropertyChangedEventArgs e ) {}

protected void CmsPosting_PropertyChanging( Object sender,
PropertyChangingEventArgs e ) {}

protected void CmsPosting_Submitted( Object sender, ChangedEventArgs e ) {}

protected void CmsPosting_Submitting( Object sender, ChangingEventArgs e ) {}
```

After registering all the available events, we can monitor the order in which they are called.

Monitoring Workflow Events

Each time an event handler is raised, we record its name and other bits of information in a log file.

First, create a new folder on your c:\ drive and name it TropicalGreenLogs. The LogEvent() method records each event as it is called in a text file called MCMSEventLog located in the c:\TropicalGreenLogs folder.

> If you are using Windows 2000, Windows Server 2003, or Windows XP with classic permissions, make sure the c:\TropicalGreenLogs folder exists and has read/write permissions assigned to the local ASPNET account. Otherwise the log file will not get written and you may get errors when executing the code below!

The LogEvent() method will accept two parameters: the name of the method being called (methodName) and the event argument of the handler (eventArgument).

Add the following code below the Global() constructor in the Global.asax.cs file:

```
//The LogEvent() method records events as they are raised
FileStream fsLog = null;
StreamWriter wLog = null;

protected void LogEvent(String methodName, Object eventArgument)
{
    fsLog = new FileStream("c:\\TropicalGreenLogs\\MCMSEventLog.txt",
                    FileMode.Append,
                    FileAccess.Write);
    wLog = new StreamWriter(fsLog);
    wLog.WriteLine("-----------------------------------------------------------");
    wLog.WriteLine(System.DateTime.Now.ToString()+" - "+ methodName);

    wLog.WriteLine(" - e (Type) "+ eventArgument.GetType().ToString());
    if (eventArgument is PublishingEventArgs)
    {
        PublishingEventArgs e = (PublishingEventArgs) eventArgument;
        wLog.WriteLine(" - e.Action: "+e.Action.ToString());
        wLog.WriteLine(" - e.Target (Type): "+e.Target.GetType().ToString());
```

```
                //Log any changes to a posting's property and custom property values
                if(e is PropertyChangingEventArgs)
                {
                   PropertyChangingEventArgs ce = (PropertyChangingEventArgs) e;
                   wLog.WriteLine(" - e.PropertyName: "+ce.PropertyName);
                   wLog.WriteLine(" - e.PropertyValue: "+ce.PropertyValue);
                }

                if(e is
                   Microsoft.ContentManagement.Publishing.Events.PropertyChangedEventArgs)
                   {
                Microsoft.ContentManagement.Publishing.Events.PropertyChangedEventArgs ce;

                   ce =
                (Microsoft.ContentManagement.Publishing.Events.PropertyChangedEventArgs) e;
                   wLog.WriteLine(" - e.PropertyName: "+ce.PropertyName);
                }

                if (e.Target is Placeholder)
                {
                   Placeholder ph = (Placeholder)e.Target;
                   wLog.WriteLine(" - Placeholder: "+ph.Name);
                   wLog.WriteLine(" - Posting: "+ ph.Posting.Path+" - State: "
                                              + ph.Posting.State);
                }

                if (e.Target is Posting)
                {
                   Posting p = (Posting)e.Target;
                   wLog.WriteLine(" - Posting: "+p.Path+" - State: "+p.State);
                }

                //Target is a channel when a posting is created
                if (e.Target is Channel)
                {
                   wLog.WriteLine(" - Channel.Path: "+((ChannelItem)(e.Target)).Path);
                   wLog.WriteLine(" - Channel (GUID): "+((ChannelItem)(e.Target)).Guid);
                }

            }
            wLog.Flush();
            wLog.Close();
            fsLog.Close();
        }
```

The result of the LogEvent() method is a series of additional information about the event that is being raised, including:

- Date and time when the event was raised
- Name of the event
- The object type of the event argument
- Name of the action
- Path and state of the posting
- Name of the placeholder (if one is being updated)

Now we will call the LogEvent() method from within each event handler, passing in the name of the event handler and its event arguments. In the following code snippet , we show how the LogEvent() method is called from within the CmsPosting_Approved() and CmsPosting_Approving() event handlers. The LogEvent() method is called in the same way for the remaining event handlers. When you have entered the code (or downloaded it from the book's companion website), save and build the solution. Add the following code to the appropriate event handlers:

```
protected void CmsPosting_Approved( Object sender, ChangedEventArgs e )
{
    LogEvent("CmsPosting_Approved",e);
}

protected void CmsPosting_Approving( Object sender, ChangingEventArgs e )
{
    LogEvent("CmsPosting_Approving",e);
}

. . . code continues . . .
```

Save the file and build the solution.

Now that we have registered all the event handlers and created the LogEvent() method to record them as they are raised, we are ready to see what happens behind the scenes as actions are performed on postings.

Sequence of Events Raised when Creating a New Page

Start by creating a new plant fact sheet. In Internet Explorer, navigate to http://localhost/ tropicalgreen/plantcatalog. Switch to Edit Site and choose to Create New Page using the Plant template. Enter some information in the placeholders and save it. Give the new posting the name EggPlant.

In Windows Explorer open the MCMSEventlog.txt file in the c:\TropicalGreenLogs folder. You should see a long list of log entries that make up a trace of the events that were raised when you created the posting.

The first events to get fired invoke the pre-event handlers:

- Creating
- Changing

They are immediately followed by the post-event handlers:

- Created
- Changed

After the posting has been created, the next events to fire are the events that update the posting's name. The same set of events is raised again to update the posting's DisplayName:

- PropertyChanging
- Changing
- PropertyChanged
- Changed

Finally, events are raised to update placeholder property values:

- PlaceholderPropertyChanging
- Changing

- `PlaceholderPropertyChanged`
- `Changed`

The last set of four event handlers is fired once for each placeholder property updated. For example, because the image placeholder has three properties, `Src`, `Alt`, and `Href`, the four event handlers are called three times.

The diagram below shows the sequence in which the events were raised.

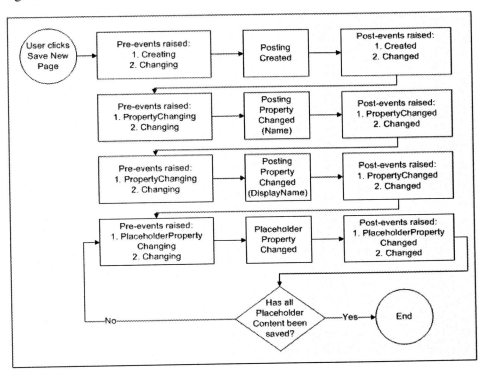

Notice that the `Changing` pre-event handler gets fired after any pre-event handler is fired. Similarly the `Changed` post-event handler is fired after any post-event handler. The `Changing` and `Changed` event handlers are known as generic event handlers and are called whenever a posting is changed. When writing code to modify the workflow, you can choose to place them in specific event handlers (such as `Creating`, `Created`) or in the generic event handlers.

> The sequence of events raised when creating a connected posting is exactly the same as that of a new posting.

Sequence of Events Raised when a Page is Saved

While still in edit site mode, open the `EggPlant` posting and edit it. Click **Save and Exit**. Open the `MCMSEventLog.txt` file, scroll to the bottom, and look at the new entries.

As compared to the case when the posting was first created, saving a posting triggers only the following events as only placeholder content and properties are saved:

- `PlaceholderPropertyChanging`
- `Changing`
- `PlaceholderPropertyChanged`
- `Changed`

The events raised are shown in the following diagram.

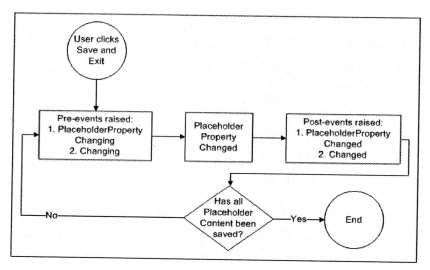

Sequence of Events Raised when a Page is Submitted, Approved, or Declined

Submit the `EggPlant` posting. Open `MCMSEventLog.txt` and observe the additional log entries.

Submitting the posting involves only four event handlers:

- `Submitting`
- `Changing`
- `Submitted`
- `Changed`

The sequence in which the events are raised is shown below.

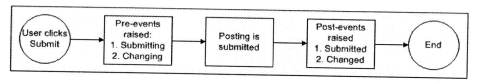

Decline and approve operations are similar. Declining a posting raises these event handlers:

- Declining
- Changing
- Declined
- Changed

Approving a posting raises the event handlers:

- Approving
- Changing
- Approved
- Changed

Sequence of Events Raised when a Page is Copied

With the EggPlant posting opened in edit site mode, click Copy. In the Copy Page dialog, select Home as the destination channel and click OK.

Notice that events recorded in the MCMSEventLog.txt file show that only the

- Creating
- Changing
- Created
- Changed

event handlers are called as shown in the diagram below.

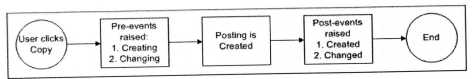

There isn't any event specifically for making copies of postings. Since copying a page is essentially creating a new page, the Creating and Created events capture it.

Sequence of Events Raised when a Page is Deleted

Delete the copy of the EggPlant posting in the Home/TropicalGreen channel. Look again at the MCMSEventLog.txt file.

Deleting a posting raises the events below:

- Deleting
- Changing
- Deleted
- Changed

The sequence in which the events are called is shown in the following diagram.

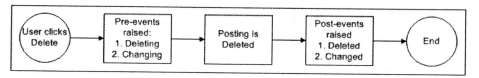

Sequence of Events Raised when a Page is Moved

Return to the EggPlant posting in the Plant Catalog channel. In edit site mode, click Move. In the Move Page dialog, choose the Home channel as the destination channel.

The events recorded in the MCMSEventLog.txt file are:

- Moving
- Changing
- Moved
- Changed

The order in which they are called is shown below.

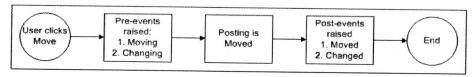

Before continuing, move the EggPlant posting back to the Plant Catalog channel.

Sequence of Events Raised when Updating Page Property/Custom Property Values

With the EggPlant posting opened, click the Page Properties link. Update Start Publishing to start immediately. Click Save.

Open MCMSEventLog.txt and look at the newly added records. They show that the events raised are:

- PropertyChanging
- Changing
- PropertyChanged
- Changed

The four event handlers are fired for each property value that is updated. If you updated two property values, like both the StartDate and DisplayName, the events would be called twice.

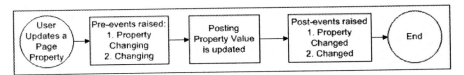

The events raised when updating a custom property follow the same concept. The events fired when a custom property value is updated are:

- CustomPropertyChanging
- Changing
- CustomPropertyChanged
- Changed

Like page properties, the set of four event handlers are called for each custom property value that is updated.

Now approve the EggPlant posting to get us back to square one.

Sequence of Events Raised when Updating Channel Properties

Click Channel Properties. Set the Start Publishing date to Immediately and save the changes.

There were no new entries logged in the MCMSEventLog.txt file. That's because event handlers only work when actions are performed on postings and are not fired when channels are created, edited, or deleted.

> MCMS does not provide workflow events for updates to channels, resources, or templates.

Now that we have learned the basics of how the event handlers work and the sequence in which they are called, we can proceed to do something useful with them. Before proceeding, comment out all of the calls to the LogEvent() method in the Global.asax.cs event handlers to prevent the log file from growing unnecessarily large.

E-mail Notification

MCMS does not ship with an e-mail notification system. Typically, authors, editors, and moderators inform one another of postings pending approval by sending e-mail to each other. The problem arises when one person forgets to send out an e-mail. The approver or author does not get notified until someone pops into the site and checks the queue in the Production Manager or Approval Assistant. The result is a pile of "forgotten" postings that languish in a Waiting for Approval or Declined state for an indefinite period of time.

Automating the e-mail notification process not only lightens the workload of authors, editors, and moderators but also ensures that the correct people are notified of postings they need to work on.

The publishing process can be modified to include an e-mail notification system as shown the diagram overleaf. In this example, after submitting a posting, the system sends an e-mail on behalf of the author to the next level of approvers. Similarly, when an editor approves a posting, and if further approval from a moderator is required, an e-mail is sent to the group of moderators assigned to the posting's channel. After being approved by a moderator, a posting may need an extra round of editor approval if the moderator modified placeholder content, posting property or custom property values (see Chapter 10 for a detailed discussion).

In cases where the editor or moderator declines the posting, an e-mail is sent to the last person who submitted the posting for approval.

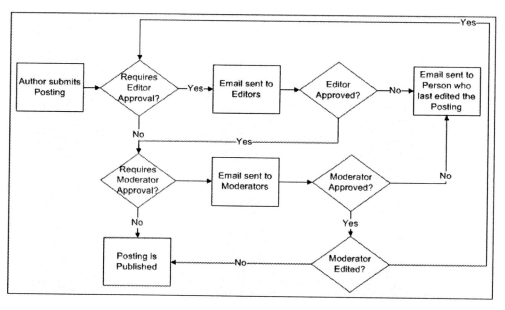

We will build the e-mail notification system using the steps outlined below.

1. Build a Notification class that takes care of the logic required to compose and send out e-mail.

2. Add logic to the Submitted event handler to send e-mail from authors to editors/moderators.

3. Add logic to the Approved event handler to send e-mail to moderators if moderator approval is required.

4. Add logic to the Declined event handler to send e-mail to the last person who submitted the posting.

The Notification Class

The Notification class will handle the logic required to send e-mail to the right person.

In order for e-mail to be dispatched, you need to be connected to a mail server. We will assume that you are online and have access to a mail server.

In Visual Studio .NET, add a new folder to the TropicalGreen project. Name the folder WorkflowManager. Within the WorkflowManager folder, add a new class file named Notification.cs.

As we are going to work with e-mail, we will use the classes in the System.Web.Mail namespace. Import the System.Web.Mail namespace above the namespace declaration.

```
using System;
using System.Web.Mail;

namespace TropicalGreen.WorkflowManager
{
    /// <summary>
    /// Summary description for Notification.
    /// </summary>
    public class Notification
    {
        public Notification()
        {
            //
            // TODO: Add constructor logic here
            //
        }
    }
}
```

Declare To, From, Subject, and Message as public variables. Best practice would be to create them as public properties with get and set accessors, but as we are not applying any extra logic, we will use the shortcut and just declare all properties as public variables. Add the following code directly below the Notification() constructor.

```
//Email address for the To: field
// Multiple addresses are separated by commas
public string To="";
public string From="";    //Email addresses for the From: field
public string Subject=""; //Text for the Subject: Field
public string Message=""; //The message within the email
```

The GetEmailAddress() method will accept a string that contains information returned from the User.ServerAccountName property (usually in the format: winNt://computername/username). In this block of code, we will rearrange the string to get the user's e-mail address in the format username@computername.net. Add the GetEmailAddress() method below the public variables declared above.

```
public string GetEmailAddress(string logonUser)
{
    string[] arrLogonUser;
    arrLogonUser = logonUser.Split('/');
    if(arrLogonUser.Length>1)
        return(arrLogonUser[arrLogonUser.Length-1] + "@" +
arrLogonUser[arrLogonUser.Length-2] + ".net");
    else
        return logonUser;
}
```

For the example in the chapter to work on your test machine, you need to send the e-mail to and from addresses on a valid domain. If the domain `computername.net` does not exist, you may get an error code `553 computername.net does not exist` error when attempting to send the e-mail. So you may need to modify the `GetEmailAddress()` method. Replace:

```
return(arrLogonUser[arrLogonUser.Length-1] + "@" +
    arrLogonUser[arrLogonUser.Length-2] + ".net");
```
with:

```
return(arrLogonUser[arrLogonUser.Length-1] + "@" + "mydomain.com");
```

Replace `mydomain.com` with a valid domain name, like your personal website.

The `Send()` method sends out the e-mail. It connects to an SMTP server and constructs a new `MailMessage` object. Add the `Send()` method below the `GetEmailAddress()` method. You will have to replace that line of code to point to an existing SMTP server capable of relaying e-mail.

```
/// Sends the email through an email server
/// using the classes in the System.Web.Mail namespace
/// </summary>
public void Send()
{
    //Replace with the name of the SMTP server you are connecting to
    string smtpServer = "127.0.0.0";

    MailMessage mail = new MailMessage();
    mail.Body = Message;       //The body of the email
    mail.From = From;          //e.g. editor1@tropicalgreen.net
    mail.To = To;              //e.g. author1@tropicalgreen.net
    mail.Subject = Subject;    //e.g. [Approved]Hibiscus

    SmtpMail.SmtpServer = smtpServer;
    SmtpMail.Send(mail);
}
```

The e-mail created will resemble this:

```
To: author1@computername.net;
From: editor1@computername.net
Datetime: 6/28/2003 11:44:31 PM
Subject: [Approved]Hibiscus
----------
Posting Name: Hibiscus
Posting Url :
/TropicalGreen/PlantCatalog/Hibiscus.htm?WBCMODE=PresentationUnpublished
State : Published
```

You probably won't have email accounts set up for the group of fictitious authors, editors and moderators of TropicalGreen. In order to see the emails that are being sent, carbon-copy all emails to your mailbox as part of the testing process. Within the `Send()` method, add the following code, replacing `myemail@mydomain.com` with your valid email address.

```
. . .code continues . . .
mail.To = To;                //e.g. author1@tropicalgreen.net
mail.CC = "myemail@mydomain.com"; //Add your email address here
mail.Subject = Subject;      //e.g. [Approved] Hibiscus
. . . code continues . . .
```

Retrieving the E-mail Address of a User from the Active Directory

You can get the e-mail address of the user based on their user name. In the example above, we rearranged the user name and domain name to form the e-mail address, such as `username@computername.net`.

While this technique may work for some cases, there are situations where you may need to retrieve the e-mail address from an external data source such as an Active Directory. You can create a helper function that accepts the user name as an input parameter and queries the Active Directory for the corresponding e-mail address, as the following code shows.

```
public string GetEmailAddress(string logonUser)
{
    //Get the user name from logonUser
    //logonUser is in the format WinNt://domain/username
    string[] arrUser;
    arrUser = logonUser.Split('/');
    string User = arrUser[3];

    string UserFilter = "(&(objectClass=user) (SAMAccountName=" + User + "))";
    //We have assumed that the user name is stored in the
    //local tropicalgreen.net domain.
    string ADConnectionString = "LDAP://CN=Users,DC=tropicalgreen,DC=net";
    DirectoryEntry dirEntry = new DirectoryEntry(ADConnectionString);
    if (dirEntry != null)
    {
        DirectorySearcher dirSearcher = new DirectorySearcher();
        dirSearcher.SearchRoot = dirEntry;
        dirSearcher.Filter = UserFilter;
        dirSearcher.SearchScope = SearchScope.Subtree;
        dirSearcher.PropertiesToLoad.Add("mail");
        SearchResult result = dirSearcher.FindOne();
        string MailAddr = result.Properties["mail"][0].ToString();
        dirSearcher.Dispose();
        dirEntry.Dispose();
        return(MailAddr);
    }
    else
    {
        return "";
    }
}
```

In order for the code to work you must add a reference to `System.DirectoryServices.dll` and import the `System.DirectoryServices` namespace. `ADConnectionString` provides the information for connecting to the Active Directory. Ideally, you should store it in a central location such as the `appSettings` section of your `web.config` file. The format for `ADConnection` string is: `LDAP://Server/CN=Users,DC=dompart1,DC=dompart2,...DC=dompartN`. The code above assumes that the user name is stored in the local domain. We look up the user in the directory and retrieve the e-mail address from the `mail` property.

The Submitted Event Handler

After the author submits a posting, an e-mail is sent to the next group of approvers in line, notifying them that there is a posting waiting for approval. The approver can be either an editor or a moderator, depending on the nature of the update performed by the author.

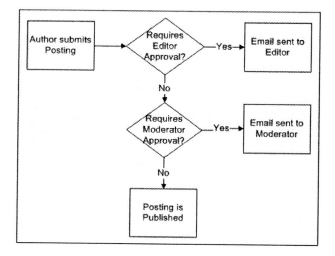

Back in the Global.asax.cs file, modify the CmsPosting_Submitted event handler as shown below.

```
protected void CmsPosting_Submitted( Object sender, ChangedEventArgs e )
{
    if(e.Target is Posting)
    {
        Posting currentPosting = (Posting)e.Target;
        if((currentPosting.State!=PostingState.Published) ||
           (currentPosting.State!=PostingState.Approved) )
        {
            ComposeMail(currentPosting,e.Action);
        }
    }

    //LogEvent("CmsPosting_Submitted",e);
}
```

The CmsPosting_Submitted event handler is raised after the posting is submitted and accepts two parameters:

- Object sender: The PostingEvents object that registered the event handler
- ChangedEventArgs e: Contains information about the event that is raised

The Target property of the ChangedEventArgs object e returns a reference to the posting being submitted. We will check the posting's state to see if it requires approval from either an editor or a moderator. If it does, we send them an e-mail by calling the ComposeMail() method.

The ComposeMail() method prepares the From, To, Subject, and Message fields of the e-mail and calls the Send() method of the Notification class created earlier. Add ComposeMail() below the Global() constructor.

```
protected void ComposeMail(Posting p, PublishingAction pAction)
{
    string to = "";
    string subject = "";

    TropicalGreen.WorkflowManager.Notification mail;
```

```
mail = new TropicalGreen.WorkflowManager.Notification();

//Prepare the To field
if(pAction == PublishingAction.Submit)
{
    foreach(User approver in p.Approvers(true))
    {
        string toAddress = mail.GetEmailAddress(approver.ServerAccountName);
        if(toAddress != "")
        {
            to += toAddress + ",";
        }
    }

    if(to.EndsWith(","))
    {
        to = to.Substring(0,to.Length-1);
    }
}
//Prepare the Subject field
if(pAction == PublishingAction.Submit)
{
    subject = "[" + pAction.ToString() + "ted]" + p.Name;
}
else
{
    subject = "[" + pAction.ToString() + "d]" + p.Name;
}
//Send the email
mail.From = mail.GetEmailAddress(CmsHttpContext.Current.User.
            ServerAccountName);
mail.To = to;
mail.Subject = subject;
mail.Message = String.Format("Posting Name: {0}\nPosting Url : "+
"{1}\nState : {2}", p.Name, p.UrlModePublished,
p.State.ToString());
mail.Send();
}
```

To get the list of approvers, the code utilizes the Posting.Approvers property. The collection returned by this property depends on the state of the posting. If the posting is Saved or Waiting For Editor Approval, Posting.Approvers returns a list of all the editors assigned to the channel. If the posting is Waiting For Moderator Approval, it returns a list of all moderators assigned to the channel. In this way, we will always get the next approvers in line regardless of whether the author changed the posting's content or properties.

The e-mail addresses of multiple approvers are stringed together using commas to separate them (e.g. editor1@tropicalgreen.net, editor2@tropicalgreen.net). You may have to change this logic (e.g. to use semicolons) depending on the conventions used to send e-mails to multiple parties in your mail system. Finally, the e-mail gets sent out.

The subject line is stamped with the Action string (Submit, Approve, or Decline) to indicate the event that triggered the mail. Before continuing, save and build the solution.

To test the code, use the technique described in Chapter 10 to configure your browser to prompt for a user name and password. Log in to the TropicalGreen site as an author (e.g. Author1). Navigate to the EggPlant posting created earlier, click Switch To Edit Site and edit the posting. Change some content and update the posting's DisplayName to EggPlants using the Page Properties. You have to update both the placeholder contents and the property for the workflow to trigger both editors and moderators.

Submit the updated posting to an editor for approval. The e-mail sent indicates that Author1 has submitted the posting for approval to Editor1 as shown below.

```
To: editor1@computername.net,
From: author1@computername.net
Datetime: 5/31/2004 2:03:58 PM
Subject: [Submitted]EggPlant
----------
Posting Name: EggPlant
Posting Url : /NR/exeres/35671882-A990-473E-B28B-
54A626B202CE.htm?WBCMODE=PresentationUnpublished
State : WaitingForEditorApproval
```

ChangedEventArgs e

The ChangedEventArgs e, of the CmsPosting_Submitted event handler contains three properties that provide useful information about the event, as detailed in the following table.

Property	Details
e.Action	Action tells you which operation is being performed on the target object. It returns an enumeration of type PublishingAction which takes on one of the following values: ○ Approve ○ Create ○ CustomPropertyChange ○ Decline ○ Delete ○ Move ○ PlaceholderPropertyChange ○ PropertyChange ○ Submit For the CmsPosting_Submitted() event, the Action property returns the value PublishingAction.Submit. This property is usually used within the CmsPosting_Changing() and CmsPosting_Changed() generic event handlers to identify the action that was performed on the posting.
e.Target	Returns a reference to the target object. In the case of the CmsPosting_Submitted() event handler, the target object is the posting that is being submitted.
e.Context	Returns the CmsContext of the target object.

ChangedEventArgs is also the type of the second parameter for the Changed, Approved, Declined, and Deleted event handlers.

The Approved Event Handler

When an editor approves the posting, one of two things can happen:

- The posting requires further moderator approval.
- The posting does not require further moderator approval and is published.

Similarly, when a moderator approves a posting, there are two possible outcomes:

- The moderator has edited the content of the posting requiring an editor to approve the changes again.
- The posting does not require further approval and gets published.

In cases where the posting needs approval from either an editor or moderator, an e-mail is sent notifying the appropriate people in the workflow. The code that does this is similar to that in the CmsPosting_Submitted() event handler. Because the e-mail is to be sent out only after the posting has been approved, enter the code in the CmsPosting_Approved() event handler as shown below. Go back to Global.asax.cs and add the following to the CmsPosting_Approved() method:

```
protected void CmsPosting_Approved( Object sender, ChangedEventArgs e )
{
    if(e.Target is Posting)
    {
        Posting currentPosting = (Posting)e.Target;
        if((currentPosting.State==PostingState.WaitingForEditorApproval)||
           (currentPosting.State==PostingState.WaitingForModeratorApproval))
        {
            ComposeMail(currentPosting, e.Action);
        }
    }
    //LogEvent("CmsPosting_Approved",e);
}
```

Modify the ComposeMail() function call to consider the approve action when preparing the list of people to mail the message to. As we did for the submit action, we send the mail to all approvers. In this case, Posting.Approvers returns a list of moderators assigned to the channel.

```
protected void ComposeMail(Posting p, PublishingAction pAction)
{
    . . . code continues . . .

    //Prepare the To field
    if(pAction == PublishingAction.Submit||pAction == PublishingAction.Approve)
    {
        foreach(User approver in p.Approvers(true))
        {
            . . . code continues . . .
        }
    }
}
```

Save and build the solution.

Log in to the TropicalGreen site with an account that has editor rights (e.g. Editor1). Navigate to the EggPlant posting submitted by Author1 earlier. The posting's state should be Waiting For Editor Approval. Approve the posting. The e-mail sent looks like this:

```
To: moderator1@computername.net,
From: editor1@computername.net
Datetime: 5/31/2004 2:17:20 PM
Subject: [Approve]EggPlant
----------
Posting Name: EggPlant
Posting Url : /NR/exeres/935F294C-A430-4318-8C59-
BB480BB7110F.htm?WBCMODE=PresentationUnpublished
State : WaitingForModeratorApproval
```

Editor1 has approved the posting. The system sees that Moderator1 is required to approve the posting and sends them a notification.

The Declined Event Handler

When the editor or moderator declines a posting, an e-mail is sent to the last person who edited it. For example, if the editor declined the posting, an e-mail would be sent to the author if he was the last person who edited it.

Since the mail is sent in response to a Declined event, we will write the code in the CmsPosting_Declined() event handler as shown below. Notice that we did not add a check for the PostingState since declined postings are always either in an Editor Declined or Moderator Declined state making such a check unnecessary.

Back in Global.asax.cs, add the following code to the CmsPosting_Declined() method:

```
protected void CmsPosting_Declined( Object sender, ChangedEventArgs e )
{
    if(e.Target is Posting)
    {
        Posting currentPosting = (Posting)e.Target;
        ComposeMail(currentPosting, e.Action);
    }

    //LogEvent("CmsPosting_Declined",e);
}
```

Modify the ComposeMail() method to consider Decline cases as shown below.

```
protected void ComposeMail(Posting p, PublishingAction pAction)
{
    . . . code continues . . .

    //Prepare the To field
    if(pAction == PublishingAction.Submit||pAction == PublishingAction.Approve)
    {
        . . . code continues . . .
    }
    else if(pAction == PublishingAction.Decline)
    {
        to = mail.GetEmailAddress(p.OwnedBy.ServerAccountName);
    }

    . . . code continues . . .
}
```

In order to get the last person who edited the posting, we used the Posting.OwnedBy property, which returns the user who last edited the posting. If the editor or moderator chose to edit the posting, the OwnedBy would contain their identity.

The Posting.OwnedBy property provides a convenient solution for getting the name of the person to direct declined postings to. However, it only works when the person who is responsible for acting on the posting is indeed the last person who edited it. If the editor or moderator declining the posting made any changes, then their name would be given by this property.

We do not use the Posting.LastModifiedBy property because the Declined operation updates the LastModifiedBy property with the name of the person declining the posting and that would *always* be the editor or moderator clicking on the Decline button.

> In most workflow systems, what we really need is the name of the person who first modified the posting. However, by default, MCMS does not record this information.
>
> In Chapter 19, we will customize the **Web Author Console** and implement a more effective way of retrieving the name of the person to send the declined notification message to.

The code is complete. Save and build the solution.

Log in to the TropicalGreen site with an account that has moderator rights in the Plant Catalog channel (e.g. Moderator1). Navigate to the EggPlant posting and choose to Decline it. An e-mail is sent with the contents:

```
To: author1@computername.net
From: moderator1@computername.net
Datetime: 5/31/2004 2:23:49 PM
Subject: [Declined]EggPlant
----------
Posting Name: EggPlant
Posting Url : /NR/exeres/935F294C-A430-4318-8C59-
BB480BB7110F.htm?WBCMODE=PresentationUnpublished
State : ModeratorDeclined
```

When Moderator1 declined the posting, a notification was sent to the person holding onto the posting's lock, which in this case is Author1.

> A word of caution: Although automating the e-mail notification process has many benefits, be on guard against an avalanche of e-mails from the system when multiple postings are submitted/approved/declined at the same time. Also, if a large group of users has been added as members of the editor and/or moderator rights groups, you will be sending out just as many e-mails to each and every one of them. That can work out to hundreds of e-mails in a single day.
>
> In this situation you might consider a solution that sends summary reports once or twice a day rather than sending an e-mail with every notification.

Now that we have covered the basics of e-mail notification, we are ready to move on to some other events. Go ahead and approve the EggPlant posting, reset your Internet Explorer security settings not to require a login, and close all open browser windows.

Canceling an Operation

Canceling an operation stops the operation from being carried out. You may need to cancel an operation when attempting to prevent authors from:

- Creating two or more postings of the same name in the channel
- Deleting postings
- Modifying certain properties with certain values (or at all)
- Carrying out just about any operation

You can cancel an operation from within the pre-event handler of this operation simply by adding the following line of code:

```
e.Cancel = true;
```

Preventing Authors from Saving Pages with Identical Names

When a channel has two or more postings with the same name, you can access only one of them using hierarchical URLs. For example, if you have three postings by the name of EggPlant in the Plant Catalog channel, entering http://localhost/tropicalgreen/plantcatalog/EggPlant.htm fetches only one of the three postings. There is no way you can view the other three postings unless you know their Unique-ID-based URLs.

To prevent such situations from happening, you need to stop authors from:

- Creating postings that share the same name as another posting within the same channel
- Updating a posting's name to one that has already been used by another posting within the same channel

An appropriate place to perform these checks is in the PropertyChanging event handler. The PropertyChanging event handler is fired once for each property that is being updated. We check the contents of e.PropertyName to see if the property being updated is the name. If it is, we retrieve the new name by retrieving the string stored in e.PropertyValue.

We look for a posting with the same name in the current channel. If one exists, we cancel the event. Back in Global.asax.cs add the following code to the CmsPosting_PropertyChanging() method:

```
protected void CmsPosting_PropertyChanging( Object sender,
PropertyChangingEventArgs e )
{
    if(e.Target is Posting)
    {
        Posting currentPosting = e.Target as Posting;
        if(currentPosting!=null)
        {
            if(e.PropertyName == "Name")
            {
                //Are there any postings in the channel that have this name?
                string newName = e.PropertyValue.ToString();
                Channel currentChannel = currentPosting.Parent;
```

```
Posting duplicate = currentChannel.GetByRelativePath(newName)
                        as Posting;

if(duplicate!=null)
{
    //Duplicate exists; Cancel the Action
    e.Cancel = true;
}
        }
    }
}
//LogEvent("CmsPosting_PropertyChanging",e);
}
```

Save and build the solution.

> Writing this code in the Creating/Created event handler will not work. That is because the Name of the posting is set between the PropertyChanging and PropertyChanged event handlers. You can't get the value of the posting's new name from the Creating/Created event handlers; if you tried, you would find that it is the name of the template it was based on. In addition, the Creating/Created event handlers are not raised when a posting is updated.

When you next attempt to create a posting with the same name as another posting in the channel, you get this error message (e.g. try creating a second posting named EggPlant):

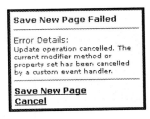

Should you attempt to change the name of an existing posting to one already taken by another posting in the same channel (e.g. try to rename the Hibiscus posting to EggPlant), you get the following error message:

Microsoft Content Management Server

Error has occured

Update operation cancelled. The current modifier method or property set has been cancelled by a custom event handler.

You can hide these error messages by setting the e.SuppressExceptionOnCancel property to true.

```
if(duplicate)!=null)
{
    //Duplicate exists; Cancel the Action
    e.Cancel = true;
    //Hides the error message
```

```
        e.SuppressExceptionOnCancel = true;
    }
```

There is a design limitation that prevents you from displaying your own custom error messages in some workflow events, especially those that perform multiple postbacks that switch to other publishing modes. You can raise an error message back to the Web Author Console, but the custom message is displayed only for a split second before it is replaced when the page reloads again on postback.

If you need to display custom error messages on the Web Author Console, consider using the techniques discussed in Chapter 19 together with the examples here to customize the console actions.

Avoiding Recursive Loops

When working with pre-event handlers, you run the risk of getting caught in a recursive loop. Imagine a scenario where you have a business process that dictates that when you delete a posting, all postings within the same channel should also be deleted. To do that, you may consider writing code within the Deleting event handler to delete all other postings in the channel. The resulting code may resemble something like this:

```
public void CmsPosting_Deleting( Object sender, ChangingEventArgs e )
{
    //Delete all postings in the same channel
    if(e.Target is Posting)
    {
        Posting currentPosting = e.Target as Posting;
        Channel currentChannel = currentPosting.Parent;

        foreach(Posting postingToDelete in currentChannel.Postings)
        {
            postingToDelete.Delete();
            e.Context.CommitAll();
        }
    }
}
```

While this may appear to work in theory, if you actually tried to run the code, you will end up with an error message that says:

Recursive event handling failed. An attempt to recursively invoke the same method or property set that invoked the event handler failed.

What actually happened here? We ended up in a recursive loop simply by calling the Posting.Delete() method within the Deleting event handler. To understand this better, step through the code in a debugger. You will find that:

1. The first call to the CmsPosting_Deleting() event handler was raised when you clicked the Delete button.
2. When looping through each posting, the Posting.Delete() method was called again for each posting in the channel.
3. Each time the Delete() method was called, the CmsPosting_Deleting() event handler was raised yet again bringing you back to step 1.

The cycle repeats itself over and over again. Fortunately, MCMS detects that it is caught in a never-ending loop and raises a PublishingEventRecursiveHandlerException.

To get around this problem, add the code that deletes the postings to the Deleted post-event handler instead of the Deleting pre-event handler. In the Deleted post-event handler, the postings are deleted before the code gets called, preventing a recursive loop.

> You may also enter a recursive loop when updating the property values of postings. This and its workaround have been documented in the online help file: http://msdn .microsoft.com/library/en-us/sitedevl/htm/ cms_sd_ext_workflow_txvk.asp.

Preventing Deletes

Earlier, in Chapter 10, we discussed how MCMS has a basic workflow in place for the creation of postings and the updating of content. This concept does not apply to deletes. As long as an author, editor, or moderator has the right to delete a posting, they can permanently take it out of production by clicking on the Delete button.

When a posting is deleted from within the Web Author Console, the only way to recover the deleted item is to restore a backed up version of the database. By the time that happens, you are probably caught between a frazzled author and a stressed database operator.

To prevent deletes, we can cancel the action in the Deleting pre-event handler in Global.asax.cs. Add the following code to the CmsPosting_Deleting() method:

```
protected void CmsPosting_Deleting( Object sender, ChangingEventArgs e )
{
    if(e.Action == PublishingAction.Delete)
    {
        e.Cancel = true;
    }
}
```

Save and build the solution. Try deleting the EggPlant posting. It won't work! You will get a Delete Failed exception in the Web Author Console:

```
Delete Failed
..............................................................................
Error Details:
Update operation cancelled. The current modifier method or property set has been
cancelled by a custom event handler.
..............................................................................
Reattempt Delete
Cancel
```

> You could also prevent deletes by removing the Delete button from the Web Author Console as discussed in Chapter 19.

By preventing all deletes, we have effectively barred authors, editors, and moderators from deleting any postings in the site. Only administrators, template designers, and channel managers can perform delete operations through Site Manager. At least, when deleting postings in Site Manager, you have the option of recovering them from the Deleted Items bin, should you need to.

Now that we have seen how deletions (and other actions) can be prevented, let's re-enable the delete function. To do so, comment out code in the `CmsPosting_Deleting()` event handler as shown below.

```
protected void CmsPosting_Deleting( Object sender, ChangingEventArgs e )
{
    /*
    if(e.Action == PublishingAction.Delete)
    {
        e.Cancel = true;
    }
    */

}
```

Generic Event Handlers

Each time a pre-event handler is called, the `Changing` event handler is also called. Similarly, each time a post-event handler is called, the `Changed` event handler is called. The `Changing` and `Changed` event handlers are known as generic event handlers because they are fired for every operation that is performed on a posting.

In the examples above, we have been writing code in specific event handlers (e.g. `Submitted`, `Approved`). When customizing the workflow, you can write code in the `Changing` and `Changed` event handlers as an alternative. The code below shows how this can be done in the `Changed` event handler. Bear in mind, however, that it is considered bad practice to do so. Generic event handlers are called each time an event is raised so placing code there incurs more overhead than putting it in specific event handlers.

```
public void CmsPosting_Changed( Object sender, ChangedEventArgs e )
{
    switch(e.Action)
    {
        case PublishingAction.Approve:
            // after a Posting has been approved
            break;

        case PublishingAction.Create:
            // after a Posting has been created
            break;

        case PublishingAction.CustomPropertyChange:
            // after a custom property value
            //of a Posting has changed
            break;

        case PublishingAction.Decline:
            // after a Posting has been declined
            break;

        case PublishingAction.Delete:
            // after a Posting has been deleted
            break;

        case PublishingAction.Move:
            // after a Posting has been moved
            break;

        case PublishingAction.PlaceholderPropertyChange:
            // after a placeholder property
```

```
                        //value has changed
                        break;

            case PublishingAction.PropertyChange:
                        // after a property value of a
                        //Posting has changed
                        break;

            case PublishingAction.Submit:
                        // after a Posting has been submitted
                        break;
        }
    }
```

Consider using generic event handlers for implementing workflow logic that is independent of the action carried out, such as code that implements an audit trail or other monitoring activities.

Summary

Once you have mastered the basics of the workflow event handlers shown in this chapter, you can customize just about any part of the publishing process.

This chapter has demonstrated how a simple e-mail notification system can be built into the workflow. When authors submit a posting for approval, an e-mail is immediately sent out to a list of approvers. Similarly, when the posting has been approved or declined, an e-mail is sent to the relevant people in the workflow.

We went on to show how operations can be canceled when certain conditions have not been met, for example, when the posting's name is not unique, or when you need to prevent users from performing certain operations such as deleting postings.

Finally, we looked at generic event handlers. While it is possible to use generic handlers instead of specific event handlers, they incur slightly higher overheads and inappropriate use is to be avoided.

17

Publishing with Authoring Connector

Authoring Connector provides the ability to upload content from Microsoft Word directly to MCMS, allowing authors to continue to work in the familiar Word environment without having to learn the technicalities of HTML or other web scripting languages. Through a simple publishing process, a Word document can be uploaded to the MCMS web server and published as a posting.

You will find Authoring Connector particularly useful when:

- Authors are not comfortable editing content in the browser and would be happier using Word instead.
- Authors require a rich editing environment that allows them to work with complex objects such as tables.
- Templates are structured to contain a single placeholder.

Authoring Connector is a client component and needs to be installed on every desktop that requires it. Once installed, it adds a **Send to MCMS** option to Word's **File** menu. Authors click on this option to upload the open document to the website.

In this chapter, we will build an additional section for the TropicalGreen site, named Columns. This new segment serves as an area for authors to upload articles they have written about fellow members, latest events, their gardening experiences, and what they've been growing in their backyards. To test the capabilities of Authoring Connector, we will use it to publish content from Word to the Columns channel.

Before We Begin

In order to complete the rest of the chapter, you must have the following software installed on your computer:

- Word XP or Word 2003
- Authoring Connector, which we will install below

You should also have completed Chapter 5.

Installing Authoring Connector

To begin, close all instances of Word on your desktop (remember to save your work first).

Insert the Microsoft Content Management Server 2002 CD into your computer. On the splash screen, choose to Install Authoring Connector. Click Next to get past the Welcome screen.

> You could also download the latest version of Authoring Connector from the official Microsoft website (http://www.microsoft.com/downloads) and store the installation file, AuthConn.exe, on a central computer for distribution to authors.

In the Customer Information dialog, enter your name and the name of your company. Choose to either add Authoring Connector options to all profiles on the computer or only to your profile. When you are done, click Next.

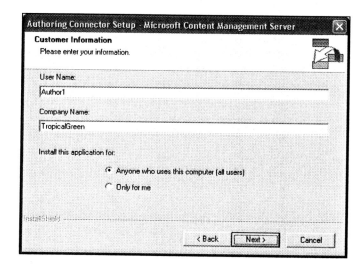

Select the Destination folder. The default folder is \Authoring Connector\ under the MCMS installation folder. If the specified folder does not exist, the installer will create it for you. When you have made your selection, click Next.

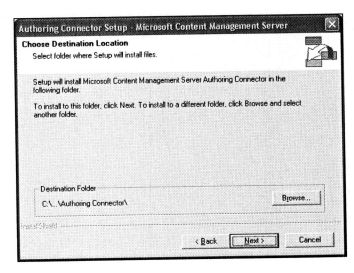

Enter the MCMS server name. Click Next when you have entered the name of a valid MCMS server, or leave it as localhost.

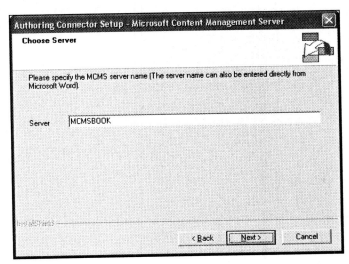

The next screen displays the name of the MCMS server name entered earlier. You can change the setting by clicking on the Back button. To begin the installation, click Install.

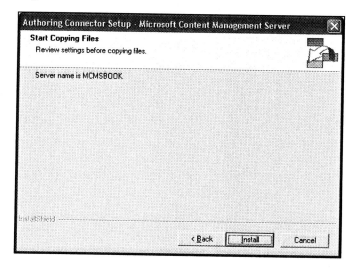

Once you have installed Authoring Connector, open Word and select File from the menu bar. You should see a new entry Send to MCMS, which expands to reveal more options.

- Create New Page
- Update Same Page
- Replace Any Page

The Update Same Page option is not available at the moment because you have not published the page to MCMS.

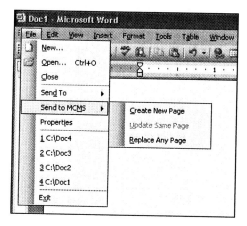

In addition, a new entry, MCMS Authoring Connector Help is added to the Help menu. The link leads to the Authoring Connector help file, which guides authors through a step-by-step tutorial on how to use Authoring Connector to publish Word documents to MCMS.

If the Send to MCMS menu item is missing or grayed out, it means that Authoring Connector was not registered properly on the client. Run the installation process again, this time:

1. Ensure that all instances of Word on the client machine have been properly closed

2. After Authoring Connector has been installed, open Word. Select Tools | Macro | Security. In the Security dialog, click on the Trusted Sources tab. Check that the Trust all installed add-ins and templates option is selected.

Columns

We will now create the new section for the TropicalGreen website, named Columns. It will be a place for listing articles about the latest news from TropicalGreen. Authors usually create articles from Word documents. A typical column runs about a page long and may include pictures at appropriate points. Here's what we will be doing:

- We will start by creating a template for our columns.
- Next, we will open an existing Word document and use Authoring Connector to create a new posting based on the template that we have created.
- Then we will use the existing Word document and test the update and replace functions of Authoring Connector.

The final part of the chapter will discuss how certain parts of the publishing process can be automated using Publishing Tasks.

We'll re-use the channel rendering script from Chapter 9 to list all articles available in the channel.

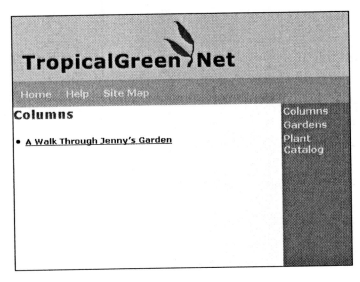

An article created for the columns section appears as shown in the following figure:

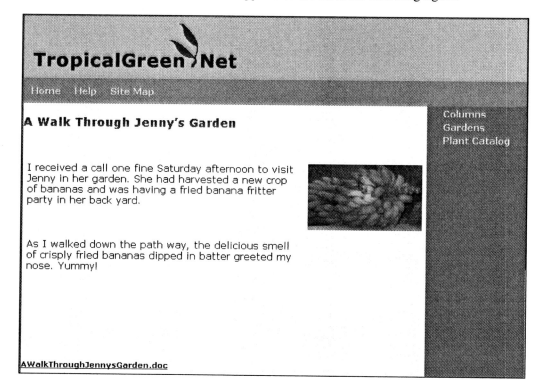

Building the Column Template

Before we can publish with Word, we need to build a template to be used by postings created using Authoring Connector. Like regular postings, a template object and template file pair will be created.

Creating the Template Object

Open the TropicalGreen solution in Visual Studio .NET.

First, create the template object. In Template Explorer, add a new template object to the `Columns` template gallery. Name the new template `Column`.

Next, in the PlaceholderDefinitions collection, add an `OfficeHtmlPlaceholderDefinition` and an `OfficeAttachmentPlaceholderDefinition` with the properties shown in the following table.

Placeholder Type	Property Name	Property Value
OfficeHtmlPlaceholderDefinition	AllowHyperlinks	True
	AllowLineBreaks	True
	Formatting	FullFormatting
	Description	Placeholder containing the story
	Name	Story
	AllowAttachments	True
	AllowImages	True
	MustUseResourceGallery	False
	UseGeneratedIcon	False
OfficeAttachmentPlaceholderDefinition	Description	Placeholder containing the story in its original Word document format
	Name	StorySource
	MustUseResourceGallery	False
	UseGeneratedIcon	False

Add a TextCustomPropertyDefinition to the custom property definition collection with the following properties:

Custom Property Type	Property Name	Property Value
TextCustomPropertyDefinition	Name	SourceOfInformation
	Value	Author's own research

Creating the Template File

Add a new MCMS template file to the Templates folder of the TropicalGreen project. Name the new template file Columns.aspx. Immediately switch the PageLayout property to FlowLayout.

Toggle back to the MCMS Template Explorer. Set the TemplateFile property of the Column template to point to the Columns.aspx template file. Check in the template object.

In Columns.aspx, switch to HTML view. Between the <head> and </head> tags, link to the stylesheet created in Chapter 7 to the template file.

```
<head>
. . . code continues . . .
<LINK href="/tropicalgreen/Styles/Styles.css" type="text/css"
rel="stylesheet">
</head>
```

Between the <form> and </form> tags enter the code below.

```
<table width="100%" border="0" cellspacing="0" cellpadding="0" height="100%">
<tr>
    <td width="100%" colspan="2" valign="top" bgcolor="#FFCC00">
        <IMG src="/tropicalgreen/images/Logo.gif">
    </td>
    <td rowspan="10" valign="top">
        (Space for Console)
    </td>
</tr>
<tr bgcolor="#66CC33">
    <td colspan="2">(Space for Top Menu)</td>
</tr>
<tr>
    <td valign="top">
        <br>
        (Space for HTML Placeholder Control)
        <br>
        (Space for Attachment Placeholder Control)
        <br>
    </td>
    <td class="RightMenuBar" width="20%" valign="top" height="100%"
align="center" rowspan="2" bgcolor="#669900">
        (Space for Right Menu Bar)
    </td>
</tr>
</tr>
</table>
```

When you have entered the HTML code, switch back to Design view. Drag and drop the following Web User Controls onto the form:

- TopMenu.ascx (built in Chapter 13) into the cell containing the words (Space for Top Menu)

- RightMenu.ascx (built in Chapter 13) into the cell containing the words (Space for Right Menu Bar)

- DefaultConsole.ascx into the cell containing the words (Space for Default Console)

From the Toolbox, drag and drop the following MCMS placeholder controls:

- HTMLPlaceholderControl into the cell containing the words (Space for HTML Placeholder Control). Set the PlaceholderToBind property to Story and the ID to ColumnStory.

- SingleAttachmentPlaceholderControl into the cell containing the words (Space for Attachment Placeholder Control). Set the PlaceholderToBind property to StorySource and the ID to ColumnStorySource.

Delete the text markers after you have dragged the controls onto the form. The completed page is shown in the following figure:

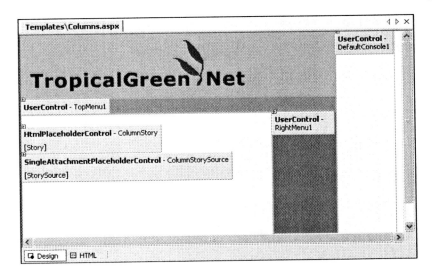

Save and build the TropicalGreen solution.

Finally, use the ChannelRenderingScript.aspx channel rendering script (created in Chapter 9) to display a list of all articles posted to the Columns channel. Open Site Manager and set the Script Url property of the Columns channel to:

```
/tropicalgreen/templates/ChannelRenderingScript.aspx
```

The OfficeHtmlPlaceholder and OfficeAttachmentPlaceholder Definitions

In the Column template, we use the two placeholder definitions shipped with MCMS that provide support for authoring from within Word:

- **OfficeHtmlPlaceholderDefinition**, which has the same properties and methods as the HtmlPlaceholderDefinition
- **OfficeAttachmentPlaceholderDefinition,** which has the same properties and methods as the AttachmentPlaceholderDefinition

When building templates that work with Authoring Connector, use the Office versions of the placeholder definitions. It is through these specialized placeholder definitions that Authoring Connector differentiates between placeholders that it needs to fill with data and placeholders that it should ignore.

To understand this better, consider the case of a template that has two placeholder definitions: The first placeholder uses the regular HtmlPlaceholderDefinition and the second, an OfficeHtmlPlaceholderDefinition. When content is published from Word using Authoring Connector, only the OfficeHtmlPlaceholder object receives the content. Authoring Connector will ignore the HtmlPlaceholder object if an OfficeHtmlPlaceholder object is available.

If multiple `OfficeHtmlPlaceholderDefinitions` or `OfficeAttachmentPlaceholderDefinitions` are added to the same template, all placeholders will receive the same content. For this reason, you can't split the content of a Word document between more than one placeholder. For example, using the standard Authoring Connector functionality, it is not possible to ensure that the title goes into the first placeholder, the abstract fills a second placeholder, and the main body goes into a third placeholder.

> Cross reference: The article, *Customizing Microsoft Content Management Server 2002 Authoring Connector*, found in the MSDN library at the URL `http://msdn.microsoft.com/library/default.asp?url=/library/en-us/dnmscms02/html/mscms_CustAuCo.asp`, suggests ways to split a Word document over multiple placeholders.

The following table summarizes how Authoring Connector saves content based on the placeholder definitions found in the template.

Composition of Template	Authoring Connector Behavior
Contains one `OfficeHtmlPlaceholder`	Authoring Connector publishes content to the `OfficeHtmlPlaceholder`.
Contains one `OfficeAttachmentPlaceholder`	Authoring Connector publishes the document as an attachment to the `OfficeAttachmentPlaceholder`.
Contains one `OfficeHtmlPlaceholder` and one `OfficeAttachmentPlaceholder`	Authoring Connector publishes the content to the `OfficeHtmlPlaceholder` and the document as an attachment to the `OfficeAttachmentPlaceholder`.
Contains more than one `OfficeHtmlPlaceholder`	Authoring Connector publishes content to each `OfficeHtmlPlaceholder`.
Contains more than one `OfficeAttachmentPlaceholder`	Authoring Connector publishes the document as an attachment to each `OfficeAttachmentPlaceholder`.
Contains no Office placeholders but contains at least one `HtmlPlaceholder`	Authoring Connector publishes content to the first `HtmlPlaceholder` it finds on the page.
Contains no Office placeholders but contains at least one `AttachmentPlaceholder`	Authoring Connector publishes content to the first `AttachmentPlaceholder` it finds on the page.
Contains no Office placeholders but contains at least one `HtmlPlaceholder` and at least one `AttachmentPlaceholder`	Authoring Connector publishes content to the first `HtmlPlaceholder` it finds on the page and saves the original Word document in the first `AttachmentPlaceholder`.
Contains at least one `OfficeHtmlPlaceholder` and at least one `AttachmentPlaceholder`/`HtmlPlaceholder`	Authoring Connector publishes content to each `OfficeHtmlPlaceholder`. No `AttachmentPlaceholder`/`HtmlPlaceholder` receives any content.
Contains at least one `OfficeAttachmentPlaceholder` and at least one `AttachmentPlaceholder`/`HtmlPlaceholder`	Authoring Connector publishes content to each `OfficeAttachmentPlaceholder`. No `AttachmentPlaceholder`/`HtmlPlaceholder` receives any content.

Publishing from Microsoft Word

Now that we have a template created, we can proceed to upload a document from Word using Authoring Connector. To begin, open a Word document. You can download the sample document from the code download section of the book's companion site or use one of your own documents. On the menu bar, select File | Send to MCMS | Create New Page. If you have any unsaved changes, Word prompts you to save them before proceeding.

The Authoring Connector Wizard dialog appears as shown in the following figure. Ensure that the Change Server Name and Path option is unchecked. Click Next to get past the welcome screen. If you have set Internet Explorer to prompt for a user name and password in the intranet zone, you will get a prompt to login at this point.

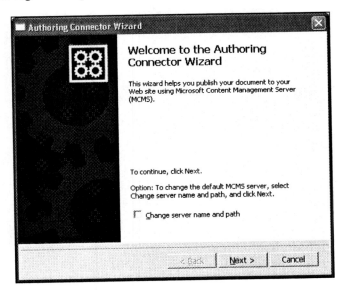

The next screen shows you a list of publishing tasks. We have not defined any so the list is empty for now (see the section *Creating Publishing Tasks* for a discussion on creating and using publishing tasks). Click Next to continue.

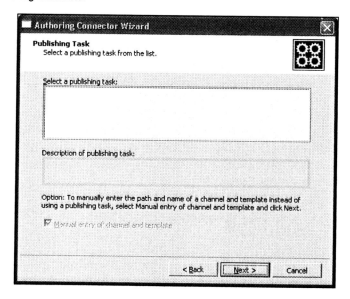

You are prompted to select the destination channel. Select the Columns channel and click Next.

If you are unable to see the channel hierarchy and can only choose the top-level channel, it means that either you do not have subscriber access to any of the second-level channels or the IE Web Controls are not correctly installed on the MCMS server.

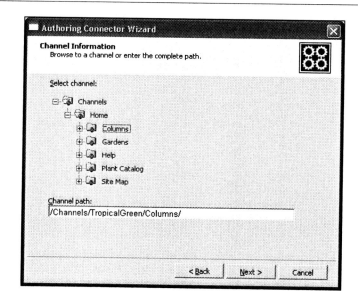

The dialog prompts you to select the template. Select the Column template and click Next.

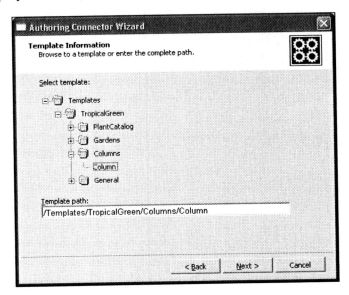

The wizard asks for the page's name, title, and description. Only the page name is mandatory. If you leave the Title to appear on Web page (which is the display name) blank, MCMS assumes that the title should take the same value as the name. Fill up the fields with the following values:

Field Name	Value
Page name	AWalkThroughJennysGarden
Title to appear on Web page	A Walk Through Jenny's Garden
Make the title the same as the page name	Unchecked
Page description	You can publish pages directly from Word to MCMS using Authoring Connector!

When you have completed all fields, click Next.

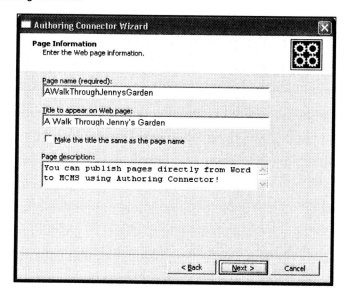

The next screen requests the start and end dates of the posting. By default, the start date is set to the current date and time and end date to never (or 1st January 3000). Accept the default values.

Ensure that the Advanced page properties option is checked and click Next.

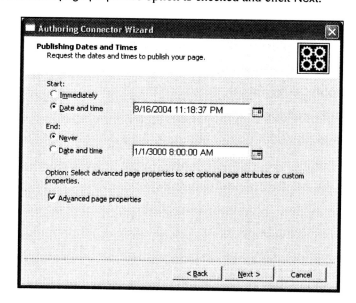

Because we have chosen to see the advanced page properties in the previous screen, the next screen shows us what these properties are. The first section displays four properties:

• Mark page as special page sets the IsImportant property of the page.

- Allow Web robots to crawl links sets the `IsRobotFollowable` property of the page.
- Hide page from subscriber when published sets the `IsHiddenModePublished` property of the page.
- Allow Web robots to index this page sets the `IsRobotIndexable` property of the page.

The second section displays a list of all custom properties assigned to the template. In this example, we have a custom text property named `SourceOfInformation`. To edit its stored value:

1. Set the Use Default property to False.
2. Enter text in the CurrentValue field e.g. (your name)'s research.

When you have set the advanced page properties, click Next.

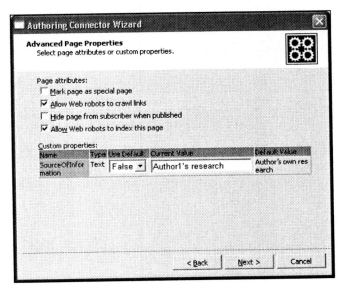

You have now entered all the necessary information to get the posting published. Click on the Preview Page button to see how the posting will appear when published. The rest of the dialog provides you with a summary of the page's name, title, destination channel, and template. These are read-only text boxes and to change any of these values, you'll need to click the Back button. Click Next to submit the page to the publishing workflow.

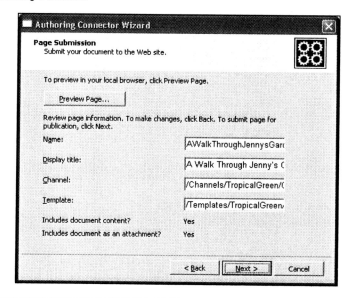

When I click Next at the Page Submission dialog, I get a pop-up dialog with a server 500 error.

You are probably using the .NET Framework 1.1. .NET 1.1 ships with a new feature that identifies potentially harmful content in POST requests. MCMS requires that this feature be disabled.

To do this, open the folder \server\MCMS under the MCMS installation folder. Turn off the read-only property of the web.config file. Then open the web.config file for editing and add the following line below the </httpModules> line at the bottom:

```
<pages smartNavigation="false" validateRequest="false" />
```

Save and close the web.config file and now you should be able to continue using the Authoring Connector.

A new posting is created in MCMS and the wizard informs you that it has been submitted to the publishing workflow. If editors and moderators have been assigned to the destination channel, the posting will not be published immediately but instead will be set to a Waiting For Editor Approval or Waiting For Moderator Approval state. Editors and moderators have to use Web Author to approve or decline a posting.

Check the Launch MCMS Web Author option and click Finish.

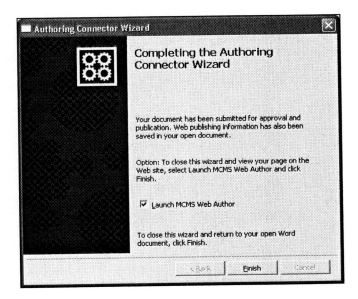

The posting has been created in MCMS and appears as shown in the following figure. Notice that it is in a Published state. That's because we have not assigned any editors or moderators to the Columns channel so any updates from authors are published without any approval required.

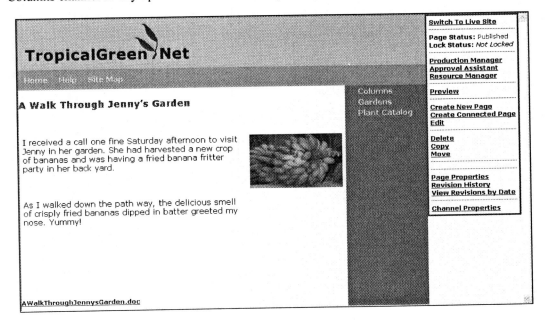

The content from the Word document has been saved to the officeHtmlPlaceholder. At the bottom of the page you will find a link to the original document that has been saved to the officeAttachmentPlaceholder. You may notice a few differences in the way the content is formatted. We will fix this in the *Maintaining a Consistent Look and Feel* section in this chapter.

Updating the Page

The first time a page is published using Authoring Connector, two properties are created within the Word document. Open the Word document. From the menu bar, select File | Properties and open the Custom tab of the Properties dialog.

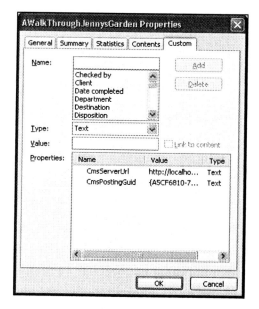

You will see two new entries:

- **CmsServerUrl** contains a string that points to the server-side component, usually in the form http://servername/mcms/cms/officeWizard/oc.aspx
- **CmsPostingGuid** stores the GUID of the MCMS posting

The **CmsServerUrl** and **CmsPostingGuid** property values are used by Authoring Connector when you decide to update the document in your MCMS repository.

To update the document and submit it for publishing, follow these steps:

1. With the Word document opened, select File | Send to MCMS | Update Same Page from the menu bar.
2. At the Welcome screen, click Next.
3. You are immediately brought to the Page Properties dialog. Notice that Authoring Connector skips the Publishing Tasks, Channel Information, and Template

Information dialogs. It already has this information from the custom property values of the Word document. In the Page Properties dialog, you can choose to amend the page name, title, and description. The previously saved property values are retrieved from the MCMS repository and displayed here. Click Next.

4. In the Publishing Date and Times dialog, you can adjust the publishing start and end dates. Click Next.

5. In the Page Submission dialog, click Next to save changes to the content repository.

6. After submitting the page, click Finish to close the Authoring Connector dialog.

Authoring Connector relies on the custom property values of the Word document to link back to the posting in the content repository. Should the posting be deleted, you will receive an error message immediately after the Welcome screen.

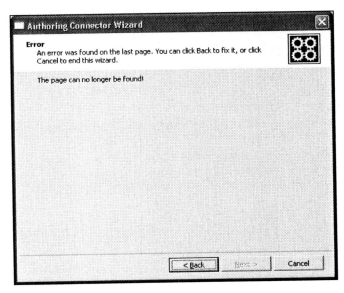

If the posting is in a state where updates are not allowed (e.g. if another author locks the posting), you will get the message The current user does not have rights to edit the requested item. when attempting to submit the posting.

If you are sure that the posting does exist on the server, choose the File | Send to MCMS | Replace Any Page option instead.

> Remember to keep the Word document updated with the latest content. Otherwise, when you next use Authoring Connector to publish the document, it overwrites all changes that were done in Web Author.

> Using Authoring Connector is a one-way road: It updates the website but it does not receive updates from the website.

> If you don't want your authors to accidentally overwrite changes made using the Web Author Console, you can set up your templates to only allow changes to come from the Authoring Connector and not allow postings to be edited using Web Author. You can do that by disabling the edit button in the Web Author. The technique is discussed in Chapter 19.

Replacing Any Page

The Replace Any Page option allows you to replace any posting in the MCMS content repository with the contents of the Word document.

You will find this option useful when:

- The posting was originally created using the Web Author Console. You have taken advantage of Word's rich authoring environment to update the posting's content and now need to synchronize your work with the online posting.

- Someone unknowingly deletes or amends the **CmsServerUrl** or **CmsPostingGuid** property values of the Word document preventing Authoring Connector from 'remembering' the location of the original posting.

To replace an existing posting:

1. Select the File | Send to MCMS | Replace Any Page option from the menu bar.
2. At the Welcome screen, click Next.
3. The next screen prompts you for the posting to replace. Navigate through the tree of channels and postings to select the posting you wish to replace. For example, choose to replace the article created earlier, AWalkThroughJennysGarden. The path of the selected posting is shown in the Web page path field. After you have made your choice, click Next.

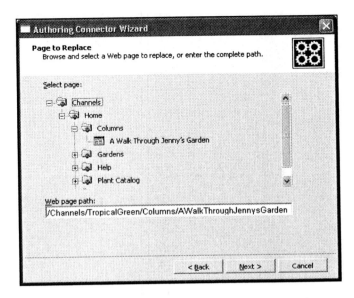

4. You are shown the Page Properties dialog. As before, you can choose to update the posting's name, title, description, start and end dates, and other properties. Click Next to accept the current values.

5. At the Page Submission screen, click Next to submit the posting.

6. Click Finish to close the Authoring Connector dialog.

Submitting Selected Text

So far, we have saved entire Word documents as postings. You can also choose to save selected portions of text instead of the complete document. This works only for an OfficeHtmlPlaceholder: an OfficeAttachmentPlaceholder will always receive the entire Word document.

Open the Word document created earlier and highlight a portion of text. From the menu bar, select File | Send to MCMS | Update Same Page.

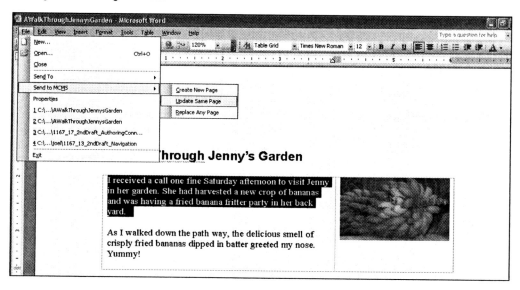

The Welcome Screen appears with a new option. You can choose to publish:

- The selected content only
- The whole document

To publish only the highlighted text, choose the Selected content only option and follow the rest of the publishing process. However, we want to keep the full text and image in our posting, so click Cancel.

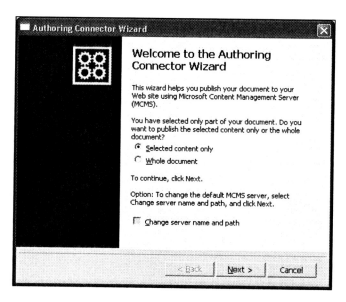

Maintaining a Consistent Look and Feel

Word uses document templates to define the styles for a document. When you first create a Word document, the default template used is the Normal template (`normal.dot`). You could change the template used in Word by selecting **Tools | Templates and Add-Ins** from the menu bar. Each document template defines the font family, font size, alignment, color, and other properties that govern the look and feel of the page.

> Document templates are files that contain the style definitions for Word documents. Documents that share the same template therefore have the same look and feel.

When Word documents are saved as postings, the look and feel of the document changes to that of the stylesheet attached to the template file. For example, when we published `AWalkthroughJennysGarden` from a Word document, our level-1 headings appeared in Arial fonts of size 16pt in Word:

A Walk Through Jenny's Garden

I received a call one fine Saturday afternoon to visit Jenny in her garden. She had harvested a new crop of bananas and was having a fried banana fritter party in her back yard.

As I walked down the path way, the delicious smell of crisply fried bananas dipped in batter greeted my nose. Yummy!

However, they display as Verdana font-size 14pt in brown once uploaded on the posting:

A Walk Through Jenny's Garden

I received a call one fine Saturday afternoon to visit Jenny in her garden. She had harvested a new crop of bananas and was having a fried banana fritter party in her back yard.

As I walked down the path way, the delicious smell of crisply fried bananas dipped in batter greeted my nose. Yummy!

Authors often get puzzled over this change in format. They get especially concerned when the change in style causes carefully positioned text and objects in the document to lose their place.

To understand this better, we need to look at what goes on behind the scenes when you publish the document using Authoring Connector. One of the tasks performed by Authoring Connector is to convert the document to a web page. To repeat this operation:

1. Open the Word document uploaded in the previous section in Word.
2. Select File | Save As Web Page from the menu bar.
3. Choose the Web Page, Filtered option in the Save as type drop-down menu.
4. The file is saved with a .htm extension.
5. Close Word.

Open the generated web page in Visual Studio .NET. Switch to HTML view so that you can see the source code. At the top of the web page the <style> tags are defined.

The following code shows a snippet of what you may see.

```
<style>
<!--
/* Style Definitions */
 p.MsoNormal, li.MsoNormal, div.MsoNormal
     {margin:0in;
     margin-bottom:.0001pt;
     font-size:12.0pt;
     font-family:"Times New Roman";}
h1
     {margin-top:12.0pt;
     margin-right:0in;
     margin-bottom:3.0pt;
     margin-left:0in;
     page-break-after:avoid;
     font-size:16.0pt;
     font-family:Arial;}
@page Section1
     {size:8.5in 11.0in;
     margin:1.0in 1.25in 1.0in 1.25in;}
div.Section1
     {page:Section1;}
-->
</style>
```

Being embedded between <head> tags, <style> tags are not imported to the placeholder when the Word document is uploaded through Authoring Connector. In order to preserve the styles and formatting from the Word document, these additional style tags must be inserted into the template. To add styles from the Word document to the Column template:

1. Open the column.aspx template file.
2. Switch to HTML view.
3. Copy and paste the contents of the <style></style> tags in the saved web page between the <head> and </head> tags of column.aspx.
4. Save column.aspx.

With the styles copied over to the template file, the look and feel of the Word document is preserved. Note the conversion from Word to HTML may not always be 100% accurate. Word may not convert complex formatting correctly to HTML. This is a limitation of Word itself. It is a good idea to remind authors to click on the Preview button in Web Author before submitting their work. Best results can often be achieved by saving the Word document as a file of the type web page, Filtered(*.htm, *.html).

> Typically, you would create a document template that shares the same style rules as the template applied on the website. Authors must then be educated to use that document template to create all documents that are to be published using Authoring Connector.

Reducing the Spacing between Line Breaks

When working in Word, you define where one paragraph ends and another begins by pressing the *Enter* key. This keystroke generates a new paragraph, introducing an extended spacing between one paragraph and the next one.

> I received a call one fine Saturday afternoon to visit Jenny in her garden. She had harvested a new crop of bananas and was having a fried banana fritter party in her back yard.
>
> As I walked down the path way, the delicious smell of crisply fried bananas dipped in batter greeted my nose. Yummy!

After being published to MCMS using the Authoring Connector, an extra line appears to have been added wherever the *Enter* key was pressed, causing the white space between paragraphs to double in size.

> I received a call one fine Saturday afternoon to visit Jenny in her garden. She had harvested a new crop of bananas and was having a fried banana fritter party in her back yard.
>
>
> As I walked down the path way, the delicious smell of crisply fried bananas dipped in batter greeted my nose. Yummy!

This is because hitting *Enter* creates a new paragraph, which is translated to a <p> tag when the document is converted to a web page. By default the <p> tag is displayed with margins that are approximately the size of two single lines.

There are several ways to get around this.

- The easiest solution is to copy the styles from the Word template document and incorporate it into the stylesheet used by the template file as described above. The

Word template document has definitions for the <p> tag to limit the margin between paragraphs.

- You could also define the margins of the <p> tag. For example, you could add in a style that says:

```
P {margin-top:10px}
```

All paragraphs would automatically have their top margins reduced to only 10px, or approximately the height of a single line. Note that if you do so, all other page design elements that use the <p> tag will be affected by this setting.

- Another option is to get authors to press *Shift + Enter* instead of just *Enter*. This introduces a line break, which gets translated to a <br> tag that has a smaller margin.

The best solution is to create your own custom Word document template that makes paragraphs show up with the margin that you want and export the styles used to the template file. That way, authors see the same formatting applied on both the Word document and the posting.

Changing the Server Name

You may have authors publishing Word documents to several MCMS sites hosted on different servers. Or perhaps the server that hosted the website has changed location and the address needs to be updated. Whatever your reasons may be, you need to point Authoring Connector to a server that was different from the one defined during the installation sequence.

The good news is that you can easily do that from Authoring Connector itself.

1. Open your Word document.
2. From the File | Send to MCMS menu, select either the Create New Page or Replace Any Page option.
3. In the Welcome screen, select the Change server name and path option.
4. Click Next and you will see the Default MCMS Server dialog as shown below. In the Server name and path field, enter the address of the oc.aspx file on the target MCMS server.
5. Click Next to save the setting or Reset to restore the previously saved settings.

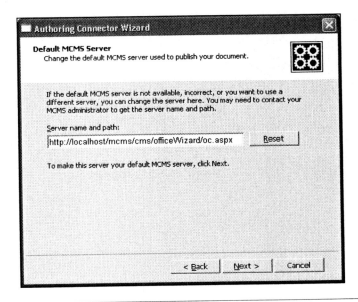

If the server name and path point to a MCMS server that is not available or if the path is not correct, you get a "requested resource not found" error message when trying to proceed from the Welcome screen to the next dialog.

Changing the Server Name for Hundreds of Documents

You may have created hundreds of documents and published them using Authoring Connector. And for reasons beyond your control, it has been decided that the server that hosts the MCMS website is to change its name. It would be a time consuming task indeed to open each document to change its server name and path.

Fortunately, you can change the name of the server using scripts. Simply update the CmsServerUrl property of the Word document. A way to achieve this could be to create a console application that references the Microsoft Word 10.0 Object Library COM object (for Word 2002/XP) or Microsoft Word 11.0 Object Library COM object (for Word 2003) or use Visual Basic for Applications (VBA). Program the script to open each document and set its custom property values appropriately.

Always test any such scripts again after applying any patches or updates from Microsoft.

Creating Publishing Tasks

Some tasks are repetitive. For instance, when authors publish columns, they need to use the Column template and choose Columns as the destination channel. The number of steps required to get the posting published from the moment the document is saved is approximately eight (one for each dialog). Authors have to remember which channels to post to or which templates to use each time they create new postings.

If they were to accidentally select a different channel, the posting would get published to the wrong place. Likewise, should they unwittingly choose another template, the format of the posting would be different from the rest. Human error will occur at some point and when that happens, someone will be called in to clean up the mess.

You can automate the process of publishing documents with Authoring Connector using Publishing Tasks. As the developer, you can specify, on behalf of authors, the destination channel and template to use within each Publishing Task.

The list of Publishing Tasks is stored as an XML file that can be found at `\Server\IIS_CMS\` `OfficeWizard\PublishingTasks.xml` under the MCMS installation folder. The following code snippet shows what a single task looks like.

```xml
<?xml version="1.0" ?>
<tasks> <!-- xmlns="http://www.microsoft.com/cmserver/ACSchema" > -->
    <task>
        <name>New Job Posting</name>
        <description>New Job Posting</description>
        <template>/Templates/General Use/Job Posting</template>
        <channel>/Channels/Intranet/Human Resources/</channel>
    </task>
</tasks>
```

Each task is made up of four elements:

- The `name` of the Publishing Task must be less than 132 characters. All text must be properly escaped HTML (e.g. < should be represented as <).

- The `description` of the Publishing Task must be less than 1024 bytes or 1024 ASCII characters. As for the `name` element, all text must be properly escaped HTML.

- The `template` or `templateGuid` is the template on which the new posting is based. You can choose to define the template from its path (e.g. `/Templates/TemplateName`) or use its GUID.

- `channel` or `channelGuid` is the destination channel of the created posting. You can choose to define the channel from its path (e.g. `/Channels/ChannelName`) or use its GUID.

Let's create a publishing task to automate the process of publishing articles to the Columns channel. Start by opening `PublishingTasks.xml` in an XML editing tool like Visual Studio .NET or Notepad. Between the `<tasks>` and `</tasks>` tags, add a new `<task>` element as shown below. When you have finished entering the task, save `PublishingTasks.xml`.

```xml
<task>
    <name>Create a new Column</name>
    <description>
        This task creates a new Column in the Columns section for the
        TropicalGreen site
```

```
    </description>
    <template>/Templates/TropicalGreen/Columns/Column</template>
    <channel>/Channels/TropicalGreen/Columns</channel>
</task>
```

Open a new Word document. Select File | Send to MCMS | Create New Page. Click Next at the Welcome screen.

The next screen displayed is the Publishing Task dialog. The task that we have created in the PublishingTasks.xml file is listed. The list only shows tasks in which the author has rights to both the template and the channel. Select Create a new Column. The description of the task is shown in the bottom panel. Click Next.

Authors can continue to manually select the template and destination channel by checking the Manual entry of channel and template option.

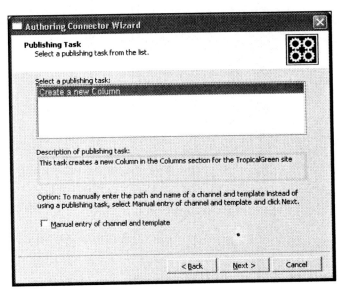

The subsequent screens take you through the rest of the publishing process. Notice that you were not asked to select the template and destination channel: This information was specified in the publishing task.

Using Publishing Tasks simplifies work, shaving off at least two steps from the publishing process. Authors need not even understand the concept of channels and templates. They simply select the task, set the page properties and submit the page for publishing.

If the new publishing task does not show up in the wizard or if the task list remains completely empty, check the following:

> Ensure that the template or channel defined exists and that the author has the rights to access these objects.
>
> Check that `PublishingTasks.xml` contains valid XML with all tags properly opened and closed and that all characters are valid.
>
> Make certain that you are amending the copy of `PublishingTasks.xml` that is specified in the `web.config` file of the Authoring Connector (discussed below).

Modifying the Location of PublishingTasks.xml and PublishingTasks.xsd

For security reasons, you may wish to change the location of the `PublishingTasks.xml` and `PublishingTasks.xsd` files. To do so, open the `web.config` file located within the `\Server\IIS_CMS\officewizard\` folder under the MCMS installation folder. Look for the following lines of code:

```
<appSettings>
  <add key="Publishing Tasks XML File Path" value="C:\secure\tasks.xml" />
  <add key="Publishing Tasks Schema File Path" value="C:\secure\tasks.xsd" />
</appSettings>
```

Move this code out of the comment area (`<!-- -->`) and replace the paths with the new location of the PublishingTasks.xml and PublishingTasks.xsd files. Don't change the value of the key attribute. It must be entered exactly as shown otherwise the new locations of the files would not be recognized.

Summary

In this chapter, we have seen how authors can publish content from Word directly to an MCMS site using Authoring Connector. Allowing your authors to continue using the tool they are already familiar with increases their acceptance of the product as well as lowering their learning curve and cranking up their productivity.

We started by creating a template for a new section of the site, which we called Columns. Next, we discussed how Authoring Connector decides which placeholder to fill in when it updates a posting. We were then ready to convert an existing Word document to a posting, using Authoring Connector. We went on to show how easily updates and replacements can be accomplished.

We also saw how formatting can be preserved by transferring the styles used in the Word document over to the template file.

Finally, we looked at how Authoring Connector can be automated and customized using Publishing Tasks. Destination channels and templates can be predefined to prevent authors from posting articles using incorrect templates or channels and to reduce the number of steps required to publish an article.

18

Implementing Forms Authentication

Windows authentication is perfect in intranet environments where everyone signs on to the website with the same credentials used to log into Windows. For sites meant for public viewing on the Internet, Windows authentication will not usually be appropriate. Visitors will be prompted for their user name and password and when they do not have an account in the specified domain (e.g. guest users), they won't be able to access content.

The good news is that there are other ways to authenticate a user. ASP.NET supports at least two alternatives. The first uses Microsoft Passport, which users may already use to authenticate against other websites. In order to implement Passport, you have to subscribe to its services, which can be too costly for a small website.

Another alternative is to use Forms authentication, which is the topic of this chapter. Users enter credentials into a form. The web application uses this information to decide whether or not the user has access to the resource they are requesting. Consider implementing Forms authentication when:

- You have portions of the site that are open to the public and portions that are meant only for a select group of people.
- You have membership details stored in an external database that contains the information required for authentication.
- When groups of users do not have Microsoft Windows accounts.
- When users have Windows accounts but are not authenticated to the same domain as the MCMS server.

About Forms Authentication

Forms authentication is a non-Microsoft-specific mechanism, which existed before ASP.NET. In those days, developers created custom forms consisting of a user name and password field. When a user clicked on the Login button, the form triggered code that checked to see if the user had access to the site. The result was usually stored as a token in the form of a cookie or a session variable. The code that did the checking involved quite a bit of logic. Not only did the developer need to ensure that the code was triggered on all pages that required authentication, he or she also had to manage the state of the token throughout the site.

Today, with ASP.NET technologies, you can find ready-to-use solutions that make implementing Forms authentication much easier. MCMS has its own flavor of Forms authentication in the form of its own set of classes in the `Microsoft.ContentManagement.Web.Security` namespace.

> Unlike ASP.NET Forms authentication, MCMS Forms authentication performs the additional step of mapping users' credentials to the rights groups they are assigned to.

As before, you still have to design the form that contains the user name and password fields. However, instead of building the logic for authenticating the user from scratch you can make use of the classes provided by ASP.NET and MCMS to do the job for you.

How It Works

In order for Forms authentication to work, IIS must allow anonymous access to resources. Otherwise, Windows authentication would take over and visitors without valid credentials would continue to get a network prompt for a user name and password.

Once anonymous access has been enabled, all requests for a page get passed on by IIS to the ASP.NET web application. The application checks to see if the page requires authentication.

> Don't forget to ensure that the files in the file system do not have restrictions that prevent the anonymous Internet user account from reading them.

When guest access has been enabled in MCMS and the guest account has been granted access to the page, the application serves the page without displaying the login page. Should the page require authentication, the application does another check to see if the user has been previously authenticated by looking for a valid ticket. If a valid ticket is not found, the user is redirected to a login form to enter a user name and password.

The logic to determine whether a user has access to the requested MCMS objects is performed by the `Microsoft.ContentManagement.Web.Security.CmsAuthorization` module. The user is granted access to a page only if:

- A valid user name and password have been entered.
- The user belongs to the group of users specified in the `<authorization>` tag of the application's `web.config` file.
- The user belongs to a subscriber/author/editor/moderator/template designer/channel manager/administrator rights group assigned to the channel of the requested page.
- Guest access has been enabled and the guest account has been granted access to the requested page.

Once the user has been successfully authenticated, a ticket is issued in the form of two cookies— an ASP.NET session cookie and an MCMS session cookie. The cookies are set on the client machine. In subsequent attempts to access other pages on the site, the browser will automatically send these cookies to the server. The ASP.NET web application checks the cookies to see if the associated ticket is still valid.

> A table that compares different authentication mechanisms for ASP.NET is available at `http://msdn.microsoft.com/library/default.asp?url=/library/enus/dnnetsec/html/SecNetAP05.asp`.

Like regular cookies, both cookies have a lifespan. Through code, you can choose to set a temporary cookie or a persistent cookie. Temporary cookies last only for the duration of the browser session. When the browser is closed, the temporary cookie is removed. Persistent cookies can endure across different browser sessions. It is the responsibility of the server to check any persistent or temporary cookie to see if it is still valid. The ASP.NET cookie has the lifespan specified in the `<forms>` tag in the `web.config` file. The MCMS cookie is kept alive for the duration of time specified in the SCA. Once either cookie expires or is deleted, the user will be directed back to the login page to get authenticated again when a page is next requested.

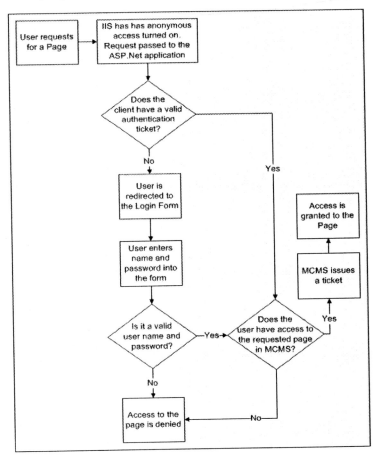

> Since cookies are required for Forms authentication to work, the user's browser must allow cookies for the site.

To implement Forms authentication, you would need to go through the following steps:

1. Configure IIS to allow anonymous access for the web application.
2. Configure the `web.config` file of the application.
3. Create the login page.

If you have portions of the site open for public viewing where it is not appropriate to authenticate users, you would need to perform these additional steps:

1. Choose or create an MCMS Guest account.
2. Turn on Guest access for the site using the SCA.
3. Assign the Guest account subscriber rights to channels meant for public viewing.

We will perform all these tasks to implement Forms authentication for the TropicalGreen site.

Configuring IIS to Allow Anonymous Access

Open Internet Services Manager by selecting Start | Programs | Administrative Tools | Internet Services Manager. In the tree on the left pane, browse to the TropicalGreen virtual directory (e.g. Computer Name | Default Web Site | TropicalGreen).

Right-click on the node that represents your website (e.g. the Default Web Site). Select Properties from the pop-up menu. The Properties dialog appears. Select the Directory Security tab and in the section labeled Anonymous access and authentication control, click the Edit... button.

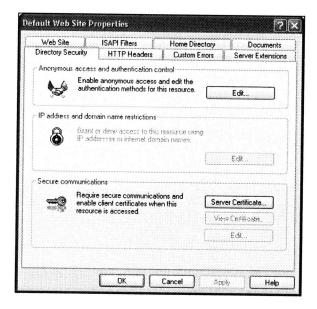

The Authentication Methods dialog opens. In the Anonymous access section, ensure that the Anonymous access option is checked.

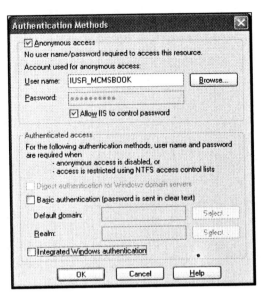

For Windows 2000, click the Edit... button in the Anonymous access section to view details of the anonymous user account. Ensure that the properties of the anonymous account are set as follows:

Property	Value
User name	IUSR_(Computername) Replace (Computername) with the name of your computer.
Allow IIS to control password	Checked

These are the default settings of IIS. Unless these settings have been changed, you should not need to set them.

With Internet Services Manager open, right-click on the TropicalGreen virtual directory. Repeat the steps above to ensure that anonymous access is configured for that virtual directory.

When you are done, close all open dialog boxes by clicking their OK buttons.

With IIS configured for anonymous access, all requests for pages of the TropicalGreen website will be passed on to ASP.NET.

Configure Settings in the Web.config File

Next we configure the web.config file of the TropicalGreen project to use Forms authentication.

Open the `web.config` file of the TropicalGreen project. Look for the `<authentication>` tag. By default, it is set to use Windows authentication. Comment out the line `<authentication mode="windows" />` and add in the code highlighted below to change the authentication mechanism to Forms.

```
<!--  AUTHENTICATION
        This section sets the authentication policies of the application.
        Possible modes are "Windows", "Forms", "Passport" and "None"
-->
<!-- authentication mode="windows" / -->

<authentication mode="Forms">
</authentication>
```

Between the `<authentication>` tags, add the `<forms>` tag. Here, we name the cookie `TropicalGreenAuthCookie`, set the login form path to `/tropicalgreen/Login.aspx` (we will build this later), configure the protection level to `all` and the cookie timeout period to 30 minutes.

```
<forms name="TropicalGreenAuthCookie"
       path="/"
       loginUrl="/tropicalgreen/Login.aspx"
       protection="All"
       timeout="30">
</forms>
```

The cookie timeout must be set to the Cookie Lifetime in minutes set in the SCA. The default setting is 30 minutes. If the two values do not match, you may run into problems when one cookie expires before the other.

> For a detailed discussion of what each attribute in the `<form>` tag means, check out the Microsoft online documentation available at `http://www.microsoft.com/resources/documentation/iis/6/all/proddocs/en-us/aaconformselement.mspx`.

Directly below the closing `</authentication>` tag, add the `<authorization>` tag (if it does not already exist). We will add the `<allow>` tag with the users attribute set to * to allow all users to access the site.

```
<authorization>
    <allow users="*"></allow>
</authorization>
```

Finally, check that the `<httpModules>` section contains a reference to the `Microsoft.ContentManagement.Web.Security.CmsAuthorizationModule` DLL. This library is automatically added to the `web.config` file if you created the project using the wizard or if the project is MCMS-enabled. It contains classes used to map authenticated users to the MCMS rights groups they are assigned to. You can remove the module only when all of the following is true:

- You have enabled guest access.

- You only expect guests to view pages on the site. The entire site—all its channels, postings, templates and resources—are available to guests, and there is no need for any kind of authentication.

```
<httpModules>
<add type="Microsoft.ContentManagement.Web.Security.CmsAuthorizationModule,
     Microsoft.ContentManagement.Web,
```

```
            Version=5.0.1200.0,
            Culture=neutral,
            PublicKeyToken=31bf3856ad364e35"
            name="CmsAuthorizationModule" />
. . . code continues . . .
</httpModules>
```

Save and close the web.config file.

Creating the Login Page

Once you have configured the TropicalGreen site to use Forms authentication, the first time you view any page within the site, you will be redirected to the form located at /tropicalgreen/login.aspx. However, that file does not exist yet! Let's create it.

With the TropicalGreen solution open in Visual Studio .NET, add a new web form to the root of the TropicalGreen project and name it Login.aspx. Set the Page Layout to FlowLayout.

Toggle to HTML view. Between the <head> tags add a link to the stylesheet created in Chapter 7.

```
<LINK href="/tropicalgreen/Styles/Styles.css" type="text/css"
        rel="stylesheet">
```

Between the <form> tags, add a table consisting of descriptive labels, textboxes for entering the domain, user name, and password, and a sign in button.

```
<div align="center">
<table>
<tr>
    <td colspan="2">
        <h1>Enter your Username and Password</h1>
            <hr noshade>
    </td>
</tr>
<tr>
    <td class="BodyText">Domain:</td>
    <td class="BodyText">
        <asp:TextBox Runat="server" ID="txtDomain" Text="">
        </asp:TextBox>
    </td>
</tr>
<tr>
    <td class="BodyText">Username:</td>
    <td class="BodyText">
        <asp:TextBox runat="server" ID="txtUsername">
        </asp:TextBox>
    </td>
</tr>
<tr>
    <td class="BodyText">Password:</td>
    <td class="BodyText">
        <asp:TextBox Runat="server" ID="txtPassword" TextMode="Password">
        </asp:TextBox>
    </td>
</tr>
<tr>
    <td></td>
    <td>
        <asp:Button Runat="server" ID="btnSignIn" Text="Sign In"></asp:Button>
    </td>
</tr>
<tr>
    <td class="BodyText" colspan="2">
```

```
            <asp:Label Runat="server" ID="lblErrorMessage" ForeColor="red">
            </asp:Label>
        </td>
    </tr>
    </table>
    </div>
```

Toggle to Design view. The form appears as shown below.

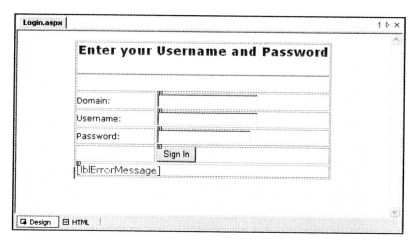

While in Design view, double-click on the form to get to the code-behind file. Import the Microsoft.ContentManagement.Web.Security namespace. This namespace contains the classes we will use to process the logic required to authenticate the user using Forms authentication. Also import the Microsoft.ContentManagement.Publishing namespace.

```
using System;
using System.Collections;
using System.ComponentModel;
using System.Data;
using System.Drawing;
using System.Web;
using System.Web.SessionState;
using System.Web.UI;
using System.Web.UI.WebControls;
using System.Web.UI.HtmlControls;

using Microsoft.ContentManagement.Web.Security;
using Microsoft.ContentManagement.Publishing;

namespace TropicalGreen
    {
        . . . code continues. . .
    }
```

Toggle back to Design view and double-click on the btnSignIn button. In the btnSignIn_Click() event handler we will string together the user name and domain in the format winNt://(domain)/(username) to form the MCMS user name. Next, we will use the CmsFormsAuthentication.AuthenticateAsUser() method to get an authentication ticket from MCMS. If the user is not a valid MCMS user, the ticket will be null. Any error messages are written to the lblErrorMessage label. Add the following code within the btnSignIn_Click() event handler:

```
private void btnSignIn_Click(object sender, System.EventArgs e)
{
    string username;
    string domain;
    string password;
    string user;

    try
    {
        username = txtUsername.Text;
        domain = txtDomain.Text.ToUpper();
        password = txtPassword.Text;

        //string the domain and userName together to get the user's account
        user = "winNt://" + domain + "/" + username;

        //get a ticket
        CmsAuthenticationTicket ticket=CmsFormsAuthentication.AuthenticateAsUser
                                       (user,password);
    }
    catch(Exception ex)
    {
        lblErrorMessage.Text = ex.Message;
    }
}
```

Once the user has been validated, we will use the RedirectFromLoginPage() method to set the cookie and send the user back to the page he or she was previously viewing. A ReturnUrl querystring is appended to the URL when the user is first brought to the Login page and stores the address of the page the user requested. The RedirectFromLoginPage() method uses the URL stored in the ReturnUrl query string to decide which page to redirect to. Add code in the btnSignIn_Click() event handler as shown below.

```
private void btnSignIn_Click(object sender, System.EventArgs e)
{
    . . . code continues . . .
    try
    {
    . . . code continues . . .

        //get a ticket
        CmsAuthenticationTicket ticket=CmsFormsAuthentication.AuthenticateAsUser
                                       (user,password);

    if(ticket!=null)
    {
      if(Request.QueryString["ReturnUrl"]!=null)
      {
        CmsFormsAuthentication.RedirectFromLoginPage(ticket,true,false);
      }
    }

        //the redirection did not occur, the user does not have access
        //to the page
        lblErrorMessage.Text = "Access denied";
    }
    catch(Exception ex)
    {
        lblErrorMessage.Text = ex.Message;
    }
}
```

The RedirectFromLoginPage() method does more than redirection. It accepts three parameters:

- **authenticationTicket** is the ticket used to generated the cookies.
- **setAspNetCookie** decides whether or not an additional ASP.NET cookie will be created. The ASP.NET cookie contains additional information that is not found in the MCMS cookie.
- **createPersistentCookie** decides whether or not the cookie will persist across browser sessions. If it is set to false, when the user closes and re-opens the browser or opens another window, he or she will get the Login page again. Once the ticket lifetime as set in the SCA has elapsed, even if createPersistentCookie is set to true, the user will be requested to login again. We are not using this feature, but you can use it to save the login for your users with some tweaking of the code.

With this information, a temporary cookie is set in the memory of the browser. Persistent cookies are stored in the file system.

Next, we will consider the case where the user navigates to http://localhost/tropicalgreen/login.aspx. Unlike the previous case, the ReturnUrl parameter has not been set and therefore cannot be used.

To handle this situation we will use the SetAuthCookie() method. This method is similar to the RedirectFromLoginPage() method, with the main difference being that the SetAuthCookie() method only sets the cookie based on the ticket. It does not perform any redirections.

Add the condition to consider the case where a ReturnUrl query string is not found. In this case, the authentication cookies will be created by SetAuthCookie(). We then explicitly call the Response.Redirect() method to bring the user to the TropicalGreen home page.

```
private void btnSignIn_click(object sender, System.EventArgs e)
{
    . . . code continues . . .
    try
    {
    . . . code continues . . .

      if(ticket!=null)
      {
        if(Request.QueryString["ReturnUrl"]!=null)
        {
          CmsFormsAuthentication.RedirectFromLoginPage(ticket,true,false);
        }
        else
        {
          CmsFormsAuthentication.SetAuthCookie(ticket,true,false);
          Channel root = CmsHttpContext.Current.Searches.GetByPath
                       ("/Channels/TropicalGreen") as Channel;
          if(root!=null)
          {
            Response.Redirect(root.Url);
          }
        }
      }
      . . . code continues . . .
    }
    . . . code continues . .
}
```

The `setAuthCookie()` method is typically used when you need to suppress the redirection. The Login page is complete. Save and build the solution. Close `login.aspx` and its code-behind file.

Since the Login page could be processed before the user has been authenticated by MCMS, ensure that the Login page:

1. Is not a posting based on a template.

2. Does not access any `CmsHttpContext` members, including references to channels, template galleries, resource galleries, postings, templates, resources, and users. If this is a mandatory requirement then you will have to use the `CmsApplicationContext` to access these items.

Otherwise, you may get an error message that says:

Guest access is not enabled for the CMS server. Access is denied.

Or, if guest access has been enabled (see the later part of this chapter for how to do this):

The current user does not have access to the requested item.

Logging on to the Site

Open Internet Explorer and navigate to `http://localhost/tropicalgreen/plantcatalog`. You should see the login box shown in the following screenshot.

Look at the address bar in Internet Explorer and you will see that the URL of the login page has been appended with a querystring holding a value for a parameter called `ReturnUrl`. The value stored in the `ReturnUrl` querystring is a URL-encoded path back to the page that you have requested to see.

> If you have set up MCMS to work within a single domain, consider storing the domain name in a centrally managed location such as an application setting in the `web.config` file. In this way, you can retrieve its value when calling the `CmsFormsAuthentication.AuthenticateAsUser()` method without users having to enter it each time they fill in the form.

Enter your administrative user name and password. For example:

Field	Value
Domain	MCMSBook (replace with the name of your computer/domain name)
UserName	Author1
Password	(the password you have set for this account)

If you have entered valid credentials, you will be brought to the Plant Catalog page. Click on any of the plant fact sheets. Notice that you are not asked to enter your credentials again: You will remain authenticated for as long as the cookie lasts.

The CmsFormsAuthentication Class

In the example above, we used the `CmsFormsAuthentication.AuthenticateAsUser()` method to get the authentication ticket. There are other ways to retrieve this ticket, detailed next.

- `AuthenticateAsCurrentUser()` logs in with the credentials of the current Windows user. Using this method, you do not have to ask for user names and passwords as these are already obtained from the `WindowsIdentity.GetCurrent()` method. However, because you have configured IIS to allow anonymous access to the site, you will always be using the credentials of the ASPNET account.

- `AuthenticateAsGuest()` logs in with the credentials of the MCMS guest account. If guest account is enabled, the user will be issued a ticket that gives access to portions of the site that are open to guests.

- `AuthenticateUsingWindowsToken()` logs in with the credentials of a Windows user. It is usually used when impersonating a logon session with a Windows account.

- `AuthenticateAsUser()` is the method used in the example above. With this method, you specify the domain, username and password of the user. The format of the user account is `WinNT://Domain/Username`.

In all these methods, you can choose to pass in optional parameters defining the client account name and client account type. For example, we can specify our own custom values for the user's client account name and client account type by calling:

```
CmsFormsAuthentication.AuthenticateAsUser
            (user,password,"MyAccountName1","MyAccountType1");
```

In this case, `User.ClientAccountName` has the value `MyAccountName1`. `User.ClientAccountType` holds the value `MyAccountType1`. This opens the possibility of having multiple users using the same Windows account but mapped to different client accounts.

What's in the Cookie

You can see the contents of the cookie by using the `GetAuthCookie()` method as shown below:

```
HttpCookie cook = CmsFormsAuthentication.GetAuthCookie(ticket,true);
Response.Write(cook.Value.ToString());
```

You will get values such as this:

zne2e42rfjou3mlrhrmpad4opbt2xacv2rq5gm4bctx77slym24ntq5ii3f6ybohuoklqpwxf3g4j

This does not tell you much because the contents have been encrypted. Be assured that the cookie only contains only information that is required for the `RedirectFromLoginPage()`, `SetAuthCookie()`, and `GetAuthCookie()` methods to work. It does not contain sensitive information like the Windows token and password, or other information that may compromise the security of the system.

When Users Do Not Have Rights to View the Requested Page

Should you visit a page you have no access to, you would be returned to the login page. Unless you enter the credentials of a user who has the rights to view the page, you will keep being returned to the login page. To provide a way out, it is a good idea to add a hyperlink that leads the visitor from the login page to the referring page or at least to a part of the site that is accessible.

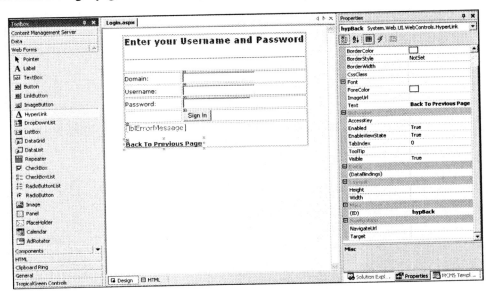

With `Login.aspx` opened in Design view, drag and drop a Hyperlink control from the Web Forms Toolbox onto the form as shown in the following figure:

Give the Hyperlink the following properties:

Property	Value
ID	hypBack
Text	Back To Previous Page

Double-click on the form to get to its code-behind file. Add logic to the `Page_Load()` event handler to populate the `NavigateUrl` property of the hyperlink with the URL of the referring page.

```
private void Page_Load(object sender, System.EventArgs e)
{
    // Put user code to initialize the page here
    if(!Page.IsPostBack)
    {
        //if there is a referring page,
        //populate the NavigateUrl property
        //of the hypBack hyperlink
        //with its URL.
        if(Page.Request.UrlReferrer!=null)
        {
            hypBack.NavigateUrl = Page.Request.UrlReferrer.ToString();
        }
        else
        {
            hypBack.Visible = false;
        }
    }
}
```

Save and build the solution. Now, when the visitor clicks on a link that leads to a page that requires authentication, the Back To Previous Page hyperlink provides a nice route out of the login page and back to wherever the visitor came from.

When the Cookie is Deleted or No Longer Valid

The cookies can cease to be valid in either of the following cases:

- If you have set the `createPersistentCookie` flag to `true` when creating the cookie, the cookie becomes invalid when the time period set for the cookie lifetime in the SCA has elapsed. This can happen when the user has been inactive but has left the browser open.

- The user clicks a button that calls the `CmsFormsAuthentication.SignOut()` method.

The cookies can be deleted by the user if:

- The user deletes cookies from their browser by selecting Tools | Internet Options ... | Delete Cookies... from the browser's toolbar.

- The browser is closed and you have set the `createPersistentCookie` flag to `false` when creating the cookie.

In either case, the cookie will be invalidated or removed. When the user next requests a page, they are once again redirected to the login page.

Welcoming Guests to the Site

Up to this point, we have configured the TropicalGreen site to use Forms authentication. All site visitors are brought to the login page to have their credentials authenticated before they are given access to view pages.

On public websites, expecting visitors to enter a user name and password (assuming anyone remembers these things) is as good as waving a huge banner with the words "We don't want you here" . Even websites that require members to enter a user name and password typically allow guests on the first page of the site at least.

In order for guests to view certain MCMS content without entering any credentials, Guest access must be enabled.

Determining or Creating the MCMS Guest Account

First, we need to decide the account that is to be used as the MCMS guest account. You can use the same IUSR_ComputerName account used by IIS. However, doing so means that if your server is on a web farm, all machines must have a user with the name IUSR_ComputerName as well.

> Don't mix up the account used to configure IIS for anonymous access (usually IUSR_ComputerName) with the MCMS guest account. They are separate accounts used for different purposes.
>
> If you do use the IUSR_ComputerName account, you must set the MCMS guest account to localmachine\IUSR_ComputerName. Note the use of the keyword localmachine.

It is for this reason that it is recommended to designate a domain user as the MCMS guest account. We aren't going to assume that you are connected to a domain right now, so we will create a local machine account for MCMS guest access. To do so:

1. Select Start | Programs | Administrative Tools | Computer Management (or Computer Manager in Windows 2000).

2. In the tree on the left hand panel, expand Computer Management (Local) | System Tools | Local Users and Groups.

3. Right-click Users and select New User.

4. Create a new account with the following properties.
   When you are done, click Create.

Property	Value
User name	MCMSGuest
Full name	MCMS Guest
Description	MCMS Guest Account
Password	(set an appropriate password)
User must change password at next logon	Unchecked
User cannot change password	Checked
Password never expires	Checked
Account is disabled	Unchecked

5. Click Close.

6. Close Computer Management (or Computer Manager).

With a designated guest account created, we are ready to assign it as the MCMS guest account in the SCA.

Turning on Guest Access in the SCA

First, open the SCA. From the Start Menu, select Programs | Microsoft Content Management Server | Server Configuration Application. In the SCA, select the Security tab. By default, the value of the AllowGuests On Site flag is set to No.

Click Configure.... The MCMS Configuration Application – Security Configuration dialog opens. Set the following properties in the guest visitors section:

Property	Value
Allow Guests On Site	Yes
Guest Login Account	DOMAINNAME\MCMSGuest
	Replace DOMAINNAME with the name of your computer or domain name.

Close all opened dialogs by clicking the OK buttons. Close the SCA. We have now configured MCMS to allow guests to all MCMS-managed websites.

Assign the Guest Account Subscriber Rights

Although we have configured MCMS to allow guests on site, guests will still not be able to view pages until we have assigned the guest account to a subscriber rights group that has access to the appropriate containers.

Follow the steps outlined in the section *Creating Rights Groups* in Chapter 10 to create a new subscriber rights group in Site Manager named Guests and assign the MCMSGuest account to it.

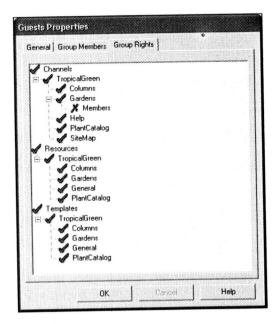

Next, give the Guests subscriber rights group access to all channels, resource galleries and template galleries that currently exist in the site, except for the Members channel (which we are reserving only for members of Tropical Green). In this way, our guests will have access to all the content in the website that we have prepared so far. Refer to the section, *Assigning Rights Groups to Containers* in Chapter 10, for a detailed discussion on how this is done.

Visiting the Site as a Guest

Let's visit the TropicalGreen site again to see the difference. Open Internet Explorer and navigate to http://localhost/tropicalgreen/plantcatalog. You did not have to log into the site!

Notice, however, that the Web Author Console is missing.

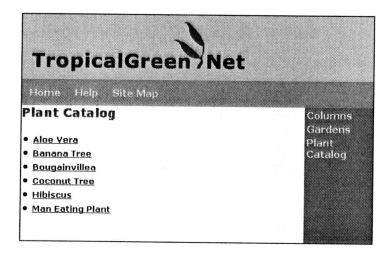

Previously, when you visited the TropicalGreen website, the server automatically identified you based on your Windows logon credentials. It knew that you were the administrator of the website and granted you full permissions, including full use of the Web Author Console.

After you implemented Forms authentication, you were shown the login page where you entered your user name and password. When you clicked on the Sign In button, the server validated your credentials and identified you as an administrator.

Now, with guest access turned on, Internet Explorer did not send your credentials over to the server so you get the view of a guest, and guests are not required to login. Yes, you are still the administrator, but the server can't identify you as such. Everyone, including authors, editors, moderators, template designers, channel managers, and administrators of the Tropical Green club will be identified as guests.

There are several ways of accessing the Web Author Console with guest access turned on:

- Create a login button somewhere in the menu to direct authors to the login page.
- Have authors bookmark the login page and use it as a start point for accessing the authoring site.
- Create a special channel to which the guest account does not have access. Assign the login page as the channel rendering script of this special channel.

Let's explore each of these options, starting with the creation of a Login/Logout button for authors.

Creating a Login/Logout Button for Authors

In the TropicalGreen project, open RightMenu.ascx (created in Chapter 13). Drag and drop a Button onto the Web User Control and give it the following properties:

Property	Value
ID	btnLogin
Text	Login

In Design view, double-click on the form to get to its code behind file. Add the `Microsoft.ContentManagement.Web.Security` namespace above the namespace declaration:

```
using Microsoft.ContentManagement.Web.Security;
```

In the `Page_Load()` event handler, add the following code.

```
//Show Login or Logout button, depending on context
if(CmsHttpContext.Current.IsDefaultGuestEnabled)
{
    if(CmsHttpContext.Current.IsLoggedInAsGuest)
    {
        btnLogin.Text = "Login";
    }
    else
    {
        btnLogin.Text = "Logout";
    }
}
else
{
    btnLogin.Visible = false;
}
```

We will first use the `IsDefaultGuestEnabled` property to see if guest access has been enabled for the site. The `IsLoggedInAsGuest` property checks to see if the user is logged in. Before the user gets authenticated, the button says Login. Once the user has logged in, the button says Logout.

Toggle to Design view and double-click on btnLogin to get to the `btnLogin_Click()` event handler. If the user is logged in as a guest we will redirect to the login page to get authenticated, attaching the current URL as the value of a `ReturnUrl` query string parameter. For requests to logout, we will call the `CmsFormsAuthentication.SignOut()` method and redirect to the published version of the page. Modify the `btnLogin_Click()` event handler as shown below.

```
private void btnLogin_Click(object sender, System.EventArgs e)
{
    CmsHttpContext cmsContext = CmsHttpContext.Current;
    ChannelItem currentItem = cmsContext.ChannelItem;
    if(cmsContext.IsLoggedInAsGuest)
    {
        Response.Redirect("/tropicalgreen/login.aspx?ReturnUrl=" +
                    Server.UrlEncode(currentItem.UrlModePublished));
    }
    else
    {
        CmsFormsAuthentication.SignOut();
        Response.Redirect(currentItem.UrlModePublished);
    }
}
```

Save and build the solution. When you next view the plant catalog, click on the Login button. Sign in with your credentials.

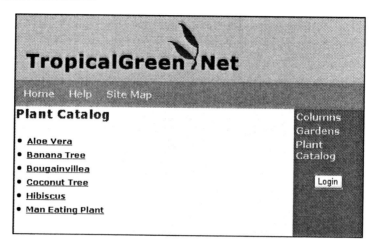

If you have been assigned to a group that has the rights to modify the site, you will be brought to the same page with the Web Author Console displayed. At the same time, the text on the button changes from Login to Logout. Click the Logout button to come back to the guest view of the page.

Creating a Login Channel for Authors

If letting regular subscribers see the Login button is not desirable, consider getting authors to bookmark the login page (`http://localhost/tropicalgreen/login.aspx`). Whenever authors require access the authoring site, they simply select this bookmark. Using this method, you don't have to create a Login button to bring users to the login page.

To make it even easier for authors to remember the URL to the login page, create a channel to which the guest account does not have access. Doing so provides a shorter and friendlier URL.

Property	Value
Name	Admin
DisplayName	Admin
Script Url	/tropicalgreen/templates/ChannelRenderingScript.aspx

Remove the Guests subscriber rights group access to this channel. When you navigate to http://localhost/tropicalgreen/admin, you will be brought to the login page.

Summary

In this chapter we looked at how Forms authentication can be used as an alternative to Windows authentication. We examined the CmsFormsAuthentication class and used it to implement Forms authentication on the TropicalGreen site. To do this, we had to configure IIS to allow anonymous access to the TropicalGreen virtual directory, and then configure the web.config file to use Forms authentication instead of Windows authentication. Finally, we created a Login page for users to enter their credentials to access to the site.

Next, we turned on guest access for the TropicalGreen site. We found that with guest access enabled, content providers were not able to see the Web Author Console and perform authoring tasks. To provide content providers with the means to log on to the site, we needed them to have access the login page. We explored the options available here, including creating a separate login button for content providers to access the authoring site and adding a special channel that does not have guest access enabled.

19

Customizing the Web Author Console

The Default Web Author Console that is provided by MCMS appears as a green box of links neatly arranged in a single-column table. More often than not, you can complete construction of your website using the Default Console. However, given the demanding nature of today's sites, we can think of a few situations where you may want to customize it:

- You have been asked to get the Web Author Console to blend in with the rest of the website. The green border and font type clashes with the well-coordinated colors used elsewhere.

- The Default Console is taking up too much screen space.

- Authors of your site have sent feedback that the choices presented on the console are confusing. They want a simpler interface with fewer buttons.

- Authors have complained that there are too many steps involved in the creation of a page. They want the Web Author Console to bypass the selection of template galleries and templates and jump straight to the creation of a posting with a system-defined template.

- You have received requests from the site owner to hide specific buttons like Delete to prevent accidental deletion of pages.

- You need to add new buttons to perform specific tasks to meet the unique business requirements of your organization. A common request is to add a Release Ownership button that allows content providers to release the lock on a posting.

Whatever reasons you may have, let's assume that you need to modify the way the Default Console looks and behaves. There are several techniques that can achieve the level of customization you require. In this chapter, we will walk you through customization tasks ranging from changing the look and feel to adding buttons and links and modifying their behavior. While the solutions presented here are specific for this site, the methods used to achieve them cover many tricks and techniques you can use on your own site.

Before We Begin

Before proceeding with the examples in this chapter, we will make a copy of the Default Console. We will modify the copy instead of the original file. Ensure that you have completed these steps:

1. In the `Console` folder of the TropicalGreen solution, create a copy of the `DefaultConsole.ascx` file. Name the copy `CustomConsole.ascx`. Do a search for all instances of the text string `DefaultConsole` and replace with `CustomConsole` in both `CustomConsole.ascx` and its corresponding code-behind file. There should only be 2-3 instances in the HTML and code-behind views. Save and build the solution.

2. Replace the Default Console in the Plant template. Open the `Plant.aspx` template file in Design view. Drag and drop the `CustomConsole.ascx` file onto the place where the Default Console is. Delete the Default Console.

3. In Solution Explorer, create a new folder in the root of the TropicalGreen project named `ConsoleButtons`. This is where we will store all the class files when we create custom action controls.

4. Create another folder named `Dialogs`. We will store all custom dialogs created in this chapter here.

The Different Faces of the Web Author Console

While working with the Default Console in previous chapters, you will have noticed how the available options change according to the actions that you choose.

- When you first log in to the site, the Web Author Console displays the Switch to Edit Site link.

- When you click on the Switch to Edit Site link, the options available in the console change, showing you a list of actions for the active posting.

- When you click on say, the Edit link, the console's options change yet again, asking you to either Preview, Save, Save And Exit, or Exit.

- Finally, should you get errors when attempting to perform an action, the error message is displayed in an Error Console.

The Console in the Seven Modes of the Web Author Context

A total of seven different Web Author context modes exist. The Web Author Console has a different display for each mode and changes from one to the other according to several factors including the state of the posting and the action performed. Here are the seven modes:

1. **AuthoringNew** is the mode while you are working on a new page.

2. **AuthoringPreview** is the mode when you preview a page by clicking on the Preview button while creating a new page or editing an existing page. The Default Console can never show any options in this mode.

3. **AuthoringReedit** is the mode while you edit an existing page. You get to this mode after selecting the Edit option in the Web Author Console.

4. **PresentationPublished** is the mode when you open a posting in its published state.

5. **PresentationUnpublished** is the mode entered when you view a posting in its unpublished state. You get to this mode immediately after clicking the Switch To Edit Site link when you first enter a site or when you click Save And Exit after creating or editing a posting.

6. **PresentationUnpublishedPreview** is the mode when you preview a posting by clicking on the Preview button on the Console in the `PresentationUnpublished` mode. The Default Console can never show any options in this mode.

7. **TemplatePreview** is the mode when you choose to preview a template from the Select Template dialog. The Default Console cannot show any options in this mode.

Besides these seven Web Author context modes, the Web Author Console recognizes error conditions. Error messages and actions to remedy the problem are displayed in the Error Console.

Using the PAPI to Determine the Current Web Author Context Mode

The current mode is determined by the result returned from the `WebAuthorContext.Current.Mode` property. The following code determines if the Web Author context is in `AuthoringNew` mode.

```
Using Microsoft.ContentManagement.WebControls;
. . .

WebAuthorContext wacContext;
wacContext = WebAuthorContext.Current;
if(wacContext.Mode == WebAuthorContextMode.AuthoringNew)
{
    // the Web Author Console is in the AuthoringNew Mode
}
```

Building Blocks of the Web Author Console

Given that the Web Author Console recognizes seven different Web Author context modes, we need to know how it is able to show different sets of controls for each mode. To understand this better, we need to look at how the Web Author Console is constructed.

The Web Author Console consists of three basic building blocks:

1. The Console Object
2. Site Mode Containers
3. Action/Status Controls

These blocks are packaged neatly into a single Web User Control, the Default Console. A good place to begin our study of the Web Author Console is to look at the copy of the Default Console that we made earlier. Open `CustomConsole.ascx` file in Visual Studio.NET and view its HTML code. Identify the basic blocks that make up the Default Console as you work through this section.

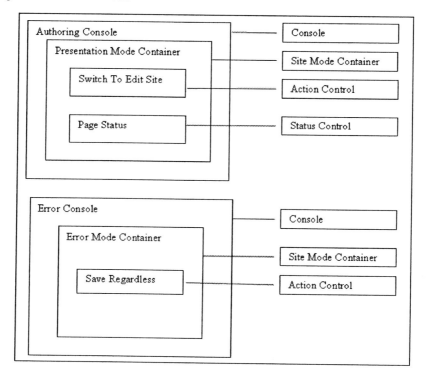

The Console Object

The Console object is the parent block that marks the beginning and end points of the Web Author Console. There are two types of Console objects:

1. **Authoring Console**: Displays the authoring and status functions of the channel and/or posting, depending on the context.
2. **Error Console**: Displays error messages generated by the Authoring Console.

The Default Console bundles both consoles together in the same Web User Control. In this way, you get to see the action buttons in the same place as the error message. The Authoring Console appears as a table with a green border and the Error Console as a table with a red border.

Although you can choose to separate these controls by creating two Web User Controls, one for the Authoring Console and another for the Error Console, it is not recommended. The Authoring and Error Consoles must be paired together. When developers forget to include the Error Console in their template files, authors encountering errors on save never see the error messages. Not being informed of the failed save attempt, they may log out and close their browsers, losing any content added or modified in that session forever. For this reason, Microsoft ships both consoles as a single control so that the chance of missing one console is very low.

Look at the HTML code of the `CustomConsole.ascx` file. Can you see where the Authoring and Error Consoles begin and end?

```
. . . code continues . . .
<CmsConsole:Console runat="server" id="Console1">
    . . . code continues . . .
</CmsConsole:Console>

<CmsConsole:ErrorConsole runat="server" id="ErrorConsole1">
        . . . code continues . . .
</CmsConsole:ErrorConsole>
```

The Authoring Console begins with the `<CmsConsole:Console>` tag and the Error Console with the `<CmsConsole:ErrorConsole>` tag.

Site Mode Containers

Nested within each Web Author Console object are multiple Site Mode Container objects. Site Mode Containers are used by the Web Author Console to hide or display options depending on the current publishing mode. A single Console object may have multiple Site Mode Container objects. There are three kinds of Site Mode Container: `PresentationModeContainer`, `AuthoringModeContainer`, and `ErrorModeContainer`.

PresentationModeContainer

Any HTML or ASP.NET Controls nested within the `PresentationModeContainer` are displayed only when the Web Author Console is in the `PresentationUnpublished` or `PresentationPublished` modes.

In HTML, they are coded as:

```
<cms:PresentationModeContainer id="PresentationModeContainer1" runat="server"
Mode="both">
<!--controls and HTML that appear only in PresentationPublished or
PresentationUnpublished modes -->
</cms:PresentationModeContainer>
```

The `Mode` attribute gives you granular control over when the content of a container should be displayed and it can take on one of the following values:

- **Published**: When `Mode` is set to `Published`, the `PresentationContainer` will be displayed only in `PresentationPublished` mode and is hidden in other modes.

- **Unpublished**: When it is set to `Unpublished`, the `PresentationContainer` will be displayed only in `PresentationUnpublished` mode and is hidden in other modes.

- **Both**: When it is set to the default value, `Both`, the `PresentationContainer` appears in both, `PresentationPublished` and `PresentationUnpublished` modes.

The Console has two `PresentationModeContainer` objects. See if you can find them.

Usage of Site Mode Container Objects is not restricted to the console. They can also be used within template files. For example, you could add the following line of code directly within the template file:

```
<body>
    <form id="Plant" method="post" runat="server">
        <cms:PresentationModeContainer id="PresentationModeContainer1"
            runat="server" Mode="Unpublished">
```

```
      This text appears only when the WebAuthorContext is in a
      PresentationUnpublished mode
         </cms:PresentationModeContainer>
      </form>
   </body>
```

Because the mode attribute is set to Unpublished, the text between the
<cms:PresentationModeContainer> tags will be displayed only when the web author context is
in a PresentationUnpublished mode. You can use this technique to display text that is seen only
by content providers and not by visitors to the site. The benefit of this method is that you can add
content to the template file without amending the code-behind file, which would require you to
recompile the project.

AuthoringModeContainer

Contents nested within an AuthoringModeContainer are displayed when the Web Author Console
is in either the AuthoringNew or AuthoringReedit mode.

The syntax is:

```
      <cms:AuthoringModeContainer id="AuthoringModeContainer1" runat="server">
   <!--controls and HTML that appear only in AuthoringNew or AuthoringReedit modes-->
      </cms:AuthoringModeContainer>
```

Like the PresentationModeContainer, the AuthoringModeContainer is fine-tuned using the Mode
attribute, which takes one of the following values this time:

- **AuthoringNew**: The AuthoringModeContainer displays its content only in the
  AuthoringNew mode. The Default Console shows the Save New Page action in
  this mode.

- **AuthoringReedit**: The AuthoringModeContainer displays its content only in the
  AuthoringReedit mode. The Default Console shows the Save and Save And Exit
  actions in this mode.

- **Both**: The AuthoringModeContainer displays its content in both the AuthoringNew
  and AuthoringReedit modes. This is the default value. The Default Console shows
  the Preview and Exit actions in this mode.

ErrorModeContainer

The ErrorModeContainer is displayed when an error is raised by an event triggered by a
placeholder control, workflow event, or other function.

In the Default Console, the ErrorModeContainer is coded as:

```
      <Cms:ErrorModeContainer id="ErrorModeContainerFailedCreate1"
         runat="server" mode="FailedSaveNewPage">
      . . .controls and HTML that appear when the an error is raised while saving a
   new page. . .
      </Cms:ErrorModeContainer>
```

Here are the possible values for the mode property:

- **FailedSaveNewPage**: The ErrorModeContainer displays its contents when an error
  has occurred while attempting to save a new page.

- **OverlappedSave**: The `ErrorModeContainer` displays its contents when an overlapped save error has been raised.

- **FailedSavePlaceholder**: The `ErrorModeContainer` displays its contents when an error has occurred while attempting to save the contents of a particular placeholder.

- **FailedSubmit**: The `ErrorModeContainer` displays its contents when an error has occurred while submitting a posting.

- **FailedApprove**: The `ErrorModeContainer` displays its contents when an error has occurred while approving a posting.

- **FailedDecline**: The `ErrorModeContainer` displays its contents when an error has occurred while declining a posting.

- **FailedDelete**: The `ErrorModeContainer` displays its contents when an error has occurred while deleting a posting.

The details of the error are retrieved from the `Error` property. You can also access the error's `Title` and `Exception` properties and display them in the error mode container. The display of an error message caused by a failed attempt to save a new page is coded like this:

```
<Cms:ErrorModeContainer id="ErrorModeContainerFailedCreate1"
    runat="server" mode="FailedSaveNewPage">
    <B><FONT color="red"><%# Container.Error.Title %></FONT></B>
    <HR>
    <FONT color="red">Error Details:<BR>
    <FONT size="-2">
    <%# Container.Error.Exception.Message %>
    </FONT></FONT>
    <HR>
</Cms:ErrorModeContainer>
```

Action/Status Controls

Action/Status Controls are server controls. These are the links you see on the console itself, for example Switch To Edit Site, Create New Page, etc. You can nest multiple Action or Status control objects within a single Site Mode Container Object. Depending on the current Web Author context mode, the state of the posting and the rights assigned to you, you will see different server controls at different times.

The Switch to Edit Site link is coded in the Default Console as:

```
<CmsConsole:SwitchToPresentationUnpublishedAction
    id="SwitchToPresentationUnpublishedAction1" runat="server">
<A id=SwitchToPresentationUnpublishedAnchor
    onclick="<%# Container.ActionJavascript %>;return false"
    href="#"
    target=_self>
<%# Container.Text %>
</A>
<BR>
</CmsConsole:SwitchToPresentationUnpublishedAction>
```

Changing the Look and Feel of the Default Console

The fastest way to customize how the Web Author Console looks is to simply amend the HTML code. While the samples here are simple, they give a taste of the customization you can perform on the Web Author Console. With basic HTML skills, you can whip up a Web Author Console that is customized to blend in with the rest of the site.

Changing Colors

A table with a green border may work well on some sites, like the TropicalGreen site. But you may want to change the colors on the Web Author Console to follow your site's color scheme.

To change the table border color and background color, start by opening `CustomConsole.ascx` in HTML view.

Change the table formatting attributes to reflect the style you want. For example, if you want an orange border with a lemon chiffon background, look for the following line of code in the `CustomConsole.ascx` file:

```
<TABLE borderColor="green" cellSpacing="0" cellPadding="5" width="100%"
border="2">
```

and change it to:

```
<TABLE borderColor="orange" bgcolor="lemonchiffon" cellSpacing="0"
cellPadding="5" width="100%" border="2">
```

Changing Fonts

To change the fonts, look for the following line of code (at approximately line 8):

```
<FONT face="Verdana,Arial,sans-serif" size="2">
```

To set the font face to Arial, simply change the `<font>` tag to:

```
<FONT face="Arial,sans-serif" size="2">
```

Save `CustomConsole.ascx`. When you next open a posting based on the Plant template for editing, you will see that the console now has an orange border, a lemon chiffon colored background, and an Arial font face. Open `http://localhost/tropicalgreen/plantcatalog/hibiscus.htm` and log in as an administrator to see the revised console.

Changing Text on Action Controls

You can also change the text label for each Action Control by amending the HTML code. For example you may want to shorten Switch To Edit Site to read simply Edit Site. To do so, simply look for the following line of code:

```
<A id=SwitchToPresentationUnpublishedAnchor
    onclick="<%# Container.ActionJavascript %>;return false"
    href="#"
    target=_self>
<%# Container.Text %>
</A>
```

and change it to:

```
<A id=SwitchToPresentationUnpublishedAnchor
    onclick="<%# Container.ActionJavascript %>;return false"
    href="#"
    target=_self>
Edit Site
</A>
```

Changing Action Controls from Hyperlinks to Buttons

You can change the Action Controls to appear as buttons instead of hyperlinks. To do so, simply replace the `<A>` tags with `<input type="button">` tags. For example, to replace the Switch To Edit Site hyperlink with a button, change:

```
<A id=SwitchToPresentationUnpublishedAnchor
    onclick="<%# Container.ActionJavascript %>;return false"
    href="#"
    target=_self>
<%# Container.Text %>
</A>
```

to:

```
<input type="button" onclick="<%# Container.ActionJavascript %>;return false"
Value="<%# Container.Text %>" id=SwitchToPresentationUnpublishedButton>
```

Now you have a Switch To Edit Site button instead of a hyperlink.

Removing Controls from the List

The easiest way to remove unwanted items from the Web Author Console is to delete their HTML code.

Simply look for the lines of HTML that display the Action Control and delete it. For example, to remove the Delete Page link, look for the following lines of code and remove everything between and including the `<CmsConsole:DeleteAction>` tag.

```
<CmsConsole:DeleteAction id="DeleteAction1" runat="server">
<A id=DeleteAnchor
    onclick="<%# Container.ActionJavascript %>;return false"
    href="#"
    target=_self>
<%# Container.Text %>
</A>
<BR>
</CmsConsole:DeleteAction>
```

Using the methods described so far, you can change the look and feel of the Web Author Console without having to re-build the project as code-behind files have not been changed.

Adding Custom Action Controls to the Console

When you actually start planning your site, you may realize that the functions available on the Default Console are still not quite enough to meet the site's requirements.

Here are just some of the common requests we have received in various projects based on MCMS.

Authors who have seen a prototype based on the Default Console have said that:

- They want to skip the Choose a Template screens when creating a new page. It does not make sense to repeat the action every time a new page is created when the same template is always used within a particular channel.

- When deleting a posting, they want all connected postings to be deleted as well.

- They want to see a list of postings that have expired.

- The Decline function is great. But the author receiving the bad news has no clue why the work has been declined. To aid editors to give a reason for declining, there should be the ability to enter a message explaining why the work was not accepted.

- Authors have asked for a button that gives them the ability to release a lock on a posting. In this way, they can get another author to work on the content before the posting is submitted for editor approval.

Your specific requirements are likely to differ in flavors and levels of complexity. Nevertheless, the Default Console does not address any of these and other issues you may have. The only way to solve these problems is to either create a new Action Control or modify the behavior of an existing Action Control.

The PAPI provides all the libraries required to extend the functionality of the Web Author Console. There are three basic classes that all Action Controls inherit from, and to create a new control, we simply sub-class from one of them. They are described in the following table:

Class	Description
BaseAction	This is the base class for both the BasePostbackAction and BaseNewWindowAction class. Inherit from this class when your custom action control does not require postback actions or the opening of new browser windows. Usually, these actions perform simple client-side JavaScript functions.
BasePostbackAction	Inherit from the BasePostbackAction class when you require scripts to be executed on the server through postbacks. The Decline, Approve, and Submit actions are three examples in the Default Console that make use of this.
BaseNewWindowAction	The BaseNewWindowAction class is used when the action requires the opening of a new browser window. There are many examples in the Default Console that inherit from the BaseNewWindowAction class, such as the Copy, Create New Page, and Page Properties actions.

Inheriting from a BaseAction Class

Let's start by tackling the first item on our list: skipping the Select a Template screens. Because we won't be performing any postbacks or opening any new windows, we'll start from the BaseAction class.

Creating a New Page with a Pre-Defined Template

In this example, we build an Action Control similar to the Create New Page option. When it is clicked, the author is brought directly to the new page based on a pre-determined template.

We start by creating a new class file. In Solution Explorer, add a new class file to the ConsoleButtons folder. Name the new class file NewFromTemplate.cs.

Above the namespace declaration add the namespaces that are required for the control to work:

```
using System;
using Microsoft.ContentManagement.Publishing;
using Microsoft.ContentManagement.WebControls;
using Microsoft.ContentManagement.WebControls.ConsoleControls;

namespace TropicalGreen.ConsoleButtons
{
    . . . code continues . . .
}
```

The class needs to inherit from the BaseAction class. Add the following statement to the NewFromTemplate class declaration to indicate that the new console action inherits from the BaseAction class.

```
. . . code continues . . .
public class NewFromTemplate: BaseAction
{
    . . . code continues . . .
}
```

Inside the NewFromTemplate class, create a TemplatePath property to store the path of the template that the developer has chosen as the default template for the channel. It is a read/write property, so developers can set its value either from the HTML on the console or from code-behind files. Add the property below the NewFromTemplate() constructor.

```
private string mTemplatePath;
public string TemplatePath
{
    get
    {
        return mTemplatePath;
    }
    set
    {
        mTemplatePath = value;
    }
}
```

The GenerateUrl() method will generate the URL of a new posting based on the specified template and the current channel. To do so, it uses the WebAuthorContext.GetAuthoringNewUrl() method which accepts two parameters: The first is the template that the posting is based on; the second is the channel that stores the posting.

Add the GenerateUrl() method below the TemplatePath public property definition.

```
private string GenerateUrl()
{
    //get the current CmsHttpContext
    CmsHttpContext cmsContext = CmsHttpContext.Current;

    //get the current Channel
    Channel c = cmsContext.Channel;

    Template t = null;
    string url = "";

    //get the pre-defined Template
    t = cmsContext.Searches.GetByPath(mTemplatePath) as Template;
```

```
//get the URL of new postings based on the Template
if(t!=null)
{
    WebAuthorContext wac = WebAuthorContext.Current;
    url = wac.GetAuthoringNewUrl(t,c);
}

return url;
}
```

Below the `GenerateUrl()` method, add the following code that overrides the existing `ActionJavascript` property of the base class. The `ActionJavascript` property contains JavaScript code that is executed on the client's browser when users click on the custom control. The returned JavaScript redirects the author to the URL returned by the `GenerateUrl()` method.

```
public override string ActionJavascript
{
    get
    {
        String url = GenerateUrl();
        string javascript = "window.location.href='" + url + "'";

        return javascript;
    }
}
```

We need to supply text to describe what the control does or MCMS will default it to `Unknown Action Text`. Below the `ActionJavascript` property, add code to override the `Text` property of the base class. You can set any text you think appropriate for your control. We will label it `Create Posting From Default Template` to differentiate it from the regular `Create New Posting` action.

```
public override string Text
{
    get
    {
        return "Create Posting from Default Template";
    }
}
```

The `Available` property of the `BaseAction` class is a Boolean that returns true when the custom control is visible on the Web Author Console, false otherwise. Override the `Available` property to return true only when the author has rights to create postings in the channel. Enter the following code below the `Text` property:

```
public override bool Available
{
    get
    {
        return CmsHttpContext.Current.Channel.CanCreatePostings;
    }
}
```

If you attempt to compile the solution now, you will get this error message:

'tropicalgreen.ConsoleButtons.NewFromTemplate' does not implement inherited abstract member 'Microsoft.ContentManagement.WebControls.ConsoleControls.BaseAction.PerformAction()'

That's because the `BaseAction` class has an abstract method called `PerformAction()`. We won't be adding any logic in this function but we still have to implement it for the code to compile.

Add the following code below the `Available` property.

```
public override void PerformAction()
{
    return;
}
```

At last, the control is complete. To add it to the Custom Control, open `CustomConsole.ascx` in HTML view. We need to register the tag prefix of the TropicalGreen solution. We will assign our custom action controls with the tag prefix `TropicalGreenConsole`. This way, we do not have to enter the full namespace when adding our controls to the console. Add this line of code at the top of the `CustomConsole.ascx` file, directly below the `<%@ Control %>` directive:

```
<%@ Register TagPrefix="TropicalGreenConsole"
Namespace="TropicalGreen.ConsoleButtons" Assembly="tropicalgreen" %>
```

Look for the closing tag of the `Create New Page` action control. (Tip: Press *Ctrl + F* and enter `CreateNewPageAction` as the search key). After the closing tag, `</CmsConsole:CreateNewPageAction>`, enter the following HTML code. The `TemplatePath` attribute contains the path to our Plant template:

```
<TropicalGreenConsole:NewFromTemplate id="CreateFromTemplate1" runat="server"
TemplatePath="/templates/tropicalgreen/plantcatalog/plant">
<A
      id=CreateFromTemplateAnchor
      onclick="<%# Container.ActionJavascript %>;return false" href="#"
      target=_self>
   <%# Container.Text %>
</A>
<br>
</TropicalGreenConsole:NewFromTemplate>
```

When you are done, save and build the solution. To test the control:

1. Navigate to the Hibiscus posting, `http://localhost/tropicalgreen/ plantcatalog/hibiscus.htm`.
2. Log in as Author1 and switch to edit site mode.
3. Click on the new Create New Posting from Default Template action.
4. You are brought to a new posting based on the Plant template.

The Select a Template dialogs have been bypassed!

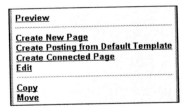

Inheriting from a BasePostbackAction Class

What happens when the customization goes beyond what you can do with JavaScript? Take our second case for example where connected postings should be deleted whenever an author deletes a posting, avoiding the hassle of having to go through deleting each connected posting one by one.

You can't perform deletes using JavaScript: A postback to the server and calls to the Publishing API are required. In cases like these, the `BasePostbackAction` class comes in handy.

Deleting All Connected Postings Together with the Original Posting

We will now create a new custom action that deletes not only the current posting, but also all connected postings, when the control is clicked.

With the TropicalGreen project open in Visual Studio .NET, create a new class file in the `ConsoleButtons` folder. Name the new class file `DeleteConnPosting.cs`.

Add the following statements above the namespace declaration:

```
using System;
using Microsoft.ContentManagement.Publishing;
using Microsoft.ContentManagement.WebControls;
using Microsoft.ContentManagement.WebControls.ConsoleControls;

namespace TropicalGreen.ConsoleButtons
{
    . . . code continues . . .
}
```

Add the name of the `BasePostbackAction` class to the `DeleteConnPosting` class declaration to indicate that the new console action inherits from it:

```
. . . code continues . . .
public class DeleteConnPosting: BasePostbackAction
{
    . . . code continues . . .
}
```

The `BasePostBackAction` class implements a `PeformActionBehaviour()` method, which you can override to include the logic that should be executed on the server. This is the method we will use to hold the logic for deleting all the connected postings.

Override the `PerformActionBehavior()` method inherited from the base class by adding the following code below the `DeleteConnPosting()` constructor:

```
protected override void PerformActionBehavior()
{
    //get the current CmsHttpContext;
    CmsHttpContext cmsContext = CmsHttpContext.Current;
    WebAuthorContext wac = WebAuthorContext.Current;

    //get the posting that is marked for deletion
    Posting deletedPosting = cmsContext.Posting;

    //delete each connected posting
    foreach(Posting connectedP in deletedPosting.ConnectedPostings)
    {
        connectedP.Delete();
    }

    //delete the posting that is marked for deletion
    deletedPosting.Delete();

    cmsContext.CommitAll();

    //get the url of the parent channel for the current Web author context mode
```

```
        string url = "";
        url = wac.GetUrlForMode(cmsContext.Channel,wac.Mode);

        //redirect to the url of the channel
        base.GenerateStartupScriptRedirect(url);
    }
```

This method first deletes all connected postings and finally the current posting. If everything goes smoothly, the deletes are committed to the database. On completion, it will redirect the author to the URL of the channel using the `GenerateStartupScriptRedirect()` method.

We need to give the control a label. To do so, override the `Text` property inherited from the base class by adding the following code directly below the `PerformActionBehaviour()` method.

```
public override string Text
{
    get
    {
        return "Delete This Posting and all Connected Postings";
    }
}
```

The control should be visible on the Web Author Console only when the author has the rights to delete the current posting. Override the `Available` property of the base class by adding the following code below the `Text` property:

```
public override bool Available
{
    get
    {
        Posting currentPosting = CmsHttpContext.Current.Posting;
        if(currentPosting!=null)
        {
            return currentPosting.CanDelete;
        }
        else
        {
            return false;
        }
    }
}
```

The control is complete. Save and build the project.

Add the new server control to `CustomConsole.ascx` in HTML view. Look for the closing tags of the `SwitchToAuthoringReeditAction` control. (Tip: Press *Ctrl + F* and use `SwitchToAuthoringReeditAction` as the search string.) After the `</CmsConsole:SwitchToAuthoringReeditAction>` and `<hr>` tags, add the following code:

```
<TropicalGreenConsole:DeleteConnPosting id="DeleteConnPosting1"
runat="server">
    <A
        id=DeleteAnchor onclick="<%# Container.ActionJavascript %>;return false"
        href="#"
        target=_self>
    <%# Container.Text %>
    </A>
    <BR>
</TropicalGreenConsole:DeleteConnPosting>
```

The class is complete. Save `CustomConsole.ascx`. To test the control:

1. Navigate to `http://localhost/tropicalgreen/plantcatalog`.

2. Switch to edit site mode.

3. Select a suitable plant fact sheet (one that you won't mind deleting).

4. Choose to Create a Connected Page.

5. Select the TropicalGreen (Home) channel as the destination channel.

6. Select the Plant template as the template to use.

7. When the posting has been created, don't enter any information into it (there's no point since we are going to delete it anyway). Click Save New Page.

8. Click Delete This Posting and all Connected Postings.

The current posting and all its connected postings are deleted in a single click. You can use Site Manager to browse to both the TropicalGreen and Plant Catalog channels to double-check that the postings have really been deleted.

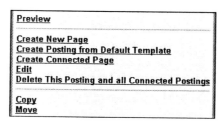

We will discuss connected postings in more depth in Chapter 20.

Raising Errors within the Error Console

Errors can occur anytime during a postback. In the example above, several things could happen:

- Another author is working on the posting to be deleted.

- The posting has been submitted/approved/declined but the changes have yet to be committed.

- You do not have rights to delete the posting. It could be one of those moments where you had the rights to delete it when the page was rendered but your rights were removed later.

If you can't fix the errors, the next best way to deal with them is to handle them in the code. For the Web Author Console, an appropriate place to display error messages is the Error Mode Container.

Catching Errors in a Try-Catch Block

The first thing we need to do is to trap any error that occurs. We will wrap the code in the PerformActionBehavior method with a try-catch block. In the catch block, we will store the raised exception in a variable named ex.

```
protected override void PerformActionBehavior()
{
    //get the current CmsHttpContext;
    CmsHttpContext cmsContext = CmsHttpContext.Current;
    WebAuthorContext wac = WebAuthorContext.Current;

    try
    {
    . . . logic to delete posting and connected postings. . .
    }
    catch(Exception ex)
    {
    }
}
```

Raising the Error

When an error occurs, we will do two things:

1. **Roll back the changes**: Call the `CmsHttpContext.RollbackAll()` method.
2. **Raise the error and display the error message on the Error Mode Container**: In order for the error to be displayed on the Error Mode Container, create a `WebAuthorErrorEventArgs` object and pass it to the `WebAuthorContext. RaiseErrorEvent` method.

In the catch block, add the following code

```
catch(Exception ex)
{
    //Deletion failed
    cmsContext.RollbackAll();

    //Raise an error to the error container
    WebAuthorErrorEventArgs e = new
        WebAuthorErrorEventArgs(ErrorModeContainer.FailedDelete,ex);
    wac.RaiseErrorEvent(e);
}
```

Now when an error occurs while deleting a posting, it will appear in the Error Mode Container as shown in the following figure.

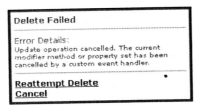

Raising Custom Error Messages

You could also display custom error messages by passing in custom exceptions to the `WebAuthorErrorEventArgs()` constructor. For example, if we wanted to display the message "Deletions of this posting and its connected pages failed", we could amend the catch block as follows:

```
catch(Exception ex)
{
    //Deletion failed
    cmsContext.RollbackAll();

    Exception exCustom = new Exception
        ("Deletion of this posting and its connected pages failed.", ex);

    //Raise an error to the error container
    WebAuthorErrorEventArgs e = new
        WebAuthorErrorEventArgs(ErrorModeContainer.FailedDelete,exCustom);
    wac.RaiseErrorEvent(e);
}
```

When an exception is raised to the Error Console, the custom error message is displayed instead.

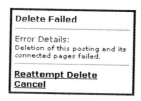

Releasing the Ownership of a Posting

Earlier, in Chapter 10, we discussed the problems faced by authors when an editor or moderator edits a posting before declining it. The editor sends an e-mail to the author, requesting that problem sections of content be reworked. However, the author finds the Edit button is not available on the Web Author Console as the posting has been locked by the editor (or moderator). The only way for the editor or moderator to release the ownership was to publish the unfinished posting.

In this example, we will provide another example derived from the BasePostbackAction class, the Release Ownership button. The button will be displayed on the Authoring Console in the PresentationModeContainer.

When the editor or moderator clicks on the Release Ownership button, the ownership of the posting is set to Everybody. With the posting unlocked, authors can proceed to edit the posting.

Add a new class file to the ConsoleButtons folder of the TropicalGreen project. Name the class file ReleaseOwnership.cs.

Above the namespace declaration, add the following statements for the namespaces of methods that will be used throughout the class.

```
using System;
using Microsoft.ContentManagement.Publishing;
using Microsoft.ContentManagement.WebControls;
using Microsoft.ContentManagement.WebControls.ConsoleControls;

namespace TropicalGreen.ConsoleButtons
{
    . . . code continues . . .
}
```

Inherit from the BasePostbackAction class:

```
. . . code continues . . .
```

```
public class ReleaseOwnership: BasePostbackAction
{
    . . . code continues . . .
}
```

Let's label the button Release Ownership. Add the Text property below the ReleaseOwnership() constructor.

```
public override string Text
{
    get
    {
        return "Release Ownership";
    }
}
```

In the overridden Available property, we shall set the button to show up only if the posting is owned by the current user.

```
public override bool Available
{
    get
    {
        CmsHttpContext cmsContext = CmsHttpContext.Current;
        Posting currentPosting = cmsContext.Posting;
        if(currentPosting!=null)
        {
            if(currentPosting.OwnedBy.ServerAccountName
                ==cmsContext.User.ServerAccountName)
            {
                return true;
            }
            else
            {
                return false;
            }
        }
        else
        {
            return false;
        }
    }
}
```

We will release the lock on the posting by calling the Posting.ReleaseOwnership() method in the overridden PeformActionBehavior() method. The ReleaseOwnership() method sets the Posting.OwnedBy property of the posting to Everybody. When the lock is released, the Page Status on the Authoring Console will contain the value Not Locked. A try-catch block wraps round the ReleaseOwnership() method to take care of exceptions such as where the person declining the posting does not own the lock. Add the PerformActionBehavior() method directly below the Available property accessors.

```
protected override void PerformActionBehavior()
{
    CmsHttpContext cmsContext = CmsHttpContext.Current;
    Posting currentPosting = cmsContext.Posting;

    //Release the lock on the posting
    //so that other authors can edit it.
    if(currentPosting.CanSetProperties)
    {
        try
        {
            currentPosting.ReleaseOwnership(false);
```

```
            cmsContext.CommitAll();
        }
        catch
        {
            //We have set the allowReleaseByNonOwner flag to false.
            //If the user does not own the lock
            //he would not be able to release it
            //and an exception would be raised.
        }
    }
}
```

The `ReleaseOwnership()` method accepts an optional input Boolean parameter, `allowReleaseByNonOwner`. By default, the value of `allowReleaseByNonOwner` is false. When set to `true`, it allows editors, moderators, template designers, channel managers, and administrators to release the lock even if they are not the owners of the posting.

Add the button to the Authoring Console. With `CustomConsole.ascx` opened in HTML view, add the following code below the closing `</CmsConsole:PostingLockingInfo>` tag.

```
<TropicalGreenConsole:ReleaseOwnership runat="server" id="ReleaseOwnership1">
    <A id="ReleaseOwnershipAnchor"
        onclick="<%# Container.ActionJavascript%>;return false" href="#">
        <%# Container.Text %>
    </A>
</TropicalGreenConsole:ReleaseOwnership>
```

Save and build the solution. Let's test it to see it in action:

1. Log in to the TropicalGreen site as Editor1.
2. Navigate to `http://localhost/tropicalgreen/plantcatalog/hibiscus.htm`. The Lock Status says Not Locked. This means that anyone with author rights to the channel can edit and save this posting.
3. Edit the posting and save it.
4. Notice that the Lock Status indicates that Editor1 is now the owner of the posting.
5. Now, imagine that Editor1 has issues with the content and wants Author1 to fix it. Author1 is unable to edit the posting because Editor1 has locked it.
6. Still logged in as Editor1, click on the Release Ownership button.
7. The lock on the posting is release and the Lock Status shows that the posting is Not Locked. Author1 can now edit the posting.

```
Switch To Live Site
‾‾‾‾‾‾‾‾‾‾‾‾‾‾‾‾‾‾‾‾‾‾‾‾‾‾‾
Page Status: Saved
Version: Page has Live Version
Lock Status: WinNT://MCMSBOOK/Editor1 Release Ownership
```

Once the lock on the posting is released and its ownership is set to `Everybody`, the posting will no longer show up in either Approval Manager or Production Manager for any user.

Inheriting from the BaseNewWindowAction Class

The BaseNewWindowAction class has a property called UrlNewWindow dedicated to the storage of the URL of the page that is to be displayed in a new window.

After setting the UrlNewWindow property, you still have to override the ActionJavascript property to add the necessary JavaScript to open the URL in a new window.

The developers at Microsoft must have thought of this because for the BaseNewWindowAction class, ActionJavascript is an abstract property inherited from the BaseAction class. You must override it for the code to compile. In that way, you won't forget to write the logic required to open the new window.

Generating a List of Expired Postings

Our next example makes use of the BaseNewWindowAction class. We will build a dialog that provides a list of all expired postings in the current channel.

In the ConsoleButtons folder of the TropicalGreen project, create a new class file. Name the new class file ListExpiredPostings.cs.

Add the following statements above the namespace declaration:

```
using System;
using System.Web;
using Microsoft.ContentManagement.Publishing;
using Microsoft.ContentManagement.WebControls.ConsoleControls;

namespace TropicalGreen.ConsoleButtons
{
    . . . code continues . . .
}
```

Add the name of the BaseNewWindowAction class after the ListExpiredPostings class declaration to indicate that the new console action inherits from it:

```
    . . . code continues . . .
public class ListExpiredPostings: BaseNewWindowAction
{
    . . . code continues . . .
}
```

In the previous examples, we have been overriding the Text property of the base class to supply the label for the action control. Another way of doing this is to assign a value to the Text property of the base class. Add the following code in the ListExpiredPostings() constructor:

```
public ListExpiredPostings()
{
    //
    // TODO: Add constructor logic here
    //
    base.Text = "List Expired Postings";
}
```

We will override the UrlNewWindow property to supply the URL of the dialog window that displays the list of expired postings (created later). The URL we want to point to is /tropicalgreen/dialogs/ListExpiredPostings.aspx (a dialog we will be building later). At the end of the URL, append a querystring generated by the

`ChannelItem.QueryStringModeUnpublished` property. With the querystring attached to the URL, we will open the dialog in the `Unpublished` mode and will able to access the current channel using the `CmsHttpContext.Current.Channel` property.

```
public override string UrlNewWindow
{
    get
    {
        string url = "";
        CmsHttpContext cmsContext = CmsHttpContext.Current;
        ChannelItem currentChannelItem = cmsContext.ChannelItem;
        if(currentChannelItem!=null)
        {
            url = "/tropicalgreen/dialogs/ListExpiredPostings.aspx?" +
                currentChannelItem.QueryStringModeUnpublished;
        }
        return url;
    }
}
```

The script in the `ActionJavascript` property calls the JavaScript `window.open()` method to open the URL specified in the `UrlNewWindow` property in a new window. Add the following code below the `UrlNewWindow` property:

```
public override string ActionJavascript
{
    get
    {
        return "window.open('" + this.UrlNewWindow + "');";
    }
}
```

In the `Dialogs` folder of the TropicalGreen project, create a new web form. Name the new web form `ListExpiredPostings.aspx` and set the Page Layout to FlowLayout.

Switch to HTML view. Between the <head> tags, link to the `styles.css` stylesheet created in Chapter 7.

```
<head>
. . . code continues . . .

<LINK href="/tropicalgreen/Styles/Styles.css" type="text/css"
rel="stylesheet">

. . . code continues . . .
</head>
```

Between the <form> and </form> tags, add a `Label`, a `DataGrid` and an HTML `Button`. The column in the `DataGrid` displays the list of expired postings as hyperlinks.

```
<h1>Expired Postings in this Channel</h1>
<asp:datagrid id="dgExpiredPostings" runat="server"
AutoGenerateColumns="False" ShowHeader="False">
<Columns>
<asp:HyperLinkColumn DataNavigateUrlField="Url"
DataTextField="DisplayName"></asp:HyperLinkColumn>
</Columns>
</asp:datagrid>
<br>
<INPUT type="button" value="Close" onclick="window.close();">
```

Toggle to Design view. The form appears as shown in the following figure.

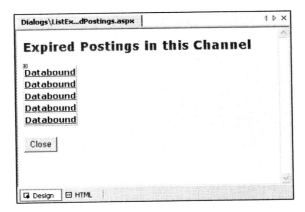

Double-click on the ListExpiredPostings.aspx file in Design view. Above the namespace declaration, import the namespaces required:

```
using Microsoft.ContentManagement.Publishing;
using Microsoft.ContentManagement.WebControls;
namespace TropicalGreen.Dialogs
{
. . . code continues . . .
}
```

The Page_Load() event handler will iterate through the list of postings in the current channel. If the posting is expired, we will extract its display name and URL and store it in a DataTable. After all the postings in the channel have been processed, the DataTable is bound to the DataGrid. In the Page_Load() event handler, enter the following code:

```
// Put user code to initialize the page here
if(!Page.IsPostBack)
{
    CmsHttpContext cmsContext = CmsHttpContext.Current;
    WebAuthorContext wac = WebAuthorContext.Current;
    Channel c = cmsContext.Channel;

    DataTable dt = new DataTable();
    dt.Columns.Add
        (new DataColumn("DisplayName",Type.GetType("System.String")));
        dt.Columns.Add(new DataColumn("Url",Type.GetType("System.String")));

    foreach(Posting p in c.Postings)
    {
        if(p.State==PostingState.Expired)
        {
        DataRow dr = dt.NewRow();
        dr[0] = p.DisplayName;
        dr[1] = "javascript:window.opener.location.href='" +
        wac.GetUrlForMode(p,wac.Mode) + "';window.close();";
        dt.Rows.Add(dr);
        }
    }
    dgExpiredPostings.DataSource = dt.DefaultView;
    dgExpiredPostings.DataBind();
}
```

Finally, we are ready to add the control to the Custom Console below the Preview Action Control. Open the `CustomConsole.ascx` file in HTML view. Look for the end tag of the Preview Control. (Tip: Press *Ctrl + F* and use `PresentationPreviewAction` as the search string.) Add the following code below the `</CmsConsole:PresentationPreviewAction>` tag:

```
<TropicalGreenConsole:ListExpiredPostings id="ListExpiredPostingsAction1"
                                          runat="server">
    <A
      id=ListExpiredPostingsAnchor
      onclick="<%# Container.ActionJavascript %>;return false"
      href="#"
      target=_self>
    <%# Container.Text %>
    </A>
    <BR>
</TropicalGreenConsole:ListExpiredPostings>
```

The control is complete. Save and build the solution. To test the control:

1. Browse to `http://localhost/tropicalgreen/plantcatalog` and log in as an administrator.

2. Open any plant fact sheet.

3. Switch to edit site mode.

4. To expire the posting, open the Page Properties and set the Stop Publishing date to the previous day, then click Save.

5. Click Approve.

6. Click on the newly added List Expired Postings link.

The dialog opens in a new window, showing the list of all expired postings in the Plant Catalog channel as shown in the following figure. Of course, if you didn't have any expired postings in the channel, the list remains empty.

Modifying Existing Actions

If you want to add additional features and functionality to an existing Action Control do you have to recreate the server control from scratch by inheriting one of the three base action classes?

You do not have to. You can inherit directly from any of the server control classes in the `Microsoft.ContentManagement.WebControls.ConsoleControls` namespace. Because all the default server controls are themselves sub-classed from the three base action classes, custom controls inheriting from them also become heir to the base action's properties, methods, and events.

Declining with Reason

One of the most sought-after features in the community is the modification of the Decline action to prompt editors for a reason. The advantage of creating a server control that inherits from the DeclineAction class is that we don't have to worry about writing the code that does the work of declining the posting. All we need to do is to add a dialog box for editors to enter remarks.

In this example, a dialog box pops up when an editor clicks on the Decline button, prompting for a reason. When the editor clicks on the OK button of the dialog, the decline reason is stored in a hidden text box within the posting. The contents are then accessed through the Request.Form collection when the CmsPosting_Declined() event handler is fired. From there the contents can be written to an external database for safekeeping or attached to an e-mail addressed to the author.

> You could also store the decline reason in a custom property of the posting. However, if you are using the Posting.OwnedBy property to decide to whom to send the decline reason, the editor will be on the receiving end instead! That's because updating a posting's custom property changes the Posting.OwnedBy property to that of the editor. In addition the posting will no longer be automatically assigned back to the author in this situation.

To begin, we will add a new class file to the ConsoleButtons folder of the TropicalGreen project. Name the new class file DeclineWithReason.cs.

Add the following statements above the namespace declaration:

```
using System;
using System.Web;
using Microsoft.ContentManagement.Publishing;
using Microsoft.ContentManagement.WebControls.ConsoleControls;

namespace TropicalGreen.ConsoleButtons
{
    . . . code continues . . .
}
```

Next change the class to inherit from the DeclineAction class:

```
public class DeclineWithReason : DeclineAction
{
}
```

Give the console button a label by adding the following code in the DeclineWithReason() constructor:

```
public DeclineWithReason()
{
    //
    // TODO: Add constructor logic here
    //
    base.Text = "Decline with Reason";
}
```

When an editor clicks on the Decline with Reason button, a dialog opens. Because scripts returned from the ActionJavascript() method are fired when the Decline with Reason button is clicked, it's the perfect place to add the JavaScript that opens the dialog. To do so, we will simply use the JavaScript window.open() method to pop up the dialog (GetDeclineReason.aspx, which we will construct in a moment).

Add the following code below the class constructor:

```
public override string ActionJavascript
{
    get
    {
        string url;
        url = Page.Request.ApplicationPath+"/Dialogs/GetDeclineReason.aspx";

        return "window.open('"+ url + "');";
    }
}
```

When the server control is loaded, it performs two tasks:

1. Create a hidden input field named DeclineReason to store the reason.
2. Register the JavaScript function, SetDeclineReason(), which stores the reason in the DeclineReason hidden input field.

Add the following code below the DeclineWithReason() constructor:

```
protected override void OnLoad(System.EventArgs e)
{
    base.OnLoad( e );
    if (this.Available == true)
    {
        //Create the "DeclineReason" hidden field
        Page.RegisterHiddenField( "DeclineReason", "" );

        //Register the javascript block that stores the
        //decline reason in the hidden field
        string reasonfunc = "<script language=\"JavaScript\">\n"+
            "function SetDeclineReason(strReason)\n"+
            "{\n"+
            "   CMS_PostbackForm.DeclineReason.value = strReason;\n"+
            "   "+base.ActionJavascript+";\n"+
            "}\n"+
            "</script>";

        Page.RegisterClientScriptBlock( "DeclineReasonScript", reasonfunc );
    }
}
```

Creating the GetDeclineReason Dialog

Next, we will create the GetDeclineReason.aspx dialog. In the Dialogs folder of the TropicalGreen project, create a new web form named GetDeclineReason.aspx. Set the Page Layout to FlowLayout.

With GetDeclineReason.aspx in HTML view, add a Label, an HTML TextArea and an HTML submit button between the <form> tags as shown below. Within the <INPUT type="submit" value="OK"> tag, add an onclick() event handler that calls our JavaScript verifyInput() method.

```
<asp:Label id="Label1" runat="server">Enter the reason for declining this
posting</asp:Label>
<br>
<TEXTAREA rows="4" cols="50" id="txtDeclineReason"></TEXTAREA>
<br>
<INPUT type="submit" value="OK" id="submit"
onclick="javascript:verifyInput();">
```

Enter the JavaScript function that updates the decline reason between the <HEAD> tags:

```
<HEAD>
. . . code continues . . .
<script language="javascript">
<!--
function verifyInput()
{
//verify that user has entered a reason
 if (this.document.all["txtDeclineReason"].value == "")
  {
    this.document.all["txtDeclineReason"].focus();
    alert("Please enter the reason for declining the post.");
    event.returnValue = false;
    return false;
  }
  else
  {
   //Store the decline reason in the hidden field created in the console
   window.opener.SetDeclineReason(this.document.all["txtDeclineReason"].value);
   window.close();
  }
}
// -->
</script>
</HEAD>
```

Toggle to Design view. The completed web form is shown below.

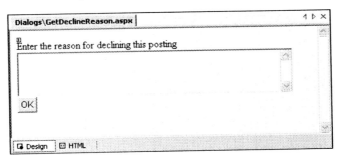

The code checks that the reason for declining has been given. Blank fields are not accepted. When the editor has typed some text into the box, the SetDecline()method of the console is called, filling the hidden field with the contents of the txtDeclineReason TextBox.

Add the control to the Custom Console below the default Decline control. Open the CustomConsole.ascx file in HTML view. Find the end tag of the Decline action control, and add the following code below the </CmsConsole:DeclineAction> tag:

```
<TropicalGreenConsole:DeclineWithReason id="DeclineWithReason1"
runat="server">
   <A id=DeclineWithReasonAnchor
        onclick="<%# Container.ActionJavascript %>;return false"
        href="#"
        target=_self>
   <%# Container.Text %>
   </A>
   <BR>
</TropicalGreenConsole:DeclineWithReason>
```

The control is complete. Save and build the solution.

Accessing the DeclineReason Field

You can find the value of the `DeclineReason` field using the `Request.Form` collection in the workflow event hooks. For example, in the `CmsPosting_Declined()` event hander you could add the following code to retrieve the reason. You can send it as part of the e-mail to the author or store it in a database for retrieval later.

```
if(Request.Form["DeclineReason"]!=null)
  {
      string declineReason = Request.Form["DeclineReason"];
      //Process the decline reason
      //You could send it as an email to the
      //author or store it in a database
      //for retrieval later
      //. . . code continues . . .
  }
```

Identifying the Person Who First Edited a Posting

Back in Chapter 16, we used the `Posting.OwnedBy` property to get the name of the last person who edited the posting. We then directed all decline notifications to the person whose user name is stored in the `Posting.OwnedBy` property.

However, that isn't always correct. More often than not, before editors and moderators decline a posting, they will take the chance to edit it, perhaps to add comments or modify parts of the content. The moment the editor or moderator saves the posting, the `Posting.OwnedBy` property contains his or her user name. And because we have programmed the decline notification to use the `Posting.OwnedBy` property to decide who the e-mail should be routed to, the editor or moderator will receive the e-mail. Not quite the result that they would expect.

In most workflow systems, what we really need is the name of the first person to modify the posting. This person could be one of the following:

- The one who created the posting and saved it for the first time
- The first person to edit and save a posting that was previously published

MCMS does not record this information. The good news is that we can capture this name by adding custom code to the workflow event handlers and modifying the behavior of the Save actions in the Web Author Console. We then record the information either in a separate database table or as a custom property value within the posting. To keep this example simple, we will store the name as a custom property value.

Creating the FirstSavedBy Custom Property Definition

First, we will create a custom property named `FirstSavedBy` in the Plant template:

1. In Template Explorer, check out the Plant template.
2. In the Properties dialog, open the Custom Property Definition Collection Editor.
3. Click Add. Give the new Custom Property the following values:

    Name = FirstSavedBy

    Value = (leave it as an empty string)
4. Click OK.

5. Check in the Plant template.

We will store the name of the first person to create/edit and save the posting in the FirstSavedBy custom property.

Capturing the Name of the First Person to Save a New Posting

The first person to save the new posting is also the person who created it. In order to capture their user name, we shall write additional code in the CmsPosting_Created() event handler. In Global.asax.cs of the TropicalGreen project, add the following code to the CmsPosting_Created() method:

```
public void CmsPosting_Created( Object sender, CreatedEventArgs e )
{
    Posting pPosting = (Posting)e.Target;
    if (pPosting.CustomProperties["FirstSavedBy"] != null)
    {
        pPosting.CustomProperties["FirstSavedBy"].Value =
                                    e.Context.User.ServerAccountName;
    }

    //LogEvent("CmsPosting_Submitting",e);
}
```

Save and build the solution. Let's test the workflow event:

1. Navigate to http://localhost/tropicalgreen/plantcatalog.
2. Log in as Editor1.
3. Click Switch To Edit Site.
4. Click Create New Page.
5. Select the Plant template in the PlantCatalog Template gallery.
6. Click Save New Page. Name the new page Ixora.

When the page has been saved, look at its page properties and observe that the value in the FirstSavedBy custom property contains the user name of the first person to create the posting.

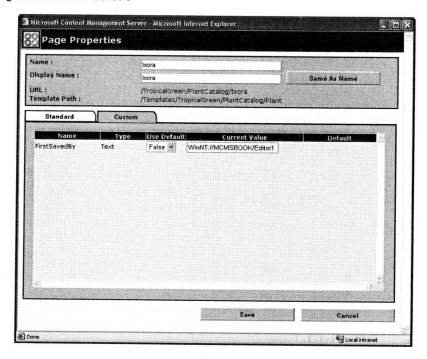

Capturing the Name of the First Person to Edit and Save a Previously Published Posting

After editing the posting, authors can choose to click either the Save button or the Save And Exit button to commit the changes to the database. There's no way to tell which button would be clicked first so we will have to modify both such that when the first author clicks on either of them, their name will be recorded in the FirstSavedBy custom property of the posting.

Modifying the AuthoringReeditSaveAndExit Action

The Save And Exit button is derived from the AuthoringReeditSaveAndExit class. We will modify it to record the name of the first person who saved the posting.

We will start by creating a new class file in the ConsoleButtons folder of the TropicalGreen project. Name the new class file ReeditSaveandExitWithAuthorTracking.cs.

Next, we will enter the following statements above the namespace declaration:

```
using System;
using System.Web.UI.WebControls;
using Microsoft.ContentManagement.Publishing;
using Microsoft.ContentManagement.WebControls.ConsoleControls;
namespace TropicalGreen.ConsoleButtons
{
    . . . code continues . . .
}
```

Our class inherits from the AuthoringReeditSaveAndExit class so add the following code after the class declaration:

```
public class ReeditSaveandExitwithAuthorTracking :
                          AuthoringReeditSaveAndExitAction
{
    . . . code continues . . .
}
```

We set the text of the console button to Save & Exit with AuthorTracking in the constructor:

```
public class ReeditSaveandExitwithAuthorTracking :
                          AuthoringReeditSaveAndExitAction
{
    public ReeditSaveandExitwithAuthorTracking()
    {
        //
        // TODO: Add constructor logic here
        //
        base.Text = "Save &amp; Exit with AuthorTracking";
    }
}
```

Finally, we will modify the behavior of the console action to write the name of the author saving the posting to the FirstSavedBy custom property. In addition, we still need to perform the default action of saving the posting and exiting from authoring view. The best way to achieve both tasks is by overriding the PerformActionBehavior() method.

Before the author edits and saves a posting that has been published previously, it is in one of the following states: Published, Approved, or Expired. As we are only interested in the first author to save a previously published posting, we only want to record the user name when the posting is in one of these three approved states. First, we will perform the default action of saving and exiting by calling base.PerformActionBehavior(). Then we will save the name of the author in the FirstSavedBy custom property.

After the posting has been saved, it will show a state of Saved and thus subsequent edits and saves to the posting will not be recorded in the FirstSavedBy custom property. For such cases, we simply perform the default save and exit actions.

Add the PerformActionBehavior() method directly below the ReeditSaveandExitwithAuthor Tracking() constructor.

```
protected override void PerformActionBehavior()
{
    Posting pPosting = CmsHttpContext.Current.Posting;
    if (pPosting.State == PostingState.Published ||
    pPosting.State == PostingState.Approved ||
    pPosting.State == PostingState.Expired)
    {
        base.PerformActionBehavior();
        if (pPosting.CustomProperties["FirstSavedBy"] != null)
        {
            pPosting.CustomProperties["FirstSavedBy"].Value =
            CmsHttpContext.Current.User.ServerAccountName;
        }
        CmsHttpContext.Current.CommitAll();
    }
    else
    {
        base.PerformActionBehavior();
    }
}
```

Modifying the AuthoringReeditSaveAction

The Save button inherits from the `AuthoringReeditSaveAction` class.

Add a new class file to the `ConsoleButtons` folder of the TropicalGreen project. Name the new class file `ReeditSaveWithAuthorTracking.cs`.

Above the namespace declarations, add the namespaces that we will be using.

```
using System;
using System.Web.UI.WebControls;
using Microsoft.ContentManagement.Publishing;
using Microsoft.ContentManagement.WebControls.ConsoleControls;

namespace TropicalGreen.ConsoleButtons
{
    . . . code continues . . .
}
```

Next, inherit from the `AuthoringReeditSaveAction` class:

```
public class ReeditSaveWithAuthorTracking : AuthoringReeditSaveAction
{
}
```

We will set the text of the console button to Save with AuthorTracking within the `ReeditSaveWithAuthorTracking()` constructor:

```
public ReeditSaveWithAuthorTracking()
{
    //
    // TODO: Add constructor logic here
    //
    base.Text = "Save with AuthorTracking";
}
```

The steps taken to modify the `PerformActionBehavior()` method differs slightly from the modified Save And Exit button we programmed earlier. The first section is exactly the same: We check the state of the posting and record the name of the author only if the posting is in the `Published`, `Approved`, or `Expired` state. Once the `FirstSavedBy` custom property has been updated with the user name of the author, we generate a JavaScript that updates the `__CMS_PageChangeToken` hidden field (generated when the posting is rendered on the browser) with the value of the posting's change token. This is required to prevent overlapping save exceptions from being raised.

Add the `PerformActionBehavior()` method directly below the `ReeditSaveWithAuthorTracking()` constructor.

```
protected override void PerformActionBehavior()
{
    Posting pPosting = (Posting)CmsHttpContext.Current.Posting;
    if (pPosting.State == PostingState.Published ||
        pPosting.State == PostingState.Approved ||
        pPosting.State == PostingState.Expired)
    {
        base.PerformActionBehavior();

        if (pPosting.CustomProperties["FirstSavedBy"] != null)
        {
            pPosting.CustomProperties["FirstSavedBy"].Value =
                CmsHttpContext.Current.User.ServerAccountName;
        }
```

```
            CmsHttpContext.Current.CommitAll();

            // We overwrite the change token rendered by the base method.
            // Without this an Overlapping Save would occur when saving twice
            string overwriteChangeToken =
                "<!-- script block generated by ReeditSaveWithAuthorTracking -->\n" +
                "<script language=\"javascript\" type=\"text/javascript\">\n"+
                "<!--\n" +
                "  __CMS_PostbackForm.__CMS_PageChangeToken.value = \"" +
            pPosting.ChangeToken.ToString()+"\";\n" +
                "-->\n" +
                "</script>\n";

            Page.RegisterClientScriptBlock("overwriteChangeToken",
                overwriteChangeToken);
    }
    else
    {
        base.PerformActionBehavior();
    }
}
```

Let's add the modified controls to our Custom Console. Open CustomConsole.ascx in HTML view and add the following code after the </CmsConsole:AuthoringReeditSaveAndExitAction> closing tag.

```
<TropicalGreenConsole:ReeditSaveWithAuthorTracking runat="server"
                                    id="ReeditSaveWithAuthorTracking1">
    <A id=ReeditSaveWithAuthorTrackingAnchor
        onclick="<%# Container.ActionJavascript %>;return false" href="#"
        target=_self>
        <%# Container.Text %>
    </A>
    <BR>
</TropicalGreenConsole:ReeditSaveWithAuthorTracking>

<TropicalGreenConsole:ReeditSaveandExitWithAuthorTracking runat="server"
                                    id="ReeditSaveandExitWithAuthorTracking1">
    <A id=ReeditSaveandExitWithAuthorTrackingAnchor
        onclick="<%# Container.ActionJavascript %>;return false" href="#"
        target=_self>
        <%# Container.Text %>
    </A>
    <BR>
</TropicalGreenConsole:ReeditSaveandExitWithAuthorTracking>
```

Save and build the solution. To test the buttons:

1. Log in as the administrator, point your browser to http://localhost/ tropicalgreen/plantcatalog/ and switch to edit site mode.

2. Approve the Ixora posting. The state of the posting is now Published.

3. Log the administrator out.

4. Log in as Author1.

5. Edit the posting. When saving click on either the Save with AuthorTracking or Save & Exit with AuthorTracking button. Look at the value of the FirstSavedBy custom property. It holds the user name of Author1, the first person to save the posting after it has been published.

To use the value stored in the FirstSavedBy custom property, modify the ComposeMail() method in Global.asax.cs to read from it:

```
else if(pAction == PublishingAction.Decline)
{
    //to = mail.GetEmailAddress(p.OwnedBy.ServerAccountName);

    CustomProperty cp = p.CustomProperties["FirstSavedBy"];
    if(cp!=null)
    {
        to = mail.GetEmailAddress(cp.Value);
    }
}
}
```

Summary

The Web Author Console is a highly customizable component. You can change its look and feel by modifying the HTML that renders the Web Author Console, or build a totally new control from scratch by following the code provided in the Default Console that ships with MCMS.

In this chapter, we created new Action Controls by creating classes that inherit from each of the BaseAction classes. We created an Action Control that bypasses the Save New Page dialogs by inheriting from the BaseAction class.

We went on to create two Action Controls that inherit from the BasePostback class: a control that deletes not only the current posting but also all postings connected to it; and a control that releases the ownership of a posting. We saw how server-side scripts can be called in postbacks by overriding the PerformActionBehavior() method.

Next, we saw how controls that open new dialog windows can also be created by inheriting from the BaseNewWindowAction class when we created a control that opened a dialog listing all expired postings in the channel.

Finally, we created several controls that were derived directly from existing Action Controls that come with the Default Console. We built a version of the Decline Action Control that captured a reason. This brought us to the same issue we faced back in Chapter 16 when we could not capture the name of the person who first saved the posting. We got around it here by creating customized versions of the Save and Save And Exit buttons.

20
Creating Connected Templates and Pages

The basic idea behind connected templates and pages (or postings) is reducing duplication of content. A common problem in pre-content management systems is managing shared content. Some pages have exactly the same content but are different in design and layout. In many cases, this leads to content being manually copied from one page to the other in the hope that no major changes to the copied code will ever be required.

This method works, if a little clumsily. Once the pages are created, updating shared content can easily become a problem. Each and every page containing certain information must be updated and kept consistent. If just one page is left out, the content on that page will be out of date.

The ability to manage shared information is a feature that is available out of the box with MCMS. Shared information is administered through connected templates and postings. When the content of one posting is updated, all connected postings are automatically updated at the same time. Authors do not have to scour the site for pages containing pieces of shared content and update each separately.

Connected templates and postings are used in situations where you need to:

- **Create pages that share content**: Your website may require pages to be created for online viewing both through a regular browser and on mobile devices like a Pocket PC. Or perhaps you just want to create a printer-friendly version of the page.
- **Create pages that are a subset of a bigger page**: An example of this is when you have pages showing both public and confidential information when viewed on an intranet but only displaying the public information when viewed via the Internet.
- **Create multiple pages with the same content but in different channels**: Perhaps you have a page that is read by both the Sales and Information Systems departments. Due to the different rights groups assigned to each department, you create two different channels and create connected postings for pages that are shared across both channels.

In this chapter, we will build a Gardens section for the TropicalGreen site. The section contains two channels, each containing a set of connected postings. One set contains confidential information to be seen only by members. The second displays the same information but with only non-confidential placeholder content shown to guests of the site. We show how connected templates and postings give authors the option to upload content once and share it across both the public and members-only channels of the Gardens section.

About Connected Templates and Postings

Connected templates and postings are useful for repurposing content without re-editing it or creating multiple copies of postings across many channels. They are different from postings created using the Copy function, which creates two completely independent postings and so changing the contents of one copy does not affect the other.

When you create a connected posting, you create postings where changes to one do affect the other. To understand this better, let's take a closer look at what connected templates and postings really are.

Connected Templates

Connected templates share the same underlying placeholder definitions. For example a template, named Public, could have the following settings:

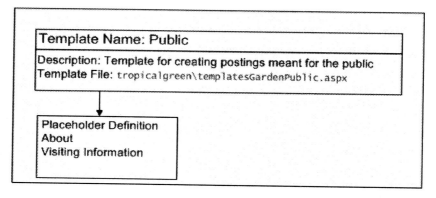

There's nothing special about the Public template. It's like any of the regular templates we have seen so far. Now, suppose we want to create a connected template based on the Public template. Let's call this new connected template as Members.

Immediately, the Members template will share the placeholder definitions of the Public template. If you were to add, edit, or remove any of these definitions from either template, the other template would be updated as well.

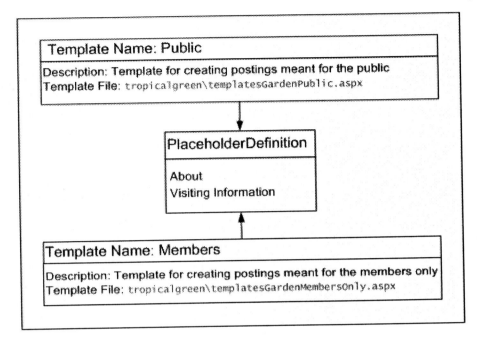

Connected templates can have their own:

- Name
- Description
- Template File
- Custom Property Definitions

The layout of a given page is defined by its template file, which is not shared among connected templates. In this way, postings created from connected templates can have a different look and feel but share the same content. By adding the same (or a different) set of placeholder controls to the connected template files, you can display the same (or a different) subset of the shared content in the connected posting.

Another point to note is that connected templates can maintain their own set of custom property definitions. However, when two or more connected templates have custom property definitions of the same name, postings that are based on them will share custom property values.

Connected Postings

Connected postings are created from either the same template as the original posting or a connected template. Connected postings share:

- All content in shared placeholders
- A common page name

- A common description
- Custom property values when you create custom property definitions with the same name on two connected templates

When authors update any of these properties, all connected postings will be automatically updated with the new values.

There is no concept of master and secondary postings. Once a posting has been connected to another, they are both considered equals and share *all* content in *all* placeholders. You can of course, choose to hide content you do not wish to show by adding different sets of placeholder controls as we will show in this chapter.

> In MCMS 2001, you could create connected postings based on any template. The concept of connected templates was introduced in MCMS 2002 and you can only create connected postings from connected templates.

Before We Begin

Before proceeding with the examples in this chapter, we strongly advise you to complete Chapter 5. Ensure that both the Gardens and Members channels have the properties described in the following table:

Channel Name	Properties	
Gardens	DisplayName	Gardens
	Path	/Channels/TropicalGreen/Gardens
	Script URL	/tropicalgreen/templates/ChannelRenderingScript.aspx
	Use channel script with Pages	No
Members	DisplayName	Members
	Path	/Channels/TropicalGreen/Gardens/Members
	Script URL	/tropicalgreen/templates/ChannelRenderingScript.aspx
	Use channel script with Pages	No

A template gallery named Gardens should already exist below the TropicalGreen template gallery (/Templates/TropicalGreen/Gardens).

Also, ensure that the Researchers author-rights group has been given the rights to create postings in both the Gardens and Members channels based on templates stored in the Gardens template gallery. Also give them access to resources in the Garden resource gallery. Make sure the rights group has all of the rights outlined in the image below.

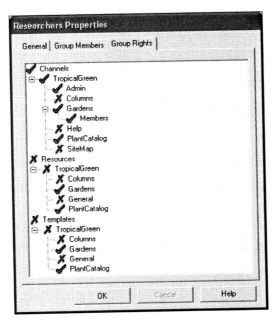

Creating Connected Templates

Now that we have prepared the workspace we can create connected templates and postings.

The First Template

To begin, we will create the template upon which all Garden postings meant only for members will be based.

Open the TropicalGreen solution in Visual Studio .NET. In Template Explorer, add a new template to the Gardens template gallery.

Name the new template Members and add the following placeholder definitions:

Type	Property Name	Property Value
HtmlPlaceholderDefinition	AllowHyperLinks	True
	AllowLineBreaks	True
	Formatting	FullFormatting
	Description	About the Garden
	Name	About
	AllowAttachments	True
	AllowImages	True
	MustUseResourceGallery	False
	UseGeneratedIcon	False
HtmlPlaceholderDefinition	AllowHyperLinks	True
	AllowLineBreaks	True
	Formatting	FullFormatting
	Description	Visiting Information
	Name	VisitingInformation
	AllowAttachments	True
	AllowImages	True
	MustUseResourceGallery	False
	UseGeneratedIcon	False

Add two TextCustomPropertyDefinitions to the custom property definition collection with the following properties. The FirstSavedBy value will be set by the CmsPosting_Created() workflow action created in Chapter 19.

Custom Property Type	Property Name	Property Value
TextCustomPropertyDefinition	Name	FirstSavedBy
	Value	(empty string)
TextCustomPropertyDefinition	Name	SourceOfInformation
	Value	(empty string)

Keep the Members template object checked out.

Add a new MCMS template file to the TropicalGreen project in the Templates folder. Name the new file GardenMembersOnly.aspx. Change the Page Layout to FlowLayout. In the MCMS Template Explorer, set the TemplateFile property of the Members template to point to /tropicalgreen/templates/GardenMembersOnly.aspx. Check in the Members template.

Switch to HTML view and add a reference to the `styles.css` stylesheet between the <head> tags.

```
<LINK rel="stylesheet" type="text/css"
href="/TropicalGreen/Styles/Styles.css">
```

Between the <form> tags, add the following HTML code. Don't forget to include the markers between the brackets.

```
<table width="100%" border="0" cellspacing="0" cellpadding="0">
<tr>
    <td vAlign="top" width="100%" bgColor="#ffcc00" colSpan="2">
        <IMG src="/tropicalgreen/images/Logo.gif">
    </td>
    <td rowspan="10" valign="top">
        (Space for Default Console)
    </td>
</tr>
<tr bgColor="#66cc33">
    <td colSpan="2">
        (Space for Top Menu)
    </td>
</tr>
<tr>
    <td valign="top" style="PADDING-LEFT:30px">
        <h1><asp:Literal ID="litDisplayName" Runat="Server"></asp:Literal></h1>
        <h2>About</h2>
        (Space for About HTML Placeholder Control)
        <h2>Visiting Information (Confidential)</h2>
        (Space for VisitingInformation Placeholder Control)
        <br>
    </td>
    <td class="RightMenuBar" width="20%" valign="top" height="100%"
            align="center" rowspan="2" bgcolor="#669900">
        (Space for Right Menu)
    </td>
</tr>
</table>
```

Toggle to Design view. Drag and drop the following Web User Controls onto the form:

- `TopMenu.ascx` (built in Chapter13) into the cell containing the words (Space for Top Menu)
- `RightMenu.ascx` (built in Chapter 13) into the cell containing the words (Space for Right Menu)
- `DefaultConsole.ascx` (found in the Console folder) into the cell containing the words (Space for Default Console)

From the Toolbox, drag and drop the following MCMS placeholder controls:

- `HTMLPlaceholderControl` into the cell containing the words (Space for About HTML Placeholder Control). Set the `PlaceholderToBind` property to About.
- `HTMLPlaceholderControl` into the cell containing the words (Space for VisitingInformation Placeholder Control). Set the `PlaceholderToBind` property to VisitingInformation.

Delete the markers after you have dragged the controls onto the form. The completed form is shown on the next page.

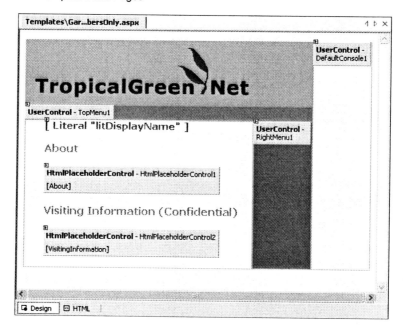

Right-click anywhere on the template file and select View Code to get its code-behind file. Above the namespace declaration, import the `Microsoft.ContentManagement.Publishing` namespace.

```
. . . code continues . . .

//The namespace of the MCMS PAPI
using Microsoft.ContentManagement.Publishing;

namespace TropicalGreen.Templates
{
    . . . code continues . . .
}
```

In the `Page_Load()` event handler, add the following code to display the posting's display name in the `litDisplayName` literal.

```
private void Page_Load(object sender, System.EventArgs e)
{
    // Put user code to initialize the page here
    CmsHttpContext cmsContext = CmsHttpContext.Current;
    Posting currentPosting = cmsContext.Posting;
    string displayName = "";
    if ( currentPosting != null )
    {
     displayName = currentPosting.DisplayName;
     litDisplayName.Text = displayName;
    }
}
```

Save and build the solution.

The Connected Template

Now that we have a Members template and template file, we can create a connected template based on it. In this section, we will create the Public template. The purpose of this template is to generate postings that contain the same information as those generated by the Members template. The only difference is that the postings from the Public template will not display the content stored in the visitingInformation placeholder.

From Template Explorer, right-click the Members template and choose the Create Connected option from the menu.

A prompt appears with the message:

Creating a template connected to 'Members' will make 'Members' and each of the templates it is connected to locked from check out by other users. Do you wish to continue?

Click Yes. This warning is necessary because connected templates share placeholder definitions. Any additions, updates, or deletions to the list of placeholder definitions to a template affect the placeholder definitions of all other connected templates as well. By locking all connected templates when you check out a template, MCMS prevents you from overwriting the changes of connected templates that other developers are working on.

Give the new connected template the name Public. Notice that the icon used to represent the Members template has changed from ☐ to ☐. It's now the template icon with a little lock on the left and a chain on the right. The chain represents the fact that this template has a connected template associated with it. The lock means that no one else can check out the template for as long as you have the Public template checked out.

Notice the following points about the properties of the Public template:

- It shares the same set of placeholder definitions as the Members template. The About and visitingInformation placeholder definitions are automatically listed in the Placeholder Definition Collection Editor.
- It does not share the same set of custom property definitions. In fact, as it is a newly created template, no custom property definitions have been defined.

> You may be tempted to remove the `VisitingInformation` placeholder definition from the Public template. Whatever you do, don't remove it. Because connected templates share placeholder definitions, deleting the `VisitingInformation` placeholder definition from the Public template removes it from the Members template as well. Doing so may cause loss of information. All content that has been stored in the `VisitingInformation` placeholder will become inaccessible.

Let's add a custom property definition that has the same name as the one found in the Members template (`SourceOfInformation`) and another that is unique to the Public template (`ContactPerson`). Add the following `TextCustomPropertyDefinitions` to the custom property definition collection with the following properties:

Custom Property Type	Property Name	Property Value
TextCustomPropertyDefinition	Name	SourceOfInformation
	Value	(empty string)
TextCustomPropertyDefinition	Name	ContactPerson
	Value	(empty string)

Keep the Public template checked out.

Since the Public version of the template file will be exactly the same as that of the Members template file, with the exception of the placeholder control that displays visiting information, we will take the shortcut. Make a copy of the `GardenMembersOnly.aspx` file. Rename the copy `GardenPublic.aspx`. Open `GardenPublic.aspx` in HTML view and replace all occurrences of the text `GardenMembersOnly` with `GardenPublic`. Repeat for all occurrences of the text in the corresponding code-behind file.

In HTML view, comment out the code that renders the `VisitingInformation` placeholder control by inserting <%-- and --%> markers around it.

```
<%--<h2>Visiting Information (Confidential)</h2>
<cms:HtmlPlaceholderControl id="HtmlPlaceholderControl2" runat="server"
PlaceholderToBind="VisitingInformation"></cms:HtmlPlaceholderControl>--%>
```

In MCMS Template Explorer, set the `TemplateFile` property of the Public template to point to `/tropicalgreen/templates/GardenPublic.aspx`. When you are done, check in the Public template. Notice that the little lock disappears from the template icon of both the Members and Public templates. It now looks like this: ▨. Keep in mind that you need to check in all connected templates before any of them can be checked out by another developer.

The completed `GardenPublic.aspx` template file is shown opposite.

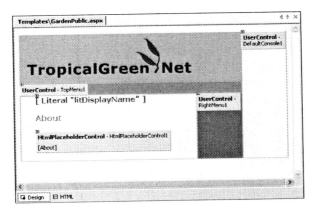

Both the Members and Public templates are complete. Save and build the solution.

Creating Connected Postings

With the templates built, we can proceed to create postings.

Creating the Original Posting

The first posting that we will create is meant only for members. Imagine that you have planted a new herb garden and have pictures to upload to the Gardens section of the TropicalGreen website. Let's create a posting about the herb garden.

1. Navigate to `http://localhost/tropicalgreen/gardens/members/`.
2. You should be prompted to log on. Log on with the credentials of `Author1`.
3. Click Switch To Edit Site.
4. Select the Create New Page option.
5. Choose Gardens template gallery to create the posting based on Members template.
6. In the About placeholder control, add some text:
    You start the day with the fresh smell of herbs growing in your garden.
7. In the VisitingInformation placeholder control, add some text:
    Visit my garden at
    10 Tropical Green

    Open on Saturdays and Sundays from 3pm - 5pm
    You can contact me at Author1@tropicalgreen.net

8. Click Save New Page. Name the page HerbGarden and set its `Display Name` to `Herb Garden (Member's View)`. Click OK.
9. Click Page Properties. Set the `Description` of the page to This is a story about my beautiful herb garden.

10. With the Page Properties dialog still open, select the Custom tab.

11. Set the SourceOfInformation custom property value to The Herb expert. Click Save.

12. Click Submit to publish the new page. Because there are no editors or moderators assigned to the channel, the page status changes from Saved to Published.

We now have a posting based on the Members template. The completed posting is shown below.

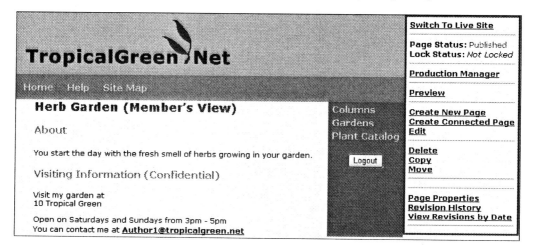

Creating the Connected Posting

In the public version of the page, we want to show the contents of the About placeholder but hide the contents of the VisitingInformation placeholder. To create a connected posting based on the HerbGarden posting, with the HerbGarden posting opened in edit mode, click Create Connected Page from the Web Author Console.

In the Select Destination Channel dialog, select /Channels/TropicalGreen/Gardens. The tree view contains a list of channels that the author has authoring rights to. Even though MCMS does not restrict you from choosing the same channel as the original posting, it is a good idea to choose a different channel. Because connected postings share the same Page Name values, you would end up having two postings sharing the same name in the same channel.

This could lead to problems when accessing the connected postings by their hierarchical URLs. MCMS would just pick one (or none) of the two postings to display, leaving the other reachable only by its Unique-ID-based URL. In addition, because rights groups are applied on a channel level and not on a page level, you can't create a 'members-only' version of the page by placing it in a channel opened to the public.

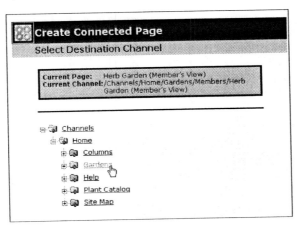

After the destination channel has been selected, the Select Template Dialog appears. In this dialog, you are shown a list that includes:

- The template on which the original posting is based (in this case, that is the Members template).
- The templates that are connected to the template on which the original posting is based. The author must be assigned rights to the template galleries of these templates in order to see them in the list.

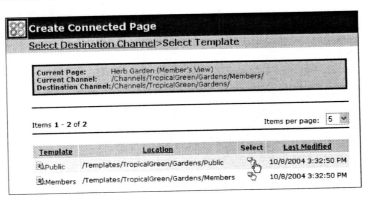

Select the Public template.

Connected Postings Share Placeholder Content

The new connected posting appears in authoring mode. Notice that:

- The About placeholder is pre-populated with the contents of the members' version of the posting.

- There is an additional icon ⊞ at the top of the placeholder. The tooltip for the icon says Placeholder is shared with other pages. When you see this icon, you know that you are working with a connected posting. Changing the contents of the placeholder would also change the placeholder content of all other connected postings.

- The VisitingInformation placeholder is not displayed.

Let's try changing the text in the About placeholder and see what happens. Add an extra line of text in the About placeholder that reads: Aloes, Basils, Mint and Curry leaves.

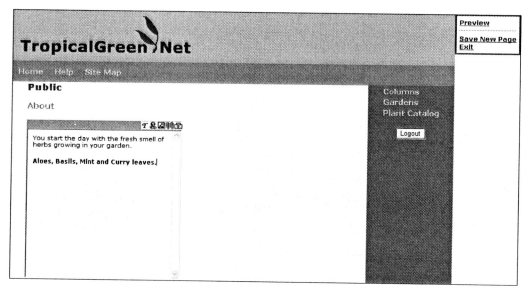

Connected Postings Have a Common Page Name

Click Save New page. In the Save New Page dialog, observe that:

- The Name of the page is automatically set to HerbGarden, the name of the original posting. The text box has been disabled. You can't change the name at this point.

- The initial value in the Display Name field is the same as that of the original posting.

Because connected postings do not share display names, you can give the public version of the page its own distinct name. Enter The Herb Garden (Public View) in the Display Name field. Click OK to save the page.

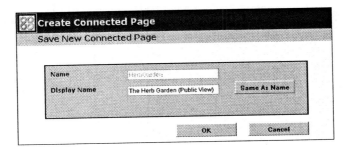

Connected Postings Have a Common Description

Back at the unpublished view of the public version of the HerbGarden posting, click the Page Properties button on the Web Author Console. The dialog looks very much like the ones we have seen so far with the exception of little icons ⊞ next to the Name and Description fields. Place your mouse cursor over these icons to reveal a tooltip, which says Shared Property.

Unlike the Save New Page dialog earlier, the Page Properties dialog allows you to change the name of the page. Note that doing so will change not only the name of the page that you are currently working on, but also the names of all pages connected to it. The description is also a shared property. The field is automatically populated with the description that we entered earlier in the original members' version of the page. Let's change it to see what happens. Change the description to read:

This is a story about my beautiful herb garden which started from a single seed.

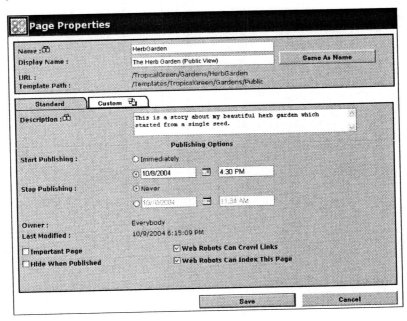

Connected Postings Can Share Custom Property Values

With the Page Properties dialog still opened, click on the Custom tab. There is an icon ▦ on the Custom tab that says Shared Property in its tooltip. Notice that:

- Although you have not entered anything into the SourceOfInformation custom property field, it is automatically set with the value entered in the member's version of the page.
- The value in the ContactPerson custom property remains empty.
- The FirstSavedBy custom property that could be seen in the member's version of the page is not displayed.

Under the hood, all connected templates share connected definitions as well. You don't see them because they are not accessible if the template does not contain a definition for it. To share custom property values, just create custom property definitions of the same name in the respective connected templates.

We did this for the SourceOfInformation custom property by creating it in both the Public and Members templates. When you set the value of the SourceOfInformation custom property in the members' version of the posting, the public version of the posting was also immediately updated.

The Public template did not have a definition for the FirstSavedBy custom property definition so there is no value for this property.

Similarly, you can set the value of the ContactPerson custom property and the text you enter there will not affect the members' version of the page.

Set the custom property values of the public version of the page as follows:

Property	Value
ContactPerson	(YourName)
SourceOfInformation	(YourName), the Herb expert

Click Save to commit the changes and close the Page Properties dialog.

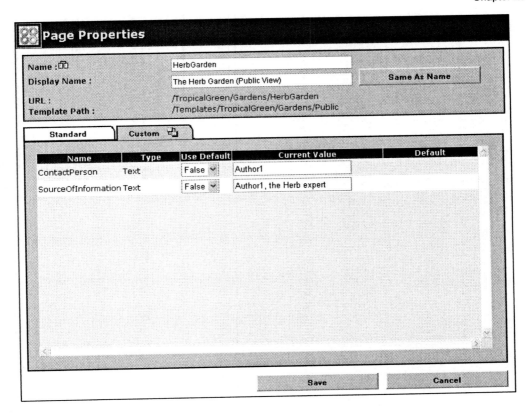

Going to a Connected Page

After you have created the connected page for the public version of the members' page, a new option in appears in the Web Author Console. The Web Author Console detects that the page you are working on is a connected page and reveals the Go To Connected Page option.

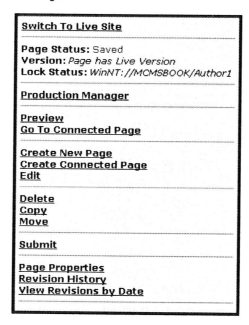

Click Go To Connected Page. The Go To Connected Page dialog shows a list of all pages that meet the following criteria:

- They are connected to the page you are currently working on.
- They are children of channels that you have been granted access rights to.

In this case, the list shows the members' version of the page. This dialog is very useful for the following reasons:

- Firstly, you can use it to see which pages are connected to the page you are working on and their locations.
- Secondly, it is often used to navigate to the other connected pages. Click the 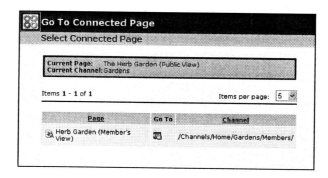 button to jump to the Herb Garden (Member's View) page.

The members' version of the page was the original posting that we based the public version of the page on. Throughout the exercises above, we have made quite a few changes to the content of the public version of the page. Let's take a look at the members' version and see how it has changed throughout the process. You should see that:

- Although we have published the members' version of the page, its status has changed from Published to Saved. This is because we have made changes to the placeholder content of the public page. Since the placeholder content is shared, the members' page receives the update as well and the changes have to be submitted again before they can be published.

- A live version of the members' page exists. This live version contains content that was published before we created and updated the public page.

- The locking owner is Author1, or the user who updated the public version of the page.

- The content of the About placeholder has been updated to contain the new text from the public version of the page. (Remember we added the line Aloes, Basils, Mint and Curry Leaves.)

- The content of the VisitingInformation placeholder remains unchanged.

- The following property values remain unchanged:
    - Display Name; it still shows as **Herb Garden (Member's View)**
    - The Start and Expiry dates
    - Important Page flag
    - Hide When Published flag
    - Web Robots Can Crawl Links flag
    - Web Robots Can Index This Page flag

- These properties are not shared by connected pages.

- The Description property, on the other hand, has been updated to show the additional line of text inserted when we updated the Description property of the public version of the page.

- Similarly, the SourceOfInformation custom property value has changed to whatever we entered on the public version of the page. It now includes your name. When connected templates have custom properties defined with the same name, the resulting connected postings will share custom property values.

Finally, because we have logged in as Author1, we are able to see both the public and members' versions of the page. If we were to log out and view the pages using the guest account, we would only be able to access the public version of the page.

Connected Postings Share Workflow Processes

We have seen how shared content gets updated to all connected postings when the posting is saved. What about getting the postings published? Do we have to visit each and every connected posting to submit them one by one before all shared content gets published?

Submission or Approval of a Posting Submits or Approves all Connected Postings

Before we began this chapter, we assigned the Researcher rights group to both the Gardens and Members channels. This means that the workflow mechanics for both the public and members' channels are the same: it is an authors-only publishing process (see Chapter 10 for details) where the posting's status changes to published/approved/expired immediately after authors submit them. The following table shows the current status of both connected pages:

Display Name	Status
Herb Garden (Member's View)	Saved
The Herb Garden (Public View)	Saved

With the members' version of the page opened, click Submit. Note the status of both postings.

Display Name	Status
Herb Garden (Member's View)	Published
The Herb Garden (Public View)	Published

When you submitted the members' page, the public page was automatically submitted along with it! You do not have to navigate to each and every page to submit them individually.

Connected Postings Follow the Workflow of the Posting that has been Submitted/Approved

Let's see what happens if we change the workflow such that the Gardens channel and the Members channel no longer share the same workflow processes. We can accomplish this by assigning different rights groups to each of the channels.

In Site Manager, add the Press Secretary rights group to the Members channel such that the rights group assigned to each channel is as shown in the table below.

Channel Name	Role	Rights Groups
Gardens	Authors	Researchers
	Subscribers	Guests
Members	Authors	Researchers
	Subscribers	Members
	Editors	Press Secretary

Using the account of Author1, edit the posting, The Herb Garden (Public View), and save it. As before, the status of both connected pages changes from Published to Saved.

Display Name	Status
Herb Garden (Member's View)	Saved
The Herb Garden (Public View)	Saved

Submit The Herb Garden (Public View). Notice that the status of both the public and members' postings change from Saved to Published.

Display Name	Status
Herb Garden (Member's View)	Published
The Herb Garden (Public View)	Published

Even though editors have been assigned to the Members channel, the members' version of the page does not require an editor to approve it. That's because the connected posting takes on the workflow of the posting that was being submitted. In this case, the public version still has an author-only workflow, so when its content was submitted and published, the members' version was submitted and published as well.

Now, try submitting the posting starting from the Members posting. Navigate to Herb Garden (Member's View). Edit the posting and save it. As before, the status of both connected postings changes from Published to Saved.

Display Name	Status
Herb Garden (Member's View)	Saved
The Herb Garden (Public View)	Saved

Submit Herb Garden (Member's View). The status of both connected postings changes from Saved to Waiting For Editor Approval. This is because we have submitted a posting in a channel that has an author-editor workflow. Even though the public version of the page has no editors assigned to it, it adopts the workflow of the connected posting that has been submitted.

Display Name	Status
Herb Garden (Member's View)	Waiting For Editor Approval
The Herb Garden (Public View)	Waiting For Editor Approval

Sign out Author1 and login as Editor1. Browse to the The Herb Garden (Public View). Notice that even though its status shows as Waiting For Editor Approval, the Approve button is not available. That's because Editor1 has not been assigned as an editor of the Gardens channel.

Navigate to Herb Garden (Member's View) and approve it. Note that both connected pages are approved and published at the same time.

Display Name	Status
Herb Garden (Member's View)	Published
The Herb Garden (Public View)	Published

Before creating a connected posting, ensure that the original posting has been published. Otherwise, you may encounter a known bug in the author-editor workflow where the status of the posting changes to `Waiting For Moderator Approval` after the editor approves the posting. This happens even when no moderators have been assigned to any of the channels.

Alternatives to Connected Postings

Apart from using connected postings and templates, there are other ways to share content across a site.

Connected postings are not the best solution when the postings to be connected have shared placeholders that contain different placeholder content. For example, you may have shared content such as legal disclaimers or the company's logo. Apart from the shared content, each posting will have its own unique content, perhaps the main body or story. In such cases, connected postings and templates will not work.

With connected templates and postings, *all* placeholder definitions and content are shared. You can't share just the legal disclaimer and have different content in other placeholders. In the example above, we have seen how updating the About placeholder content automatically updates the About placeholder content of all connected postings.

In this situation you need to use other ways to tackle shared content. You could retrieve placeholder content programmatically by using the techniques in Chapter 12 (or try the sample on GotDotNet at
`http://www.gotdotnet.com/Community/UserSamples/Details.aspx?SampleGuid=1045e51d-f83d-4caf-99b9-8b395b722f24`) to read the placeholder contents of a posting and display it on any other posting that requires the information.

If you are concerned about inflating the number of postings in the site, another alternative is to employ 'template switching' techniques. Instead of creating a connected posting each time you require the use of a different template file, you simply modify the URL and specify the template file the posting is based on.

Creating Printer-Friendly Pages with Template Switching

Let's try out template switching by creating a printer-friendly version of the garden pages using template switching.

First, we will create a connected template for the printer-friendly page.

1. Right-click either the Public or Members template object in Template Explorer and select Create Connected.

2. Name the new template `PrinterFriendly`.

3. Right-click `PrinterFriendly` and select **Save**. Keep `PrinterFriendly` checked out.

Next, we will create a template file to define the layout of the printer-friendly page.

1. Add a new MCMS Template File in the `Templates` folder of the TropicalGreen project.

2. Name the new template file `GardenPrinterFriendly.aspx` and set its **PageLayout** to FlowLayout.

3. When the template file has been created, assign `/tropicalgreen/templates/ GardenPrinterFriendly.aspx` to the **TemplateFile** property of the `PrinterFriendly` template object. Check in the `PrinterFriendly` template.

4. In HTML view, add a reference to the stylesheet between the `<head>` tags:

```
<LINK href="/tropicalgreen/Styles/Styles.css" type="text/css"
         rel="stylesheet">
```

5. Between the `<form>` tags, add a `Literal` control to display the page title and an `HtmlPlaceholder` control to show the contents of the `About` placeholder as shown in the code below. Set the `PlaceholderToBind` property of the `HtmlPlaceholderControl1` control to `About`.

```
<form id="GardenPrinterFriendly" method="post" runat="server">
    <h1><asp:Literal id="litDisplayName" runat="server"></asp:Literal></h1>
    <br>
</form>
```

6. Toggle to Design view. Drag an `HtmlPlaceholderControl` from the Toolbox and drop it below `litDisplayName`. Set the `PlaceholderToBind` property of the `HtmlPlaceholderControl1` control to `About`.

7. While in Design view, double-click on the template file. In the code-behind file, import the `Microsoft.ContentManagement.Publishing` namespace.

```
. . . code continues . . .

//The MCMS PAPI
using Microsoft.ContentManagement.Publishing;

namespace TropicalGreen.Templates
{
. . . code continues . . .
}
```

8. In the `Page_Load()` event handler, load the page title into `litDisplayName` literal.

```
private void Page_Load(object sender, System.EventArgs e)
{
    // Put user code to initialize the page here
    litDisplayName.Text = CmsHttpContext.Current.Posting.DisplayName;
}
```

9. Save and build the project.

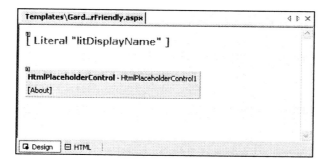

Now that we have created the PrinterFriendly template and template file, we are ready to generate printer-friendly pages. Instead of creating connected postings using the Web Author Console, we are going to generate them on the fly.

Open GardenPublic.aspx in Design view. Drag and drop a HyperLink on to the form. Give the HyperLink the following property values:

Property	Value
ID	btnPrinterFriendly
Text	Printer Friendly Version
Target	_blank

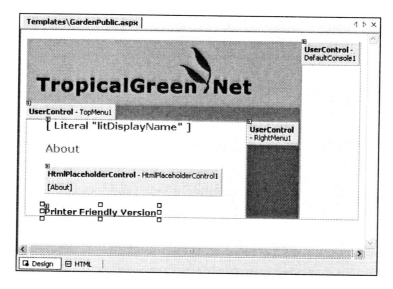

Double-click on GardenPublic.aspx to open its code-behind file. In the Page_Load() event handler, add code that populates the NavigateUrl property of btnPrnterFriendly with that of the current posting and the printer-friendly template.

```
private void Page_Load(object sender, System.EventArgs e)
{
    CmsHttpContext cmsContext = CmsHttpContext.Current;
    Posting currentPosting = cmsContext.Posting;
     string displayName = "";

    if ( currentPosting != null )
    {
        displayName = currentPosting.DisplayName;
        litDisplayName.Text = displayName;

        //1. Get the template that the current posting is using
        Template currentTemplate = currentPosting.Template;
        if(currentTemplate != null)
        {
            //2. See if the user has the rights to see the PrinterFriendly template
            Template printerFriendly =
                    currentTemplate.ConnectedTemplates["PrinterFriendly"];
            if(printerFriendly != null)
            {
                //3. Ensure that the PrinterFriendly template has a SourceFile
                if(printerFriendly.SourceFile != "")
                {
                    //4. Set the NavigateUrl property to the sourcefile of the
                    //PrinterFriendly template append information about
                    //the current posting as querystrings to the
                    //redirected URL
                    btnPrinterFriendly.NavigateUrl = printerFriendly.SourceFile + "?"
                                        + Request.QueryString.ToString();
                }
            }
        }
    }
}
```

The first step gets a reference to the current posting. In this case, that's the public version of the garden page. We also check:

- If the user has the rights to see the PrinterFriendly template
- If the PrinterFriendly template is connected to the currently used template
- If the PrinterFriendly template has its TemplateFile property set (known as SourceFile in the PAPI)

If all three conditions are met, we set the NavigateUrl property of btnPrinterFriendly to a URL composed of the path to the SourceFile of the PrinterFriendly template and the querystring containing information about the current posting. The resulting URL resembles this:

```
http://localhost/TropicalGreen/Templates/GardenPrinterFriendly.aspx?
NRMODE=Published&NRORIGINALURL=%2fTropicalGreen%2fGardens%2fHerbGarden.htm&NRNODEG
UID=%7b2D50F608-8F28-4AB7-B7C4-A62B83FC7628%7d&NRCACHEHINT=NoModifyGuest
```

Based on this information, MCMS is able to put together information from the posting using the template to deliver an alternative view of the posting! If you entered the URL directly into the address bar of the browser, you would see the printer-friendly version of the page too.

Save and build the solution. Navigate to the public The Herb Garden (Public View) page and click on the Printer Friendly Version link button. You will see the page with the same content but without menu bars.

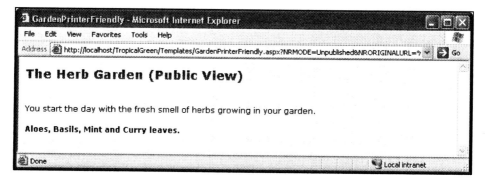

Summary

When used correctly, connected templates and postings are good productivity boosters. You can write content to a single posting and when it is saved, all connected postings are updated at the same time.

In this chapter, we looked at how connected templates and postings are created. We saw how easy it is for authors to administer shared content through connected postings. We also looked at the workflow implications for connected postings when they are stored in channels that have been assigned different rights groups.

Finally, we looked at an alternative to creating connected postings by employing template switching techniques to create a printer-friendly version of a posting.

21
Aggregating Content

We are coming into the final stretch of development for the TropicalGreen site. We have the main sections of the site built, the workflow set up, the Authoring Connector in place, and the login page working. From a high-level perspective, it seems that we are just about done!

But wait! If we go to `http://localhost/tropicalgreen/` what do we see?

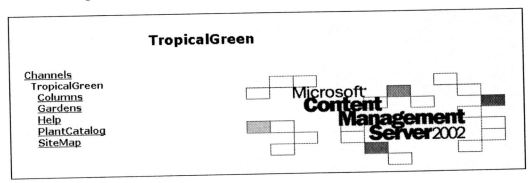

The standard MCMS cover page shows a simple channel listing and the MCMS 2002 logo. We need to replace it with a proper home page for the TropicalGreen website, one that will serve as a starting point to all other areas of the site. While the look of the pages is important, we will not focus on the design. Instead, we will show you how to write code to pull information from different areas of the site for display on a single page. We choose the front page because it is usually the most prominent page where information should be aggregated. Of course, you can apply these techniques to any section within the site.

In this chapter we will build a channel rendering script for the TropicalGreen home page. The home page will include a list of our sections and an area to list recently added content. This will give us a better understanding of how you can use the MCMS Publishing API (PAPI) to access and aggregate content. The completed home page is shown overleaf.

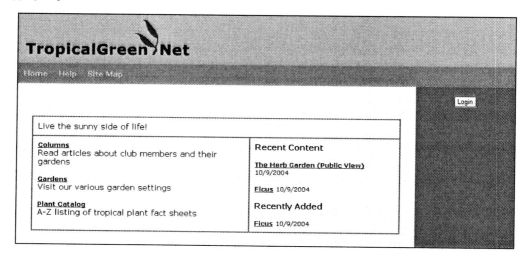

Create the Channel Rendering Script

Before we get started, we need to create the channel rendering script file and assign it to our TropicalGreen channel.

1. Open the TropicalGreen solution in Visual Studio .NET.

2. In the TropicalGreen project, add a new web form file to the `Templates` folder. Call it `HomePage.aspx`.

3. When the template appears in Design view, change the `PageLayout` property to FlowLayout.

4. Switch to HTML view and add the following reference to the TropicalGreen stylesheet between the `<head>` tags:

    ```
    <LINK rel="stylesheet" type="text/css"
        href="/TropicalGreen/Styles/Styles.css">
    ```

5. Inside the `<form>` tags, add the now-familiar TropicalGreen layout table:

```
<table width="100%" border="0" cellspacing="0" cellpadding="0">
    <tr>
        <td width="100%" colspan="2" valign="top" bgcolor="#FFCC00">
            <IMG src="/tropicalgreen/images/Logo.gif">
        </td>
        <td vAlign="top" rowSpan="10">
            (Space for Default Console)
        </td>
    </tr>
    <tr bgColor="#66cc33">
        <td colSpan="2">(Space for Top Menu)</td>
    </tr>
    <tr>
        <td vAlign="top" align="center" style="PADDING:30px">
            <p> </p>
            <table cellspacing="0" cellpadding="10" border="1"
                    bordercolor="#669900">
                <tr vAlign="top">
                    <td colSpan="2">
```

```
                    (Space for Description)
                </td>
            </tr>
            <tr>
                <td vAlign="top">
                    (Space for Summary of Sections)
                </td>
                <td vAlign="top">
                    (Space for Recently Added)
                </td>
            </tr>
        </table>
    </td>
    <td class="RightMenuBar" width="20%" valign="top" height="100%"
        align="center" rowspan="2" bgcolor="#669900">
        (Space for Right Menu)
    </td>
    </tr>
</table>
```

6. Switch back to Design view and drag-and-drop the `TopMenu.ascx`, `RightMenu.ascx`, and `DefaultConsole.ascx` Web User Controls onto the web form in the appropriate locations. Delete the (Space for ...) placeholder text for those three areas.

7. From Solution Explorer, open the `RightMenu.ascx` control and switch to Code view.

8. Inside the `Page_Load()` event handler, add an `if` statement around the `foreach(Channel subChannel in tropicalGreen.Channels)` loop. This will hide the right menu on the home page but allow it to appear on all other pages. We do not want to see the right menu on the home page because it would duplicate the Summary of Sections navigation we are adding to the center of the page.

```
if (cmsContext.Channel != tropicalGreen)
{
    foreach(Channel subChannel in tropicalGreen.Channels)
    {
        . . . code continues . . .
    }
}
```

9. Close `RightMenu.ascx` and its code-behind file.

10. Save and build the solution.

11. Open Site Manager, right-click on the TropicalGreen channel, and select Properties.

12. Go to the Publishing tab and click Select... under the Channel Rendering section.

13. In the Script URL field, type in `/tropicalgreen/templates/HomePage.aspx`. Click OK and close all open dialogs.

14. Go to Internet Explorer and refresh the `http://localhost/tropicalgreen/` page.

The structure for the home page is in place. Now we need to enhance it just a bit.

Adding the Summary of Sections

Since the list of sections is only to appear on the home page, we are going to add the code directly to the HomePage.aspx file instead of creating a separate control. If you need similar logic on multiple templates or channel rendering scripts in your site, you can create a control or even a Web Control Library project for sharable controls.

In our case, we will drop a PlaceHolder ASP.NET server control from the Web Form section of the Toolbox (be sure not to use an MCMS content placeholder) onto our channel rendering script and write some code-behind logic to populate the PlaceHolder with a list of our main content sections, similar to the sections listed in the right-hand menu.

1. Back in Visual Studio .NET, make sure you are in Design view for HomePage.aspx.
2. Drag-and-drop a Label control into the (Space for Description) area. Delete the (Space for ...) text.
3. Set the ID and Text properties of the new Label to lblDescription.
4. Drag-and-drop a PlaceHolder ASP.NET server control from the Web Forms section of the Toolbox onto the template in the (Space for Summary of Sections) area. Delete the (Space for ...) text.
5. With the new PlaceHolder selected, change its ID to phSummaryOfSections.
6. Double-click on the web form to bring up the HomePage.aspx.cs code-behind file.
7. Above the namespace declaration, import the Microsoft.ContentManagement.Publishing namespace:

```
. . . code continues . . .
using Microsoft.ContentManagement.Publishing;

namespace TropicalGreen.Templates
{
    . . . Code continues . . .
}
```

8. In the Page_Load() event handler, add the following code to iterate through the TropicalGreen channels and display links and descriptions to just the main channels that are shown in the right menu with the MenuLocation custom property set to right (remember that we created this custom property in Chapter 13 to decide whether to

display the channel in the top or right menus). It will also populate the Description label.

```
private void Page_Load(object sender, System.EventArgs e)
{
    //Put user code to initialize the page here
    CmsHttpContext cmsContext = CmsHttpContext.Current;

    //Since we are in the TropicalGreen root,
    //we can use the current context to create the list of sections.
    Channel tropicalGreen;
    tropicalGreen = cmsContext.Channel as Channel;

    //Show the description of the TropicalGreen channel.
    lblDescription.Text = tropicalGreen.Description;

    //Display a title, link, and description of the main channels
    foreach(Channel subChannel in tropicalGreen.Channels)
    {
        CustomProperty menuLocation =
            subChannel.CustomProperties["MenuLocation"];

        if(menuLocation != null)
        {
            if(menuLocation.Value.ToLower() == "right")
            {
                HtmlGenericControl section = new HtmlGenericControl("p");
                HtmlAnchor sectionLink = new HtmlAnchor();
                HtmlGenericControl sectionTitle =
                    new HtmlGenericControl("b");
                HtmlGenericControl sectionDescription =
                    new HtmlGenericControl("span");

                sectionLink.InnerHtml = subChannel.DisplayName;
                sectionLink.HRef = subChannel.Url;
                sectionTitle.Controls.Add(sectionLink);
                sectionDescription.InnerHtml = "<br>" +
                    subChannel.Description;

                section.Controls.Add(sectionTitle);
                section.Controls.Add(sectionDescription);
                phSummaryOfSections.Controls.Add(section);
            }
        }
    }
}
```

9. Save and build the solution.

If you do not have descriptions for the three main channels, go to Site Manager and edit the Description property to match the following table:

Channel	Description
Columns	Read articles about club members and their gardens
Gardens	Visit our various garden settings
Plant Catalog	A-Z listing of tropical plant fact sheets

> Alternatively, you could navigate to each channel in your browser and use the Web Author Console to modify the Description property for each channel. Make sure you log in with a template designer, channel manager, or administrator account, though. Only those users can edit the Description property of a channel.

Go back to Internet Explorer and refresh the `http://localhost/tropicalgreen/` page. We are about halfway there!

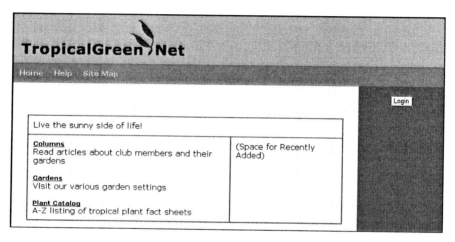

Recent Content

Now that we have a nice listing of the main sections of the TropicalGreen site, we want to add a listing of the most recent content. For that we will use the `Searches.NewPostings()` method from the MCMS PAPI. This method gets a collection of postings that have their ChangeDate property within a specified number of days.

1. Back in Visual Studio .NET, make sure you are in Design view.

2. Drag-and-drop a PlaceHolder ASP.NET server control from the Web Forms section of the Toolbox onto the template in the (Space for Recently Added) area. Delete the (Space for ...) text.

3. With the new PlaceHolder selected, change its ID to `phRecentContent`.

4. Double-click on the web form to open up the `HomePage.aspx.cs` code-behind file.

5. Below any existing code in the `Page_Load()` event handler, add the following code that gets the postings that have changed in the last five days as a `PostingCollection`, and writes a listing of links to the new `phRecentContent` `PlaceHolder`.

```
private void Page_Load(object sender, System.EventArgs e)
{
        . . . code continues . . .

    //Show the Recent Content postings and sort them
    //by descending change date
```

```
//Get last five days worth
PostingCollection recentPostings = cmsContext.Searches.NewPostings(5);
recentPostings.SortByChangeDate(false);

HtmlGenericControl recentIntro = new HtmlGenericControl("p");
recentIntro.InnerHtml = "<b>Recent Content</b>";
phRecentContent.Controls.Add(recentIntro);

foreach(Posting posting in recentPostings)
{
    HtmlGenericControl recentPosting = new HtmlGenericControl("p");
    HtmlAnchor recentLink = new HtmlAnchor();
    HtmlGenericControl recentTitle = new HtmlGenericControl("b");
    HtmlGenericControl recentDate = new HtmlGenericControl("small");

    recentLink.InnerHtml = posting.DisplayName;
    recentLink.HRef = posting.Url;
    recentTitle.Controls.Add(recentLink);
    recentPosting.Controls.Add(recentTitle);
    recentDate.InnerHtml = " " +
        posting.ChangeDate.ToShortDateString();
    recentPosting.Controls.Add(recentDate);
    phRecentContent.Controls.Add(recentPosting);
}
}
```

6. Save and build the solution.

Now when you navigate to http://localhost/TropicalGreen/ you will probably not see anything listed under the Recent Content area (unless you have edited a posting within the last five days).

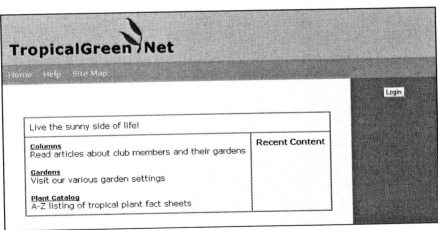

If you do see some items listed, that means you have created or modified the specified postings within the last five days. It might also mean that you have changed the StartDate of the parent channel of the postings.

In order to see some recent content, do the following:

1. Log in to the TropicalGreen site as the administrator.

2. Go to the Plant Catalog channel and create and approve a new posting called Ficus using the Plant template.

3. Go to the Gardens channel and edit The Herb Garden (Public View) posting and approve it.

Stay logged in and navigate back to the TropicalGreen home page. You should see three items under the Recent Content.

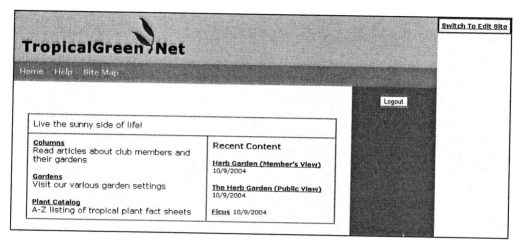

So, what happened here? We just added one new posting and modified one other posting, yet we have three postings listed. Well, since The Herb Garden is a pair of connected postings with a public posting and a member's posting, the process of editing the public version of the page also changed the member's version.

Click Logout and you should now only see two items under Recent Content, as the TropicalGreen guest subscriber does not have rights to the /Gardens/Members channel.

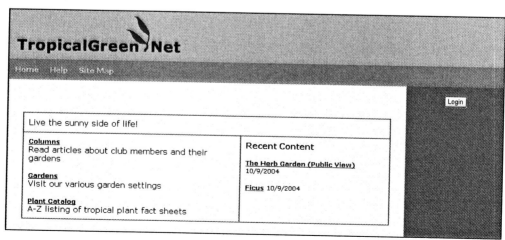

Well, we got all of the areas of the home page working. The only thing left to do is to get the Recent Content area to work the way we want it to. We want it to display a list of postings that have been added to the site in the past five days. The Searches.NewPostings() method is a misnomer. According to the MCMS documentation, "This search returns Posting objects for which the property ChangeDate is within the last [n] days." This means anything that has *changed* is included in the collection, not just *new* postings with recent start dates.

The ChangeDate of a posting is decided based on one of the following properties:

1. LastModifiedDate
2. StartDate and ExpiryDate (if they are less than the current date)
3. StartDate and ExpiryDate of the parent channel (if they are less than the current date)

The property with the most recent date determines the ChangeDate. So, for example, if today is July 15, 2004 and your posting was last modified on July 1, 2004 (LastModifiedDate), but the StartDate of the posting or the channel was set to July 15, 2004, then the ChangeDate would be July 15, 2004, not July 1, 2004.

So let's try another method.

How to Get a List of Recently Added Postings

There are a few ways to get what we want. One way is to use the Union() method, another way is to continue using the NewPostings() method and add logic to filter out the unwanted postings.

> The ChannelCollection.Union() and PostingCollection.Union() methods from the PAPI are used to combine ChannelCollection or PostingCollection members together. So, for example, you could use the Union() method to combine the postings of two or more channels together in one collection.

We will use the PostingCollection.Union() method to combine channel collections and get a list of the three most recent postings by StartDate instead of ChangeDate.

1. Back in Visual Studio .NET, make sure you are in Design view.
2. Drag-and-drop a PlaceHolder ASP.NET server control from the Web forms section of the Toolbar onto the template below the phRecentContent PlaceHolder.
3. With the new PlaceHolder selected, change its ID to phRecentlyAddedContent.
4. Double-click on the web form to bring up the HomePage.aspx.cs code-behind file.
5. In the HomePage class below the Page_Load() event handler, add the following iterative method that will combine postings from all channels together using the Union() method.

```
//CombineAllPostings creates a PostingCollection of all postings
//in the baseChannel and below
private PostingCollection CombineAllPostings(Channel baseChannel)
{
    PostingCollection basePostingCollection;
    basePostingCollection = baseChannel.Postings;
```

```
        //Interatively call CombineAllPostings for each sub-channel
        foreach(Channel channel in baseChannel.Channels)
        {
            basePostingCollection =
                basePostingCollection.Union(CombineAllPostings(channel))
                as PostingCollection;
        }

        return basePostingCollection;
    }
```

6. In the Page_Load() event handler, add the following code below the existing code. This will iterate through all TropicalGreen postings and only list those with a start date between today and five days ago.

```
private void Page_Load(object sender, System.EventArgs e)
{
    . . . code continues . . .
    //Show the Recently Added postings and sort them
    //by descending change date
    //Get last five days worth
    //Get the PostingCollection of everything below TropicalGreen
    PostingCollection tropicalGreenPostings =
        CombineAllPostings(tropicalGreen);
    tropicalGreenPostings.SortByStartDate(false);

    HtmlGenericControl recentlyAddedIntro =
        new HtmlGenericControl("p");
    recentlyAddedIntro.InnerHtml = "<b>Recently Added</b>";
    phRecentlyAddedContent.Controls.Add(recentlyAddedIntro);

    TimeSpan subtractDays = new TimeSpan(5,0,0,0);
    foreach(Posting posting in tropicalGreenPostings)
    {
        //List posting only if its StartDate is between today
        //and five days ago
        //Otherwise, break the loop
        if(posting.StartDate >= DateTime.Now.Subtract(subtractDays))
        {
            HtmlGenericControl recentlyAddedPosting =
                new HtmlGenericControl("p");
            HtmlAnchor recentlyAddedLink = new HtmlAnchor();
            HtmlGenericControl recentlyAddedTitle =
                new HtmlGenericControl("b");
            HtmlGenericControl recentlyAddedDate =
                new HtmlGenericControl("small");

            recentlyAddedLink.InnerHtml = posting.DisplayName;
            recentlyAddedLink.HRef = posting.Url;
            recentlyAddedTitle.Controls.Add(recentlyAddedLink);
            recentlyAddedPosting.Controls.Add(recentlyAddedTitle);

            //Use the StartDate instead of the ChangeDate
            recentlyAddedDate.InnerHtml =
                " " + posting.StartDate.ToShortDateString();
            recentlyAddedPosting.Controls.Add(recentlyAddedDate);

            phRecentlyAddedContent.Controls.Add(recentlyAddedPosting);
        }
        else
        {
            break;
        }
    }
}
```

7. Save and build the solution.

Now go back to your browser and reload the TropicalGreen home page. You should see only the Ficus posting listed under Recently Added, and two postings listed under the Recent Content area.

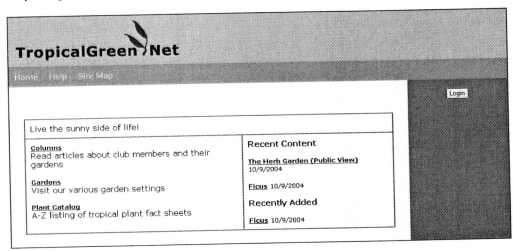

We should mention here that `Union()` is a powerful yet dangerous method. If your site grows to hundreds or thousands of channels and postings, this method could get very expensive to operate, which would be especially noticeable if used on the home page in this manner.

In cases where your site contains more than a few dozen channels, it is a good idea to break out calls to the `Union()` method into smaller chunks, or use the `Searches.NewPostings()` method, custom properties, or another method for achieving the same functionality. For example, in the Recently Added scenario above, we can actually achieve the functionality we want and reduce the processing overhead of the page by changing one line of code and removing the `combineAllPostings()` method from the code-behind file.

Replace this line:

```
PostingCollection tropicalGreenPostings = combineAllPostings(tropicalGreen);
```

with:

```
PostingCollection tropicalGreenPostings = cmsContext.Searches.NewPostings(5);
```

Since our code checks the `startDate` of each posting as it writes out the content to the RecentlyAddedContent `PlaceHolder`, we would only see a list of postings with start dates equal to or less than five days ago. This would reduce the processing load on our site, as the `Union()` method would no longer be necessary. This change to the code would work for our particular scenario, but sometimes you may need to use the `Union()` method to create a more fine-grained aggregate of content on your site, for instance to summarize a particular channel and its sub-channels. For other options, see the *Alternative Functionality* section below.

> On a related note, the home page is a strong candidate for the use of output caching, which we will discuss in Chapter 22.

From this point you can decide whether you want to use the `Searches.NewPostings()` method, the `PostingCollection.Union()` method, or another method to create your aggregated content listing. Each method does its job well, but a given website's requirements will dictate which method works best. For the TropicalGreen site, we will leave both in place.

Alternative Functionality

Other options for achieving aggregate content listings on an MCMS website include:

- Using a database to index postings and their metadata. You can implement some form of indexing that provides a quick lookup mechanism, and some search engines can do this as well.

- Create a static snapshot of the home page on a regular basis, say at the start of each day. The static page is then used for that day rather than re-generating it each time a user requests it.

- Pulling and pushing content from MCMS to non-MCMS sources using Web Services. See *Using Microsoft Content Management Server 2002 and Web Services* on MSDN (found at `http://msdn.microsoft.com/library/en-us/dnmscms02/html/cms_2002webservices.asp`).

Examples of these methods and others can be found by searching the resources listed in Appendix B.

Summary

In this chapter, we demonstrated some of the ways that you can aggregate content from MCMS as we built up the TropicalGreen home page from scratch. We learned how to create a list of sections and lists of recently changed and recently added content. We started by working with a collection of channels, listing channels and their descriptions in the Summary of Sections area of the home page.

Next, we used the `Searches.NewPostings()` method to get a list of postings that have been modified in the last five days and listed them in the Recent Content section. We went on to show an alternative method of retrieving a collection of postings that were added in the last five days by combining a list of all postings under the TropicalGreen channel and sorting them by their start dates. We checked their start dates to see which postings were added within the last five days and added them to the Recently Added section of the home page.

Finally, we suggested alternative ways to aggregate content for a home page, including creating a separate database index, use of static pages, and pulling content from other sources.

22

Enhancing Performance with Caching

Caching is a general term that describes the technique of keeping data that is likely to be needed in a format or location that speeds up access to that data. For example, your PC stores information about running programs in the semiconductor devices known as Random Access Memory (RAM) chips, and computers today can have many hundreds of megabytes of this memory. RAM chips are fast, but modern motherboards invariably come fitted with a smaller amount of even faster memory chips, called the RAM cache.

When a running program is working with an item held in RAM, the whole block of memory around that item is transferred to the RAM cache, vastly speeding up subsequent accesses to that same data item or its neighbors. It works because programs often access items that are near to each other in RAM. Items in a collection, for instance, are usually all held in the same area of RAM, so you can imagine the speed benefits that caching brings when iterating through a collection.

So that's the principle of caching: store items that are likely to be used in the near future somewhere quick and easy to get to. MCMS uses both RAM and hard drive space to cache content from the MCMS-managed database. Microsoft recommends at least one gigabyte of RAM for a production MCMS server. For sites with tens of thousands of postings, much more than one gigabyte of RAM will be necessary to keep the site from slowing down significantly.

The processor and database are still very important components in MCMS, and you should not neglect the recommended minimums there. But the caching components—mainly RAM—are some of the most important parts of the MCMS system.

How MCMS Works with Caching

Back in Chapter 1, we saw how MCMS renders content. MCMS does not produce static HTML pages anywhere on the server's hard disk, even though when you view the source of an MCMS posting in your browser you will see plain HTML. MCMS assembles this HTML for postings on the fly from template files and content in embedded MCMS placeholders. While dynamically generating pages ensures flexibility in the design of the application, it incurs processing overheads. More time is taken to generate and deliver dynamic pages as compared with static pages, which are delivered without any processing by the server.

MCMS optimizes site performance with four caching mechanisms:

- **Disk cache.** When accessed for the first time, MCMS resource gallery items and local attachments are pulled from the database and stored on disk in the MCMS disk cache. Subsequent requests for cached resources can then be pulled from the disk cache instead of rebuilding them from the database.

- **Node cache.** When accessed for the first time, properties and placeholder content are pulled from the MCMS database and stored in the memory as node memory cache; subsequent requests for cached content are pulled from RAM instead of the database.

- **ASP.NET output cache.** The ASP.NET Output Cache engine is used to cache entire or sections of a page.

- **SQL Server cache.** As SQL Server is used as the back-end content repository, its built-in caching mechanisms will also be used.

When a posting is requested by a user's browser, the HTML that MCMS builds for that posting, based on the content in the database, is actually held in RAM, not on the hard disk, before being output to the end user. When the HTML is sent to the user's web browser by IIS (the Windows web server), the page consists of nothing more than standard HTML, links, and images, with a little JavaScript perhaps.

While the URL of a posting on an MCMS site looks like a URL for any regular static web page, in reality the "page" does not exist anywhere as a complete object with the name given in the URL, except perhaps in the web browser cache on the visitor's computer (and possibly proxy server caches along the way). Don't bother looking for pages with the names of postings under the IIS wwwroot folder on your MCMS server.

> The database is not involved in processing requests for content that has been cached either in RAM or the file system, until the content is invalidated, the cache is full, or the server is restarted.

What MCMS Caches by Default

Without any effort on your part, MCMS already caches a whole bunch of stuff. This caching is probably enough for most websites. We'll go over the default caching features, and in the next section we'll see what you can do to enhance your website with custom ASP.NET output caching.

The Disk Cache

When a visitor to your MCMS website accesses a page, ASP.NET receives the request (or ASP if you are working with legacy templates), accesses the content, and compiles it in RAM, combining it with your template code (from the file-system) and any posting-specific MCMS content (such as placeholder content). Local attachments and resource gallery items used within postings are not saved in RAM but instead saved in the MCMS disk cache.

The disk cache for MCMS is contained in the /NR/rdonlyres/ virtual directory. Embedded resource gallery items and local attachments (JPGs, GIFs, DOCs, PDFs, etc.) are copied here from the database the first time they are accessed, and if the items are updated and re-requested. This speeds up access to the resources but also keeps them under the control of MCMS.

The size (in megabytes) and location of the disk cache are configurable using the Server Configuration Application (SCA). It must be at least 50 MB in size.

See Chapter 4 for instructions on how to empty the disk cache.

The Node Cache and High-Level Caches

MCMS caches node objects in RAM by default, to lighten the load on the database and greatly speed up access to content (as RAM is so much quicker than the disk). Accessing content in RAM is much faster than accessing it from the disk, and way quicker than regenerating each posting from the database for every request.

There are multiple memory caches in MCMS. The most important is the Node Cache. It prevents the database from being accessed over and over for the same content. A single node is one object in the MCMS system, like a posting, channel, or template item. While there is no way to determine the actual contents of the Node Cache (you can't see what has been cached and what hasn't, either programmatically or otherwise), you do need to understand that it is very important in the smooth functioning of MCMS.

Besides the Node Cache, there are other caches often referred to as high-level caches. For example, placeholders can hold MCMS-managed links that need to be changed during run time with the current URL. One of the other high-level caches stores this information to avoid the need to needlessly repeat processing and database access every time the placeholder is accessed. Another high-level cache stores the group membership information for MCMS users. So if the same user accesses the site more than once, the user's rights do not need to be looked up more than once. Probably the most important high-level cache is the friendly URL to internal URL cache, which translates the human-readable URLs to the ugly-looking Unique ID based URLs that MCMS needs.

All high-level caches are automatically flushed when anything changes in the MCMS database, for example, when a new posting is created or content in a posting is changed and saved. They are flushed because it would be too complicated to track exactly which information was used to build the content in the high-level caches. This does not affect site performance very much because the high-level caches can be rebuilt using the Node Cache without accessing the database. Unlike the high-level caches, the Node Cache is not automatically flushed when the database is changed.

So once an object is in the Node Cache, it stays there until one of the following happens:

- The cache is cleared manually using the SCA.
- The process that holds the cache is restarted (INETINFO.EXE, ASPNET_WP.EXE or W3WP.EXE, and DLLHOST.EXE).
- The object is updated.
- An additional item is requested that needs to be added to the cache but no free cache space is available. In this case, random objects would be released from the cache to

make way for newly requested objects. The Node Cache is optimized to work in scenarios where no items need to be kicked out, so it does not track ages of objects.

Clearing the memory cache can be automated by running a script that loads and closes this page on the server:

`http://localhost:<SCA_port>/NRConfig/MemoryFlush.asp?ResServerIndex=0`

This script can only run locally on the server so your website visitors cannot access it to clear your cache. Because the page is protected by IIS and the file system to allow only local administrators, the script must be run in the context of an administrator.

This is the same script that is run when clicking on the Clear Memory Cache button on the Cache tab in the SCA.

Tuning the Node Cache

The size of the Node Cache is configurable using the SCA. Typically, the Maximum Nodes in Memory Cache setting in the SCA should be set to more than the total number of active nodes in the system. This can be checked by using a SQL script.

For read-only sites, the following SQL query statement calculates the number of items to set as the maximum for the node cache. It already contains a 30% allowance for new items to be added in the future.

```
SELECT ceiling(count(*) * 1.3) FROM node
WHERE (archivedwhen IS null)
AND (deletedwhen IS null)
AND datediff(hour, expirydate,    getdate())  < 1
AND (datediff(hour, effectivedate, getdate()) > 1
    OR effectivedate IS null)
AND (datediff(hour, approvedwhen,  getdate())  > 1
    OR (type >= 65535 AND approvedwhen IS null))
```

Estimating the number of nodes required for read-write sites is trickier as all possible nodes could be used as part of the authoring process. However, unless you have very active authors working on the server, items will be read more often than they get updated. You can use the same formula as for the read-only site. The additional 30% allowance would also cater for additional nodes that may be used by authors.

Depending on how much RAM is available on the server, the Node Cache setting may need to be lower than the total number of active nodes. Generally, a node cache that stores more than 35,000 nodes should be stress-tested before being implemented on a production server. This is because massive paging with virtual memory may occur, which likely will result in even lower performance. Also, the more memory used up by the Node Cache, the less there is available for ASP.NET output caching, so a balance must be attained.

In addition, a node does not have a fixed size in bytes. Placeholder content, if retrieved, is added to a posting node in the cache and will increase the size of a node. So if placeholders contain a lot of content, fewer nodes can be stored in the same amount of RAM than if the placeholders contain less content.

Unfortunately there is no common agreement on how to set the node option in the SCA in a situation where more nodes exist in the database than can be stored in memory. It often requires trial-and-error and load testing to fine tune.

Improving Performance with ASP.NET Output Caching

Accessing many objects at once can be a high-processing task, so some sort of programmatic caching is recommended in addition to the internal caching mechanisms discussed above for templates that access many objects via the Publishing API. The preferred method of caching for MCMS is ASP.NET output caching. This will reduce the number of objects that MCMS must compile when a page is requested, therefore reducing the amount of processing required.

ASP.NET output caching is used to store content created by dynamic pages. Instead of assembling the page over and over again, the content is retrieved from the cache. There are two types of ASP.NET output caching:

- Page caching
- User control caching (also called ASP.NET fragment caching)

If you are using legacy ASP-based templates from MCMS 2001, you cannot utilize ASP.NET output caching. However, MCMS 2001 includes its own fragment caching feature for ASP-based templates. We will not cover this caching mechanism here, but you can find more information at http://msdn.microsoft.com/library/en-us/dnmscms01/html/cmsperfoc.asp. A downside to ASP-based fragment caching is that it is nearly impossible to customize different "views" of the cache for different users, for example if personalization is used on the site. The fragment cache is created the first time a user hits a particular page that includes the caching. The subsequent users will see the same content, even if they do not have rights to that content. In this case, either no caching should be used or you should move to ASP.NET output caching for greater control.

Output caching is useful in many situations, as it is very useful whenever the cost of rendering the page is high and the page is hit frequently. It is especially useful when your pages or user controls use the MCMS searches methods to retrieve content, as our navigation controls did in Chapter 13, especially custom property searches. The Searches methods are very expensive for the system to process. Navigation is another place where output caching can come in handy. The execution of navigation code can instantiate many objects, yet navigation does not change often so it's a ripe candidate for caching.

You can learn more about ASP.NET output caching on MSDN or in any of the many books on ASP.NET. In this chapter we'll be trying out some of the features that MCMS adds to the basic ASP.NET output cache functionality.

MCMS adds the following VaryByCustom options to output caching:

- CMSPosting caches each posting separately.
- CMSControl caches each control independent of the current posting.
- CMSRole caches different versions of the posting or control for each user role.

- CMSUser caches different versions of the posting or control for each user.

You can use combinations of CMSPosting or CMSControl along with CMSRole or CMSUser, for example CMSPosting;CMSUser or CMSControl;CMSRole.

Enabling ASP.NET Output Caching

Before we begin, we need to tell our project that we are inheriting from CmsHttpApplication so that the MCMS extensions to the output caching work properly. Do the following:

1. Open the TropicalGreen project in Visual Studio .NET, and open the Global.asax file. Double-click on the web form to open the code-behind file.

2. Change the public class Global to inherit from the CmsHttpApplication:

```
public class Global : Microsoft.ContentManagement.Web.CmsHttpApplication
{
    . . . code continues . . .
}
```

Now we are ready to add some output caching!

Caching the Plant Fact Sheet

In the Plant Catalog channel, we have created several plant fact sheets. For as long as the content of each fact sheet does not change, we can take advantage of ASP.NET output caching to serve the same version of each page without re-generating them whenever they are requested. This makes the plant fact sheets good candidates for caching at the page level.

Caching at the Page Level

Let's add page-level output caching with personalization to our Plant template.

1. Open the /Templates/Plant.aspx template file in Visual Studio .NET.

2. Switch to HTML view.

3. At the top of the page, add the following directive:

```
<%@ OutputCache Duration="30" Location="Server" VaryByParam="None"
VaryByCustom="CMSPosting" %>
```

4. Switch back to Design view.

5. Drag and drop a Label control onto the form and place it under the RightMenu.ascx User Control. Change the Label's Text property to Last Updated and change the ID property to lblLastUpdated.

6. Double-click the new Label. This will bring you to the code-behind page. In the Page_Load() event handler add the following code:

```
private void Page_Load(object sender, System.EventArgs e)
{
    . . . code continues . . .
    lblLastUpdated.Text = "Last Updated: " + DateTime.Now.ToString();
}
```

7. Save and build the solution.

Setting the `varyByCustom` attribute to `CmsPosting` ensures that each posting that is based on the same template file is cached separately. In this case, we have set the page to remain in the cache for 30 seconds.

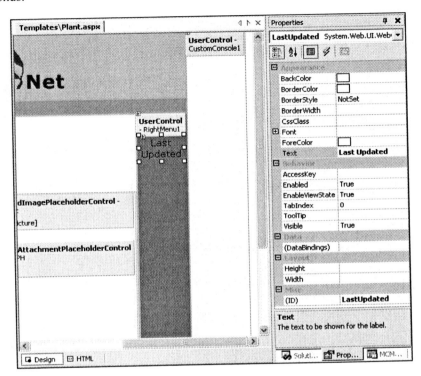

Navigate to `http://localhost/tropicalgreen/plantcatalog/`. Click on any of the plant fact sheets. Note the time displayed on the Last Updated label.

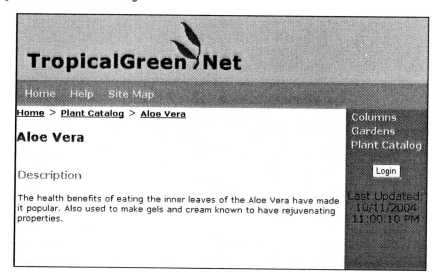

Now hit the Refresh button in your browser. Notice that the time does not increment. You can keep hitting refresh for thirty seconds before the time will change, as your page is now saved in the output cache for 30 seconds! Once 30 seconds is up, the object will be released and a new version of the page will be saved to the cache the next time the page is accessed.

Log in as an administrator and click Switch To Edit Site. Notice that the Last Updated time for the page in edit site view is different from the Last Updated time for the page in live site view. Switch back to live site view and then quickly switch back to edit site view, refreshing each time. You should see yet a different time in edit site view. This is because by default, MCMS automatically disables output caching when you are in unpublished (edit) or authoring mode.

Any time the user switches to edit site view the output cache is not used for the page or any of its controls. This is necessary to ensure that the latest content is always displayed to authors rather than a possibly out-of-date cached version.

> In fact, all of the pages based on a particular template share the same URL (for example, behind the scenes all Plant fact sheets really have a URL of `/tropicalgreen/templates/Plant.aspx`). However, MCMS appends a querystring with the parameter `NRNODEGUID=XXXX` to the path to differentiate one page from another.
>
> For example, if you take your browser and have a look at the HTML source for one of the plant pages in live site mode, you will see a `<base>` tag similar to this:
>
> ```
> <base
> href="http://localhost/TropicalGreen/Templates/Plant.aspx?NRMODE=Published
> &NRORIGINALURL=%2fTropicalGreen%2fPlantCatalog%2fBananaTree%2ehtm&NRNODEGU
> ID=%7b3413AEF2-4BBC-48A8-9C1E-BBFCB739F685%7d&NRCACHEHINT=ModifyLoggedIn">
> ```

This is the "true" URL of the page—the one that contains instructions to fill a particular template file with placeholder content from the repository. Notice that the querystring behind each URL is different.

If you do not choose a VaryByCustom value (or VaryByParam value if you want to), the unique querystrings will not be taken into account when a page is cached. So, all pages based on a particular template will share one output cache entry in live site mode.

•

Although query strings are an essential part of the URLs in edit site mode as the following example shows, MCMS is smart enough to know not to use output caching in edit site mode.

```
<base
href="http://localhost/TropicalGreen/Templates/Plant.aspx?NRMODE=Unpublish
ed&NRORIGINALURL=%2fNR%2fexeres%2f3413AEF2-4BBC-48A8-9C1E-BBFCB739F685%2cf
rameless%2ehtm%3fNRMODE%3dUnpublished%26WBCMODE%3dPresentationUnpublished%
26wbc_purpose%3dBasic&FRAMELESS=true&NRNODEGUID=%7b3413AEF2-4BBC-48A8-9C1E
-BBFCB739F685%7d&NRCACHEHINT=ModifyLoggedIn&wbc_purpose=Basic&WBCMODE=Pres
entationUnpublished">
```

MCMS is smart enough to know not to use the output caching in edit site mode.

If you use more than one URL to access your site, you may run into trouble with output caching. For example, as a developer you can access the TropicalGreen site via http://localhost/ or http://computername/ (e.g. http://mcmsbook/). The <base> tag is rendered with the full path, so this can cause a problem for users who cannot, say, use localhost as the URL.

In that case, the VaryByHeader="Host" attribute in the OutputCache directive will solve this problem by keeping separate versions of the page for each URL. For example:

```
<%@ OutputCache Duration="30" Location="Server" VaryByHeader="Host"
VaryByParam="None" VaryByCustom="CMSPosting" %>
```

Caching the Site Map

Earlier in the book, we created the site map as a channel rendering script. Open your browser and access the current site map at http://localhost/tropicalgreeb/sitemap/.

The site map is a perfect candidate for caching because it contains a navigation user control that could become quite a cumbersome processing task as the site grows larger and larger and contains more channels and postings.

With the site map tree expanded, the page should look something like this:

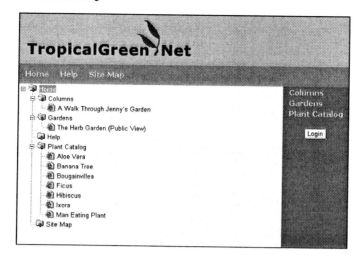

Caching at the Channel Level

We have now seen caching on the page level and we know that MCMS also supports caching at the control, user, and role levels. If you consider the various combinations of caching, something seems to be missing. What if you had a navigation control, say a breadcrumb trail that displays the same set of links for each posting within the same channel, but shows a different set of links for postings in another channel? We could get around this by setting the varyByCustom property to CMSPosting;CMSControl. However, that would mean storing cached versions of the same control for each posting. It would be more efficient to store only one instance of the control for each channel instead.

As MCMS does not support caching at the channel level by default, we are going to demonstrate how MCMS allows us to extend the default set of caching options with our own rule. We will add a new caching option, CMSChannel, to our project so that we can also assign output caching at the channel level.

1. You should still have the Global.asax code-behind file, Global.asax.cs, open. If not, open it again.

2. Check that the following namespace has been added to the top of the page:
   ```
   using Microsoft.ContentManagement.Publishing;
   ```

3. Inside the Global class, add the following code below the public Global() method:
   ```
   protected override string GetVaryByCustomStringToken(HttpContext context,
                                                         string token)
   {
       if (token.ToLower() == "cmschannel")
           return CmsHttpContext.Current.Channel.Guid;
       else
           return base.GetVaryByCustomStringToken(context,token);
   }
   ```

   This code will enable our new CMSChannel VaryByCustom caching option.

4. Save and close the Global.asax and Global.asax.cs files.

We are going to try channel-level caching on the site map (a channel rendering script) by setting VaryByCustom to our new parameter, CMSChannel. Let's get started!

1. Open the /Templates/SiteMap.aspx file in Visual Studio.

2. Switch to HTML view.

3. At the top of the page, add the following directive:

```
<%@ OutputCache Duration="30" Location="Server" VaryByParam="None"
    VaryByCustom="CMSChannel" %>
```

4. Switch back to Design view.

5. Drag and drop a Label control from the Web Form section of the Toolbox onto the form and place it under the RightMenu User Control. Change the Label's Text property to Last Updated and change the ID property to lblLastUpdated.

6. Double-click the new Label. This will bring you to the code-behind page. In the Page_Load() event handler add the following code:

```
private void Page_Load(object sender, System.EventArgs e)
{
    // Put user code to initialize the page here
    lblLastUpdated.Text = "Last Updated: " + DateTime.Now.ToString();
}
```

7. Save and build the solution.

Open your browser and navigate to http://localhost/tropicalgreen/sitemap/. You should see something like this:

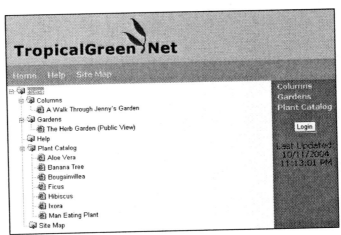

For the next 30 seconds, hitting the Refresh button in your browser won't increment the timer as we have set the page to be cached for 30 seconds. On the 31st second, the timer gets updated once again as the cache period expires.

Caching at the Control Level

Let's proceed to add output caching to the `SiteMapTree.ascx` control. We are going to show how the page and control can have different levels of caching.

1. First, open the `/UserControls/SiteMapTree.ascx` file (not the `/Templates/Sitemap.aspx` file!) in Visual Studio.

2. Switch to HTML view.

3. At the top of the page, add the following directive:

```
<%@ OutputCache Duration="60" VaryByParam="None"
VaryByCustom="CMSChannel;CMSControl" %>
```

4. Switch back to Design view.

5. Drag and drop a Label control onto the form and place it under the TreeView control. You may need to hit *Enter* to add a carriage return. Change the Label's Text property to Last Updated and change the ID property to `lblLastUpdated`.

6. Double-click the new Label. This will bring you to the code-behind page. In the `Page_Load()` event handler add the following code below the `CreateTree()` method call:

```
private void Page_Load(object sender, System.EventArgs e)
{
    . . . code continues . . .
    CreateTree(tropicalGreen,node);

    lblLastUpdated.Text = "Last Updated: " + DateTime.Now.ToString();
}
```

7. Save and build the solution.

Go back to your browser and navigate to `http://localhost/tropicalgreen/sitemap/`. With the tree collapsed, you should see something like this:

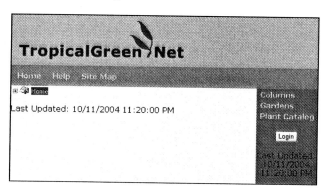

Notice that both Last Updated times are the same. Keep hitting the Refresh button in your browser for about thirty seconds. At that point you should notice that the page level instance of the Last Updated time changes but the Last Updated time for the `SiteMapTree` control does not. Since the `SiteMapTree` cache duration was set to sixty seconds, this control will continue to be cached for twice the length of time as the parent channel rendering script.

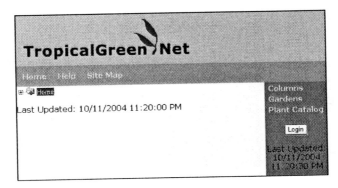

Now that we've learned the basics of output caching in MCMS, let's try some more advanced caching features—personalization and invalidation.

Personalization and Invalidation

Two things that MCMS brings to the caching table are personalization and invalidation.

- **Personalization** enables different versions of pages to be cached for each user or role group. If you didn't use personalization, every user might see the same version of a page. This could be a problem if an editor is the first one to access a page and fill the output cache. If a subscriber comes along and accesses the same page they may see content that was not meant for public consumption! In fact, this will happen with the caching we added for the site map above! You might also have problems with caching when pages contain content specific to a particular user, like something as simple as showing the user's name on the page.

- **Invalidation** is a simple concept—each time an object is added or changed in the MCMS content repository, the output cache is flushed. It is a simple concept yet it has great consequences. On one hand, your site would never have outdated content on it. On the other hand, if your site is updated often then the output cache may be constantly flushed and recreated. Depending on the type of site you have, this may or may not be a good idea. Alternatively, setting an output cache duration of only a few minutes could achieve similar functionality without necessitating clearing the output cache completely.

ASP.NET 1.0 and 1.1 do not have automatic invalidation for user web controls or server controls, only for complete web forms. For this reason invalidation will only invalidate channel rendering script and posting content but not user controls or server controls. This can have a significant impact on your site, since cached navigation controls cannot be automatically invalidated.

Personalization

First, let's add output caching with personalization to our Plant template.

1. Open the /Templates/Plant.aspx template file in Visual Studio .NET.

2. Switch to HTML view.

3. At the top of the page, add `CMSRole` to the `varyByCustom` attribute:

```
<%@ OutputCache Duration="30" Location="Server" VaryByHeader="Host"
    VaryByParam="None" VaryByCustom="CMSPosting;CMSRole"%>
```

4. Save the template.

Go back to your browser. You should still be on the site map. Expand the Tropical Green and the Plant Catalog channels and choose the Hibiscus posting. You should see the Last Updated date and time appear in the right-hand navigation column.

Now we want to see if another user sees the same output cache. In a new instance of Internet Explorer, navigate to `http://localhost/tropicalgreeb/plantcatalog/hibiscus.htm`. Log in using the Author1 account we set up in Chapter 10. Note the Last Updated time. Now click the Logout button.

Click Login again. This time, log in using your administrator account. You should see a different Last Updated time! The posting is cached differently for the author and administrator role groups. In addition, the cache for the posting will remain valid for 30 seconds for each role group.

> Be aware that *all* role memberships are taken into account when using `CMSRole`. This means if a user is member of a specific author group and a subscriber group while another user is only a member of the author group each will receive different cached instances of the page. Two users will only see the same cached instance if they belong to exactly the same MCMS user groups.

It would be a good idea at this point to go back to your `sitemap.aspx` page and add the `CMSRole` option to the output cache directive of both the ASPX page and the ASCX control.

Invalidation

First, let's change the Plant template to cache content for ten minutes instead of 30 seconds.

1. Go back to `Plant.aspx` in Visual Studio .NET and switch to HTML view.

2. Modify the `OutputCache` directive by changing the `Duration` to 600 (ten minutes):

```
<%@ OutputCache Duration="600" Location="Server" VaryByHeader="Host"
    VaryByParam="None" VaryByCustom="CMSPosting;CMSRole" %>
```

So now if you went ahead and edited the Hibiscus posting, approved the change, and navigated back to `http://localhost/tropicalgreen/plantcatalog/hibiscus.htm`, you would still see the cached version of the posting without the changes you just made. Go ahead and try it:

1. Click the Switch To Edit Site link.

2. Click the Edit link.

3. Add some text to the Description placeholder.

4. Click Save And Exit and then Approve the posting.

5. Click Switch To Live Site.

Right after you switch to live site view you may actually see the changed version of the posting. This is because you are not in the true live site view of the posting. You are in a live site view using a Unique ID based URL, and this view has a separate page cache instance from the hierarchical URL view that your visitors would use. Notice the URL in your browser looks something like this: `http://localhost/NR/exeres/109A19D4-0E8B-402C-A76D-31CCFC7EAA3,frameless.htm?NRMODE=Published`.

To see the posting in the true live site view, browse to `http://localhost/tropicalgreen/plantcatalog/hibiscus.htm`, then refresh your browser. Notice that the content that you just added does not appear! This is because the content you see is still the cached version and the ten minutes we have set for the cache to expire is not up yet. For the latest content to show, we need to invalidate the cache.

Let's add the invalidation code and try it again:

1. Go back to the `Plant.aspx` template file in Visual Studio .NET. Switch to the code view.

2. Add the `Microsoft.ContentManagement.Web.Caching` namespace to the list at the top of the `Plant.aspx.cs` code-behind file:

   ```
   using Microsoft.ContentManagement.Web.Caching;
   ```

3. In the `Page_Load()` event handler, add the following line at the top of the method:

   ```
   private void Page_Load(object sender, System.EventArgs e)
   {
       // Put user code to initialize the page here
       CmsHttpCachePolicy.Current.AddValidationCallbackAllCmsContent();
       . . . code continues . . .
   }
   ```

4. Save and build the solution.

Refresh `http://localhost/tropicalgreen/plantcatalog/hibiscus.htm` in your browser. Then go through the process of editing the posting, adding some content, and approving it, then navigate back to `http://localhost/tropicalgreen/plantcatalog/hibiscus.htm`. Your changes will now appear even though the duration of the output cache was not exceeded!

If you want other types of pages invalidated at the same time, you must include the call to `CmsHttpCachePolicy.Current.AddValidationCallbackAllCmsContent()` in any ASPX template or channel rendering script that you want invalidated. Thus you would need to add that line along with the `Microsoft.ContentManagement.Web.Caching` reference to the `sitemap.aspx` file as well; otherwise its content will not be invalidated when a change is made to content in the system.

Keep in mind that all web form content from the output cache was invalidated when you edited the Hibiscus posting, even cached content from other plant postings. So although this appears as though it would be detrimental to the caching on your site, it is a useful feature to have. The reason you might want to use invalidation is because, for example, if you change the name of the root channel of your site, all links on the site immediately become invalid. Or, if you change the start date for a channel, items beneath it may no longer be visible so links to those items would become invalid.

If you have a web farm that contains multiple servers configured as read-write sites, timed output caching may not work perfectly as the memory cache is not shared. So it's best not to have MCMS servers on a web farm configured using timed output caching. If you have a web farm consider using invalidation instead of timed output caching.

Proving that Caching Enhances Site Performance

You can use MCMS performance counters to compare results before and after output caching is enabled. The counters can be configured in the Performance Logs and Alerts | Counter Logs section of the Computer Management Console in Windows.

Create a new Counter Log by right-clicking and choosing New Log Settings... Name the new log and click Add Counters.... Choose the CMS Performance Counters from the Performance object drop-down list.

You can also create a new Alert to monitor whether the counters go above or below a set threshold. Here is a list of the available counters:

Counter	Description
AE Node objects	Number of active MCMS COM objects on the server
AE Node objects created/sec	Number of AE node objects created per second
Authenticated sessions	Number of authenticated sessions connected to the server
Authenticated sessions/sec	Number of authenticated sessions opened per second
Cache hits/sec	Rate of cache hits on the master cache
Cache misses/sec	Rate of cache misses on the master cache
CMS Connections opened/sec	MCMS connections opened per second
Data access operations/sec	Number of data access operations executed per second
Edit sessions	Authoring or development sessions connected to server
Edit sessions opened/sec	Authoring or development sessions opened per second
Exceptions thrown	Number of exceptions thrown by server
Guest sessions	Number of guest sessions on the server
Guest sessions/sec	Number of guest sessions per second
ISAPI sessions	Number of ISAPI sessions opened by the server
ISAPI sessions/sec	Number of ISAPI sessions opened per second
Master cache nodes	Number of items in the internal MCMS master cache—not the same as the Node Cache
Number of CMS connections	Number of open MCMS application connections
Shared nodes	Number of items/nodes referenced by server, including master cache items
Shared nodes/sec	Shared nodes created per second

What does AE stand for? Well, MCMS was originally built by a small company in Vancouver, British Columbia, and it was first called Active Enterprise. The name eventually changed to NCompass Resolution. Microsoft purchased NCompass in 2001 and the Resolution product became Microsoft Content Management Server. You may notice references to both AE and NR throughout MCMS.

Load-testing software like the Application Center Test product that is part of Visual Studio .NET Enterprise Architect should also be used to gauge effectiveness. We strongly recommend that you load-test any website before it is released to production, whether or not you use output caching!

A good reference for performance optimization is the online book available at `http://msdn.microsoft.com/library/en-us/CMS2002_GB/htm/ mcms2002_perf_deploy_abstract_msdn_xugb.asp?frame=true`.

Summary

In this chapter, we reviewed the default caching features in MCMS and discussed why caching is important. We learned how caching works in MCMS and ASP.NET. We went over the things that MCMS caches, from the disk cache, to the Node Cache and high-level caches. We also showed you how you can tune your MCMS server for optimal performance.

Then we tried out a few different ways to use ASP.NET output caching with MCMS templates, channel rendering scripts, and user controls. We also tried out the personalization and invalidation features of ASP.NET output caching in order to keep content personal and fresh for our users.

Lastly, we mentioned that you can and should use the CMS Performance Counters to ensure that caching is working well on your site, and also help you optimize your code.

23

Site Deployment

At some point in time, you will be faced with the task of moving objects from one MCMS database to another. You may wish to deploy the application from a development server to a production server, either because the first version is ready to go live or perhaps because a new version of the site has been completed. Part of your plan will be to synchronize database objects in the development site with the objects in the production site.

Or your environment has been designed to work with a staging server. Authors update content on a staging server. Once postings have been approved and published, they are deployed to a production server on a regular basis.

Another possibility might be the need to move objects around when you have several installations of MCMS in your intranet. As part of an effort to share information across departments, different sites exchange information.

Usually, you would create a web service to make the same content available to all servers, but there may be some instances where you would want to duplicate content.

There are many other possible situations we haven't mentioned here. Fortunately, you don't have to write your deployment scripts from scratch. There are three different options to transport database objects stored in the MCMS repository from one server to another:

- **Database backup and restore**. If the destination environment is a fresh setup, the easiest way to get everything across is to move the entire database. This technique uses standard SQL backup and restore procedures. The only thing you need to do after deployment is ensure that the SQL and MCMS user accounts are valid for the destination domain.

- **MCMS Site Deployment Manager**. When deploying only selected sections of the site, use Site Deployment Manager. You get to pick and choose which objects you want transported to the destination server and which objects to leave behind.

- **MCMS Site Deployment Scripts**. You can automate incremental deployments by writing scripts using the Site Deployment API (SDAPI). Note that the SDAPI does not cover the same functionality as Site Deployment Manager. See the *Differences between the Site Deployment API and the Site Deployment Manager* section later in this chapter.

When deploying entire websites based on MCMS, there are three areas to consider:

1. Database objects
2. File system objects
3. Configuration settings in the IIS Metabase

For a website to be moved completely, each of these must be duplicated on the production server.

In this chapter, we will focus on how we can safely transport database objects across servers using either the MCMS Site Deployment Manager or MCMS Site Deployment Scripts.

We will not cover how to use database backup and restore, or how to move the file system objects and other configuration settings, since those methods are not specific to MCMS.

A good reference on deploying ASP.NET applications is available on Microsoft's website: `http://msdn.microsoft.com/library/en-us/dnbda/html/DALGRoadmap.asp`.

For large websites involving multiple servers in a cluster, you can ease deployment by using Microsoft Application Center.

There is a useful article on Microsoft's site, at `http://www.microsoft.com/technet/ prodtechnol/cms/deploy/cmsdes01.mspx`, which contains information on how Application Center can be used to deploy entire MCMS websites.

Using the Site Deployment Manager

You can use Site Deployment Manager to:

1. Create a package to be exported to another MCMS server
2. Import an existing package to the MCMS server you are currently logged in to

> Only MCMS Administrators are able to launch Site Deployment Manager.

In this section, we will first create a package containing objects to be exported to another MCMS database. We will then import the package that we have created into the second MCMS database.

To begin, let's open Site Deployment Manger.

From the Start menu, select Programs | Microsoft Content Management Server | Site Manager.

Log in using an administrator account. From the menu bar, select Tools | Options....

Ensure that all export package defaults are checked. We will see what each option means as we work through the chapter.

Click OK to close the Options dialog.

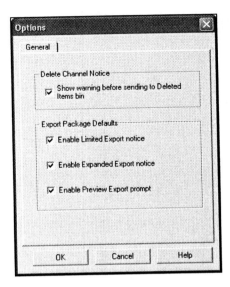

Site Deployment Manager is used to transport objects from one MCMS database to another. When deploying MCMS objects, Site Deployment Manager exports all selected items to the file system—placeholder content and metadata are transformed into XML files; resources are added as binaries.

It packages them into a container known as the Site Deployment Object File (or SDO file for short). On the destination server, Site Deployment Manager unpacks the content and imports it into the database.

Opening the Site Deployment Export Dialog

Open the Site Deployment Export dialog by selecting File | Package | Export... from the menu bar.

By default, the content of the Item Selection tab is displayed.

The top half of the Item Selection tab consists of two areas.

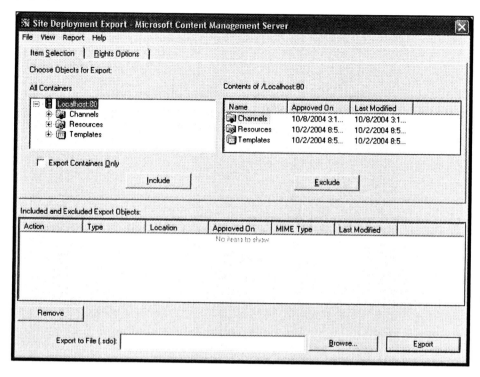

The area on the left-hand side, labeled All Containers, lists the containers (channels, resource galleries, and template galleries) stored in the MCMS repository. They are presented as a tree. You can expand and collapse the tree to reveal sub-containers.

On the right-hand side, the Contents of /Localhost area lists the contents of the selected container.

To see what's in each container, you can:

- Click on a container in the All Containers box.
- Double-click on any container in the Contents of /Localhost box. Note that choosing this option also adds the container to the Included and Excluded Export Objects list.

The bottom panel, labeled Included and Excluded Export Objects, shows a list of objects included or excluded for export. Items to be included will be listed with a green check mark and items to be excluded show up with a black cross. The list is currently empty as we have not selected any objects for export.

Choosing Objects for Export

The Include button adds items for export. Included items are displayed in the Included and Excluded Export Objects box with a green check mark next to them.

To choose an object for export there are two choices:

- Highlight the container in the All Containers box and click Include.
- Highlight the container/object in the Contents of ... box and click Include.

If the object has already been added, you can:

- Right-click the object in the Included and Excluded Export Objects list and select Include from the context menu.

Let's try including a posting. In the All Containers box, select Channels | TropicalGreen | PlantCatalog.

Observe that the listing shown in the right-hand box changes to reflect the contents of the PlantCatalog channel.

In the Contents of box, select the CoconutTree posting and click Include.

The Coconut Tree posting is added to the Included and Excluded Export Object list with a green check mark.

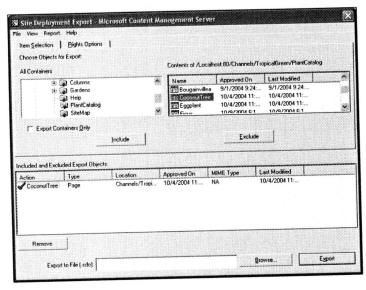

Instead of adding objects one by one, you can also choose to add entire containers of objects.

In the All Containers box, expand the Channels container and select TropicalGreen.

Click Include.

The TropicalGreen channel is listed in the Included and Excluded Export Objects list with a green check mark.

All descendants of the TropicalGreen channel will be exported.

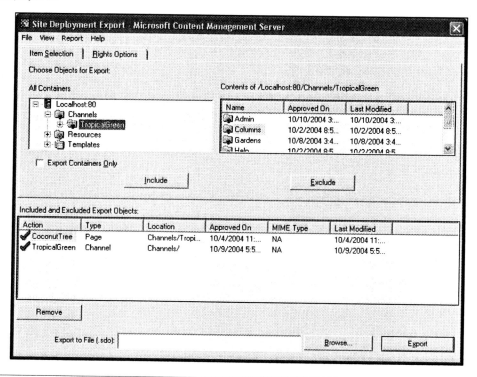

Only the latest approved version of postings can be exported. Postings that have not been published or that are waiting for moderator approval will not be exported.

Excluding Objects from the Export Package

You can select specific items to be excluded from the site deployment file. This feature is very useful when you have certain areas of the website that are not ready to be exported. Or perhaps you have content that should remain on the development server and not on the production server.

To exclude specific items you can either:

- Highlight the container in the All Containers box and click Exclude, or
- Highlight the container/object in the Contents of ... box and click Exclude

And if the object has been previously included in the Included and Excluded Export Objects list, you could:

- Right-click the object in the Included and Excluded Export Objects list and select Exclude from the context menu.

Excluded items are listed in the Included and Excluded Export Objects list with an X next to them.

Let's choose not to export any of the sample postings created for the members section of the Gardens channel. In the All Containers box, select Channels | TropicalGreen | Gardens | Members. Click Exclude.

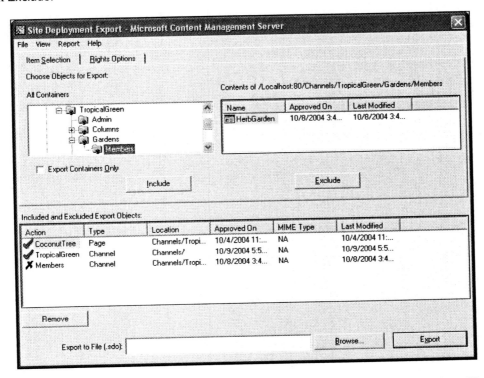

If you wish to exclude only selected postings, select the postings in the Contents of... box. You can select multiple postings by clicking on the first item, pressing the C*trl* button and clicking the other items. With all the postings selected, click Exclude.

Although MCMS gives you the flexibility to choose objects that you wish to exclude, it automatically includes them in the package if other objects depend on them. A typical example is that of a posting based on a template. If you include say PostingA, which was built upon TemplateA, excluding TemplateA would have no effect. MCMS is intelligent enough to identify that PostingA is dependent on TemplateA and adds TemplateA into the package regardless of whether the template has been excluded or not.

Exporting Containers Only

To export only containers (channels, resource galleries and template galleries), check the Export Containers Only option.

Check the Export Containers Only option. An alert box appears with the message Non-container objects in the Export List will be ignored. You can prevent the warning message from appearing in future by checking the Do not show me this message again option. If you have accidentally turned off the warning message and would like to get it to show up again, check the Enable Limited Export notice option in the Options dialog (accessible by selecting Tools | Options... in Site Manager's menu bar).

Click OK to close the alert box. Notice that the posting that we included in the earlier exercise has been grayed out.

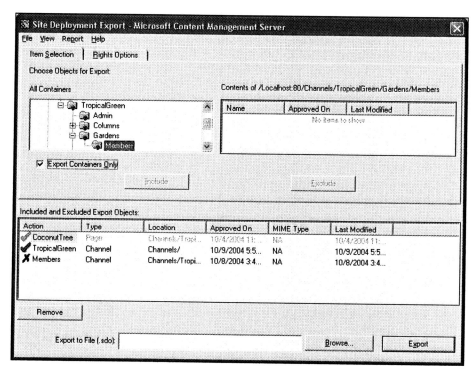

Uncheck the Export Container Only option. An alert box appears again; this time it carries a different message: Currently selected containers will be exported with all their non-excluded contents. Similarly, you can turn the warning message on or off by checking or unchecking the Enable Expanded Export notice option in the Options dialog (accessible by selecting Tools | Options... from Site Manager's menu bar).

The included postings in the list are no longer grayed out.

Viewing Template Dependencies

The dependency report shows a list of all postings that make use of a particular template. In this example, we will generate a list of plant fact sheets that are based on the Plant template. In the All Containers box, expand the tree and select the Templates | TropicalGreen | PlantCatalog node. In the Contents Of... box, select the Plant template. To generate a dependency report you could choose to:

- Select Report | Dependency from Site Deployment Export dialog toolbar.

- Right-click on the Plant template in the Contents of ... box, and select the Dependency Report option.

The Dependent Report is generated and displayed within a new browser window:

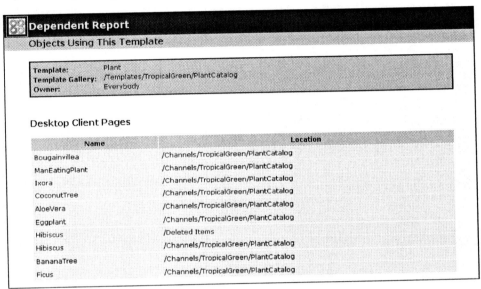

The report shows the name of the template, the path of the template gallery it belongs to, and the owner. More importantly, it lists all postings that use the template.

If the Dependency Report option is grayed out, it means that the template has been checked out.

In addition, you can run a Dependent Report in Site Manager in the normal Template Gallery view by right-clicking on any template and selecting Dependent Report.

Removing Objects from the Included and Excluded Export Objects List

To remove an object from the Included and Excluded Export Objects list:

- Select the item from the Included and Excluded Export Objects list and click the Remove button. Using this method, you can remove multiple items from the list by selecting more than one item. You can select multiple items by using Ctrl + left mouse button or Shift + left mouse button.

- Right-click the item in the Included and Excluded Export Objects list and select the Remove option.

Let's remove the CoconutTree posting from the list. In the Included and Excluded Export Objects box, right-click on the CoconutTree posting and select the Remove option from the context menu. The object is removed from the list.

Exporting Rights Groups and Users

The Rights Option tab provides options to include, within the export package, both rights groups and their users.

The Rights Options screen shows two options:

- Export Rights Groups includes the rights groups in the export package without their members.
- Export Users includes the rights groups in the export package with their members. This option is disabled by default. To enable it, check Export Rights Groups.

By default, both options are unchecked. Click the Rights Option tab and check both the Export Rights Groups and Export Users options.

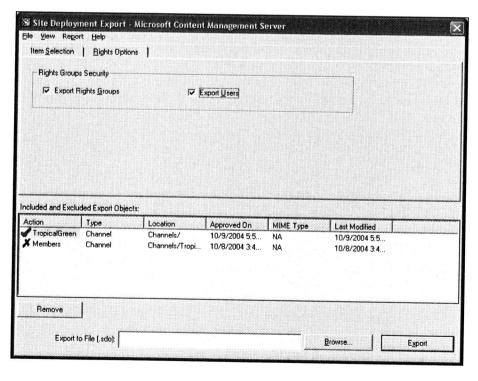

Specifying the Location of the Export Package

You need to specify the location in which the export package will be created. To do so, click the Browse... button in the Export to File (.sdo) field.

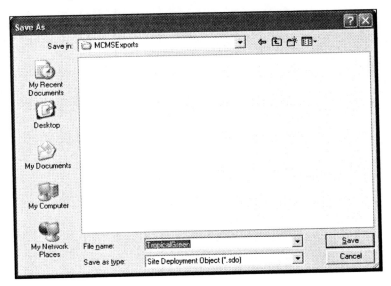

In the Save As dialog, select an appropriate location on your hard disk to save the export package to (e.g. c:\MCMSExports). Create the folder first if it does not exist. Name the Site Deployment Object file TropicalGreen.sdo. When you are done, click Save.

> All Site Deployment Object files have the extension *.sdo.

Saving an Export Profile

After having selected which objects to include or exclude from the export package, save your settings by selecting File | Save Export Profile from the toolbar.

In the Save Export Profile dialog, find a suitable location in your hard disk (e.g. c:\MCMSExports) to save the profile and name the export profile TropicalGreenExport.sde. Site Deployment Export Profiles are saved with the extension *.sde.

Previewing the Contents of an Export Package

Once you have selected the objects to be included or excluded, you are ready to create the export package. Before you do so, it is a good idea to preview its contents.

Generate a preview report of the export object by selecting Report | Export Preview from the toolbar. The job that generates the report starts, and its progress is shown in a dialog containing a progress bar.

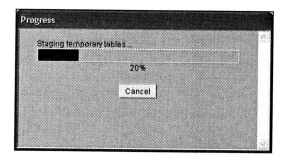

When it has completed, you will receive a report presented as an HTML page in a new browser window. The report is divided into five sections:

- Report Information
- Selected Export Parameters
- Selected Containers and Items
  - Channels and Pages
  - Template Galleries and Templates
  - Resource Galleries and Resources
  - User Rights Groups
- Selected Export objects not currently available for Export
- Selected objects containing Broken Links

Report Information

This section displays general information about the report including:

- **Package file**
  The name of the site deployment object file and its path. If the Export to file field was left blank, the value shown here will be None Specified.

- **Generated on**
  The date and time that the report was generated.

- **Report generated by**
  The user account of the person who generated the report.

- **Client Machine**
  The name of the machine that generated the report.

- **Client Version**
  The version number of the MCMS server on the machine that generated the report.

- **Server URL**
  The address of the server that contains the objects to be exported. In our case, it shows `localhost` because we are creating the site deployment object on the same server in which the preview report is generated.

- **Server Version**
  The version number of the MCMS server on the machine that contains the objects to be exported.

Report Information

Package file:	C:\MCMSExports\TropicalGreen.sdo
Generated on:	10/12/2004 11:34:33 AM
Report generated by:	WinNT://MCMSBOOK/Administrator
Client Machine:	MCMSBOOK
Client Version:	5.0.4484.0
Server URL:	http://localhost:80/NR/System/Marshalling/
Server Version:	5.0.4484.0

Selected Export Parameters

The selections made in the Rights Options tab are shown in this section of the report. Because we selected to export rights groups and users, these are marked as being `Exported`.

The CreatedBy Specifier states that when the object has been exported, the `createdBy` property will not be exported to the destination server. You can't change this value using Site Deployment Manager (but you can do so using the Site Deployment API as we shall see later in this chapter).

Selected Export Parameters

General

Security Parameters:

User Rights Groups:	Exported
Users:	Exported
CreatedBy Specifier:	NOT Exported

Selected Containers and Items

This section of the report lists all the selected channels, postings, resource galleries, resources, template galleries, templates, user rights groups, and users that have been included in the package. The objects that you have added to the Included and Excluded Export Objects list are bolded.

MCMS automatically adds all dependent items to the list. These dependent items are listed in normal font weight, not in bold. Examples of dependent items are:

- Sub-containers and objects (channels, postings, resource galleries, resources, template galleries, and templates) that are descendants of selected objects
- Templates used by descendent postings and their corresponding template galleries
- Resources used by descendent postings and their corresponding resource galleries
- If you've selected the option to include rights groups in the package, all rights groups assigned to selected containers will be exported as well.

For example, although we did not instruct MCMS to export template galleries and templates, they have been included in the package anyway. That's because when we included the TropicalGreen channel object, MCMS exported all its descendants as well, including postings in the site. Templates are considered dependencies because postings require them to work correctly, and so they are exported as well. Template galleries are required to hold the templates and are therefore also included in the export object.

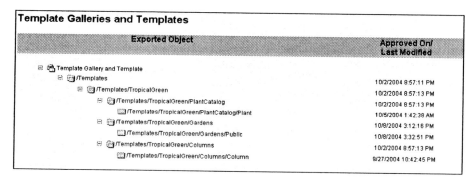

Selected Export Objects Not Currently Available for Export

Site Deployment Manager does not export postings that do not have approved versions, especially those in a Waiting For Moderator Approval state. Between the time a posting is included on the list of objects to be exported and the time the report was generated, an author could have changed the posting's properties and submitted it to a moderator for approval. While waiting for moderator approval, the page does not have an approved version and Site Deployment Manager is not able to export it.

Similarly, postings based on templates that do not have approved versions will not be exported. For example, when a new template is created and saved, all new postings based on it will not be exported until the template is checked in.

Usually, you would see a single word, None, printed in this section. As an example, we have set the Hibiscus posting to a Waiting For Moderator Approval state and added it to the Included and Excluded Export Objects list to show you how the report looks when there are objects not available for export:

```
┌──────────────────────────────────────────────────────┐
│ Selected Export objects not currently                  │
│ available for Export:                                  │
│                                                        │
│   Posting    /Channels/TropicalGreen/PlantCatalog/Hibiscus │
└──────────────────────────────────────────────────────┘
```

Selected Objects Containing Broken Links

The final section of the report shows objects with broken links. Broken links are typically caused by postings with hyperlinks to other postings that have not been included in the export job. As before, your report probably has the word None written in this section. (That's good news, you have no broken links between your MCMS objects!)

The example below shows a case in which the Banana Tree page contains a link to the Hibiscus page. When the Hibiscus page is not included in the export job, it is listed as a missing link within the Banana Tree page.

Creating the Export Package

If all looks well on the Export Preview report, you are ready to create the export package. Back at the Site Deployment Export dialog, click Export.

If you did not see the Export Preview Report, you will be prompted to view it now. You can choose to suppress the warning message from appearing in future by checking the Do not show me this message again option. If you have previously suppressed the message and would like to get it to show again, choose the Enable Preview Export prompt option from the Options dialog (accessible by selecting Tools | Options... from the menu bar in Site Manager). Click Yes to start the export process.

A progress bar appears showing you how the export is progressing. The export process goes through five stages:

- Staging Temporary Tables
- Generating XML (which includes exporting resources)
- Compressing the Object Package
- Generating Report
- Export Successful

When completed, a message appears telling you that the export was a success together with a Show Report button. Click Show Report. The report displayed should be the same as the one generated in the preview.

The generated SDO file essentially consists of XML files that provide the import/export instructions to MCMS as well as all images and resource files. You can view the contents of a *.sdo file using software like WinZip. On Windows XP or Windows Server 2003, you can simply rename the extension to *.cab and open it like a folder to see its contents.

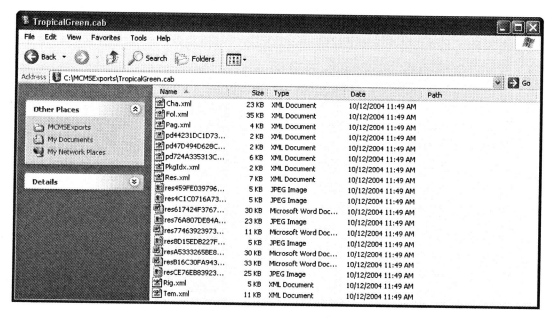

Importing Packages

To test how packages are imported and to simulate the movement of data across machines, you would need todo one of the following:

- Have a second MCMS test machine
- Simulate a "second" database for testing purposes

Creating a Fresh Database for Testing Import Jobs

Let's create a fresh database to test the import process.

1. Close Site Manager.
2. From the Start menu, select Programs | Microsoft SQL Server | Enterprise Manager.
3. Expand the nodes Microsoft SQL Servers | SQL Server Group | (Server Name) | Databases. Right-click on the Databases folder and select New Database....
4. In the Database Properties dialog, name the new database TropicalGreen2.
5. Click OK to close the dialog.
6. Add the MCMS System Account as a user of the database (we discussed how this can be done in detail in Chapter 3).

7. Close Enterprise Manager.

With the database created, use the Database Configuration Application to point MCMS to it. We now have a blank MCMS database to import the objects into.

Opening the Site Deployment Import Dialog

Open Site Manager on the destination MCMS server (in our case, localhost) and login using an account that has administrator rights. Select File | Package Import from the toolbar. The Site Deployment Import Dialog opens as shown below.

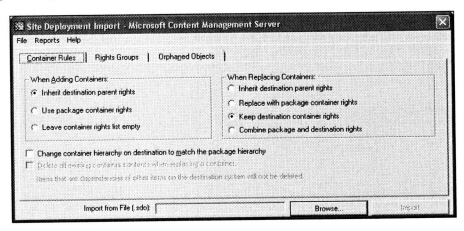

There are three tabs in the Site Deployment Import dialog:

- **Container Rules**
  First displayed when opening the Site Deployment Import dialog. It specifies the rules applied for channels, resource galleries, and template galleries.

- **Rights Groups**
  Contains options that instruct MCMS whether to import rights groups and users.

- **Orphaned Objects**
  Specifies the containers to place objects with no parents.

Let's look at each of these options in turn.

Container Rules

This tab provides several options to choose from that will determine how MCMS imports container objects. The top panel is made up of two sections:

- The panel on the right is labeled When Adding Containers. It provides options to specify the rights groups assigned to new objects.

- The panel on the left is labeled When Replacing Containers and provides options to specify the rights groups assigned to objects that are being replaced.

When Adding Containers

MCMS recognizes containers by their GUID. If it can't find an object with a matching GUID on the destination server, the container is considered new.

When MCMS imports a new container to the destination, it needs to know what kinds of rights it needs to apply to the imported container. You can choose to:

- **Inherit destination parent rights.** This is the default setting. When checked, MCMS automatically assigns the new container the same rights as its parent on the destination server.

- **Use package container rights.** Checking this option has the effect of retaining the rights groups that have been assigned to the container on the source server. In order for this option to be meaningful, the site deployment object file must contain information about rights groups. The Export Rights Group option must be checked when creating the export object.

  There is a possibility that these rights group have not been created on the destination server and have not been included in the object file. When MCMS encounters such situations, it is not able to apply the rights group to the new container.

- **Leave container rights list empty.** This option instructs MCMS not to assign any rights group on the new container after import.

To understand this better, consider the case of an object called ContainerB. ContainerB does not exist on the destination server and is therefore considered by the import job to be a new container. In the export file, ContainerB has a rights group called SourceGroup assigned to it. The table below lists the possible outcomes of importing a new container. The rights group assigned to each container is shown in brackets.

Option	Scenario	Source	Destination
Inherit destination parent rights	Before Import	ContainerA **(SourceGroup)**	ContainerA **(DestinationGroup)**
		ContainerB **(SourceGroup)**	

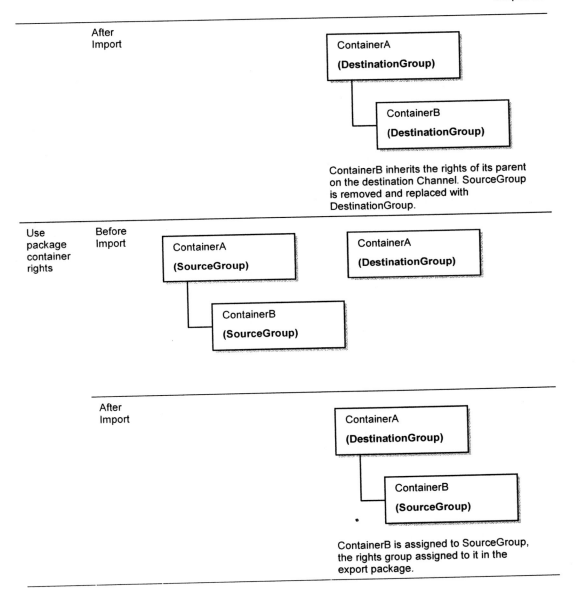

After
Import

ContainerA
(DestinationGroup)

ContainerB
(DestinationGroup)

ContainerB inherits the rights of its parent on the destination Channel. SourceGroup is removed and replaced with DestinationGroup.

Use package container rights

Before Import

ContainerA
(SourceGroup)

ContainerB
(SourceGroup)

ContainerA
(DestinationGroup)

After
Import

ContainerA
(DestinationGroup)

ContainerB
(SourceGroup)

ContainerB is assigned to SourceGroup, the rights group assigned to it in the export package.

Leave container rights list empty	Before Import	

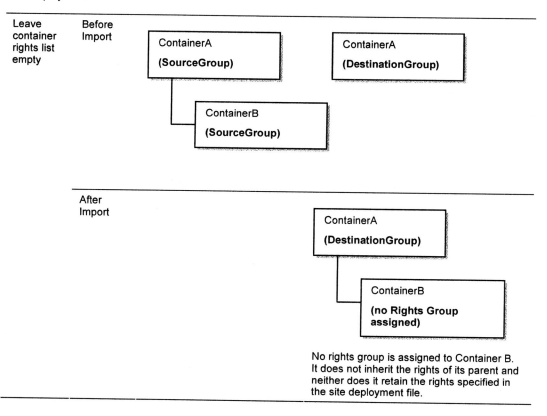

No rights group is assigned to Container B. It does not inherit the rights of its parent and neither does it retain the rights specified in the site deployment file.

When Replacing Containers

When the import job sees an object on the destination server that shares the same GUID as an object in the package, it replaces it.

These rules apply when MCMS detects that you are attempting to replace an existing container on the destination server. There are four options to choose from:

- **Inherit destination parent rights**
  When imported, the container will inherit the rights of its new parent container on the destination server.

- **Replace with package container rights**
  Check this option only if you want to replace all rights groups of the existing container on the destination with those of the imported container from the source.

- **Keep destination container rights**
  By default, this is the selected option. It's also the safest. The replaced container's rights are kept in tact. Nothing gets changed. All information about rights carried by the source is ignored.

- **Combine package and destination rights**
  This adds the source rights to the destination rights, merging them together.

In a real production environment, be careful when selecting the Replace with package container rights and Combine package and destination rights options, especially when deploying from test setups. You would not want to have rights groups used for testing purposes assigned to channels in production. And should you specify users to be imported (and if they have been included in the export package), you may end up having test users on your production site as well!

The table below summarizes the before and after results of each import option for replaced containers. In each scenario, both ContainerA and ContainerB are part of the package to be imported from the source server.

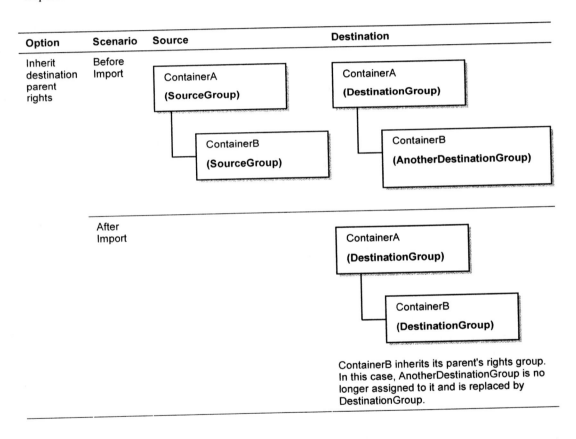

Option	Scenario	Source	Destination

ContainerB inherits its parent's rights group. In this case, AnotherDestinationGroup is no longer assigned to it and is replaced by DestinationGroup.

Site Deployment

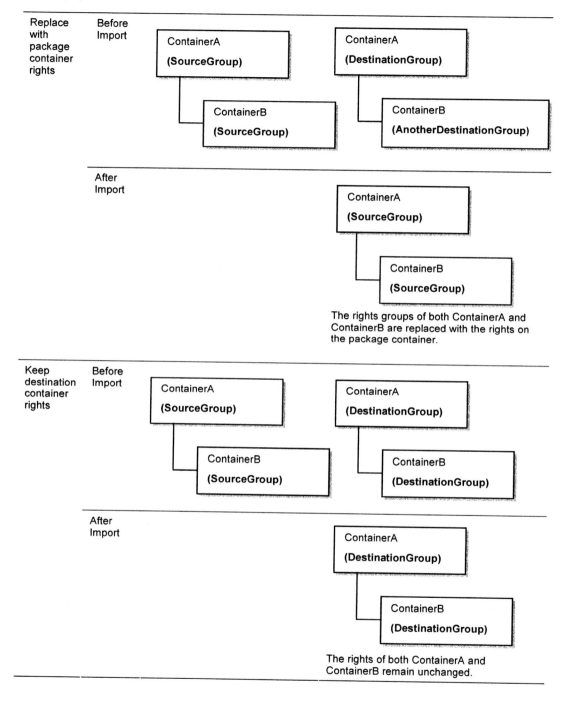

The rights groups of both ContainerA and
ContainerB are replaced with the rights on
the package container.

The rights of both ContainerA and
ContainerB remain unchanged.

576

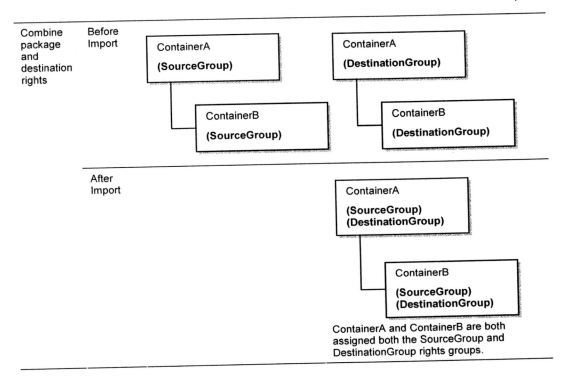

Combine package and destination rights

Before Import

After Import

ContainerA and ContainerB are both assigned both the SourceGroup and DestinationGroup rights groups.

Changing Container Hierarchy on Destination to Match the Package Hierarchy

By default, the Change container hierarchy on destination to match the package hierarchy option is not checked. Check this option to apply the hierarchy that has been defined in the package. This is handy when you have moved objects on the source server and want to change the structure on the destination server too. Otherwise, MCMS will follow the existing hierarchy defined on the destination server.

Selecting this option automatically enables the option below it: Delete all existing container contents when replacing a container.

Deleting all Existing Container Contents when Replacing a Container

The Delete all existing container contents when replacing a container option instructs the import process to delete all child objects in the destination container before repopulating it with objects defined in the package.

For example, when importing a channel that already exists on the destination server, say the PlantCatalog channel, the import process will delete all postings in the destination's PlantCatalog channel first. After the import process is complete, only plant postings found within the package will exist on the destination server.

Anything to do with deleting objects on the production server should ring a few warning bells. While this option is essential for removing postings that have been deleted on the source server, it is important to understand what this does and when to use it, or you may get nasty surprises in the production environment in the form of "missing objects".

One particularly undesirable effect may arise if you have moderators as part of your workflow processes. Recall that the package contains only postings with an approved version. Postings in a Waiting For Moderator Approval state are not included in the package even if they have been published before. Therefore, when the container's objects are replaced, these postings go missing.

Rights Groups

The second tab, Rights Groups, contains several options related to how rights groups are imported. There are two panels:

- Select how Rights Groups are imported
- Select how Users are imported

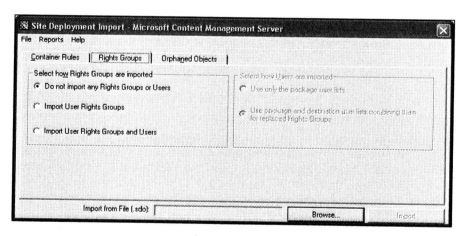

Select how Rights Groups are Imported

This section provides options that instruct MCMS how to handle rights groups defined in the package. Three options are available:

- **Do not import any Rights Groups or Users.** Instructs MCMS to ignore any rights groups defined in the package.

- **Import User Rights Groups.** This option is enabled only if MCMS detects that the package contains rights groups. Choose this option to import the rights groups containers only (no users will be imported).

- **Import User Rights Groups and Users.** This option is enabled only if MCMS detects that the package contains both rights groups and users. Choose this option to import rights groups containers as well as all user members defined within the group.

Select how Users are Imported

This option is enabled only if you have instructed MCMS to import users by checking the Import User Rights Groups and Users option. Two options are available:

- **Use only the package user lists.** Check this to replace the list of users for the corresponding rights group on the destination server with that found in the package.

- **Use package and destination user lists combining them for replaced Rights Groups.** When replacing a rights group on the destination server, MCMS will merge the users on both the replaced rights group as well as users in the package.

The table below shows how users are imported to the user rights group based on the option selected in the Select how Users are imported panel.

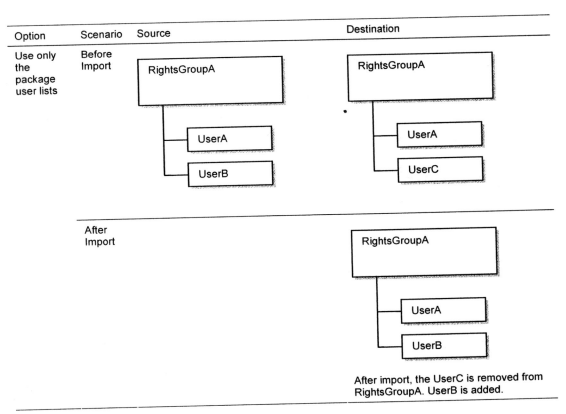

Option	Scenario	Source	Destination

After import, the UserC is removed from RightsGroupA. UserB is added.

Use package and destination user lists combining them for replaced Rights Groups	Before Import	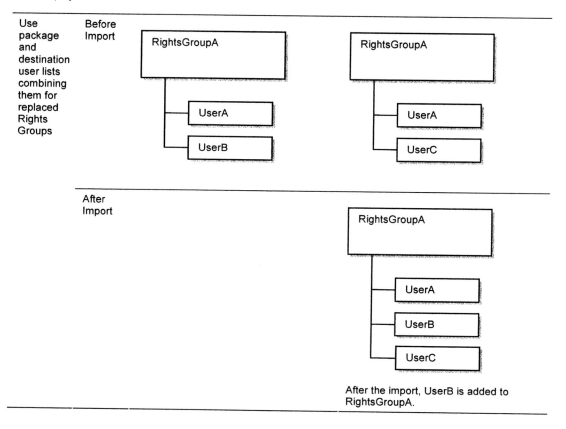

After the import, UserB is added to RightsGroupA.

Orphaned Objects

Sometimes, MCMS is unable to locate the parent on the destination setup. When this happens, the imported object is **orphaned**.

An orphan is an object within the package whose parent has not been:

- Deployed to the destination server
- Included as part of the import package

If both conditions are met, the object would not have a parent on the destination server and is considered an orphan.

Should the parent container not exist on the destination server, you can't simply create a new channel with the same name and properties. Doing so would merely create a similar channel but with a different GUID. The imported objects would not become its children and would still be considered orphans. The only way to prevent orphans is to include the parent channel as part of the package or deploy it earlier.

By default, orphaned objects are imported to the root container objects. Change the containers where orphaned objects are imported to by clicking on the ellipses.

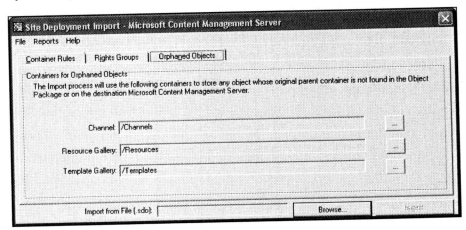

Importing an Existing Site Deployment Object File

We are going to import the objects exported earlier in the TropicalGreen.sdo site deployment object file. In Site Deployment Import, click Browse.... In the Select SDO File for Import dialog, locate the TropicalGreen.sdo file created earlier and click Open.

Set the following property values in the Import dialog:

Property	Value
Container Rules	
When Adding Containers	Use Package container rights
When Replacing Containers	Combine package and destination rights
Change container hierarchy on destination to match the package hierarchy	Unchecked
Rights Groups	
Select how Rights Groups are imported	Import User Rights Groups and Users
Select how Users are imported	Use package and destination user lists combining them for replaced Rights Groups
Orphaned Objects	
Channel	/Channels
Resource Gallery	/Resources
Template Gallery	/Templates

When you are done, click Import. A confirmation alert appears warning you that once started, the import process cannot be terminated. It also recommends that you back up the Microsoft Content Management Server database before proceeding. This is excellent advice. If you have not created a backup of the database, consider doing so before proceeding. Click Import Preview to preview the objects that would be imported to the database.

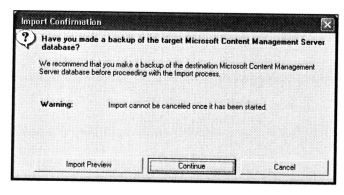

Previewing the Contents of an Import Package

You can also generate the import report by selecting Reports | Import Preview from the toolbar. The import report consists of five sections:

- Report Information
- Import Parameters
- Object Placement from Source to Destination Server (Imported Objects)
  - Channels and Pages
  - Template Galleries and Templates
  - Resource Galleries and Resources
  - User Rights Groups
- Destination Objects that will be Deleted on Import
- Destination Objects that may Contain Broken Links after Import

Report Information

The first section of the report is similar to the Report Information section of the export report that we saw earlier in the section, *Previewing the Contents of an Export Package*, with some key differences:

- **Package file.** The name of the temporary site deployment object file and its path. The file specified in the Import from File field is first uploaded to this temporary location before being processed by the import process.
- **Client Machine and Version.** This refers to the machine running Site Manager used to start the import process.

- **Server URL and Version.** This refers to the destination MCMS server where the import process runs.

Report Information

Package file:	C:\PROGRA~1\MIB84C~1\Server\Temp\sdupload.sdo
Generated on:	10/13/2004 11:38:04 AM
Report generated by:	WinNT://MCMSBOOK/Administrator
Client Machine:	MCMSBOOK
Client Version:	5.0.4484.0
Server URL:	http://localhost:80/NR/System/Marshalling/
Server Version:	5.0.4484.0

Selected Import Parameters

This section displays options that were selected in the Site Deployment Import dialog.

The Set Created By on imported objects to parameter will always have the value Set to current user. You can't change this value. This means that all imported objects will have the `CreatedBy` property changed to the user ID of the person who ran the import process (but you can change this using the Site Deployment API as we shall see later in this chapter).

Import Parameters

Containers

When Adding Containers:	Use package container rights
When Replacing Containers:	Combine package and destination rights
Change container hierarchy on destination to match the package hierarchy:	No
Delete all existing container contents when replacing a container:	No

Rights Groups

Select how Rights Groups are imported:	Import User Rights Groups *and* Users
When and how Users are imported:	Use package and destination user lists, combining them for replaced Rights Groups
Set Created By on imported objects to:	Set to current user

Orphaned Objects - destination containers

Channel:	/Channels
Template Gallery:	/Templates
Resource Gallery:	/Resources

Object Placement from Source to Destination System (Imported Objects)

This section of the report lists all the selected channels, postings, resource galleries, resources, template galleries, and templates that have been imported. The figure overleaf shows an example of the Resource Galleries and Resources section of a particular import. The first column shows

583

the path of the object being imported and its last modified date. The second column provides an indicator that shows if the object is New or Same. Finally, the last column states the destination path of the imported object.

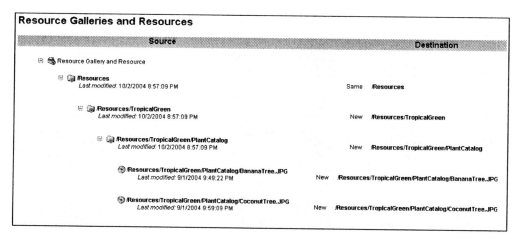

Destination Objects that will be Deleted on Import

Some objects may get deleted after the import job. This may happen when you have selected the Delete all existing container contents when replacing a container option in the Import dialog. When that option is checked, objects found on the destination server but not in the site deployment file are deleted.

In addition, export packages created using the SDAPI would automatically contain information about deleted items that are listed in this section.

If this is the first time you are running the import job on a fresh database, this section of the report will simply state None (being a fresh database, there is nothing to delete anyway), which means that no objects on the destination server will be deleted at the end of the import process.

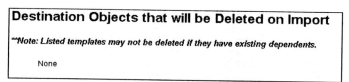

Let's see how the report looks when there are objects to be deleted. Let's say there is a channel called Admin and a resource called eggplant.gif on the destination server. And for the purpose of this example, suppose that these two objects have not been added to the import package. When the import job runs with the Delete all existing container contents when replacing a container flag turned on, both the channel and the resource will be deleted on the destination server.

The note Listed templates may not be deleted if they have existing dependents simply means that even though templates could be marked for deletion, they will not be deleted if there are postings on the destination server that make use of them.

Destination Objects that will be Deleted on Import

"Note: Listed templates may not be deleted if they have existing dependents.

Channel   /Channels/Admin

Resource   /Resources/PlantCatalog/eggplant.gif

Destination Objects that may Contain Broken Links after Import

This is a list of objects that reference other objects that are not found in the destination server or object file.

For example, Posting A links to Posting B. For some reason (possibly it was deleted, possibly it was not published), Posting B is not found on the destination server after the import. MCMS will list Posting A in this section of the report with a remark saying that there was a missing link caused by Posting B.

Starting the Import Process

To start the import process, close the report and click the Continue button.

A progress dialog keeps you updated on the progress. If you are fast enough, you can catch the different stages of the import process:

- Initializing...
- Staging Rights Groups and Users
- Staging Resource Galleries and/or Resources
- Staging Template Galleries and/or Templates
- Staging Channels and/or Postings
- Preparing Data
- Merging Data
- Generating Report
- Import Successful

When the import is complete, you receive an alert. Click Show Report to see the objects that have been imported. The Import Report is displayed in a separate window and is similar to the one seen in the preview.

Running Import Processes on a Live Production Site

Running the import process on a live production site has very little impact on the availability and performance of the site. Even when running lengthy import jobs, there is only a small chance that visitors to the site may get HTTP 404 (not found) or occasional HTTP 500 errors (internal server error). In fact, with a generously sized Node Cache, the chance of this happening is as close to zero as you can get.

MCMS 2001 administrators may remember how the import process used to lock up the database preventing anyone from reading or writing in it. Authors were not able to write to the repository and fresh content could not be served. Only content in the MCMS cache would be delivered until the import process completed. Requests for content not already in the cache resulted in HTTP 404 or HTTP 500 errors.

In MCMS 2002, the logic used to perform imports has been improved over previous versions. Locks are released during the import process instead of at the end. Today, site-availability issues rarely surface and administrators can safely perform lengthy import jobs on live production sites. Nevertheless, it is still considered good practice to work with small deployment packages whenever possible.

Before We Continue

Close Site Manager and use the DCA to reconnect to the original TropicalGreen database.

Automating Deployment Using the Site Deployment API

On certain occasions, it's perfectly normal to have someone sitting in front of the server, clicking buttons, exporting and importing objects across MCMS databases. However, it wouldn't be productive to do that when you have regular incremental updates to the site.

MCMS provides an option to create scripts for incremental updates to allow automatic deployment using the Site Deployment API (SDAPI). With the SDAPI, we can write scripts that automate the process of exporting objects from the source server and importing them on the destination server.

The SDAPI is packaged as a COM-based application programming interface. There are two sets of objects in the SDAPI:

- Objects that support server-side site deployment. Scripts built on this API are executed on the source MCMS server for exports and destination MCMS server for imports.

  The required library file is located at:
  `<install directory>\server\bin\NRSiteDeployServer.dll`.

- Objects that support client-side site deployment. Scripts built using the client-side API run on the client machines that connect to a remote MCMS server.

  The client needs to have HTTP (or HTTPS) access to the remote MCMS server. It is not necessary to have the MCMS server components running on the machine executing the client-side site deployment scripts. Only Site Manager has to be installed on this machine.

The required library file is located at:
`<install directory>\client\NRSiteDeployClient.dll`.

Differences between the Site Deployment API and the Site Deployment Manager

Before we go any further, it is important to understand that the SDAPI does not provide the same functions as site Deployment Manager. It was not built as a replacement for the Site Deployment Manager, but rather to complement it.

SDAPI	Site Deployment Manager
Designed for incremental exports. Channels and postings that are not modified during the specified interval would not be exported.	**Designed for full or selected exports.** Objects added to a list can be included or excluded in the export package regardless of whether they have been modified.
Does not export specific resources and templates. For example, you can't select a single template or resource to be deployed. It only selects channels and postings that have changed since the last deployment or according to the time interval specified. Resource galleries, resources, template galleries, and templates are exported only if the exported postings have dependencies to these items.	**Can be used to export specific objects including resources and templates.** You can select a single object or a group of objects (including template gallery items and resource gallery items) to be deployed.
Automatically deletes objects that have been deleted on the source server. If a channel or posting has been deleted on the source server (and does not sit in the Deleted Items bin), the SDAPI will delete the corresponding object on the destination server.	Only when the Delete all existing container contents when replacing a container option is checked would objects that not found in the site deployment file be deleted on the destination server.
Has the ability to export/import rights groups and users without any other objects. You can back up the entire collection of rights groups and users and restore them on the destination server.	You can only export and import rights groups and users assigned to other container objects in the site deployment file.
Has the option to include CreatedBy user information in the exported package. Similarly, you can choose whether or not to import the CreatedBy user information to the destination server (if the information can be found in the package).	The CreatedBy user is never included in the export package. When the import process completes, the CreatedBy information on the destination object is that of the user account running the import job.
When performing server-side imports, automatically creates a container named "CMS Default SiteDeploy Destination" to store orphans. For client-side imports, the root container is used.	Allows you to select the channel, template gallery, and resource gallery to hold orphaned objects.

Like Site Manager, the SDAPI does not deploy files or anything else that is not in the MCMS repository. Both are tools for transporting database objects between two MCMS servers. You still need to transfer such file system objects through other means.

Writing a Server-Side Export Script

Let's write a console application using C# to export the TropicalGreen database objects to an SDO file. This gives us the flexibility of working with a language and development environment that we are already familiar with. You could also do the same tasks with VB.NET or shell scripting languages (such as VBScript).

First, create a new Visual C# Console Application in Visual Studio .NET. Give it the name ExportServerSide. Rename class1.cs to ExportScript.cs.

Next, we need to add a reference to the MSCMS Site Deployment (Server-side) component, NRSiteDeployServer.dll. Right-click the References folder in Solution Explorer and select Add Reference. In the Add Reference dialog, select the COM tab. In the list of available components, scroll till you find MSCMS Site Deployment (Server-Side). Watch out for the name here—there's an S in MSCMS in the server-side component.

After you have selected the component, click Select and then click OK to close this dialog.

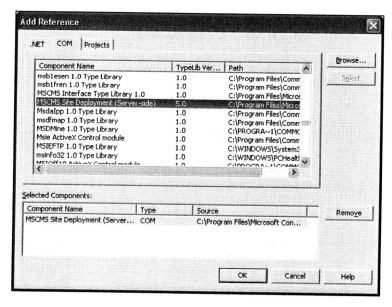

Import the SITEDEPLOYSERVERLib namespace by adding the appropriate statement above the ExportServerSide namespace declaration. In the Main() method, create a new instance of the CmsDeployExportClass.

```
using System;
using SITEDEPLOYSERVERLib;

namespace ExportServerSide
{
    . . . code continues . . .
    static void Main(string[] args)
    {
```

```
//
// TODO: Add code to start application here
//
CmsDeployExport exportJob = new CmsDeployExportClass();
    }
}
```

Authenticating the User Running the Export Process

We need to authenticate the user whose account is to be used to run the export process. The user account used for authentication must belong to either the MCMS administrator group or a group that is linked to a channel manager role. Note that if the user is a channel manager, then the SDAPI will only export objects they have been assigned to.

Authentication is performed using one of the three methods available:

- `AuthenticateAsCurrentUser()`:
  Uses the account information of the user running the script.

- `AuthenticateAsUser()`:
  Allows you to specify a separate user name and password.

- `AuthenticateUsingUserHandle()`:
  Allows you to specify a Windows User handle. This option is typically used when attempting to run the export process from an ASP.NET application where the `AuthenticateAsCurrentUser()` method will not work.

We are going to assume that the account that runs the console application is an MCMS administrator. To keep things simple, we will use the `AuthenticateAsCurrentUser()` method. Add the following line of code to the `Main()` function.

```
static void Main(string[] args)
{
    //
    // TODO: Add constructor logic here
    //
    CmsDeployExport exportJob = new CmsDeployExportClass();
    exportJob.AuthenticateAsCurrentUser();
}
```

Specifying Export Options

The SDAPI provides two options to configure how objects are packaged in the SDO file:

- `IncludeCreatedBy`
- `IncludeRightsGroup`

The IncludeCreatedBy Option

Every object has a `CreatedBy` property. When the export job runs, you can use the `IncludeCreatedBy` option to decide whether or not `CreatedBy` property values are exported.

Enum Value	Integer Value	CreatedBy property
CMS_EXPORT_NOT_INCLUDE_CREATED_BY_USER	1	The CreatedBy value of each object is not included in the package.
CMS_EXPORT_INCLUDE_CREATED_BY_USER	2	This is the default setting. The CreatedBy property of each object is included in the package.

To specify the IncludeCreatedBy option, we could use either the integer value or its 'friendly' name from its enumeration. In the example below, we will use its enumeration name (provided by the CMS_EXPORT_CREATED_BY_SPECIFIER enumeration). Add the following code within the Main() method.

```
static void Main(string[] args)
{
    . . . code continues . . .
    //Specify the include rights group option
    CmsDeployExportOptions exportOptions = exportJob.Options;
    exportOptions.IncludeCreatedBy = (int)
        CMS_EXPORT_CREATED_BY_SPECIFIER.CMS_EXPORT_INCLUDE_CREATED_BY_USER;
}
```

The IncludeRightsGroup Option

The IncludeRightsGroup option provides instructions to specify whether or not user rights groups and their members are exported. This is similar to the options available in the Rights Options dialog in the Site Deployment Export dialog.

The table below summarizes what it does:

Enumeration Value	Integer Value	Include Rights Group	Include Members of Rights Groups
CMS_EXPORT_RIGHTS_GROUPS_NONE	1	No	No
CMS_EXPORT_RIGHTS_GROUP_WITHOUT_MEMBERS	2	Yes	No
CMS_EXPORT_RIGHTS_GROUP_WITH_MEMBERS	3	Yes	Yes

The enumeration value can be accessed through the CMS_EXPORT_RIGHTS_GROUPS enumeration. By default, the option is set to CMS_EXPORT_RIGHTS_GROUP_WITH_MEMBERS.

In this example, we will set the script to include rights group and their members. Add the following code within the Main() method.

```
exportOptions.IncludeRightsGroups = (int)
    CMS_EXPORT_RIGHTS_GROUPS.CMS_EXPORT_RIGHTS_GROUP_WITH_MEMBERS;
```

Calling the Export Method

In order to execute the Export() command, we will need to supply it with three variables:

- **PackageFileName.** A string containing the path and name of the generated site deployment object file.

- **TimeInterval.** An integer storing a number of minutes. Only objects that have been modified in that number of minutes would be exported.
- **ParentChannel.** A string containing the GUID of the parent channel whose child channels and postings you wish to export. Leave it as an empty string if you wish to export the entire website, starting from the root channel.

We will declare three variables, `packageFileName`, `timeInterval`, and `parentChannel`, before using them in the `Export()` method later.

Specifying the Package File Name

We will store the generated SDO package in the `c:\MCMSExports` folder on the local machine. (Change this to a suitable location on your hard disk drive, which you probably created earlier.)

The directory specified must exist before the export process runs or the script will generate an error message saying:

```
The specified path c:\MCMSExports\TropicalGreenExportSS.sdo for
the Object Package is not valid.
Specify a valid path and perform this operation again.
```

We will name our SDO package `TropicalGreenExportSS.sdo`. You can name it anything you like, as long as it is a valid Windows file name. At the end of the `Main()` method, add the following lines of code.

```
static void Main(string[] args)
{
    . . . code continues . . .
    //Specify the package file name
    string packageFileName;
    packageFileName = @"c:\MCMSExports\TropicalGreenExportSS.sdo";
}
```

Specifying the Time Interval

The second variable stores the number of minutes. What it does is to instruct MCMS to export only objects that have changed during the last x minutes.

Setting it to a value of 0 imports all objects that have changed since the last deployment and are in the `Approved` or `Published` state.

In this example, we'll set the `timeInterval` to 60. This means that only channels and postings that have been modified in the past 60 minutes will be included in the site deployment object file. At the end of the `Main()` method, add the following lines of code:

```
static void Main(string[] args)
{
    . . . code continues . . .

    //Specify the time interval
    int timeInterval = 60;
}
```

Specifying the Parent Channel

You can specify that the script deploys objects starting from a specified channel that's not the root. For example, to export only the channels and postings in the PlantCatalog channel, we set this variable to the GUID of the PlantCatalog channel. You can obtain the channel's GUID by using the `Channel.Guid` property of the Publishing API.

We will set this variable to an empty string to start the export process from the root channel. Add the following code at the end of the `Main()` method:

```
static void Main(string[] args)
{
    . . . code continues . . .
    //Specify the parent channel
    //to start from a specific channel, uncomment the code snippet below
    string parentChannel = "";

    /*
    CmsApplicationContext cmsContext = new CmsApplicationContext();
    cmsContext.AuthenticateAsCurrentUser(PublishingMode.Published);
    Channel parent = cmsContext.Searches.GetByPath(
                            "/Channels/TropicalGreen/PlantCatalog")
                                            as Channel;
    if(parent!=null)
    {
        parentChannel = parent.Guid;
    }
    */
}
```

The commented-out portion of the code provides an example on how you can go about obtaining the GUID of a specific parent channel (in this example, we show how to get the GUID of the PlantCatalog channel) should you wish to deploy only specific sections of the site.

The Completed Script

Once all three variables have been declared, we use them as input variables to the `Export()` method. The `Export()` method returns a string that contains the URL of the generated Export Report. To display the report, we start an Internet Explorer process from code.

The code below shows the completed `Main()` method. Make sure to add in the highlighted parts.

```
public static void Main(string[] args)
{
    //
    // TODO: Add constructor logic here
    //
    CmsDeployExport exportJob = new CmsDeployExportClass();
    exportJob.AuthenticateAsCurrentUser();

    //Specify the include rights group option
    CmsDeployExportOptions exportOptions = exportJob.Options;
    exportOptions.IncludeCreatedBy = (int)
        CMS_EXPORT_CREATED_BY_SPECIFIER.CMS_EXPORT_INCLUDE_CREATED_BY_USER;
    exportOptions.IncludeRightsGroups = (int)
        CMS_EXPORT_RIGHTS_GROUPS.CMS_EXPORT_RIGHTS_GROUP_WITH_MEMBERS;

    //Specify the package file name
    string packageFileName;
    packageFileName = @"c:\MCMSExports\TropicalGreenExportSS.sdo";

    //Specify the time interval
    int timeInterval = 60;

    //Specify the parent channel
    string parentChannel = "";
```

```
//Execute the job
string reportUrl = "http://localhost";
reportUrl += exportJob.Export(packageFileName,timeInterval,parentChannel);

System.Diagnostics.Process.Start("iexplore.exe",reportUrl);
}
```

Save and build the ExportServerSide solution. Run the console application (you may want to double-check that you are connected to the TropicalGreen database first). The SDO file is created in the location specified in the packageFileName variable. When the job completes, Internet Explorer will open, displaying the Export Report.

Writing a Server-Side Import Script

Now that we have created the site deployment file using a server-side export script we can choose to import the object to the destination server using Site Deployment Manager, or write a script based on the SDAPI to automate the task. In this example, we write a script to perform the import.

Create a new Visual C# Console Application in Visual Studio .NET. Name the new application ImportServerSide. Rename Class1.cs to ImportSS.cs.

Add a reference to the MSCMS Site Deployment (Server-side) component found in the COM tab of the Add Reference dialog.

Add the SITEDEPLOYSERLib namespace above the ImportServerSide namespace declaration and create a new instance of the CmsDeployImportClass within Main() as shown in the code below:

```
using System;
using SITEDEPLOYSERVERLib;

namespace ImportServerSide
{
    /// <summary>
    /// Summary description for ImportSS.
    /// </summary>
    class ImportSS
    {
        /// <summary>
        /// The main entry point for the application.
        /// </summary>
        [STAThread]
        static void Main(string[] args)
        {
            //
            // TODO: Add code to start application here
            //
            CmsDeployImport importJob = new CmsDeployImportClass();
        }
    }
}
```

Authenticating the User Running the Import Process

The import job runs only if the user that is authenticated to do so belongs to the MCMS Administrator group.

> While export jobs can also be done by a channel manager (as long as they have access to the relevant items) import jobs can only be performed by an MCMS administrator.

You can choose any of the authentication methods described in the previous section, *Authenticating the User Running the Export Process*. In this example, we will assume that the user running the script has administrator privileges and use the `AuthenticateAsCurrentUser()` method. Add the following code within the `Main()` method:

```
static void Main(string[] args)
{
    //
    // TODO: Add code to start application here
    //
    CmsDeployImport importJob = new CmsDeployImportClass();

    //Authenticate the user running the import job
    importJob.AuthenticateAsCurrentUser();
}
```

Configuring Import Options

The `CmsDeploymentImport` class contains four options that allow us to specify how objects are imported to the destination:

- `IncludeCreatedBy`
- `IncludeRightsGroup`
- `RightsOnAdd`
- `RightsOnReplace`

The IncludeCreatedBy Option

The `IncludeCreatedBy` option is similar to the `IncludeCreatedBy` option in the `CmsDeployExportOptions` class. It specifies with which of the following the `CreatedBy` property values on the destination object are replaced:

- The user name of the account used to run the import process
- The `CreatedBy` property values in the site deployment file

Enumerated Value	Integer Value	CreatedBy property
CMS_IMPORT_CREATED_BY_CURRENT_USER	1	This is the default setting.
		The CreatedBy value in each object imported is replaced with the user name of the account that running the import job.
CMS_IMPORT_CREATED_BY_USE_PACKAGE	2	The CreatedBy value in each object imported is replaced with the CreatedBy property value found in the site deployment file.

Assign the `options.IncludeCreatedBy` property either the enumerated value or its integer equivalent. The enumerated value can be accessed from the `CMS_IMPORT_CREATED_BY_SPECIFIER` enumeration as shown. Append the line below the existing code within `Main()`.

```
static void Main(string[] args)
{
    . . . code continues . . .

    //Specify the import options
    importJob.Options.IncludeCreatedBy = (int)
        CMS_IMPORT_CREATED_BY_SPECIFIER.CMS_IMPORT_CREATED_BY_USE_PACKAGE;
}
```

The IncludeRightsGroup Option

The IncludeRightsGroup option provides settings to determine whether user rights groups and their members are imported. The options available here are similar to those found in the Rights Options | Select how Rights Groups are imported tab of the Site Deployment Import dialog.

Enumerated Value	Integer Value	Includes Rights Groups	Includes Members of Rights Groups
CMS_IMPORT_RIGHTS_GROUPS_NONE	1	No	No
CMS_IMPORT_RIGHTS_GROUP_WITHOUT_MEMBERS	2	Yes	No
CMS_IMPORT_RIGHTS_GROUP_WITH_MEMBERS	3	Yes	Yes

By default, the option is set to CMS_IMPORT_RIGHTS_GROUP_WITH_MEMBERS. Assign the Options.IncludeRightsGroup property either the enumerated value or its integer equivalent. The enumerated value can be accessed from the CMS_IMPORT_RIGHTS_GROUPS enumeration as shown below. Append the line below the existing code within Main().

```
static void Main(string[] args)
{
    . . . code continues . . .

    importJob.Options.IncludeRightsGroups = (int)
        CMS_IMPORT_RIGHTS_GROUPS.CMS_IMPORT_RIGHTS_GROUP_USE_PACKAGE_MEMBERS;
}
```

The RightsOnAdd Option

The RightsOnAdd option provides instructions similar to the options available on the Container Rules | When Adding Containers section of the Site Deployment Import dialog. The table below summarizes what each of the three options do.

Enumerated Value	Integer Value	Description
CMS_IMPORT_RIGHTS_ON_ADD_NO_RIGHTS	1	New containers added by the import job will not have any Rights Group applied to them.
CMS_IMPORT_RIGHTS_ON_ADD_INHERIT_FROM _PARENT (default)	2	New containers added by the import job will inherit rights group from the parent container of the destination server.
CMS_IMPORT_RIGHTS_ON_ADD_USE_PACKAGE	3	New containers added by the import job will be assigned rights groups as specified in the site deployment object file.

By default, the option is set to CMS_IMPORT_RIGHTS_ON_ADD_INHERIT_FROM_PARENT. Assign the Options.RightsOnAdd property either the enumerated value or its integer equivalent. The enumerated value can be accessed from the CMS_IMPORT_RIGHTS_ON_ADD enumeration as shown below. Append the line below the existing code within Main().

```
static void Main(string[] args)
{
    . . . code continues . . .

    importJob.Options.RightsOnAdd = (int)
        CMS_IMPORT_RIGHTS_ON_ADD.CMS_IMPORT_RIGHTS_ON_ADD_USE_PACKAGE;
}
```

The RightsOnReplace Option

The RightsOnReplace option provides instructions similar to the options available on the Container Rules | When Replacing Containers section of the Site Deployment Import dialog. The table below summarizes the available options and what they do.

Enumerated Value	Integer Value	Description
CMS_IMPORT_RIGHTS_ON_REPLACE_KEEP_EXISTING	1	Does not import the rights groups for containers that are replaced by the import job.
CMS_IMPORT_RIGHTS_ON_REPLACE_USE_PACKAGE	2	Updates the rights group assigned to the replaced containers based on the rights specified in the site deployment object file.

By default, the option is set to CMS_IMPORT_RIGHTS_ON_REPLACE_KEEP_EXISTING. We can assign the Options.RightsOnReplace property either the enumerated value or its integer equivalent. The enumerated value can be accessed from the CMS_IMPORT_RIGHTS_ON_REPLACE enumeration. Append the line below to the existing code within Main().

```
static void Main(string[] args)
{
    . . . code continues . . .

    importJob.Options.RightsOnReplace = (int)
        CMS_IMPORT_RIGHTS_ON_REPLACE.CMS_IMPORT_RIGHTS_ON_REPLACE_USE_PACKAGE;
}
```

Calling the Import Method

In order to call the Import() method, we need to supply it with the path of the SDO package to be imported. In our example, the site deployment file created earlier resides in the c:\MCMSExports\ directory and has the name TropicalGreenExportSS.sdo. If you specified a different location just change the value of the input parameter accordingly.

The Import() method returns a string containing the URL of the generated import report. Once the import job completes, the script opens an instance of Internet Explorer to display the report. Append the following code after the existing code within Main().

```
static void Main(string[] args)
{
```

```
. . . code continues . . .

//Call the import method
string reportUrl = "http://localhost";
reportUrl +=
    importJob.Import(@"c:\MCMSExports\TropicalGreenExportSS.sdo");

System.Diagnostics.Process.Start("iexplore.exe",reportUrl);
}
```

The Completed Script

The completed script is shown below:

```csharp
using System;
using SITEDEPLOYSERVERLib;

namespace ImportServerSide
{
    /// <summary>
    /// Summary description for ImportSS.
    /// </summary>
    class ImportSS
    {
        /// <summary>
        /// The main entry point for the application.
        /// </summary>
        [STAThread]
        static void Main(string[] args)
        {
            //
            // TODO: Add code to start application here
            //
            CmsDeployImport importJob = new CmsDeployImportClass();

            //Authenticate the user running the import job
            importJob.AuthenticateAsCurrentUser();

            //Specify the import options
            importJob.Options.IncludeCreatedBy = (int)
                CMS_IMPORT_CREATED_BY_SPECIFIER.CMS_IMPORT_CREATED_BY_USE_PACKAGE;
            importJob.Options.IncludeRightsGroups =   (int)
                CMS_IMPORT_RIGHTS_GROUPS.CMS_IMPORT_RIGHTS_GROUP_USE_PACKAGE_MEMBERS;
            importJob.Options.RightsOnAdd = (int)
                CMS_IMPORT_RIGHTS_ON_ADD.CMS_IMPORT_RIGHTS_ON_ADD_USE_PACKAGE;
            importJob.Options.RightsOnReplace = (int)
                CMS_IMPORT_RIGHTS_ON_REPLACE.CMS_IMPORT_RIGHTS_ON_REPLACE_USE_PACKAGE;

            //Call the import method
            string reportUrl = "http://localhost";
            reportUrl +=
                importJob.Import(@"c:\MCMSExports\TropicalGreenExportSS.sdo");

            System.Diagnostics.Process.Start("iexplore.exe",reportUrl);
        }
    }
}
```

Save and build the ImportServerSide solution. When the console application is executed, the site deployment object file in the specified location is imported to the destination MCMS server. To import the objects to a separate MCMS database, run the script on a separate MCMS server that points to another database or use the DCA to point your MCMS server to another database. On completion, Internet Explorer launches and displays the import report.

The source and destination servers are usually separate machines. For the server-side import script to work, you need to transport the SDO package from the source server to the destination server using standard techniques like File Transfer Protocol or XCopy. In the section *Server-Side Deployment Scripts vs. Client-Side Deployment Scripts*, we will discuss how you can avoid moving SDO files from source to destination using the client-side SDAPI.

Writing a Script to Back up and Restore Rights Groups and Users

There may be occasions when you just want to back up or restore rights groups and users without changing the assignment of rights on containers. The CmsUserGroupBackupRestore class of the SDAPI allows you to:

- Back up the entire collection of rights groups and users to an SDO file
- Restore the created SDO file to a destination server

In this way, you can synchronize rights groups and users between two MCMS servers. You could do the same thing by importing channels, template galleries, or resource galleries but that may mean modifying existing content on the destination server.

Creating a Backup of Rights Groups and Users

To test this, create a new Visual C# Console Application named BackupUserGroupServerSide. Rename Class1.cs to BackupUserGroup.cs.

Select Project | Add Reference and add a reference to the MSCMS Site Deployment (Server-side) COM component.

Modify the code in BackupUserGroup.cs as shown below. We first create an instance of the CmsUserGroupBackupRestore class. Next, we authenticate with the MCMS server using the credentials of the user running the script. Finally, we call the Backup() method, passing in the path and name of the SDO file to be created. The Backup() method returns the URL of the generated report, which is opened in Internet Explorer.

```csharp
using System;
using SITEDEPLOYSERVERLib;

namespace BackupUserGroupServerSide
{
    /// <summary>
    /// Summary description for BackupUserGroup.
    /// </summary>
    class BackupUserGroup
    {
        /// <summary>
        /// The main entry point for the application.
        /// </summary>
        [STAThread]
        static void Main(string[] args)
        {
            //
            // TODO: Add code to start application here
            //

            CmsUserGroupBackupRestore backupJob;
            backupJob = new CmsUserGroupBackupRestoreClass();
```

```
            backupJob.AuthenticateAsCurrentUser();

            string reportUrl = "http://localhost";
            reportUrl += backupJob.Backup(@"c:\MCMSExports\usergroup.sdo");

            System.Diagnostics.Process.Start("iexplore.exe",reportUrl);
        }
    }
}
```

Build the solution and execute the console application. When it completes, look at the generated report. In the Parameters section of the report, it says that both user rights groups and users are exported. This is the default setting and there is no way to change it. Using this method, you can't export rights groups without users.

Parameters

General

Security Parameters:

User Rights Groups:	Exported
Users:	Exported
CreatedBy Specifier:	NOT Exported

Restoring Rights Groups and Users

Restoring the SDO file containing the collection of rights groups and users can be carried out either through Site Manager Import or by calling the CmsUserGroupBackupRestore.Restore() method.

The Restore() method accepts two parameters:

- The fully qualified path of the SDO file.
- A Boolean named RemoveUsers that indicates what the restore job should do when adding users to the rights group on the destination server. When it is set to true, all users from existing rights groups are removed before users found in the package are added. False combines the users on both the destination server and the package.

Note that the Restore() method does not change the assignment of rights groups to containers.

To test the Restore() method, create a new Visual C# Console Application and name it RestoreUserGroupServerSide. Rename Class1.cs to RestoreUserGroup.cs.

Select Project | Add Reference and add a reference to the MSCMS Site Deployment (Server-side) COM component. Modify the code in RestoreUserGroup.cs as shown below. First we create an instance of the CmsUserGroupBackupRestore class, and then authenticate with the MCMS server using the credentials of the user running the script. Finally, we call the Restore() method, passing in the path and name of the SDO file to be restored.

```
using System;
using SITEDEPLOYSERVERLib;

namespace RestoreUserGroupServerSide
{
    /// <summary>
    /// Summary description for RestoreUserGroup.
    /// </summary>
    class RestoreUserGroup
    {
        /// <summary>
        /// The main entry point for the application.
        /// </summary>
        [STAThread]
        static void Main(string[] args)
        {
            //
            // TODO: Add code to start application here
            //

            CmsUserGroupBackupRestore restoreJob;
            restoreJob = new CmsUserGroupBackupRestoreClass();
            restoreJob.AuthenticateAsCurrentUser();

            string reportUrl = "http://localhost";
            string packageFileName = @"c:\MCMSExports\usergroup.sdo";
            reportUrl += restoreJob.Restore(packageFileName,false);

            System.Diagnostics.Process.Start("iexplore.exe",reportUrl);
        }
    }
}
```

Build the solution. If you can, run the console application on a separate MCMS server that points to second database or point your MCMS server to a another database you would like to import the objects into. When it completes, the Restore() method returns the URL of the generated report, which is opened in Internet Explorer.

> Users from the MCMS Administrator Group are never removed. The job will always combine administrators from the package with those that already exist on the destination.

Server-Side Deployment Scripts vs. Client-Side Deployment Scripts

Use client-side deployment scripts when attempting to run the export/import process from a remote client machine. A typical use case scenario is when you plan to run all jobs on the same machine. For example you may plan to:

1. Run a server-side export script on the source server, ServerA, to create the SDO file.
2. Run a client-side import script that connects to the destination server, ServerB, from ServerA to import the objects in the SDO file.

In this way, you eliminate the need to transfer the SDO file from ServerA to ServerB (usually using FTP or XCopy). To write client-side scripts, add a reference to the MCMS Site Deployment (Client-side) component (which has the namespace SITEDEPLOYCLIENTLib). One major difference between the client-side and server-side versions of the API is in the authentication methods:

- The client-side API does not have the `AuthenticateUsingUserHandle()` method.

- The remaining `AuthenticateAsCurrentUser()` and `AuthenticateAsUser()` methods have an additional input parameter: a string holding the name of the remote source/destination MCMS server in the form `http://servername:portnumber`. If the port number is 80 you can omit it. For example, to authenticate with the server named MCMSBook when scripting the export job, you can call:

```
exportJob.AuthenticateAsCurrentUser("http://MCMSBook");
```
or:
```
exportJob.AuthenticateAsUser("http://MCMSBook",username,password);
```

The properties and methods of both objects are otherwise very similar.

Planning for Contingencies

As in all deployment jobs, be prepared to slam on the brakes should something not go right. Here are some tips to enable you to roll back a bad deployment.

- Perform regular backups of the database. Preferably back up the database before every import job.

- When scheduling scripts, do not let batch jobs overlap.

- Although the jobs are automated, monitor them. When an error occurs, have the system notify someone.

- Keep site deployment files as small as possible. If you need to do a large update, chop it up into smaller jobs.

- Ensure that site deployment jobs do not run at the same time as background processing is scheduled. Otherwise background processing will not run and database clean-up will not happen.

Summary

In this chapter, we looked at two ways of transferring MCMS objects from one server to another.

The first method used the Site Deployment Manager—an interactive graphical user interface that allows administrators to create export packages. The same interface is used to import these objects to a separate destination server.

The second method we looked at was how incremental updates to a site can be scripted as console applications using the Site Deployment API. Once written and compiled, the executable file can be run on a scheduled basis. We wrote scripts to perform incremental exports and imports as well as backups and restores of rights groups and users. We also discussed some differences between using the Site Deployment Manager and the Site Deployment API.

Finally, we compared the server-side deployment API and the client-side deployment API. Both essentially provide the same functionality with the exception that the server-side API is run on the local machine while the client-side API is run from a remote client machine. We also provided some food for thought when planning for contingencies.

24
Hosting Multiple Websites and Adding SSL Security

Here is a scenario that you might identify with: having completed the TropicalGreen website and deployed it, the owners of TropicalGreen.net sit you down and tell you they need another website, InternationalGreen.net. In addition, a portion of the site must be secured using Secure Sockets Layer (SSL).

Immediately, sirens go off in your head. Wait, you think, we only have servers set up to host a single MCMS website. Another website would require another set of servers and licenses. Plus, MCMS uses channels that are not part of the file-system and not managed by IIS, so how can they be secured by SSL?

Don't panic. In this chapter, we will show you how to host multiple websites on a single server and how to implement SSL security without the need for more equipment or MCMS licenses.

We will go over three primary ways you could host different, separate MCMS websites on a single MCMS server. We will review each method and come to a conclusion for the best method for creating the InternationalGreen.net website. In addition, we will show you how to use SSL to encrypt channels in MCMS to secure parts of your website rather than requiring the whole site to use SSL.

> We assume that you are not working with the Standard Edition of MCMS. The Standard Edition does not support host header mapping, which is necessary for the examples in the chapter to work.

Hosting Multiple MCMS Websites

While it may at first seem impossible to host more than one website on an MCMS server, in fact it is quite possible. In order to determine the best solution for the scenario we detailed above, we will consider the following three main options:

- Multiple top-level channels, (each leading to a different website) and one MCMS application

- Multiple top-level channels and multiple MCMS applications
- Mapping top-level channel names to host header names

> All of these methods require some discipline when creating navigation, as some of the MCMS Web Author Console dialog boxes might show channels from the other websites. Creative coding can prevent users of each site from seeing channels from the other sites, or a simple "do not touch" might be sufficient.

We consider these options in the following sections.

Multiple Channels and One MCMS Application

The quickest way to host multiple "sites" on a single MCMS server is to create separate channels in Site Manager for each site. Suppose we wanted to create the InternationalGreen website. Directly below the root Channels channel, you would add a new channel named InternationalGreen. This method allows you to use your single MCMS application to host more than one website.

You would access each site via its Uniform Resource Locator (URL).

- For the main TropicalGreen site, navigate to:
  www.tropicalgreen.net/tropicalgreen/.
- For the InternationalGreen site, navigate to:
  www.tropicalgreen.net/internationalgreen/.

You could also use URL forwarding in IIS to create alternative Domain Name Service (DNS) entries for each site, so that a call to www.tropicalgreen.net/ would forward to www.tropicalgreen.net/tropicalgreen/, and a call to www.internationalgreen.net would forward to www.tropicalgreen.net/internationalgreen/ (or it could even be www.internationalgreen.net/internationalgreen/), etc.

In Site Manager, the sites would be listed like this:

This method can work in some situations, but for our InternationalGreen site it will not be acceptable. The reasons for this include:

- Users may see www.tropicalgreen.net in the address bar of the browser. Accessing the International Green site via the tropicalgreen.net URL is undesirable.
- Using URL forwarding is undesirable, as it can confuse site visitors and reduce trust ("Why is my browser redirecting me?"), and adds unwanted double-hits to the server.

- All templates, controls, and other code files are shared between the various channels, which may be a problem if the sites look very different and/or have divergent functionality.

Multiple Channels and Multiple MCMS Applications

If you create multiple channels for each website, you could also create multiple MCMS applications using Visual Studio .NET. This would allow you to keep the template files, controls, and other code files for each site separate (but you can still share common Web Custom Controls between your projects).

While this method solves the problem of shared templates, controls, and other code files, it does not avoid the need to use www.internationalgreen.net as the direct URL for the new InternationalGreen site.

Mapping Channel Names to Host Header Names

The last method uses the concept of mapped host headers, MCMS-style. While host headers are not an MCMS creation, MCMS uses them in a slightly different way than normal.

Host headers allow you to assign more than one domain name to a single IP address and port number and have the web server display different websites for each domain name. The use of host headers requires HTTP/1.1, but all modern-day browsers support this.

With mapped host headers, you can access:

- The TropicalGreen site, by navigating to www.tropicalgreen.net (instead of www.tropicalgreen.net/tropicalgreen/)
- The InternationalGreen site, by navigating to www.internationalgreen.net (instead of www.tropicalgreen.net/internationalgreen/ or www.internationalgreen.net/internationalgreen/)

Thus we will not have the problem of the new InternationalGreen site sharing its URL with the existing site, and neither do we have to redirect to an InternationalGreen channel.

> The Standard Edition of MCMS does not support MCMS host header mapping.

Turning on MCMS Host Header Mapping

IIS has the Host Header Names feature in the Web Site Properties dialog under the Advanced... button on the Web Site tab. However, this cannot be used to host multiple MCMS websites on a single server (although it is possible to use it together with MCMS mapped host headers).

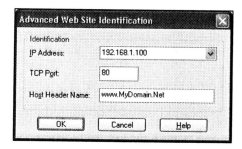

For MCMS to host multiple sites, we need to use the Server Configuration Application (SCA) to turn on the MCMS Map Channel Names to Host Header Names feature.

To configure host header mapping in MCMS we need to perform the following steps in the SCA:

1. Open the SCA by going to Start | Programs | Microsoft Content Management Server | Server Configuration Application.
2. On the General tab, click the Configure... button.
3. Change the value of the Map Channel Names to Host Header Names to Yes.
4. Click OK.

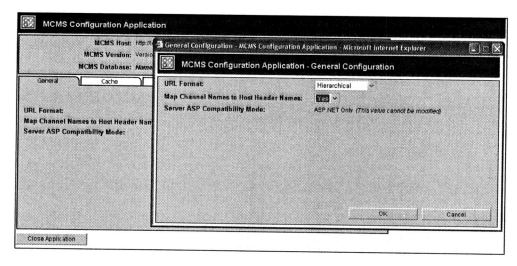

Now that the SCA is configured for mapped host headers, we need to make the following changes in Site Manager.

Configuring Channel Names in Site Manager

In order for our two sites to live separately from each other, we need to change the top-level channel name of our TropicalGreen site and add a new channel for InternationalGreen.

1. Open Site Manager, and expand the root channel, Channels.

2. Rename the TropicalGreen channel as www.tropicalgreen.net.

3. Add a new channel under Channels called www.internationalgreen.net, or rename the InternationalGreen channel if you have created it already.

You should end up with two channels like this:

When using MCMS host headers, the top-level channels in Site Manager must be named according to the desired host header name. The host header name can be a fully qualified domain name, a NetBIOS name, or a name maintained by another name service on your network.

A **fully qualified domain name** (or **FQDN**) consists of a **host** and **domain name**, including the **top-level domain**. For example, www.tropicalgreen.net is a fully qualified domain name. www is the host, tropicalgreen is the second-level domain, and net is the top-level domain. An FQDN always starts with a host name and continues all the way up to the top-level domain name.

So if the host name is europe, europe.tropicalgreen.net is also an FQDN. A **NetBIOS** name is the name registered to your server on your Windows intranet, typically using the Windows Internet Name Service (WINS). If your server is called tropicalgreen, you could access the web server via http://tropicalgreen/, but only on your intranet as NetBIOS does not propagate outside of your company's local or wide area network.

Register Sites with Name Resolution Service

Typically, the FQDNs you are using would be registered with your DNS service and assigned to the IP address of your server. The problem now is we do not have either www.tropicalgreen.net or www.internationalgreen.net mapped to the IP address on our machine! Even if these were the URLs of our production server, each developer would not be able to use the URLs to test the site locally. So what do we do? This is not a problem at all. We will use the TCP/IP hosts file to assign these URLs to our localhost (127.0.0.1). The hosts file allows you to specify which IP addresses go with FQDNs and NetBIOS names, so your machine does not have to access the DNS to resolve server names. You can also use the hosts file to define or override DNS names, as we are going to do.

1. Open the hosts file using Notepad. The location of the hosts file differs according to the operating system. Refer to the table below to find out where you can find it.

Operating System	Location of hosts file
Windows 2000 (and XP/Server 2003 systems upgraded from Windows 2000)	C:\WINNT\system32\drivers\etc\hosts
Windows XP/ Windows Server 2003	C:\WINDOWS\system32\drivers\etc\hosts

2. Add the following two highlighted lines below any existing entries in the hosts file:

```
# Copyright (c) 1993-1999 Microsoft Corp.
#
# This is a sample HOSTS file used by Microsoft TCP/IP for Windows.
#
# This file contains the mappings of IP addresses to host names. Each
# entry should be kept on an individual line. The IP address should
# be placed in the first column followed by the corresponding host name.
# The IP address and the host name should be separated by at least one
# space.
#
# Additionally, comments (such as these) may be inserted on individual
# lines or following the machine name denoted by a '#' symbol.
#
# For example:
#
#       102.54.94.97      rhino.acme.com         # source server
#       38.25.63.10       x.acme.com             # x client host

127.0.0.1    localhost
127.0.0.1    www.tropicalgreen.net
127.0.0.1    www.internationalgreen.net
```

3. Save and close the hosts file.

Now you should be able to point your browser to www.tropicalgreen.net or
www.internationalgreen.net and see the home page for either site. Give it a try. Type
http://www.tropicalgreen.net/ into your browser. (You may need to close and re-open your
browser for the new settings to take effect.) If all goes well, you will see the following Object
reference not set to an instance of an object error message:

Don't worry... this is to be expected!

Upon further investigation, you will find that this error is caused by the following line in the
UserControls/TopMenu.ascx.cs file:

```
string path = "/Channels/TropicalGreen/";
```

As you can see, the `TopMenu.ascx` control uses the `Searches.GetByPath()` method to access the root channel of the TropicalGreen site. Since we just changed the name of the root channel it is little surprise that we receive an error message!

To fix this, change `TropicalGreen` to `www.tropicalgreen.net`:

```
string path = "/Channels/www.tropicalgreen.net/";
```

At the same time, you need to change a few other controls on the site. Here is a summary of all required changes:

Control Code-Behind	Old Code	Revised Code
`RightMenu.ascx.cs` Approx. line 29	`string path = "/Channels/TropicalGreen/";`	`string path = "/Channels/www.tropicalgreen.net/";`
`SiteMapTree.ascx.cs` Approx. line 32	`Channel tropicalGreen = cmsContext.Searches. GetByPath ("/Channels/TropicalGreen/") as Channel;`	`Channel tropicalGreen = cmsContext.Searches.GetByPath ("/Channels/www.tropicalgreen.net/") as Channel;`
`TopMenu.ascx.cs` Approx. line 28	`string path = "/Channels/TropicalGreen/";`	`string path = "/Channels/www.tropicalgreen.net/";`

One way to prevent the need for these changes is to use `Searches.GetByGUID()` instead of `Searches.GetByPath()`. It would not then matter if the name of the root channel changes, as the GUID of an object in MCMS never changes (unless you delete it and re-create it).

Another way to avoid these changes to the code is to use an `<appSettings>` key for your root site name in the `web.config` file, so if the site name changes you just need to modify the value of the key and it will propagate throughout your site.

So, in the `web.config` file you would add a line something like the following within the `<configuration>` section:

```
<appSettings>
    <add key="tgRoot" value="/Channels/www.tropicalgreen.net/" />
</appSettings>
```

Then in your code you would add `using System.Configuration;` to your list of namespace declarations and change the code from:

```
string path = "/Channels/www.tropicalgreen.net/";
```

to:

```
string path = ConfigurationSettings.AppSettings["tgRoot"];
tropicalGreen = cmsContext.Searches.GetByPath(path) as Channel;
```

After making the changes, save all open files and build the TropicalGreen project. Now open up your browser again and access `http://www.tropicalgreen.net/`. The home page should appear as normal, but this time without requiring the `/tropicalgreen/` path as part of the URL!

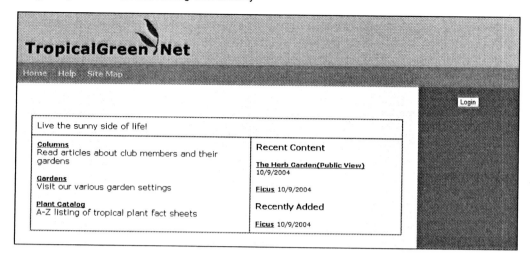

Now try http://www.internationalgreen.net/ in your browser. The default MCMS channel rendering script should appear.

You've just added a second website to your MCMS server! Of course, now you would need to code all of the templates, add the channels, and assign rights to the new site. But you already know how to do that!

You can now create a new Visual Studio .NET solution to hold the template files and controls for the new site, or you can add template files and controls in the TropicalGreen solution. You also need to create the channel, template gallery, and resource gallery structures for the new website and assign role groups and users.

Depending on how the new site is going to look and act, you may want to create a new solution. If required, you can reference the TropicalGreenControlLib project and/or the TropicalGreenPlaceholderDefinition project. Apart from that, the code will be separate between your two sites making it easier to keep each site apart and consistent.

If the new site is going to look and act similarly to the existing site, go ahead and use the same project to avoid duplicating code.

MCMS Host Header Caveats

While using host headers in MCMS is a great way to run multiple websites on a single MCMS server, there is one important thing to consider:

- You cannot have more than one FQDN per site, as each site is a different channel and a channel can only have one name, which needs to be identical to the FQDN. For example, you can't have both www.tropicalgreen.net and www.international green.net pointing to the tropicalgreen channel.

Luckily, there are workarounds for this issue, such as:

- Using a redirect from one domain to the MCMS domain. This would be noticeable to the user. This can be as simple as a Response.Redirect() from one site to the other.
- Using an ISAPI rewrite filter or HTTP module. This would not be noticeable to the user. Search for "ISAPI rewrite" in your favorite search engine. A good example can be found at www.isapirewrite.com.

Another Benefit of Host Headers

Besides using MCMS host headers for hosting multiple websites on a single server, you can also use the feature to avoid the need to add the MCMS top-level channel to your website, even if you have just one website. So, with the TropicalGreen site we can eliminate the need to visit http://www.tropicalgreen.net/tropicalgreen/. Instead we can simply enter http://www.tropicalgreen.net/ in our browser's location bar.

Adding SSL Security

There are many reasons you might want to secure traffic to and from your website using SSL. One reason is to secure the login credentials of your users. Another reason is that restricted areas of your website might contain confidential information. Without SSL security, HTTP traffic traveling between the server and your users is passed as unencrypted plain text and binary data, and can be intercepted by packet sniffers or other network applications. SSL encrypts the HTTP traffic to ensure that only two parties can send and read data in the current session: the server and the client.

There are many ways that SSL security can be added to an MCMS website. For example, you can secure your entire website simply by setting the Secure communications options on the Directory Security tab in IIS to require SSL. However, securing the entire site would mean longer page processing times and possible barriers for search robots trying to index the site. In most real-world scenarios, your site will probably be divided into a secured area, and an unsecured area containing public information.

In the case of our new InternationalGreen site, we only need to secure a channel called Secure. In order to secure just one channel rather than the whole website, we need to write some code that will redirect the user to a secure connection for a channel that is marked as requiring SSL. We will use a custom property named RequireSSL. When it has the value yes, the channel will be secured.

Using a custom property is a benefit because, if we wish to secure more channels later, we can simply set the custom property value using Site Manager without having to modify and re-compile our code. Since you probably do not have an SSL certificate installed on your machine, we will not be able to get the secure connection fully functioning right now. But we will get everything ready for when you get that certificate installed!

> Certificate Authorities such as Verisign (`www.verisign.com`) provide free trial certificates, which you can use to try out the example in this section.
>
> For instructions on how to obtain and install a certificate, see the IIS product documentation at:
> `www.microsoft.com/resources/documentation/iis/6/all/proddocs/en-us/sec_auth_certificate.mspx`

We will create an HTTP module to handle all requests that are coming in. If the request is for a channel that requires SSL, we will simply perform a redirect to the URL of the channel, pre-pended with `https`; if the request is for a channel that does not require SSL, we will make sure that the URL is pre-pended with `http`, so that the request will be handled as it would be without SSL. HTTP modules are well suited for this purpose because they are activated for all requests made to the web application. First, let's create the HTTP module to handle the redirect.

1. With the TropicalGreen solution open in Visual Studio, add a new **C# Class Library** project called `TropicalGreenHttpModules`. Set the location to `c:\`.

2. Using the **Add Reference...** feature, add the references to the following .NET assemblies to the project:
   `System.Web.dll` and
   `Microsoft.ContentManagement.Publishing.dll`. (You will need to need to Browse... to `\Server\bin\Microsoft.ContentManagement.Publishing.dll` in the MCMS installation folder.)

3. Delete the `Class1.cs` file and create a new class file named `CmsSslHttpModule.cs`.

4. Add the following namespaces to the new file:

```
using System;
using System.Web;
using Microsoft.ContentManagement.Publishing;

namespace TropicalGreenHttpModules
{
    . . . code continues . . .
}
```

5. Inherit from `IHttpModule`:

```
public class CmsSslHttpModule : IHttpModule
```

6. Replace all of the code inside the `public class CmsSslHttpModule` with the code shown below. This code checks the custom properties of the current channel to see if there is a `RequireSSL` custom property. If there is and it is set to a value of `yes`, the module will redirect the user to an HTTPS connection, otherwise it will use an HTTP connection. It also ensures that the friendly URLs are retained when switching to the secure connection:

```
. . . code continues . . .
class CmsSslHttpModule : IHttpModule
{
    //IHttpModule members
    public void Init(HttpApplication httpApp)
    {
        httpApp.PreRequestHandlerExecute +=
            new EventHandler(this.OnPreRequestHandlerExecute);
    }

    public void Dispose()
    {
        //Nothing to do
    }
    public void OnPreRequestHandlerExecute(object o, EventArgs e)
    {
        HttpApplication httpApp = (HttpApplication) o;
        HttpContext ctx = HttpContext.Current;
        CmsHttpContext cmsContext = null;

        //Try-catch to prevent access denied exception during forms login.
        try
        {
            cmsContext = CmsHttpContext.Current;
        }
        catch
        {
            //Nothing to do...
        }
        if (cmsContext != null)
        {
            if (cmsContext.Channel != null)
            {
                bool RequireSSL = false;
                if (cmsContext.Channel.
                    CustomProperties["RequireSSL"] != null)
                {
                    RequireSSL =
                        (cmsContext.Channel.
                        CustomProperties["RequireSSL"].Value).ToLower()
                        == "yes";
                }

                string Url = "";
                string UglyUrl = ctx.Request.Url.PathAndQuery;

                if(cmsContext.Mode == PublishingMode.Published)
                {
                    if(ctx.Request.QueryString["NRORIGINALURL"] != null)
                    {
                        Url = ctx.Request.QueryString["NRORIGINALURL"];
                    }
                }

                if(Url != "")
                    Url = ctx.Request.Url.Host+Url;
                else
                    Url = ctx.Request.Url.Host+UglyUrl;

                if (RequireSSL & !ctx.Request.IsSecureConnection)
                    ctx.Response.Redirect("https://"+Url);
                if (!RequireSSL & ctx.Request.IsSecureConnection)
                    ctx.Response.Redirect("http://"+Url);
            }
        }
    }
}
```

7. Save and build the TropicalGreenHttpModules project.

8. In the TropicalGreen project, select Project | Add Reference. In the Add References dialog, click on the Project tab. Select the TropicalGreenHttpModules project created earlier. Click Select then click OK.

9. In the web.config file in the TropicalGreen project, add the following line between the <httpModules> tags:

```
<add type="TropicalGreenHttpModules.CmsSslHttpModule,
     TropicalGreenHttpModules" name="CmsSslHttpModule" />
```

10. Save and build the TropicalGreen solution.

Now that the module has been created and referenced from our TropicalGreen project, we can create the Secure channel and mark it as requiring SSL:

1. Open Site Manager.

2. Add a new channel below the www.internationalgreen.net channel called Secure.

3. Right-click on the new Secure channel and select Properties.

4. In the Custom tab, add a new Custom Property called RequireSSL and set the value to yes.

5. In the Publishing tab, click Select... under the Channel Rendering section and set the Script URL to /tropicalgreen/Login.aspx.

6. We need a channel rendering script (or to add a posting to the channel) because the HTTP module does not work if the default MCMS channel rendering script is used.

Now we can try out the new Secure channel. Open your browser and navigate to http://www.internationalgreen.net/secure/. If all goes well, the URL should get redirected to an HTTPS URL, https://www.internationalgreen.net/secure/. Unfortunately, you probably do not have an SSL certificate installed on your machine, so you should get a Cannot find server or DNS error or The Page cannot be displayed message. But that's OK; the point here is to demonstrate how the redirection to HTTPS works.

Summary

In this chapter, we learned a few ways to host more than one MCMS website on a single server. We saw how multiple top-level channels can be created, each one corresponding to a single MCMS website. Then we turned on MCMS host header mapping which allowed us to access our websites using fully qualified domain names.

We also created an HTTP module to allow us to require SSL for certain MCMS channels. The module handles all requests, and looks for a channel custom property named RequiresSSL. If the custom property value is set to yes, the visitor will be redirected to the page using HTTPS.

Upgrading from MCMS 2001 to MCMS 2002

This appendix covers the basic steps you will need to follow to upgrade an MCMS 2001 website to MCMS 2002.

If you are upgrading your site, the advice in this appendix should be mixed in with Chapters 2, 3, and 4. So instead of installing a site from scratch, you would take your old site, upgrade the MCMS software, upgrade the database, and then decide how to upgrade your templates.

In fact, those are the basic steps for moving from MCMS 2001 to MCMS 2002:

- Backing up the old site's files and database
- Upgrading the MCMS software (uninstalling MCMS 2001 and installing MCMS 2002) or creating a new MCMS server to house the upgraded site
- Upgrading the database using the DCA
- Deciding whether to move to ASP.NET templates or stick with ASP templates

Backing Up the MCMS 2001 Site

Before making any changes to your current MCMS 2001 site, make a full backup of all of your custom code files (ASP and HTML), include files, image files, changes made in the `<InstallDrive>:\Program Files\Microsoft Content Management Server\Server\ IIS_NR\System\WBC\Customizable\` folder (workflow, console, and other changes to the ASP Web Author Console), and anything else you added to the file system.

Also make a full backup of the MCMS 2001 database using SQL Server Enterprise Manager.

It is assumed that you will be doing the upgrade in your development environment, where the database may not have all of the current production content. That's OK. All that matters at the moment is that the template objects are the same. Once the upgrade is complete, the production database can be upgraded and the upgraded template objects can be deployed to the production site along with your files.

> We suggest that you should keep the old MCMS 2001 development server intact, in case you need to update the current site while you are upgrading your site to MCMS 2002.
>
> Therefore, it's best to set up a brand new development server to handle the task of upgrading your site. On the new server, you can install MCMS 2002 from scratch instead of needing to uninstall MCMS 2001 first. You can copy your custom files over to the new server after MCMS 2002 is installed and then follow the steps below.
>
> *Be sure to fully test the site on the current development server before doing the upgrade.* This will help you isolate any problems and determine whether they were caused by the upgrade process or not.

Upgrading the MCMS Software

Before you upgrade a server to MCMS 2002, you actually need to uninstall MCMS 2001 first.

The most reliable way of uninstalling MCMS 2001 is to run the MCMS 2001 install program from the CD or MSI package and choose the Remove option.

See Chapter 2 for how to install MCMS 2002. Also read the information at http://www.microsoft.com/cmserver/default.aspx?url=/cmserver/techinfo/productdoc/2002/upgrade_guide.htm and http://msdn.microsoft.com/library/en-us/dnmscms02/html/cms_2002migrationnet.asp for directions on how to upgrade.

> If you are creating a new server to use for your MCMS 2002 site, you do not need to worry about the MCMS software upgrade process. You can install MCMS 2002 from scratch as described in Chapter 2, and just make a copy of your MCMS 2001 files and database for the new server and DCA upgrade process to use.

Upgrading the Database

After the MCMS 2002 installation is complete, you will need to run the Database Configuration Application (DCA). In the database selection dialog, choose the MCMS 2001 database you wish to upgrade from.

This will modify the schema in the database, and also extract the template and channel rendering script (also known as the navigation template) code to the file system. This code will be copied into the `Templates` and `Channel_Rendering_Scripts` folders under the `Server\IIS_NR\exeres` subdirectory of the MCMS installation folder.

During the upgrade, the DCA will create a `MigrationReport.txt` file in the MCMS `LogFiles` folder located in the MCMS `LogFiles` directory. This report outlines any changes that were made, including the location of the templates and channel rendering scripts listed above, as well as any placeholders that may have changed.

Once the DCA has completed its job, your site should generally be working again under MCMS 2002. But we need to check a few things just in case.

Noticing the Differences

Before we check your site, we'd like to point out a few things that differ between MCMS 2001 and MCMS 2002. Besides the fact that you can now use both managed and unmanaged code (ASP.NET and ASP, respectively) to access MCMS content, the revised user and administrative interfaces take some getting used to.

Site Manager Replaces the Site Builder

The change of name indicates its new role in MCMS. It has evolved to become more of a *manager* than a *builder*. Site Manager is the main interface for Site Administrators to manage the structure of the website channels, resource galleries, and template galleries, as well as to add role groups and assign user rights. It's also used by channel managers to modify the structure, and by template designers to maintain the template galleries.

Site Manager no longer allows authors and editors to add or edit content, or perform other content management or workflow-related functions such as adding or editing resources or approving postings. That task is now relegated exclusively to the Web Author Console.

> Site Builder will not work with the new MCMS 2002 site, and Site Manager will not work with your old MCMS 2001 site. Furthermore, you can only have one or the other installed on your machine at a time. Thus if you are managing the old site while developing the new site, you'll need access to Site Builder on another machine or use a package such as VMware® Workstation or Microsoft Virtual PC to host multiple desktop environments on your machine.

Visual Studio .NET for Templates

During the upgrade process, the code for all of your templates and channel rendering scripts (formerly known as navigation templates) was moved to the file system. This is a great thing: Now you no longer need to use Site Builder to make changes to the code in these objects.

> One thing you might miss is the Resource window from Site Builder. This window allowed you to drag items from the Resource Gallery directly into your templates. You can still do this, but you'll need to do it with code using either `Searches.GetByGUID()` or `Searches.GetByPath()`.

You can leave the files in the default location, `exeres` (paths mentioned above), or move them to your project area. If you move them, you'll need to change the template location path of the template objects using the Visual Studio Template Explorer. Refer to Chapter 6 to find how to access the Template Explorer in Visual Studio .NET.

Visual Studio .NET is the suggested means of creating and editing templates and channel rendering scripts from now on. You can use your current editor, like Dreamweaver or FrontPage, but you will not have access to the Template Explorer. You will need to use Visual Studio .NET to add and edit template objects.

If you want to, you could write your own Template Explorer that runs independently of Visual Studio .NET. A sample is available on GotDotNet:

```
http://www.gotdotnet.com/Community/UserSamples/Details.aspx?SampleGuid=69fef7c
e-5447-4c3a-b91c-355569563507
```

A template designer will still need to use the Site Manager to manage channels, assign channel rendering script to channels, and create resource galleries. These functions cannot be performed in Visual Studio .NET.

> The Navigation URL field is a deprecated property used for framed sites in MCMS 2001, and does not work with ASP.NET-based templates. The template designer must go through each channel to store this information in the Script URL field or its PAPI equivalent, the outerScriptFile property, and use the Use channel script with Pages property if necessary.

Web Author Console

MCMS 2002 has pretty much the same Web Author Console functionality as MCMS 2001, but you may notice that some of the dialog boxes look a little different.

If you are still using ASP templates you may notice that some dialog boxes have been re-written in ASP.NET, while others still run as ASP. If you move to ASP.NET templates, you will see all ASP.NET dialog boxes.

> It should be noted here that support for video both in the resource gallery and as attachments to postings has been removed in MCMS 2002.

ASP or ASP.NET?

The last step of the upgrade is determining which path you want to take: stick with your classic ASP templates or migrate your code to ASP.NET.

Staying with ASP

Sticking to ASP is the fastest and easiest way to go. Little work is needed after this point. However, if you stick with ASP you will not be able to take advantage of all of the cool new features of the ASP.NET Publishing Application Programming Interface (PAPI), and the next version of MCMS will most likely no longer offer support for classic ASP at all. However, for the short term you will be able to use your existing, time-tested code while still reaping some of the benefits of the better performance of the newer version of MCMS.

Also, if you are using the MCMS Site Stager you will need to stick with ASP templates until you can migrate from Site Stager, as Site Stager does not work with ASP.NET MCMS sites.

While trying to stage the site using Site Stager, I keep getting this error message in the log files: Failed to connect to MSCMS server, probably due to user authentication error. Please check the Stage As User Name and Password in the staging profile. **Site Stager is not able to proceed.**

If you are using Site Stager in MCMS 2002, make sure you do the following:

1. Check that the StageAs user name and password are valid and map to an MCMS user account (at least subscriber access) with rights to the channels that you wish to stage.

2. Add the StageAs user to a new template designer role group. There is a design limitation in the Site Stager that prevents your site from being staged unless the Site Stager user is in a template designer role group. The role group does not require any permissions.

An alternative is to migrate to ASP.NET and create your own site stager application. A sample site stager for ASP.NET sites is available on GotDotNet:

```
http://www.gotdotnet.com/Community/UserSamples/Details.aspx?SampleGuid=153B8D2
0-EE51-4105-AAEF-519A7B841FCC
```

If you decide to stick with ASP, then be sure to do the following.

Fixing the Customizable Files

When running the upgrade, MCMS will overwrite all of the files under the MCMS Server\IIS_NR\System\WBC\Customizable\ folder. This is not documented anywhere, which is why we tell you to backup this folder before running the upgrade.

After the upgrade, you will need to go into each file under the Customizable folder and copy your customized code into the new files in Customizable. DO NOT OVERWRITE THE NEW FILES! Go into each file individually to examine what changes Microsoft has made to them, and incorporate your code into them. If you copy your files over the new files, you will have problems.

Checking Your Other Code

The Customizable folder is the only area MCMS will touch during the upgrade process. However, you still need to go into your other code, as well as your template code, to be sure all of your functionality is still working. You should create a test plan to ensure that all necessary features of your site are working as designed.

Test! Test! Test!

We really can't overemphasize how you should test everything thoroughly to be sure it's working as designed.

Go for Broke: ASP.NET

Moving your site to ASP.NET is not as quick and easy as leaving it in ASP, but once the migration is complete, you have a much richer PAPI and better performance. Once you get used to ASP.NET you'll probably be able to code new functionality even faster than doing it in ASP!

If you plan on moving to ASP.NET, we recommend you do the entire site at once instead of doing a portion at a time. One reason is that you will find that ASP and ASP.NET pages will lead to different user experiences, which may cause unnecessary confusion to your users. So, if you can, do a complete redesign and move everything to ASP.NET all at once. Don't worry, the content repository (database) can be reused; only the code needs to be upgraded (templates, channel rendering scripts, workflow, etc.).

Nevertheless, you may wish to gradually migrate sections of your site from ASP to ASP.NET. This may work well for larger sites containing multiple departments or sub-sites that may include hundreds or thousands of templates. This may also work for situations where some departments are not ready to move to ASP.NET right away, or are slow at adopting the new platform.

In either case, just follow Chapters 5 through 23 to create the new ASP.NET templates, channel rendering scripts, placeholder controls, workflow, Web Author Console customizations, site deployment, and performance enhancements.

You can probably transfer a lot of your logic and design from your ASP code to ASP.NET, but the actual coding syntax will be different. A good architecture, design, and migration plan will make the transition much easier.

More help can be found at:

`http://msdn.microsoft.com/library/en-us/dnanchor/html/contentmanagementserver.asp`

Summary

In this appendix we discussed how to upgrade your MCMS 2001 to MCMS 2002. We went over the four main steps for moving to MCMS 2002: backing up the old site files and database, upgrading the MCMS software, upgrading the database, and deciding whether to move to ASP.NET templates or stick with ASP templates. Upgrading to MCMS 2002 takes some planning, some guts, and some time. But once you have done it, you will reap many rewards for the effort.

B
References

Microsoft Resources

- MCMS Product Website:
  `http://www.microsoft.com/cmserver/`
- Microsoft's MCMS FAQ maintained by Stefan Goßner:
  `http://download.microsoft.com/download/4/2/5/4250f79a-c3a1-4003-9272`
  `-2404e92bb76a/MCMS+2002+-+(complete)+FAQ.htm`
- MCMS User Samples on GotDotNet:
  `http://www.gotdotnet.com/community/usersamples/Default.aspx?`
  `ProductDropDownList=Content+Management+Server`
- Microsoft MCMS Public Newsgroups:
  `http://www.microsoft.com/cmserver/default.aspx?url=/CMServer/community`
- MCMS Whitepapers and other documents:
  `http://blogs.msdn.com/stefan_gossner/articles/271524.aspx`
- MCMS on MSDN:
  `http://msdn.microsoft.com/library/en-`
  `us/dnanchor/html/contentmanagementserver.asp`
- MCMS on TechNet:
  `http://www.microsoft.com/technet/prodtechnol/cms/default.mspx`
- Microsoft Content Management Server 2002 Product Documentation:
  `http://www.microsoft.com/cmserver/default.aspx?url=/cmserver/techinfo/`
  `productdoc/2002/2002doc_help.htm`
- Windows Update:
  `http://windowsupdate.microsoft.com`
- Microsoft Internet Explorer:
  `http://www.microsoft.com/windows/ie/`
- Microsoft SQL Server:
  `http://www.microsoft.com/sql/`
- Microsoft Visual J# .NET Version 1.0 Redistributable Package:
  `http://go.microsoft.com/fwlink/?LinkId=14506`
- Microsoft Visual J# .NET Version 1.1 Redistributable Package:
  `http://go.microsoft.com/fwlink/?LinkId=16283`
- Internet Explorer Web Controls for Content Management Server 2002 with SP1a:
  `http://www.microsoft.com/downloads/details.aspx?FamilyID=fac6350c`
  `-8ad6-4bca-8860-8a6ae3f64448&DisplayLang=en`

- Visual SourceSafe:
  `http://msdn.microsoft.com/vstudio/previous/ssafe/`

- Microsoft Download Center:
  `http://www.microsoft.com/downloads`

Knowledge Base Articles Referenced in the Book

- How to Install and Use the IIS Lockdown Wizard:
  `http://support.microsoft.com/default.aspx?id=325864`

- FIX: Virtual directories disappear from the IIS 5.1 snap-in:
  `http://support.microsoft.com/?id=308179`

MSDN and TechNet Articles Referenced in the Book

- Visual Studio Debugging:
  `http://msdn.microsoft.com/library/default.asp?url=/library/en-us/vsdebug/html/vc_Debugging_Your_Application_home_page.asp`

- Preparing to Migrate to MCMS 2002 and ASP.NET:
  `http://msdn.microsoft.com/library/en-us/dnmscms02/html/cms_2002migrationnet.asp`

- Changing Property Values within Event Handlers:
  `http://msdn.microsoft.com/library/en-us/sitedev1/htm/cms_sd_ext_workflow_txvk.asp`

- Customizing Microsoft Content Management Server 2002 Authoring Connector:
  `http://msdn.microsoft.com/library/default.asp?url=/library/en-us/dnmscms02/html/mscms_CustAuCo.asp`

- Building Secure ASP.NET Applications: Authentication, Authorization, and Secure Communication:
  `http://msdn.microsoft.com/library/default.asp?url=/library/en-us/dnnetsec/html/SecNetAP05.asp`

- ASP.NET Settings Schema Reference <forms> Element:
  `http://www.microsoft.com/resources/documentation/iis/6/all/proddocs/en-us/aaconformselement.mspx`

- Using Microsoft Content Management Server 2002 and Web Services:
  `http://msdn.microsoft.com/library/en-us/dnmscms02/html/cms_2002webservices.asp`

- Performance Optimization and Capacity Planning:
  `http://msdn.microsoft.com/library/en-us/dnmscms01/html/cmsperfoc.asp`

- Performance Planning and Deployment with Content Management Server 2002:
  `http://msdn.microsoft.com/library/en-us/CMS2002_GB/htm/mcms2002_perf_deploy_abstract_msdn_xugb.asp?frame=true`

- Deploying .NET Framework-based Applications:
  `http://msdn.microsoft.com/library/en-us/dnbda/html/DALGRoadmap.asp`

- Deploying MCMS Sites - Using Application Center 2000:
  `http://www.microsoft.com/technet/prodtechnol/cms/deploy/cmsdes01.mspx`

- Certificates:
  `http://www.microsoft.com/resources/documentation/iis/6/all/proddocs/en-us/sec_auth_certificate.mspx`

- Upgrade Guide for Content Management Server 2002:
  http://www.microsoft.com/cmserver/default.aspx?url=/cmserver/techinfo/productdoc/2002/upgrade_guide.htm

Author Blogs

- Mei Ying's blog:
  http://meiyinglim.blogspot.com/

- Joel's blog:
  http://joelsef.blogspot.com/

- Stefan's blog:
  http://blogs.msdn.com/stefan_gossner/

Community Resources

- Angus Logan's blog:
  http://www.anguslogan.com/

- Spencer Harbar's MCMS Resource Site:
  http://www.mcmsfaq.com/

- Arpan Shah's Blog:
  http://weblogs.asp.net/arpans/

- Mark Harrison's Blog:
  http://blog.markharrison.co.uk/

Other References from the Chapters

- Telerik r.a.d.editor for Content Management Server:
  http://www.telerik.com/mcms/

- GotDotNet User Sample: RenderPlaceholderServerControl:
  http://www.gotdotnet.com/Community/UserSamples/Details.aspx?SampleGuid=1045e51d-f83d-4caf-99b9-8b395b722f24

- Regular-Expressions.info:
  http://www.regular-expressions.info/

- Helicon Tech ISAPI_Rewrite:
  http://www.isapirewrite.com/

About Tropical Plants

- USDA Plant Hardiness Zone Map:
  http://www.usna.usda.gov/Hardzone/

Index

A

R

Printed in the United States
29602LVS00007B/11-12